DESIGNING PUBLIC POLICY

A Casebook on the Role of Policy Analysis

LAURENCE E. LYNN, Jr.

with the assistance of

Stephanie G. Gould

GOODYEAR PUBLISHING COMPANY, INC.

Santa Monica, California

GOODYEAR PUBLIC POLICY ANALYSIS AND MANAGEMENT SERIES
Arnold J. Meltsner and Mark H. Moore, Editors

DISCOVERING WHETHER PROGRAMS WORK: A GUIDE TO STATISTICAL
METHODS FOR PROGRAM EVALUATION
Laura Irwin Langbein

GETTING THE FACTS: A FIELDWORK GUIDE FOR EVALUATORS
AND POLICY ANALYSTS
Jerome T. Murphy

Library of Congress Cataloging in Publication Data

Lynn, Laurence E., Jr.   1937–
    Designing public policy.

    1. Policy sciences—Case studies.   2. Public
administration—Case studies.   3. United States—
Politics and government—Case studies.   I. Gould,
Stephanie G., joint author.   II. Title.
H62.L84   309   79-21000
ISBN 0-8302-2183-2

Current printing (last digit):
10 9 8 7 6 5 4 3 2 1

ISBN: 0-8302-2183-2

Printed in the United States of America

Contents

Preface   v

Case Acknowledgements   vii

1 Analysis and Policymaking   1

Introduction   1
Education for Public Management   2
Management and Analysis   3
Policy Analysis for Decisionmaking   5
Acquiring the Analytic Habit   7

2 The Policymaking Process   9

Introduction   9
A Framework for Analysis   10
The Individual Decisionmaker   11
Groups and Groupthink   14
The Political Process   17
Economy, Society, and Culture   21
So What?   21

3 The Central Utah Project (A)   24

Appendix: Responsibilities of
    Interior Officials   46

4 The Central Utah Project (B)   54

Sequel   81

**5 Caspar Weinberger
and Welfare Reform**   82

Appendix A: Major Characteristics of
    the Welfare System   98
Appendix B: Staff Paper on Welfare
    Objectives   102

6 Detroit: A Statistical Profile   104

7 The Detroit Fiscal Crisis (A)   133

Appendix A: Charting the Tragedy of
    the Lower East Side   141
Appendix B: Detroit . . . A City Being
    Destroyed   145

Appendix C: Detroit: That Sinking
Feeling   147

Appendix D: The Positive Side of
Detroit's Situation   149

8   The Detroit Fiscal Crisis (B)   152
Sequel   173

9   Atlanta: A Statistical Profile   176

**10   Expanding Atlanta's City
Limits (A)**   204

Appendix: The City of Atlanta's
Non-General Fund Expenditures   218

**11   Expanding Atlanta's City
Limits (B)**   225

Appendix A: Research Atlanta's
Methodological Considerations   240
Appendix B: A Critique of the Research
Atlanta Study   246
Sequel   256

12   Public Policy for Day Care   258
Sequel   274

**13   Federal Financial Aid for
Postsecondary Education**   279
Sequel   296

14   High Mountain Sheep Dam   308

Appendix A: Present Value Calculations   322
Appendix B: Analysis of Sensitivity of
Thermal Power Costs to Technological
Change Parameters   323
Appendix C: Analysis of Sensitivity of
Wilderness Value Estimates to Demand
Shift and Technological Change
Parameters   323
Sequel   324

**15   Automobile Emissions Control:
The Sulfates Problem (A)**   326

Appendix A: Chronology of Events:
The Sulfates Problem   341
Appendix B: Alternative Engine
Systems   342

**16   Automobile Emissions Control:
The Sulfates Problem (B)**   345
Sequel: Later Research on Sulfates   365

17   The C–5A (A)   366

Appendix: Historical Role of the
Secretary   384

18   The C–5A (B)   386

Appendix A: Operation of the Cost
Overrun and Repricing Formulae   403
Appendix B: The Cover-Up Controversy   404

**19   The Connecticut Enforcement
Project (A)**   405

**20   The Connecticut Enforcement
Project (B)**   425

**21   The Connecticut Enforcement
Project (C)**   441

Appendix A: An Evaluation of   452
Civil Penalties
Appendix B: Conclusions Drawn from   455
the Limited Application of a
Civil Penalties Program in the
State of Connecticut

**22   Income Transfers vs. the   462
Public Provision of Goods
and Services In-Kind**

Preface

The cases in this book were initially developed for use at Harvard University's John F. Kennedy School of Government. Shortly after joining the School's faculty in 1975, I assumed responsibility for a required first-year course in the two-year program leading to a Master's Degree in Public Policy. The objective of the course, called "Workshop," was to give students practice in applying the concepts and methods of policy analysis to actual policy issues. The curriculum included the study of a variety of cases and case-like materials and the completion of group projects and exercises. Professor Richard E. Neustadt, Chairman of the Executive Committee of the School's Case Program, encouraged me to develop whatever new cases might be needed for this course, drawing as appropriate on my own government experience.

Developing cases is like eating salted nuts—you cannot stop with one or two. With support, encouragement, and advice from the Kennedy School case community—colleagues who were also developing and teaching cases—the initial cases (The Central Utah Project case was the first) gradually became a sizable group dealing with policy analysis and policymaking. Among them are the cases included in this book. At the same time, the concept of the course in which they are taught evolved from "merely" illustrating the uses of analytic concepts to defining the role of analysis and analysts in the policymaking process and to establishing criteria for judging the quality of analytic products. The ideas underlying this course form the basis for the first two chapters of this book.

Each case has been used several times in the professional schools and programs of Harvard University, and many have been used in other schools and universities. Drafts of each case were read by experts in the field and by many of the public officials and others whose actions are described in the case. Where not available on tapes of interviews, all quotations and references to personal recollections or opinions were checked with the authors. The final texts of the cases have benefitted from reactions, suggestions, and criticisms obtained from students, expert critics, and participants who have used or reviewed them.

Stephanie G. Gould, Editor for the Kennedy School's Case and Curriculum Development Program has been indispensable to the development of these cases. This type of case tends to be overlong—after going to the trouble of getting the information, case writers and their professors are loathe to leave anything out—and she has muscled them into their present state of clarity and conciseness against all opposition. Beyond that, she has consistently approached these cases as a student would. A case that is satisfactorily developed to a trained eye, may be incomprehensible to an inexperienced student. Stephanie Gould thus deserves substantial credit for the extent to which the cases actually fulfill their teaching objectives. She has also contributed useful ideas to the first two chapters of the book. I am also indebted to Chris Argyris, Robert F. Coulam, Alexander L. George, and Judith K. Larsen for their valuable comments on earlier drafts of Chapter 2. Alicia McFall oversaw the assembly and final preparation of the case materials, and worked far beyond the call of duty in correcting galley and page proofs. Marci Hazard, my secretary and administrative assistant, did her usual superb job in preparing the manuscript for publication.

Case Acknowledgements

All cases were prepared under the supervision of the author, assisted by Stephanie G. Gould, Editor of the Kennedy School of Government Case and Curriculum Development Program. They were copyrighted by the President and Fellows of Harvard College and are published here with their permission. Primary responsibility for the research, writing, and financial support for each case should be credited as follows:

The Central Utah Project (A) and *(B)* was initially prepared by Theodore J. Bogosian, and revised by Deborah Harrity and William J. Mates. *The Central Utah Project Sequel* was prepared by William J. Mates.

Caspar Weinberger and Welfare Reform was prepared by Cynthia L. Horan. Support for case development was provided in part by the Alfred P. Sloan Foundation.

A Statistical Profile of Metropolitan Detroit was compiled by William B. Mates.

The Detroit Fiscal Crisis (A) was prepared by William J. Mates and William B. Marcus. *The Detroit Fiscal Crisis (B)* and *Sequel* were prepared by William B. Marcus.

A Statistical Profile of Metropolitan Atlanta and *Expanding Atlanta's City Limits (A)* were prepared by William B. Marcus. Funds for the development of the cases were provided in part by the Alfred P. Sloan Foundation.

Expanding Atlanta's City Limits (B) and *Sequel* were prepared by Theodore J. Bogosian and William B. Marcus. Funds for their development were provided in part by the Alfred P. Sloan Foundation.

Public Policy for Day Care was prepared by Anngail A. Croswell.

Federal Financial Aid for Postsecondary Education was prepared by Robert B. Knauss and supported in part by a grant from the Alfred P. Sloan Foundation.

Federal Financial Aid for Postsecondary Education in the Seventies Sequel and *Public Policy for Day Care Sequel* were prepared by J. Bradley O'Connell.

High Mountain Sheep Dam and *High Mountain Sheep Dam Sequel* were prepared by William B. Marcus.

Automobile Emissions Control: The Sulfates Problem (A) and *(B)* were prepared by Theodore J. Bogosian and William J. Mates. Funds for case development were provided in part by the Executive Programs in Health Policy and Management, Harvard School of Public Health under DHEW Contract No. 1-AH-44105.

The C-5A (A) and *(B)* were prepared by Kathleen G. Heintz. Funds for case development were provided in part by the Alfred P. Sloan Foundation.

The Connecticut Enforcement Project (A) was prepared by William B. Marcus and William J. Mates. Donald J. Gogel also assisted with Part *(B)*, and Theodore J. Bogosian with Part *(C)*. Funds for the development of this case were provided in part by the Public Policy Curricular Materials Development Program, administered by the Duke Institute of Policy Sciences and Public Affairs and the Rand Graduate Institute, and in part by the Executive Program in Health Policy and Management, Harvard School of Public Health, under DHEW Contract No. 1-AH-44105. William Drayton, Jr. provided valuable advice during the preparation of the case.

1

Analysis and Policymaking

INTRODUCTION

The steady growth in the number, variety, complexity, and social importance of policy issues confronting government is making increasing intellectual demands on public officials and their staffs. What should be done about nuclear safety, teenage pregnancies, urban decline, rising hospital costs, unemployment among black youth, violence towards spouses and children, and the disposal of toxic wastes? Many of these subjects were not on the public agenda twenty years ago. They are priority issues now, and new ones of a similar character emerge virtually every year. For most elected and appointed officials and their staffs, such complicated and controversial questions are outside the scope of their judgment and previous experience. Yet, the questions cannot be sidestepped; government executives are expected to deal with them responsibly and effectively.

To aid them in thinking about and deciding on such matters, public officials have been depending to an increasing extent on knowledge derived from research, policy analysis, program evaluations, and statistics to inform or buttress their views. Elected and appointed officials in the various branches and levels of government, from federal judges to town selectmen, are citing studies, official data, and expert opinion in at least partial justification for their actions more often than in the past. Their staffs, which have been increasing in size and responsibility in recent decades, include growing numbers of people trained in or familiar with analytic techniques to gather and evaluate information. Increasing amounts of research, analysis, and data gathering are being done. The federal government alone, which spent $40 to $50 million a year on social science research and statistics in the late 1930s, now spends about forty times that much on social R&D.

Developments such as these hardly mean that we are witnessing a sudden and unique transformation of American government. Charles E. Lindblom has observed that "In all governments all over the world, a

1

standard routine for reaching a policy decision is to gather and analyze facts, doing so with at least implicit theory."[1] Nor has the U.S. Government only recently come to appreciate the potential role of knowledge in policymaking. Our history is studded with examples: President Thomas Jefferson's commissioning of the Lewis and Clark Expedition to gather data for policy in the West; President Herbert Hoover's creation of a Committee on Recent Social Trends; President Franklin D. Roosevelt's establishment of the National Resources Planning Board; the spread of policy analysis at President Lyndon B. Johnson's instigation.

Moreover, this growing dependence on organized knowledge production is not such that "science" is replacing "politics," that self-interest is giving way to objectivity in policymaking, or that technocrats and policy analysts are now running the government. Conventional explanations of political behavior—pluralism, incrementalism, bureaucratic politics—built around concepts of power, partisanship, cooperation, and compromise are not outmoded, as chapter 2 will make clear. Nonetheless, the policy game is changing. Political success depends more and more on familiarity with, if not mastery of, complex substantive issues. Because the power to influence policy is widely shared in our system of government, public officials seeking to influence policy—to play the policy game well—must be persuasive. Because of the changing character of policy issues, it is probably harder to be persuasive than it used to be. Seniority, affability, and clever "wheeling and dealing" may be relatively less influential than being generally knowledgeable and tough minded, having the ability to offer ideas and solutions that can attract a wide following, or having a reputation as a well-informed critic. Increasingly, officials from the President on down lose influence in policy debates when they cannot get their numbers right or when their ideas and arguments are successfully challenged by opposing experts. Indeed, thorough and detailed command of an issue or problem is often mandatory. Legislatures are requiring executives to be experts in the programs and issues under their jurisdiction. Judges are requiring detailed proof that administrative decisions are not arbitrary and capricious. Budget officials demand positive program evaluations. The public demands accountability. Thus the dynamic processes whereby our political system confronts social problems are perceptibly, if not dramatically, raising the standards of substantive and managerial competence in the performance of public responsibilities.

EDUCATION FOR PUBLIC MANAGEMENT

Substantive competence in the performance of public responsibilities is an elusive concept. Incompetence may be easier to identify, if not to define. While working in and around government, you will often hear public officials characterized in various unflattering ways. You will hear, for example, of those who:

"shoot from the hip" or decide on the basis of "gut reactions";

base their decisions on "which way the wind is blowing";

take the advice of the last person who spoke to them, are "over their heads," or are unable to "get on top of the problem";

get "bogged down in the details," cannot "find the handles" on an issue, or cannot make a decision;

are "lightweights" or fail to "do their homework."

Officials who get tagged with such epithets are usually ones who are unable or unwilling to figure out in a systematic way how to ask good questions, to use their own or their staff's time efficiently in studying issues, or to evaluate evidence and arguments. They are unable to cope with the complexity of the issues they must confront on a daily basis. As a result, their performance as policymakers and managers may become disorganized or desultory. They may be driven to seeking paths of least resistance through the daily morass of irritants and frustrations, such as making snap judgments, deferring to someone else, or procrastinating. They are not regarded as competent. They appear to contribute little to policy.

There are a wide variety of explanations for the types of official behavior we observe, many of which will be discussed further in chapter 2. In brief, individuals may differ widely in how they think and learn, in how they process and evaluate incoming information, and in how they cope with pressure and stress. These differences are rooted in the cognitive processes of the mind and in emotional makeup. An individual who, for example, is essentially intuitive and non-quantitative may not do well, and may experience genuine anxiety and stress, if confronted with a problem requiring methodical assessment of large amounts of disparate data. A systematic, precise, low-key official may perform poorly when in a fast-moving situation that places a premium on quickness and creativity. One implication of this observation is that not just anyone can do any job; it is important to match intellectual style and capacity with the demands of the position, all other things equal. Furthermore, some individuals may naturally do better in some situations than in others, a factor which should be taken into account when assigning work or responsibility.

Despite the prevalence of individual differences in native "analytic ability," this book has as its purpose the improvement of your ability to cope with the complexity of public policy issues by helping you acquire the ability to be analytical about them. Its premise is that public officials and their staffs *should* be unself-consciously, habitually analytical in dealing with the issues they face. For some, this may come naturally; for others it may be difficult to acquire new and unfamiliar modes of thinking and responding to problem situations. For all, however, it is an important ingredient of effectiveness.

Analytic ability does not mean technical facility with specific analytic tools and techniques, such as micro-economic theory or linear programming, though such facility can be important in the analytic process. It means, rather, being able to think systematically and clearly about a complex or unfamiliar policy problem and form an independent and competent view of the issues, alternatives, and likely consequences of different actions, all within an unpredictable, distracting, and highly charged political environment. It means having confidence in your ability to think and act sensibly in the face of uncertainty, incomplete information, multiple and competing objectives, value conflicts, and irresolvable disagreements over what should be done. Throughout the book we will refer to this type of intellectual activity and motivation as "policy analysis," but you should be clear that the reference is to an attitude and an approach, rather than to a body of specific methods.

The fundamental orientation of the book is practical, rather than academic. It is intended as an aid to practitioners rather than to scholars. The book is designed to serve three specific purposes:

> to help you acquire the habit of being analytical in the most general sense in confronting the types of problems found in government;

> to increase your facility in using analytic concepts and techniques—for example, microeconomic theory, decision analysis, and statistical inference —to address public policy problems; and

> to familiarize you with the role of the analytically-trained professional within the institutional and political context of public policymaking.

These purposes, especially the second one, may raise questions about the audience for these materials. Is the book intended primarily for people who will become practicing policy analysts and planners, who must be familiar with analytic methods? Or is it, as the earlier discussion implied, to prepare people for public management, elective office, or senior policymaking and advisory positions, where a mastery of technique may not seem to matter?

The ultimate purpose is to help you develop skills needed in reaching decisions about complex policy issues from positions of middle- and high-level responsibility in the executive, legislative, and judicial branches of government. However, senior positions are often attained only after a suitable apprenticeship as a staff analyst in a planning office, special assistant to a senior executive, legislative aide, staff lawyer in a regulatory agency, staff member in a management consulting firm, or project officer in an operating agency—that is, in positions for which technical analytical competence is much more clearly in the line of duty. People who are effective in such early career positions are increasingly viewed as a primary source of candidates for top-level positions.

Hence the skills that are the concern of this book are important to entry-level, mid-career, and even later success in government.

MANAGEMENT AND ANALYSIS

The pressure on public officials to know more and have competent ideas about public policy has created demands on the educational and scientific communities. In response, both a profession—public management—and a discipline—policy analysis—are emerging. They will be of growing importance in developing ideas and approaches to aid public managers.

Public Management[2]

Depending on one's perspective, the profession of public management either is replacing or is a lineal descendent of the venerable profession of public administration. With its early roots in the reform-minded Progressive era, public administration, both as a profession and as a special field of study within the academic discipline of political science, developed in association with the growth of the civil service system to rescue the performance of regular government functions from spoils system politics. Gradually the President came to be viewed as an administrator as well as the nation's top elected politician, and the civil servant as a technician and professional instead of merely as a clerk. The biggest boost to the notion of the President as chief executive came when Congress passed the Budget and Accounting Act of 1921, creating the executive budget and giving the President a special staff for overseeing it.

Through the first few decades of the twentieth century, the central ideas of public administration as a field of study became the separation of the practice of administration from politics and efficiency as the goal of administrative practice. The development of the social sciences during this period was consistent with the idea that administration could be "scientific" and value free—similar developments were occurring in the field of business administration—or at least rational. Further development of this notion has extended through the postwar development of public management systems such as Planning-Programming-Budgeting (PPB), Management-by-Objectives (MBO), and Zero-Base-Budgeting (ZBB). Indeed, the rationale for some of these ideas has been almost delightfully naive concerning the role of politics in the decision-making of public managers.

Criticisms of the dichotomy between public administration and politics were inevitable. The dichotomy is false. Such criticisms probably have their roots in the administration of President Franklin D. Roosevelt. The concomitant emergence of unprece-

dented social distress, wholesale innovations concerning the role of government in human affairs, and the vital importance of the political process in shaping governmental roles and functions—not to mention the growing role of intellectuals in government—stimulated "the interpenetration of administration and politics," propelling orthodox public administration, with its emphasis on politically neutral efficiency, into a decline from which it has never really recovered. Moreover, the forces that precipitated this decline have never abated. The steady, if disorderly, growth of the public sector since World War II and, along with it, the growth in executive responsibility and accountability, have continued to focus attention on the political executive and the functions of management in the highly complex, steadily changing, intrinsically political federal system. Indeed, it was in the early part of this period, 1952, that the intellectual forebear of this book, Harold Stein's *Public Administration and Policy Development: A Case Book*, appeared.[3] In it he stated that "to neglect [the administrator's relations with his political environment] is to study public administration in a political vacuum—a realm where public administration does not exist."[4]

Right now, thinking and research on topics related to public management/public administration are scattered among professional schools of public policy, public administration, management, and business administration, and among academic disciplines such as political science, sociology, economics, and social psychology. A view enjoying increasing popularity is that public management requires specialized skills different from the skills needed in private management. These specialized skills have to do with designing and executing public policies within the framework of a partisan political process. This competes with the view that the similarities in public, private, and non-profit management greatly outweigh the differences, that management is the same in any large organization. Eventually, a single profession of management may emerge. If it does, it will probably be because the regulation and bureaucratization of private activity will blur distinctions between "public" and "private," "political" and "non-political."

Policy Analysis

Policy analysis, too, is in an early stage of definition and development, and later it may succumb to or merge with concurrent developments in the social sciences that emphasize the importance of the content and formation of public policy. For now, however, policy analysis refers to the analysis of public policy problems with the aim of clarifying issues, alternatives, and consequences and thus improving the basis for policy decisions.

Just as the evolution of public management reflects the increasing professionalization and centralization of government activities, the emergence of policy analysis reflects in significant measure the growing demands placed on public officials by the complexity of the issues they face. It must be pointed out that there is something uniquely American about this development. Other Western democracies facing similar social problems have far less developed policy analysis capabilities. Our separate institutions sharing power, the pluralism of our political process, the permeability of the American civil service, and the democratization of higher education all help explain the unique popularity of policy analysis in American policymaking. Whatever the institutional and cultural explanations for the use of policy analysis, the demand for it originates in the kinds of issues with which public officials must contend.

Despite the evidence that these developments in the role of policy analysis are reflections of broad social changes in the role and character of government, they have not been uncontroversial. The principal challenge to them has been most clearly and consistently expressed by Professor Laurence H. Tribe of the Harvard University Law School.[5] In this view, policy analysis, with its methodological bias in favor of economic models and concepts, reflects a "wants orientation" to public choices and a value system built on ever-changing perceptions of immediate self-interest, of benefits and costs expressed in monetary terms. Tribe believes that public policy should be founded on bodies of principle to which we are committed or obligated rather than on calculations of who gains and who loses by specific government actions. The discovery and integration of our values rather than repeated references to analytic frameworks built on self-interest should lie at the heart of policymaking.

This type of concern must be taken seriously by any advocate for analysis. A narrow dependence on benefit-cost calculations to guide policy choice *would*

be inappropriate. This view should not be allowed to obscure a central point, however, which is that the sensitive and sophisticated use of policy analysis can indeed *improve* the bases on which public policy decisions *are made*. They are seldom made on the basis of reflective thought about the proper role of the state, holistic theories about social process, and mature consideration of what social justice requires. Rather they are usually based on incomplete, hasty, and often mistaken formulations of the issues and alternatives. This kind of decisionmaking can be improved by policy analysis. To "improve" in this sense means to make complex issues more intelligible, the range of alternatives more appropriate, and the social consequences of each alternative more evident than they would be if such skills were not used. It is not mere sophistry to suggest that the discovery of those principles that ought to govern particular choices will occur through an analytic process that reveals what is truly at stake.

This, then, is the test of policy analysis: Does it improve the basis for making a decision? If an analysis ignores—or even worse, distorts or dismisses—important issues of principle that policymakers could be expected to recognize and take into account, the analysis itself should be ignored; it will not improve the basis for policy choice. It is often precisely when issue debates are dominated by opposing principles, conflicts over facts, and disagreements over consequences—when policymakers are frozen into fixed positions, paralyzed by doubt, or mesmerized by the struggle for power—that analysis can help most by clarifying issues and by yielding ideas for identifying and better preserving that which we value most. Possession of the ability to know when this is the case is one of the important skills of public management, and one of the subtlest aspects of analytic craftsmanship.

POLICY ANALYSIS FOR DECISIONMAKING

You will learn a great deal about government just by reading the materials in this book. However, the book is not a self-contained text or a primer on policy analysis and its applications; no case book can be. It is assumed that you have acquired or are acquiring a grasp of basic analytic tools and concepts in other courses or from other sources. It is further assumed that you will be studying these cases as part of an organized course or curriculum in which you will be aided by a teacher in working through these materials. The purpose of this book, then, is to help you translate your grasp of technical material into practical, on-the-job skills, whether you aspire to be an analyst or a manager drawing from time to time on the products of analysis.

Not everyone agrees that the practical, professional aspects of policy analysis can be learned in a classroom. Many teachers and practitioners believe that the "non-academic," non-technical aspects of policy analysis are best learned on the job. Indeed, some go farther and assert that the factors that distinguish a competent academic technician from a successful practitioner in government are for the most part intangible and unteachable, rooted as they are in personality, motivation, and styles of organization. Good training, in this view, is a necessary but not a sufficient condition for achieving professional competence; you must also go to work.

There is no substitute for working experience. However, this case book is founded on a different view of what professional education in policy analysis should and can accomplish. This view begins with the observation that every public policy decision is a part of a psychological, social, and political process encompassing far more than the issue at hand. The essence of analysis, as we have stressed, is to use analytic skills to improve the bases on which actual decisions are reached. This requires an understanding not only of the logical structure of policy problems, the usual emphasis of technical training in analytic methods, but also of the decisionmaking processes and the factors shaping them. Analysts who neglect this latter type of understanding tend to produce work that is regarded by decisionmakers as misguided and irrelevant even if it is technically competent.

Mere understanding of decisionmaking contexts is not enough, however. The analyst must design and conduct his or her work in the light of that understanding. Real policy problems typically are messy, ill-defined, and resistant to the straightforward application of formal analytic techniques. An effective policy analysis will be eclectic and *sui generis*, designed to suit the problem and the needs of the decisionmaker who faces it. Coming up with such designs requires cleverness and imagination more than mastery of technique. The policy analyst is properly viewed as a craftsman, creating a useful and stylish product from appropriate materials—data, analytic tools, common sense, non-quantitative evidence—rather than as an applied social scientist or technocrat. A good

analyst will never be perceived as a "hammer looking for a nail." His or her analyses of problems will not be predictable: always in the form of a decision tree, or a benefit-cost analysis, or an econometric model, or a market-failure perspective. Their character will vary with the nature of the task at hand.

Some elaboration of this point of view will be helpful. When first considering a policy issue, an "academic" policy analyst is apt to seek the early identification of a conceptual framework, a formal model if possible, that aids in understanding the fundamental logic of the problem and that provides a frame of reference for selecting policy objectives, identifying alternatives, and assessing their consequences. The analyst attempts to subdue the riot of details attending real world problems into manageable formations as promptly as possible, to view the world through conceptual constructs such as "market failure," "constrained optimization," "benefit-cost analysis," and the like. The analyst working in this tradition is warned that failure to impose these conceptual constructs at a very early stage in decisionmaking leaves him or her vulnerable to the anarchy of "particulars."

An analytic craftsman will begin with a different motivation. The initial question will be: What is the problem as the decisionmaker is likely to view it? What is the decisionmaker's reality that I must address? How is the decision likely to be reached? What are the "particulars"? The analytic craftsman will also want to obtain a conceptual grasp of the problem, but not before obtaining a feel for the texture of the problem, insights into the complex blend of factors that enter into the decisionmaker's natural frame of reference. The approach rests on the belief that attention to concrete details can unleash considerable creative power and artistry and that the resulting analysis is far more likely to help the decisionmaker choose than analysis designed primarily for its logical or methodological appeal.

The point of view of this case book is that fulfillment of these purposes—understanding policymaking contexts and using that understanding in the design, conduct, and use of policy analysis—must be a goal of formal professional education in policy analysis or public management.

ACQUIRING THE ANALYTIC HABIT

An effective means of achieving this educational objective is working through cases of the type included in this book.

The cases cover a wide range of issues of continuing interest, e.g., welfare reform, urban policy, environmental protection, day care, water resources development. They encompass a variety of decision-making contexts: federal, state, and local government; program and regulatory agencies; senior management and staff responsibilities; internal decisionmaking and complex involvements with outside constituencies. They pose intellectual challenges of varying degrees of difficulty, from simply sorting out the issues to assessing a body of conflicting and incomplete data to deciding on the proper role of government. All cases depict actual events and circumstances. The names have *not* been changed, nor has controversial or sensitive material been censored. Every effort has been made to convey accurately the decisionmaking contexts as the participants experienced them.

The use of these cases will enable you to gain practice in defining or conceptualizing policy problems in a way that will aid decisionmakers, choosing analytic approaches from among those you know or are learning or designing new ones, identifying relevant information, constructing persuasive policy arguments, and communicating findings and recommendations in a style suitable to actual decision-making contexts. Cases can help you appreciate the pressures of real time constraints on public officials, the need to make decisions whether or not a scientific and complete understanding of the problem has been achieved, the messiness and ill-defined character of most policy problems, and the extent to which policy decisions are embedded in larger political, bureaucratic, and social contexts. Cases confront you with the real world tensions you must resolve, e.g., between the abstract and the concrete, the objective and the subjective, one social or policy goal and another. By repeatedly working with cases you will come to understand that the domain of ideas and the domain of action are neither separate nor separable and that craft skills are what enable you to relate the one to the other.

There are other advantages to working through these cases. Although cases cannot fully capture the feel of an actual situation—the pressure of deadlines, the subtle influences of personality and interpersonal chemistry, the nuances of political negotiations and bargaining, the frustrations wrought by bureaucratic confusion, conflict, and inertia—they nevertheless provide valuable vicarious experience with governmental situations. Further, a case often provides a fuller and more sharply drawn picture of the realities and nuances of a situation than individual participants had at the time. Learning about government through these kinds of cases may aid you in acquiring more sophisticated standards concerning what ought to be taken into account when approaching complex policy issues than you could get with on-the-job training or an apprenticeship.

The use of cases to teach the uses of analysis in decisionmaking is not without pitfalls. You may wonder if being repeatedly forced to "make decisions" and "make recommendations" after a relatively few hours of study is not an encouragement to superficiality, the policy analysts' version of "shooting from the hip." Would time be better spent on studying analytic methods or on studying fewer issues in greater depth? Perhaps, though this danger has been minimized by structuring the cases so that superficial thinking does not suffice in grappling with the issues they raise. Greater pitfalls, however, lie either in your acquiring technical analytic skills without having to recognize that their ultimate use is in the service of political processes or, worse, in your believing that analytic sophistication has no bearing on effectiveness in the political world. These pitfalls are often encountered when policy analysis and analytic techniques are taught strictly as an academic discipline without constantly testing the principles and methods against the kinds of messy real world situations that cases depict.

REFERENCES

1. Charles E. Lindblom, *The Policy-Making Process* (Englewood Cliffs, New Jersey: Prentice-Hall, Inc., 1968), p. 6.
2. For further discussion of these points, see, for example, Alan Altschuler, "The Study of American Public Administration," in Alan Altschuler, ed., *The Politics of the Federal Bureaucracy* (New York: Dodd, Mead and Co., 1968), pp. 55-72; Harold Seidman, *Politics, Position, and*

Power (New York: Oxford University Press, 1975); and Herbert Emmerich, *Federal Organization and Administrative Management* (University, Alabama: The University of Alabama Press, 1971).

3. Harold Stein, editor, *Public Administration and Policy Development: A Case Book* (New York: Harcourt, Brace and Company, 1952). The introduction to this book is still a fresh and vital essay on public administration, well worth reading.

4. *Ibid.*, p. xii.

5. See, for example, Laurence H. Tribe, "Policy Science: Analysis or Ideology?" *Philosophy and Public Affairs,* Vol. 2, No. 1, Fall 1972, pp. 66–110, and "Ways Not to Think About Plastic Trees," in Laurence H. Tribe, Corinne H. Schelling, and John Voss, editors, *When Values Conflict: Essays on Environmental Analysis, Discourse, and Decision* (Cambridge, Massachusetts: Ballinger Publishing Company, 1976), pp. 61–91.

2

The Policymaking Process

INTRODUCTION

It is common in political debate to hear the assertion, "This country needs a comprehensive national policy on [fill in the blank: youth unemployment, energy conservation, urban development, arms control, you name it]." Assertions such as these are usually buttressed by discussions of the actions of government that relate to the subject at issue but which have conflicting, vague, or undefined goals and uncoordinated, inconsistent, and often ineffective administration. Why should one federal department campaign against smoking while another subsidizes the growing of tobacco? To clear up the confusion, to bring order to program administration, and to increase the scope and effectiveness of government effort, it is said, we need policy.

We should expect a long wait for policy of this character to materialize. Occasionally—the Social Security Act of 1935, the Employment Act of 1946, the so-called Humphrey-Hawkins Act of 1978—Congress legislates what seems to be definitive and unambiguous policy. Even in these cases, however, decisions concerning why and how government shall carry out its putative intent usually raise more questions than answers concerning precisely what policy is. Observe a city government deciding on salary increases for municipal employees, a state legislature reviewing welfare policy, or the federal government choosing means to increase employment and contain inflation. You will not fail to notice that the process of deciding is complex and disorderly, with "no beginning or end, and . . . boundaries . . . which are most uncertain."[1] The parties to decisionmaking often have quite different objectives and dissimilar ideas about what the problem is. Further, decisions may leave the question of objectives unresolved. Even if clear agreement is reached on goals or objectives, the means chosen to carry them out may seem inadequate or inappropriate. In short, the government may have taken action, but what is the policy?

This state of affairs raises problems for the policy analyst. What does it mean to say that analysis should be designed on the basis of an intimate grasp of the policymaking context when such contexts are so muddled and disorderly? How does an analyst of policy choices adapt to circumstances in which clear-cut choices are deliberately (or unconsciously) avoided or obfuscated? One answer, usually offered by successful practitioners, is that you learn by doing; experience is the best teacher of craft skills. If an analyst has good training, the right frame of mind, and perhaps a check list of mistakes to avoid, practice on the job—as with practice teaching, a legal clerkship, or a medical internship—will lead to personal self-confidence and professional competence in dealing with the shapeless character of real decisionmaking. Things may look disorderly at first (or from the outside), but experience will teach one how to be effective.

This view is correct as far as it goes. It is virtually impossible to recreate in a classroom the feel of an actual situation—the pressures and the frustrations associated with confusion, fatigue, conflict, and inertia—and such factors manifestly do affect decisions. Nevertheless, you will learn much more from your experience on the job if you have as much understanding as possible of the nature of the policymaking process before you plunge into it. Much of what appears disorderly and confusing is actually quite explainable, even justifiable, if you begin with realistic expectations concerning the policy process. Helping you appreciate this point is the purpose of this chapter.
the purpose of this chapter.

The volume of literature bearing on policymaking is large and growing. Moreover, studies vary widely in purpose, approach, and quality. In a single chapter we cannot hope to provide a comprehensive assessment of the many important ideas and findings produced by practitioners and researchers over the last few decades. Rather than attempt the impossible, we instead set forth a simple framework of the policymaking process, then use it to review and interpret some of the salient literature on how analysts and analysis relate to that process.

A FRAMEWORK FOR ANALYSIS

The definition of policymaking begins with "*individuals* who often come together in *small groups* within the framework of an *organization* that is characterized by hierarchy, division of labor, and specialization."[2] This formulation, even though restricted, is useful in the analysis of decisionmaking by large executive branch organizations, such as the U.S. Department of Defense or a state department of offender rehabilitation. For the most part, however, no single organization has the authority or power to determine the policy of the government. In our system, power is shared among the numerous entities that comprise the different branches and levels of government. Indeed, even though the power to influence policy may not include each of us as individuals, it surely includes individuals in key positions and individuals who organize themselves around particular interests.

If we employ the overworked term "actor" to characterize an individual, group, or organization with the power to influence policy in some, albeit limited, way, we can say that the policymaking system comprises (a) *actors*, the *sources of their power*, and their *interests*; and (b) the *rules and practices* governing the formal and informal relationships among actors. *Policy* can be viewed as the output of this policymaking system.

Already we have used several undefined terms: policy, power, and interests. We could follow custom and rely on the reader's common sense to define them, but we shall instead offer definitions of these three terms—though with the caution that the definitions are intended as aids to using the materials in this book, not as authoritative statements. *Interests* are occurrences or circumstances that an actor regards as beneficial. *Power* is the ability to bring about, or measurably increase the likelihood of, beneficial occurrences via government action. *Policy* is a specific set of government actions that will, *by design or otherwise,* produce a particular class of effects.

Thus an actor, say the National Organization for Women, will seek policies, say federal financing of day care centers serving all working women, that will advance its interests, say wider work opportunities for women with children. The organization has power to the extent that it can, for example by offering or threatening to withhold electoral support, sway enough congressional votes to increase the chances that day care legislation will pass.

Many other definitions of these concepts are to be found in the policy studies literature. Definitions of policy, for example, range from relatively simple ones similar to the above (political scientist Thomas R. Dye defines public policy as "whatever governments choose to do or not to do"[3]) to elaborate formulations such as "a particular object or set of objects which are intended to be affected . . . [together with] a desired course of events . . . a selected line of action . . . a declaration of intent . . . and an implementation of intent. . . ."[4] The definition used here is unencumbered by concepts such as "choosing" or "intent" which are ambiguous and, further, are difficult if not impossible to observe in practice. It is especially helpful in interpreting the character of government actions.

If policy is viewed as government actions that are associated with particular kinds of effects, it follows that government at all levels is continuously "producing" policies. These policies may lack certain desirable properties. Government actions producing similar effects, say increased use of day care by working women, may not be well coordinated. Their precise intent may not be clear. They may appear to be based on differing views of the problem to which they are a response. As a result, some people, though apparently needy, may be ineligible for benefits. But these government actions, despite their collective shortcomings, constitute policy nonetheless. The policymaking process, then, is that process by which the character of government actions is determined.

In the following sections, we shall attempt to present salient ideas concerning how key elements of the policymaking "system" influence policy.

THE INDIVIDUAL DECISIONMAKER

As the discussion in chapter 1 indicated, the purpose of this book is to equip you to use analytic skills to improve the basis for policy decisions. A decisionmaker will not inevitably make better choices just because he or she is presented with a sophisticated, "rational" policy analysis. The extensive literature, originating in several disciplines, on individual decisionmaking reveals a wide variety of perspectives on how people think about and reach decisions. To give you a sense of the implications of this literature for policymaking and for the role of analysis, we first sketch the model of decisionmaking that undergirds much of the policy analysis literature. Then we create a contrasting perspective by drawing on research on decisionmaking from various disciplines.

The Rational Actor

Much of the literature on the practices and techniques for analyzing policies is based explicitly or implicitly on a model of policymaking that has come to be known as the "rational actor" model.[5] In this model, actors—for example, a commissioner of youth services, the administrator of the U.S. Environmental Protection Agency, a city manager, or the head of the National Organization for Women—are assumed to behave purposefully and rationally. That is, their actions are: (a) oriented toward explicit, consciously chosen goals; (b) mutually consistent; and (c) designed to enhance, perhaps maximize, the achievement of their interests.

In the political process, actors with shared interests are assumed to combine their power to bring about policies to their liking, compromising where necessary to obtain the best possible outcome. Thus, the National Organization for Women, the Child Welfare League, the AFL–CIO, and the American Public Welfare Association might join forces to seek passage of comprehensive day care legislation. They would work with supportive legislators, seek to persuade uncommitted legislators, and mobilize public support for the most effective government action they can obtain.

Policy analysis is central to policymaking when decisionmakers are assumed to be rational. The role of the analyst, or of the analytically-minded actor, is to identify government actions that will "maximize benefits," achieve an optimal outcome in meaningful terms, or at least unambiguously improve the extent to which policy goals are achieved. The analyst seeks to specify goals, clarify issues, design alternative courses of action, and assess the possible consequences of each alternative in order to facilitate rational choice. Powerful analytic tools can, if appropriate, be mobilized for these purposes. Indeed, it is important to increase the power of these tools—i.e., the speed and precision with which complex problems can be analyzed—because the rationality of choice will thereby be increased. For example, a detailed computer simulation model may reveal more of the complex effects of a decision, thereby aiding the decisionmaker in making a more rational choice.

Needless to say, policies are not typically the product of clear-cut choice and cooperative action. The usual situation is one of conflict among actors based on differences in interests, objectives, and perceptions of the situations in which they find themselves. Increasingly, scholars of decisionmaking within the rational actor framework have focused on collective decision situations characterized by conflicting interests and perceptions, by high degrees of uncertainty, severe limitations on the availability of information, and cognitive complexity, by reliance on different kinds of decision rules, such as voting procedures, and by complex interactions among the actions of some individuals and the effects these actions have on others. Much of the didactic literature on policy analysis duly notes the recurrence of situations involving bargaining, compromise, and interactions among actors and suggests models and other approaches for dealing with them.

Some powerful propositions with important policy implications emerge from this work. For example, perfectly rational behavior by individuals may lead to results that virtually all regard as unsatisfactory.[6] (The corollary proposition is that the collective outcome you observe is not necessarily the outcome any individual prefers or believes is the best that can be attained.) Voting by individuals, each of whom can consistently rank alternatives, may produce collective rankings of the same alternatives that are inconsistent. In general, as a field for further work, procedural rationality, i.e., determining which procedures for choosing among alternatives will lead to good choices, is thought by some researchers to be more promising than substantive rationality, i.e., determining which set of government actions maximizes benefits.[7]

Whatever the intellectual structure of the problem, the rationalist view is that "problems"—matters about which public officials must decide—are a product of the organizational, political, and socioeconomic environment. Things are not as they should be. A public official and his or her staff become aware that a problem exists and immerse themselves in it in order to bring matters into sharp focus. They study the problem, then either decide, or choose a strategy, or prepare to react to events, or do whatever is rational under the circumstances.

The Cognitive-Emotional Actor*

An altogether different picture of how actors make choices and decisions results from taking into account the psychological dimensions of decisionmaking. Cognitive psychology suggests the value of viewing the human mind as an information-processing system. Over time, a person, for the most part quite unconsciously, develops patterned ways of processing incoming information. Because of the complexity of this information, the processes for storing, evaluating, and using it necessarily involve the devising of structures that order and simplify the world. These structures take the form of beliefs, images, or other models and ideas about reality that become the basis for interpreting sensory data. The individual needs such mental constructs in order to make sense of what would otherwise be an overwhelming amount of information.

Individuals differ widely in how they process information. They differ in the types and complexity of the structures they use and in the ways by which they create, modify, or validate these structures, i.e., learn. James L. McKenney and Peter G. W. Keen have developed what they call a "model of cognitive style."[8] Their idea is that people differ fundamentally both in how they process and in how they evaluate information. With respect to processing, *preceptive* individuals test incoming sensory data against preformed concepts, whereas *receptive* thinkers focus more on the details and are more inductive in interpreting them. With respect to evaluation, *intuitive* thinkers employ trial-and-error methods and respond to cues in ways they are not always able to verbalize; *systematic* thinkers structure and analyze information using explicit methods or algorithms. The authors' central argument is that:

> decisionmaking is above all situational and, therefore, includes problem finding. The manager scans his environment and organizes what he perceives. His efforts are as much geared to clarifying his values and intents as to dealing with predefined problems.[9]

McKenney and Keen further postulate that thinkers of a particular type are better suited to some

---

*Use of this term in this context has been suggested to me by Chris Argyris.

management contexts than to others. For example, intuitive thinkers may have trouble mastering details that must be understood in methodical sequences, but they may perform well when information is lacking, problems are unstructured, and uncertainties are dominant. At times, policy analysts may be tempted to regard intuitive, less systematic thinkers as less competent or intelligent, but this is a mistake. Exceedingly bright officials may nevertheless be intuitive and preceptive and react with impatience to carefully structured, systematic staff work. They may be the ones who *appear* to shoot from the hip or who quickly and restlessly toss out ideas and proposals and who make up their minds in a seemingly unsystematic way. Their solutions may nonetheless be good ones, even inspired ones considering the complexity and pressure of many decision situations.

Whatever their style, human beings in decisionmaking and choice situations will be seeking to fulfill certain cognitive and emotional needs. Individuals typically strive for certainty, stability, simplicity, and consistency in their images of reality and their beliefs about the world. They will employ a variety of psychological and other means to protect themselves from threats to these highly valued states of mind.

When faced with complexity and uncertainty, for example, decisionmakers will resort to their belief systems or cognitive maps of reality when designing their reactions. If the designs are to work, they must be considered valid, so certainty is imputed to them. Further, relatively simple and unambiguous belief systems will be preferred to complicated formulations that heighten awareness of uncertainty and conflicts among values or goals.

Incoming information is likely to be processed in a way that preserves stability and continuity of beliefs.[10] A decisionmaker may ignore facts or events of obvious importance, be unwilling to consider opposing arguments or views, or shift ground repeatedly in maintaining commitment to a course of action that is consistent with ingrained beliefs or images of reality. Thus problems, the existence of complex tradeoffs, and evidence inconsistent with a chosen course of action may go unrecognized or literally unrecorded in the decisionmaker's mind. Whereas all of us have psychological tendencies of this kind, some

people exhibit these tendencies in more extreme form. These tendencies may serve them well, as when they persevere in the face of numerous distractions to reach a solution that works, or they may lead to outcomes that are self-destructive because of the decisionmaker's inability to change his or her views or alter incorrect beliefs.

There may be a fundamental difference, moreover, between the approaches to decisionmaking public officials say they use—their "espoused theories"—and the approaches they actually employ—their "theories in use." Chris Argyris and Donald Schön argue, for example, that whatever their espoused theories, most people have the same theory-in-use.[11] According to their model, people behave in ways that are consistent with four governing values: they want to achieve their purposes; they want to win, not lose; they want to suppress negative feelings; and they want to emphasize rationality. In pursuit of these values, people tend to seek control—literal psychological and hierarchical control—over their environment and to regulate incoming information. The result is that they erect barriers to real learning. People will not submit their ideas to potentially disconfirming tests, to feedback which might be critical or pose problems; they "will tend to play it safe; they are not going to violate their governing values and upset others, especially if the others have power";[12] and they will process only that information which is within "acceptable" limits, i.e., they will engage in the kind of mechanical learning characteristic of servo-mechanisms. Though done for self-protection, this behavior can lead to precisely the kinds of negative consequences they are seeking to avoid: fundamental discontinuities between their actions and the realities to which these actions are a response.

Confronted with complexity, conflict, and uncertainty, a decisionmaker may experience genuine stress, frustration, anxiety, and self-doubt. These emotional responses to the situation may not be evident to staff or colleagues, but their underlying presence may explain much of the decisionmaker's observed behavior. For example, induced by stress a decisionmaker may ignore or deny the existence of a value conflict, or even abandon or downgrade one of the values at stake. In the face of uncertainty, and the realization that calculated risks must be taken, a decisionmaker may procrastinate, hoping that something better will turn up. Alternatively, the decisionmaker may make a decision prematurely, hoping to eliminate the stressful situation, or decide in effect to see only the advantages of one particular course of action and only the disadvantages of others, thus minimizing the painfulness of the choice and the perceived magnitude of the risks. He or she may adopt a wide variety of rationalizations that distort or bias the assessment of available information, all toward the end of increasing confidence that the chosen course of action is clearly the right one.

In short, decisionmakers may unconsciously employ a variety of psychological ploys or props to alleviate stress and eliminate self-doubt. These psychological tendencies, which are present in everyone, are magnified and shaped by attributes of personality, emotional state, intelligence, motivation, and cognitive style. They may lead to individual leadership or managerial performance that ranges from brilliant to ineffective and completely inconsistent with the nature of the problem at hand.

Real Actors

It should be clear from the discussion so far that some public officials will be much more receptive to systematic analysis, and more likely to rely on it when facing critical choices, than others. However, even officials whose cognitive style is receptive and systematic may resist ideas and information inconsistent with what they believe or know to be true. Even if they say they are suspending judgment and want to hear all sides of an issue, their values and beliefs are coming into play constantly in sorting and evaluating what they hear and read. They may have preconceptions about the social goals of government action (or inaction), the ways in which people and institutions behave and the reasons for their behavior, and the procedures that ought to be followed in making decisions. For some officials, such preconceptions may be merely starting points in the thought process; such individuals may be quite flexible and adaptive, especially when they are addressed from within a frame of reference they can readily understand. For others, such preconceptions may be filters for dissonant information; their eyes may glaze over as discussion wanders away from familiar ground.

Stress may reinforce existing tendencies or introduce unpredictable elements into a decisionmaking situation. Afflicted with doubt, an official may seek to shore up self-confidence by exaggerated activity, speeded-up round-the-clock group discussions, demands for complicated analysis within tight deadlines, numerous phone calls to friends or experts, emotional exhortations to staff, or abrupt changes of direction as new thoughts are injected into the process. Pressure, or the perception of it, can bring out the best or the worst in an official.

In fact, it would be quite irrational—another appropriate term is non-functional—for a decisionmaker to suppress emotional, needs-based reactions to a problem situation, that is, to ignore internal, latent, personal goals and focus only on external, impersonal, "analytical" ones. As Herbert Simon has noted, "Almost all explanations of pathological behavior in the psychoanalytic literature . . . explain the patient's illness in terms of the functions it performs for him."[13] The rational actor in the simplistic sense described on pages 11–12 above—an official whose decisionmaking performance is not affected by cognitive limits, needs for stability and assurance, and preference for single-valued criteria for choice— does not exist.

An important implication of these considerations is that the "problems" on which policy analysts work should not be viewed as malfunctions in social arrangements that any "objective" official will see in the same light: leaking social pipes that need government repair. More often than not problems are highly subjective interpretations of reality by individual officials. The analyst-as-craftsman cannot define the "problem" to be addressed by a policy analysis without taking into account the perceptions of the audience for the analysis. The policy analyst must attempt to see the world as the decisionmaker sees it and design the analysis with his or her concerns explicitly in view. If the analyst believes that significant changes in a decisionmaker's perspectives are needed to achieve an improvement in the policymaking process, considerable thought must be devoted not only to how the analysis is designed, but also to how its conclusions are presented or discussed. An analyst who fails to recognize a decisionmaker's cognitive style and characteristics risks being ignored.

GROUPS AND GROUPTHINK

Individuals involved in policymaking often find themselves participating in small groups. They may be compelled to be involved by external authority—the governor or the agency head convening a task force, executive committee, or working group—or they may choose to create or be part of a group in order to get emotional or cognitive assistance in solving a problem. Small groups are pervasive in policymaking.

It is often assumed for convenience that whatever is said about individual actors as decisionmakers also holds for groups, or even for organizations. This assumption obscures an important fact. Group processes often have a distinctive, even a decisive, influence on policy quite apart from the characteristics of individual members.

A small group may bring together people with different perceptions, perspectives, and specialized knowledge, and interactions among them may produce a much better analysis of the problem than any individual could produce in the same amount of time. Indeed, this often happens. As anyone who has participated in group problem-solving or decisionmaking can testify, however, other things happen in groups, and the whole is not always greater than the sum of the parts. Some research has shown, for example, that individual decisions are more creative, but group decisions tend to be more thorough in that they leave out fewer important considerations and explore implications more thoroughly. However, all of the psychological and emotional factors discussed above are likely to become involved when members of a group interact with one another, and the results may vary widely.

One of the most popular theses concerning group performance is that of Irving L. Janis.[14] Based on his study of public policy "fiascos," he coined the term "groupthink," which "refers to a deterioration of mental efficiency, reality testing, and moral judgment that results from in-group pressures."[15] Groups that are especially vulnerable in groupthink are those that are cohesive, screened from outside scrutiny, and strongly led. Victims of groupthink fail to analyze all the relevant alternatives, are biased in assessing evidence, seek little outside help or advice, fail to reexamine early agreements or choices, and neglect implementation problems. They seek mutual concurrence—unanimity, conformity—and reject threats to achieving it. Why? A likely reason is that groupthink is a device for alleviating the stresses of decisionmaking induced by a situation that creates self-doubt, anxiety, or threats to the self-esteem of group members. This is especially likely in situations where a practical decision may appear to violate a humanitarian ideal or principle. The kinds of psychological props and ploys that an individual would employ in such circumstances are reinforced by the concurrence-seeking behavior of the group.

The pressures to conform are apparently more general than those characteristic of groupthink situations. Alexander George states that:

> [Some] kind of bargaining process is likely to operate within the group, even if members are unaware of it. . . . Typically this bargaining process works in the direction of conformity, with group members interacting to reduce variances in behavior and to crystallize attitudes and beliefs.[16]

Unless they possess great status or prestige, dissidents, whatever the merits of their views, may find themselves under pressure to moderate their views, perhaps under the implied threat of expulsion from the group. The warnings or skepticism that dissidents often contribute, and which can be so important to high quality analysis of a problem, may be ignored or worse: discredited.

The need-fulfilling view of individual decisionmaking might be interpreted to predict that some groups will be hard pressed to accomplish anything.

> [The] role of bargaining as traditionally understood will be sharply diminished. . . . The limited outcome calculations, the single-value focus, and the dependence on selected feedback channels, should all retard the process of accommodation. If, because of the peculiarities of a given decision problem, conflict among the separate actors is relatively intense, then the overall decision process should display less coherence than that produced by mutual accommodations among analytic actors.[17]

The nature of the group process is not independent of the attitudes and behavior of the group's leader or of the authority that convened it. An executive can establish norms or decision rules that will affect the group's behavior. If he or she indicates a preference for unanimity over conflict and disagreement, shows a liking for views that are consistent with previously stated beliefs, or abhors numbers, economic arguments, or the invocation of moral imperatives, the group may well go along, especially if one of the members steadfastly enforces such standards. If the leader communicates no particular expectations or norms, however, rank or status differentiation, or dominant ideologies within the organization, are likely to be reflected in the group's behavior. Thus an "in-house" group established "to critically review our whole policy" may be incapable of doing any such thing.

Still other research has shown the influence of whether the group is well-established or has been newly created and of whether there is high or low internal conflict.[18] On the one hand, internal conflict may be much more threatening to an *ad hoc* group and can lead to recommendations or solutions that represent compromise for its own sake. In an established group, on the other hand, conflict can be productive of uniquely creative solutions to a problem because individual members do not feel that the cohesiveness of the group is threatened by sharp disagreements.

Thus a group product can be greater than the sum of its individual parts, or considerably less, depending on a wide range of variables. A group may enhance the influence of an individual's creative ideas or suppress any kind of dissidence, creative or not. A group may promote action or retard it. A policymaking process that involves group effort is likely to produce different policy ideas, recommendations, or decisions than one that does not.

What does this mean to the practicing policy analyst? A staff analyst may come into contact with group processes in several ways. The analyst's "client," the audience for the analysis, may be involved in a group decisionmaking process. The analyst may be part of a staff group drawn from within his or her office, from within the agency, or from several agencies. These groups may be tightly knit, with the members expected to function as a team, or they may be confederations of autonomous agency representatives. Whatever the variant, the analyst must interact with others and confront their ideas, perspectives, cognitive processes, and approaches to analysis. This is likely to require social and intellectual skills of a much higher order, and a greater tolerance for give-and-take, than those needed to produce an individual staff analysis and explain it to a single superior.

The Bureaucratic Influence

Individuals and groups function within the context of an organization which is typically characterized by hierarchy, division of labor, and specialization. We have already suggested that the organizational context can influence individual and group behavior. Organizations are more than mere collections of individuals.[19] A variety of accounts and propositions concerning life and behavior within organizations—Parkinson's Law, the Peter Principle, Michael Maccoby's *The Gamesman*,[20] and Anthony Downs' *Inside Bureaucracy*,[21] for example—have contributed to the widespread popular impression that organizational contexts powerfully shape how people act. Indeed, the aphorism "Where you stand depends on where you sit" suggests the limitations on the free will of an executive. What in general can be said about the relationships between organizational context and individual or group decisionmaking?

In *The Essence of Decision*, Graham Allison fashioned what he termed the "organizational process model" of policymaking. Instead of viewing policy decisions as the product of rational choice by an actor, this model views them as the outputs of large organizations functioning according to regular or routinized patterns of behavior. This formulation is suggestive of the relationships we are looking for.

Individuals and groups are participants in, and their behavior presumably reflects at least in some measure, the organization's internal processes. One form of individual and group influence on the organization, then, is their success in modifying or circumventing these standard or routine processes. Circumvention can be quite simple: An agency head may ignore standard consultation processes and publicly commit his or her agency to a position on an issue. Such actions are also risky; the "organization," i.e., subordinate units hostile to the action, may be defiant and notify political opponents of the decision that standard procedures were violated—e.g., "the professionals were not consulted"—and possibly undermine the agency head. To avoid such risks, the agency head may employ more complicated devices to modify routine such as establishing a small group, the real purpose of which is to reallocate access to the decisionmaking process by admitting members who would have been cut out of the regular routines.

The reverse can also occur: The influence may flow from the organization to the individuals. This proposition can be developed on several levels. On an instrumental level, organizational routines may be designed to minimize the influence on decisions of particular individuals or groups or to guarantee a kind of internal equilibrium among competing interests. Early studies in the field of administrative science might be interpreted as directed at the goal of designing standard operating procedures for government agencies that would guarantee efficient programs no matter who is running the place. At a more organic level, many of the more recent studies of organizations view the development of internal organizational arrangements as reflections of human cognitive processes. The human mind seeks to order reality in ways that will reduce uncertainty, complexity, and instability. Internal organizational arrangements are designed to do the same things. James G. March and Herbert A. Simon state the proposition that "the basic features of organizational structure and function derive from the characteristics of human problem-solving processes. . . ."[22] That is, organizational functions become routinized, specialized, and compartmentalized and decisionmaking becomes standardized according to relatively simple decision rules. From then on, in Robert F. Coulam's expression, "the organization regiments the belief structures of those who comprise it."[23]

The effects of the internal structure of an organization are likely to have a considerable influence on policymaking because of their effects on the flow of information. Hierarchy, for example, produces a phenomenon called "uncertainty absorption":

> a marked tendency for the critical uncertainties identified in policy analyses provided by experts at lower levels of the organization to be left out, de-emphasized, or presented in an oversimplified or one sided manner when summaries of these analyses are transmitted upward to top level officials. . . . The inadequacies of such summaries can easily reinforce rather than counter-balance the psychological tendency of policy-makers to deal with complex issues by squeezing them into pre-existing but perhaps inappropriate cognitive categories and repertoires of action.[24]

Specialization produces a tendency on the part of specialized units to hoard information and use it selectively to achieve power and position.[25] The size of an organization—the "height" of its hierarchies, width of the top official's span of control, the numbers and complexity of internal processes—matter, too; communication problems are greater in larger, more complex organizations. An analyst, whose business it is to obtain information and use it to inform policy choices, will be affected by all of these factors.

Thus, a practicing policy analyst, in addition to being intellectually and socially skillful, must be a good bureaucrat. He or she must have some understanding of how the organization actually functions, of who has power, of who has information, and of the incentives to which people with power and information respond. To cite just one example, the professional employees of a subordinate bureau may have a stronger identification with their profession than with the narrow interests of their bureau. By understanding this and approaching them as professionals, a policy analyst may unlock important sources of advice and information. If this is not the case, a very different approach to obtaining the needed help may be required.

The general point is that a policy decision is the product of an interplay of intrapersonal and interpersonal factors, of factors relating to individual, group, and organizational behavior. The effects of these considerations on the role and use of policy analysis and analytic approaches to policy decisions are obvious, but exceedingly complex and therefore difficult to categorize in any neat way. But we are not done yet. There is the matter of the political system.

THE POLITICAL PROCESS*

Some governmental organizations have apparently unlimited power to take certain actions with external impact: making grants, issuing permits, awarding contracts, establishing certain rules or regulations, and the like. For most actions, however, including virtually all matters of significance, government agencies are not autonomous; their actions are subject to review, modification, or veto by others: other executive agencies, the legislature, the courts, powerful associations, even the voters aroused to action by administrative ineptitude. Even when an organization apparently has the unrestricted power to act, it usually must be mindful of the reactions of those affected, lest restrictions later be imposed. Thus, with respect to the

---

*In the preparation of this section, I have benefitted from the ideas of Michael H. Madow.

achievement of policy objectives, power is shared, and organizations must be viewed as part of a wider political system. Just as the decisions of an individual both influence and are influenced by group and organizational dynamics, the outputs or decisions of organizations both influence and are influenced by the political system. The question is, what can we say *in general* about these interrelationships?

As we have seen, generalizing about individual, group, and organizational behavior and the interactions among them is hard enough. As we move out of the confined contexts of organizations into the political system, the difficulties of generalizing are compounded. Political processes, and the social, cultural, and economic milieu within which they are embedded, are so complex that simplifying concepts or models often seem too abstract or limited to be helpful. Indeed, it may seem fruitless to look for rules encompassing direct, instrumental connections between social and political forces, on the one hand, and specific organizational decisions and the analyses that inform them, on the other.

Before endorsing this view, however, it will be helpful to survey briefly some of the approaches that have been taken on this subject to see if helpful generalizations exist. This is not an easy task. As an aid to sorting through them, we shall reformulate our problem and our questions in the following way.

We are interested in how the *content of policy*, i.e., the specific character or design of governmental actions that advance certain interests, is determined. What is the role of specific actors in policy determination?

Academic interest in studying the content of policy is of relatively recent origin. Nevertheless, several distinct types of approaches have emerged.

Models of Bureaucratic Politics

Organizations such as the federal Department of Health, Education and Welfare, a state department of environmental protection, or a city sanitation department are not autonomous. Their concerns and activities often overlap with those of other agencies or departments at the same or other levels of government. They are subject to various policies, resource constraints, and procedural requirements emanating from the central authority: the President, the Governor, or the Mayor. Thus leaders and other key members of each organization have necessarily become involved with a variety of other actors in the course of policymaking. Graham Allison has observed:

> This milieu necessitates that government decisions and actions result from a political process. In this process, sometimes one group committed to a course of action triumphs over other groups fighting for other alternatives. Equally often, however, different groups pulling in different directions produce . . . a resultant—a mixture of conflicting preferences and unequal power of various individuals—distinct from what any person or group intended.[26]

Sometimes the playing out of bureaucratic politics resembles the group processes discussed above. This kind of process is apt to occur when the President or the Governor assembles his or her top advisers on an issue and asks them to agree on a matter. More often, the process is less tightly knit and varies with such factors as the hierarchical structure of the relationships among the actors, the familiarity of the participants with each other, the extent to which authority is decentralized, and the penetration of the process by outside influences.

From an organization's perspective, a variety of unwelcome things can happen to a policy proposal as it is processed by "the administration." More powerful advocates may smother it. It may be so quickly accepted that its flaws remain hidden until a later, more inconvenient time. It may be modified or amended along lines that substantially weaken it from the proposing organization's perspective. It may, accidentally or otherwise, be labelled or advocated in misleading ways and therefore be decided or amended on the wrong grounds. Important qualifying or supporting arguments may be omitted from the discussion leading to misperceptions and erroneous judgments by the decisionmaker.

From the chief executive's standpoint, the possible malfunctions associated with bureaucratic politics are likely to be viewed quite differently. A chief executive may not hear all the alternatives or be able to appraise them fully if none of the parties has an interest in seeing things precisely his or her way. Issues or conflicts may be deliberately suppressed or glossed over. Unpopular, threatening, or disruptive ideas may never be mentioned. All may fall victim to groupthink.

Perhaps the salient difference between an intra-organizational and an inter-organizational decision-making context, however, is the participants' ties, informal and otherwise, to external constituencies and to partisan, legislative politics. Objectives, issues, alternatives, evaluations, and choice—all the elements of a policy analysis—are interrelated in various ways with the wider political process. The next few sections outline several approaches to thinking about this process.

Systems Models

Systems approaches to policy determinations are founded on the work of political scientist David Easton.[27] These approaches seek to explain policy outputs—variously defined as government expenditures on welfare, education, highways, and the like—in terms of the social/political/economic environment (e.g., the level of education of the citizenry, degree of urbanization, per capita income or wealth) and of characteristics of the political process (e.g., party structure and competition, legislative apportionment among different classes of voters, and voter participation). The basic questions raised by this approach are: How do environmental factors affect the character of the political system? How do characteristics of the political system affect the content of public policies? How do environmental factors directly affect the content of public policy?[28] Empirical studies in this tradition generally seek statistical associations among environmental, process, and output variables for different political jurisdictions—states, counties, and localities—at a given point in time. (A typical question is, will a more educated citizenry, or will the level of economic development more generally, be associated with higher levels of spending on public welfare?)

Many of these studies have found significant correlations between environmental factors, primarily the level of social and economic development, and policy outputs such as expenditures on public services, but little correlation between environmental and process variables or between process and output variables. A recent study by Harold L. Wilensky, for example, compared health and welfare policies among sixty-two countries with different political systems and levels of economic development and concluded that "economic growth is the ultimate cause of welfare state development."[29] The implication of such findings is that the political process is a "black box" that is largely irrelevant to the determination of policy outputs as defined in the studies. The political system is a neutral transmission mechanism without any significant effect on policy outputs.

Such studies have been criticized on a variety of grounds, many of them technical. In a substantive vein, investigators have argued that more sophisticated definitions of policy outputs and the characteristics of political processes will reveal complex interrelationships among them. One study, for example, showed that city expenditures on planning and amenities are greatly influenced by policymakers' value orientations, their perceptions of the city's problems, their predelictions, their beliefs about the future, and so on.[30] That is, the cognitive approaches of individual policymakers discussed above may well matter.

Power Models

An analytically and methodologically distinct set of approaches focuses directly and in a detailed way on the political process and the loci of power within it. Perhaps the dominant approach within this set is associated with the term "pluralism." According to pluralists, policy is determined largely by the competition among "groups" pursuing specific interests according to "rules" governing the political process. (The term "group," as used here, in contrast to its use above, refers to an association of relatively like-minded people pursuing a specific interest or set of interests.) A compact characterization of pluralism is that it focuses "on *behavior* in the making of *decisions* on *issues* over which there is an observable *conflict* of (subjective) *interests*, seen as express policy preferences, revealed by political participation."[31]

The dominant method of study employed by pluralists has been the case study. Such studies typically identify an important and controversial issue or decision, identify the individuals and interest groups involved in its resolution, study the behavior of all involved parties, and make inferences about the relative influence of these parties on the basis of observed behavior and the resulting outcome.

A contrasting approach is associated with the term "elitism." Elitists see public policies as the product, not of a polycentric bargaining process, but of the interests and values of ruling or governing elites which are relatively immune from popular influence and which exercise authority in a hierarchical fashion. According to this view, changes in policy reflect changes in the interests or values of powerful elites. Earlier versions of elite theory stressed the central importance in resource allocation of those who control large organizations—corporations, the military, private associations, government agencies. More recent versions see elite influence as a more subtle phenomenon involving controls over the policy agenda, i.e., the power to exclude issues from serious public debate or to define issues in ways that do not threaten elite interests. By focussing on what has happened, proponents of this view will say, pluralists fail to notice the importance of factors which prevent things from happening, thereby missing the vital but submerged role played by powerful elites.

Policy Content Approaches

Still another category of approach is founded on the view that the process of policy determination depends on the characteristics of the policy being studied. Theodore Lowi, for example, distinguishes policies in terms of their expected short-run impact on society.[32] His categories include: distributive policies—those perceived as providing tangible benefits to identifiable interest groups; redistributive policies—those perceived as equalizing the availability of benefits by shifting resources from some groups to others; regulatory policies—those that establish rules or procedures governing the activities of public and private organizations and individuals; and constituency policies—those perceived as benefitting identifiable constituents. The thesis is that there is no single theory of politics or policy determination. Policies determine political relationships rather than the other way around. Lowi argues, for example, that distributive policies differ from redistributive policies in the locus and nature of decisionmaking. Distributive decisions are made in congressional committees and within administrative agencies through a process of log-rolling and mutual non-interference; redistributive decisions are a product of bureaucratic conflict in the executive branch involving clashes among classes and ideologies.

The idea that the content of policy is an independent as well as a dependent variable is not necessarily inconsistent with systems, pluralist, or elitist approaches. One study in the systems tradition, for example, provides evidence that party competition, a characteristic of the political process, is more important to policy determination if the policy issue is perceived as being associated with the struggle between "haves" and "have nots."[33]

Analytic Approaches

A final category of approaches we shall mention is distinguished mainly by their reliance on non-operational analytic frameworks within which policy outputs can be explained. A good example is Anthony Downs' "issue attention cycle."[34] Public cnosideration of certain issues proceeds through the following cycle: (1) a "pre-problem state," the period just prior to which the public has become aware of an undesirable social condition; (2) a period of "alarmed discovery and euphoric enthusiasm," during which there is widespread determination to do something about the condition; (3) a period during which there is "realization of the cost of significant progress" and of the tradeoffs that solving the problem would require; (4) "gradual decline of intense public interest" as discouragement, boredom, or reluctance take hold; and (5) "the post-problem state" during which the issue moves into "a prolonged limbo—a twilight realm of lesser attention or spasmodic recurrences of interest." The issues that are most likely to go through this cycle are those which (a) involve a problem affecting only a minority of the public, (b) require actions that are perceived to impose costs on the majority, and (c) have no intrinsically exciting qualities.

A different way to think about policy issues is offered by Roger W. Cobb and Charles D. Elder.[35] Focussing on the question of how a policy issue can attract wide public attention, they argue that policy issues can be characterized in terms of five "dimensions": (1) "specificity"; (2) "social significance"; (3) "temporal relevance," that is, its perceived timeliness; (4) "complexity"; and (5) "categorical precedence," that is, the novelty of the actions needed to address it. For an issue to gain mass recognition, they advise, it "should be defined or redefined . . . as ambiguously as possible, with implications for as many people as possible, involving issues other than the dispute in question, with no categorical precedence, and as simply as feasible."[36]

Still a different approach is that of James E. Anderson, who views policymaking as a "sequential pattern of activity (that is, a process) in which a number of functional categories of activity can be distinguished."[37] These categories are: (1) "problem formation and agenda setting," (2) "policy formulation," (3) "policy adoption," (4) "policy implementation," and (5) "policy evaluation." "In actuality," he says, "policy-making often does follow in sequence the pattern of activities listed above."[38]

Approaches such as these attempt to impose some explanatory order on a reality that is exceedingly complex. From the perspective of this book, they suffer from the defect that their analytic categories are vague, overlapping, and difficult to verify operationally. They do not yield a wealth of useful prescriptions to practitioners. Their main value is in providing a variety of ideas and insights that may prove helpful in explaining what is happening in specific cases. In the Connecticut Enforcement Project case for example, participants were aware that they were in a period of "gradual decline of intense public interest" in environmental protection, and their ideas and tactics were chosen accordingly. Other applications will occur to you as you read the cases.

ECONOMY, SOCIETY, AND CULTURE

For all that has been said about the actors, institutions, and procedures of the policymaking process, little or nothing has been said about the basic character of the American state and how it influences policy, or more appropriately, how policy reflects our character as a people, our methods of self-government, and basic changes in society and the economy. The fragmented, disorderly, and incremental character of American policy has its tap root in the Constitution, with its separation of powers, federal organization, checks and balances, and other features that define our political processes. Periods of increasing birth rates can be expected to be followed by gradually increasing priorities for education; declining birth rates and increased longevity will gradually shift attention to the older population. Deeply ingrained beliefs that the able-bodied should work will limit the range of possibilities for reforming the welfare system. A deteriorating physical housing stock will lead to pressures for renewal, relocation, or reforms. An increasing ratio of retired to employed workers will affect the financial viability of pension plans. When

air and water pollution become patently offensive, people will demand action.

Not all policymaking involves the wider society, engages our most deeply held values and beliefs, and becomes the subject of sustained media coverage and public debate. A great many issues engage the attention primarily of our elected and senior appointed officials. At the federal level, issues such as labor law reform, aid to education, and community development, to name a few, are of this character.

There is still a third level of policymaking, moreover. It centers at the middle management level of executive agencies, the senior aide level in legislatures, the special assistant level to elected chief executives, and relatively senior levels of budget, financial management, and personnel offices. Issues at this level are for the "specialists." Such issues typically concern the technical design features of policies—definitions of eligibility, income, residence, disability, household, etc. These issues can have price tags of hundreds of millions or even billions of dollars, and they must usually be ratified by constitutionally designated officials. But their substance is thrashed out at much lower levels of government, a simple necessity in a government as complex as ours.

As you might expect, the adept political operator or advocate will seek to have his or her issue dealt with at the level where favorable action is thought to be most likely. This can mean either taking the issue to the people—farmers or the poor marching on Washington—or working out a deal among the specialists.

This framework suggests a rather elaborate set of possibilities for explaining political behavior, which we will not be able to discuss here. Suffice it to say that the play of power, and the role of analysis, will be different depending on whether the wider public, the elected officials, or the specialists are the key actors.

SO WHAT?

If you have come this far, you may be tempted to believe that cognitive styles, groupthink, elite domination of policy agendas, issue-attention cycles, and demographic shifts constitute an impenetrable, trackless thicket. To hack a pathway through such concepts while also trying to get the numbers right may seem futile, or worse: beside the point. For the analyst-as-craftsman to clarify issues and alternatives through artistry and imagination in using concepts and data, discrimination and good taste are essential. Does one really need to rummage among the journals to find out why a cabinet officer may prefer to get truth from *The Readers' Digest*?

A good way to clarify the purpose of this collage of ideas and findings is to note a common occurrence in the analytic community. Policy analysts or analysts-as-managers who have become capable craftsmen often present their work to predominantly academic audiences. Their discussions are not uncommonly met with sharp criticism or even incredulity on the part of researchers who find the analysts' work lacking in refinement, elegance, completeness, or sufficient appreciation of the shortcomings of models, methods, or data. "This is really a programming problem, isn't it?" "You ignored several interesting objectives." "These data hardly constitute proof." "Why assume the financing formula can't be changed?"

Leaving aside instances of sheer incompetence, the differences between a policy analysis done to meet an official's needs and one done primarily to satisfy the internal logic of particular analytic approaches may be substantial. Indeed, the former may appear somewhat misshapen, oblate instead of round, with some of the primer showing and a "ding" or two on the surface.

The reason is, simply, that analysis done intentionally for use by a real decisionmaker will be shaped—occasionally battered—by the kinds of factors catalogued in this chapter. Stories of how this happens are legion. A cabinet officer was given ten charts to brief the President on the strategic balance between the United States and the Soviet Union. Never having used charts before, he stood uncertainly in front of ten chart-holding easels, strolled over to number 7, and said, "This looks interesting. Let's start with this one." Another top official directed all supporting analysis for important meetings, no matter how complex the subject, to be on one side of one page. Thereafter, all pica type was changed to elite, regular size paper was converted to legal size, margins disappeared, and paragraph indentations were reduced to two spaces. These are minor matters and merely hint at serious considerations. As you work through these cases, you will find that each one affords you

the opportunity to assess the possible influence of some of the factors discussed in this chapter. For example:

• How might the cognitive maps or belief systems of Russell Train (Automobile Emissions Control: The Sulfates Problem), Rogers C. B. Morton (The Central Utah Project), or Caspar Weinberger (Caspar Weinberger and Welfare Reform) affect their approach to the issues in the case? How would knowledge of their preconceptions affect a policy analyst?

• If Robert S. McNamara (The C-5A) had convened a small staff group to advise him on the award of the C-5A contract, how might it have affected the decision? What contribution could the policy analyst have hoped to make in a small group setting?

• Could Dan Lufkin (The Connecticut Enforcement Project) have succeeded in his objectives had he relied on an interagency task force instead of a group of outside consultants? Would in-house people have analyzed the problem the same way?

• Do the developments in Atlanta (Expanding Atlanta's City Limits) and Detroit (The Detroit Fiscal Crisis) give credence to the pluralist model of policy determination? How could policy analysis influence policy outcomes in these cities?

The policymaking process has many dimensions, many textures. The analyst-as-craftsman should welcome their contribution to his or her art.

REFERENCES

1. Lindblom, *op. cit.*, p. 4.
2. Alexander L. George, "Introduction and Overview," in *The Use of Information*, Appendix D to the Report of the Commission on the Organization of Government for the Conduct of Foreign Policy (Washington, D.C.: U.S. Government Printing Office, 1975), p. 10. I have drawn on this Appendix at numerous points in this chapter. A useful review of social psychological approaches to decisionmaking is that of Samuel A. Kirkpatrick, "Psychological Views of Decision-Making," in C. P. Cotter, editor, *Political Science Annual,* Vol. 6 (Indianapolis: Bobbs-Merrill, 1975), pp. 39–112.
3. Thomas R. Dye, *Understanding Public Policy* (Englewood Cliffs, New Jersey: Prentice-Hall, Inc., 1972), p. 1.
4. Austin Ranney, "The Study of Policy Content," in *Political Science and Public Policy*, Austin Ranney, editor (Chicago, Illinois: Markham, 1968), p. 7. For a review of policy definitions and a perceptive discussion of the problems of theorizing about the policymaking process,

see George G. Greenberg, Jeffrey A. Miller, Lawrence B. Mohr, and Bruce C. Vladeck, "Developing Public Policy Theory: Perspectives from Empirical Research," *The American Political Science Review* 71:4 (1977), pp. 1532-1543.

5. For example, in their recent text *A Primer for Policy Analysis* (New York: W. W. Norton & Co., Inc., 1978), Edith Stokey and Richard Zeckhauser state: "The approach to policy analysis throughout this *Primer* is that of the rational decision maker who lays out goals and uses logical processes to explore the best way to reach those goals." (p. 3.) In his seminal article, "The Science of Muddling Through" (*Public Administration Review,* Vol. XIX, Spring 1959, pp. 79–88), Charles E. Lindblom termed this approach to policymaking the "rational-comprehensive" method.

6. For a fascinating discussion of these possibilities, see Thomas C. Schelling, *Micromotives and Macrobehavior* (New York: W. W. Norton and Company, Inc., 1978).

7. Herbert A. Simon, "Rationality as Process and as Process of Thought," *Proceedings of the American Economic Association* 68:2 (May 1978), pp. 1–16.

8. James L. McKenney and Peter G. W. Keen, "How Managers' Minds Work," *Harvard Business Review* (May–June 1974), pp. 79-90.

9. *Ibid.,* p. 81.

10. John D. Steinbruner, *The Cybernetic Theory of Decision: New Dimensions of Political Analysis* (Princeton: Princeton University Press, 1974). See also Robert F. Coulam, *Illusions of Choice: The F-111 and the Problem of Weapons Acquisition Reform* (Princeton: Princeton University Press, 1977).

11. See Chris Argyris and Donald Schön, *Theory in Practice* (New York: Jossey-Bass, 1974). A brief overview is in Chris Argyris, "Leadership, Learning, and Changing the Status Quo," *Organizational Organisms* 4:3 (Winter 1976), pp. 29–43.

12. *Ibid.,* p. 32.

13. *Ibid.,* p. 3.

14. Irving L. Janis, *Victims of Groupthink* (Boston: Houghton Mifflin Company, 1972). See also I. L. Janis and L. Mann, *Decision Making* (New York: Free Press, 1977), which provides interesting material on many of the subjects discussed in this chapter.

15. *Ibid.,* p. 9.

16. *Ibid.,* p. 44.

17. Steinbruner, *op. cit.,* p. 147.

18. Jay Hall, "Decision, Decisions, Decisions," *Psychology Today* (November 1971), p. 51ff.

19. For a useful, brief typology of research on organizational learning, a theme that underlines this section, see Chris Argyris and Donald A. Schön, *Organizational Learning: A Theory of Action Perspective* (Reading, Mass.: Addi-Wesley Publishing Company, 1978), pp. 319–329.

20. Michael Maccoby, *The Gamesman* (New York: Simon and Schuster, 1976).

21. Anthony Downs, *Inside Bureaucracy* (Boston: Little, Brown and Company, 1967).

22. James G. March and Herbert A. Simon, *Organizations* (New York: John Wiley & Sons, Inc., 1968), p. 169.

23. Coulam, *op. cit.,* p. 27.

24. George, *op. cit.,* p. 43.

25. Harold L. Wilensky, *Organizational Intelligence* (New York: Basic Books, Inc., 1967), p. 48.

26. Allison, *op. cit.,* p. 145.

27. See David Easton, *The Political System* (New York: Knopf, 1953); *A Framework for Political Analysis* (Englewood Cliffs, New Jersey: Prentice-Hall, 1965); *A Systems Analysis of Political Life* (New York: John Wiley & Sons, 1965).

28. Dye, *op. cit.*

29. Harold L. Wilensky, *The Welfare State and Equality: Structural and Ideological Roots of Public Policy* (Berkeley, University of California Press, 1975), p. 24.

30. Heinz Eulau and Robert Eyestone, "Policy Maps of City Councils and Policy Outcomes: A Developmental Analysis," *American Political Science Review* 62:1 (March, 1968), pp. 124–143.

31. Steven Lukes, *Power: A Radical View* (New York: Macmillan, 1974), p. 15.

32. Theodore J. Lowi, "American Business, Public Policy, Case-Studies, and Political Theory," *World Politics* (July 16, 1964), pp. 677–715.

33. Charles F. Cnuddle and Donald I. McCrone, "Party Competition and Welfare Policies on the American States," *American Political Science Review* (1972) 63 (Sept. 1969) pp. 858–866.

34. Anthony Downs, "Up and Down with Ecology–The 'Issue-Attention Cycle'," *The Public Interest* (Summer 1972), pp. 38–50.

35. Roger W. Cobb and Charles D. Elder, *Participation in American Politics: The Dynamics of Agenda Building* (Boston: Allyn & Bacon, 1972).

36. *Ibid.,* p. 162.

37. James E. Anderson, editor, *Cases in Public Policy Making* (Holt, Rinehart, and Winston, 1976), p. 5.

38. *Ibid.,* pp. 5–6.

3

The Central Utah Project (A)

The Central Utah Project is a complex $2.1 billion multi-purpose water resource project conceived in 1950 by the Bureau of Reclamation (BuRec) of the U.S. Department of the Interior (see Exhibit 3.1). As originally envisioned by the Bureau, the project would involve the construction of a number of water transfer and storage systems intended to alter the natural distribution of Utah's water. These systems would regulate and store water from the mountain streams in northeastern Utah and make this water available to the populous central area of the State for municipal and industrial uses, irrigation, recreation, and power development.

Like other large-scale water development projects, the Central Utah Project (CUP) has received increasing publicity in the last decade. Predictions of severe water shortages and periodic droughts in the West have focused national attention on the problem of inequitable distribution of water resources—a problem most severely felt in the Western states. Each year these states divert and store 100 million acre-feet (a.f.)* of water for irrigation purposes, compared to a national total of 140 million. Of this diverted water, the West consumes 55 million a.f. in irrigation, a large portion of the national total of 78 million. Such a high level of consumption, combined with the nation's fastest growing population and its lowest rainfall, creates water management problems for the area. One frequently proposed solution for these problems is the large-scale transfer of water from one basin to another, as in the CUP; but this solution has proved increasingly controversial and by the mid-1960's, the future of such projects was by no means assured.

In the case of the CUP, controversy centered on one of the largest components of the project, the "Bonneville Unit," designed to divert water by gravity flow from the Uinta Basin across the Wasatch Mountains into the populous Bonneville Basin, where Salt Lake City and County are located (see Maps 3.1

---

*a.f.—acre-foot, the amount of water that would cover one acre to a depth of one foot.

and 3.2). Congress first appropriated funds for construction of the Bonneville Unit in 1965. Funding in subsequent years, however, was delayed and erratic, as debates over the merits of the project mounted. The estimated costs of the CUP mounted also, to levels unacceptable to many critics. In terms of irrigation, the capital investment increased from $1,298 to $1,405 per a.f.–about $28 per a.f. per year of the project's life, excluding operation and maintenance costs. (This cost, if borne totally by irrigators, would be prohibitive, according to a study of direct irrigation benefits for a similar arid environment in the Texas high plains.) One study shows direct benefits of irrigation water in nearby parts of the state as ranging from $0–15 per a.f. Other studies suggest that development of alternative water sources could yield water for irrigation at a cost much lower (less than half) than the Bonneville Unit.

Controversy over the Bonneville Unit was not confined to project costs. As construction progressed, an alliance of sportsmen and environmentalists both in and out of government began to organize opposition to the CUP. Then, in January 1970, the National Environmental Policy Act (NEPA) became law; under NEPA, federal agencies responsible for actions that may affect the environment must prepare and consider "environmental impact statements" assessing the impacts of those actions. In compliance with the requirements of the act, BuRec prepared a draft environmental impact statement for the CUP, released on August 14, 1972 and followed by a public hearing on the project. Sixteen years and $84 million into the CUP, the Bureau of Reclamation found itself under severe pressure at the hearing from environmental critics, including two federal agencies and the Sierra Club, who objected to such predicted effects of the CUP as reduced streamflows, the disappearance of certain blue-ribbon trout streams, the destruction of wildlife habitats in several lakes and basins, the encouragement of potentially destructive land use and population growth patterns in the already heavily populated Bonneville Basin (Salt Lake City) area, and the increased salinization of the Colorado River. Nonetheless, the Governor of Utah reaffirmed the state's support of the CUP and construction of the Bonneville Unit continued after the hearings were completed.

A further complication for the future of the CUP and the Bonneville Unit was the Indian Deferral Agreement, signed on September 20, 1965, by the United States, the Ute Indian Tribe, and the Central Utah Water Conservancy District.* According to the provisions of the agreement, the Indians agreed to temporarily suspend their water rights and to defer irrigation of some of their lands in order to allow diversion of water to the Bonneville Unit. The Indians entered the agreement with the expectation that eventual recognition of their water rights with the completion of CUP construction would enable greater development of Indian-owned land. The future of the Indians' water rights, however, was by no means settled by the signing of the agreement, and in 1967, Palmer DeLong, BuRec project manager for the CUP, cast some doubt on that future when he questioned whether enough water was available in the Colorado River system to complete the Project. At a news conference, DeLong said that the largest single unit of the Central Utah Project, the Ute Indian Unit, depended upon the availability of water in the Colorado River. It was not clear, in light of projected industrial water needs in the Uinta Basin, that water supplies to construct the Ute Indian Unit would be available, nor was it clear that construction of that unit of the CUP would ultimately satisfy the specific conditions set up under the Indian Deferral Agreement.

* * * *

In the summer of 1973, at about the same time as the release of the final environmental impact statement (EIS) on the Bonneville Unit, the Interior Department began a general review of water resource projects at the request of Under Secretary John Whitaker and the Office of Management and Budget (OMB). Under Interior Department procedures, the Assistant Secretary for Program Development and

---

*The Central Utah Water Conservancy District (CUWCD) is a special-purpose governmental organization set up under Utah law to promote reclamation of arid land in central Utah. It has the authority to set rates for use of CUP water, to propose tax assessments to finance operation of CUP and repay federal construction loans, and to negotiate with BuRec on repayment terms. The organization has also taken on the job of lobbying Congress for completion of the CUP. CUWCD is governed by a 17-member elected board representing the seven counties in which initial CUP construction is located.

Budget and the Solicitor had responsibility for approving the EIS, but before contracts could be let on a project, the Secretary of the Interior himself had to give his approval. Assistant Secretary for Program Development and Budget* Laurence E. Lynn Jr. took advantage of the circumstances to insist on a full review of the CUP by Secretary Morton.

Thus, in the fall of 1973, Secretary of the Interior Rogers C. B. Morton faced a decision on the question of completing the Bonneville Unit of the CUP. Currant Creek Dam and Reservoir were the features scheduled for immediate construction in the Bonneville Unit (see Maps 3.3–3.6), at an estimated cost of $5 million. These features, with a capacity of 14,500 a.f., would receive and store water impounded by the Strawberry Aqueduct, the 37-mile long interceptor of Rock Creek and seven other streams tributary to the Duchesne River, and would deliver water to the Strawberry Reservoir for subsequent transfer to the Bonneville Basin. The Strawberry Aqueduct (or the portion of it comprised of Currant Creek and Strawberry Reservoir and the connecting tunnels) would be able to function alone as a separate unit in the event that Bonneville Unit construction was discontinued.

In September 1973, Assistant Secretary for Program Development and Budget Laurence E. Lynn Jr. asked Assistant Secretary for Land and Water Resources Jack Horton to prepare for Secretary Morton

---

*This title has subsequently been changed to Assistant Secretary for Policy, Budget and Administration.

a Program Decision Options Document (PDOD) on the next phase of CUP construction. (A PDOD, required by Interior Department procedures for any major Secretarial action, identifies the issues which a decision maker faces, provides background and analysis of these issues, and gives arguments for and against the available alternatives.) Lynn then circulated the PDOD among the following parties for comment:

> NON-INTERIOR ENTITIES:
> State of Utah

> INTERIOR ENTITIES:
> Bureau of Reclamation
> Assistant Secretary for Land and Water Resources
> Assistant Secretary for Fish and Wildlife and Parks
> Assistant Secretary for Program Development and Budget
> Assistant to the Secretary for Indian Affairs
> Assistant Secretary for Energy and Minerals
> Solicitor

(See the Appendix for a description of the functions of the Interior officials.) After receiving the comments of these officials, Lynn forwarded the PDOD and the comments to Secretary Morton, together with a cover memorandum. These documents, which are attached to this case, summarize the information available to Secretary Morton as he prepared to decide whether to authorize continuation of CUP construction.

<u>MEMORANDUM</u>

October 19, 1973

TO: Secretary
THROUGH: Under Secretary
FROM: Assistant Secretary — Program Development and Budget
SUBJECT: Bonneville Unit, Central Utah Project

Attached at Tab A is the PDOD on the Bonneville Unit. The Bonneville Unit is one of six units of the Central Utah Project (CUP). It is by far the largest of the four units of the initial phase of CUP and is the only unit of the initial phase which affects both the Bonneville Basin and the Uinta Basin. The other units are in the Uinta Basin. The final phase consists of the large Ute Indian Unit and the Uinta Unit.

Briefly, the Bonneville Unit develops water from two sources: the Strawberry Aqueduct in the Uinta Basin; and Utah Lake in the Bonneville Basin. The water is used for two purposes: approximately one-third for M&I* and two-thirds for irrigation.

Another aspect of the Bonneville Unit is the Indian Deferral Agreement which recognizes water rights on 15,000 acres but defers the irrigation of the acreage until the Ute Indian Unit is constructed.

At present, the following issues are unresolved:

— What is the best way to meet the Salt Lake County demand for M&I water?
— What should be the amount of bypass flows in the Uinta Basin streams for fishery purposes?
— How can the Department best meet its obligation to the Ute Indians that result from the Indian Deferral Agreement?

The immediate decision to be made is whether we should:

(a) continue with the Strawberry Aqueduct by going ahead with construction of Currant Creek Dam while trying to resolve the outstanding issues; or

(b) not continue the Strawberry Aqueduct until we can resolve the above issues and reformulate the Bonneville Unit, if necessary.

The positions of the interested parties in the Department are summarized on the following page; their complete comments can be found at the designated Tab.

Page 1

---

*M&I—municipal and industrial, which includes household uses.

<u>MEMORANDUM</u> — Page 2

POSITIONS OF INTERESTED PARTIES

<u>Bureau of Reclamation</u>: Continue construction on Strawberry Aqueduct System but provide supplemental environmental assessments on remaining features for Secretarial action before proceeding further. (Comments in PDOD at Tab A.)

<u>Assistant Secretary — Land and Water Resources</u>: Recommends ". . . that construction of the Currant Creek Dam of the Strawberry Aqueduct be approved, but with a reconsideration of the future use of the water in both the Uinta and Bonneville Basins" prior to any further construction on the Strawberry Aqueduct. (Comments at Tab B.)

<u>Assistant Secretary for Fish and Wildlife and Parks</u>: Does "<u>not</u> believe that Currant Creek Dam construction should proceed prior to any re-evaluation." (Comments at Tab C.)

<u>Assistant Secretary — Program Development and Budget</u>: The Bonneville Unit should be reformulated with emphasis placed on the orderly development of M&I water for Salt Lake County, developing a firm plan for providing water to the Ute Indians, and ensuring water availability for energy development in the Uinta Basin. (Comments at Tab D.)

<u>Assistant to the Secretary for Indian Affairs</u>: "It appears to us that action leading to diversion of water to the Bonneville Basin without assurance that the Ute Tribe will get the full benefits of the Central Utah Project as contemplated by the agreement and the authorization Act of Congress would not be in the Tribe's best interest . . . we are certain you will want to delay a decision until this consultation (with the Tribe) has been completed." (Comments at Tab E.)

<u>Assistant Secretary — Energy and Minerals</u>: Commenting on the availability of water for future oil shale development in the Uinta Basin, he stated that "Water from the Bonneville Unit was considered in the Department's final environmental statement for the currently proposed oil shale leasing program. The conclusion of this environmental study was that adequate water based on present plans would be available for the one-million-barrel-per-day output envisioned for 1985." (Comments at Tab F.)

<u>Solicitor</u>: Within the Solicitor's office there appear to be differences of opinion about the legal position of the Department with respect to the Indian Deferral Agreement. The Solicitor will resolve the differences in time for the decision meetings.

Laurence E. Lynn, Jr.

Enclosures

ENCLOSURE – Page 1   **A**

PROGRAM DECISION OPTION DOCUMENT

Bonneville Unit – Central Utah Project

ISSUE: What position should the Department adopt regarding further development of the Bonneville Unit?

ALTERNATIVES: (1) Stop construction.

(2) Delay construction on the project collection system until a further evaluation has been made of the project.

(3) Continue construction (award new contracts) on Strawberry Aqueduct system but provide supplemental environmental assessments on remaining project features for Secretarial action before proceeding further.

Background Analysis:*

[As first considered by Congress, the CUP was divided into two phases, and subsequently into six separate units for planning and construction. The initial phase, consisting of construction of the Jensen, Vernal, Upalco and Bonneville Units, was authorized by Congress in 1956, as part of the Colorado River Storage Project Act. The Vernal Unit of the initial phase has been constructed and is now in operation, and the Bonneville Unit is about 18% complete. Funds have been made available to start the Jensen and Upalco Units.]

[The second phase of the project includes the Uinta and Ute Indian Units, neither of which has been built. The Uinta Unit was authorized by Congress in 1968 and final construction plans are now being prepared. The Ute Indian Unit is still the subject of feasibility studies, which are a prerequisite for congressional authorization. These studies are scheduled to be completed in 1978. The Ute Indian Unit, now under study, will encompass and tie together all other units, at a cost in excess of $600 million (in 1971 dollars). By the year 2000, when it is expected to be phased into the project, it will be the source annually of an estimated 700,000 a.f. of water, including 123,000 a.f. of water from the Colorado River. The Jensen, Vernal, Uinta and Upalco Units are relatively small and are situated entirely within the Uinta Basin. The Bonneville and Ute Indian Units involve both the Uinta Basin and the Bonneville Basin and are very complex in plan, extensive in scope, and expensive.]

*Because the authors of the PDOD assumed that Secretary Morton was generally familiar with the background of the CUP, the PDOD did not include the following bracketed information, which has been added so that the reader can better understand the discussion that follows it.

ENCLOSURE — Page 2

The Bonneville Unit was authorized for construction as a participating project of the Colorado River Storage Project in April 1956. It includes developments in both the Uinta and Bonneville Basins with a diversion of water from the sparsely populated Uinta Basin to the more densely populated Bonneville Basin (Salt Lake City). The unit would develop 99,000 acre-feet annually for municipal and industrial purposes. It will also develop 112,000 acre-feet to supply supplemental water to an existing 213,000 acres of irrigated lands and 95,000 acre-feet to supply 29,370 acres of non-irrigated lands. The remaining 6,500 acre-feet would be used for streamflow for fishery. Hydroelectric power generation of 133,500 kw is planned. Facilities include 10 new reservoirs and the enlargement of two existing reservoirs; more than 140 miles of aqueducts, tunnels and canals; and three powerplants [and nine pumping plants and 200 miles of pipe drains].

The Bonneville Unit would utilize 160,000 acre-feet of Utah's share of the Colorado River out of a total allocation of 1.3 million acre-feet. Present estimates of the unit's impact on the Colorado River water quality, excluding future salinity control measures, show an increase in salinity of 12 mg/l at Imperial Dam by 1985.

Construction of the Bonneville Unit was started in 1967 and is now about 18% complete. Fifteen of the proposed 21 miles of the Jordan Aqueduct which delivers municipal and industrial water into Salt Lake County is completed. A $9 million water purification plant, financed and constructed by the Central Utah Water Conservancy District on the Jordan Aqueduct, is expected to be completed in early 1974. Starvation Dam (near Duchesne) and Soldier Creek Dam (to enlarge Strawberry Reservoir) are constructed. The Strawberry Aqueduct is complete between Strawberry Reservoir and Currant Creek. Construction has not started on features required to deliver water from Strawberry Reservoir into the Bonneville Basin.* About $18 million, including $2 million of Congressional write-in, is budgeted for F.Y. 1974.

Based on an estimated cost of $490 million and an interest rate of 3.2%, the project had a benefit cost ratio of 1.5 to 1 in 1972. Of the $250 million allocated to irrigation, $13 million is expected to be repaid directly by unit irrigators; $41 million will be paid from ad valorem taxes by irrigators and non-irrigators. Of the $142 million allocated to M&I, $94 million will be repaid directly by water users and $48 million from ad valorem taxes.

*This sentence should read, "Construction has not started on features required to deliver water from *the enlarged* Strawberry Reservoir into the Bonneville Basin." The original Strawberry Reservoir was completed in 1912 as a component of BuRec's Strawberry Valley Water Project. The Project now operates at full capacity and annually delivers over 60,000 acre-feet of water to the Utah County area for irrigation and power production. The Project consists of Strawberry Dam, a 71-foot high structure at the Reservoir's southeastern corner, and a four-mile diversion tunnel running from the western edge of the Reservoir to the head of Diamond Fork Canyon. The Strawberry Reservoir was enlarged by the completion of the Starvation Dam. Water from the enlarged reservoir will be delivered to the Bonneville Basin via the Syar Tunnel and the Wasatch Aqueduct, CUP features which will be completed by the mid-1980s. Currant Creek Dam and Reservoir will supply water to the enlarged reservoir via Currant, Layout, and Water Hollow tunnels. These tunnels were under construction in 1973.

<u>ENCLOSURE</u> – Page 3

Costs allocated to power ($71 million) would be repaid from power revenues. Any reimbursable costs ($164 million) not paid by water users and ad valorem tax revenues would be repaid by revenues from Bonneville Unit powerplants and from Utah's share of revenues from the Colorado River Storage Project basin fund. Non-reimbursable cost allocations for flood control, recreation, fish and wildlife, etc., total approximately $59 million (about 10%).

The repayment contract, dated December 28, 1965, between the United States and the Central Utah Water Conservancy District was endorsed by a general election with a vote of 13 to 1 in favor of the project. The contract covers the repayment by the conservancy district of an obligation of $130,673,000 (with provisions for an increase), plus interest on the unpaid portion of this obligation for municipal and industrial water. Under the contract, a development block notice would be issued by the United States to the district as water becomes available for sale.

Development Block Notice No. 1 (Duchesne area) was issued to the conservancy district on June 19, 1970. This notice was for 21,400 acre-feet of irrigation water from Starvation Reservoir. On June 10, 1971, the Salt Lake County Water Conservancy District petitioned the Central Utah Water Conservancy District for a perpetual allotment of 50,000 acre-feet of water annually from the Bonneville Unit. The initial delivery of 3,000 acre-feet was requested during calendar year 1974, and the total allotment would be used by about 1990.

The draft environmental impact statement was filed with CEQ on August 14, 1972. A public hearing was held on September 22 and 23, 1972. The final environmental impact statement was filed with CEQ on August 2, 1973. It contains a full disclosure of known environmental impacts of the Bonneville Unit with a commitment to prepare supplemental impact statements on features in the Bonneville Basin.

The Bonneville Unit plan was concurred in by State and Federal agencies in 1964. Recently, environmental interests have reiterated concern about the reduction of stream-flows below reservoirs and diversion points along the Strawberry Aqueduct. The State of Utah continues to support present plans for these diversions as evidenced by the Governor's letter of November 1, 1972, and the Utah Board of Wildlife Resources resolution dated September 6, 1973. Continued construction of this system except for reservoir inundation need not constitute an irretrievable or irreversible commitment because of the large by-pass capacity that will be incorporated into the diversion structures. The Bureau of Reclamation and the Central Utah Water Conservancy District have agreed to develop aqueduct operating criteria consistent with obligations to the water users, keeping in mind minimizing the adverse impacts on streams with recognition of stream accretions, winter conditions, and other factors affecting the ecosystem.

<u>ENCLOSURE</u> – Page 4

A major environmental issue not yet resolved is the magnitude of streamflows below reservoirs and diversion points on the Strawberry Aqueduct and the loss of habitat on Utah Lake. Under the present plan for the Strawberry Aqueduct system there would be an irretrievable loss of 20 miles of stream by inundation. About 143 miles of stream would be subjected to reduced flows of which 113 miles are of significant importance to the State fishery resource. Of that 113 miles, 46 miles of stream habitat would be severely reduced in quality.

Most of the Strawberry Aqueduct system is located on national forest land. The Forest Service recommends 26,300 acre-feet minimum by-pass for fish to streams within the forest; 3,500 acre-feet of by-pass are provided in the project plan. The proposed plan would include diking of Provo Bay and Goshen Bay of Utah Lake in the Bonneville Basin. The marshes of Provo and Goshen Bays presently constitute about 25,000 acres of primarily waterfowl nesting habitat and some nesting-feeding habitat. According to the State Division of Wildlife Resources the drainage of these bays would destroy much of this habitat. The Bureau of Reclamation is committed by the final environmental impact statement to perform additional studies and prepare necessary environmental impact statements regarding the diking.

In 1965, the Indian Deferral Agreement (Contract No. 14-06-W-194) was executed among the United States (Bureau of Reclamation and the Bureau of Indian Affairs), the Ute Indian Tribe, and the Central Utah Water Conservancy District. Indian interests agreed to defer irrigation on certain blocks of Indian lands and allow diversion of water to the Bonneville Basin in order to satisfy immediate needs. The agreement was negotiated with a spirit of cooperation intended to permit a systematic and optimum development for both Indian and non-Indian interests within the Uinta Basin. Under the terms of the deferral agreement, the Indians will be allowed to develop the water to which they are entitled under State and Federal water laws and the "Winters Doctrine."* It was agreed that the year 2005 would be the maximum date of deferral or equitable adjustment would need to be made to permit the immediate Indian use of the water so deferred. The agreement was approved by the Secretary of the Interior and subsequently acknowledged by Congress in the Colorado River Basin Act of September 1968.

The Ute Tribe and the Bureau of Indian Affairs have always looked to the Ute Indian Unit (ultimate phase of the Central Utah Project) to provide for their maximum water

---

*The usual rule in water law in the western states is that the first person to put a water resource to productive use is the owner of that resource, even if the water lies on or flows through land belonging to another. However, in *Winters v. United States*, 297 U.S. 564 (1908), the Supreme Court held that a different rule applied to water found on Indian reservations, *viz.*, that the grant of lands for a reservation included the right to such water as would be necessary for the tribe's future needs, regardless of present use patterns. What neither the *Winters* case nor subsequent cases have made entirely clear is how those future needs are to be quantified, although one measure that has been used in a number of cases is the amount of reservation land that would be arable if irrigated.

<u>ENCLOSURE</u> — Page 5

resource development in the Uinta Basin. This potential for greater development and the recognition of their water rights was the incentive and basis for their acceptance of the deferral concept. The obligation to develop Indian water resources in the Uinta Basin was recognized by the Congress in its authority and directive to perform feasibility investigations of the Ute Indian Unit. Congress directed that these investigations be completed by 1974 with the intent of meeting the conditions expressed in the deferral agreement. Various alternatives for developing the water resources in the Uinta Basin for Indian benefit will be outlined in the investigations.

Full development of the Ute Indian Unit to include importation of water from Flaming Gorge Reservoir and expanded transmountain diversions from the Uinta Basin to Bonneville Basin would not be required to provide an opportunity for the Ute Tribe to develop a water supply equivalent to the amount deferred in 1965. Funds to accomplish this minimum development would be approximately the same as the amount that would have been required had the use not been deferred.

Nine applications for oil and gas exploration leases are under consideration in the vicinity of Utah Lake. Interest in oil and gas potential in this area has increased significantly in recent years. About one half of these applications are within the lake proper and presently include restrictions on drilling activity. Development of the Bonneville Unit would be compatible with these activities. BLM is currently preparing a Management Framework Plan for the Utah Lake area and the Bureau of Reclamation will cooperate in its preparation.

Future development of the Uinta Basin would be largely associated with utilization of raw materials, including oil, gas, oil shale, phosphate, and forest and agricultural products. The Uinta Basin contains a significant portion of the nation's known oil shale. The importance of the oil shale resource is more fully known today than ever before, but data relative to the timing, process, and resources necessary for development are not yet available. Water requirements for municipal and industrial use in the Uinta Basin have been projected by the State Department of Natural Resources to increase from 20,000 acre-feet annually to about 130,000 acre-feet by 2020. This increase in requirement could be met in the following ways: (1) Utah's share of the Colorado River (on the basis of 5.8 million acre-feet available to the Upper Basin States) is 1,322,000 acre-feet. Present use, including net evaporation charge on the river is 818,000 acre-feet, leaving 504,000 acre-feet for future uses. Current estimates of committed future use total 397,000 acre-feet, which leaves 107,000 acre-feet uncommitted and available for oil shale development. Estimates of committed future use were derived as follows:

ENCLOSURE — Page 6

Bonneville Unit	160,000 acre-feet
Emery County Project	6,000 acre-feet
Jensen Unit	15,000 acre-feet
Upalco Unit	10,000 acre-feet
Uinta Unit	30,000 acre-feet
Indian Lands	50,000 acre-feet
Kaiparowits Power Project	102,000 acre-feet
Huntington Canyon Powerplant	24,000 acre-feet
Total Estimated Future Uses	397,000 acre-feet

(2) Under terms of the October 2, 1969, contract with the developers of the Kaiparowits Project, priority to 102,000 acre-feet presently reserved for the project will be subordinated to the Central Utah Project beginning in 2010. The total amount to be relinquished periodically in blocks, would be available by 2030. (3) As explained in the Oil Shale Environmental Statement, "Additional water can be made available if the States permit the [oil shale] industry to purchase some of the water rights from those presently using water and if the use category is changed from some of the future commitments."

Augmentation of Colorado River Basin water supplies by importation from other basins, desalination, or weather modification would increase the water supply available for oil shale development in Utah, Colorado, and Wyoming.

Municipal and industrial water supply envisioned by the project is an important part of the total M&I demand in that it firms up additional local supplies by releases to meet peak requirements during the year and needs during drought periods that occur periodically. It is estimated that the 99,000 acre-feet scheduled for M&I deliveries would be fully utilized before the turn of the century, probably by 1995. The various techniques of population projection vary somewhat, but the divergence in estimates for 1995 is minimal. That is, the possible error in projection would be only three or four years in terms of being behind or ahead of projections.

The projections for M&I water needs within the Bonneville Unit do not consider any water savings from an increase in water rates. It is difficult to determine the amount of reduction in municipal water consumption in the Bonneville Unit area which would result from increased water charges. Completed studies indicate that many variables affect this reduction. These studies indicate that a significant increase in water charges would cause an initial reduction in use, but continued increases in cost would not reduce uses very much. Some studies indicate that this reduced use would only be temporary and use would tend to return to original levels after a short period of adjustment to the new prices.

<u>ENCLOSURE</u> — Page 7

Conversion of water from irrigation to M&I use is permissible under Utah law with just compensation. Collection of potential converted water, regulation, and delivery into the water systems to meet demand patterns would be required along with extensive water treatment to meet minimum State standards. Importation of water for M&I use from river basins to the north of the Bonneville Unit was considered, but the cost would be prohibitive. Northern water sources probably would be only temporary because requirements in those areas are expected to grow in near future years.

Other alternatives such as reuse and recycling present water quality problems. Local stream development is limited in quantity, 50% more costly, and would require reservoirs and aqueducts with possible environmentally damaging effects.

<u>Discussion of Alternatives</u>

1. <u>Stop Construction</u>

    <u>Arguments For:</u>

    No additional Federal expenditures for unit facilities ($400 million).

    Avoid additional changes in the natural environment, such as the reduction of natural flows in some 198 miles of streams, diking of Utah Lake, land disturbances from constructed facilities, and increased land use.

    <u>Arguments Against:</u>

    253,000 acre-feet of water including 99,000 acre-feet for municipal and industrial use would not be available for use in the Bonneville Basin.

    133,500 kw of hydroelectric power would not be developed by the Federal Government.

    Approximately $70 million worth of partially constructed facilities would not be usable.

    $9 million water purification plant, non-Federal investment not usable.

    Legal action could be initiated by State officials for not meeting Federal contractual commitments.

    Economic loss to State from lack of construction employment.

    Delay in economic benefits of resource development.

2. <u>Delay construction on the project collection system until a further evaluation has been made of the project.</u>

<u>ENCLOSURE</u> — Page 8

<u>Arguments For:</u>

Provide time for reformulation of the unit.

Could result in a reduction of $400 million in Federal expenditure.

<u>Arguments Against:</u>

Delay in meeting M&I water needs in the Bonneville Basin by 1976.

Delay in developing 133,500 kw hydroelectric power output.

Construction deferral resulting in higher project costs.

$70 million of completed Federal facilities not usable.

$9 million water purification plant, non-Federal investment, not usable.

Plan reformulation may result in reduced benefits to water users and necessitate renegotiation of agreements with the Central Utah Water Conservancy District, Ute Indian Tribe, and Salt Lake County Water Conservancy District.

Possible legal action for not meeting contractual obligations.

3. <u>Continue construction (award new contracts) on Strawberry Aqueduct System but provide supplemental environmental assessments on remaining features for secretarial action before proceeding further.</u>

<u>Arguments For:</u>

Unit water development goals and objectives would be met upon a reasonable schedule, particularly permitting the delivery of M&I water into the Bonneville Basin.

Partial water delivery revenues would be realized.

Time available to perform environmental studies relating to Provo and Goshen Bay Dikes, and other features in the Bonneville Basin.

Construction can proceed on a reasonably efficient schedule on the Strawberry Aqueduct System.

Avoid argument that Federal Government is delaying development.

<u>Arguments Against:</u>

Unavoidable environmental impacts upon Uinta Basin trout streams.

Risk legal action by environmental interests.

If no other features are constructed, investment in Strawberry Aqueduct System is not usable in Bonneville Basin.

<u>ENCLOSURE</u> — Page 9

<u>BUDGET EFFECT</u>

Alternative	1973	1974	1975	1976	1977	1978	1979
(1)	$29M	$ 5M	0	0	0	0	0
(2)	$29M	$ 6M	$ 1M	$ 1M	$ 1M	?	?
(3)	$29M	$18M	$23M	$27M	$36M	$44M	$41M

M E M O R A N D U M   **B**

September 21, 1973

TO: The Secretary

THROUGH: Assistant Secretary — Program Development and Budget

FROM: Assistant Secretary — Land and Water Resources

SUBJECT: Central Utah Project

Following an analysis of the Bureau of Reclamation Environmental Impact Statement and PDOD for the Bonneville Unit of the Central Utah Project, I recommend that construction of the Currant Creek Dam of the Strawberry Aqueduct be approved but with a reconsideration of the future use of the water in both the Uinta and Bonneville Basins. I base this recommendation on the following conclusions:

1. Approximately 100,000 of the 135,000 acre-feet of water to be diverted to the Bonneville Basin is allocated to M&I purposes, and that allocation should have the highest priority in terms of the use of the water.

2. The remaining 35,000 acre-feet is allocated to irrigation purposes in the Bonneville area and should have a lower priority.

3. A difference exists between the recommendation of the Forest Service that about 18,000 acre-feet a year be guaranteed to safeguard the stream flow in the Uinta watershed and the Bureau of Reclamation, which is guaranteeing a minimum flow of about 6,000 acre-feet.

My recommendation on a go-ahead on the Strawberry Aqueduct is conditioned with the firm assurance that there will be no construction beyond Currant Creek Dam and no commitment of the use of the additional 35,000 a.f. of water until the Governor of Utah, the U.S. Forest Service, and the Bureau of Reclamation have reexamined and reached a decision as to the proper use of this water.

It is important to realize that if any portion of the 35,000 a.f. is not diverted to the Bonneville area, it would not be lost to the State of Utah but could be efficiently and effectively used in eastern Starvation Dam. There are reasons to think that a better use for a portion of the 35,000 a.f. might be to more optimally balance population growth, with particular reference to the land exchange now being examined between the State and BLM for oil shale development in the eastern portion of the State.

In summary, I am suggesting a go-ahead on actions which would provide M&I water to the Salt Lake area but delay a commitment for additional (non M&I) waters to that area

Page 1

<u>MEMORANDUM</u> — Page 2

until subsequent discussions and agreements have been reached among the Forest Service, Bureau of Reclamation, and the Governor of Utah to fully protect the stream flows in the Uinta watershed.

Following the advice to you of the Assistant Secretary for Program Development and Budget, the Assistant Secretary for Fish and Wildlife and Parks, and the Under Secretary, I would be happy to undertake the actions that I have recommended, particularly the reexamination of the use of the water which presently is planned to be diverted to the Bonneville Basin for irrigation purposes.

(sgd) JACK O. HORTON

M E M O R A N D U M **C**

October 2, 1973

TO: Assistant Secretary — Program Development and Budget

FROM: Assistant Secretary for Fish and Wildlife and Parks

SUBJECT: Bonneville Unit — Central Utah Project (Your memorandum of
September 24)*

A preliminary draft of the attached memorandum to you from my office was prepared and transmitted by the Bureau of Sport Fisheries and Wildlife in my absence last week. I am forwarding it to you with the following additional comments:

First, I want to support Assistant Secretary Horton's suggestion that use of Uinta Basin water in eastern Utah might be a better use of such water.

Second, I strongly share BSFW's concern that their agency should be a partner in the reevaluation and review, particularly in determining appropriate stream flows for the project.

Finally, I do _not_ believe that the Currant Creek Dam construction should proceed prior to any reevaluation.

Nathaniel P. Reed

*The reference is to Assistant Secretary Lynn's request for comments on the PDOD.

MEMORANDUM

TO: Assistant Secretary — Program Development and Budget
FROM: Assistant Secretary for Fish and Wildlife and Parks
SUBJECT: Bonneville Unit — Central Utah Project (Your memorandum of
             September 24)

We have reviewed the latest version of the Program Decision Option Document for the subject project.

The recent rewrite differs slightly from that submitted to us for review on July 20. Our memorandum of August 6 sets forth our reasons for rejection of the option to "Complete work on the Collection System and reformulate other systems of the Unit." It is apparent that the concerns of the Bureau of Sport Fisheries and Wildlife have been given scant consideration in revising the document.

Assistant Secretary Horton's memorandum of September 21 recognizes the interests of the Forest Service and the State of Utah in the matter but totally ignores the responsibilities of the Bureau of Sport Fisheries and Wildlife, the agency which provides Departmental expertise on fish and wildlife matters. The memorandum presents an alternative plan that has not been fully aired or appraised.

The continued "shuffling of cards" and modification of statements and plans make it abundantly clear that the Central Utah Project has many elements that are subject to question.

The Bureau of Reclamation has provided no indication that streams in the Uinta Basin will receive water needed to sustain their values. The decision to divert water from the Uinta Basin was made at a time when environmental matters were given little consideration. To proceed with construction of Currant Creek Dam and the Strawberry Aqueduct will only indicate to the conservationists that it is "business as usual."

The main point of issue relative to this decision is the magnitude of stream flows in the Uinta Basin. The disagreements are:

a. Forest Service recommends 26,300 acre-feet of water be by-passed to the Uinta streams.

b. BSFW recommends 89,353 acre-feet of water be by-passed to maintain fishery value.

c. Reclamation's plan provides for 6,500 acre-feet of storage for minimum flows.

d. The State of Utah is recommending 37,000 acre-feet for minimum flows.

<u>MEMORANDUM</u> — Page 2

Our analysis of August 6 recommended the formation of a Task Force to be charged with the resolution of the problems related to the Central Utah Project. This suggestion has not been followed, and it would be well to settle the in-house disagreements.

Without the benefit of adequate consideration of environmental concern, we must continue our objection to any furtherance of construction on the Bonneville Unit. Among other things adequate assurance should be provided for the maintenance of water flows in streams affected by the project.

In summation, to allow the project to go forward without resolution of the problems will only demonstrate to the concerned conservation interests, and the Nation, that this Department is placing undue bias on development to the detriment of environmental concerns. I firmly believe that the Department will err if it continues to push for further construction of the Bonneville Unit as presently conceived.

Kenneth E. Black

<u>M E M O R A N D U M</u>   **D**

October 19, 1973

TO: The Secretary
THROUGH: The Under Secretary
FROM: Assistant Secretary — Program Development and Budget.
SUBJECT: Bonneville Unit, Central Utah Project

Our analysis of the Bonneville Unit, and our examination of the immediate proposal to award a contract for construction of Currant Creek Dam, have led to the following conclusions:

Most of the problems with the continuation of the Bonneville Unit stem from the diversion of Uinta Basin water to the Bonneville Basin: high quality fisheries would be damaged, problems of replacing the deferred Indian water have not been faced, and major energy development possibilities such as oil shale, oil field development and refining, and thermal power would be foregone. On the other hand, incremental supplies of M&I water can be developed in the Bonneville Basin by features of the Bonneville Unit and other alternatives to meet the needs of Salt Lake County until well into the next century.

Furthermore, it is our understanding that we can even meet our short term commitments to provide M&I water because the existing portions of the Strawberry Aqueduct are yielding about 4,000 a.f. per year, which is being stored in Strawberry Reservoir.

Therefore, I recommend that you elect to reformulate the Bonneville Unit. The future emphasis should be placed on the orderly development of M&I water for Salt Lake County, developing a firm plan for providing water to the Ute Indians, and ensuring water availability for energy development in the Uinta Basin.

Laurence E. Lynn, Jr.

<u>M E M O R A N D U M</u>   E

September 26, 1973

TO: Secretary of the Interior
THROUGH: Assistant Secretary — Program Development & Budget
FROM: Assistant to the Secretary for Indian Affairs*
SUBJECT: Bonneville Unit — Central Utah Project

The Act of September 30, 1968, 82 Stat. 885, 897 includes the following proviso:

> That the planning report for the Ute Indian Unit of the Central Utah participating project shall be completed on or before December 31, 1974, to enable the United States of America to meet the commitments heretofore made to the Ute Indian Tribe of the Uintah and Ouray Indian Reservation under the agreement dated September 30, 1965 (Contract Numbered 14-06-W-194).

The Tribe regards this language as a ratification of the Agreement by the Congress and as a commitment to implement its provisions. It is our understanding that because of environmental considerations the Central Utah Project may not proceed according to schedule and, indeed, there is a strong possibility it will not be completed.

The Ute Indian Tribe of the Uintah and Ouray Reservation entered into the Indian Deferral Agreement in 1965. By this Agreement irrigation of certain Indian lands was deferred to allow diversion of water to the Bonneville Basin in order to satisfy immediate needs of non-Indians. The Ute Indian Unit is the final phase of the Central Utah Project. It appears to us that action leading to diversion of water to the Bonneville Basin without assurance that the Ute Tribe will get the full benefits of the Central Utah Project as contemplated by the Agreement and the authorizing Act of Congress would not be in the Tribe's best interest.

Before we make a recommendation in this matter of vital concern to the Tribe, we believe it should be consulted to obtain its views. We are, therefore, starting the consultation process. We are certain you will want to delay a decision until this consultation has been completed.

M. R. Franklin

---

*At the time of the events described in this case, the post of Commissioner of Indian Affairs was vacant, and the Assistant to the Secretary for Indian Affairs was acting as a *de facto* Commissioner.

<u>M E M O R A N D U M</u>   **F**

September 26, 1973

TO: Assistant Secretary — Energy and Minerals
THROUGH: Deputy Assistant Secretary for Energy and Minerals
FROM: Director, Bureau of Mines
SUBJECT: Bonneville Unit — Central Utah Project

The uncertainties involved in projecting future water needs in the Uinta Basin for possible oil shale developments in Utah make it difficult, if not impossible, to arrive at adequate decisions on how alternatives now being considered for the Bonneville Unit project will affect potential oil shale needs. Little information is available on the hydrology of the Utah oil shale area. There are uncertainties as to how much of a future oil shale industry might locate in Utah.

The present project as planned will provide 107,000 acre-feet of water downstream of the Strawberry Reservoir for other uses, essentially including that for oil shale development. Water from the Bonneville Unit was considered in the Department's final environmental statement for the currently proposed oil shale leasing program. The conclusion of this environmental study was that adequate water based on present plans would be available for the 1 million barrel per day output envisioned for 1985.

J. D. Morgan
Acting Director

APPENDIX

Responsibilities of Interior Officials

The responsibilities of the Department of the Interior include the administration of federal lands, including Indian reservations; the conservation and development of minerals, water resources, fish and wildlife; mine safety; outdoor recreation programs; administration of scenic and historical areas; reclamation of arid western lands through irrigation; the management of hydroelectric power systems; and the social and economic development of Indians.

The Assistant Secretary for Fish and Wildlife and Parks is responsible for programs relating to the development, conservation and use of fish, wildlife, outdoor recreation, and historical and national parks.

The Assistant Secretary for Energy and Minerals oversee programs related to mineral resources, mine safety, electric power, topographic and geologic surveys, and ocean mineral resources.

The Assistant Secretary for Land and Water Resources, who prepared the PDOD for the Central Utah Project, has responsibilities in the area of land use and water planning, public land management, construction and operation of dams and other water projects, and marketing of water and hydroelectric power. The Bureau of Reclamation is under this Assistant Secretary; the Commissioner of Reclamation's responsibilities include the location, construction, operation and maintenance of public works that store, divert and develop water for the reclamation of arid and semi-arid land in the western states.

The duties of the Assistant Secretary for Program Development and Budget (now Policy, Budget and Administration) include budget management, comprehensive planning, policy analysis, economic analyses of Interior programs and natural resource issues, and management of interagency and interdisciplinary departmental programs.

The Bureau of Indian Affairs, under a Commissioner, has as its responsibilities the economic and social development of American Indians and Alaskans, including assisting those groups in managing their own affairs. The Bureau also acts as trustee for Indian and Alaskan lands and monies held in trust by the United States.

The Solicitor is the Secretary's principal legal advisor and the department's chief law officer, overseeing all of Interior's legal work except for the Office of Hearings and Appeals.

All of the officials described here are on the same organizational level of the Interior Department except for the Commissioner of Reclamation, who reports to the Assistant Secretary for Land and Water Resources.

Source: United States Government Manual

EXHIBIT 3.1   Department of the Interior Organization

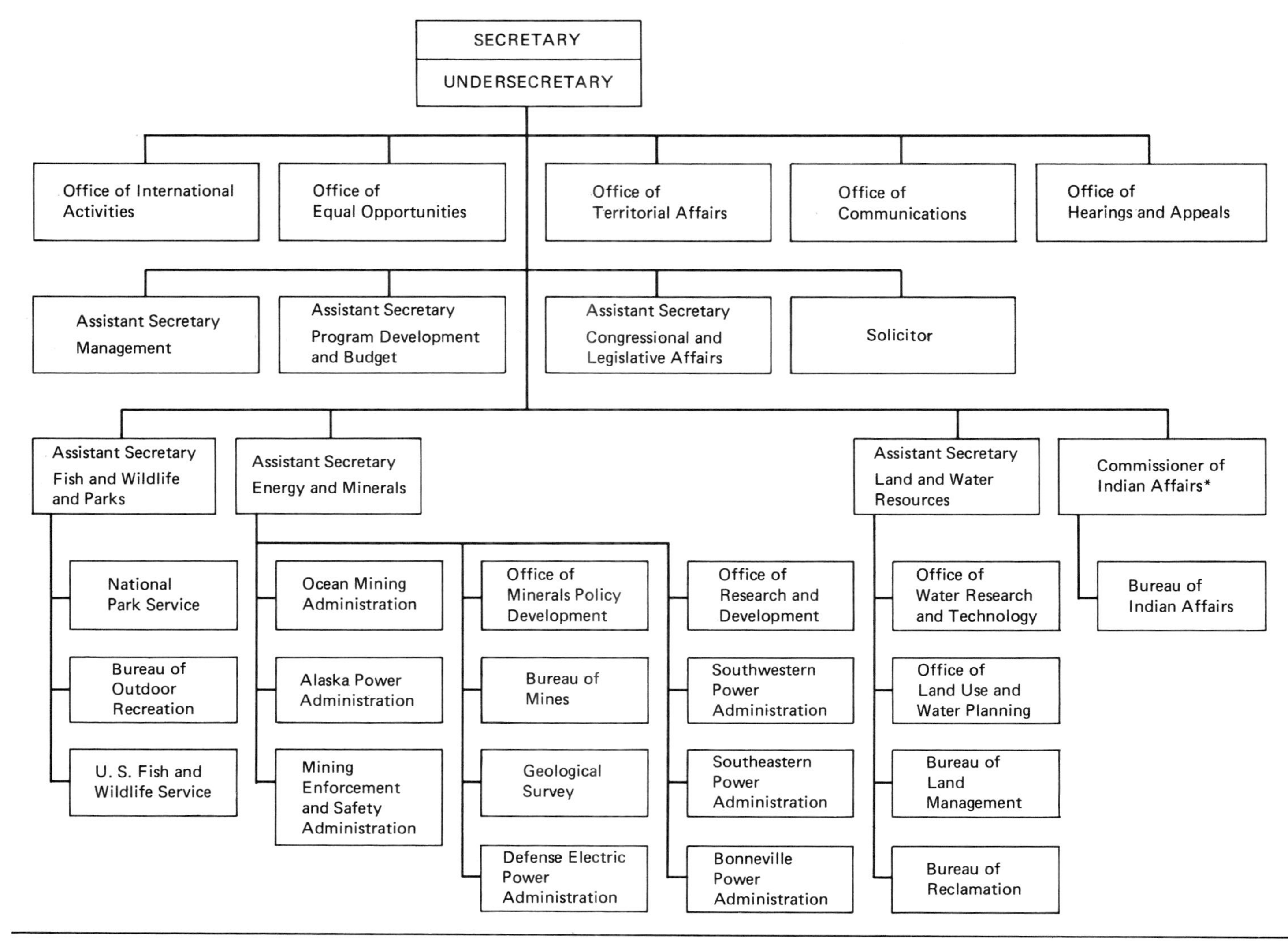

*At the time of the events described in this case, the post of Commissioner of Indian Affairs was vacant, and the Assistant to the Secretary for Indian Affairs was acting as a *de facto* Commissioner.

MAP 3.1: Utah

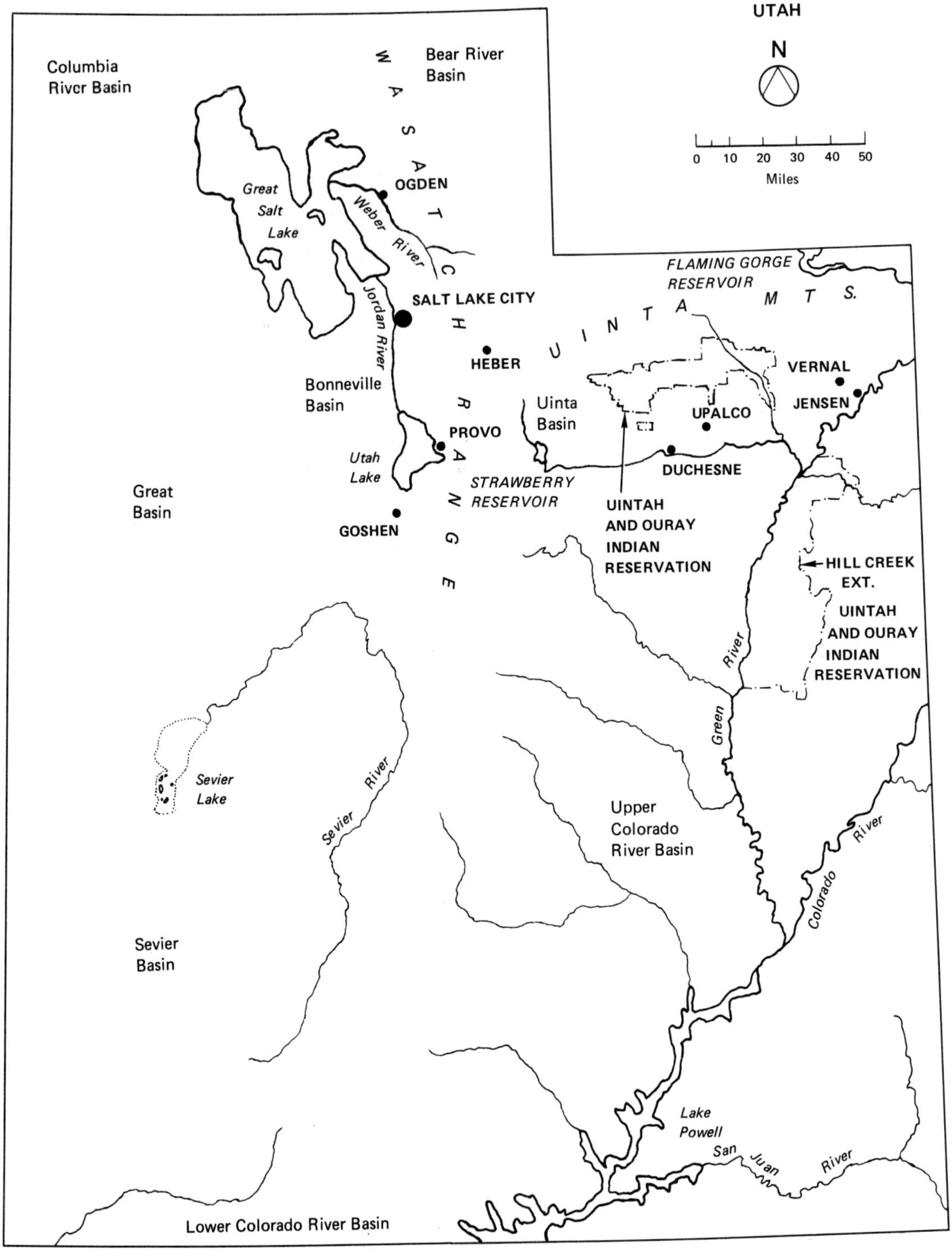
UTAH
N
0 10 20 30 40 50
Miles
Columbia River Basin
Bear River Basin
WASATCH RANGE
Great Salt Lake
OGDEN
Weber River
Jordan River
SALT LAKE CITY
FLAMING GORGE RESERVOIR
UINTA MTS.
HEBER
VERNAL
JENSEN
UPALCO
Uinta Basin
Bonneville Basin
PROVO
Utah Lake
STRAWBERRY RESERVOIR
DUCHESNE
UINTAH AND OURAY INDIAN RESERVATION
GOSHEN
Great Basin
HILL CREEK EXT.
UINTAH AND OURAY INDIAN RESERVATION
Green River
Sevier Lake
Sevier River
Upper Colorado River Basin
Colorado River
Sevier Basin
Lake Powell
San Juan River
Lower Colorado River Basin

MAP 3.2:   State of Utah—Counties

MAP 3.3:   Bonneville Unit, CUP

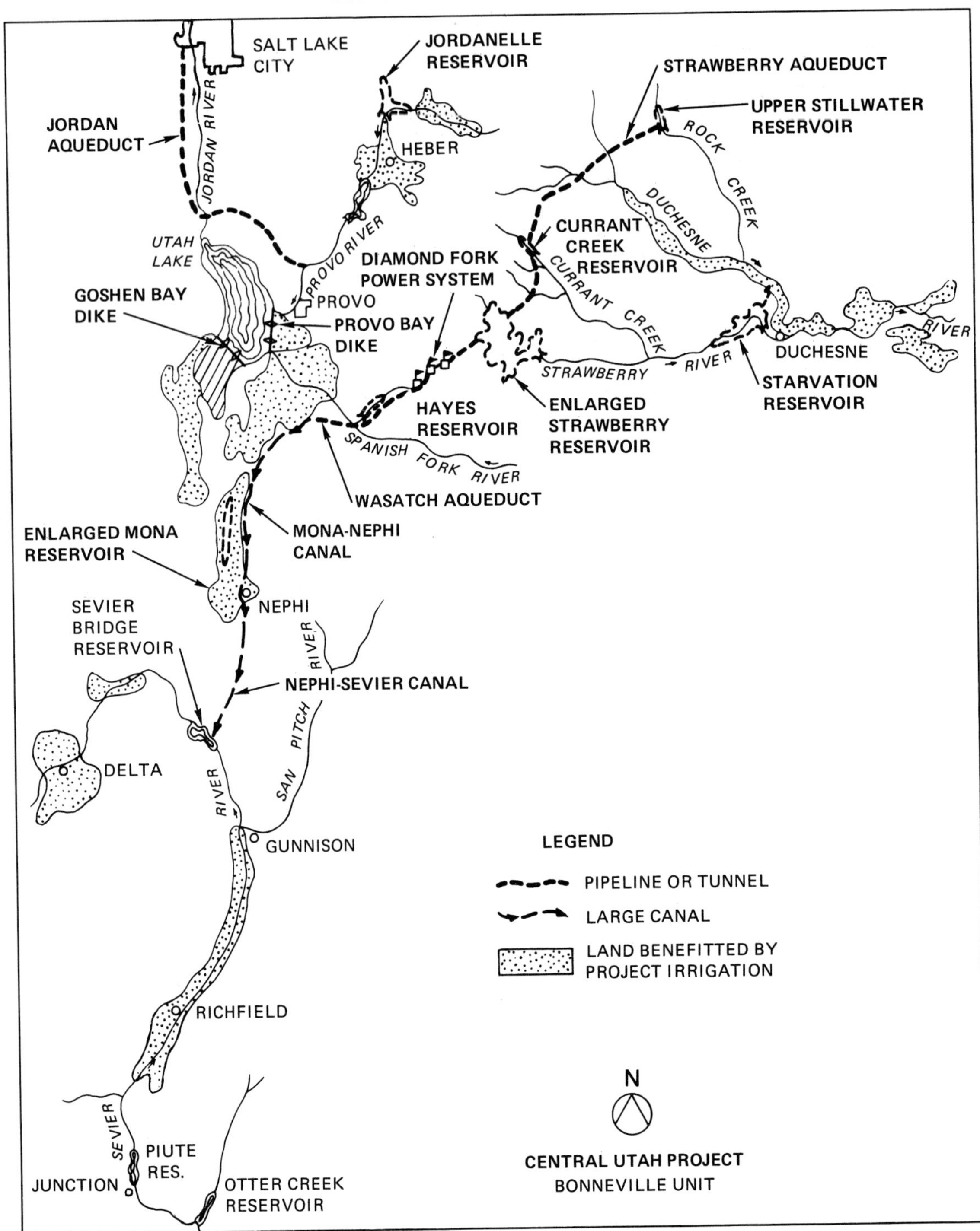

**MAP 3.4: Bonneville Unit
Schematic of Water Flows**

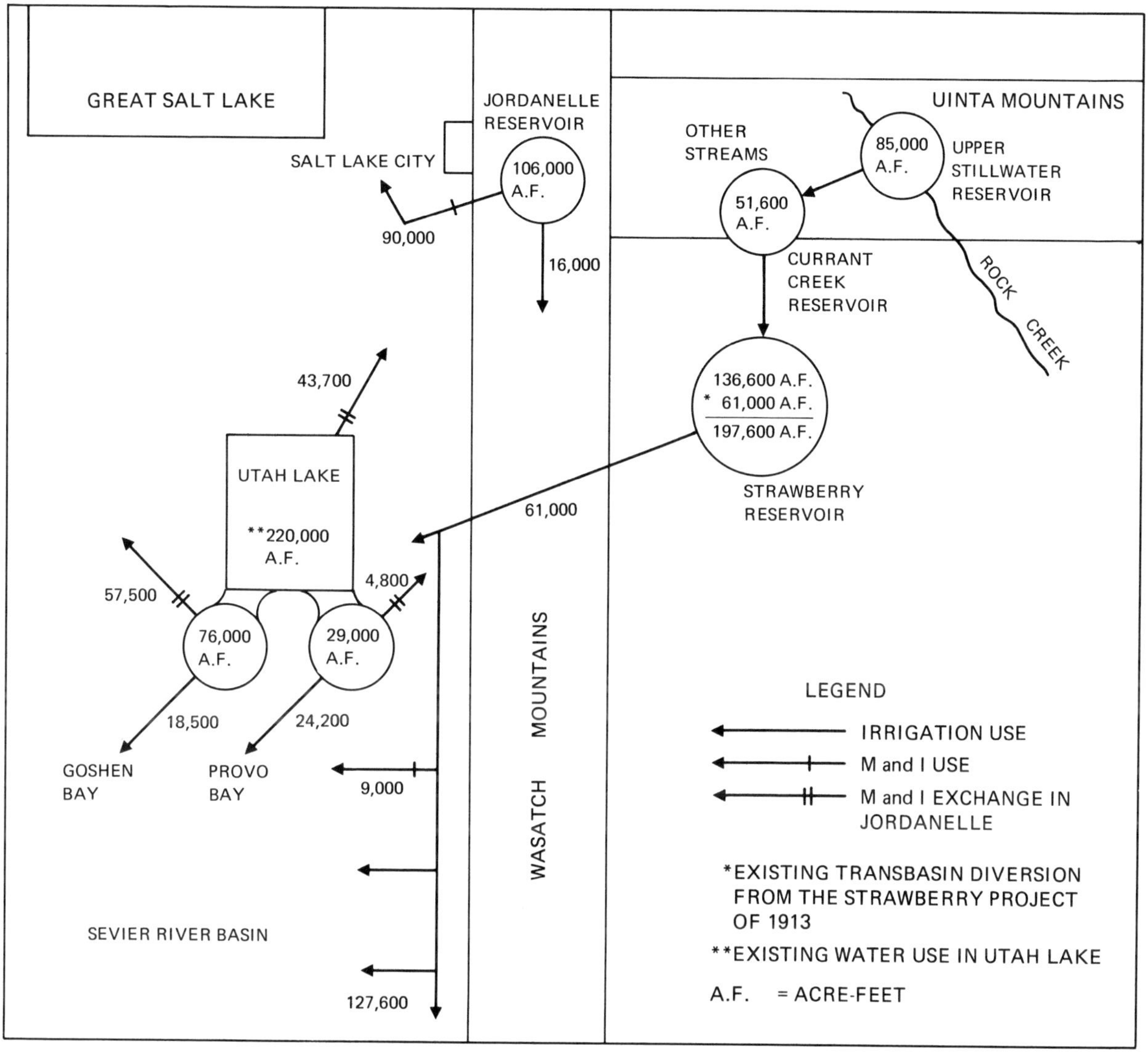

*Existing transbasin diversion from the Strawberry Project of 1913.

**Existing water use in Utah Lake.

A.F.—Acre-feet
Res.—Reservoir
Mtns.—Mountains

MAP 3.5:   Strawberry Aqueduct and Collection System

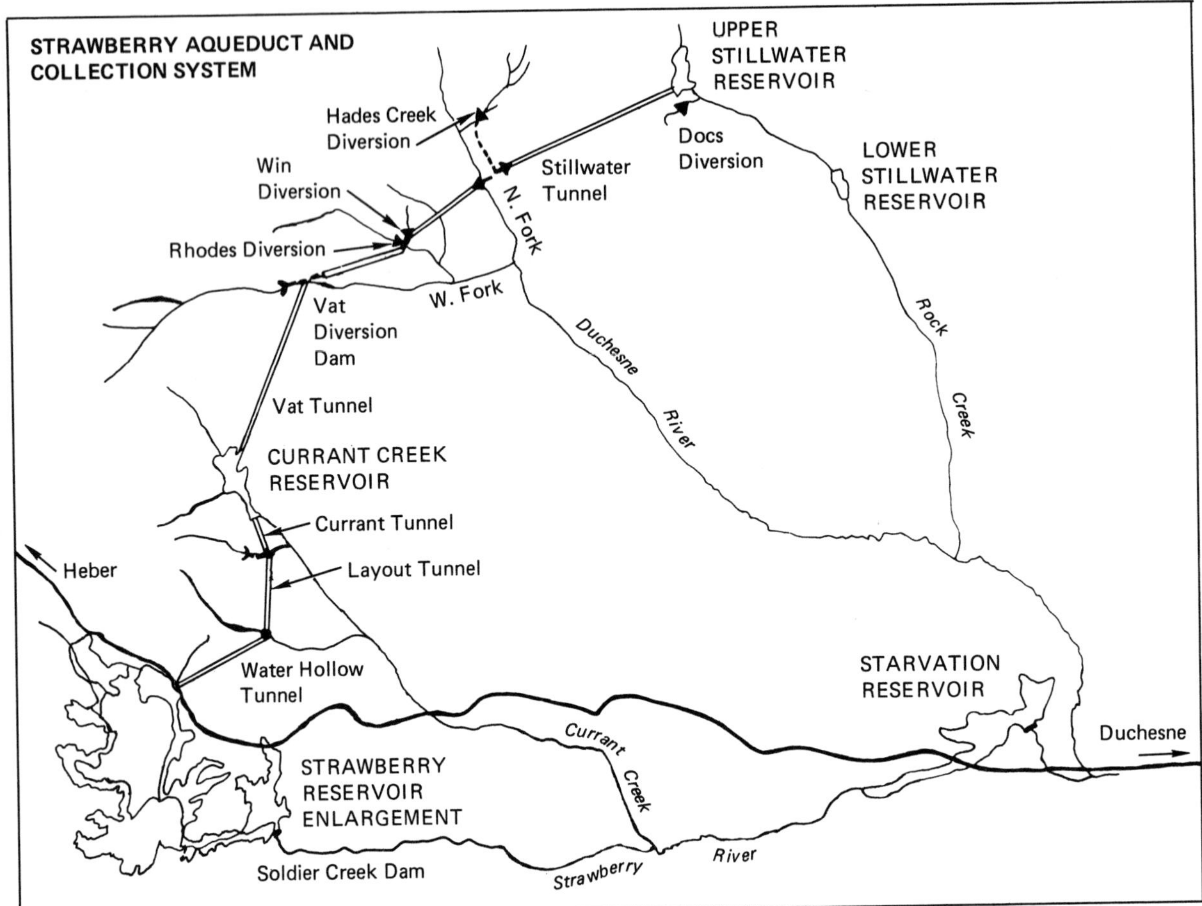

Construction on the Bonneville Unit commenced on March 29, 1967. The Starvation Dam and Reservoir complex was completed in September 1970. The Soldier Creek Dam, creating the enlarged Strawberry Reservoir, was completed in November 1973. The segment of the Strawberry Aqueduct System from the enlarged Strawberry Reservoir to Currant Creek, comprising the Water Hollow, Layout and Currant Tunnels, has been completed.

Source: Central Utah Conservancy District Manual, March, 1975.

MAP 3.6:   Currant Creek Reservoir

CURRANT CREEK RESERVOIR

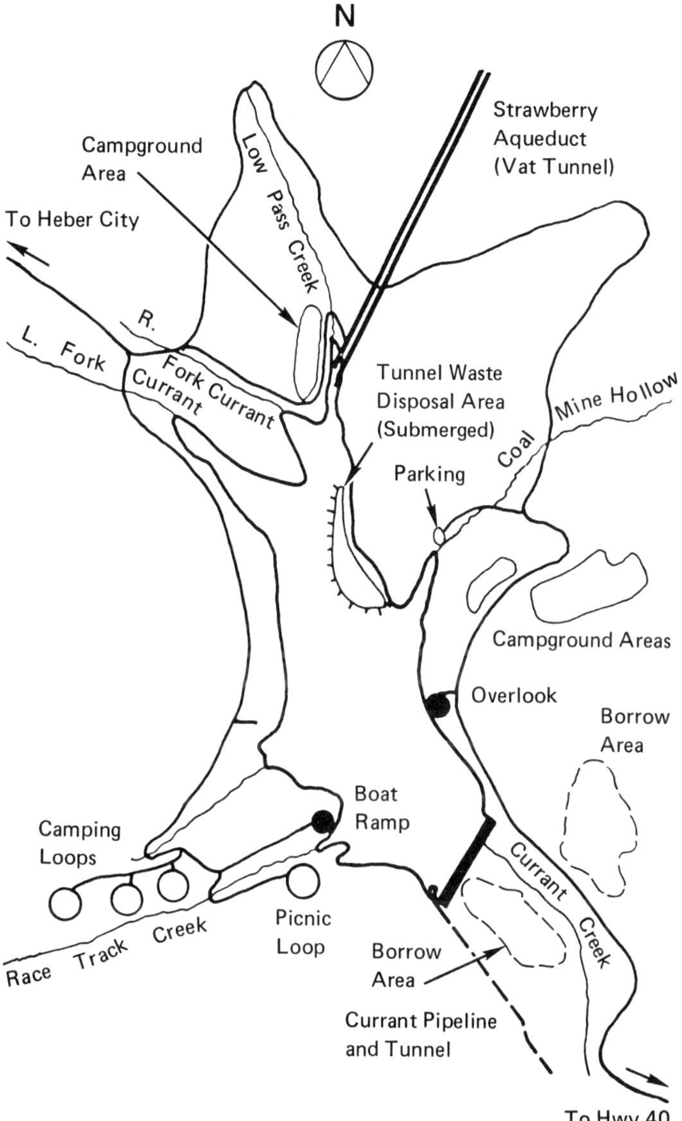

Currant Creek Reservoir will form an open water connection between the Vat Tunnel and Currant Creek pipeline portion of the Strawberry Aqueduct. It will divert water from Currant Creek and five of its smaller tributary streams into the Aqueduct.

Source: Central Utah Conservancy District Manual, March, 1975.

4

The Central Utah Project (B)

In the fall of 1973, Secretary of the Interior Rogers C.B. Morton faced a decision about whether to proceed with construction of the "Bonneville Unit" of the Central Utah Project (CUP). The CUP, a billion-dollar-plus water resource project, had been conceived in the 1950s by the Bureau of Reclamation in the Department of the Interior; the Bonneville Unit, one of the largest components of the project, was intended to augment the manageable water supply in the populous Bonneville Basin (where Salt Lake City is located), principally by transferring water into the basin from the mountain streams in the northeastern part of the state (see Maps 3.1 and 3.2). At the time of Morton's decision, the project had been under construction for about fifteen years and the Bonneville Unit was about 18% complete. The next features of the unit scheduled for construction were the Currant Creek Dam and Reservoir, which would receive and store water from the Strawberry Aqueduct and deliver water to the Strawberry Reservoir for subsequent transfer to the Bonneville Basin (see Maps 3.3–3.6). (The features necessary to effect this transfer—the Wasatch Aqueduct and Syar Tunnel—had not yet been built, but the Strawberry Reservoir enlargement was otherwise complete, and, with the construction of Currant Creek Dam, would be able to function independently in the event that further construction of the Bonneville Unit were discontinued.) Although Morton's immediate decision was simply whether to authorize construction of Currant Creek Dam, his decision would have obvious ramifications for the future of the entire Central Utah Project.

This case examines the CUP as a vehicle for resolving Utah's water problems. In particular, the case outlines the water needs to which the CUP is addressed; the history and scope of the project (and, more specifically, of the Bonneville and Ute Indian Units, the two most expensive components of the project); the possibilities for meeting Utah's water needs without massive relocation of supplies; and the conflicting concerns surrounding Secretary Morton's decision on continuing construction.

UTAH'S WATER NEEDS

Utah is the second driest state in the Union, receiving an average of 13 inches or 59 million acre-feet* of precipitation annually. Of this amount, an estimated 7.7 million a.f. or 13% enters Utah's rivers and streams and thus constitutes the state's total manageable water supply; the rest is lost through (for example) evaporation, plant transpiration, and contamination (as in the Great Salt Lake). Rainfall varies from year to year and season to season; and although Utah has not experienced a serious drought in more than a decade, the threat of a water shortage is very real to many citizens of the state. As one active proponent of water reclamation commented:

> . . . if we had two or three dry years in a row [that were] no more severe than some we had in the sixties, we would have water rationing in Salt Lake County, with problems of low pressure for fire protection and some areas periodically out of water.

The Bonneville Unit Definite Plan Report, prepared in 1964 by the Bureau of Reclamation (BuRec) with the assistance of a federal-state inter-agency task force, estimated the supply of water renewable through precipitation in the Bonneville Basin** at 2,263,000 a.f.; and all subsequent BuRec planning and appropriations requests for the Bonneville Unit were based on this estimate. The Bonneville Unit Plan estimated the 1965 demand for water in the Bonneville Basin at 2,634,000 a.f., meaning that 371,000 a.f. had to be diverted into the Basin from outside. The plan anticipated this "diversion requirement" to increase substantially by the year 2020, as Exhibit 4.1 shows. The various components of demand on which these estimates were based are outlined below.

Municipal and Industrial Water Needs

Municipal and industrial—or M&I—water, used for drinking, watering lawns, commercial and industrial purposes, and so forth, is a much smaller component of Utah's total water "budget" than irrigation uses, but it is also growing at a much faster rate. The 1970 Interim Report on the State of Utah Water Plan contained the following estimates for the state as a whole:

Use	1965	2020	% Increase
Irrigation	2,010,000	2,510,000	+ 25
M&I	150,000	800,000	+433

The estimated increase in M&I water needs is principally attributable to projected population growth, extrapolated from historical growth data. The 1930–70 annual population growth rate for all of Utah was about 1.9%,*** as compared to 2.2% for the densely populated Wasatch Front area (the area along the western edge of the Wasatch mountains), which by 1970 contained 77.6% of the state's population. (Utah's rural counties experienced a decrease in population of 0.8% annually during the same period.)

Utah's population and the attendant demand for M&I water are expected to continue to grow rapidly. BuRec's final Environmental Impact Statement for the Bonneville Unit contains the following population information:

> All projections made to date indicate a positive growth rate for the State of Utah, particularly during the period 1970–2020. The Harline study was conducted for the Bureau of Reclamation in 1964 by the Bureau of Economic and Business Research of the University of Utah. This projection was used in the Bonneville Unit Definite Plan Report because it was the most current projection available at the time. Since that time, several other projections have been made. The most recent is a 1971–1972 State of Utah study

---

*One acre-foot (a.f.) is the amount of water needed to cover an area of one acre to a depth of one foot; it is a standard measure of water supply.

**The Bonneville Basin is defined here as the drainage areas for the Jordan and Sevier Rivers; it thus excludes the Weber River drainage area, which lies just north of the Salt Lake City portion of the Wasatch Front area (see Map 3.1).

***This annual growth rate amounts to a total growth of 108% over the forty-year period, compared to 65% for the United States as a whole.

made by an interdisciplinary Federal-State agency task force brought together for the express purpose of deriving an up-to-date population projection for the state. This population projection and others [Exhibit 4.2] vary by about one million persons by the year 2020. Since all projections indicate a substantial growth and a related water requirement, the amount of water provided by the Bonneville Unit could only supply the requirement for a specific time period, depending on the actual population growth. For example, according to the 196[4] Harline curve, Bonneville Unit water would be required for Salt Lake County about 1972 and would satisfy the requirements until about 1990. According to the more conservative 1971 Utah State (OBERS)* curve, Bonneville Unit water would not be required until about 1980 and would fulfill the needs until about 2005.

The most significant factor in Utah's past and projected population growth is the state's high birth rate—currently the second highest in the nation. (Three-fourths of Utah's population belongs to the Church of Latter Day Saints, which opposes birth control. In the words of one church administrator: "Curtailment of birth is an abomination in the eyes of the Lord. . . . We must multiply and replicate as stated by the Lord.") Also, the higher estimates of population growth incorporate projections of more rapid economic growth in Utah than in the rest of the United States, in consequence of the state's low energy costs, abundant energy resources, and relatively low labor costs. Although BuRec noted that projections of Utah's population and need for M&I water vary widely, the Bureau continued to use the 1964 Harline projection in planning for the Bonneville Unit. (The Sierra Club has pointed out that use of the lower 1971 OBERS projection would reduce estimated water demand for the year 2020 by 372,000 a.f.)

Irrigation Water Requirements

In outlining the need for increased irrigation capacity offered by the Bonneville Unit, the Bureau of Reclamation observed that:

> . . . irrigation will continue to be the major use of water in the future in terms of water diverted

and consumptive use. The major irrigation water need is for supplemental service to presently irrigated lands to stabilize existing agricultural production and the development of full service to new land areas to offset those lands being taken out of agricultural production by industrialization and urbanization. By maintaining the existing agricultural base, adequate greenbelt areas could be preserved. Stabilizing the farm economy also reduces an outmigration trend from rural to urban areas. Development of Bonneville Unit water for irrigation purposes, as discussed above, is in harmony with the planning principle of the State Water Plan. The plan states that sufficient water should be provided, where financially possible, for (1) supplemental water needs for those irrigated lands having a reasonably high level of productivity or the irrigation of new good-quality lands when such irrigation would stabilize and strengthen existing farm units and (2) to the extent that water is available, the permanent irrigation of new lands in those areas where the net return, considering all costs, would be the greatest. The State Water Plan also recognizes the temporary interim use of water for irrigation until needed on a permanent basis for municipal and industrial use. The projected requirement for irrigation by the time frames and the amount that could be supplied by the Bonneville Unit, according to the Bonneville Unit Plan, is included in the totals given in [Exhibit 4.1].

Recent evidence disputes the need for increased irrigation acreage and more water for irrigation, especially in a state such as Utah, which has a short growing season and limited water resources. In 1972, the National Water Commission's Report (the product of a five-year, $5 million water resource study authorized by Congress and approved by President Nixon) contained this statement:

> Results of the agricultural forecasting studies indicate that food and fiber demands in the year 2000 could be met by returning land now idled under government programs to production and by using less irrigated land than at the present without placing undue strain on either the total available water supply in the West or the food producing capacity of U.S. agriculture. Under all of the alternative futures considered, consumptive use of water in agriculture would be less than

---

*OBERS is an acronym for Office of Business Economics, Department of Commerce and Economic Research Services, Department of Agriculture.

at present. In the event of future water scarcities, especially in the West, agriculture need not use more water but could actually release a fairly large supply of water for industrial, urban, and other uses. The transfer of water from agriculture to other uses would not put pressure on the nation's food supplies or export possibilities. Neither would it have other than minimal effects on the cost of food to the nation's consumers.

With a change in the life styles and eating habits of consumers to reduce demand for beef, even more water and land would be surplus in 2000. With a relatively mild level of substitution of soy protein meats for part of the beef consumption in 2000, the productive capacity of U.S. agriculture could surpass any level previously experienced in this nation. Large amounts of both water and land would be surplus, as far as agricultural needs were concerned. At the same time, farm prices would be substantially depressed below recent levels.

In a 1974 Ralph Nader Task Force Report entitled *Damming the West,* a USDA economist stated:

We would have a hard time defending the need for more irrigated land. About one-third or 160,000,000 acres of cropland in the U.S. are presently idle. Of this idle acreage, about 50,000,000 acres lie idle as a result of government expenditures to take farmland out of production.

According to the Interim Report on the State Water Plan (March 1970) done by the development-oriented Utah State Division of Water Resources, opportunities exist within Utah for more efficient irrigation. The report noted numerous possibilities in most areas of the state to increase the effectiveness and productivity of irrigation through more intensive land use, land reclamation and drainage procedures, the transfer of water to more productive lands, and other means. As an example, the Report cited a 1969 USDA study of the Sevier River Basin which concluded that a 10% increase in the efficiency of use of irrigation water would make up that basin's currently estimated 78,000 a.f. deficiency (a deficiency currently proposed to be made up with Bonneville Unit water).

According to a 1971 BuRec study, 245,000 acres of new land to serve irrigated agricultural purposes will be needed by 2020 because approximately 239,000 acres of irrigated land are expected to be lost to urban, industrial, and other uses. However, the Sierra Club pointed out in 1973 that the development of such substantial new irrigated acreage appeared unlikely in view of the conclusions of the National Water Commission report (cited above) and in view of a growing movement to require beneficiaries of federal public works projects to pay the full cost through user charges and market interest rates. Should the associated water rights of this irrigated acreage be totally reallocated to M&I uses, about 956,000 a.f. of water would be made available (on the basis of current United States Department of Agriculture (USDA) estimates of four acre-feet used per acre of irrigated land).

Other Water Needs

In addition to the projected growth in municipal, industrial, and irrigation demands for water, growth of other—and to some extent competing—needs for water can be anticipated in the future. Recreational uses already have a well-established constituency, which can be expected to grow with future population growth. Also, the conservation of existing streams and wetlands for ecological purposes has attracted increasingly vigorous support.

Often competing with recreational and ecological demands on the water supply is demand for hydroelectric power. Since 1938, the demand for electrical energy has doubled every ten years in the state of Utah: in 1938 Utah used 800 million kilowatt-hours of electricity compared to more than 6,000 million kilowatt-hours used in 1968. In this same period, generating capacity requirements increased from about 150,000 kilowatts to over one million kilowatts. Consequently, water development projects like the CUP have a strong appeal to those concerned with future energy shortages. (The Bonneville Unit alone, for example, will produce 320 million kilowatt-hours of electrical energy annually from hydroelectric power plants having an installed capacity of 133,500 kilowatts.)

Competition between demands on water supply—not unique to the state of Utah—has been increased by the recognition of the possible importance of developing oil shale as an energy source, for which development large amounts of water are necessary.

The Uinta Basin (from which the Bonneville Unit will draw much of its water supply) is estimated to contain 15% of the world's known oil shale deposits (equivalent to 80 billion barrels of oil) plus small amounts of oil and natural gas. Presently, there are oil wells operating and being drilled in the Uinta Basin, but the oil is shipped to the Bonneville Basin for refinement because the water needed for refineries is not available at the Uinta Basin, since it is already being withdrawn by the Bonneville Unit. The surface water being removed from the Uinta Basin (135,000 a.f.) by the Bonneville Unit is equivalent to that required for the processing of 900,000 barrels per day of oil from shale. Water for oil shale development is intended to come from the Ute Indian Unit, the final phase of the CUP.

THE CENTRAL UTAH PROJECT

In 1950, a 96-page interim report from the Regional Director to the Commissioner of Reclamation contained the first outline of what is now known as the Bonneville Unit of the Central Utah Project (see Maps 3.3 and 3.4). BuRec described the project as follows:

> *Central Utah Project, Utah.* The comprehensive Central Utah Project, a large multiple-purpose development, is of such magnitude that it has been planned in two parts—the initial phase, a unified portion that could operate independently, and the ultimate phase. Only the initial phase is included in the group recommended for initial participation in the Upper Colorado River Account.
>
> The initial phase would intercept the flow of streams on the south slope of the Uinta Mountains as far east as Rock Creek and would convey the water westward by gravity flow for use in the Bonneville Basin. Water for replacement and expanded irrigation in the Uinta Basin would be provided by storage in local streams. Several regulatory reservoirs would be required in both the Bonneville and Uinta Basins, the principal one being the enlarged Strawberry Reservoir on the Strawberry River. By construction of Soldier Creek Dam the capacity of the reservoir would be increased from 283,000 acre-feet to 1,360,000 acre-feet. The initial phase would provide for the irrigation of 26,614 acres of new land and 163,957 acres now irrigated but in need of more water or improved water regulation. It would also provide 47,000 acre-feet of water annually for

municipal, industrial, and related uses. It would generate each year approximately 383,100,000 kilowatt-hours of firm energy, and 3,600,000 kilowatt-hours of nonfirm energy.

In 1951, a supplemental congressional report on the Central Utah Project offered additional information on the consideration of alternative plans within the project definition:

> After the general scheme for the Central Utah Project had been outlined, alternative means of accomplishing certain objectives still remained. In each instance it had been necessary to choose between alternatives in order to set up the plan. . . . The Central Utah Project has evolved from previous investigations of various independent projects. . . . The project would achieve and enlarge upon the water development objectives of practically all of the earlier plans, although by generally different means. Because of its larger, more flexible operation, it would provide more complete and efficient utilization of the available water supply than would the several independent developments and would provide more benefits for the costs involved.

As first considered by Congress, the CUP was divided into two phases, and subsequently divided into six separate units for planning and construction. The initial phase, consisting of the Jensen, Vernal, Upalco, and Bonneville Units, was authorized in 1956 as a part of the Colorado River Storage Project Act. At that time, the cost of the initial phase was estimated at $231,044,000. The Vernal Unit is now in operation, and the Bonneville Unit, largest in the CUP, is about 20% complete. Funds have been made available to start the Jensen and Upalco Units.

The second phase of the project includes the Uinta and Ute Indian Units, neither of which have been built. The Uinta Unit was authorized by Congress in 1968 and final construction plans are now being prepared. The Ute Indian Unit is still the subject of feasibility studies, which are a prerequisite for congressional authorization and are scheduled to be completed in 1978.

The Bonneville Unit

The Bonneville Unit, now under construction, is the largest and most comprehensive of the authorized units in the initial phase of the Central Utah Project. When completed, the unit would make available a total of 313,000 a.f. of water annually. This water would be stored and transported by a complex system involving construction of ten new reservoirs and the enlargement of two existing reservoirs; more than 140 miles of aqueducts, tunnels, and canals; three power plants; nine pumping plants and 200 miles of pipe drains.

Crossing the high flank of the Uinta Mountains, the Strawberry Aqueduct, about 37 miles long, will intercept the flows of Rock Creek and several other tributaries to the Duchesne River. Upper Stillwater and Currant Creek Reservoirs will serve as storage reservoirs along the aqueduct. Water will flow by gravity through the aqueduct to the enlarged Strawberry Reservoir. The completed Soldier Creek Dam (about seven miles downstream from the existing Strawberry Dam) has already increased the potential capacity of Strawberry Reservoir from 283,000 to 1,100,000 acre-feet (see Maps 3.5 and 3.6).

The 6.5 mile-long pressurized Syar Tunnel will divert storage water from Strawberry Reservoir through the Wasatch Divide between the Uinta and Bonneville Basins. Approximately 197,000 acre-feet will be released annually through the tunnel, including 61,000 acre-feet of present yield from the existing Strawberry Reservoir. Water descending about 2,000 feet to the Bonneville Basin floor will flow through the Syar, Sixth Water and Dyne power plants of the Diamond Ford Power System. The plants will have a total generating capacity of about 133,000 kilowatts.

During the nonirrigation season, about 97,000 acre-feet of water released to turn the power plant turbines, if not required for other uses, will be stored in either Utah Lake, the 51,500 acre-foot capacity Hayes Reservoir on Diamond Fork, the enlarged Mona Reservoir, or the existing Sevier Bridge Reservoir. Water stored in these reservoirs is to be used during the irrigation season. About 100,000 acre-feet of water released through the power plants during the irrigation season will be diverted directly onto project land or used for municipal and industrial purposes. Wasatch Aqueduct, Mona-Nephi Canal and Nephi-Sevier Canal will convey irrigation water from the power plants and reservoirs to lands in Utah and Juab Counties and the Sevier River Basin. Municipal and industrial water released from Strawberry Reservoir will be used in south Utah and Juab Counties.

Provo and Goshen Bays will be separated from Utah Lake by dikes to reduce evaporation losses. Part of the project water collected in Utah Lake will be exchanged upstream on Provo River for water that presently flows into Utah Lake. The replaced Provo River water will be stored in the 320,000 acre-foot capacity Jordanelle Reservoir to be constructed seven miles north of Heber City. Water from Jordanelle Reservoir will be used for some irrigation in the Heber area but primarily for municipal and industrial purposes in northern Utah and Salt Lake Counties. Distribution of the municipal and industrial water will be by the Jordan Aqueduct System.

Through Utah Lake diking and Jordanelle Reservoir Storage and other minor in-basin developments, another 116,000 a.f. will be added to the Bonneville Basin supply, bringing the total Bonneville Unit additions to about 313,000 a.f.

Diversion	197,000 a.f.
Addition	116,000 a.f.
	313,000 a.f.

Exhibit 4.3 shows the allocation of this water between the Bonneville and Uinta Basins (see also Map 3.4).

This 313,000 a.f. of water will be made available annually by the Bonneville Unit for the following purposes:

High quality municipal and industrial water	99,000 a.f.
Supplemental and full service irrigation	207,500 a.f.
Stream flows for fishery	6,500 a.f.
	313,000 a.f.

More than two-thirds of the 313,000 a.f. made available by the completed Bonneville Unit will be allotted to supplemental and new irrigation water. Of that share (206,500 a.f.), 112,000 a.f. will supply supplemental irrigation for 213,000 acres of previously irrigated lands in the Bonneville Basin, and 95,000 a.f. will supply irrigation for 30,000 acres of previously unirrigated lands in the basin.

The cost of providing 99,000 a.f. of M&I water to the Bonneville Basin has most recently been estimated in excess of $71 million or $15/a.f. annually over the 50-year life of the project (exclusive of average annual operating and maintenance costs of over $85,000), although other estimates have ranged as high as $60/a.f. of M&I water.

In 1964, BuRec estimated the direct benefit-cost ratio of the Bonneville Unit to be 1.30.* The Bonneville Unit investment in irrigation is about $1,300 per acre, or over 50% of its total cost of over $400,000,000 in 1974 dollars. The farmer's repayment contract insures a return of $2.10 per acre. A special property tax covering all residents in the project area will return $2.43 per acre. The remaining amount will be paid for by power revenues from federal projects. Users of M&I water must pay the full cost—with interest—of that water, but irrigators cannot be charged more than the Secretary of the Interior determines they are able to pay.

The Ute Indian Unit

The Ute Indian Unit is designed to further increase the supply of water diverted to the Salt Lake City area from the Uinta Basin and to make more water available for use in the Uinta Basin itself. Increased irrigation, municipal, and industrial water will be made available, as well as additional power and recreational opportunities. When the demand for water exhausts the supply of the initial phase of the Central Utah Project, the Ute Indian Unit will then—as presently planned, close to the year 2020—be phased into the project to meet the demand. The Ute Indian Unit is expected to yield 700,000 a.f. at a cost of $500,000,000.

Two major aqueducts, the principal features of the Ute Indian Unit, will make Colorado River water readily available to both the Bonneville and Uinta Basins. The Uinta Aqueduct will be an extension of the Strawberry Aqueduct being constructed as part of the Bonneville Unit, and will collect water from Uinta mountain streams and transfer it to the enlarged Strawberry Reservoir and on into the Bonneville Basin. The Flaming Gorge Aqueduct will convey water from Flaming Gorge Reservoir into the Uinta Basin to replace water that has been released to the Bonneville Basin through the Uinta Aqueduct, and to provide additional quantities of water to the Uinta Basin—123,000 a.f. of Colorado River water.

The potential benefits from development of the Ute Indian Unit are great and will have a significant

bearing on future state water planning. Realization of this potential, however, depends heavily on the determination of whether or not the unit will be permitted to draw upon Utah's entitlements to Colorado River water. To date, many possibilities for developing these entitlements have been explored, yet no plan has been completed and the possibilities remain mired in competing needs. Recent energy requirements, for example, have placed new emphasis on the development and use of water resources for power generation, and as other water needs increase beyond the readily available water supply, the competition among users will intensify and the priorities will become more difficult to define.

The task of planning the Ute Indian Unit to accommodate these diverse needs has been assumed by the Bureau of Reclamation, with the concurrence of the state. In 1973, the federal government endorsed the Water Resources Council's proposed Guidelines for Implementing Principles and Standards for Multi-objective Planning of Water Resources; and thus, the Ute Indian Unit must be formulated and evaluated in accordance with these new planning procedures. As required by the procedures, a multi-objective planning (MOP) team is in the process of organization, and will be representative of interested state and federal planning agencies, the Ute Indian Tribe and the public. The guidelines also require that due consideration be given to prior commitments, economic justification, repayment capabilities and other requirements imposed on all proposals. In addition, alternative sources of water, weather modification, and water saving practices must be fully explored and evaluated. The Ute Indian Unit investigations and planning report are tentatively scheduled for completion during FY 1978.

ALTERNATIVES

Because the Bonneville and Ute Indian Units involve such great expense and environmental upheaval, both proponents and opponents of the project have had to concern themselves with possible alternative methods of meeting Utah's future water needs. Parcels of water in the Bonneville Basin, both natural and man-made, have yet to be fully used, and Utah's own State Water Plan lists "more effective use of locally available water supplies" as one of three

---

*In 1956, BuRec estimated the benefit-cost ratio of the Bonneville Unit to be 1.8 to 1, but rising costs have since reduced this ratio. Many critics, disputing BuRec's determinations of costs and benefits, contend that the ratio should be still further reduced.

approaches to meeting the state's water needs (the others are public works such as CUP and better state planning and management). Numerous proposals have been put forward for "more effective use of locally available water supplies." In comments on the 1973 draft Environmental Impact Statement (EIS) for the Bonneville Unit, for example, the Sierra Club noted that BuRec had not considered the following possibilities for substantially increasing the Bonneville Basin water supply: increasing the efficiency of Sevier Basin (see Map 3.1); diking Utah Lake to reduce water loss from that source; and recycling and treating waste water in Salt Lake City, to comply with state water quality laws. The Club cited various estimates from federal agencies indicating that these measures could add 293,000 a.f. to the Bonneville Basin water supply. Although the practicality of these and other such prospects for developing untapped water resources have not been examined in great detail, the following alternatives to inter-basin transfers appear at least technically feasible:

Groundwater. Groundwater sources may be developed to meet further needs in the Wasatch Front. BuRec's EIS on the Bonneville Unit acknowledges the potential availability of 30,000 a.f. annually of high-quality water from groundwater wells. Tests performed by the Utah Department of Natural Resources indicate that a considerable increase in the use of groundwater is scientifically feasible, and that the present groundwater yield could be increased by 50,000 a.f. annually with no serious adverse environmental effects. The Salt Lake Water Conservancy District has drilled approximately 30 wells, and towns surrounding Salt Lake City are drilling wells from year to year as more water is needed.

Even more optimistically, the U.S. Geological Survey and the Utah State Division of Water Resources have indicated the availability of additional groundwater up to 150,000 a.f. per year in the Wasatch area. Mining groundwater is considerably less expensive than the $1,500 per acre-foot development cost of the Bonneville Unit. However, experts have testified that many of the groundwater wells west of the Jordan River are really not available for use because they are contaminated by chemicals from nearby industry and are below state health standards.

Recycling. Utah water pollution laws require that all waters in the Bonneville Basin be Class C (culinary quality) by 1978. According to EPA estimates, the advanced wastewater treatment and recy-

cling necessary to implement the pollution laws will make over 100,000 a.f. of M&I water available. The State Division of Water Resources has studied the recycling of Wasatch Front M&I water and has shown that it is economically feasible (less expensive than Bonneville water) and practical.

Phreatophyte Control. Phreatophytes, meaning "well plants," depend on groundwater which lies within reach of their roots. These succulent plants, which grow in areas of high water table, have no agricultural use but do store a large amount of water. Phreatophyte control, especially around Utah Lake, could result in savings of 56,400 a.f. per year according to 1969 reports of Utah state water agencies. Phreatophyte control costs are much lower than Bonneville Unit costs.

Reservoirs. The proposed Little Dell and existing Deer Creek Reservoirs could provide an additional 75,000 a.f. in arid years if their capabilities were maximized. In 1971, the U.S. Army Corps of Engineers authorized a reservoir on Little Dell Creek to provide Salt Lake with 30,000 a.f. of high quality M&I water. However, the project has not been built, largely because of expected evaporation losses. In addition, Salt Lake City has 47,200 a.f. per year available from Deer Creek Reservoir. From 1964–72, the city has needed only 24% of its allotment from Deer Creek, leaving 47,200 a.f. of M&I water annually untapped.

Rivers. There are 65,000 a.f. of water available from the completed Weber Basin Project in northwest Utah. The project, built by BuRec with public funds, is uneconomical and underused at present because irrigators will not buy its expensive water; but this water could be marketed in Salt Lake City at less expense than Bonneville Unit water. Also, according to the Interior Department's Bureau of Sport Fisheries and Wildlife (BSF&W) (later renamed the Fish and Wildlife Service [F&WS]), "There is a potential for development of 110,000 a.f. of M&I water in the Bear River drainage" which could be delivered to Salt Lake City.

Pricing. Despite its aridity, Utah has the nation's second lowest water prices ($.25/first 1000 gallons, $.17/1000 gallons after that), which encourage water use. Salt Lake City residents use more M&I water per capita than people in Tucson, despite the latter's hotter, drier climate. Salt Lake City, for example, uses more than 56,000 a.f. per year for watering municipal lawns and gardens.

CONFLICT OVER THE CUP

Despite the scale of the CUP, the availability of (largely unexplored) alternatives, and the size of the environmental and economic commitment represented by the project, the project encountered no serious resistance until well into the 1960s. The problems that materialized at that time centered on financing, environmental impact, and Indian water rights.

Financial Problems

On January 21, 1964, President Johnson sent to Congress a proposed budget which included $600,000 for planning the final phase of the CUP and which omitted the Bonneville Unit from the "new starts" list. The *Deseret News*, Utah's Mormon newspaper, responded:

> For the time being, Utah may be able to make due with no new reclamation starts. But because our long-range future depends more on the development of water—with the industry and jobs it brings—than on a defense industry subject to sudden changes, we can't afford to relent in our efforts to make the desert bloom.

On March 2, 1964, in response to this threat to reclamation, the Central Utah Water Conservancy District (CUWCD) came into being as a private organization for the promotion of reclamation in Central Utah. Edward W. Clyde, a Salt Lake City attorney, drafted the petition for formation of the CUWCD and remained the vital force in the District's organization. As outlined in the petition and approved by the District Court, the CUWCD—whose 17 board members represent the seven Utah counties in which the initial phase of the CUP would be built*—has two basic responsibilities. First, it will set rates for water use and propose tax assessments to finance operation of the project and repay federal loans; and second, it will negotiate with BuRec on repayment terms. The organization has also assumed for itself the responsi-

---

*These seven counties include nearly 80% of Utah's population.

bility of lobbying Congress for appropriations to complete the initial phase of the CUP. Utah state officials greeted word of the CUWCD's creation with enthusiasm. As Governor George D. Clyde commented:

> It's the best piece of news I've heard in a long time. I commend all the counties concerned for the diligence, patience and care they took to form this district.

On October 10, 1964, Palmer DeLong, CUP manager for the Bureau of Reclamation, told the CUWCD that plans were far enough developed that construction could begin on the Bonneville Unit as soon as Congress appropriated the money.

In February 1965, the Senate eliminated Bonneville Unit construction funds in its budget for FY 1966. Senator Wallace Bennett (R-Utah) lashed out at his colleagues after the cut:

> Initially, the budget contained $3.6 million to begin construction of the Bonneville Unit, but then the reclamation program was slashed by President Johnson to divert funds to the so-called poverty programs. Can it be that good, solid reclamation projects that pay for themselves are to be pushed aside for state welfare doles?

On October 14, 1965, after both House and Senate Appropriations Committees had heard testimony from the Utah congressional delegation, state officials, and BuRec representatives, a Senate-House Conference Committee approved a $3.5 million appropriation for the start of construction on the Bonneville Unit.

While Congress considered the question of federal contributions to the project, the CUWCD was seeking approval of a repayment contract from voters within the District. The CUWCD's public information committee used an advertising agency to promote the CUP and to "pre-sell the favorable decision of the voters in the conservancy district." The election by which the voters (property taxpayers) would authorize the CUWCD to execute the repayment contract with the Bureau of Reclamation was held on December 14, 1965. In the weeks prior to the election, voters were subjected to a media blitz promoting ratification. The vote was 15 to 1 in favor of the CUP, with six of the seven counties voting to ratify. The seventh county, Uintah County, narrowly defeated the proposal on the basis that it did not want its high quality mountain stream water—which would be diverted to the Bonneville Basin—to be replaced by low quality Green River water.

Work began on the Bonneville Unit in 1969. After the groundbreaking on May 31, construction started simultaneously on the three projects which composed the Starvation Complex of the Unit. Although work continued in fiscal years 1968-70, appropriations decreased—from $11.8 million in FY 1968 to $7.6 million in FY 1969 and only $5.6 million in FY 1970. In December 1970, the Nixon Administration put a freeze order on $31.7 million worth of Bureau of Reclamation projects, including the $2.0 million appropriated by the Congress for the CUP in FY 1971.

Utah's congressional delegation appeared before both Senate and House Appropriations subcommittees on May 20, 1971 in an urgent appeal for at least $20 million for the Bonneville Unit in the FY 1972 budget. (The Nixon Administration had earlier recommended $10.2 million.) The Utah delegation vehemently objected to any limitations on funding for the unit:

> If funding continues at this rate it will be 60 years before the Bonneville Unit is completed. I submit this is false economy. This is no pork-barrel project.
>
> —Senator Bennett

> We have four million acres of arid lands suitable for raising crops which could be made fertile by irrigation.
>
> —Senator Moss

> Those who complain of high costs must be reminded there are a number of areas where you can't put a dollar value. One unit of the project is going to help the Ute Indians.
>
> —Representative McKay

> A more efficient agricultural water supply will be an incentive for our young people to stay on the farm instead of moving to already overcrowded and troubled urban areas.
>
> —Clyde Ritchie
> CUWCD President

In October 1971, a Senate Appropriations subcommittee met to consider supplemental spending on reclamation projects, including the CUP. The Washington correspondent of the *Deseret News* made the following report:

It is hinted that the Nixon Administration might spend another $5.5 million on CUP if Congress votes it. It may be significant that Senator Wallace Bennett, Utah's Republican senior Senator, is doing much of Nixon's work in the Senate on economic policy, and Senator Bennett's position could be influential.

Indications are that water project money will be flowing freely in the next few months, particularly in the West.

On November 17, the Nixon Administration requested —and received—$5.5 million for the CUP in a supplemental budget request for FY 1972. Appropriations for the project rose the next year to $29.4 million, but declined again in FY 1974, to $6.3 million.

As this brief history of CUP appropriations suggests, Congress has in the last analysis come through with the funds needed to continue construction, although the level of congressional support—and of funding—has fluctuated. Palmer DeLong, BuRec project manager for CUP, noted in an address to the CUWCD's annual meeting in April 1973 that "more progress was made on the CUP during 1972 than in any year" since it began. But DeLong went on to say that the main threat to continued construction had become the controversy over the environmental impacts of the Bonneville Unit.

Environmental Impacts

As the construction of the Bonneville Unit proceeded, environmental complaints began to be registered against the CUP. On New Year's Day 1966, the *Deseret News* published the following article:

The Wildlife Management Institute, headquartered in Washington, D.C., has taken exception to recreation propaganda published by the CUWCD. The District and BuRec also found strong objections from Utah sportsmen recently for statements painting the CUP as a "recreation gain."

. . . Coming under heavy censure was the bureau's statement that they were "providing 6,500 acre-feet of water for fish life" when in fact they were not "providing" it but leaving that small amount after receiving most of the stream . . .

There are a number of things the CUWCD doesn't say. No mention is made that the ultimate phase will dry up 6 of the 9 best trout streams in Utah or that BuRec is planning to allow only 6,500 a.f. of water per year for fish-life in the initial phase. That is barely enough water to wet the rocks on a couple of the streams.

Omitted, too, is mention of the fact that the CUWCD has the power to tax real estate to pay for non-reimbursable costs of the project. Thus, a Salt Lake City fly fisherman could pay a tax on his home to help deny water to his favorite trout stream.

These complaints, and those of the Sierra Club, Trout Unlimited, and the U.S. Forest Service, failed to produce a closer examination of CUP's environmental impacts.

NEPA. In December of 1969 the National Environmental Policy Act (NEPA) was passed "to establish a national policy for the environment, to provide for the establishment of a Council on Environmental Quality (CEQ), and for other environmental purposes." The newly-created CEQ was composed of a three-member council appointed by the President, included in whose duties were:

> . . . a review of the programs and activities of the federal government . . . with particular reference to their effects on the environment and on the conservation, development, and utilization of natural resources . . .

Section 102 (2)(c) of NEPA states that the Congress "authorizes and directs that to the fullest extent possible . . . all agencies of the Federal Government shall . . ."

> (c) include in every recommendation or report on proposals for legislation and other major Federal actions significantly affecting the quality of the human environment, a detailed statement by the responsible official on—
> (i) the environmental impact of the proposed action;
> (ii) any adverse environmental effects which cannot be avoided should the proposal be implemented;
> (iii) alternatives to the proposed action;
> (iv) the relationship between local short-term uses of man's environment and the maintenance and enhancement of long-term productivity; and
> (v) any irreversible and irretrievable commitments of resources which would be involved in the proposed action should it be implemented.

Prior to making any detailed statement, the responsible Federal official shall consult with and obtain the comments of any Federal agency which has jurisdiction by law or special expertise with respect to any environmental impact involved.

On April 23, 1971, the CEQ provided guidelines for preparing environmental impact statements that had particular application to the Bonneville Unit, since the guidelines interpreted the application of Section 102 (2)(c) of NEPA to existing projects and programs.

> To the maximum extent practicable the section 102(2)(c) procedure should be applied to further major Federal actions having a significant effect on the environment even though they arise from projects or programs initiated prior to enactment of the Act on January 1, 1970. Where it is not practicable to reassess the basic course of action, it is still important that further incremental major actions be shaped so as to minimize adverse environmental consequences. It is also important in further action that account be taken of environmental consequences not fully evaluated at the outset of the project or program.

In accordance with these guidelines, the Bureau of Reclamation began to compile information for the preparation of an environmental impact statement in June 1971.

By autumn 1971, more concerned individuals and environmental groups had expressed a need for further reexamination of the CUP.

> The Sierra Club opposes further funding of the Central Utah Project and urges a comprehensive re-evaluation of it be made by independent, qualified and disinterested experts.
> —Sierra Club Resolution
> September 26, 1971

> Every possible alternative should be explored before diverting so many biologically high quality streams in the Central Utah Project. The public does not realize the irreversible process involved here. All of BuRec's technological skill should be called upon to avoid the loss of these streams where possible.
> —David Gillespie, PhD
> Aquatic Biologist

The CUP should be reappraised on the grounds that it would concentrate too much population and economic growth in Salt Lake City when such growth should be spread throughout the state.

—Gary L. Gregor, PhD
Sociologist,
University of Utah

The Planners have never told the whole story to the public. The original plans of the CUP are entirely out of date with present environmental values. We need more information.

—David L. Freed
Trout Unlimited

Draft EIS. On August 14, 1972, BuRec released the first draft of its Environmental Impact Statement (EIS) to CEQ and the public, as required by NEPA. A public hearing on the project was held on September 22-23. Sixteen years and $84 million into the CUP, the Bureau of Reclamation and the CUWCD found themselves under severe pressure at the hearing from environmental critics which included two federal agencies and the Sierra Club.

On Friday, September 22, an audience of about 1,000, including pep clubs and school bands, listened to the proponents of the CUP discuss the project. Clyde Ritchie, CUWCD president, concurred with other government leaders that the Draft EIS prepared by BuRec was "adequate, complete, and in full compliance with the National Environmental Policy Act."

On Saturday, 60 people—mostly participants—attended the hearings as those in opposition expressed their views. David C. Raskin, Conservation Chairman of the local chapter of the Sierra Club, and a professor of psychology at the University of Utah, led the dissent. Dr. Raskin attacked the Draft EIS as "woefully inadequate" and "nothing more than a crude attempt to provide justification for an environmentally unsound, economically outrageous project." In a lengthy statement, he said his club objected to the project on the grounds that many miles of streams in the Uintah Mountains would be destroyed due to insufficient water releases. Raskin also objected to the brief consideration of alternatives in the EIS draft. He called for a full development of Wasatch Front Streams, development of ground water and a campaign to change the consumption patterns of water users.

The League of Women Voters joined the Sierra Club in dissent. Speaking for the League, Emily Hall observed that the League had supported the CUP at its inception in 1956, "but we have since grown older and wiser." Hall questioned the ability of BuRec to act as its own judge and recommended that impartial, disinterested parties, such as geologists, engineers, conservationists and experts in population trends, conduct new studies. She also recommended the consideration of alternatives such as water well drilling, better farming methods, and raising water prices for consumers.

Herbert Frost of the American Audubon Society said his organization was concerned about the proposed diking of Utah Lake at Provo and Goshen Bays. He warned of considerable destruction of valuable waterfowl nesting areas if these bays were drained and converted to farmland.

The hearings ended on Saturday afternoon after 100 people had testified. The balance between the number of proponents and critics who testified was even, and building of the Bonneville Unit continued to gain momentum after the hearings were completed. The State of Utah reaffirmed its total support of the CUP in a letter from Governor Rampton to David Crandall, regional BuRec director.

Criticism of the Draft EIS. Within the agencies of the federal government, the Draft EIS received mixed reviews. The task of compiling an environmental statement on such a complex project in which some features are completed, others underway, and the rest in the final planning stages, was universally recognized as monumental.

In a memorandum to the Commissioner of Reclamation, the Director of the Interior Department's Bureau of Sport Fisheries and Wildlife, Willis King, was particularly critical of the Draft EIS's treatment of environmental effects:

> In most cases, the description of the environment and environmental effects is entirely too sketchy. . . . We would like to see the [EIS] be objective. Throughout we find numerous insertions, opinions, and qualifying phrases which lead the reader to question the credibility of the impact statement. . . .
>
> In summary, the plans for the Bonneville Unit do not adequately provide for the fish and wildlife of the area. It is essential that modifications be made in project plans that recognize the need for fish and wildlife values as well as irrigation and M&I purposes.

On December 19, 1972, BuRec Commissioner Ellis Armstrong received a seven-page letter from John A. Green, Regional Administrator of the Environmental Protection Agency which contained EPA's review of the Draft EIS. Mr. Green concluded the letter with the following paragraph:

In accordance with the rating system which EPA uses to categorize the nature of its comments on environmental statements, the Bonneville Unit EIS has been placed in Category 2. More information is needed to fully assess the environmental impacts of the proposed action.

On January 19, 1973, Rogers C. B. Morton, the Secretary of the Interior, received the following letter from Russell Train, head of the CEQ:

Dear Rog:

On August 14, 1972, we received the Bureau of Reclamation's draft environmental impact statement on the Bonneville Unit of the Central Utah Project. I understand that work on the final statement is being completed and that it will be filed in the near future. The impact statement indicates that the Bonneville Unit is about 14% complete and will take about 25 years to complete, at a cost currently estimated at $500 million.

It appears from comments from agencies and organizations outside the Bureau that the environmental impacts of this Unit will be major and severe. Because of the magnitude of this project and the developing controversy, a full environmental assessment of the Unit and the cumulative impacts of the other Units should be available before additional work is performed. In this connection, the section on environmental impacts makes reference to numerous on-going studies, including water quality, recreation potential, flora and fauna, downstream flows, and mitigation measures in the project area. These and other studies referred to in the statement should be concluded and findings and recommendations included in the final statement.

Another area of concern is the Unit impact on the increasing salinity problem of the lower Colorado River. The impact statement states that although the Unit would add to the problem, "a salinity control program for the entire Colorado River Basin is in progress." While salinity control measures are under study in the Bureau, no implementation program has as yet been recommended for authorization and reference to the

program in this context is misleading. In light of the current work being conducted by the Brownell Task Force in an effort to provide the President with a permanent solution to the Colorado River salinity problem with Mexico, a thorough appraisal of the Unit's impact on this problem should be included in the final statement.

Preparing an impact statement on a project of this complexity is of course a difficult undertaking. However, I believe that the inclusion of the aforementioned items will considerably strengthen the Bureau's final statement.

Sincerely,

Russell E. Train
Chairman

On March 26, Russell Train received a reply to his letter to Rogers C. B. Morton from W. W. Lyons, Deputy Secretary of the Interior. Mr. Lyons wrote that BuRec had reviewed the draft to see if all of the studies mentioned there would be concluded before the final EIS was completed in mid-summer 1973. BuRec placed the studies in three categories: (1) studies completed and to be used in the final EIS; (2) incomplete studies, most of which would not be completed for several years; and (3) studies that are currently underway on features of the project not yet constructed and that will be helpful in preparing detailed future environmental statements. Lyons also commented that:

The Department of the Interior as well as the Bureau of Reclamation, shares your concern about the increase in salinity of the Colorado River from development and use of the water supply in the river. We also recognize that the present program to study the Colorado River water quality problems is investigative in nature and that no implementation program has yet been recommended. We will certainly make a thorough appraisal of the unit's impact on this problem in the final environmental statement.

We appreciate receiving your suggestions for strengthening the final environmental statement on the Bonneville Unit. It is expected that the statement will be fully responsive to the major environmental factors involved in this large and complicated water resources development project.

Major contract awards on the Bonneville Unit scheduled to start in Fiscal Year 1973 [the Currant Creek Dam, Vat and Stillwater Tunnels] have been delayed until Fiscal Year 1974. This was necessary in view of the environmental concerns as well as the present limitations on Federal funding for the Reclamation program.

The opposition, meanwhile, continued to mount. On May 23, 1973, David Raskin of the Sierra Club testified before the House and Senate Public Works Appropriations Subcommittees and expressed his concern about continued development of the CUP. Citing the potential for enormous rapid development in the Uinta Basin, Dr. Raskin argued that leaving the water in the Uinta Basin rather than diverting it to the Bonneville Basin would best satisfy the state's competing water needs. Raskin also outlined the Sierra Club's view of the environmental losses associated with the CUP.

> The environmental losses from this project are staggering. The Bonneville Unit alone will destroy 223 miles of trout streams, including 11% of the blue-ribbon trout streams remaining in Utah. This will produce a loss of 99,000 man-fishing days on quality trout streams. The diking of Provo Bay and Goshen Bay on Utah Lake will eliminate 25,000 acres of marsh and water habitat which will destroy the highly productive warm-water fishery, eliminate 3,950,000 water-fowl days and 18,000 hunting days. In addition, 9,400 acres of important wildlife habitat will be inundated by the reservoirs at Strawberry, Upper Stillwater and Currant Creek. The Upper Stillwater Valley is considered by many to be the most beautiful place on the south slope of the Uinta Mountains and is heavily used for recreation. The construction of the additional units of the CUP will produce even greater stream fishery losses than those planned for the Bonneville Unit. The net result of the CUP will be to force all future growth in Utah to occur along the populous Wasatch Front. Already, Salt Lake City has one of the most severe air pollution problems in the nation, and the additional growth will only increase the problems of air pollution, congestion, and decreased quality of life. Furthermore, future growth and development in the Uinta Basin will be prevented, forcing a continuation of the present problem of migration from rural to urban areas in Utah. Finally, the Uinta Basin is already experiencing water rationing as a result of the appropriation of all of the water for the CUP.

Under pressure from Utah's congressional delegation, state government, and the CUWCD, for issuance of a final EIS, Jack Horton, Assistant Secretary of the Interior for Land and Water Resources, explained the delay as follows in a letter to Governor Rampton:

> [After the Draft EIS hearings] more than 1,500 written and oral comments were received. Each comment had to be considered in preparing the final statement. This has required considerable research and study in order to insure that the environmental aspects of the project [are considered] as well as negotiation toward resolution of the differences in views and objectives of the Federal, State, and local entities.
>
> We will undertake every effort to expedite the review of the proposed statement. Furthermore, we will give due consideration to requesting a waiver of the 30-day waiting period if the review should be delayed.

Governor Rampton replied to Horton's letter on July 17.

> On May 22, 1973, I met with Secretary Morton in his office and he promised me at that time that the statement would be filed within two weeks. It was not, and I again went to Washington, and on June 19, 1973, I, along with members of Utah's congressional delegation and representatives of the Central Utah Project, met with Commissioner Stamm in his office. After a discussion of the matter, Mr. Stamm told us that while he had some misgivings about some parts of the environmental statement, if we were satisfied with it, he would not require further review and would see that it was forthwith filed. For you now to impose a further indefinite delay on this matter is certainly a violation of good faith.

One week later, Assistant Secretary Horton received a memo from the Assistant Secretary for Fish and Wildlife and Parks, Nathaniel Reed. Following a recent affirmation by BuRec Regional Director Crandall that the Bonneville Unit plan was not now open to modification except by Secretarial intervention, Reed and his staff provided an environmental reanalysis of the Unit in hopes of mitigating adverse impacts on fish, wildlife, and recreational resources.

The reanalysis included a criticism of Fish and Wildlife and Parks' own lackadaisical environmental posture in the 1960s, as a result of which the Assistant Secretary's office failed to set forth a clean, objective evaluation of the major impacts of the Bonneville Unit on fish and wildlife. In consequence:

> Our recommendations for adequate stream flows, for example, were continually rejected by the Bureau of Reclamation and when the State went along with Reclamation's plan for the unit, the Bureau of Sport Fisheries and Wildlife followed suit. The result was the unacceptable fish and wildlife losses reflected in the current plan. Consequently, the confidence of the environmental community in Utah and of State resource agencies in the ability of this Bureau to meet its responsibilities for protecting the Nation's interests in fish and wildlife resources has been seriously impaired.

The reanalysis focused in considerable detail on four major areas of environmental impact where modification of the current plan was judged critical. Those areas include:

(1) Preservation of stream fish in Rock Creek, Strawberry River, Currant Creek, and the West Fork of the Duchesne River.
(2) Preservation of the natural marsh environment of Provo Bay.
(3) Preservation of fish spawning habitat in Goshen Bay.
(4) Establishment of multi-purpose management for the enlarged Strawberry River and associated lands.

Final EIS. On August 2, the Bureau of Reclamation released its Final Environmental Impact Statement to the CEQ and the public. The Final EIS and its appendix (which included almost 1,500 written and oral comments submitted at the public hearings on the Draft EIS) are enormous documents about the size of the Boston Yellow and White Pages, respectively. While the 900-page document defies easy summary, BuRec did attempt a sort of summary in its one-page preface to the document:

> *Summary of Environmental Impacts and Adverse Environmental Effects:*
> Construction and operation of the Bonneville Unit would cause significant changes in the natural environment of the area. In 11 Uinta Basin streams there would be a reduction of flows in about 100 miles of waterway, sometimes below minimums suggested by fishery biologists. A sig-
> nificant amount of quality fishing and stream recreation would be lost. The diking of two Utah Lake bays to reduce evaporation losses would reduce lake area by one-third and adversely affect a substantial amount of high quality fish and wildlife habitat. Additional fish and wildlife habitat would be lost by reservoir inundation of 22,000 acres of land and 10 miles of streams. Conversely, reservoir fishing and related water-oriented sports would be substantially increased. Construction of some features would cause extensive land disturbance and would permanently alter existing esthetics. Salinity of the Colorado River would be increased (1) by diversion to Bonneville Basin and increased consumptive use in Uinta Basin which would deplete the river supply and (2) by increased salt load of return flows in the Uinta Basin. Recreational use of National Forest land would increase as a result of improved access and additional facilities provided by Unit development.
> The Bonneville Unit would facilitate continued industrial and population growth in the Wasatch Front portion of the Bonneville Basin. Attendant to the growth would be an increase in social and pollution problems related to population concentrations. Distribution of water by the Unit could also influence growth and development of other areas of the State, particularly the Sevier River and Uinta Basins.

According to the 1973 CEQ guidelines 10(b), "administrative action cannot be taken sooner than 30 days after the final text of an environmental statement (together with comments) has been made available to the public." At the end of the 30-day waiting period or at any later time, the Department of the Interior could decide whether to continue the project as planned, modify it, or halt it. The waiting period is intended to provide time for comment on the final EIS by the public, and by state, local and federal agencies. However, if Secretary Morton allowed construction to proceed—even after the 30-day comment period—he could be sued under NEPA for failure to "adequately" consider the environmental impacts.

On September 6—35 days after the report was filed—Grace Reppert, CEQ staff member responsible for reviewing the EIS, told the *Deseret News* that only two comments on the impact statement had been received to date. One of the comments came from David Raskin, who observed that:

> The extreme length and complexity of the final EIS together with the great amount of new information contained, makes it virtually impossible for the public to provide thorough and meaningful comments within the brief period of 30 days.

The Interior Department took no formal actions on Raskin's request for an additional 30-day comment period, but neither did it approve the project plans. Objections, meanwhile, continued to accumulate.

Because 85 percent of the usable water for the Bonneville Unit comes from National Forest Lands in Utah, the U.S. Forest Service was concerned that many of the CUP features to be constructed on National Forest Lands would be irreversible and irretrievable commitments to the use of the lands. In a September 11, 1973 memo to BuRec Commissioner Gilbert Stamm, John McGuire, Chief of the U.S. Forest Service, urged that more studies be done.

> We are seriously concerned that a full and complete environmental analysis has not been attained in many respects. . . . We suggest a joint meeting with the Bureau of Reclamation, CEQ, and Forest representatives prior to any action on the project. At such a meeting, we would propose going into more detail in an effort to reach a better base of understanding and to resolve existing conflicts.

The Assistant Secretary for Fish and Wildlife and Parks shared the concern of the Forest Service regarding environmental impacts:

> The Bonneville Unit, if constructed as now planned, will have the following major impacts on fish, wildlife, recreational, and environmental resources: (1) damage or destroy 223 miles of fishing streams, including 57 miles (11%) of Utah's Blue Ribbon trout water; (2) eliminate 25,000 acres of marsh and water habitat in Provo Bay and Goshen Bay of Utah Lake; (3) result in major fish and aesthetic losses within the Upper Stillwater Reservoir site in Rock Creek Canyon; and (4) eliminate a total of 9,400 acres of wildlife habitat by inundation resulting from construction and operation of Soldier Creek Dam (Strawberry Reservoir enlargement), Upper Stillwater Dam, and Currant Creek Dam.

On September 11, 1973, the U.S. Forest Service summarized the issue of the magnitude of stream flows below reservoirs and diversion points on the Strawberry Aqueduct.

> The State of Utah has only 61.8 miles of class I fishing streams and 450.9 miles of class II fishing streams as classified by the Utah Division of Wildlife Resources. These 512.7 miles represent only 10% of Utah's 5,377 total miles of fishing streams. Approximately 2,109 miles of former trout habitat have already been eliminated in Utah. The Bonneville Unit of the Central Utah Project will reduce 8.1% of class I, and 10.5% of the class II fishing streams within the State. With all the present reservoirs and natural lakes in the State, there appears to be a significant imbalance of flat water recreation in relation to the ever-diminishing resource of stream-type recreation in Utah.

When all streams are considered, the Forest Service and Utah State recommendations call for around 40,000 a.f. of stream flows for fishing bypasses. Meeting this stream flow requirement would decrease the yield of the Strawberry Aqueduct by 25,000 a.f. The Bureau of Sport Fishing and Wildlife, meanwhile, recommends almost 50,000 a.f. more water for stream bypass flows (see Exhibits 4.4, 4.5, and 4.6).

The Forest Service is requesting:

> . . . minimum flows necessary to sustain the aquatic habitat and preserve the natural fisheries . . .
>
> The objective to retain sufficient streambottom coverage and a favorable depth for existing pools is not intended to imply the fisheries will remain the same after the streams are altered. Retention of at least 80% of the low flow aquatic habitat does not guarantee 100% or even 80% retention of the fishery.

In contrast, the BSF&W recommendation:

> . . . represents the best available estimate of the flow regimens required to maintain the existing habitat and preserve the existing aquatic ecosystems; i.e., flows that will provide for successful spawning, incubation and growth of fish necessary for the support of a high quality fishery.

A range in flow may be essential to preservation of the stream ecosystem. For example, occasional high, wild flows are necessary to flush silt from spawning gravels and to replenish spawning gravels from upstream sources. Water of a certain depth and velocity over spawning areas is required to insure successful incubation and hatching of trout eggs.

The Forest Service requested that its proposal for an increase in bypass flows be discussed prior to any decision about completion of the Strawberry Aqueduct. Assistant Secretary Horton of Land and Water Resources recommended that negotiations on the issue be held concurrent with the construction of Currant Creek Dam, a structure which would create a reservoir for the flows of Rock Creek and other streams which would be intercepted by the Strawberry Aqueduct.

Indian Deferral Agreement

On September 20, 1965, the United States, the Ute Indian Tribe, and the Central Utah Water Conservancy District entered into an agreement—the "Indian Deferral Agreement"—concerning the water rights of the Ute Indian Tribe. Under the agreement, the United States, the Ute Indian Tribe, and the Central Utah Water Conservancy District recognized and confirmed the right of the Ute Indians to the use of water on 21,208 acres of Indian water right land in the Uinta Basin. (This land was given to the Indians on October 3, 1861 by President Lincoln.) The agreement further provides that the use of water on another 15,242 acres of Indian-owned land (which had no prior history of irrigation but which the Indians claimed under the Winters Doctrine*) would be deferred "upon the condition that said lands be included in the final phase of the Central Utah Project." Through this provision, the Indians were provided assurance of future water service for these lands upon the completion of the ultimate phase of the Central Utah Project.

*In 1908, the Supreme Court propounded a doctrine of Indian Water Rights in the case of *Winters v. U.S.* The court ruled that Indians reserve, by inference, rights to water on their lands even though water rights are not mentioned in any particular treaty or other official document, and that when the Indians reserved rights to use of water for themselves or when the Congress or Executive Branch reserved it for them, the rights thus reserved must be sufficient to satisfy the Reservation's future needs.

However, if the final phase of the CUP was unable to supply water service to the Indians for these 15,242 acres by the first day of January 2005, the Deferral Agreement provides that "equitable adjustment will be made in accordance with said reserved and perfected water rights of the Tribe to permit the immediate Indian use of the water so reserved."

The effect of this provision is to require the CUWCD and the United States to reduce CUP water use by others to the extent necessary to restore the use of water to the Indians for the 15,242 acres. In approving a September 2, 1965 memorandum executing the agreement, Interior Secretary Stewart Udall indicated his understanding that this provision was a legally enforceable right of the Indians. The memo read:

> If the Indian needs are not met by the timely construction of additional facilities, water to satisfy Indian requirements could come from the Bonneville Unit of the CUP. We regard this eventuality as unlikely; however, caution dictates term contracts with water users in the Bonneville Unit so approximately 60,000 acre-feet annually can be made available to meet the Indian commitment if necessary.

In a memorandum to Secretary Udall, an expert on Indian water rights in the Solicitor's Office of the Interior Department urged that the Deferral Agreement be reexamined prior to being executed. William H. Veeder, described by opposition attorneys as the "crazy man of Indian water rights," concluded the following:

> Irreparable damage may well be experienced by the Ute Indians if the Agreement is executed. Not only is there grave doubt as to the power of the Conservancy District to enter into the Agreement, [but] the vague and illusory terms [of the agreement might] result in loss or serious impairment of [Indian] rights if they . . . should be tested in a court proceeding. Numerous questions remain unanswered.

Veeder's memorandum contained the following recommendations:

> (1) The Commissioner of Indian Affairs should refrain from executing the Four Party Agreement absent an opinion from the Solicitor expressly

approving the contract both as to the form and content of it; declaring that the Conservancy District is empowered to execute it, making it binding in every regard and binding upon "all the world."

(2) Delay in the Project need not necessarily ensue. Stipulations in proper form to protect the rights of the Indians, binding upon the State of Utah, the State Engineer, and all interested parties could be entered into which might well be affirmed by a court decree, either by modification of existing Federal decrees, if that course is open, or by a friendly proceeding which would be in the nature of a suit for declaratory judgment confirming and establishing the rights of the Indians.

On September 20, 1965, the Indian Deferral Agreement was signed by N. B. Bennett, Jr., Acting BuRec Commissioner, John O. Crow, Deputy Commissioner of the Bureau of Indian Affairs, Francis Wyasket, Chairman of the Ute Indian Tribe of the Uintah and Ouray Reservation, and Sterling D. Jones, President of the CUWCD. John Boyden, Sr., a Mormon, was the Utes' attorney and negotiated the agreement for the tribe.

The signing of the agreement did not settle the future of the Indians' water rights, however. In 1967, Palmer DeLong, BuRec project manager for the CUP, questioned whether enough water was available within the Colorado River system to complete the Project. At a news conference, DeLong said that the largest single unit of the Central Utah Project, the Ute Indian Unit, depended upon the availability of water in the Colorado River. Citing then current proposals to increase the availability of Colorado water to Arizona and Southern California for the development of power plants and irrigation, DeLong said:

The availability of sufficient water to carry out the Ute Indian project will be even more in doubt. Once water rightfully Utah's is put into use in Arizona it will never be available for beneficial use in this state. The far greater supply promised by the Ute Indian Unit—700,000 a.f. to be made available at a $500 million cost—which is needed for the next century still depends in considerable measure on what happens to water supplies of the Colorado system.

Since no statutory authority existed under which the Utes might convey their water rights, the agreement required formal ratification by the Secretary of the Interior in the form of a special act: the Act of September 30, 1968 (82 Stat. 855). The September 1968 Act contained the following provision:

That the planning report for the Ute Indian Unit of the CUP shall be completed on or before December 31, 1974, to enable the United States to meet the commitments made to the Ute Indian Tribe under the agreement dated September 20, 1965.

The agreement enabled the CUP to proceed while at the same time notifying the Utes that their *Winters* doctrine rights were recognized and it promised "that all phases of the CUP will in good faith be diligently pursued to satisfy all Indian water rights at the earliest possible date."

By 1973, the issues raised by the Indian Deferral Agreement were becoming increasingly difficult to ignore. The further construction of the Strawberry Aqueduct collection system was dependent upon the diversion to the Bonneville Basin of 61,000 a.f. of water from Indian lands. In the agreement, the Bureau of Reclamation and the CUWCD promised to replace the water by the year 2005, through either the construction of the Uinta Unit and the Ute Indian Unit, the return of water "borrowed" for the Bonneville Unit, or the implementation of "unspecified" projects.

The Indians were satisfied with the 1965 Agreement because it promised water for Indian lands that had no previous history of irrigation and gave the Indians access to more water than they had prior to the agreement. It was becoming clear, however, that by 1973 there was a real question about the availability of Colorado River water for the Ute Indian Unit. According to the State Division of Water Resources, Utah had only 123,000 a.f. of uncommitted Colorado River water, and demands for oil shale development in the Uinta Basin will require an additional 480,000 a.f. of Colorado River water. Thus, there would apparently not be enough water for the completion of the Ute Indian Unit.

In an October 2, 1973 resolution, the Indians called upon the Secretary of the Interior, Rogers Morton,

. . . to reaffirm the commitments of the United States, or to inform the tribe as to how the United States could feasibly discharge its additional trust responsibility to assist the tribe in applying to beneficial use the water rights of the tribe without the Central Utah Project as contemplated by said agreements.

Within the Interior Department, there was a great deal of discussion on the Indian issue. Specifically, the discussion focused on two points: (1) whether the Bureau of Reclamation had the legal authority to promise replacement water from a project (the Ute Indian Unit) which had not been approved by Congress and the President; and (2) whether the Indian Deferral Agreement effectively committed the federal government to building the Ute Indian Unit before its economic or environmental implications were fully evaluated.

The Indians supported continuation of the Bonneville Unit because they felt that it was the best way for them to get their water; that is, "They feel they are a part of a total Utah package and that their best chance for obtaining the water for Indian lands comes from not breaking the relationship which has been established thus far with the non-Indians. . . . They would not be competing for water by themselves," according to a source within the Interior Department. The Utes have never contended that they were ready to develop the Indian-owned lands which are mentioned in the Deferral Agreement, nor that the Bonneville Unit interfered with the development of these lands.

On September 21, 1973, Assistant Secretary for Land and Water Resources Jack Horton recommended construction of Currant Creek Dam (a portion of the Bonneville Unit which would collect and divert Uinta Basin water to the Bonneville Basin) and to "reconsider the future use of water in both the Uinta and Bonneville Basins." Reid Chambers, Associate Solicitor for Indian Affairs, warned that the action recommended by Horton contemplated modification of the plan presented to the tribe in the Deferral Agreement, since Horton's "reconsideration" was unilateral. In a memorandum to the Solicitor, Ken Frizell, Chambers wrote:

> . . . the tribe could sue to enjoin diversions from the Bonneville Basin. Changes in the terms of the contract cannot be made unilaterally by one of the parties. It is not a matter to be resolved only among the Governor of Utah, the U.S. Forest Service, and BuRec.

The tribe agreed to defer use of their water

rights on the promise that "all phases" of the CUP be "diligently pursued." Any reconsideration or modification of CUP plans violates the agreement.

In response to Horton's recommendation, the Indians drew up their resolution of October 2. It appears that the Indians' fears that the Deferral Agreement was just another white man's promise were not unfounded. In a memorandum to Assistant Secretary Lynn, Roland G. Robinson, Acting Associate Solicitor in the Division of Energy and Resources, had the following comments on the Deferral Agreement.

> It was not the intent of the agreement to create in the Indians a legal right to have the facilities constructed by the United States. But even if such had been the intent, the United States could not be judicially compelled to complete the project. A possibility that should not be discounted is that the Indians may repudiate the deferral arrangement if it should appear that the United States does not intend to complete the project. In that event, the United States could as a last resort, acquire the Indians' water rights by condemnation if they were essential for any phase of the project. This last alternative, however, would not be necessary until the Indians' water rights were being or could be put to beneficial use by them.

THE POLITICAL CONTEXT

In reaching his decision on the future of the Central Utah Project, Secretary of the Interior Morton had to take into account not only the views of the Interior Department Staff, but also the political considerations surrounding the CUP issue—in particular, the future of Utah's Senate seat then held by Wallace Bennett. Bennett, a conservative Republican, had decided earlier in 1973 that he would not seek reelection. The 76-year-old Senator had won only 54% of the vote in his 1968 election, and his son Robert had been the proprietor of the CIA-run public relations agency which had been the apparent employer of Howard Hunt at the time he was engaged by the Nixon White House. His chances of getting reelected to a fifth term were regarded as slim by most political observers.

Bennett hand-picked Salt Lake Mayor Jake Garn as his successor. Garn, a solidly conservative Republican, was expected to run unopposed in the state's

GOP primary in 1974 and to face a formidable opponent in Democratic Congressman Wayne Owens. Two years earlier, Owens had defeated Republican Congressman Sherman Lloyd in a campaign that was highlighted by the 35-year-old Owens' 689-mile hike the length of the state. Youthful and fit, Owens had served on the staffs of both Robert and Edward Kennedy, and his devout Mormonism insured his appeal with conservative Utahans. Owens was expected to win his party's nomination overwhelmingly.

The election had particular importance because of Utah's history of reelecting incumbent Senators. Utahans value seniority in politics as well as in the Mormon church and, with the single exception of Senator Moss's first victory in 1958, no incumbent Utah Senator has been beaten since 1950. Morton, a five-time Republican Congressman from Maryland's

Eastern Shore region and a highly respected man in GOP circles, was aware of the significance of the Utah Senate race. Garn expected that Owens' campaign would emphasize environmental issues and that Owens would have the support of members of the Sierra Club and other conservation groups in his fund-raising effort. Garn's best prospects seemed to lie in backing the Central Utah Project and other state development efforts which were popular with Utah voters, thus forcing Owens to take a stand that might split his broad coalition of support. Any decision by Morton which would prevent the Central Utah Project from becoming an issue in the upcoming Senate campaign might effectively destroy Garn's chances and would improve the prospects of a Democratic hold on Utah's Senate seats for many years to come.

D E P A R T M E N T   O F   T H E   I N T E R I O R

OFFICE OF THE SECRETARY

For Release November 8, 1973

**SECRETARY MORTON ANNOUNCES CONSTRUCTION OF
BONNEVILLE UNIT IN UTAH WILL PROCEED**

Secretary of the Interior Rogers C. B. Morton announced today that the Bureau of Reclamation will soon call for bids for construction of the Currant Creek Dam and Reservoir, features of the Bonneville Unit, Central Utah Project.

"In response to the need and desires of the local communities and the State of Utah," said Secretary Morton, "Reclamation will proceed with construction of the Currant Creek Dam and Reservoir, which is the next step in the construction of the Strawberry Aqueduct System.

"We anticipate funding in Fiscal Year 1975 to continue construction of the Strawberry Aqueduct.

"In the meantime, the Department will refine and resolve two important issues which have been extensively analyzed and discussed during the past three months. These issues deal with the streamflows in the Uinta Basin and the irrigation of Indian lands of the Ute Tribe."

Unresolved differences exist with the Forest Service regarding the Bureau of Reclamation's proposed releases from the Strawberry Aqueduct to the Uinta streams for maintenance and protection of existing fisheries. The Department plans to meet with concerned parties to determine the most equitable solution to the streamflow issue.

With regard to Indian irrigation, the Ute Tribe entered into a four-party agreement in 1965 with Central Utah Conservancy District, the Bureau of Reclamation, and the Bureau of Indian Affairs. Under that agreement the Ute Indians agreed to the deferment of the use of a certain amount of (Indian) water in return for recognition of rights to that water. The deferment continues until 2005, at which time either the ultimate phase of the Central Utah Project will be completed and the deferred water replaced, or "equitable adjustment" will be made.

The Ute Indians, on October 2, 1973, adopted a resolution which "calls upon the Secretary of the Interior to reaffirm the commitments of the United States, or to inform

Page 1

DEPARTMENT OF THE INTERIOR MEMORANDUM — Page 2

the Tribe as to how the United States could feasibly discharge its additional trust responsibility to assist the Tribe in applying to beneficial use the water rights of the Tribe
without the Central Utah Project as contemplated by said agreement."

Secretary Morton said, "I have informed the Tribal officials that the Department will
begin immediately to work with them to evaluate the alternatives available to assist the
Indians as laid out in their resolution."

The Bonneville Unit is a major trans-basin diversion project to develop 160,000 acre-feet
of water from Utah's share of the Colorado River in the Uinta Basin and transport a large
portion of that water to the Salt Lake City area.

Under the authorized plan, additional water is expected to be developed in the Utah Lake
area but additional study is required before construction of that portion of the project
can be started.

The total cost of the Bonneville Unit is estimated to be about $500 million, and in total
it would provide about 313,000 acre-feet of water annually. While the major portion of
the ultimate water supply would be used for irrigation, 99,000 acre-feet in the first phase
is reserved for municipal and industrial use.

Commissioner of Reclamation Gilbert G. Stamm said that several features, including
Starvation Dam, Strawberry Reservoir enlargement, and the Jordan Aqueduct, are already
completed or under construction for which nearly $100 million has been expended. The
construction of Currant Creek Dam and Reservoir is expected to require about $5 million
in FY 1974, with these funds presently available.

EXHIBIT 4.1: Bonneville and Uinta Basin Water Supply and Demand
(000 acre feet)

Bonneville Unit Area	Water Supply	Total Demand**				Unsatisfied Demand***			
		1965	1980	2000	2020	1965	1980	2000	2020
Bonneville Basin									
Great Salt Lake (includes only the Jordan River drainage portion of the Wasatch Front)	1,338	1,357	1,421	1,577	1,926	19	83	239	588
Sevier Lake (includes Sevier River drainage area)	925	1,277	1,279	1,282	1,286	352	354	357	361
TOTAL	2,263	2,634	2,700	2,859	3,212	371	437	596	949
Uinta Basin									
Uinta Basin (includes Duchesne River drainage only)	390*	282	283	283	344	0****	37	37	98

*This water supply would be reduced by 149,000 a.f. by 1980—the amount of the proposed diversion from the Uinta Basin to the Bonneville Basin under the Bonneville Unit Plan. However, BuRec did not add that amount to the Bonneville Basin supply.

**Approximately half of all water used is consumed so that it is not available for further use. The unconsumed portion is available for re-use if facilities are available to satisfy the time, place, and quality requirements of the next use.

***According to BuRec, 149,000 a.f. of Uinta Basin water will be diverted to the Bonneville Basin by 1980 by the Bonneville Unit of CUP; however, the Bureau did not reflect this increased supply in its calculations of unsatisfied demand for the Great Salt Lake and Sevier Lake areas.

****In calculating the unsatisfied demand, BuRec did not use negative numbers or show surpluses; if it had, the unsatisfied demand in the Uinta Basin in 1965 would be -108,000 a.f., i.e., there would be a surplus.

Source: BuRec, Bonneville Unit Definite Plan Report, 1964, excerpted in BuRec, Bonneville Unit Final Environmental Statement, 1973, p. 6 (headings and notes modified).

EXHIBIT 4.2:   Population Projection for Utah

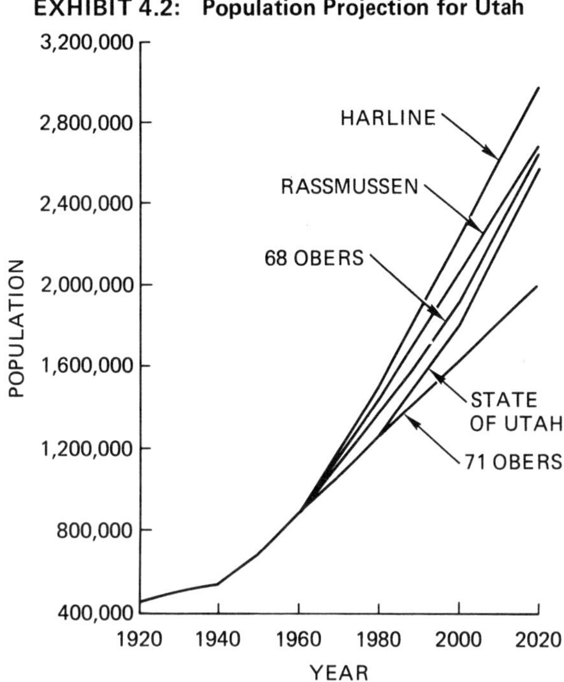

Source: *Bureau of Reclamation,* Bonneville Unit Final Environmental Statement, *1973, p. 9.*

**EXHIBIT 4.3:   Diversion Requirements (1,000 Acre-feet)
Satisfied by the Bonneville Unit**

Bonneville Unit Area	Unsatisfied Diversion Requirement (by year)[1]				Req. Satisfied by Bonneville Unit[2]	Remaining Unsatisfied Diversion Req. (by Year)			
	1965	1980	2000	2020		1965	1980	2000	2020
Great Salt Lake (includes only the Jordan River Drainage of the Wasatch Front area)	19	83	239	588	255	19	0	0	333
Sevier Lake (includes Sevier River Drainage)	352	354	357	361	30[3]	352	324	327	331
Uinta Basin (includes Duchesne River Drainage only)	0	37	37	98	28	0	9	9	70
TOTALS	371	474	633	1047	313	371	333*	336*	734

[1] Includes water requirements for irrigation, municipal and industrial, and existing wetland uses.

[2] Part of Bonneville Unit supply assumed to be available by 1980.

[3] Represents only about 10% of the diversion requirement; however, this amount would allow flexibility in the Sevier River system that would permit a more efficient use of the total water supply of the basin.

*In deriving the figures for unsatisfied diversion requirements in 1980 and 2000, BuRec ignored negative numbers. For example, for 1980, a Great Salt Lake requirement of 83,000 a.f. minus a Bonneville Unit contribution of 255,000 a.f. yields a "surplus" of 172,000 a.f., not zero. For this reason, the asterisked numbers do not equal the Unsatisfied Diversion Requirements minus the Bonneville Unit contributions.

Source: Final Environmental Impact Statement for Bonneville Unit (BuRec).

**EXHIBIT 4.4:   Bypass Flows and Their Result on Stream Fisherman Days:
Recommended Strawberry Aqueduct Fishery Bypasses**

	BuRec*	Forest Service	Utah State Division of Wildlife	BSF&W
Rock Creek	3,500	14,300	18,100	47,400
Wolf Creek	—	2,400	**	—
West Fork Duchesne River	—	5,900	5,900	14,500
Currant Creek	—	3,700	4,300	10,300
Strawberry River	3,000	**	8,700	17,300
TOTALS	6,500	26,300	37,000	89,500

*Expected spills and irrigation bypasses may add 6,000 a.f. to the bypasses effective for fisheries.

**No recommendation.

Source: Interior Department Memorandum, September, 1973.

EXHIBIT 4.5:   Fisherman Days

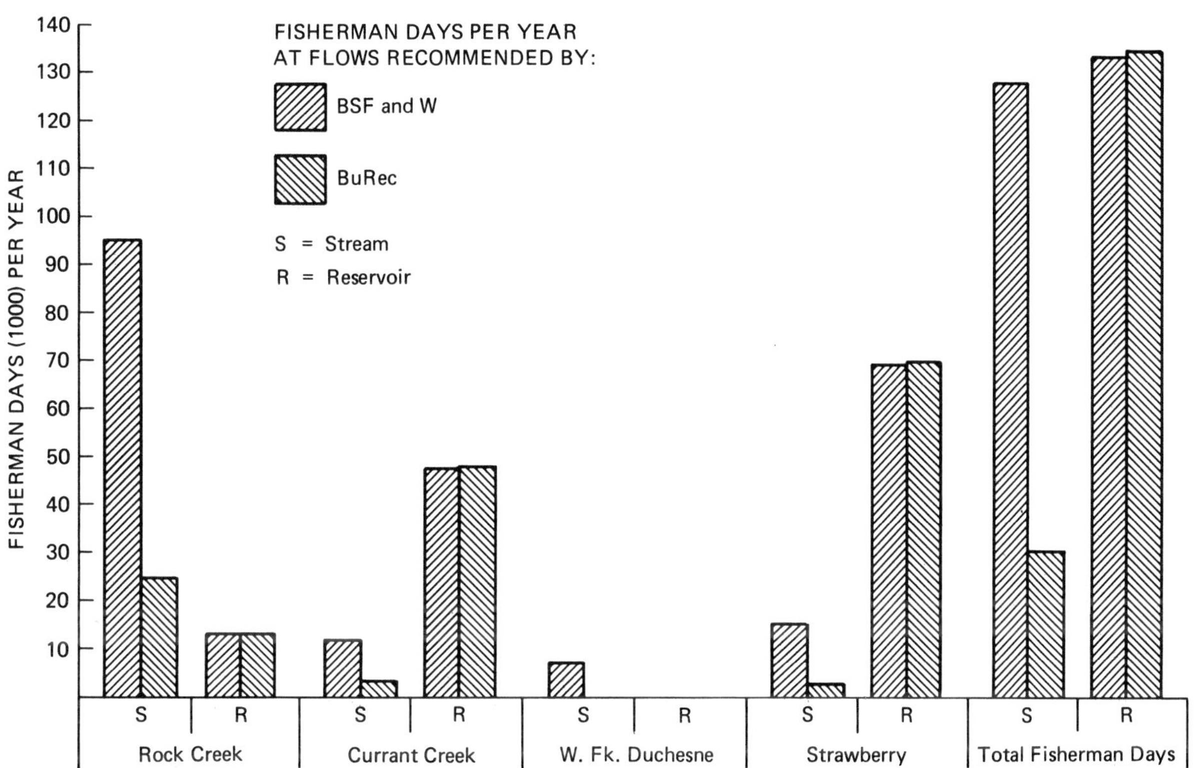

Source: Interior Department Memorandum, September, 1973.

EXHIBIT 4.6: Rock Creek at Upper Stillwater Dam

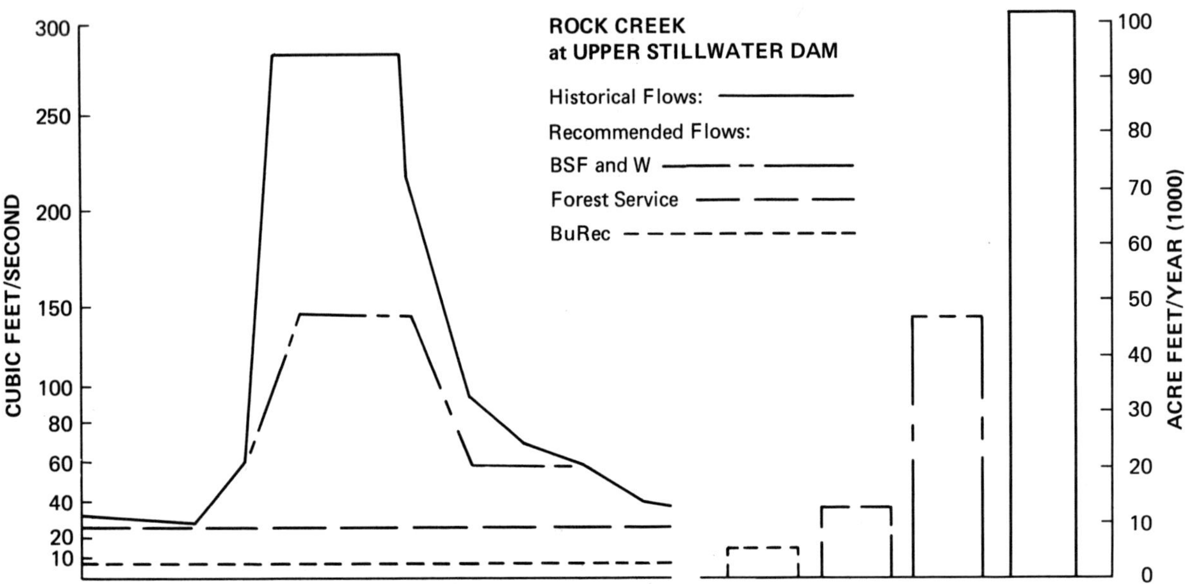

Source: Interior Department Memorandum, September, 1973.

THE CENTRAL UTAH PROJECT: SEQUEL

On November 8, 1973, Interior Secretary Rogers C. B. Morton announced that the Bureau of Reclamation would soon call for bids for construction of Currant Creek Dam and Reservoir; the text of the Secretary's announcement is reproduced in the memo at the end of this sequel. In deciding to proceed with Currant Creek Dam, Morton was in agreement with Assistant Secretary for Land and Water Resources Jack Horton; but while Horton had recommended that construction of Currant Creek Dam be accompanied by "a reconsideration of the future use of the water in both the Uinta and Bonneville Basins . . . [before any] construction beyond Currant Creek Dam," Morton merely said that he "anticipate[d] funding in Fiscal Year 1975 to continue construction of the Strawberry Aqueduct."

Morton's decision to allow construction of the Bonneville Unit of the Central Utah Project to proceed did not end the controversy over the project. In 1977, President Carter asked Congress to delete from the FY 1978 budget funds for the CUP and eighteen other water resource projects which he regarded as "unsupportable on economic, environmental and/or safety grounds." Congress refused to go along with the President's recommendation on the CUP and a number of other projects, although funds for half of the projects on Carter's "hit list" were eliminated from the FY 1978 budget. Both the President and Congress vowed to continue to give close scrutiny to such projects and to proposals to terminate them, and with over $600 million worth of Bonneville Unit construction left, there will doubtless be further challenges to the project.

Changing economic conditions have led to a reconceptualization of the ultimate phase of the CUP. When Congress authorized construction of CUP's initial phase in 1956, most of Utah's economic activity was located along the Wasatch Front; the Uinta Basin apparently had little need for large amounts of new water (and had an insufficient tax base to pay for it), and accordingly the main thrust of the entire CUP was to divert water from the Uinta Basin to the Bonneville Basin.

However, by 1978 the energy crisis of the seventies and the Interior Department's decision to grant oil shale development leases in Duchesne County had fundamentally altered this picture. The assessed valuation of Duchesne County (located in the Uinta Basin) went from $11 million in 1965 to $151 million in 1976 as oil production and other industrial facilities located in the area. The need for municipal and industrial (M&I) water in the Uinta Basin increased substantially, and at its January 1976 meeting, the Central Utah Water Conservancy District voted that the Ute Indian Unit (still in the planning stage) should not be planned so as to provide for any transbasin diversion. One expert estimates that, as a result, the 136,000 acre-feet of Utah's Colorado River entitlement originally planned to constitute the initial diversion of water from the Uinta to the Bonneville Basin will in fact constitute the entire diversion; planning for the development of the rest of Utah's unused Colorado River entitlement, estimated at 450,000 acre-feet, will probably focus on M&I uses in the Uinta Basin.

These developments did not affect construction of the Bonneville Unit. As of early 1978, Currant Creek Dam was complete, though not yet operational. Work had begun on tunnels upstream from the dam. Features such as the Syar Tunnel, which will carry Strawberry Aqueduct water across the Wasatch Divide, were still in the planning stages. The Jensen unit of the CUP was also under construction, but the Upalco and Uinta Units were not, although the local Indian tribes were pressing for Congress to authorize funds to start the Uinta unit. Feasibility studies on the Ute Indian Unit were still being conducted and the unit's future remained in doubt. Groups such as the Sierra Club had not dropped their opposition to the CUP, nor had other Utahans wavered in their support of the project.

5

Caspar Weinberger and Welfare Reform

On November 28, 1972, 21 days after his landslide victory over George McGovern, Richard M. Nixon announced the appointment of Caspar W. Weinberger as Secretary of the Department of Health, Education and Welfare. The President's choice of HEW head seemed to embody his pre-election pledges to cut back social programs and to dismantle big government. In his two and a half years at the Office of Management and Budget (as Deputy Director from 1970 to 1972 and Director in 1972), Weinberger had earned the sobriquet of "Cap the Knife" for his institution of tough new budget review procedures and his role in the Administration's tight fiscal policies, including impounding $8 billion in congressional appropriations in 1972.

HEW was an obvious target for Nixon's fiscal conservatism. Its 1973 budget was expected to exceed $83 billion,* thus becoming the largest of any depart-

*The following table compares budget outlays for HEW and the Department of Defense.

| | HEW | | DOD | |
	budget outlay (000)	% change	budget outlay (000)	% change
1968	40.576		77.373	
1969	46.854	16	77.872	.006
1970	52.249	11	77.150	−.009
1971	61.249	18	74.546	−.03
1972	71.780	16	75.151	.008
1973 (est.)	83.850	16	74.200	−.0007
1974 (est.)	93.822	12	78.200	5.0

Source: OMB, Budget in Brief, 1974.

ment; yet even liberals were conceding its social programs were falling far short of their goals. Moreover, HEW administered the AFDC program—the principal welfare program and a lightning rod for antigovernment sentiments. The number of AFDC recipients had doubled between 1965 and 1970; the number of food stamp recipients had climbed from two million in 1968 to 13 million in 1973. While welfare rights organizations were winning legal battles to liberalize welfare regulations and were organizing people to get on the rolls, the press was highlighting program abuses and many governors were blaming welfare for state fiscal problems.

Since the Administration had been unsuccessful in its previous attempt to solve the welfare problem through structural overhaul—the Family Assistance Plan—a second term strategy of cleaning up the system through aggressive tight-fisted management appeared inevitable. As Nixon observed in his 1973 State of the Union address:

> With the failure of the past two Congresses to enact my proposals for fundamental reform of the Nation's public assistance system, that system remains as I described it in a message last year—"a crazy quilt of injustice and contradiction that has developed in bits and pieces over the years."
>
> The major existing program, Aid to Families with Dependent Children (AFDC), is as inequitable, inefficient, and inadequate as ever. . . .
>
> Since the legislative outlook seems to preclude passage of an overall structural reform bill in the immediate future, I have directed that vigorous steps be taken to strengthen the management of AFDC through administrative measures and legislative proposals.
>
> Under these reforms, Federal impediments to efficient State administration of the current AFDC system will be removed wherever possible. Changes will be proposed to reduce the complexities of current eligibility and payment processes. Work will continue to be required of all those who can reasonably be considered available for employment, while Federal funds to help welfare recipients acquire needed job skills will increase.
>
> One thing is certain: the welfare mess cannot be permitted to continue. A system which penalizes a person for going to work and rewards a person for going on welfare is totally alien to the American tradition of self-reliance and self-respect. That is why welfare reform has been and

will continue to be one of our major goals; and we will work diligently with the Congress in developing ways to achieve it.

In Weinberger Nixon seemed to have found a like-minded "reformer." In an interview shortly after taking over at HEW, he stated his intention to strengthen welfare management, noting the "substantial reluctance on the part of a great many people to push very hard for plans that have the effect of bringing very large numbers of additional people onto the welfare rolls. . . . Some very fundamental work has to be done in the welfare reform field before we are ready to come through with additional plans." Weinberger cited with approval welfare management and mandatory work reforms instituted by his former boss, conservative California Governor Ronald Reagan, and he stated his intention to encourage such reforms in other states.

Eight months after his appointment, on November 6, 1973, Weinberger presented the President with a memo rejecting "minor tinkering or sequential change" and advocating welfare overhaul based on Milton Friedman's negative income tax concept. The reform included the elimination of AFDC, Food Stamps, the newly enacted Supplementary Security Income program (SSI), and the integration of the welfare and tax systems. By mid-July 1974, Weinberger's proposal was fully developed into the Income Supplement Program (ISP) which would have placed all citizens into family units either paying taxes or receiving cash payments, depending on the unit's composition and income. For each family unit, a level of income would be established by the sum of its personal tax exemptions plus the standard deduction; families with income below this level would receive cash supplements ($3,600 a year was to be provided to a family of four with no income; if such a family unit were headed by a wage earner, it could receive cash supplements up to an income level of $7,200). The ISP was initially estimated to add $3 to $5 billion to welfare program costs.

This was the most sweeping welfare reform proposal ever advocated by a cabinet officer. The fact that Weinberger was proposing a reform long associated with liberals took his conservative colleagues by surprise. Liberal politicians were equally perplexed. When the President announced his support of Weinberger's cash assistance welfare strategy in February 1974, the *New York Times* quoted one former Johnson Administration official as remarking:

> If a Democratic administration had made some of the proposals this Republican administration is making, the Democrats would have been run out of town. President Nixon's proposals would bring about social reform and social mobility that would be unprecedented. They are radical, yet they are conservatism at its best. They represent the point where radicalism and conservatism converge.[1]

This case describes the process of welfare policy-making initiated by Secretary Weinberger at HEW in 1973. It focuses especially on Weinberger's adoption of a negative income tax approach to welfare reform and the role that the Office of the Assistant Secretary for Planning and Evaluation played in the Secretary's decision.

NEW STRATEGIES FOR WELFARE REFORM

Welfare reform had been the first major domestic policy initiative of the Nixon Administration. After a long and heated Executive Branch debate, the Administration proposed its Family Assistance Plan to Congress in 1969. Passed by the House in 1971 and (in a slightly different version) in 1972, the legislation was defeated in the Senate Finance Committee* by an alliance of conservatives fearing reduced work incentives for the poor and liberals judging benefit levels too low. The 1972 version of the Family Assistance Plan (HR 1) would have grouped families into two categories: those with unemployable heads (mothers with children under three years of age), who were to

receive cash assistance, and those with employable heads, who would be required to register for work as a condition of receiving the equivalent level of assistance. FAP would have provided a $2400 benefit level for a family of four with no other income; would have permitted a 67% benefit reduction rate after a $750 earnings disregard; would have required extensive state supplementation of benefits; and would have been jointly administered by HEW and the Department of Labor. According to various estimates, FAP could have increased the number of public assistance recipients from 11 to 24 million and could have cost an additional $4 billion a year. By 1972 the Administration had dropped its advocacy of FAP, viewing it as a political liability in an election year.

Regardless of its inconclusiveness, the FAP debate did demonstrate that earlier approaches to eliminating welfare dependency through services such as compensatory education, job training and child care had been challenged by a strategy focusing on direct cash assistance to poor people. One of the most often advanced of such strategies was the negative income tax (NIT), generally regarded as the brainchild of University of Chicago economist, Milton Friedman. NIT involved the abolition of existing income and in-kind transfer programs and the provision of a guaranteed income to all persons through the tax system. Similar approaches were advocated by prominent liberal economists such as James Tobin and Robert Lampmann. The negative income tax had also become popular with some analysts associated with "the War on Poverty": in 1965, OEO's Office of Research Plans, Programs and Evaluations proposed a negative income tax as the income maintenance component of its first ten-year anti-poverty plan and continued to advocate a negative income tax as part of its annual anti-poverty planning effort. In November 1968, under Assistant Secretary Alice Rivlin, HEW's Office of Planning and Evaluation issued a "Program Memorandum on Income Maintenance and Rehabilitation Services Program" proposing several cash assistance alternatives including a negative income tax. (Both OEO and HEW undertook large experiments to evaluate the effect of a negative income tax on work behavior.) Although all these comprehensive cash strategies were rejected by the Johnson Administration, negative income tax advocates remained in HEW after Nixon's inauguration and played a major role in structuring the Family Assistance Plan.

---

*FAP's key congressional antagonist was Senator Russell Long (D-La.), Chairman of the Senate Finance Committee, who drafted his own income supplement proposal, to reflect congressional concern about the matter of work incentives. Long, as well as many others in Congress, found FAP's work provisions inadequate; as he commented: "I don't see why anybody is going to work for that money if he's never worked before anyway, and he can get just as much without working."[2] Long's own plan would require all AFDC recipients except mothers with children under six to accept (federally guaranteed) jobs.

Outside of the government, support for cash payments to recipients was even more consistently voiced. In May 1968, for example, numerous prominent economists urged adoption of a negative income tax at the Joint Economic Committee's hearing on Income Maintenance programs. In November 1969 the President's Commission on Income Maintenance Programs (Heineman Commission) issued its report recommending "a universal income supplement program financed and administered by the Federal Government, making cash payment to all members of the population with income needs."

In conjunction with the growing debate on welfare reform, a large body of data was being produced on the characteristics of the poor and on the effectiveness of various government transfer programs. This data was incorporated piecemeal into congressional reforms of welfare during the decade. For instance, evidence on the work disincentives of AFDC 100% benefit reduction rates on earnings underlay the 1967 Amendments to the Social Security Act permitting AFDC recipients who worked to retain one-third of their earnings and deduct a certain amount of their work-related expenses. Analysis of the inadequacies of payment level, geographic differences in benefits and other program inequities supported the federalization of the adult categories of welfare in 1972.* Congress had been conducting hearings on welfare programs since 1968, and in 1972 the Joint Economic Committee's Subcommittee on Fiscal Policy initiated a major evaluation of income transfer programs. The issue of welfare reform had thus remained on the political agenda.

Even before Weinberger was sworn in as Director of OMB on June 12, 1972, his name had become synonymous with the Administration policy of impounding money appropriated by Congress, a policy which congressmen of all persuasions saw as an abuse of Presidential power and liberals saw as an attack on social programs. In April 1971, before the Senate Appropriations Committee, Weinberger had observed:

---

*HR 1 eliminated three state administered categorical assistance programs—Aid to the Blind, Aid to the Permanently and Totally Disabled and Old Age Assistance—replacing them with the federally administered Supplementary Security Income (SSI) on January 1, 1974.

My experience in government has been an unceasing attempt to reduce government expenditures at all levels. . . . The whole nature of the appropriations process is such that Congress is, in one way or another, virtually prevented from having—or at least from taking—an overall look at the effect of their total actions. . . . There is only one agency in government that has, in a sense, the overall responsibility or at least does look at the overall picture at any given time. . . .

Elsewhere he noted:

There is a prevalent myth that Congress finds hard to resist, and that is that you demonstrate your commitment to a particular program, and your support for it, by the amount of other people's money you're willing to spend on it. If you don't vote for excessive spending, the theory seems to be that you're opposed to such things as welfare or health or education.

So the pressures for spending are all upwards. There are very few downward pressures, except the vaguely expressed feeling throughout the country that we are spending too much and that we should do something about it. But that feeling is rarely focused. What *is* focused on Washington is the pressure from groups that want their particular program funded more heavily than it is.[3]

Weinberger's HEW confirmation hearings before the Senate Committee on Labor and Public Welfare in January 1973 demonstrated congressional hostility to Weinberger's role in Nixon's impoundments policy and suspicion that Weinberger was being nominated as HEW Secretary chiefly to eliminate social programs. In Senator Jacob Javits' words, Weinberger was being called to account for having been the "ax man of the Administration." Weinberger himself denied that the President had saddled him with any "axing" mandate for HEW. He offered this view of his HEW responsibilities to the Committee:

A lot of the thrust and the lesson for the budgetary decisions this year seems to have been ignored, and that was quite simply to try to free existing resources, within a total that the President and others determined would not be inflationary or require higher taxes, so that we could do a better job for the people who most need it within that total. I do not think we serve those people whose needs are primarily designed to be taken care of by the Department of Health, Education and Welfare and other departments if we permit a program that will result in heavy inflation—that cuts income in those fields more quickly and more drastically than others—or if we get ourselves in a situation where the level of the productive capacity and potential of the country are dried up. . . .

William H. Taft, IV, who worked with Weinberger at the FTC and OMB and became his Executive Assistant at HEW, commented on liberal reaction to Weinberger's appointment as HEW Secretary.

> I think had he been appointed Secretary of Defense, he would have been greeted over there with exactly the same outlook. And certainly had he gone to Agriculture, which we tried to cut like crazy and failed, he would have been viewed in exactly the same way. That would have been true no matter what cabinet post he had taken.

Weinberger appointed two former associates of Ronald Reagan, James S. Dwight, Jr. and Robert B. Carleson, to oversee the operation of HEW welfare programs. Both men were strong advocates of state control over welfare.* In March 1973, he nominated Dwight to be Administrator of Social Rehabilitation Services (SRS),** which administered categorical grants under Aid to the Blind, Aid to the Permanent and Totally Disabled, Old Age Assistance, AFDC, and Medicaid. (Transfer of the first three programs to the Social Security Administration was to occur with the implementation of the Supplemental Social Security Income (SSI) on January 1, 1974.) In that same month, Robert Carleson became a Special Assistant to the Secretary and requested that Weinberger make him Commissioner of Welfare, a title which had previously been abolished. (After Weinberger's departure from HEW, the title was once again abolished.)

---

*States maintain great freedom to shape their own welfare programs, and to set payments and needs standards. The primary federal control over the states was Social and Rehabilitation Services' authority to review state welfare plans and to reject these on the basis of non-compliance with federal regulations. A variety of formulas govern the federal-state allocation of funds for different welfare programs. For AFDC, the largest welfare program, the federal government paid 55% of the total costs of $7.8 billion in 1973. (The Agriculture Department pays 100% of the program costs for food stamps although administrative costs are shared.)

**The SRS was abolished as part of the reorganization of HEW in 1977 and its functions were transferred to other components of the department.

Dwight had been Deputy Director of the California Department of Finance from 1967 to 1972 and thus had worked with Weinberger in California. He came to Washington in August 1972 to become Associate Director for Management at OMB. Although he had not been responsible for welfare programs in California, Dwight had been part of a state administration bent on welfare reforms. He began to examine the issue while at OMB:

> There was a popular view in both OMB and in HEW in the summer of 1972 that the states lacked the capacity to deal with the management of these programs. I assumed this was the foundation of the FAP and SSI development. When I came to OMB, I challenged that presumption. The response to my challenge was to cite the lack of evidence that the states were effectively doing nothing but squandering their own money and federal money.

Carleson's appointment signalled even more clearly Weinberger's strong commitment to cleaning up the existing system.[4] Formerly Commissioner of the California Department of Social Welfare, Carleson had designed and implemented the state's controversial Welfare Reform Act of 1971, an act which Governor Reagan had called "the most comprehensive welfare reform legislation ever attempted by any state." The subject of a heated legislative battle before becoming law in September 1971, the Act was designed to halt the number of persons coming onto the welfare rolls—particularly the AFDC-UF (Unemployed Fathers) rolls—through numerous changes in existing law. Almost all the Act's major provisions were challenged (but ultimately upheld) in court on constitutional grounds or on grounds that they were inconsistent with federal regulations; and the California Welfare Rights Organization attacked the community work program (employable welfare recipients were required to work at public service jobs) as "slave labor." Reagan himself agreed that many provisions were not in compliance with HEW regulations but asserted they were consistent with "Congressional intent." By the end of 1972, Carleson and Reagan claimed the legislation was saving the state from bankruptcy. The state's total welfare caseload had nearly doubled from December 1967 to December 1970, but by June 1972 it had declined by 185,000 persons.

Moreover, although total grant payments had stopped rising by September 1972, average benefits in all welfare categories had risen. Reagan announced to Californians in March 1972:

> Without our reforms there would now be more than a half million more Californians drawing welfare benefits than there actually are, at an increased cost to our taxpayers of $1.1 billion this year and next. We've turned the welfare monster around in California and we're convinced that our approach to reform is the right answer to the problem.*

Carleson saw his appointment as HEW Welfare Commissioner and Special Assistant to the Secretary as a green light to promulgate his California policies nationally. Carleson viewed Weinberger as an ally in his continuing fight against federalization of AFDC; and Nixon's 1973 State of the Union Address confirmed to Carleson that his own view was the Administration's policy. As California Welfare Commissioner, he had argued with HEW officials over the constraints of federal regulations and had come to believe they were purposely continuing the AFDC "mess" to make a political case for federal takeover of AFDC:

> I set out to help put out the fire for federalization by demonstrating that the states could bring the system under control. I got myself appointed as Special Assistant to be within the Office of the Secretary, allowing me to bypass the federal welfare bureaucracy and to act as a personal representative to the governors and other state officials. In addition, being in the Office of the Secretary enabled me to oversee the implementation of SSI.

Within HEW Dwight and Carleson were initially perceived as representing Weinberger's views on welfare. One official recalled the general impression. "Ye

---

*Critics disputed Reagan's claims, arguing that the state's declining birth and immigration rates and, most importantly, lower unemployment rate were the major sources for caseload decline. However, the *California Journal*, a political monthly initially not sympathetic to the Welfare Reform Act, noted in December 1972:

> The conclusion seems inescapable that the reform programs have had a very significant impact on welfare costs and caseloads in California and that the Reagan administration has to a large extent succeeded. . . .

gods, here come the Californians and Weinberger's another one of them."[5] Another remembered:

> Carleson was perceived at a distance as a fellow who had accomplished quite a lot in California, had cut down the ineligibles, cut down the error rate and permitted within a fiscal constraint even larger benefits to be paid to the residual caseload. Here was a fellow who had satisfied the intellectual interests of both the conservative and liberal camps. Through good management he had brought all of this off, [so] by God, bring him into the federal government, and teach both the feds and other states how to do it. This was on the surface an appealing argument no matter where you stood on the spectrum.

A NEW ROUND OF WELFARE REFORM?

Despite his "State of the Union" focus on management, the President remained interested in considering new ways to reform welfare programs. Weinberger shared Nixon's view that some kind of reform was a necessity:

> I thought welfare reform needed doing. I was never satisfied with the Family Assistance Plan. It seemed to me that FAP had a lot of real deficiencies. It didn't have a strong work requirement for people able to work. I thought some of the things the governor had done in California, such as the distinction between people able to work and people not able to work had worked well. I was worried about the total cost of welfare and what seemed to me much more worrisome, future projections of cost. Along with that, I was worried that it did not seem to me we were accomplishing anything with what we had for the people who needed it most. And I had spent a lot of time in state government working on government organization, and was grievously offended by the total lack of organization of welfare. It's just a full spread of programs. . . . There is no agency to look at what they accomplish, or to look at whether they're all needed or whether there's duplication. Nobody looks at anything like uniform eligibility requirements or uniform administration or any one of a number of things.

Weinberger directed his HEW Undersecretary Frank Carlucci to establish a Welfare Reform Interagency Task Force. Carlucci had been Weinberger's OMB Deputy Director and also Assistant Director of the Office of Economic Opportunity from 1969 to 1970 and its Director in 1971. Carlucci recollected Weinberger's mandate:

> My instructions from Cap in initiating the welfare reform effort were very broad. . . . Both he and I agreed from the outset that the existing system was a mess and that true reform could only be achieved by a massive overhaul. In our various discussions on this subject I had gained some insight into his general philosophy.
>
> He approached the subject, I would say, with only three biases: One was that the existing system was a total failure and that while tightening it up could help, the only solution was to substitute it with something much less bureaucratic, and much more targeted on the real poor; he felt strongly that the states had to play an important role in the new system; he felt equally strongly that a work requirement was essential. . . .
>
> I had felt from my OEO days that total overhaul was necessary. I think it is fair to say that I had been more sympathetic to FAP than Cap, but I had not really delved into it deeply enough to take a strong position one way or the other. I felt less compulsion about building in a strong role for the states, although I agreed philosophically with Cap's thesis that the central government was running far too many programs that might be better run at the local level. As far as the work requirement was concerned I felt from my OEO experience that the cost of such a requirement frequently outweighed the benefits gained, particularly since a relatively small percentage of the poor were actually able to work and did not want to. My experience had been that most poor people wanted a job, and they preferred it to welfare.

The Task Force was to include Assistant Secretaries from the agencies involved in welfare programs: Agriculture, the Council of Economic Advisors, Social Security Administration, SRS, HUD, Department of Labor, Manpower Administration (renamed the Employment and Training Administration in 1975), and OMB. One of the participants recalled the Task Force's initially vague mandate:

> It was communicated to us that Nixon wanted to reexamine the area of welfare reform, that he was unhappy that nothing for the non-aged population had happened during the previous round. He wanted something done and he wanted Weinberger in his role as Counselor and Secretary of HEW to restudy the issue and come back to him with a proposal that could be passed. He was concerned about political feasibility as well as capitalizing on all the knowledge that was generated in the previous debate.

Carlucci assigned primary responsibility for coordinating the effort and for directing the analysis to William A. Morrill, a former colleague at OMB, who had been appointed Assistant Secretary for Planning and Evaluation. Despite Carleson's position as Commissioner of Welfare, Carlucci believed that the Office of Planning and Evaluation was the place to consider the broad issues of welfare reform.

> Carleson's charter from the outset was to make recommendations on tightening up the existing system. . . . In my judgment Carleson had a number of valid points to make on the existing system, and as I recall I ruled in his favor on those issues more often than not. It was on the general issue of welfare reform in its broad outlines that Bob was weakest. When Cap and I discussed the issue of reform I recommended that Morrill be given the central responsibility, while admitting of course that Carleson should be brought in. Cap had absolutely no problem with that. . . .
>
> There was no commitment made to Bob Carleson that he would be the czar in such matters as welfare reform. . . . Not that Bob recognized this as a limiting factor on his charter. . . . When he discovered that Bill Morrill and his people would be working on welfare reform he came immediately to me to express his concern that the bureaucrats were going to work us over and we should be careful. FAP would be resuscitated. It was important that he be included in any meetings which discussed issues of welfare reform. I agreed.

Morrill assigned the issue to the Office of Income Security Policy, headed by John L. Palmer. Morrill himself had little experience in welfare policy. He described his own attitude toward welfare reform:

> I knew a little bit about it, but I really came to the subject with no predispositions whatsoever.

I had more than average concern, I suppose, about the underlying issues—poverty, and what have you. I had been an activist in my non-professional life, I've been on [community action] boards of directors, and I had dealt with the poverty issue in Fairfax County [where he had been Deputy County Executive]. So I was not indifferent about it. I just wasn't terribly smart about the subject when I started out. But, I did feel the system ought to be tightened up.

He was, however, well aware of the political pitfalls of welfare reform. For instance, in organizing a new process of welfare policy-making, Morrill "resisted bringing in the FAP planners who were lurking about in HEW who thought they would have another go at it."

Although Palmer had been in Planning and Evaluation since 1971 and had worked on the welfare component of "the MEGA proposal,"* he had not been involved with FAP. Morrill saw him as having "no particular strong intellectual commitment to any viewpoint." (Palmer described himself as having the "technical expertise to understand welfare" but lacking any real substantive experience with it.) Morrill was aware that Senator Russell Long's suspicions that the Office of Planning and Evaluation was too liberal and pro-recipient might eventually hinder any reforms proposed by it, yet he believed pulling the welfare issue out of Planning and Evaluation would be a mistake. Establishing a separate group to address only the welfare question would negate the presidential thrust to centralize domestic policy-making under Secretary Weinberger. Planning and Evaluation was the Secretary's planning and analytic office. Moreover, Morrill needed good issues to attract a "solid staff." Finally as one observer noted, there was a widespread attitude that trying to placate Long was hopeless—"There was no place in HEW we could organize a welfare reform effort and make Russell Long love it."

---

*Formally titled "Comprehensive HEW Simplification and Reform Plan," the MEGA proposal was developed by the Office of Planning and Evaluation in 1972 to overhaul HEW's programmatic structure. Its welfare component would have divided families into employable and unemployable members providing cash assistance according to the number of unemployable mothers and excluding employables from such assistance.

Morrill and Palmer assigned primary responsibility for the staff work to Michael Barth, an analyst at OEO (which was being disbanded that spring). Palmer had known Barth's work at OEO and considered him knowledgeable about welfare issues and an able researcher. He asked Barth for some assistance and, after Barth's transfer from OEO to the National Institute of Education (NIE) in the spring of 1973, Barth was loaned to HEW by NIE. Like Palmer, Barth was a Ph.D. economist. Although he had worked on issues of labor supply, migration and family stability, he had not been directly involved in developing welfare policy.

> The problem was that Palmer and I didn't know very much about welfare. In other words, we had our strengths, I guess, as labor economists who understood the interaction between income maintenance and labor markets and who had fairly strong views on the issue. In addition, maybe we were good analysts, straight thinkers, or something like that. But we didn't know that much about welfare and we were really very sensitive about that.

Morrill also hired George Carcagno, a consultant from Mathematica, Inc., who had considerable knowledge of both AFDC and of the welfare system in general, and Palmer recruited several other staff who were leaving OEO.

One participant characterized the initial planning as "a massive touchy-feely." Palmer described it more concretely:

> There was never much said about a schedule, other than it is an important issue and let's move ahead, but it gave us in the office a chance to structure the process in a way that we thought made sense without being in the position of having a very short time to do it. I think the most important thing was the process that we defined. There was a general recognition that first of all the President and Weinberger really wanted to go back to ground zero to reexamine the whole question. And, there was a whole new set of actors throughout the government because there was a big changeover at the end of the first Nixon Administration. There were new people in the Labor Department, new people on the

Domestic Council, new people within the Department of HEW, new people in OMB. Wherever you looked in terms of key actors, there was a whole new group of people on the policy-making level, the assistant secretary level and up, to educate and to bring along in terms of them getting to the point where they could formulate their own views about welfare reform. And knowing what a terribly controversial issue it is and how it immediately evokes people's passions and prejudices, we felt that it was far better not to immediately jump in and examine programmatic alternatives but to really go back as close to ground zero as possible and present, or structure, a study of the current welfare system: what it was like, what was wrong with it, what objectives one would want to see embodied in welfare reform, what the major issues were that would have to be confronted. We wanted to determine what types of analysis and what other kinds of information could be brought to bear on major issues. We would try to deal as much as possible with this non-controversial background material and get everybody up to speed on that before jumping into the program alternatives on which there was clearly going to be a lot of dispute.

There were many areas where the tools that we had to work with and the kinds of evidence that we could bring to bear on critical questions was the real difference between what went on with FAP and this is the difference between night and day. There was a tremendous amount of research done in the intervening five years.*

Palmer, who was involved in other activities, relied heavily on Barth to organize the staff work and identify the crucial issues. The basic work schedule evolved into an interagency production of background papers on technical issues (such as the transfer efficiency of means tested programs, the evaluation of

the impact of manpower programs, the coverage of the transfer system), an overview paper to be developed by Barth's staff (which would describe the present transfer system, establish goals for a transfer system and alternative ways to modify the existing system) and a final design of the Secretary's preferred alternative reform option(s). Barth and Carcagno worked throughout May and June to produce the overview paper (which was subsequently lauded by the Institute for Research on Poverty for its comprehensiveness and objectivity). One of Barth's staff remembered his early perceptions of the Task Force effort:

> We started off with this overview paper. I guess most of us expected that we were heading towards another FAP. MEGA was not discussed. . . . We all pretty much favored comprehensive reform; some were in favor of a negative income tax if it were feasible but most of us considered it infeasible. We thought we'd end up with FAP.

At least some observers tended to discount the reform orientation of the Task Force. After learning that HEW was again developing reform strategies, an aide to Senator Abraham Ribicoff commented:

> I wouldn't hold my breath with what they're going to come up with. Reform means money and HEW is full of the Reagan-California clique that is intent on cutting costs.[6]

WEINBERGER STEPS IN

Although staff work on the background papers continued, by summer the Interagency Task Force itself had lapsed, after only one or two formal meetings. (Its demise may be at least in part attributed to the growing controversy over Watergate and the focus of the Nixon White House on that issue. The Senate hearings on Watergate began in the summer of 1973.)

By early July the overview paper was completed and the Secretary decided to involve himself directly in the welfare reform process. This was a decision Carlucci and Morrill both supported. Carlucci noted:

> Neither of us had any doubt from the outset that the study would produce a real reform proposal. Cap liked bold initiatives but we also knew he would be hard to convince if the proposal seemed to (a) involve more money, (b) mean more bureaucracy, (c) move towards greater centralization, or (d) resemble FAP. Yet we knew we had

---

*This research included the results of the New Jersey Income Maintenance Experiments indicating that receipt of guaranteed income does not result in reduced work effort by primary wage earners; information on the income stability of the poverty population compiled by the Panel Study of Income Dynamics at the University of Michigan Survey Research Center; the 1971 AFDC sample produced by the National Center for Social Statistics; and information on income transfer programs being put together by the staff of the Joint Economic Committee's Subcommittee on Fiscal Policy.

great advantages in that Cap was a conservative in the truest sense. He disliked bureaucracy intensely but he had great faith in the poor people themselves. He felt the existing system cheated them. We knew that if we could demonstrate something simpler and better targeted that it would appeal to his instincts. At the outset we gambled a bit on him but it was not too long before we were certain that the merits of our case would be strong enough to convince Cap if we could just set in motion a process whereby he could become totally acquainted with all the facts. Hence, the idea of setting up a series of briefing sessions.

Despite his strong criticisms of FAP, Weinberger recognized his knowledge of welfare was impressionistic and second-hand. He respected his staff, and trusted them to produce the kind of documentation he needed to "sort out his thinking process." He directed Morrill and Palmer to conduct a series of briefings for the Department designed to describe existing income maintenance programs, their inadequacies and alternatives for reform:

> I laid out certain things that I wanted. One of them was a definite cost factor. I wanted to know what each option would cost and whether we could secure any saving. I wanted a strong work requirement for people who could work. I wanted some evidence that what we're doing was going to benefit the people who needed it most. . . .
>
> I wanted a better administrative structure. Very irrelevant considerations were determining amounts and directions and results of these programs. And so I wanted to get some logic into the administrative structure. Programs should be consolidated so the whole array of welfare programs could be looked at together. There was the congressional habit of responding to what appeared to be a crisis and enact a new program. But there would never be the slightest consideration of what the effect of that new program was on either the Treasury or on the other programs or on individuals receiving benefits.
>
> Also I wanted to start with the idea that welfare should not be used as a means of redistributing income. Welfare should be used to help those who needed help while they needed help. But it should not be looked upon as a permanent way

of life or as an attempt to equalize income or to give people money because it was unfair that they didn't have it.

Palmer planned a series of ten briefings (ultimately only eight were held), lasting 90 minutes each and attended by Secretary Weinberger, HEW Assistant Secretaries, the Commissioner of Social Security, William Taft, Robert Carleson, and James Dwight. Although both Palmer and Morrill were coming to favor the negative income tax,* they were concerned to maintain a purely educational process and to structure the analysis to meet the concerns of the Secretary:

> Our conscious effort was not to push a viewpoint, but to present as broadly and objectively as possible the background information that the Secretary needed. You can't entirely separate out *what* and *the way* you present things, but Bill Morrill was one of those people who could really stand back and objectively present alternatives and present the full range of views and not put himself and his own views into it until he was asked to do so. This is one of his real strengths and that's why Weinberger placed a lot of confidence in him. . . . I think we all felt that the correct reading of certain background issues tended to lead you to a negative income tax, but we weren't saying that to Weinberger.
>
> We had some sense for what his instincts and views were and there was no question that we had to structure the information to be responsive to these. There were certain kinds of questions that he was going to ask; obviously you

---

*Palmer related: "I'm personally convinced, and I've seen it time and time again, that for the most part, when somebody really takes the time and trouble to learn the details well, they tend to get led to the negative income tax approach as a solution, because it makes some sense, and it makes more sense than a lot of other approaches."

Barth recalled the development of his thinking:

> I had never really thought about the negative income tax from the point of view of alternative policies. I suppose that when I arrived at HEW I had the standard economist's notion that the negative income tax was the thing to do. It's a reasonable compromise between trade-offs; it maximizes the use of the market. A similar situation arises if you ask most economists whether free trade is a good idea. They haven't really thought about it; they're not trade specialists but they think it's a good idea. I didn't really know the nuts and bolts of welfare. I really learned a lot. The process convinced me, but I suppose I would say that I was a pushover to start with.

tried to anticipate those questions so that you were doing good staff work for him and giving him what he wanted. For example, you could predict that he was going to be very concerned about the disincentive effects of something. So, we put a lot of effort into really pulling together all the models of behavioral responses, and in trying to illuminate the whole work incentive issue in the briefings. Three or four years ago, if you had a much more liberal secretary he might not have been concerned about work incentives, and you would know that, and therefore, you wouldn't spend a lot of time and staff resources trying to prepare material.

Background material on the substance of the briefing was prepared and distributed to participants in advance with additional notes and handouts distributed at the meeting. Palmer and Barth would then make a formal presentation. They first described four transfer programs (AFDC, Food Stamps, Medicaid, and the adult categories of welfare); provided information on the incidence of poverty and the poverty population; and evaluated the coverage of both welfare and social insurance programs by family type. (See Appendix A for excerpts from the analysts' evaluation of the existing welfare system.)

The meetings turned to defining the structure of a "good" welfare system in order to identify where existing programs fell short. Here, as Palmer pointed out, the values of the analysts and the Secretary were stated openly:

I think the one place where value judgments clearly had to enter explicitly into the process was in the criteria that we laid out for what a welfare system ought to do. After all, you have to have some objectives in mind initially which you try to get people to accept at a broad and general level. So, we put forward what we thought were the important objectives. But then Weinberger had a chance to interact with us on those and to say, "I don't consider this important." "Let's not worry about it." Or, "What about . . . ?" for example, we clearly laid out the conventional objectives of work incentives, adequacy, horizontal and vertical equity, family stability, and so on. I know one that we didn't initially mention was fiscal control—the notion that you'd want the system to be designed in a way that policy-makers could really have a firm hand on how much money was going through it.

I doubt that we put as much emphasis on administrative efficiency initially as we did ultimately because that was an important concern of the Secretary.

The welfare objectives eventually emerging from the discussions are outlined in Appendix B.

By this point in the briefings, the analysts had established some understanding of the operations and failures of the existing welfare system. They had also outlined possible objectives to which individual programs might be addressed. They then began to examine the trade-offs among the various objectives posed by the different types of programs. As they summarized their thinking:

Benefits can be transferred in three basic forms:

—Cash, as in AFDC,
—Voucher, as in Food Stamps, or
—Goods and services, as in public housing.

There is no reason why the three cannot be used simultaneously, if that arrangement best fulfills policy goals. Generally, cash is the most efficient transfer device and maximizes the options of the recipient. Vouchers (including insurance) are useful to direct consumption and can be used to effect a national policy of equal access to a particular good or service while leaving the consumption decision within this category of goods or services up to the individual. Direct provision of goods or services controls consumption more directly and is useful when the supply of the good or service in question is not responsive to market demand, and the government thus has an interest and a responsibility for maintaining efficiently functioning markets. . . .

The adoption of a mix of cash and in-kind programs precludes a simple administrative structure. Such a course also requires that much attention be given to the question of how a variety of means-tested programs, targeted at the same population, should be related. Care should be taken that neither basic benefits nor benefit reduction rates be permitted to cumulate to undesirably high levels. . . . [S]trong political pressures surround noncash transfer programs, making it difficult to alter them or cash them out. Finally . . . moving from a simple universal cash transfer to a mixed cash in-kind system with a work requirement introduces administrative complexities and inequities. That is, program structures become more complex and the degree to which the primary policy goals are successfully fulfilled is reduced as the system is asked to address many concerns simultaneously.

From this general review of program alternatives, the analysts turned to a more detailed examination of the conflicts/compromises among objectives posed by specific program reform options. They divided these options into two classes: those which could (and in their view, should) be pursued immediately regardless of any long-term shift in welfare policy; and those—labelled "major structural reform"—which would require very consequential and explicit policy choices. Under the first class, they considered various labor market strategies and administrative reforms intended to facilitate the operation of existing programs. Although they regarded many of these limited-scope reforms as necessary prerequisites for public acceptance of more large scale reform, they did not view these reforms as—by themselves—adequate.

Under the class of "major structural reform options," the analysts examined four possibilities:

(1) A national minimum benefit for AFDC
(2) An earnings supplement
(3) An in-kind strategy
(4) Two types of cash transfer programs: a variation of the Family Assistance Plan and a Friedman-type of tax system reform.

Although Palmer and Barth did not recommend any of these alternatives to the Secretary, Dwight and Carleson objected strongly to the content and policy implications of the briefings and saw this "educational process" as one inevitably pushing the Secretary to welfare overhaul. Carleson especially argued strenuously with Palmer and Barth. Dwight's deputy, John A. Svahn characterized the briefings as "a selling job" with high level HEW staff there only to impress the Secretary and to be seen participating in what was clearly a priority departmental discussion. According to Svahn, most of those attending probably could not even understand the numbers and statistics being presented. Barth disputed this:

> Even if we had set the briefings up to be purely a selling job which we did not, Carleson and Dwight

were present. I will never forget one of the first briefings. We had prepared briefing notebooks. I was sitting next to Carleson. On one page of the notebook, he had 18 points to make. And he marched through every one of them. We were supposed to be giving the briefing. He would just interrupt in the middle of the sentence and say, "Well, Cap." The secretary would ask questions but he didn't challenge us a lot. On the other hand, the meetings were contentious. He was always listening to a debate.

Carleson recalled his surprise at the content of the meetings since he had assumed that Weinberger had initiated the welfare reform planning process merely at the behest of the President and was not himself committed to structural reform:

> The impressions I had were that Cap was favorably disposed to the negative income tax even at the early meetings. At that time I concluded it was because all the information he was getting was from one side. All of the information was coming up through Morrill's shop. If I didn't know anything about welfare and I read that information, I would think it was great because they were very good at couching all of this in conservative language: things like reducing overlapping and duplication; getting rid of all of this administrative overhead; simplifying it; getting rid of all those hard to use food stamps. For example, when they said "strong work incentives," they meant no work requirement because the words "incentive" and "strong" mean permitting an even lower benefit reduction rate—in other words, going from a two-thirds to 50% benefit reduction rate. If you ask the average fiscal conservative who doesn't know welfare and if you use the words "strong," "work," and "incentives," they're all good words to him. Most fiscal conservatives like "incentives"; they like "work"; and they like "strong." But those three words mean just the opposite of a stronger work requirement.
>
> What's attractive about the negative income tax is that it gets it all down in dollars. It's no longer food stamps, housing, or jobs. And if it's in dollars and you know how many people, then as a good budgeter you know how much it's going to cost. This has an awful lot of appeal to somebody who wants to run a very orderly program. It also has an appeal to those people who

believe in running things from headquarters. I think one of the reasons that big business goes for it is because they run their own operations from headquarters. You can run it from Washington; you don't have to have fifty different state systems; this sounds like a logical way. The trouble is that when you're dealing with welfare you are dealing with problems. Each individual in each family probably has a little different solution to get off welfare. The only way you're going to solve the welfare problem for each individual or each family is to look at each individually and you can't do that from Washington.

I sent Cap a memo where I laid out what I thought were the dangers of the negative income tax. I argued about the fallacies of federalization: the fact that it would not solve the welfare problem but aggravate it because the truly needy wouldn't receive adequate benefits and therefore they would either slip through the cracks or else there would be tremendous state requirements to make up the slack. Or, on the other side of the fence, that the national benefit levels would eventually grow so high in order to take care of the truly needy that they would cover vast amounts of non-needy and, that once you establish a national benefit, there would be tremendous political pressure on the one decision point, Congress, to continually increase the national benefit. This would be particularly true if the national minimum were financed by the federal government and particularly true if it were being administered by the federal government because pressure would be coming from the recipients and from the states which would have to be picking up the slack for people requiring benefits in excess of the national minimum.

Dwight was also skeptical of the briefings. Even before they began, he had recognized the differences between his position on welfare and that of Palmer's staff. In his effort to draw up new regulations tightening welfare management, Dwight was meeting with vociferous departmental opposition from the Income Security Office. The staff saw the regulations as hurting welfare recipients since they often eliminated client-oriented procedures. Dwight, however, saw the conflict as one between his responses to state requests for administrative changes in order to identify ineligi-

ble clients and to reduce fraud and those of the traditional HEW welfare bureaucracy—which often knew little about the actual operation of the welfare system. Dwight recognized early on that his assumptions about welfare were profoundly different from those implicit in the Palmer and Barth presentations:

> I held two basic convictions against reform: I felt that the quality of the existing system was an unknown, largely because there had never been a concerted effort over a long period of time to clean it up. I believed it could be improved. The comparisons were invalid. In other words you couldn't compare with a clean existing system because nobody knew exactly what that was. Second, we couldn't afford reform. There were a lot of theoretical proposals which were bantered around, but the base case is that if you're going to substantially increase the benefit levels, you're going to do two things: one, the average cost of the program is going to be greater because you're increasing the amount of the benefit; secondly you're going to substantially expand the number of people receiving benefits because of the way you determine eligibility—if you raise the standard it just means that more people are going to become eligible.

Dwight also distrusted the numbers presented to the Secretary:

> Their information was all speculative. Factually we were dealing with the same information. But as you look into the future, it becomes a matter of speculation. We differed on what the trends were going to be and what it was going to cost if we maintained the status quo and what it was going to cost if we embraced structural reform. . . .
>
> And [costs] was an issue where I finally just gave up. I told Cap, "I could go off, I could manufacture facts just like Palmer and Barth. I can go out and get you some numbers that will produce a different result but it's a futile effort because the issue is not facts, but a basic disagreement about assumptions."

These objections did not trouble the analysts since Carleson and Dwight did not counter with analysis of their own nor did they demand information to support their positions. Barth remembered:

> Carleson really had a shot at the Secretary. After all, he had a relationship with the Secretary that

Palmer and I didn't. Morrill almost would never take Carleson on in those settings. It was just bad tactically to argue with him because eventually you gave him enough rope and he hung himself. And I think that was largely because he kept arguing almost at an emotional level.

I never understood the situation. Both Carleson and Dwight were smart. It seemed to me their strategy was wrong: they would never force a debate on the merits of the issue in front of Weinberger. They would always come on with statements such as "It's not the right way to do it," "The country's going to fall apart," or something like that. It seems to me they didn't have the respect for Weinberger's intellect that was required; either they weren't sure of him intellectually or they didn't have respect for his intellect. There was never debate on the merits. They would never give you a chance to reply. Especially Carleson. And I don't understand why because he made some good arguments. And he really knows the welfare system.

An especially troublesome issue for the analysts was the inclusion of a work requirement in any proposal. Barth recalled:

Our real fear was that work relief would somehow get into the proposal. Work relief is a system where recipients must work for their benefit and receive no added benefit for working. The cash benefit is divided by—say 80—and the recipient must work 80 hours a month. Bob Carleson was a strong advocate of work relief. He said it had worked very well in California. We disagreed very strongly. We constantly asked him for evidence. None was ever forthcoming.

I had very strong feelings against work relief. A lot of people who were poor really wanted to work, and were already horribly stigmatized. To put them in a situation like work relief was just the wrong way to do it. . . . I remember writing up a memo to Morrill to that effect. . . . I knew Morrill didn't like work relief but this was a touchy point where Carleson was clearly scoring some points. We had won on everything else.

The staff was devoting a large part of its analytic effort to discussions of the work requirement, work incentives and various work conditioned programs to "get behind the rhetoric on work requirements."

Knowledgeable of the growing evidence confirming or suggesting the strong labor force attachment of the poor, and armed with the results of the New Jersey experiment, the analysts presented this information to the Secretary:

What we argued was that while the experimental results were not conclusive, they were consistent with the cross-sectional results. In other words, a totally different methodology yielded similar results. Viewed in isolation the New Jersey results were not that influential, but viewed in the context of a whole range of evidence, they're one more factor that seems to indicate that large scale withdrawal from the labor force or work reduction is probably not going to result. You can't argue that it's 10% nor 15%, but the biggest fear in the sixties was a picture of massive withdrawal from the labor market. I think the New Jersey experiment pretty conclusively put the fear to rest.

Analysts running the New Jersey project were invited to give a briefing to the Secretary. In addition, Palmer's office presented arguments on the high costs of manpower programs and their typically poor results. Despite the strong conviction of the analysts, Morrill, Taft and Carlucci, that a work requirement was a costly, administratively inefficient and unnecessary addition to an income transfer program, Weinberger insisted that a work requirement was integral to welfare programs:

I felt that the work requirement was essential from a number of points of view, one of which was the way the public would view it. I thought that regardless of how much you could demonstrate through the New Jersey and other experiments that a guaranteed income did not necessarily reduce the work effort, you were not invalidating the basis for a work requirement. One of the essentials for a welfare reform program is public acceptance and in order to get public acceptance you have to have a work requirement. I thought this was basically right as long as it was required only of people who were fully able to meet it. I did not believe that the work requirement should be met by public service employment.*

____

*The final ISP proposal included an optional state work registration requirement for all unemployed recipients without child care responsibilities. Recipients refusing to cooperate with the state employment service assisting them in finding jobs would lose their benefits.

Although Carleson's and Dwight's objections obviously troubled him, Weinberger impressed the staff with his commitment to reading and understanding the analyses and information. Palmer came to believe that the Secretary's intellectual openness was crucial to the development of the policy-making process.

> Weinberger was a guy who often shot from the hip. . . . [But] he was open to evidence and analysis and, in my own view, would come out more right than wrong once he actually spent more time with an issue. Not moving to get a fast decision on welfare reform turned out to be important in terms of getting him to the point where he really knew it well enough to make a decision that was based less on instincts and prejudices and more on a full understanding of the issue.

MILTON FRIEDMAN

In late August, Weinberger and Taft left on a diplomatic trip to the USSR. Palmer's staff began to develop in detail the reform options presented to the Secretary in the briefings. At Carlucci's request, a copy of Friedman's article, "The Case for a Negative Income Tax" was pouched to Weinberger in the Soviet Union, where he and Taft spent much time discussing welfare reform.

Carlucci recalled that he and Morrill were becoming concerned that the briefings were breaking down:

> Bill and I were discussing the lack of progress that had been made in the last one or two briefing sessions. Bob Carleson had developed a tendency to interrupt the briefers at every sentence, and it was clear to me that this was even beginning to frustrate Cap. At this rate, it would take us forever to get through the issues we had to address. We were looking for some dramatic way of achieving a breakthrough. Bill had been in touch with Milton Friedman and his name came up. We both agreed that it might be desirable to have a session with Milton. Bill wondered if he should go out and see him, and one of us suggested it might be a good idea to get him into HEW for a briefing. Who actually said it, I don't recall, but we both thought we had hit on something good.
>
> In any event the idea turned out to be the best one we had. Friedman was absolutely brilliant and covered in five minutes what it might have taken us months to cover. . . .

To many of the participants, Friedman's appearance at this point was critical. (Weinberger already knew Friedman through their mutual friend and colleague George Schultz, then Secretary of the Treasury, who had been a strong supporter of FAP and had consistently advocated overhaul of AFDC.) Palmer recalled the meeting as finally decimating the lure of Carleson's conservative arguments:

> Friedman was someone that Weinberger knew and certainly respected and believed had similar viewpoints to his own. We had a session where Friedman came and met with the same set of actors who were in the briefing sessions. Basically Weinberger asked Friedman, "What do you think we ought to do?" And, Friedman was extremely articulate and convincing about the negative income tax as differentiated from FAP. That, of course, was one of the options in the memo we were working on. My recollection is that Weinberger more or less made up his mind subsequent to that session. That is, he didn't really make up his mind on the basis of carefully studying the things that we prepared as much as on having been moved along, having gone through an evolution in his understanding of the issue.

Morrill remembered a combination of intellectual virtuosity and committed conservatism:

> Friedman's contribution to all of this process was an important one—less to the ultimate persuasion of Cap than in dealing more with Cap's own underlying reservations in a couple of areas. Friedman literally not only moved Cap across some threshold but changed an attitude of acceptance of what was necessary into a very strong positive enthusiasm.
>
> There were two issues with which Cap struggled the hardest. One was, could you do it with jobs? This was an issue where what we knew was not all that strong. The other issue was the work requirement. Cap kept saying, "I'd rather do welfare reform with a jobs route. How much can we do?" And what we had to tell him was, "We don't think you can do it without getting into a public service job program, and from everything we know you can't do that without running up the costs fairly substantially." And because we

couldn't deal with those two points, he moved away from what was intrinsically his preferred ideological position. I think Friedman dealt with those issues pretty successfully by saying, "Look that's an interesting question, but it's just irrelevant"—that is, politically, the work requirement had to be there but conceptually it was not the guts of the debate. Out of all that we kept coming back to the issue not as "welfare reform" but more nearly as "tax reform."

Paul O'Neill, Assistant OMB Director for Human Resource Programs, had kept in touch with Morrill and Carlucci on the welfare policy process, although he had not attended prior HEW briefings. O'Neill had also worked with Weinberger at OMB and had known the strong objections Weinberger had to FAP. He recalled the impressions Friedman made on the Secretary at the meeting. Friedman stressed that the negative income tax would abolish large bureaucracies, concentrate funds on the poorest and promote work through permitting recipients to retain portions of their earnings. He also answered Weinberger's concern that the negative income tax would become fiscally uncontrollable since the states would have no fiscal stake in it and thus would not serve as counterweights to inevitable political pressures for continually higher benefit rates. By integrating the tax and transfer system, Friedman pointed out, fiscal control over welfare spending would be augmented: any increase in breakeven level of income would simultaneously require an increase in tax exemption for tax purposes and this in turn would require higher taxes on higher incomes.*

THE MEMO TO THE PRESIDENT

Three weeks later on November 6, Secretary Weinberger sent a memo to the President, titled "Major Domestic Programs and Tax Reform." Initially drafted by Morrill the memo advocated the integration of the tax, welfare and domestic assistance programs along the general line of Friedman's negative income tax scheme. The memo recommended to the President the establishment of a small working group to develop a detailed proposal. In the memo (a copy

of which was obtained from former staff), Weinberger outlined the reason for his recommendation:

When I step back from the details of the problems which your major reforms have encountered, I find a common set of issues and obstacles which have impeded them:

- Although the approach to broad social problems which relies on a multiplicity of narrow categorical assistance programs has been widely recognized as a failure, or at least not effective, recommendations to eliminate these assistance programs in favor of direct assistance to individuals, or revenue sharing, is usually not well received. Without a broad based understanding and support, we have been left to do battle one at a time with particular recipients, interest groups and Congressional committees with a strong stake in the existing structure of such categorical programs. This posture is not a winner.

- The interrelationships of the domestic assistance programs have become as important as the content of each one. To ignore these interrelationships is to pile one program on top of another with undesirable, unintended and costly results. Congresswoman Griffiths' ongoing studies have been documenting this fact in excruciating detail in the public welfare area. The involvement of 19 different Congressional committees in various income security programs does not help. In retrospect, your Family Assistance Plan probably ran into as much trouble for what it did not address as for what it contained.

- There has been no assured means of linking domestic assistance programs—reformed or otherwise—with fiscal sanity. The piecemeal approach to expenditures and taxes in the Congress, and the schizophrenic public attitudes of support for specific programs and distaste for the total bill must be addressed with some specific linkages. Your 1974 budget engendered a growing concern with this issue in the Congress, and attempted to deal with it by means of a ceiling. Governor Reagan, with the same consideration in mind, has proposed a specific Constitutional ceiling in California.

---

*Friedman's article "The Case for a Negative Income Tax" concludes: "The cost of the payments is in one lump sum that can be calculated and that will be painfully obvious to every taxpayer. It will be obvious that every rise in the rate applied to negative taxable income raises the cost."

- We have not really come to grips with public frustration and dissatisfaction with the performance and size of the Federal bureaucracy and a related, growing dissatisfaction with the equity of the tax system. Much of the latter stems, I believe, from disillusionment about results achieved for taxes paid. While you have made consistent efforts to reduce the Federal payroll, improved efficiency is swamped by program additions and changes. Only major structural reforms are likely to make more than a marginal difference.

If I were persuaded that the disorder and costs of the present programs could be contained or somewhat improved, I might be tempted to recommend a series of modest improvements in welfare for you to present the Congress and the country. My assessment is to the contrary. A more modest approach just does not address the fundamental issues, and does not provide promise of success. Time is not on our side. Left alone or altered modestly, the present situation will inexorably get worse, making fundamental reform even more difficult later.

A few examples in the welfare system may undergird this assessment. Food stamps costing about $2.2 billion in FY 1974 are now projected to cost about $6 billion—perhaps more—by FY 1976. Our efforts to cash them out for a part of the low income population—the aged, blind and disabled—is rapidly eroding to nothing. Senator Long is gaining support for his work bonus which would pay a modest benefit to low income workers covered by the payroll tax. Appropriate in purpose, the Long proposal trivializes a good idea in a way that is likely to create more problems than it solves, since it adds yet another means-tested transfer program to the existing system. The drumbeat of social security increases, which puts you in an impossible position, continues apace. The list could go on and on.

You are slowly but surely being pushed into a corner of choosing between tax increases and an economically sane budget without attaining reform. Minor tinkering or sequential changes do not seem to work with the Congress and, in any event, do not deal with fundamental structural problems and program interrelationships. Only a major reform initiative seems to offer a way out.

Unaware of the Secretary's decision Barth and his staff were still working on an options paper outlining the programmatic alternatives for welfare reform and their costs. Barth recalled with surprise learning of the Secretary's memorandum:

After the briefings we started to work on an options paper which never saw the light of day. . . . I realized later it was a smokescreen for this memo to the President. I don't know when Morrill conceived it or how. . . . And then I thought, this is fascinating; the whole town thinks we're doing this options paper and they're doing an end run around the system.

APPENDIX A

Major Characteristics of the Welfare System

GEOGRAPHIC DIFFERENCES

Interstate and intrastate differences in eligibility, benefit levels, and administration are perhaps the inevitable (and not necessarily undesirable) result of the decentralized federal-state structure that characterizes much of the current welfare system. As indicated earlier, the practical effect of this structure is that similar families in similar circumstances can receive very different treatment depending solely on their place of residence. Differences are primarily based on the relative desires and capabilities of political subdivisions to assist their needy populations and only partially on cost of living differentials. Many observers have been concerned that this large variance in benefit levels has affected the migration patterns of the poor, although there is little conclusive evidence to that effect.

The variation in average monthly AFDC benefits per recipient has been noted, from $82.71 in New York to $14.40 in Mississippi in April 1973. Under the Medicaid program, estimated average yearly medical payments per family ranged from $1,150 in California to $50 in Mississippi. In the past there has been some variation in the eligibility requirements and income definitions for the food stamp program; however, in 1971 eligibility requirements, income definitions, and the benefit structure were made uniform throughout the country. Under the public housing program the local authorities have the sole authority for defining income for the purposes of eligibility and rental charges, and thus the net benefit structure; housing benefits are, however, systematically related to local housing costs.

The desirability of eliminating interstate differences depends in part on attitudes toward decentralization and federal-state relationships, in part on concerns for equity among recipients, and in part on the degree of interest in ensuring that any additional federal dollars are targeted on the most needy of recipients. (Should the federal government be spending transfer dollars on families with incomes at the $10,000 level in New York while not doing so for those at the $2,000 level in Mississippi?) It seems that a decision must be made among options that range from complete decentralization (as in General Assistance), to partial decentralization (AFDC), to federal standards (food stamps), and to complete federalization (SSI) with state supplementation possible.

THE IMPACT OF CATEGORIZATION

The purpose of categorization is target efficiency, that is, to assure that the benefits of a program are received, to the extent possible, by that group presumed to be in need. The exclusion of certain groups is thus a natural consequence of this approach.* Categorization can be useful to the extent that a target group can be separated from the rest of the population; at the same time incentives for undesirable "self-selection" into the target group should be prevented. The latter is one of the serious problems that can accompany categorization.

SSI can be relatively effective in categorization because the target group is defined by relatively objective criteria (age, blindness, disability) that are directly related to a person's ability to earn. Furthermore, it is unlikely that many persons would or could change their characteristics to become eligible for SSI.

---

*Palmer and Barth presented data indicating that while 97% of the aged poor receive some form of transfers, 20% of the poor receive no transfers and 51% of families with children headed by an able man receive no transfers.

On the other hand, the AFDC categorization process is less effective. As explained earlier, AFDC benefits are provided only to a certain category of poor persons: families in which there is a dependent child who has been deprived of parental support. Single persons and childless couples are not eligible. Intact families with heads who work more than 100 hours a month at low wages—the working poor— are also not eligible for benefits. In 27 states, welfare benefits are not provided to intact families with unemployed heads. In the 23 states with the AFDC-UF program, benefits are not provided to an unemployed father if he is eligible for unemployment compensation. These eligibility criteria are not directly related to ability to earn, and because they are more easily manipulated, incentives are created for people to alter their behavior in order to qualify for benefits. The head of an intact family, for example, can increase his family's income by leaving home, thus making the family eligible for benefits. There is very little evidence, however, on the extent to which the categorical nature of AFDC actually leads to family breakup or fewer family formations. It is also not clear what effect more vigorous attempts to obtain child support from absent fathers would have on preventing family breakups. California has recently instituted several measures aimed at this problem. The cost-effectiveness of this approach should be evaluated.

Categorization can also result in gaps and overlaps in coverage. In the current system there is no cash assistance available to the working poor family with a head who works full time though the income of this family may be less than the income of an AFDC family with a nonworking head. . . .

Another problem sometimes results from differences between eligibility for admission to a program and eligibility for continued participation. For example, assuming the presence of a dependent child and assets below the allowable limit, eligibility for AFDC is determined by comparing current income to the needs standard. If a female family head is employed and earning more than the needs standard, her family is ineligible for benefits. She may, however, be working alongside a woman with the same earned income and family size who receives AFDC benefits because she was on AFDC before starting work. The income disregards any work-related expense deductions that enable her to earn income well beyond the needs standards. Such results may provide the person without eligibility with strong incentives to leave work (at least temporarily) in order to achieve eligibility.

DISINCENTIVES

Work disincentives have been a major concern of the welfare reform effort. Few would argue with the notion that the welfare system should be designed to encourage those who can work to do so. While there is an argument as to the proper mix of market incentives and work requirements, it seems reasonable to expect that a welfare recipient who works should increase his disposable income as a result of his efforts. In fact, the system has certain features that actively discourage work. These take two forms: "notches," and high cumulative benefit reduction rates. A notch . . . occurs when a small change in income results in a precipitous change in benefits. . . .

Notches do, however, have a rationale. First, they can limit costs by limiting coverage. Second, within these cost constraints they can enable full benefits to be provided to everyone on welfare; as in the case of Medicaid, there is no benefit decline as income rises. Third, they can avoid the extension of benefits to certain persons above the poverty level. Against these arguments must be weighed the negative impact of the notches on work incentives, promoting a response to the system that is directly counter to its objectives. The equity of providing extensive benefits to some persons and none to others who are at substantially the same income level, should also be considered.

Linking benefits more closely to income, an approach not in use in some programs, provides a partial solution to this problem. Program benefits, rather than being "on-off," decline gradually as income rises. This type of benefit structure is a part of most of the major programs—AFDC, food stamps, public housing—and is a major feature of the Administration's new health insurance proposal. However, this solution only partially alleviates the work disincentive problem, since a family that participates in several programs also faces several benefit reductions as a result of an increase in earnings. A reduction in AFDC benefits, increases in food stamp purchase price and the public housing rent, along with other net benefit reductions can take a very large bite out of increased

earnings, and can, in fact, have the net effect of reducing disposable income. Consider an intact family of four in New York City that participates in the cash assistance program (AFDC-UF and New York City Home Relief, in this example), food stamps, school lunch, Medicaid, and public housing. The family head works part time and earns $3,000. If he earns an extra $1,000, family disposable income will be reduced by $231. If he reduces his earnings by $1,000, the net loss of disposable income will be only $60. Over the range of earnings from zero to $5,000, a $1,000 increase in earnings will increase disposable income by at most $91. The cumulative benefit reduction rate in this example is an extremely high one. However, such a high rate does not apply to the overwhelming majority of families currently receiving transfer payments. But it does apply to some. Moreover, if programs continue to expand and proliferate as they have in the past, the example will apply to many more families.

BENEFITS IN CASH OR IN-KIND?

Inefficiencies due to the form of the transfer benefits (relative to the need presumably being met) are undoubtedly prevalent in the welfare system. However, measuring precisely the degree of inefficiency is difficult. Would it be more cost-effective to provide vouchers to welfare recipients who request them for child care and let the market operate, or to provide the care directly through the public sector? The existence of a multiplicity of programs each providing a different type of transfer to overlapping target populations is probably not the result of a process in which the needs of these populations as a whole were considered and in which the most efficient set of transfer forms and related programs was structured to meet these needs. The existence of different programs with different transfer forms may be explained in part by several factors: by the historical timing of both the manifestation of a particular concern of society and the existence of sufficient resources to meet the concern; by the desire to restrict recipients' use of public transfer dollars to particular purposes; by the lobbying strengths of various interest groups; and by the vagaries of the agency structure of the executive branch and the committee structure of Congress. In any event, whatever the reasons and rationales for their existence, the present multiplicity of transfer forms must be considered undesirable when viewed from the various perspectives involved.

ADMINISTRATIVE EFFICIENCY

Another characteristic of the present welfare system is administrative overlap and inefficiencies among programs comprising the system. These problems can be viewed partly as a consequence of the categorical strategy and the multiplicity of transfer benefits provided, but they result as well from the independence, subjectivity, and lack of coordination among the various programs. . . .

Our current system of multiple, loosely coordinated programs compounds administrative effort. The AFDC program uses one set of eligibility criteria and income definitions, the food stamp program uses a second set, and public housing a third. This inefficiency may be acceptable if for some reason it is necessary. However, eligibility criteria and income definitions do not always differ among programs for rational reasons. Differences emerge primarily because the programs were created and structured independently without much regard for the administrative efficiency that could be realized through common eligibility criteria and common program definitions, where feasible and desirable. Further, common information gathering could be established even where differential application is necessary.

When combined with the complex and subjective criteria for eligibility and benefit determination that exist in individual programs, uncoordinated and duplicative administration increases the likelihood of undetected error and fraud—although fraud, as legally defined, does not appear to be substantial. Errors in eligibility determination and benefit calculations are more serious, and work to increase and reduce benefits. The Department of Health, Education, and Welfare has launched a major effort to reduce errors in AFDC by streamlining procedures and instituting the Quality Control Sampling System. While this will reduce the errors resulting from the internal complexities of AFDC, it will have less impact on errors that result from uncoordinated and duplicative administration of overlapping programs. Those problems are best addressed by better program integration.

TARGET INEFFICIENCIES

As previous discussion and data have indicated, the monies expended through the welfare system, while providing very substantial income supplementation to the poor, are not very target efficient. The effects of geographical variations, categorization, and multiple program participation were elaborated on above. In addition, some of the programs, particularly food stamps and AFDC, contain very liberal disregards for certain types of income that can result in a family of four retaining eligibility at income levels in excess of $10,000 per year.

Finally, target inefficiencies have been introduced into the transfer system as a whole (social insurance and welfare) as a result of the utilization of the social insurance system as a vehicle to accomplish welfare objectives. This has occurred largely because of the inadequacies of our welfare system. The existence of higher minimum benefit levels and the loosening of eligibility criteria in both the UI and OASDI systems beyond those easily justifiable as social insurance objectives were partially a result of the lack of adequate coverage by the welfare system of the aged and intact family heads and a result of the desire to remove as large a proportion of the aged as possible from the need to undergo a means test. However, because the social insurance programs are not income-tested to any great extent, they are inefficient vehicles for achieving welfare objectives. Most increases in such programs, even if used to increase minimum benefit levels or extend eligibility to groups with less previous attachment to the labor force, will go to families well above the poverty level. Equivalent increased benefits in welfare programs would be highly targeted on needy families or individuals.

Providing smaller benefits to the near poor than to the poor is not necessarily target inefficient if the goal is a more equal distribution of income (as opposed to the alleviation of poverty) or replacement of interrupted earnings. In the case of UI and Social Security, however, the benefits are going to only some of the near poor, and these benefits are often larger than the benefits that go to the poor. In fact, some of the poor continue to receive no transfers at all.

GENERAL

Due to the multiplicity of programs comprising the welfare system, many with overlapping target populations, its overall effects are difficult to understand and, in many cases, are not those intended by the designers of some of its components. Furthermore, many different Congressional committees have oversight of its various components, and few of them need concern themselves explicitly with the overall resource constraints of the total system. Thus, it is virtually impossible to promulgate a coherent strategy for the whole system, one that reflects a considered compromise among the somewhat conflicting objectives and the limited resources available to achieve them.

APPENDIX B

Staff Paper on Welfare Objectives

ADEQUACY

An income-tested transfer system should be designed in tandem with the employment and social insurance systems so that people who can work and people who cannot work have access to a level of income that provides some minimum level of adequacy. (Unfortunately, adequacy is not only hard to agree upon, it is hard to measure.) The design of the system has to reflect a realistic assessment of what our employment and social and private insurance systems are accomplishing—and can be expected to accomplish.

TARGET EFFICIENCY

Benefits should be accurately targeted on those most in need. Within a given budget constraint, greater benefits should be transferred to those with lower incomes. Tradeoffs between possible increases in certain kinds of expenditures on social insurance programs (those directed specifically at low-income groups) or income-tested transfer programs should be carefully considered in this regard.

ADMINISTRATIVE EFFICIENCY

The system should obtain its objectives at a minimum cost. It should be straightforward to administer, combining administrative functions into a single unit, when possible. If multiple programs are required, then a high degree of coordination and integration should exist among programs serving the same populations. These measures would control administrative costs and make the system more manageable and accessible. It is important to note that simplicity for the recipient is as desirable as for the administrators; both should be implemented, if possible.

HORIZONTAL EQUITY

People in similar circumstances should be treated similarly. Categorization is one way of defining similar circumstances; yet as has been seen, administrative discretion and program rules can cause inequities. Wide interstate benefit differentials might also be considered inequitable. In addition, gaps in categorical coverage, which have left some families and individuals ineligible for assistance while others with generally similar characteristics are eligible for benefits, should be remedied. Such horizontal inequities and ineffective categorization can create incentives for undesirable behavior, such as family splitting. The total income of families with the head working full time should be greater than that of families not putting out any work effort but who are receiving income-tested transfer income.

VERTICAL EQUITY

Persons and families who earn more should receive more total income than those earning less. Those with relatively greater needs should receive relatively greater assistance. This principle of vertical equity must be carefully integrated with the following principle.

WORK INCENTIVES

People who are able to work should find it strongly in their interest to do so. The system should encourage self-sufficiency. Thus, those who work and earn more should have substantially higher disposable incomes. Recipients who work should not be penalized for working as has been the case due to notches and high cumulative benefit reduction rates in the present welfare system. On the other hand, the basic benefit level of an income supplementation plan for those already working may be a partial disincentive to work (at least for secondary workers), even if marginal benefit reduction rates are kept low.

FAMILY STABILITY INCENTIVES

Any new system should minimize disincentives to family formation and eliminate possible incentives for family break-up. As noted, one of the serious problems that can accompany a categorical program is that people may be encouraged to "self-select" themselves into the target group.

INDEPENDENCE

Promotion of independence for the recipient, while often considered a most important goal of an income-tested transfer system, is difficult to translate into operational terms. However, the system ought to be structured in such a way that it aids and encourages individuals and families who are able to become self-sufficient, so they will no longer require assistance.

COHERENCY AND CONTROL

The system as a whole should be understandable in its operation and effect, should have the effect intended, and should be subject to policy and fiscal control.

REFERENCES

1. *New York Times,* February 5, 1974.
2. Quoted in *National Journal,* September 8, 1973, p. 1316.
3. *U.S. News and World Report*, July 17, 1972.
4. This description of the Welfare Reform Act is based on articles in the *California Journal*, July-August 1971, June 1972, and December 1972.
5. The *New York Times,* April 5, 1973, p. 91.
6. Quoted in *National Journal*, September 18, 1973.

6

Detroit: A Statistical Profile

A STATISTICAL PROFILE OF METROPOLITAN DETROIT

The *statistical profile* on metropolitan Detroit comprises data on population, age distribution, and population migration patterns broken down by SMSA, Detroit, and suburban areas; education, employment, and income, including income distribution and welfare caseload; price indices; crime; fire and fire alarms; housing; business activity; government revenues and expenditures; and comparative national statistics. A map is included. Unless another source is given, all tables are constructed from census data, including the 1950, 1960, and 1970 censuses of population and the 1958, 1963, 1967, and 1972 censuses of manufacturers and of business. Other sources include *Detroit Financial Populations,* 1977–1982, published by the city of Detroit's Budget Department including Bureau of Labor Statistics data.

By analyzing these data you will be able to identify the major trends affecting the economy of the city.

TABLE OF CONTENTS

Population

6.1 Population
6.2 Age distribution of population
6.3 Migration patterns

Education, Employment, and Income

6.4 Schooling of population over 25
6.5 Labor force participation and employment by type
6.6 Unemployment, 1967–1976
6.7 Employment by industrial group
6.8 Location of jobs in the metropolitan area; place of work by place of residence
6.9 Income distribution and median income; family income by race
6.10 Welfare caseload, 1961–1976

Prices

6.11 Price indices

Crime

6.12 Selected major crime statistics
6.13 Fire alarms

Housing

6.14 Housing conditions
6.15 Construction and demolition of housing units

Business

6.16 Business statistics: retail trade, wholesale trade, selected services, manufacturing
6.17 Manufacturing by Standard Industrial Classification, 1967

Government

6.18 City of Detroit, appropriations
6.19 City of Detroit, projected revenue sources, 1976–77
6.20 City of Detroit, tax revenues and state tax-sharing aid revenues
6.21 City of Detroit, property tax base, tax rate, and revenues

Comparative Statistics

6.22 Comparative national statistics

Regional Map

6.23 Detroit and its principal suburbs

EXHIBIT 6.1: Population

	SMSA*	Detroit	Wayne County	Wayne Suburbs	Oakland County	Macomb County	Total Suburbs	State of Michigan
1950								
Total	3,016,197	1,849,568	2,435,235	585,667	396,001	184,961	1,166,629	6,371,766
White	2,654,270	1,545,847	2,096,269	550,422	377,539	180,462	1,108,423	5,917,825
Non-white	361,927	303,721	338,966	35,245	18,462	4,499	58,206	453,941
% non-white	12.0%	16.4%	13.9%	6.0%	4.6%	2.4%	5.0%	7.1%
1960								
Total	3,762,360	1,670,144	2,666,297	996,153	690,259	405,804	2,092,216	7,823,194
White	3,195,372	1,182,970	2,130,185	947,215	666,181	399,006	2,012,402	7,085,865
Non-white	566,988	487,174	536,112	48,938	24,078	6,798	79,814	737,329
% non-white	15.1%	29.2%	20.1%	4.9%	3.5%	1.7%	3.8%	9.4%
Growth 1950–60								
Total	24.74%	−9.70%	9.49%	70.09%	74.31%	119.40%	79.34%	22.78%
White	19.10%	−23.47%	1.62%	72.09%	76.45%	121.03%	81.56%	19.74%
Non-white	56.66%	60.40%	58.16%	38.85%	30.42%	51.10%	37.12%	62.43%
1970								
Total	4,199,931	1,511,482	2,666,751	1,155,269	907,871	625,309	2,688,449	8,875,068
White	3,419,720	838,877	1,928,500	1,089,623	875,664	615,556	2,580,843	7,843,805
Non-white	780,211	672,605	738,251	65,646	32,207	9,753	107,606	1,031,263
% non-white	18.6%	44.5%	27.7%	5.7%	3.6%	1.6%	4.0%	11.6%
Growth 1960–70								
Total	11.63%	−9.50%	0.01%	15.97%	31.53%	54.09%	28.50%	13.45%
White	7.02%	−29.10%	−9.47%	15.03%	31.45%	54.27%	28.25%	10.70%
Non-white	37.61%	38.06%	37.70%	34.14%	33.76%	43.47%	34.82%	39.86%
1973 Total**	4,196,511	1,409,973	2,600,322	1,190,349	941,709	654,480	2,786,538	9,064,979
1975 Total**	4,154,464	1,335,085	2,517,726	1,182,641	966,625	669,813	2,819,379	9,116,699
Growth 1970–75	−1.08%	−11.67%	−5.59%	2.37%	6.47%	7.12%	4.87%	2.64%

*SMSA stands for Standard Metropolitan Statistical Area. The definition of the Detroit SMSA used consistently in these materials includes Wayne, Oakland and Macomb Counties, despite a change in the definition by the Census Bureau in 1971.

**Racial statistics not available for 1973 and 1975.

EXHIBIT 6.2:   Age Distribution of Population

	SMSA			Detroit			Suburbs		
	Total	White	Black	Total	White	Black	Total	White	Black
1960									
% of population between									
0–5	12.42%	12.11%	14.18%	10.32%	8.76%	14.09%	14.10%	14.08%	15.73%
5–14	20.43%	20.02%	22.70%	18.13%	16.37%	22.40%	22.27%	22.17%	24.97%
15–19	6.56%	6.58%	6.55%	6.65%	6.79%	6.32%	6.49%	6.46%	7.15%
20–44	33.44%	33.19%	34.72%	31.62%	30.18%	35.09%	34.89%	34.96%	33.54%
45–64	19.99%	20.42%	17.49%	23.80%	26.30%	17.74%	16.94%	16.97%	14.84%
65+	7.16%	7.66%	4.32%	9.48%	11.59%	4.37%	5.30%	5.35%	3.77%
Median age	29.4	30.0	26.1	33.2	36.4	26.5	26.4	26.4	24.8
1970									
% of population between									
0–5	9.01%	8.60%	10.91%	8.80%	7.15%	10.91%	9.13%	9.08%	10.86%
5–14	21.26%	20.88%	23.02%	18.32%	14.84%	22.78%	22.92%	22.86%	24.63%
15–19	9.35%	9.13%	10.35%	8.96%	8.01%	10.17%	9.58%	9.50%	11.57%
20–44	31.44%	31.41%	31.60%	29.70%	28.19%	31.66%	32.42%	32.46%	31.17%
45–64	20.83%	21.42%	18.11%	22.77%	26.15%	18.43%	19.73%	19.87%	15.88%
65+	8.10%	8.56%	6.03%	11.46%	15.66%	6.04%	6.22%	6.23%	5.88%

Median age data unavailable for 1970.

EXHIBIT 6.3: Migration patterns

Residence 5 years previously	Current Residence					
	SMSA	Detroit	All suburbs	Wayne suburbs	Oakland County	Macomb County
1960						
Population over 5	3,296,267	1,497,744	1,798,523	858,762	597,533	342,228
Same house	52.84%	55.41%	50.70%	52.44%	50.07%	47.41%
Different house:						
Detroit	23.72%	34.33%	14.89%	15.88%	10.62%	19.88%
suburbs	14.92%	3.27%	24.62%	22.11%	28.73%	23.75%
outside SMSA	5.95%	4.08%	7.51%	7.08%	8.53%	6.82%
Northwest	4.26%	2.40%	5.81%	5.37%	6.79%	5.18%
South	1.69%	1.68%	1.71%	1.71%	1.75%	1.63%
abroad	0.98%	0.96%	0.99%	0.96%	0.85%	1.32%
Moved, old location not reported	1.58%	1.94%	1.28%	1.53%	1.20%	0.82%
1970						
Population over 5	3,821,825	1,378,989	2,442,836	1,054,981	826,958	560,897
Same house	56.18%	54.68%	57.01%	61.15%	52.00%	56.63%
Different house:						
Detroit	15.02%	27.00%	8.27%	7.90%	7.65%	9.90%
Suburbs	15.71%	4.20%	22.21%	19.56%	25.81%	21.88%
outside SMSA	7.38%	6.66%	7.79%	6.99%	9.69%	6.50%
North & West	5.17%	3.64%	6.03%	5.23%	7.77%	4.98%
South	2.21%	3.02%	1.76%	1.76%	1.92%	1.52%
abroad	1.09%	1.17%	1.04%	1.00%	0.97%	1.21%
Moved, old location not reported	4.62%	6.29%	3.68%	3.40%	3.88%	3.88%

EXHIBIT 6.3 (continued)

Residence 5 years previously	White Migration Current Residence			Black Migration Current Residence		
	SMSA	*Detroit*	*Suburbs*	*SMSA*	*Detroit*	*Suburbs*
1960						
Population over 5	2,809,709	1,079,253	1,730,456	486,558	418,491	68,067
Same house	54.98%	61.59%	50.86%	40.52%	39.50%	46.73%
Different house:						
Detroit	20.11%	28.25%	15.04%	44.60%	50.03%	11.23%
Suburbs	16.41%	3.61%	24.40%	6.30%	2.39%	30.30%
outside SMSA	6.13%	3.88%	7.53%	4.94%	4.60%	7.05%
abroad	1.09%	1.23%	1.01%	0.29%	0.25%	0.53%
Moved, old location not reported	1.27%	1.44%	1.17%	3.35%	3.22%	4.16%
1970						
Population over 5	3,147,220	790,310	2,356,910	674,605	588,679	85,926
Same house	58.37%	61.84%	57.21%	45.94%	45.09%	51.74%
Different house:						
Detroit	11.43%	21.10%	8.18%	31.83%	34.91%	10.72%
Suburbs	18.02%	5.36%	22.27%	4.93%	2.63%	20.69%
outside SMSA	7.19%	5.43%	7.78%	8.28%	8.30%	8.14%
North & West	5.55%	3.84%	6.14%	3.38%	3.37%	3.41%
South	1.63%	1.60%	1.64%	4.90%	4.93%	4.73%
abroad	1.24%	1.78%	1.06%	0.38%	0.35%	0.58%
Moved, old location not reported	3.75%	4.49%	3.50%	8.64%	8.72%	8.13%

EXHIBIT 6.4:   Schooling of Population over 25

	SMSA	Detroit	Wayne County	Wayne Suburbs	Oakland County	Macomb County	All Suburbs
1960							
8th grade or less	35.85%	42.53%	38.52%	30.98%	26.31%	32.76%	29.77%
1–3 years high school	23.24%	23.06%	23.24%	23.57%	22.06%	25.40%	23.41%
4 years high school	25.89%	22.10%	24.49%	29.00%	29.61%	29.72%	29.33%
1–3 years college	8.11%	6.98%	7.61%	8.80%	10.84%	6.98%	9.13%
4+ years college	6.91%	5.33%	6.13%	7.65%	11.17%	5.13%	8.35%
1970							
8th grade or less	24.93%	32.88%	28.43%	22.19%	16.93%	20.83%	20.09%
1–3 years high school	22.93%	25.32%	24.08%	22.34%	19.19%	23.31%	21.48%
4 years high school	33.12%	28.10%	31.27%	35.70%	34.62%	39.51%	36.19%
1–3 years college	9.48%	7.48%	8.48%	9.88%	12.82%	9.05%	10.70%
4+ years college	9.53%	6.21%	7.74%	9.89%	16.44%	7.28%	11.55%
% high school graduates	52.1%	41.8%	47.5%	55.5%	63.9%	55.9%	58.4%

	White			Black		
	SMSA	Detroit	Suburbs	SMSA	Detroit	Suburbs
1960						
8th grade or less	33.85%	40.72%	29.04%	48.11%	47.82%	49.98%
1–3 years high school	22.88%	22.17%	23.38%	25.49%	25.67%	24.29%
4 years high school	27.21%	23.59%	29.76%	17.72%	17.75%	17.47%
1–3 years college	8.48%	7.35%	9.26%	5.86%	5.88%	5.67%
4+ years college	7.57%	6.17%	8.55%	2.83%	2.87%	2.58%
1970						
8th grade or less	23.24%	32.54%	19.60%	33.66%	33.45%	35.20%
1–3 years high school	21.66%	22.74%	21.24%	29.51%	29.61%	28.81%
4 years high school	34.44%	29.19%	36.53%	26.36%	26.30%	26.76%
1–3 years college	10.00%	7.86%	10.85%	6.77%	6.85%	6.16%
4+ years college	10.65%	7.67%	11.82%	3.70%	3.79%	3.07%
% high school graduates	55.1%	44.8%	59.1%	36.8%	36.9%	36.1%

EXHIBIT 6.5: Labor Force Participation and Employment by Type

	SMSA		Detroit		Suburbs	
	Male	*Female*	*Male*	*Female*	*Male*	*Female*
1960						
Population over 14	1,254,305	1,325,819	585,049	633,334	669,256	693,485
% in labor force	80.4%	32.9%	77.5%	35.8%	83.0%	30.2%
% of labor force unemployed	7.6%	8.0%	10.2%	9.2%	6.3%	5.8%
Number of employed	927,024	401,711	406,247	206,048	520,777	195,663
% of employed						
Professional & technical	11.92%	12.54%	9.39%	11.31%	13.89%	13.84%
Managers, proprietors	9.30%	3.09%	7.51%	2.94%	10.70%	3.24%
Clerical	7.67%	34.40%	8.26%	33.12%	7.21%	35.75%
Sales	7.42%	9.58%	6.93%	8.78%	7.81%	10.42%
Crafts & foremen	22.15%	1.18%	19.16%	1.22%	24.49%	1.14%
Operatives	25.59%	11.68%	28.33%	11.93%	23.45%	11.41%
Laborers	5.49%	0.61%	6.45%	0.64%	4.75%	0.58%
Service workers	5.94%	14.91%	7.69%	15.56%	4.57%	14.23%
Private household	0.11%	6.49%	0.14%	7.32%	0.08%	5.62%
Not reported	4.40%	5.51%	6.13%	7.17%	3.05%	3.70%
1970						
Population over 16	1,353,699	1,482,922	501,649	570,068	852,050	912,854
% in labor force	79.5%	40.0%	73.3%	41.7%	83.1%	39.0%
% unemployed	5.3%	6.4%	6.9%	7.7%	4.9%	5.5%
Number of employed	1,015,407	555,546	341,944	219,240	673,463	336,306
% of employed						
Professional & technical	14.90%	14.69%	10.21%	13.23%	17.27%	15.63%
Managers, proprietors	9.30%	3.07%	5.80%	2.83%	11.08%	3.22%
Clerical	7.60%	38.91%	8.38%	37.33%	7.20%	39.93%
Sales	6.33%	8.59%	4.55%	6.82%	7.24%	9.75%
Crafts, foremen	22.65%	1.74%	19.15%	1.86%	24.42%	1.66%
Operatives	25.53%	11.25%	33.69%	12.25%	21.39%	10.59%
Laborers	5.93%	0.97%	7.62%	1.17%	5.07%	0.84%
Service workers	7.71%	18.16%	10.52%	20.37%	6.28%	16.72%
Private household	0.05%	2.62%	0.08%	4.12%	0.03%	1.65%

EXHIBIT 6.5 (continued)

| | White Employment by Type | | | | | |
| | SMSA | | Detroit | | Suburbs | |
	Male	Female	Male	Female	Male	Female
1960						
Population over 14	1,080,354	1,134,770	435,270	466,717	645,084	668,053
% in labor force	81.1%	32.4%	77.8%	35.8%	83.5%	30.1%
Unemployment rate	6.6%	6.6%	7.7%	6.8%	5.9%	6.5%
Number employed	819,284	343,622	312,477	155,643	506,807	187,979
% of employed						
Professional and technical	13.04%	13.35%	11.20%	12.38%	14.16%	14.16%
Managerial	10.25%	3.40%	9.14%	3.49%	10.94%	3.33%
Clerical	7.94%	37.79%	8.96%	38.99%	7.31%	36.80%
Sales	8.12%	10.72%	8.34%	10.68%	7.98%	10.75%
Craftsmen and foremen	23.47%	1.24%	21.30%	1.35%	24.80%	1.16%
Operatives	23.90%	11.58%	25.34%	11.69%	23.01%	11.48%
Service	5.25%	13.28%	6.69%	12.74%	4.36%	13.71%
Private household	0.06%	3.57%	0.06%	2.53%	0.07%	4.44%
Laborers	4.39%	0.50%	4.30%	0.44%	4.45%	0.55%
Not reported	3.59%	4.58%	4.67%	5.74%	2.92%	3.62%
1970						
Population over 16	1,128,375	1,225,867	304,587	344,717	823,788	881,150
% in labor force	80.6%	38.8%	72.5%	39.1%	83.6%	38.8%
Unemployment rate	4.8%	5.3%	5.1%	5.2%	4.7%	5.4%
Number employed	865,797	450,817	209,583	127,692	656,214	323,125
% of employed						
Professional and technical	16.59%	15.44%	13.42%	14.31%	17.60%	15.88%
Managerial	10.44%	3.35%	7.71%	3.50%	11.31%	3.29%
Clerical	7.72%	40.90%	9.29%	41.89%	7.21%	40.50%
Sales	7.06%	9.67%	6.07%	8.78%	7.38%	10.02%
Operatives	22.03%	10.62%	25.83%	11.30%	20.81%	10.36%
Other blue collar*	29.11%	2.57%	27.71%	2.72%	29.50%	2.50%
Service	7.02%	16.14%	9.91%	16.23%	6.10%	16.11%
Private household	0.03%	1.31%	0.05%	1.27%	0.03%	1.33%

*Craftsmen, Foremen, and Laborer categories combined.

EXHIBIT 6.5 (continued)

| | Black Employment by Type | | | | | |
| | SMSA | | Detroit | | Suburbs | |
	Male	Female	Male	Female	Male	Female
1960						
Population over 14	173,351	192,049	149,779	166,617	24,172	25,432
Labor force participation	75.9%	35.9%	76.7%	36.0%	71.1%	35.0%
Unemployment rate	18.4%	15.6%	18.3%	15.9%	18.8%	13.7%
Number employed	107,740	58,089	93,770	50,405	13,970	7,684
% of employed						
Professional and technical	3.44%	7.78%	3.37%	8.03%	3.85%	6.08%
Managerial	2.08%	1.25%	2.06%	1.25%	2.24%	1.25%
Clerical	5.63%	14.38%	5.95%	15.03%	3.52%	10.10%
Sales	2.14%	2.86%	2.22%	2.93%	1.59%	2.38%
Craftsmen and foremen	12.15%	0.81%	12.01%	0.81%	13.09%	0.82%
Operatives	38.44%	12.28%	38.30%	12.67%	39.41%	9.71%
Service	11.17%	24.59%	11.03%	24.27%	12.10%	26.78%
Private household	0.46%	23.77%	0.40%	22.13%	0.89%	34.51%
Laborers	13.91%	1.25%	13.63%	1.26%	15.79%	1.22%
Not reported	10.57%	11.02%	11.02%	11.61%	7.52%	7.14%
1970						
Population over 16	225,342	257,855	197,062	225,351	28,262	31,704
Labor force participation	74.0%	45.7%	74.6%	45.7%	69.9%	45.8%
Unemployment rate	10.3%	10.8%	10.0%	11.1%	12.7%	9.2%
Number employed	149,610	104,729	132,361	91,548	17,249	13,181
% of employed						
Professional and technical	5.12%	11.46%	5.13%	11.72%	5.03%	9.60%
Managerial	2.75%	1.85%	2.78%	1.90%	2.52%	1.49%
Clerical	6.87%	30.34%	6.93%	30.98%	6.40%	25.89%
Sales	2.12%	3.96%	2.15%	4.09%	1.90%	3.03%
Operatives	45.82%	13.93%	46.14%	13.58%	43.35%	16.36%
Other blue collar*	25.51%	3.34%	25.28%	3.47%	27.29%	2.50%
Service	11.69%	26.84%	11.48%	26.14%	13.29%	31.67%
Private household	0.13%	8.28%	0.12%	8.11%	0.22%	9.45%

*Craftsmen, Foremen, and Laborer categories combined.

EXHIBIT 6.6:   Unemployment 1967–1976

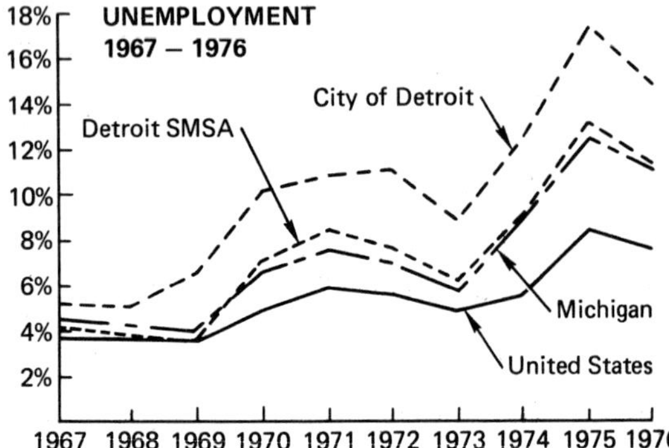

Source: City of Detroit, Budget Department, Detroit Financial Projections, 1977–1982, *December 27, 1976, p. 30.*

**EXHIBIT 6.7:   Employment of SMSA, Detroit,
and Suburban Residents, by Industrial Group**

	SMSA		Detroit		Suburbs	
	1960	*1970*	*1960*	*1970*	*1960*	*1970*
Total number employed	1,328,735	1,570,953	612,295	561,184	716,440	1,009,769
Construction	53,588	67,810	20,237	19,546	33,351	48,264
Manufacturing:	541,418	587,981	228,806	201,445	312,612	386,536
Transportation equipment	252,487 }	505,596	109,686 }	170,730	142,801 }	334,866
Other durables	190,973 }		73,388 }		117,585 }	
Non-durables	97,958	82,385	45,732	30,715	52,226	51,670
Communications, utilities, sanitation	32,300	42,599	14,540	16,354	17,760	26,245
Wholesale trade	42,917	65,698	20,230	22,187	22,687	43,511
Retail trade	195,638	246,027	92,122	82,908	103,516	163,119
Health	35,536	89,642	17,387	37,695	18,149	51,947
Education	60,701	104,921	24,696	32,210	36,005	72,711
Other professional services	50,003	58,920	23,884	22,633	26,119	36,287
Public administration	49,782	63,729	27,916	30,563	21,866	33,166
Other	266,852	161,241	142,477	95,643	124,375	65,598

EXHIBIT 6.8:   Location of Jobs in the Metropolitan Area

Place of Employment	Total Number of Jobs Held by Residents of SMSA by Place of Employment		
	1960	*1970*	*Growth 1960–1970*
Total employed	1,300,984	1,525,548	17.26%
Detroit	692,704	537,373*	−22.42%
Wayne suburbs	269,626	367,266	36.21%
Oakland County	158,020	299,231	89.36%
Macomb County	102,374	188,804	84.42%
Outside SMSA	23,370	35,694	52.73%
Not reported	54,890	97,180	77.04%

*80,274 employed in Central Business District; 457,099 in the rest of the city.

Place of Employment	Place of Residence					
	SMSA	*Detroit*	*All Suburbs*	*Wayne Suburbs*	*Oakland County*	*Macomb County*
1960						
Detroit	53.24%	77.24%	32.87%	37.17%	24.84%	36.22%
Wayne suburbs	20.72%	11.03%	28.96%	53.45%	7.08%	6.22%
Oakland County	12.15%	2.98%	20.59%	1.81%	56.77%	4.06%
Macomb County	7.87%	2.20%	12.02%	1.41%	5.78%	49.44%
Outside SMSA	1.80%	0.96%	2.51%	3.37%	2.06%	1.11%
Not reported	4.22%	5.60%	3.05%	2.79%	3.48%	2.94%
1970						
Detroit	35.22%	59.63%	21.94%	25.21%	16.31%	24.12%
CBD*	5.26%	8.55%	3.47%	4.28%	2.55%	3.32%
Rest	29.96%	51.08%	18.47%	20.94%	13.76%	20.81%
Wayne suburbs	24.07%	16.23%	28.35%	56.19%	7.59%	6.77%
Oakland County	19.61%	7.84%	26.03%	6.54%	61.24%	10.39%
Macomb County	12.38%	5.90%	15.90%	2.95%	7.17%	53.27%
Outside SMSA	2.34%	1.35%	2.88%	4.22%	2.37%	1.11%
Not reported	6.37%	9.06%	4.91%	4.88%	5.31%	4.35%

*Central Business District

EXHIBIT 6.9:　Income Distribution and Median Income

Family Income							
	SMSA	Detroit	Wayne County	Wayne Suburbs	Oakland County	Macomb County	All Suburbs
1959							
less than $2,000	8.22%	11.90%	9.36%	4.98%	5.47%	5.35%	5.21%
$2,000–3,000	5.30%	7.13%	5.90%	3.77%	3.71%	4.06%	3.80%
$3,000–5,000	14.26%	17.36%	15.20%	11.47%	11.50%	12.73%	11.72%
$5,000–7,000	24.30%	23.69%	24.23%	25.15%	23.13%	26.75%	24.79%
$7,000–10,000	26.00%	22.07%	24.92%	29.81%	27.35%	30.88%	29.20%
$10,000–15,000	15.77%	13.05%	14.87%	18.01%	18.86%	16.41%	17.98%
$15,000+	6.16%	4.78%	5.52%	6.81%	9.97%	3.83%	7.29%
Median income	$6,825	$6,069	$6,597	$7,466	$7,576	$7,091	$7,460
1969							
less than $3,000	6.40%	10.73%	7.86%	4.15%	3.92%	3.77%	3.99%
$3,000–5,000	6.02%	9.23%	7.14%	4.45%	4.19%	3.94%	4.24%
$5,000–7,000	6.83%	9.83%	7.86%	5.32%	5.24%	4.77%	5.17%
$7,000–9,000	10.35%	13.13%	11.35%	9.07%	8.49%	8.82%	8.81%
$9,000–12,000	19.71%	19.67%	20.19%	20.87%	17.75%	20.55%	19.73%
$12,000–15,000	17.67%	14.77%	16.86%	19.54%	17.10%	22.01%	19.27%
$15,000–25,000	25.97%	18.90%	23.46%	29.34%	30.13%	30.90%	29.97%
$25,000+	7.00%	3.74%	5.27%	7.24%	13.18%	5.24%	8.81%
Median income	$12,117	$10,045	$11,493	$12,799	$13,826	$13,110	$13,253
Growth in median income 1959–1969	77.50%	65.51%	59.06%	71.43%	82.50%	84.88%	77.65%

Family Income by Race					
	SMSA		Detroit		Suburbs	
	White	Black	White	Black	White	Black
1959						
less than $2,000	5.55%	23.29%	7.80%	23.65%	4.72%	20.78%
$2,000–2,999	4.36%	10.61%	5.93%	10.58%	3.52%	10.83%
$3,000–4,999	12.27%	25.10%	14.71%	24.96%	11.05%	26.06%
$5,000–6,999	24.64%	22.39%	24.20%	22.24%	24.84%	23.48%
$7,000–9,999	28.40%	12.48%	25.44%	12.45%	29.86%	12.64%
$10,000 and over	24.74%	6.12%	21.93%	6.11%	26.03%	6.21%
Median income	$7,259	$4,385	$6,770	$4,366	$7,577	$4,492
1969						
less than $3,000	4.26%	15.77%	6.62%	15.86%	3.53%	15.12%
$3,000–4,999	5.02%	10.42%	8.26%	10.44%	3.99%	10.22%
$5,000–6,999	5.78%	11.44%	8.50%	11.49%	4.92%	11.07%
$7,000–8,999	9.25%	15.17%	11.65%	14.98%	8.49%	16.59%
$9,000–9,999	6.16%	6.89%	6.64%	6.95%	6.01%	6.48%
$10,000 and over	69.48%	40.31%	58.33%	40.28%	73.05%	40.52%
Median income	$12,910	$8,643	$11,168	$8,645	$13,445	$8,638
Growth in median income 1959–1969	77.8%	97.1%	65.0%	98.0%	77.4%	92.3%

**EXHIBIT 6.10: Welfare Caseload
City of Detroit
1961–1976**

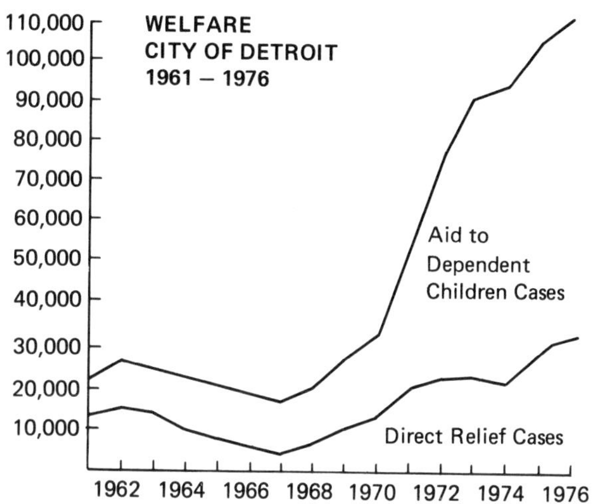

Source: City of Detroit, Budget Department, Detroit Financial Projections, 1977–1982, *p. 35.*

EXHIBIT 6.11: Price Indices

Year	Consumer Price Index for Detroit (1967 = 100)	National Non-food Wholesale Price Index (1967 = 100)
1956	83.8	90.8
1957	86.2	93.3
1958	87.5	93.6
1959	87.4	95.3
1960	88.2	95.3
1961	88.7	94.8
1962	88.9	94.8
1963	89.8	94.7
1964	90.5	95.2
1965	92.6	96.4
1966	96.7	98.5
1967	100.0	100.0
1968	104.3	102.5
1969	110.6	106.0
1970	117.4	110.0
1971	121.7	114.0
1972	126.2	117.9
1973	134.5	125.9
1974	149.0	153.8
1975	160.1	171.5

Source: Bureau of Labor Statistics.

EXHIBIT 6.12: Selected Major Crime Statistics

	Murder	Rape	Robbery
1967	281	733	11,973
1968	389	954	13,774
1969	439	913	17,419
1970	495	816	23,038
1971	577	853	20,752
1972	601	818	17,170
1973	672	1,148	16,249
1974	714	1,260	29,190
1975	637	1,425	21,343

Source: City of Detroit, Budget Department, Financial Projections 1977–1982, *Detroit (December, 1976), p. 33.*

EXHIBIT 6.13: Fire Alarms

	Total Fire Alarms	Fires	False Alarms
1960	24,292	20,446	3,846
1965	34,270	28,660	5,610
1970	62,792	40,493	22,299
1975	58,016	34,015	24,001

Source: City of Detroit, Budget Department, Detroit Financial Projections 1977–1982, *p. 34.*

EXHIBIT 6.14: Housing Conditions

	SMSA	Detroit	Wayne County	All Suburbs	Wayne Suburbs	Oakland County	Macomb County
1960							
Number of units (thousands)	1,153	553	835	600	282	204	113
% vacant	6.30%	6.94%	6.06%	5.71%	4.33%	7.67%	5.63%
Median number of rooms per housing unit	5.2	5.1	5.1	5.2	5.2	5.3	5.1
% of overcrowded units*	9.90%	8.76%	9.54%	10.92%	11.03%	9.83%	12.70%
white	8.66%	6.17%	NA**	10.46%	NA	NA	NA
black	17.72%	16.74%	NA	24.78%	NA	NA	NA
Median monthly rent (renter-occupied)	$66	$65	$64	$74	$65	$90	$74
Median house value (owner-occupied)	$13,300	$12,000	$13,000	$14,100	$14,100	$13,900	$14,200
% of owner-occupants:							
All families	71.0%	58.2%	66.0%	82.8%	81.0%	83.3%	86.2%
white	75.8%	64.7%	71.6%	83.5%	81.9%	84.3%	86.6%
black	41.0%	38.9%	40.5%	56.3%	58.9%	51.1%	56.7%
1970							
Number of units (thousands)	1,334	525	879	809	354	277	178
% vacant	5.04%	5.08%	5.51%	5.01%	6.14%	4.55%	3.47%
Median number of rooms per housing unit	5.2	5.1	5.2	5.3	5.3	5.4	5.3
% overcrowded units*	7.80%	7.54%	7.94%	7.96%	8.53%	6.36%	9.29%
white	7.28%	6.39%	NA**	7.75%	NA	NA	NA
black	11.75%	10.79%	NA	16.74%	NA	NA	NA
Median monthly rent (renter-occupied)	$92	$80	$84	$116	$96	$150	$143
Median house value (owner-occupied)	$19,600	$15,600	$18,100	$21,500	$21,100	$23,000	$22,600
% owner-occupants:							
All families	72.1%	60.0%	67.9%	79.9%	79.6%	78.3%	83.1%
white	76.1%	66.0%	73.5%	80.5%	80.6%	78.7%	83.5%
black	52.3%	51.1%	51.8%	62.0%	61.0%	65.9%	55.6%

*More than one person per room.

**NA—data not available.

**EXHIBIT 6.15:   Authorized Dwelling
Unit Construction-Demolition
1960–1975**

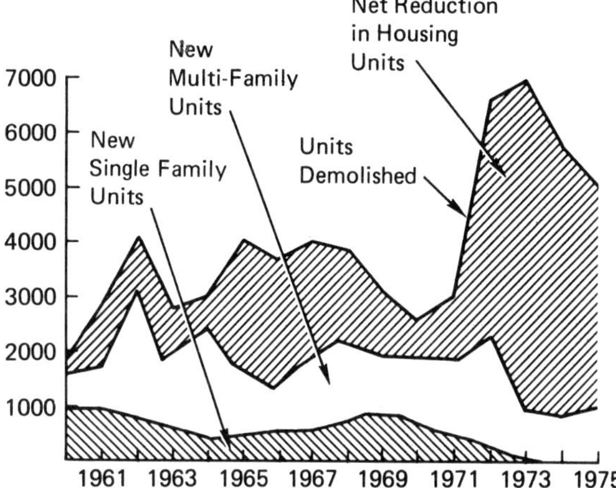

Source: City of Detroit, Budget Department, Detroit Financial Projections, 1977–1982, *December 27, 1976, p. 37.*

EXHIBIT 6.16: Business Statistics

Retail Trade

	SMSA			Detroit			Detroit as % of SMSA		
	Sales ($mil.)	Payroll ($mil.)	No. of Emps.	Sales ($mil.)	Payroll ($mil.)	No. of Emps.	Sales	Payroll	No. of Emps.
1958									
Food	1,139.9	72.3	27,621	537.2	34.9	13,465	47.1%	48.2%	48.7%
Automotive	785.0	70.5	14,328	376.6	34.2	7,079	48.0%	48.5%	49.4%
Service stations	322.3	27.3	10,000	153.0	13.2	4,856	47.5%	48.3%	48.6%
Department stores	450.4	80.2	28,137	319.5	65.1	21,814	70.9%	81.2%	77.5%
Other retail trade	1,750.5	254.5	93,114	888.0	133.0	47,286	50.7%	52.3%	50.8%
Total	4,448.1	504.8	173,200	2,274.3	280.4	94,500	51.1%	55.5%	54.6%
1963									
Food	1,236.9	90.6	26,912	502.8	37.8	11,348	40.9%	41.7%	42.2%
Automotive	1,218.3	97.5	15,028	579.8	45.7	7,088	47.6%	46.9%	47.1%
Service stations	383.0	33.7	11,078	150.3	13.7	4,454	39.2%	40.7%	40.2%
Department stores	719.5	81.3	27,093	269.9	34.4	10,579	37.5%	42.3%	39.0%
Other retail trade	1,835.3	262.1	85,706	800.5	118.3	38,680	43.6%	45.1%	45.1%
Total	5,393.0	565.2	165,817	2,303.3	249.9	72,149	42.7%	44.2%	43.5%
1967									
Food	1,606.0	117.8	30,965	558.6	41.9	11,066	34.8%	35.6%	35.7%
Automotive	1,426.5	127.7	18,420	545.7	48.7	7,178	38.3%	38.1%	39.0%
Service stations	472.3	39.6	12,182	164.6	13.7	4,371	34.9%	34.6%	35.9%
Department stores	1,135.8	142.4	34,336	335.5	47.7	11,328	29.5%	33.5%	33.0%
Other retail trade	2,412.7	368.2	100,892	941.7	150.2	41,386	39.0%	40.8%	41.0%
Total	7,053.3	795.7	196,795	2,546.1	302.2	75,329	36.1%	38.0%	38.3%
1972									
Food	2,153.0	189.6	32,191	607.1	52.5	8,993	28.2%	27.7%	27.9%
Automotive	2,120.4	196.5	18,620	584.1	56.6	5,341	27.5%	28.8%	28.7%
Service stations	636.0	58.1	15,077	179.7	16.0	4,221	28.3%	27.4%	28.0%
Department stores	1,481.6	193.0	34,018	290.0	46.3	7,771	19.6%	24.0%	22.8%
Other retail trade	3,619.2	560.1	120,135	1,063.3	171.6	36,485	29.4%	30.6%	30.4%
Total	10,010.2	1,197.3	220,041	2,724.2	343.0	62,811	27.2%	28.6%	28.5%
Wholesale Trade									
1958	8,251.9	345.3	61,635	6,458.8	258.9	45,722	78.3%	75.0%	74.2%
1963	9,952.0	438.0	65,008	6,827.0	294.1	44,615	68.6%	67.1%	68.6%
1967	13,321.1	623.0	77,373	7,573.2	354.9	44,753	56.9%	57.0%	57.8%
1972	18,407.5	843.7	75,770	6,089.1	362.7	33,691	33.1%	43.0%	44.5%

EXHIBIT 6.16 (continued)

| | Selected Services | | | | | | | | |
| | SMSA | | | Detroit | | | Detroit as % of SMSA | | |
	Sales ($mil.)	Payroll ($mil.)	No. of Emps.	Sales ($mil.)	Payroll ($mil.)	No. of Emps.	Sales	Payroll	No. of Emps.
1958									
Hotels & tourist	46.3	15.6	6,329	35.5	13.2	5,346	76.67%	84.62%	84.47%
Auto repair	79.2	21.0	6,775	53.7	14.5	4,484	67.80%	69.05%	66.18%
Business services	492.0	82.4	16,850	425.8	69.4	14,041	86.54%	84.22%	83.33%
Other	344.4	110.9	38,342	220.6	76.0	27,218	64.05%	68.53%	70.99%
Total	961.9	229.9	68,296	735.6	173.1	51,089	76.47%	75.29%	74.81%
1963									
Hotels & tourist	50.6	15.4	6,100	33.5	11.7	4,697	66.21%	75.97%	77.00%
Auto repair	134.6	30.4	7,961	71.7	16.8	4,445	53.27%	55.26%	55.83%
Business services	628.0	110.9	22,803	514.4	83.5	17,211	81.91%	75.29%	75.48%
Other	412.8	129.4	34,197	228.7	78.2	20,485	55.40%	60.43%	59.90%
Total	1,226.0	286.1	71,061	848.3	190.2	46,838	69.19%	66.48%	65.91%
1967									
Hotels & tourist	88.3	27.1	8,298	49.0	16.8	5,270	55.49%	61.99%	63.51%
Auto repair	167.0	38.5	7,777	92.4	20.5	4,103	55.33%	53.25%	52.76%
Business services	825.7	187.6	32,861	606.0	123.4	23,130	73.39%	65.78%	70.39%
Other	555.9	186.2	38,349	285.1	104.6	20,329	51.29%	56.18%	53.01%
Total	1,636.9	439.4	87,285	1,032.5	265.3	52,832	63.08%	60.38%	60.53%
1972									
Hotels & tourist	104.5	32.2	7,315	39.5	13.9	3,124	37.80%	43.17%	42.71%
Auto repair	281.9	64.1	9,772	116.1	26.4	4,113	41.19%	41.19%	42.09%
Business services	1,145.7	282.6	40,135	671.9	147.1	22,789	58.65%	52.05%	56.78%
Other	759.0	236.0	38,463	295.5	100.2	15,281	38.93%	42.45%	39.73%
Total	2,291.1	614.9	95,685	1,123.0	287.6	45,307	49.02%	46.77%	47.35%

EXHIBIT 6.16 (continued)

| | Manufacturing | | | | | | | | |
| | SMSA | | | Detroit | | | Detroit as % of SMSA | | |
	Value Added	Payroll	No. of Emps.	Value Added	Payroll	No. of Emps.	Value Added	Payroll	No. of Emps.
1958									
Transportation equipment*	1,586	844	141.5	(NOT AVAILABLE)			(NOT AVAILABLE)		
Other	2,726	1,636	263.5	(NOT AVAILABLE)			(NOT AVAILABLE)		
Total	4,312	2,480	405.0	2,087	1,226	204.4	48.40%	49.44%	50.47%
1963									
Transportation equipment	2,862	1,208	152.9	(NOT AVAILABLE)			(NOT AVAILABLE)		
Other	3,838	2,279	341.0	(NOT AVAILABLE)			(NOT AVAILABLE)		
Total	6,700	3,487	493.9	2,814	1,497	200.6	42.06%	42.93%	40.62%
1967									
Transportation equipment	3,075	1,441	166.5	1,112	471	52.4	36.16%	32.69%	31.47%
Other	5,423	3,778	418.0	2,297	1,382	157.3	42.36%	36.58%	37.63%
Total	8,498	5,219	584.5	3,409	1,853	209.7	40.11%	35.50%	35.88%
1972									
Total	11,792	7,175	555.6	4,049	2,224	180.4	34.34%	31.00%	32.47%

(Transportation equipment not available for SMSA in this year because of possible disclosure of individual corporation's business positions. Value added and payrolls in millions of dollars; number of employees in thousands.)

*Includes only industry code 37. Excludes data from other industry codes on certain components of transportation equipment, machinery necessary to produce transportation equipment, etc. It thus understates the role of the auto industry in the Detroit area.

**EXHIBIT 6.17: Manufacturing in Detroit SMSA,
by Standard Industrial Classification, 1967***

Industry Code & Description	Value of Shipments	Value Added in Manufacturing	Payroll	Number of Employees
20 Food and kindred products	955	327	154	20.8
21 Tobacco products		(NOT AVAILABLE)		
22 Textile mill products		(NOT AVAILABLE)		
23 Apparel, other textile products	209	147	84	11.9
24 Lumber and wood products	62	29	13	2.1
25 Furniture and fixtures	47	26	15	2.4
26 Paper and allied products	172	68	36	5.1
27 Printing and publishing	388	249	141	17.9
28 Chemicals and allied products	651	321	129	15.5
29 Petroleum and coal products	212	69	13	1.3
30 Rubber and plastics products	268	132	78	11.0
31 Leather and leather products		(NOT AVAILABLE)		
32 Stone, clay, and glass products	372	193	84	10.7
33 Primary metal industries	2,161	833	431	48.6
34 Fabricated metal products	2,142	1,130	619	76.6
35 Machinery, except electrical	2,682	1,625	905	93.8
36 Electrical equipment	255	136	75	9.6
37 Transportation equipment	9,452	3,075	1,441	166.5
38 Instruments and related products	54	30	17	2.2
39 Miscellaneous	84	50	26	3.7
Administrative & auxiliary	—	—	922	80.7
Other (21, 22, 31)	290	58	36	4.1
Total	20,456	8,498	5,219	584.5

Value of shipments, value added, and payroll in millions of dollars; number of employees in thousands.

*1967 used as base year because later data does not separate automotive industry because of disclosure of operations of industrial companies.

EXHIBIT 6.18:   City of Detroit, Appropriations

Fiscal Year	Total Approps.	Non-capital Approps.*	Net Approps.**
1962–63	295.77	265.43	190.97
1963–64	306.96	287.23	201.53
1964–65	306.11	286.43	219.40
1965–66	326.07	298.74	235.54
1966–67	348.82	316.86	252.97
1967–68	355.12	333.08	259.85
1968–69	391.95	378.96	280.08
1969–70	444.32	413.64	304.08
1970–71	492.07	459.73	345.02
1971–72	528.03	494.09	370.47
1972–73	589.36	553.61	407.33
1973–74	617.70	580.82	431.52
1974–75	622.62	623.93	467.70
1975–76	665.82	630.14	465.30
Expenditure Growth Trends			
1962–67	17.94%	19.38%	32.45%
1967–72	51.38%	55.93%	46.45%
1972–76	26.10%	27.54%	25.60%
1962–76	125.11%	137.40%	143.65%

All appropriations in millions of dollars.

*Non-capital appropriations include all appropriations for current expenses and exclude long-term capital projects financed by the sale of bonds.

**Net appropriations exclude all capital appropriations and also exclude all revenue earned by specific departments (e.g., bus fares, sale of power by the Public Lighting Department to other levels of government, categorical state grants for specific Health Department programs). Net appropriations are the amount of appropriations that must be financed by taxes or general state and federal aid.

**EXHIBIT 6.19:   City of Detroit, Projected Revenue Sources
1976–77**

Source	Amount (current $ millions)	% of Total Tax-supported Budget****	% of Total Tax-supported**** Budget for Current Expenditures
Taxes			
Property*	187.36	22.0%	22.8%
Income	111.80	13.1	13.6
Utility excise	28.25	3.3	3.4
Total taxes*	327.41	38.4%	39.8%
State Aid			
State income tax	29.80	3.5%	3.6%
State sales tax	27.78	3.3	3.4
Intangibles & single			
business tax*	18.52	2.2	2.3
Gas & weight taxes**	24.70	2.9	3.0
Total state aid*	100.80	11.9%	12.3%
Federal Aid			
Revenue sharing	40.40	4.8%	4.9%
Community development	31.61	3.7	3.9
CETA#	71.29	8.4	8.7
Total federal aid	143.30	16.	17.5%
User Charges***	119.71	14.1%	14.6%
Miscellaneous Revenue for Current Use	128.98	15.2%	15.7%
Total Revenue for Current Use	820.20	96.4%	100.0%
Sale of Bonds for Capital Improvement	30.28	3.6%	
Total revenue	850.48	100.0%	

Source: City of Detroit, Budget Department, Detroit, Financial Projections 1977–1982, December 27, 1976, p. 1.

  *The State Single Business Tax Act, effective in early 1976, eliminated local property taxes on business inventories. The law required the state to furnish aid to municipalities to reimburse them for this diminution in local taxes. The $19.79 million paid to Detroit for this reason was included in local property tax collections and excluded from State Single Business Tax aid, to permit comparability with years prior to 1976–77.

  **Gas and weight taxes are earmarked for street and highway-related improvements.

  ***Included in this category are fees charged by Detroit General Hospital, bus fares collected by the Department of Transportation, and money received for the sale of electric power by the Public Lighting Department to other units of government. Other minor user charges are included in "Miscellaneous Revenue for Current Use."

****The "tax-supported budget" is the budget for all city activities which are not supported fully by user charges and which do not earn a profit (e.g., water is excluded).

#Comprehensive Employment and Training Act, a public employment program.

**EXHIBIT 6.20: City of Detroit,
Tax Revenues and State Tax-Sharing Aid Revenues**

Year	Property Tax	Income Tax	Utility Tax	Total Local Taxes	Sales Tax	Intangibles Tax	Income Tax	Gasoline Tax*	Total State Aid
1961–62	119.42	—	—	119.42		(NOT AVAILABLE)			
1962–63	112.76	35.0	—	147.76	11.94	2.03	—	10.59	24.56
1963–64	110.08	39.5	—	149.58	12.69	2.03	—	11.03	25.75
1964–65	109.34	38.2	—	147.54	13.81	2.03	—	11.57	27.41
1965–66	105.45	43.3	—	148.75	15.43	2.03	—	12.34	29.80
1966–67	101.93	52.0	—	153.93	16.00	2.03	—	12.66	30.69
1967–68	112.17	48.5	—	160.67	16.93	2.03	1.27	14.12	34.35
1968–69	115.41	89.9	—	205.31	18.72	2.03	5.46	19.50	45.71
1969–70	121.99	92.8	—	214.79	18.74	2.03	6.65	19.29	46.71
1970–71	140.40	96.1	17.5	254.00	16.24	1.61	4.96	19.29	42.10
1971–72	148.39	96.1	17.5	261.99	18.23	9.06	15.97	20.32	63.58
1972–73	152.34	93.6	17.1	263.04	20.11	8.44	18.65	22.02	69.22
1973–74	152.72**	106.5	18.6	277.82**	21.53	9.70	21.98	24.83	78.04
1974–75	155.17	116.8	19.7	291.67	23.70	10.81	24.79	24.75	84.05
1975–76	161.43	110.8	24.3	296.53	29.42	17.68	24.33	25.00	92.43
1976–77	187.36***	111.8	28.25	327.41	27.78	18.52***	29.80	24.70	100.80

All numbers in millions of dollars.

*Gasoline tax-sharing revenues are earmarked for road improvements and (after 1973) for mass transportation.

**Excludes $18.69 million imposed for one year only to pay for contributions withheld from the Department of Street Railways pension fund and ordered to be paid by Wayne County Circuit Court.

***The State Single Business Tax Act of 1976 provided an additional $19.79 million in state aid to replace local property tax revenues lost when the state eliminated local taxes on business inventories. To maintain comparability with earlier years, the amount is excluded from state aid and included in local property taxes, since Detroit would have levied an additional $19.79 million in taxes without the law.

**EXHIBIT 6.21:   City of Detroit,
Property Tax Base, Tax Rate, and Revenues**

Fiscal Year	Tax Rate (Mills)	Tax Base	Budgeted Revenue
1962–63	21.891	5,285.4	112.76
1963–64	21.455	5,264.6	110.08
1964–65	21.452	5,229.9	109.34
1965–66	20.848	5,196.9	105.45
1966–67	20.983	4,991.1	101.93
1967–68	23.972	4,807.7	112.17
1968–69	24.071	4,925.6	115.41
1969–70	24.153	5,188.2	121.99
1970–71	27.100	5,306.3	140.40
1971–72	26.587	5,719.3	148.39
1972–73	27.040	5,770.6	152.34
1973–74	26.942*	5,806.7	152.72*
1974–75	27.568	5,762.4	155.17
1975–76	28.512	5,792.1	161.43
1976–77	33.183	5,754.4**	187.36**
Net Change:			
1962–67		−5.57%	−9.60%
1967–72		14.59%	45.58%
1972–77		0.61%	26.26%
1962–77		8.87%	66.16%

*Excludes 3.218 mills levied for one year only to satisfy a Circuit Court judgment that the city must pay back pensions for the Department of Street Railways. The 3.218 mills raised an additional $18.69 million in revenue which is also excluded.

**Includes $707.9 million in the tax base for business inventories, and $19.79 million in state aid to the city (equal to the city's property tax rate times this tax base). The state provided this aid to all municipalities after the State Single Business Tax Act prohibited municipalities from taxing inventories. This inclusion makes 1976–77 comparable to all previous years.

EXHIBIT 6.22:   Comparative National Statistics

Population (thousands)

	1950	1960	Growth 1950–60	1970	Growth 1960–70	1975	Growth 1970–75
Total	150,697	179,326	19.0%	203,210	13.4%	213,137	4.9%
White	133,217	158,832	19.2%	178,128	12.6%	195,198	4.0%
Non-white	17,480	20,491	17.2%	25,082	22.4%	27,940	11.4%
% non-white	11.6%	11.4%		12.3%		13.1%	

Age Distribution

	1960			1970		
	Total	White	Black	Total	White	Black
Under 5	11.3%	11.0%	14.1%	8.8%	8.3%	12.3%
5–13	18.4%	18.1%	21.5%	18.4%	17.5%	22.7%
14–19	8.9%	8.8%	10.0%	11.2%	10.9%	12.8%
20–44	32.0%	32.1%	31.3%	31.4%	31.5%	29.9%
45–64	20.3%	20.7%	17.0%	20.6%	20.9%	16.1%
65 and over	9.0%	9.4%	6.3%	9.7%	10.9%	6.2%
Median age	29.4	30.1	23.5	28.2	29.3	21.4

Schooling of Population over 25 in 1971

	Total	White	Black
8th grade or less	26.7%	25.2%	41.7%
1–3 years high school	16.8%	16.2%	23.5%
4 years high school	34.4%	35.5%	24.2%
1–3 years college	10.6%	11.1%	6.0%
4 years or more, college	11.4%	12.0%	4.5%
Median years completed	12.2	12.2	10.0

Family Income in 1969 Dollars

	1959			1969		
	Total	White	Black	Total	White	Black
less than $3,000	16.4%	14.0%	40.8%	9.3%	8.1%	21.4%
$3,000–4,999	14.0%	13.3%	21.8%	10.7%	9.6%	19.8%
$5,000–6,999	19.0%	19.2%	17.9%	12.3%	11.8%	17.4%
$7,000–9,999	23.6%	24.7%	12.2%	31.7%	21.9%	19.6%
$10,000–14,999	17.2%	19.3%	6.1%	26.7%	27.9%	14.7%
$15,000–24,999	6.7%	7.1%	1.2%	15.6%	16.6%	6.5%
$25,000 and over	2.2%	2.4%	0.1%	3.6%	4.0%	0.6%
U.S. median income	7,058	7,360	3,721	9,433	9,793	5,998
Median income in metropolitan areas	7,880	8,566	4,768	10,261	10,646	6,836

1970 Housing

% owner occupied:		% overcrowded:	
total	62.87%	total	7.96%
white	65.24%	white	6.91%
black	37.86%	black	19.06%

EXHIBIT 6.22 (continued)

Male Labor Force Participation and Type of Employment

	1960			1970		
	Total	*White*	*Black*	*Total*	*White*	*Black*
Population over 16 (thousands)	56,576	51,039	5,030	65,236	59,947	6,119
% in labor force	78.6%	79.1%	74.5%	76.2%	76.8%	72.4%
Unemployment rate	5.1%	4.7%	9.6%	4.1%	3.8%	6.8%
% of employed						
Professional and technical	10.9%	11.6%	3.3%	14.1%	14.8%	5.8%
Managerial	11.3%	12.2%	1.4%	14.4%	15.4%	4.1%
Clerical	7.6%	7.7%	6.1%	7.5%	7.4%	8.6%
Sales	7.0%	7.5%	1.6%	5.7%	6.1%	1.6%
Craftsmen	20.4%	21.3%	10.0%	19.9%	20.6%	14.2%
Operatives	20.9%	20.5%	27.0%	19.9%	18.9%	30.6%
Non-farm laborers	7.1%	5.6%	24.3%	6.8%	5.7%	18.9%
Service workers	6.3%	5.5%	15.6%	6.6%	6.0%	11.7%
Farmers and farm laborers	8.4%	8.1%	10.6%	5.1%	5.2%	4.5%

Female Labor Force Participation and Type of Employment

	1960			1970		
	Total	*White*	*Black*	*Total*	*White*	*Black*
Population over 16 (thousands)	64,961	58,087	5,925	73,852	65,421	7,317
% in labor force	34.5%	33.6%	43.0%	42.6%	41.9%	49.1%
Unemployment rate	5.3%	4.8%	9.6%	5.7%	4.9%	8.5%
% of employed						
Professional and technical	15.0%	14.6%	7.0%	13.8%	15.5%	10.0%
Managerial	4.4%	4.4%	0.7%	4.0%	4.7%	1.4%
Clerical	34.2%	34.9%	8.1%	31.9%	36.1%	18.9%
Sales	6.7%	8.8%	1.3%	7.9%	7.3%	2.5%
Craftsmen	1.1%	1.4%	0.9%	1.3%	1.1%	0.8%
Operatives	14.7%	16.7%	14.0%	16.5%	14.5%	16.8%
Non-farm laborers	0.4%	0.5%	0.8%	0.5%	0.4%	0.9%
Service workers*	22.1%	17.2%	63.7%	22.4%	18.8%	48.1%
Farmers and farm laborers	1.4%	1.5%	3.6%	1.5%	1.5%	0.5%

*Includes private household workers (1960: 8.0% of total, 4.0% of whites, 40.3% of blacks; 1970: 5.5% of total, 3.7% of whites, 19.1% of blacks).

EXHIBIT 6.22 (continued)

Retail and Wholesale Trade

	1958			1963		
	Sales	*Payroll*	*Employees*	*Sales*	*Payroll*	*Employees*
Food	49,022	3,232	1,326	57,079	4,249	1,274
Automotive	31,807	3,030	721	45,376	4,111	794
Service stations	14,178	1,133	466	17,760	1,510	520
Department stores	13,359	2,218	808	20,537	2,942	970
Other	91,280	11,976	4,590	103,450	14,820	4,852
Total retail	199,646	21,589	7,911	244,202	27,632	8,410
Wholesale trade	284,970	13,199	2,797	358,385	18,101	3,089

	1967			1972		
	Sales	*Payroll*	*Employees*	*Sales*	*Payroll*	*Employees*
Food	70,251	5,543	1,444	100,719	8,820	1,722
Automotive	55,631	5,256	907	90,030	8,622	1,035
Service stations	22,709	1,898	575	33,655	2,974	748
Department stores	32,344	4,673	1,174	51,083	7,226	1,437
Other	129,279	18,805	5,281	183,353	27,730	6,269
Total retail	310,214	36,175	9,381	458,840	55,372	11,211
Wholesale trade	459,476	23,922	3,518	695,224	36,893	4,026

Sales and payrolls in millions of dollars; number of employees in thousands.

Selected Services

	1958			1963		
	Sales	*Payroll*	*Employees*	*Sales*	*Payroll*	*Employees*
Hotels & tourist services	3,888	1,145	502	5,049	1,440	526
Auto repair	3,852	854	256	5,444	1,135	288
Business services	9,897	2,578	616	15,193	4,103	874
Other services	14,739	4,429	1,133	18,900	5,514	1,574
Total selected services	32,376	9,006	2,507	44,586	12,192	3,262

	1967			1972		
	Sales	*Payroll*	*Employees*	*Sales*	*Payroll*	*Employees*
Hotels & tourist services	7,039	1,990	617	10,638	2,971	726
Auto repair	7,028	1,468	316	12,081	2,553	392
Business services	22,595	6,699	1,212	37,802	12,250	1,759
Other services	23,880	7,367	1,696	33,350	9,758	1,838
Total selected services	60,542	17,524	3,841	93,871	27,532	4,715

Sales and payroll in millions of dollars; number of employees in thousands.

EXHIBIT 6.22 (continued)

Manufacturing	Total Value of Shipments	Manufacturing Value Added in Manufacturing	Payroll	Number of Employees
1958	326,723	141,271	73,750	15,394
1963	420,973	192,083	99,899	16,958
1967	557,398	261,984	132,208	19,323
1972	756,467	353,973	174,187	19,026

Value of shipments, valued added, and payroll in millions of dollars; number of employees in thousands.

National Manufacturing by Industry, 1967				
Industry Code & Description	Total Value of Shipments	Value Added in Manufacturing	Payroll	Number of Employees
20 Food and kindred products	83,975	26,621	10,077	1,650
21 Tobacco products	4,903	2,032	377	75
22 Textile mill products	19,815	8,153	4,391	929
23 Apparel, other textile products	21,327	10,064	5,582	1,356
24 Lumber and wood products	11,206	4,973	2,799	554
25 Furniture and fixtures	7,750	4,170	2,258	425
26 Paper and allied products	20,970	9,756	4,436	639
27 Printing and publishing	21,738	14,355	7,152	1,031
28 Chemicals and allied products	42,148	23,550	6,443	841
29 Petroleum and coal products	22,043	5,426	1,216	142
30 Rubber and plastics products	12,759	6,800	3,286	517
31 Leather and leather products	5,169	2,626	1,459	329
32 Stone, clay, and glass products	14,449	8,333	3,826	590
33 Primary metal industries	46,731	19,978	9,851	1,281
34 Fabricated metal products	34,578	18,043	9,320	1,342
35 Machinery, except electrical	48,477	27,836	14,226	1,864
36 Electrical equipment	43,361	24,487	12,968	1,875
37 Transportation equipment	68,512	28,174	15,174	1,834
38 Instruments and related products	9,907	6,418	2,822	394
39 Miscellaneous	17,578	10,187	5,819	824
Administrative & auxiliary			8,728	830
Total	557,396	261,982	132,210	19,322

Value of shipments, value added, and payroll in millions of dollars; number of employees in thousands.

EXHIBIT 6.23:   Detroit and Its Principal Suburbs

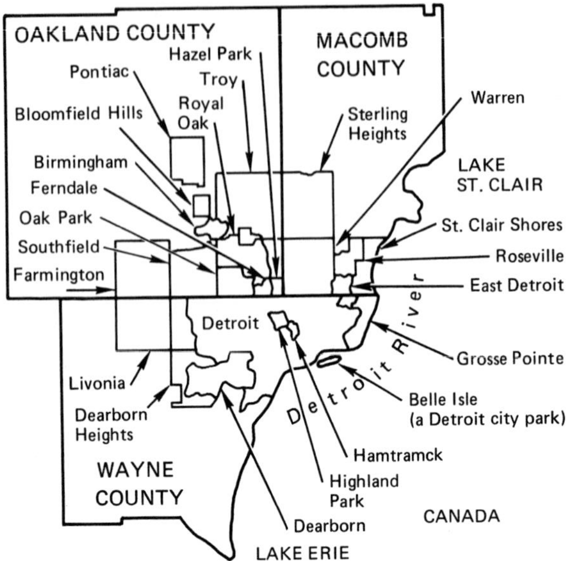

7

The Detroit Fiscal Crisis (A)

By the beginning of 1976, the city of Detroit faced a major fiscal problem. In the fiscal year ending June 30, 1975, Detroit had a cumulative operating deficit of $16.4 million (out of a total tax-supported budget* of $616.5 million). Expectations of new taxing authority and state aid that never materialized, a shortfall in tax revenue from earlier projections, and inflation requiring payment of cost-of-living allowances to employees above budget estimates resulted in a December 1975 projection of a cumulative $43.3 million deficit for fiscal 1975–76. Worse still, without new revenues from taxes, aid from other levels of government, and/or service cutbacks, the cumulative deficit was expected to rise to $112.7 million by fiscal 1976–77, and annual deficits averaging over $117 million were expected in each of the following four fiscal years for a cumulative deficit of over half a billion dollars by fiscal 1981–82.[1]

Meanwhile, banks were demanding a high (7.75%) interest rate on short-term tax-exempt city notes and bid on only $27 million of the $40 million which the city wanted to sell; Standard and Poor's bond rating service downgraded the city's long-term bonds so that interest rates on these bonds rose to 9%.[2] The Federal government threatened to withdraw funds from the Comprehensive Employment and Training Act's (CETA) public employment program in Detroit unless the program was no longer used to return laid-off employees to their jobs.[3] In short, the government was facing eventual insolvency unless increased revenues from new taxes and aid from other levels of government were forthcoming and strict controls on spending were instituted.

But the city's fiscal problem was in large part the result of social and economic problems. During the 1975 recession, the average unemployment rate

---

*The "tax-supported budget" excludes activities such as water supply which are totally supported by user charges and which are operated on a non-profit basis.

among Detroit residents was approximately 20%, compared to a state unemployment rate of 13.7% and a national rate of 8.5%. Employment within the city had fallen by nearly 20% in the five years from 1969 to 1973 as businesses and jobs moved to the suburbs, and the population of Detroit fell from 1,511,000 in 1970 to 1,335,000 in 1975.[4] In addition to the long-term movement of population and jobs from Detroit to its suburbs, the recession of 1974–76 had a disproportionate impact on the city relative to the rest of the country because of its effect on the automobile industry. The number of cars produced in the Detroit Standard Metropolitan Statistical Area (SMSA) decreased from 2.23 million units in the 1973 model year to 1.92 million in the 1974 model year and only 1.58 million in 1975.[5] Many autoworkers were laid off, and Ford and Chrysler paid out so much money in Supplemental Unemployment Benefits (designed to provide laid-off workers with 95% of their regular after-tax-take-home pay) that these benefit funds were exhausted for a time in 1975, further reducing purchasing power in the city and state.

Part A of this case, which is presented in this chapter, together with chapter 6, "A Statistical Profile of Metropolitan Detroit" is intended to provide an introduction to the history and problems of the City of Detroit and its government. Part B of the case, chapter 8, discusses the city's fiscal problem in greater detail.

HISTORICAL BACKGROUND[6]

The French established Detroit at the beginning of the 18th century as a fort to control the fur trade of the Great Lakes region. The site selected was ideal for the purpose: Detroit is situated on the Great Lakes east-west water route at the narrowest point of the Detroit River and on several important land routes, including major Indian trails. (See Exhibit 7.1 for a map.) Detroit's initial growth in the 18th century was thus as a center of trade and transportation, although its pre-eminence in the Great Lakes region began to wane by mid-century as other regional centers and transport routes grew in importance. After Detroit passed to British and American control, its settlers came mainly from New York and New England.

In the half-century from 1850 to 1900, Detroit became an important center of industrial production, and its population grew from 21,000 to 285,000. The newcomers tended to be from northern and western Europe (Germans, Dutch, Irish, Swedes, Norwegians, Finns) and Italy. Unincorporated villages began to sprout just outside Detroit; by the 1890s, many of these had been connected to the city via interurban railways. During this half-century, the expansion of the central business district (CBD) had led some higher income families to move to the city's outskirts, and Detroit's first slums began to appear near the waterfront.

Shortly after the turn of the century, Detroit almost overnight became the center of the American automobile industry. Population went from 285,000 in 1900 to 466,000 in 1910. Problems of overcrowding, traffic congestion, pollution and noise made their appearance, and the growth of factory districts further displaced upper-income residents. They were replaced by lower-income European immigrants, and Detroit's slums expanded steadily. However, the city's income continued to increase.

Between 1910 and 1930, Detroit became the automobile capital of the world, as the car evolved from a luxury for the elite to a convenience for the many. The city's wealth and population increased rapidly (466,000 in 1910 to 994,000 in 1920 to 1,569,000 in 1930). The greater mobility provided by the automobile linked more closely the central city and outlying areas. Lack of available land produced a period of "vertical" development: most of Detroit's skyscrapers were built in the 1920s. The problems of urban decay, pollution, and noise continued to increase, and for the first time, the wealthier residents abandoned the city for the nearby suburbs of Grosse Pointe, Birmingham, Bloomfield Hills, and Dearborn. They were replaced by Poles and other Eastern Europeans drawn to the booming auto factories and, after 1920, by an increasing number of Southern blacks and whites.

By 1950 Detroit's economy was firmly wedded to a single economic activity—the manufacture of automobiles. (In 1950, the automobile industry provided 53.2% of the city's manufacturing employment.) Because cars are one of the most easily postponed consumer purchases, this dependence has made Detroit especially vulnerable to economic downturns. During the 1930s, the city's population grew very slowly—from 1,569,000 in 1930 to 1,623,000 in 1940—as did that of the SMSA—from 2,177,313 to 2,377,329. The war revitalized the area's economy, and the population of the Detroit SMSA rose from 2,377,329 in 1940 to 3,016,197 in 1950.* The number of cars registered in the area also soared, and the construction of Detroit's first freeways began. The city's housing stock continued to deteriorate and the slums expanded substantially. Upper income residents continued their flight from the city; immigrants of European stock moved out from the central city, to be replaced by large numbers of Southern blacks drawn by the wartime boom. Service and commercial activities and corporate headquarters also began their outward movement.

Beginning around 1950 (and continuing to the mid-seventies), the rate of urban decay accelerated. The auto industry began to relocate outside Detroit (and indeed, outside Michigan).** Other industries began to move in, and overall growth continued (SMSA population up 24.8% to 3,764,131 in 1960; aggregate income up 48.6%). But this overall growth only thinly concealed a serious decay in the city's physical environment and social fabric. Between 1950 and 1960, the number of automobiles registered in the Detroit SMSA rose 37% to 1,631,000; freeways and other highways were extensively developed; and traffic congestion, parking problems, pollution and noise increased markedly. Middle income descendants of European immigrants began to move to the suburbs in increasing numbers; the central business district and municipal services continued to decay; and the central city became increasingly a poor, non-white enclave. Major developments such as shopping centers occurred in the suburbs, and aggregate income in the central city declined.

---

*The expansion of Detroit's population from 1940 to 1950 was due in part to annexation of surrounding areas by the central city.

**Michigan employment in motor vehicle production declined from 468,000 in 1950 to 351,000 in 1972—before the mid-seventies' recession. The percentage of American-made automobiles constructed in Michigan remained fairly constant at about one-third over the late sixties and early seventies, ranging from 31.09% in 1971 to 35.08% in 1967. However, if a trend toward small cars develops, Michigan is likely to be hurt, since many Michigan plants are old and currently used for large car production and might well close.

DETROIT IN 1976[7]

By 1976, the forces described above had created a series of major problems for the city of Detroit.

Natural Environment

Detroit's problems, like its opportunities, begin with its natural environment. Located at the center of a market area of some 35 million people, Detroit has the potential to become a major center for trade, transportation and services, although the harsh climate and the declining importance of water transport reduce these advantages somewhat.***

But Detroit has not followed that path; instead, it has concentrated on manufacturing (as of 1960, Detroit had the highest concentration of manufacturing employment of all important Great Lakes SMSAs) to the detriment of the natural environment. Urban "sprawl" has eaten up open land, including agricultural and scenically attractive land, and the ample supply of recreational land that remains is largely outside the central city, away from the mass of people.**** There is an abundant water supply, but water quality is steadily deteriorating due to the discharge of industrial wastes. Air pollution too is serious in the central city area, although much of this pollution drifts in from nearby industrial suburbs; Detroit itself has a relatively strong city enforcement program dating from the 1950s.

Man-Made Environment

The man-made environment also suffers from major problems. Highways and parking lots have divided many neighborhoods, contributing to spreading physical decay and policing problems. At the same time, the widespread reliance on private automobiles creates major traffic problems. It has been estimated that as of 1970, 14% of Detroit's housing stock was blighted, and little new construction or maintenance was underway: 60% of Detroit's houses were built before 1939, and over a third were more than 50 years old.[8] Urban "renewal" programs sponsored by

---

***The completion of the St. Lawrence seaway in 1957 partially offset the long-term decline in Great Lakes water transport.

****Belle Isle Park, located in the Detroit River near the downtown area, is an exception, but enforced fiscal austerity has left the park seriously under-maintained.

the federal Department of Housing and Urban Development (HUD) had destroyed more housing than they had created. Existing transportation facilities such as the Port of Detroit and Detroit Metropolitan Airport were also inadequate to the city's needs. The Detroit Budget Department described the results of physical decay as follows:

> The visible signs of decline are everywhere. . . . [Even some major streets] have large sections punctuated by boarded, burned or vandalized buildings. Merchants have been forced out by a fear of crime or the bad economics of business in a poor neighborhood. The decay of some commercial streets is obvious to the most casual observer. When that observer leaves the major arteries, he sees abandoned homes and vacant lots in what once were pleasant neighborhoods.[9]

Appendix A contains a graphic description of the results of decay in one Detroit neighborhood and describes some of the governmental policies that have contributed to the blight.

Demography

The City of Detroit has been losing population since 1950: the city's population declined 9.7% between 1950 and 1960, by 10.4% between 1960 and 1970, and by 11.7% between 1970 and 1975. The Detroit SMSA, which grew by some 40% from 1950 to 1970, declined by 1% from 1970 to 1975. In part these decreases were due to falling birthrates—which have affected the entire nation—but the major part has been due to net out-migration, which entails loss of income, business and vitality. The population that remains has become steadily older and less educated; by 1976 the median age of city residents was 30.1 years, as compared to 27.5 for the SMSA as a whole. In 1960 the average Detroiter 25 years of age or older had 10.0 years of schooling, compared to 10.7 years for all U.S. central cities; in 1970 the median number of years of school was 11.0 for city residents versus 12.1 years for Detroit SMSA residents.[10]

Socioeconomically, the city has problems retaining a middle class. The school system, which had been 61% black in 1968, was 81% black by 1976;* and although the number of black pupils in the system had increased by 8% over that period, the number of

whites declined by 62%. (The system as a whole lost 19% of its students.) A busing program has been implemented under court order to eliminate the few remaining white schools.** The school system is underfunded,*** inefficient, and has difficulty attracting good teachers to an urban setting. Many middle-class professionals, black and white, feel that they must either send their children to private schools or leave Detroit because of the quality of education in the city.

By 1975 Detroit had also become more racially divided. The city's population went from 29% black in 1960 to 44% black in 1970 to majority black by the early seventies, even while the city's population as a whole declined—indicating that the great outflux of the 1960s was predominantly white. Housing patterns within the city and the metropolitan area have become highly segregated. The population is also poorer: from 1961 the number of households receiving Aid to Families with Dependent Children (AFDC) rose almost 400% to over 110,000 cases; direct relief cases were also up by over 40%.[11]

In the mid 1970s, Detroit had the highest murder rate of any major American city and high crime rates for other categories of offenses. The crime rate has nearly doubled since 1967, although police pressure has caused it to drop slightly since 1974. The number of fires increased by two-thirds from 1960 to 1975 (to 34,015) and the number of false alarms grew fivefold (to 24,000).[12] Crime (and the threat of fire) acts as another deterrent to economic growth, as persistent fear deters people from living, working, or seeking recreation in the central city. The widely reported exploits of youth gangs have further increased fear among city residents,[13] and together with neighbor-

---

**Cross-district busing with the suburbs was ordered by a District Court Judge in 1971, affirmed by the Circuit Court of Appeals in 1972, but reversed by the U.S. Supreme Court in 1973. The trial and appellate courts found state action to encourage segregation and ordered cross-district busing, but the Supreme Court ruled that the suburbs were not themselves directly guilty, so that cross-district busing was not an appropriate remedy.

***Michigan law requires that voters approve all increases in property taxes and that tax levies must be renewed at five to ten year intervals. Many of the Detroit school system's financial problems result from the failure of voters to approve tax increases or renewals, combined with the low property tax base (see Part B, chapter 8).

---

*The city as a whole was still 40–45% white in 1976, but many whites were older and did not have children in school.

hood deterioration and school and unemployment problems, is causing a continuous movement of the middle class—white and black—away from the city. Appendices B and C contain two widely read—but in the view of city officials, one-sided—accounts of violence in Detroit.

But probably the most well-known incident of violence in Detroit was the 1967 riot, in which 43 persons were killed, 7,200 arrested, and close to $45 million in property damage inflicted. National Guardsmen and Regular Army troops were required to restore order. The 1967 riot led to a major population outflow to the suburbs, particularly of well-to-do Jewish families who had remained in the city until then. By 1975, such extreme tensions appeared to have eased; but as the articles reprinted in Appendices B and C indicate, many felt that a climate of fear still pervaded the city.

The Economy

Detroit's heavy reliance on manufacturing—and its consequent neglect of the rapidly growing services sector*—have made it extremely vulnerable to economic downturns, particularly since so many of its products are durable goods (such as cars), the purchase of which is the first to be postponed by consumers when times are hard. As noted at the outset of this case, unemployment in Detroit was almost two and a half times the national average in the 1975 recession; the same was true of earlier recessions, such as the one in 1958–1960. Detroit's work force contained a lower percentage of white collar workers than the country as a whole or other major urban areas; and as noted above, the city's educational attainments also suffered in comparison. The relocation of industry and population has led to declines in many economic indicators, such as per capita incomes and retail sales. However, these declines have not been spread evenly among the population; autoworkers have a strong union and are generally well paid, and the declines are felt hardest among other groups, e.g. inner-city blacks.

The Positive Side

If Detroit had problems it also had opportunities. The fifth largest city in America, it had a combination of financial, managerial, and transportation resources which could make it a service and trade center for its 35 million person market area. Aggregate investment in Detroit has been estimated at roughly $15 billion,[14] and by the mid-seventies the city had begun to attract a more diversified mix of enterprises.

The availability of a large federal mass transit grant to build a light rail system connecting various points in Detroit and connecting Detroit to its suburbs (and yielding major increases in employment) was announced late in 1975, contingent on the state's producing matching funds. A program to provide the $12 million in annual local money and $25 million in state funds necessary to bring in the $160 million annual federal grant passed the State Senate overwhelmingly in June 1976 but was defeated in the House on a 65–28 vote. Suburban legislators opposing new taxes for Detroit joined with real estate interests who opposed the increase in real estate transfer taxes that was the keystone of the plan.[15] However, it appeared possible to resurrect the plan if it were scaled down to exclude subway services and if it were based on different taxes.

Private development, particularly along the Detroit riverfront, began accelerating in the mid-seventies, providing hopes for a new economic nucleus for the city. Henry Ford II organized a consortium of Detroit business leaders to build the Detroit Renaissance Center, a downtown riverfront complex consisting of a 70-story hotel (the world's tallest hotel, with 1434 rooms) and four 39-story office towers. The hotel, three blocks from Cobo Hall, the city's convention center, was expected to stimulate Detroit's convention trade, which had been reasonably large throughout the 1960s, and the office buildings in the project were expected to slow or even partially reverse the movement of office jobs to the suburbs. However, as of July 1976, with the first tower due for completion in September, only the Ford Motor Company, which committed itself to space for 1,000 workers, had moved jobs from the suburbs to the city, although several smaller firms indicated that they were going to the Renaissance Center from other downtown offices rather than to the suburbs. The city's Community and Economic Development Department predicted that the Renaissance Center would lead to "more competitive leasing

---

*By 1960 Detroit had the lowest services sector among SMSAs and the highest manufacturing sector of any major SMSA.

postures by existing . . . buildings, a gradual filtering of tenants up from lower class [office] buildings, and poor survival potential for older, poorly located, ill maintained buildings."[16]

Other riverfront office and industrial development is also planned; for example, early in 1976 the Detroit *Free Press* announced plans to build a new riverfront headquarters and move from its old downtown office. Residential development was also being planned. Early in 1976, Max Fisher, the developer of several suburban shopping malls, urged the enactment (by the state) of a twelve-year property tax exemption on new apartment buildings (keeping taxes at the level of their previous use) so that he could construct a large area of upper-middle-class apartments on vacant riverfront land half a mile west of the downtown area, then a lightly used industrial zone.* Supporters of the exemption claimed that the city would lose very little in taxes, since the land was currently assessed at a low value and future development was unlikely without the exemption; they argued that it would create construction jobs in the interim (bringing in income tax revenues) and would provide attractive safe living space for young professionals who would then contribute to the income tax base. Then after 12 years, property taxes would be collected from this valuable asset.

Behind these construction projects lay a city with much vitality and diversity, as Appendix D describes. But to be effective, Detroit's material and human resources would need to be effectively marshalled by strong leadership, and it was unclear where such leadership would come from. The heads of the automobile companies and unions necessarily gave first attention to the problems of their industry; and by 1975, the city's government—divided among racial and economic groups and lacking any coherent plan for the city's future—faced eventual insolvency. Before Detroit's political leaders could develop a plan for the city's revitalization, they had to find ways to maintain such essential services as police and fire pro-

tection. Whether they could accomplish that "lifeboat" operation was unclear; whether they could move beyond factionalism to point Detroit toward a better future was even less certain.

POLITICS AND GOVERNMENT IN DETROIT[17]

As in any complex community, a number of different groups could be expected to wield power—and to bear responsibility for that exercise—in Detroit. This section sketches the principal groups relevant to Detroit politics as of the mid-seventies.

Automakers and Autoworkers

Any sketch of Detroit politics must begin with the major economic actors who have shaped the city's economy: the automobile manufacturers and the United Auto Workers Union (the UAW). The "Big Three" of the auto industry—General Motors, Ford and Chrysler**—are the first, third and fifth largest industrial corporations in the United States. General Motors, with roughly half the industry output, employed (as of 1969) some 750,000 people and had a gross income larger than the budget of any country in the world save the United States and the Soviet Union. Together, the Big Three accounted for 10-15% of the country's gross national product, and automaking is the country's largest manufacturing industry.

In the view of many critics, of course, this enormous power has not been matched by a like responsibility, especially in such fields as auto safety, pollution control, national transportation planning, energy conservation and minority hiring. In the view of at least one observer, the industry has begun to move "aggressively" in these areas under the prodding of activists of all stripes;[18] especially after the 1967 riot, the Big Three began determined minority recruitment efforts, and some of the results were impressive: high UAW-won wages created a stable middle class in the Detroit area, and many inner-city residents who had been considered unemployable found themselves hired.[19] But an industry that was hard hit by the 1975 recession and by foreign competition and one that is increasingly relocating elsewhere in the country could only contribute so much to Detroit's revival, and by the mid-seventies some observers felt that "Black recruitment and hiring at major Detroit area

---

*A similar tax exemption for new industrial facilities in Detroit and other Michigan cities had been approved by the state legislature in 1974; Fisher's proposal was to broaden the scope of this exemption.

**American Motors runs a poor fourth.

industries ha[d] dropped off."[*20] Moreover, with the exception of Henry Ford II, industry executives have not really made their power felt in efforts to help Detroit.

The auto executives were for a long time confirmed supporters of the Republican Party, and executives were expected to contribute to the GOP. Although bipartisan contributions are now the rule, at least on paper, the money still goes disproportionately to the Republicans.

The natural counter to the automakers is the autoworkers' union, the UAW. Michigan has the most powerful union movement in America: as of 1972, one of every 17 unionists hailed from the state and Michigan factory workers have secured wages one third above the national average.[22] Under Presidents Walter Reuther and Leonard Woodcock, the UAW developed a reputation for liberalism among unions; for example, while AFL-CIO President George Meany supported the American war effort in Vietnam, Reuther and Woodcock opposed it.[**] The UAW has traditionally been Democratic; in 1968, a strong drive by UAW leaders stemmed a rank and file George Wallace movement and saved Michigan for Humphrey.

However, the strong Wallace showing and Gerald Ford's victory in Michigan in 1976 point to fundamental changes in the UAW and Michigan's other unions. First, the unions' traditional demand—"more" —has been somewhat blunted by prosperity among highly unionized workers. Second, union leaders no longer command the automatic loyalty of rank and file members, many of whom are younger and concerned with new issues such as job safety and assembly line boredom. Third, many union members are now in effect middle class, white suburbanites who want no part of the poor, increasingly black inner city. Issues such as city-suburban busing of school children and locating low-income housing in the suburbs have strained the traditional Democratic loyalties of union members.

---

*As in most American cities black unemployment rates in Detroit—especially among teenagers—are higher than those for whites, although the published rates are only rough estimates. Even under the "aggressive" minority recruitment programs of the late sixties, "few blacks . . . won promotion to management in the auto industry."[21]
**The UAW withdrew from the AFL-CIO in 1968.

Whites and Blacks

As has just been suggested, a second important cleavage in Detroit's politics is racial. Detroit achieved a majority black population in the early 1970s, and in 1973 Detroit elected its first black mayor, Coleman Young. Young was controversial from the outset (see Appendices B and C), and his aggressive use of the largely white police force to preserve order in black neighborhoods drew sharp criticism and seemingly exacerbated racial tensions. However, there are also precedents for interracial cooperation in the city; for example, a Black-Polish Conference on Greater Detroit in 1969, oriented mainly towards social affairs where "fried chicken coalesced with sausage and sauerkraut," received widespread support. More lastingly, the New Detroit Committee, a biracial group of community leaders formed after the 1967 riot, has helped focus public attention on constructive proposals for improving life for the city's disadvantaged residents.

City, Suburbs and Countryside

The racial and economic cleavages discussed above are reflected in the divisions between Detroit and the rest of Michigan. As noted above, Detroit was 44% black in 1970, but the state as a whole was only 11.2% black. Some of the city's suburbs are working class (Warren, Royal Oak, Troy) and some upper class (Grosse Pointe, Birmingham, Bloomfield Hills), but all are opposed to penetration by lower income persons—or blacks. Dearborn counted 13 blacks in 1970 out of a population of 104,199; Warren had 28 black families, and more may have been discouraged from moving in by incidents such as a 1967 mob attack on a house bought by a mixed couple. In short, Detroit's suburbs are not sympathetic to the city's needs.

The rest of Michigan consists of small cities such as Lansing (the state capital) and Grand Rapids, small towns, farm country, and sparsely populated northern Michigan and the Upper Peninsula. The small towns and rural areas have generally high incomes (except for the northern areas), low crime rates, easily available recreational facilities, and in general the kind of more relaxed living many Americans say they want; they have witnessed steady population growth and by 1976 comprised 57% of the statewide vote. These areas were traditionally Republican, but just as "social" issues like busing and abortion have shaken the Democratic loyalties of blue collar workers, so have other issues—like Vietnam—shaken the Republican allegiance of outstaters.

Professors, Pressmen and Politicians

Influence in Michigan and Detroit must also be accorded to three other groups: the major universities, the local newspapers, and elected officeholders. Michigan has the 11th, 14th and 19th largest (in full-time enrollment) universities in the country: Michigan State at East Lansing, the University of Michigan at Ann Arbor, and Wayne State University in Detroit. Wayne State (34,000 students) is largely a commuter school; it is supported by the state. By the start of the 1970s, Wayne State had the largest black enrollment of any predominantly white university (15%), and it has striven to provide legal, medical and manpower training services to its neighbor ghetto areas. The University of Detroit, a commuter school affiliated with the Catholic Church, is also a large institution.

Detroit has two major daily papers, the somewhat conservative *News* and the more liberal *Free Press*, of which the *News* has the larger circulation. However, the *News* alienated many blacks by its coverage of crime news and, symbolically, has walled in the groundfloor windows of its downtown offices and instituted a security pass system for visitors. Detroit also has a black newspaper, the *Michigan Chronicle.*

The State Level.   The state legislature was split fairly evenly between Democrats and Republicans until the 1974 Watergate-influenced election: most of the period from 1966 to 1974 saw Democratic control of the House and Republican control of the Senate. The Governor has been a liberal Republican since 1962—first George Romney, then William Milliken—although Milliken had a close call in 1970, winning by only 1 to 1½% of the vote over Democrat Sander Levin, a state legislator and brother of Detroit City Council president Carl Levin. (The issue of state aid to parochial schools cost Milliken outstate support in 1970 which he regained in 1974.) The Democrats captured the state legislature by wide margins (68–42 in the House, 25–15 in the Senate) in 1974 and retained control in 1976.

Michigan's parties are coalitions of ideologically disparate groups. The Democrats are split between conservative working-class white homeowners (who support anti-open housing, anti-property tax and pro-

police movements*) and liberal black/progressive middle-class groups. Bitter battles were fought among Republicans in the mid-sixties between right-wing and moderate groups for control of the party; at one point Goldwater backers controlled the party machinery in several districts and used it to attack Romney supporters. Both of Michigan's statewide parties were heavily liberalized by two modern governors—Democrat G. Mennen Williams (1948-1960) and Romney (1962-70)—who refocused their parties on issues instead of patronage. But with Romney's departure and the growing conservative suburban and outstate vote, the Republicans began to drift to the right again in the early seventies.

An equally important and still emerging split is that between cities and suburbs on issues such as state aid to Michigan's increasingly hard-pressed municipalities, and coalitions are beginning to develop among legislators from Detroit, Flint, Muskegon, Ann Arbor, and other cities against suburbanites and rural/small town legislators. This development is beginning to break down party lines on issues such as aid to Detroit: two of Detroit's staunchest backers from 1972 to 1974, when Republicans controlled the State Senate, were Republican legislators from Benton Harbor (a small city, but one with a growing black population) and Ann Arbor, who chaired influential Senate committees. From 1971 to 1974, the House Speaker was a Detroit Democrat. He voluntarily resigned in 1975 in order to devote more time to urban issues and was replaced by an outstate urban Democrat. The Senate Democratic leader has been a Detroiter for many years: Coleman Young held that position before running for mayor in 1973 and has since been succeeded by two white Detroiters, one of whom has been a militant advocate of state aid to the city.

As of 1977, Michigan's two United States Senators were conservative Republican Robert Griffin and liberal Democrat Donald Riegle. The Michigan Congressional delegation split 10-9 Republican after the 1972 election, in which the threat of cross-district busing worked to the advantage of the Republicans

---

*The Detroit Police Officers' Association (DPOA) has forcefully entered city politics on several occasions when it believed its interests were at stake.

(an ultra-conservative was elected from a Detroit suburban district). But the delegation turned 12-7 Democratic in 1974 and retained an 11–8 Democratic edge in 1976, as Gerald Ford's old seat was won back by a Republican. As of 1977 the members of the Detroit contingent on the delegation were John Conyers and Charles Diggs, Jr. (both black Democrats) and Lucien Nedzi and William Brodhead (white Democrats). Detroit lost half a seat to the suburbs after the 1970 census, as a district that had previously been totally urban was split between Detroit and its suburbs, and will lose either a half or a whole seat in the 1980 reapportionment, in which Michigan is expected to lose one of its 19 representatives.

The Local Level. Detroit has a "strong mayor" form of government: the elected mayor has authority over all city agencies and appoints department heads, while the nine-member city council passes the budget and enacts local ordinances.* (Elections in Detroit are on a non-partisan basis, and city council members are elected at large.) In 1975, the council consisted of four blacks and five whites, described by many observers as four liberals, three conservatives and two swing members.

The history of recent mayoral and council elections has mirrored the changing power alignments in the city. The city government was white and conservative throughout the late 1940s and 1950s; for example, Mayor Albert Cobo won election in 1949 on a platform of keeping public housing projects segregated and instituted the first urban "renewal,"

---

*An independent elected general school board and a number of district school boards oversee the city's schools.

which consisted of tearing down a large amount of low-income housing and leaving the land empty. Cobo was succeeded in 1957 by a more moderate conservative, Louis Miriani, who temporarily instituted the practice (later found illegal) of avoiding deficits by failing to fund pensions as legally required. Miriani in turn was defeated in 1961 by a political unknown, Jerome P. Cavanagh; in that same election, the city elected its first black councillor. Cavanagh attempted to gain control of the local Democratic Party on a base of conservative, Catholic white ethnic workingmen while maintaining ties to liberal blacks; in this, he was strongly resisted by the UAW and some black leaders, although he won reelection in 1965 by a large margin, enabling him to make a unsuccessful Senate race in 1966 and to be in office during the 1967 riot.

In 1969, Cavanagh did not seek reelection and white Wayne County Sheriff Roman Gribbs and black Wayne County Auditor Richard Austin—both Democrats—contested the mayoralty; Gribbs was supported by Cavanagh's Catholic coalition, including various white "homeowners" groups and the DPOA, while the UAW backed Austin. Gribbs won by 8,000 votes of 450,000 cast. Meanwhile, the number of black councillors had increased to two in 1965, three in 1969 and four in 1973; the Council also gained a tenuous liberal majority in 1969. Gribbs decided not to seek a second term, and in 1973 State Senator Coleman Young contested the mayoralty with Gribbs' white police commissioner John Nichols, winning by a slim margin to become Detroit's first black mayor; in the same election the council retained its uncertain liberal majority.

APPENDIX A

Charting the Tragedy of the Lower East Side— A Fifth of It Has Vanished

by Jim Neubacher and Ellen Grzech

On a cold fall day when a light snow covers the bare ground, the land looks much as it must have looked 150 years ago, when a Frenchman named St. Jean owned it. Except for the refrigerator.

The ungainly box lies on its side, rust showing through the white enameled exterior. Ahead, looking south, is a house, quiet on a quiet morning. Too

quiet. The windows and doors of the house are covered with plywood.

To the left is a long, open and unobstructed line of sight. Homes that once stood in the way are gone now.

Across the street, to the right, is a house at 1607 Lillibridge. It is not boarded up, it is burned

---

Source: Detroit Free Press, *December 11, 1977, pp. 1B, 4B. Reprinted by permission.*

and charred, and open to the elements. A rookie fireman died in that house in October, fighting the fire that gutted the structure.

To the north? More and more and more of the same.

It is the heart of a 14-square mile area on Detroit's lower east side, an area characterized by pervasive blight, decay and poverty. No other large section of the city is so dismal.

In these neighborhoods are 9,000 vacant lots; nearly 20% of the once-occupied residential land in the area is empty.

In the same area, another 1,000 homes—enough to populate 25 square blocks of the city—stand vacant and boarded up. They exist on the hope someone will once again occupy them before they are vandalized, burned or ultimately demolished like the thousands before them.

In some large areas within this section of Detroit, vacant homes and vacant lots now account for four of every 10 parcels.

"It looks like Hiroshima out there," said one city official.

ONCE A POPULATION THE
SIZE OF BATTLE CREEK

In better Detroit days, on almost all of those 9,000 vacant lots stood homes and flats, built all at once in a city that grew all at once in the automobile-spawned boom after World War I.

Today, those homes and more have been forsaken by people who are unable—or unwilling—to live in them.

The vacant and demolished homes in the lower east side area once housed a population of 40,000, the equivalent of a city the size of Battle Creek.

The 9,000 empty parcels—if they were put together—would cover an area of almost two square miles, or more than Belle Isle.

In the area surveyed by the *Free Press,* no house or lot is more than 3.5 miles from either the affluent Grosse Pointe or the Renaissance Center. Five minutes to the north is the convenience of the Ford Freeway. Five minutes to the south are the pleasures of the river and Belle Isle.

Indian Village and several other elegant subdivisions are in this area of Detroit. A half-dozen parks dot the riverfront.

Yet within the last three years some land in this area has changed hands for the equivalent of an incredibly low $500 an acre. There is no visible, realistic market for much of the land in this section of Detroit, and much of it has fallen into the hands of the owner of last resort—the public.

There is so much vacant land in Detroit that city officials admit candidly that they not only don't know what to do with it, they are not even sure where it all is. Russ Chambers, property inventory manager for the city's Community and Economic Development Department (CED), says an estimated 35,000 of the 425,000 assessable parcels of land in Detroit are believed to be vacant.

He estimates the city owns 10,000 of these, and says another 100 a month are coming into city hands just from the U.S. Department of Housing and Urban Development—the bitter fruits of a spectacularly unsuccessful federal homeloan insurance program.

The amount of vacant land on the lower east side will continue to grow for years. There is no significant amount of money available to carry out an east side redevelopment plan, say Chambers and Tom Cunningham, CED's community development coordinator.

And, they add, there is no plan, either.

Without a plan for the future of the lower east side there can be no predictions of any certainty about the future of Detroit, or even the chances for successful reconstruction of other decayed urban areas in Michigan and the U.S.

The manner and degree in which the lower east side is redeveloped will affect the city for generations. The mix of races, economic classes, business and residences that results will set a pattern that will have an impact into the next century.

Here are some of the factors that could determine what the future will hold:

—*The city government will undoubtedly have an upper, if not ruling, hand in the redevelopment process. Private developers are almost totally hamstrung by policies, laws and economics that prevent them from undertaking even modest-sized redevelopment programs.*

Prior to 1973, an opinion by the Detroit corporation counsel—the city's own attorney—said it was illegal for the city to "landbank," acquire land without a definite and declared purpose in mind.

That opinion changed in 1973, however, clearing the way for the city to receive thousands of property deeds that were flooding the scandal-ridden HUD office in Detroit. Until that arrangement with HUD, the federal agency was desperately attempting to reduce its inventory of properties by selling vacant lots to the first comer for a minimum bid of $50. Speculators bought many of the lots at the minimum price.

An inspection of neighborhoods on the east side and discussion with private and public real estate men give no indication that any major private assemblage of land or rebuilding occurred because of that program. So far, no one has made any financial killing in HUD lots.

A DAMPENING EFFECT
ON PRIVATE INVESTMENT

And since mid-1975, those lots have been coming directly to one landlord—the city of Detroit. Not only has this stopped acquisition of HUD lots by all but a few private citizens, it has dampened private speculation and investment in much of the city and particularly on the lower east side.

There are at least two reasons for this: An investor who tied up all but the city-owned parcels in one neighborhood would have to deal with the city, largely on city terms, before he could acquire the rest of the land. While that may not be all bad, some developers don't consider it to be all good, either.

One east side developer, who would like very much to build a community of townhouses along one of the canals that leads to the Detroit River, says that even if he managed to acquire all the privately-owned land along the canals—a difficult task—he would have to find some way to acquire the city-owned land.

If he approached the city, officials could not merely sell the land to him on request. It would have to be put out for bids, or the area would have to be designated as official renewal area. In the latter case, the townhouse project would have to meet with citizen approval, as well as follow city, state and even federal guidelines covering almost every conceivable aspect of the development.

Secondly, says the same developer, city homeowners on the lower east side who have watched the "total clearance/urban removal" programs of the '50s and '60s that levelled entire residential neighborhoods in Detroit expect the same thing to happen in their neighborhoods in the indefinite future.

And they are aware that significant re-location benefits might be available to them if that happens.

"I can't afford to compete with those benefits," says the investor.

—The citizens who have been able or willing to remain on the lower east side will be a crucial factor: Will they pull themselves together and organize to demand a say in the rebuilding process, or will they be cleared aside?

Francis Mills, the director of the southeast Detroit Neighborhood City Hall, says she has noticed increased cooperation among east side block clubs which are uniting to solve problems.

For this, ironically, she thanks the violent 1976 summer of youth gang troubles, worst on the lower east side. "When East Siders were threatened by their kids," she says, they began to work together on community problems.

Ms. Mills calls her lower east side constituents "unsophisticated" in urban organizing. "They're sitting here thinking 'we're all going to have to go.'"

But she sees a new awareness slowly evolving in the neighborhoods her office serves.

"Two years ago, this looked like a war zone," she says. "But there's been a lot of demolition since."

First, she says, she got calls demanding that decayed homes be razed. "Then they called wanting to know why the city didn't cut the weeds. The weeds were cut and they called wanting to know why the city didn't stop garbage dumping on the lots. The garbage got cleaned up and now people are thinking, 'What are they going to do with these lots?'"

Residents of the lower east side are taking increasing advantage of a city program that allows a homeowner to buy a vacant lot next door to his property for about $250, she says.

Barbara Wright, a 31-year-old cafeteria worker at Michigan Bell Telephone, lives with her two children in one of the most depopulated areas of the lower east side.

Her house, south of Jefferson, is the only home on the block. But she bought the lot next door from the city in May 1976.

"So far I haven't done anything with it, even put a fence around it," she says. "It had been vacant quite a while, and some of the people around here were putting junk on it."

Now, she says, she can and has told them to get the junk off the property—her property. She plans to stay in her house.

"Right now, I can't do any better. I'm on a low-paying job. If something turns in my favor, or if someone comes along to buy us up, I would be willing to move. But right now I can afford my mortgage note with what I make," says Mrs. Wright.

CED's Chambers says the city sells up to 25 lots a week citywide to homeowners under the "lot next door" program.

FEDERAL FUNDING WILL
REVIVE EXISTING PROGRAMS

—Increased funding for urban rebuilding programs—something which has already begun under the Carter administration—will be necessary if the city is to tackle the immense program of blight that plagues it.

For nearly five years, after the initiation of revenue sharing formulas by the Nixon administration, federal funds to Detroit for uban renewal programs decreased steadily while the cost of rebuilding rose.

Next year, the federal funding will more than double, from $28 million to $58 million, and to an estimated $65 million by 1980–81.

But CED's Cunningham said most of the new money will be used to revive existing programs that were slowed by the funding lag in recent years.

Even if significant amounts were made available for new programs on the lower east side of the city, he says, it would take several years to select target areas, develop reconstruction priorities that win community approval, and do the actual planning for the renewal.

In the far southeast corner of the lower east side of Detroit—in a neighborhood called Jefferson-Chalmers—a redevelopment program has gone through millions of dollars in seven years and is only just now reaching the point where the first new roads and housing will be built.

Experience in that area, and in post-riot 12th St. and Lafayette Park renewal programs, has shown it takes 10 years from the beginning of a major renewal program before the first tangible results are seen.

NEW STATE LAWS SHOULD HELP

—New state laws giving cities more power in redevelopment programs and speeding up land condemnation could save not only time but millions of dollars. A more liberal condemnation law which allowed the city to condemn land for a private developer who would build something of economic benefit to the city as a whole could attract the private dollars that have been missing from much of the city's efforts to rebuild, Young administration officials believe.

One of the few certainties about any renewal program in Detroit is that it will include only a few, if any, single family homes. Instead, renewal will depend on development of wide areas of townhouses, apartments and condominiums—such as the Elmwood Park Development which has moved eastward from Lafayette Park.

Just last week, Mayor Young revealed that the city lost the chance for a $500 million Ford Motor Co. transmission plant because it could not assemble the necessary 250-acre parcel of land in six to nine months.

Young has said he will lobby for stronger city development and land use powers and also ask the City Council for $10 million to begin a program of landbanking parcels for industrial use.

To condemn land now, the city must declare the land is needed for a public project. It is illegal to condemn land for the private use of any person or group.

What that means is that developers or businesses must wait for the city to acquire land, then propose programs for the land. There is little incentive for the private market to become involved in re-construction programs until the groundwork has all been laid by the city. If the city's vision does not match the developers', it may be too late for him to do anything but take his money elsewhere.

Years will go by before these problems are solved, and years more will pass before anything tangible happens to most of the 9,000 vacant lots on the lower east side of Detroit. By that time, there may be another 9,000 vacant parcels.

Children who now race through the decaying streets after elementary school recesses each day will graduate from high school before Detroit officials can make a major move to rebuild their crumbling neighborhoods.

Barbara Wright will continue to live on an empty block next to a factory and watch her neighborhood disintegrate. Engine blocks and enough other automotive litter to build entire cars will continue to fill some of the vacant lots.

Like an animal herd which has become too big for its range, east side Detroiters will continue to thin their once dense ranks. Fewer and fewer men in their 20s will bend over the hoods of their cars on east side streets on Indian Summer mornings for do-it-yourself repair. Fewer middle-aged women will sit quietly on their east side porches watching the world go by.

Detroit has never had a neighborhood disappear due to natural causes.

People in Detroit neighborhoods in the past have been bought out, scared out, shoved out and pushed around, but they have never just walked out.

Will the land they leave behind become, in 20 years, a monument to the ability of a city to revive itself and face a new century?

Or will it go barren, like poisoned cropland, and become a symbol of a society's inability to cope with what it has made?

APPENDIX B

Detroit . . . a City Being Destroyed

Law and Government Fail Miserably and This Should Worry the Rest of America

William Serrin

DETROIT—I am outraged and so is everyone I know. The city is in desperate condition. It may, in a real sense, be dead—the first dead large city in the nation.

Young black hoodlums control many streets. People are held up. Homes are broken into. People are murdered.

Victims are told if they go to the police they will be killed. Street after street is lined with abandoned, vandalized stores. Houses and buildings have been burned by arsonists. Streets are filled with litter and walls are painted with slogans, obscenities, and the names of gangs, the Black Pillars, the Coney Oneys, the Errol Flynns.

The city and the Detroit schools are broke. Police are laid off and called back with Federal money. First-grade classes will go only half days. Fall athletics are out. Other classes are cut back. Hundreds of good people are putting their homes up for sale. Buyers can't be found, and people take what they can get and leave.

The tragedy is that there are so many good people here. You can drive through the town and see people clipping hedges on hot, treeless streets. Old ladies pull weeds and almost get run down by beer-drinking fools in their big, hot cars. People mow grass while across the street there are empty gray lots, the abandoned houses knocked down, finally, by the Federal government. Law and government policies have miserably failed these people, and the only thing you can do when you see them working on their homes is cry.

This is a city seemingly without law. People can do just about anything they want and not get punished. They throw McDonald's wrappers and beer cans from cars. Police see it and do nothing. People run stop signs. People harrass you. Nothing can be done. The young, black toughs swagger about the city with their Borsalino hats and canes. Sharp dudes. So cool. Black teenagers ran amok at a concert. Young blacks slashed people with knives and stole billfolds. People were beaten. One woman was raped, another molested. The courts considered the hoodlums minors and soon they were out on the streets. Law—society— has broken down, and it will be a long time before the city recovers. I do not think it will.

I know who is guilty, and it is not just the black hoodlums.

Source: This article appeared in the Boston Globe, *August 31, 1976, p. 19. William Serrin describes himself as "a journalist who has been writing about Detroit for eleven years." Reprinted by permission of the* Detroit Free Press, *in which this article first appeared.*

The mayor, Coleman Young, is a sharp talker who uses the street idioms that play well in the paper. He is a man of immense style, with handsomely cut suits, but he thinks more of power than action and likes his comfort. He issues ultimatums to the gangs and the gangs keep acting up. People are afraid to speak out against him because he is a black and vindictive. He goes on vacation.

I watched the Republican convention. The governor, William Milliken, placed President Ford's name in nomination for the Presidency. He suggested Ford is a fine President. I am outraged by the governor's actions. The governor tried to get Republicans to adopt a resolution that the United States needs a Marshall Plan for the cities, but it is the state that is fighting court efforts to make it pay part of the costs of funding the Detroit school integration plan. Milliken is afraid to fight for equal school funding, although he knows this is the fair way to provide for education. The President is from this industrial state. Assumedly he knows the plight people face. He does nothing for Detroit.

The Democratic nominee, Jimmy Carter, has been in Plains, Ga., where expert after expert briefed him on problems that confront this nation. They come to his farm like freshmen rushing a fraternity. "Governor, it is an honor to be here. I should be clear, Mr. Carter, that we have no long-term energy policy. The housing policy, Governor . . . the employment situation . . . the transportation needs . . . Governor, as you can see from these charts. . . ."

How much money must be spent on studies, how many briefings must be made? Carter should come to Detroit and walk Mack Avenue from Woodward Avenue on to the Grosse Pointes. All America's problems are clear on that street. Lawlessness, housing, law enforcement, unemployment, preoccupation with sex and alcohol, drugs, abandonment of buildings and land, and more. This country will solve the problems of Mack Avenue or solve no problems and it should take no briefers from the Brookings Institution to tell Carter that.

But the problem is one of private people, too. The black youths did not learn what they know by themselves. Magazines said that wearing wide-brim hats and carrying canes was black cool. The basketball player, Walt Frazier, who did not sweat, was cool. Frenchy Fuqua, the running back who wore live goldfish in the heels of his shoes, was cool. Black people like Fred Williamson and Jim Brown found they could make a bundle making violent, sex-filled movies. And the young blacks started acting in the fashion of the Hollywood actors and it was no longer acting. It was violence and death on the Detroit East Side.

But if this is, in such a large part, a city without values, then, so, too, is the rest of this country. For the sprawling, dirty, ugly, violent city is nothing if not a metaphor for the rest of America.

Taking the money and running is an old game in this country. It was not invented by the black gangs on the Detroit East Side. Old Henry Ford took his money and ran to Dearborn a long time ago and the big merchants in downtown Detroit have been doing it for years. This is the way this nation was built. This is a country of selfish people seeking money and comfort. That is what is wrong in Detroit and this is what is wrong in this country.

Today, only the small merchants express outrage when the black gangs terrorize downtown. For the rest, the violent actions are only justifications to use when they announce what they decided a long time ago to do, move to the suburbs.

Soon the police will get a hold on the black gangs. Things are bad, so the cops probably will be allowed to bang a few heads. The stories will disappear from the newspapers and magazines. But nothing will change. No matter if the mayor works hard for a while. No matter who is elected this November. Nothing is going to happen in Detroit and cities like it across the nation. Those of us here know it, and that is why we are in such despair.

APPENDIX C

Detroit: That Sinking Feeling

While other cities struggle with unemployment and economic crises, Detroit seems in a desperate class by itself. On top of the familiar catalog of urban problems, the city is experiencing a wave of crime and violence verging on anarchy in the downtown streets. This summer, a succession of assaults, robberies and murders–led principally by rampaging youth gangs–terrorized the city like nothing since the 1967 riots. A remedial curfew imposed on Detroit's teen-agers heightened racial tensions. Meanwhile, the police department itself has been tainted by intimations of scandal involving high-level heroin trafficking –climaxed last week by the apparent suicide of a deputy chief. As a result, nervous citizens are wondering whether the 33-month-old administration of Coleman A. Young, 58, the city's first black mayor, can cope with the city's ills. Newsweek correspondent Jon Lowell has had a close-up view of Motown's misery over the past dozen years. His report:

A car was parked near the city's criminal courts on a recent morning, with a HAPPY BIRTHDAY, AMERICA sticker on its windshield. Someone pegged a rock at it, shattering the windshield and neatly shredding the birthday greeting.

If there can be a single symbol of what is happening to Detroit, that one will do. How else can you begin to describe a disaster the size of the nation's sixth largest city? One out-of-town newspaper even called it a "disease"–but in fairness, Detroit is a victim, not a carrier of the disease. Like so many major American cities, it is past its industrial prime and tumbling quickly downhill. No one looks for a dramatic new expansion of the automobile industry here and the surge in unskilled job opportunities it might bring–or for any miracle infusion of new revenues. At night, the city hollows out: all you can see are the tail lights of the middle class, taking their spending money – and much of the city's tax base–to the suburbs.

Vandalism. The blight left behind adds about 800 abandoned properties a month to a wasteland that already numbers thousands of vacant and vandalized homes. The rest of the economic landscape is equally stark: unemployment among inner-city youth in excess of 50 percent, 4,000 city workers (including hundreds of police) laid off, municipal services reduced to an austere minimum and–in the past few weeks–a United Auto Workers strike making money even scarcer.

But above all, there is Detroit's lawlessness. The city's 1.3 million people are as inured to the common run of city crime as any other urbanites. But this summer it turned epidemic, spilling over into some of the best downtown streets and even the freeways. Roving bands of teen-agers assaulted stalled motorists and robbed passengers on a bus. The director of the city's neighborhood legal services had his leg broken by an auto thief who ran him over with his own car.

In August, a group of black youths went on a violent rampage, harassing, robbing and bloodying patrons at a Cobo Hall rock concert (*Newsweek,* Aug. 30). Public outrage hit a peak shortly afterwards when a well-known priest was murdered during a robbery in his rectory. Mayor Young risked his solid standing with civil libertarians to tell citizens in a special television address: "I will not permit anyone, young or old, black or white, to take our city over because they can't find a job, or didn't finish school, or can't find a park to play in . . . We will stand for it no longer." Under intense pressure to halt the violence in the streets, Mayor Young recalled 450 laid-off cops and ordered a 10 p.m. curfew on youths under 18. But in a city where the black poor appear to be a majority, and the police force is still 78 percent white, the aggressively enforced curfew was racial tinder.

In the opening days, police convoys swept up young violators by the dozens, some of them repeatedly. One night as I watched, a police car caught up with three black teen-agers scuttling down a side street. "How come you're hassling us?" one of the three demanded. "Because after 10, the streets belong to us," police officer Fred Bullis answered with a tight grin. Two of the trio were promptly released, but the third, a suspected gang member, was hauled to the station house for a $50 curfew violation ticket. The mass arrests brought a sharp protest from rights groups and another smudge on Detroit's sooty national image.

Raided.   The police, lately, have come under still another cloud. Amid rumors of a narcotics scandal two weeks ago, the Federal Drug Enforcement Administration—assisted by Detroit police chief Philip G. Tannian—raided the home of executive deputy chief Frank Blount, the department's No. 2 man. The investigators carted off files without, apparently, finding any of the drug paraphernalia cited in their search warrant. Mayor Young, furious at not being informed in advance of the raid, fired Tannian last week and replaced him with police veteran William L. Hart—who became the first black to head the department. A day later, another top-ranking police official was found shot to death in his home. It was an apparent suicide, and it may or may not have been connected to the drug investigation.

While the appointment of Hart no doubt strengthened Young's support among blacks, it scarcely improved his standing with the white power groups who have never fully trusted him. Almost from the time he took office, the gray-haired Young has been a focal point of the city's crisis. He is thought by many whites to run the city in an offhand way and his style has a "cool" that some whites take for arrogance.

'Recycling.'   But Young's worst problems are not of his own making. When he took over city hall after lengthy service as one of the more left-of-center members of the state senate's Democratic caucus, he inherited a city already suffering from the steady erosion of its tax base. Then came the economic downturn of 1974–75, which put Detroit into its worst tailspin since 1932—with auto industry unemployment topping 30 percent. In the midst of all this, his administration was drawing up a blueprint for "recycling" the city—a document spelling out Detroit's problems and needs that he served on the White House with a burst of fanfare in April 1975.

The blueprint was bluntly eloquent in detailing the city's crisis in housing, industry, jobs and law enforcement. But probably its most impressive statistic was the cost of renewal—an estimated $2 billion—and so

far, the Ford Administration has responded with words of sympathy and praise, but no cash. The magnitude of the city's needs spurred Young's early-on endorsement of Jimmy Carter. "The train's pulling out, and we're going to be on it," he told his liberal supporters who were reluctant to go for Carter. He was hoping, of course, that a Carter victory would mean a new era of goodwill, and Federal largesse, for the cities.

Meanwhile, Detroit's surprising number of loyal boosters, black and white, complain that the press exaggerates the city's troubles. "Christ, this isn't Abilene, Kansas, in 1880—it isn't that bad," says Walter M. McMurtry, Jr., president of Detroit's Inner City Business Improvement Forum. By next spring, the city may have something it can point to with deserved pride: the $337 million Renaissance Center of offices, shops and restaurants. It is the largest private development in U.S. history, featuring a spectacular 70-story John Portman hotel. And city leaders hope a restored trolley line downtown will help attract out-of-town visitors and conventioneers.

Change.   But Detroit's endemic problems are staggering, decaying schools, housing and transportation, armies of unemployed, and (according to the Detroit *Free Press*) the highest per capita rate of violent crime among 35 major American cities. Even such local free-enterprise champions as General Motors, Ford and Chrysler say a renaissance is beyond the capacity of private capital. Like most cities past their prime, Detroit has to change its economic base or perish. "We have to make the conversion from industrial to commercial and financial," says Deputy Mayor William Beckham, Jr. In the meantime, he suggests, the nation's major cities have already become the wards of the Federal government—welfare clients unable to help themselves. And barring Federal help, the question is whether Coleman Young, or any other big-town mayor, can reverse this disastrous downward spiral.

APPENDIX D

The Positive Side of Detroit's Situation

Detroit is a paradox. In order to understand the condition of the city, both sides of the paradox must be explored.

One side of the paradox is growth and development: Renaissance Center; the Civic Center Plaza; plans for a riverfront arena; plans for a massive public works program and a rapid transit system; the establishment of the Downtown Development Authority and the Economic Growth Council; active community organizations; strong and dedicated leadership; the Medical Center Complex; viable, expanding universities; the Art and Historical Museums and the Detroit Symphony; one of the finest Libraries in the world; a huge apartment complex planned for the riverfront, the Woodward Mall project; Elmwood, III. The litany could go on and on.

The other side of the paradox is decline and decay: declining population, the exodus of industrial and retail activity, blighted commercial streets and neighborhoods, high crime rates, increasing fire incidence, increasing welfare.

To view only the negative side of the paradox is to fail to see Detroit's future. Both sides must be examined. We must not minimize our very real problems, but they must be seen in perspective. If action is taken now, we are at the threshold of making Detroit a great city of the future—the not-too-distant future.

This City is a great City. It is great because of its people—strong workers, active citizens, concerned parents. It is great because of its traditions—this is the automobile capital of the world, the arsenal of democracy. It is great because of its cultural institutions—the Art Museum, three Historical Museums, the Zoological Park, the Detroit Symphony. It is great because of its ethnic diversity—riverfront festivals, restaurants, and churches reflecting dozens of nationalities and heritages.

Detroit is a huge, throbbing, vibrant city. Downtown is being reborn—Renaissance Center, the Plaza and Dodge Fountain, the Arena, and a huge apart-ment complex on the river. Some neighborhoods are shaking off their age and decay—Virginia Park, University City #2, and Jefferson-Chalmers. Commercial areas are stepping out of yesterday and into tomorrow —Washington Boulevard, Woodward Avenue, Chinatown, and Greektown. Belle Isle, gleaming in a clean Detroit River, is showing off the effects of a $10 million improvement program. Soon there will be linked parks on the riverfront, and a new Science Center.

* * *

The attraction and retention of middle income groups has begun. Right now, the potential home buyer can find more house for the money in Detroit than anywhere else. Community groups in areas like Indian Village work hard to maintain the quality of life in their neighborhoods. Old "Black Bottom" has been transformed into a modern housing complex for mixed-income residents. A huge apartment complex planned for the riverfront will represent an additional major boost for the downtown area.

Industry has begun to demonstrate its faith in Detroit. Many, many firms have invested substantially in the future. Renaissance Center is the most dramatic affirmation of faith in a city anywhere, but lesser examples are legend.

* * *

This City is at the turning point. There is abundant promise in Detroit. We have the potential for growth and development and economic vitality, and the mechanisms to grasp that dream. But, it takes money, massive amounts of money.

The revenues we can generate from existing sources are not sufficient. We cannot cross the threshold into a brighter tomorrow until we can control the problems of today. Detroit has major problems. We must recognize those problems and find the revenues necessary to deal with them.

Source: City of Detroit, Budget Department, Detroit Financial Projections *1977–1982, December 27, 1976, pp. 22, 26.*

REFERENCES

1. City of Detroit, Budget Department, *Detroit Financial Projections 1977-1982,* December 27, 1976, p. 1.
2. "Detroit Banks Buy Some City Notes, Urge Action in Fiscal Crisis," *Wall Street Journal,* March 25, 1976, p. 25.
3. Ellen Grzech, "City Going Ahead with 1188 Layoffs; Rehiring Uncertain," *Detroit Free Press,* April 2, 1976, pp. 2A, 12A.
4. City of Detroit, Mayor's Task Force on City Finances, "Report," February 24, 1976, p. 1.
5. *Ward's Automotive Yearbook,* 1976, pp. 90-91; 1975, pp. 91-92; Michigan State University, Graduate School of Business Administration, *Michigan Statistical Abstract,* 1974, p. 402.
6. This section draws heavily on Constantinos A. Doxiadis *et al., Emergence and Growth of an Urban Region: The Developing Urban Detroit Area* (The Detroit Edison Company, 1970), vol. 3, pp. 129-144.
7. This section draws heavily on Doxiadis *et al.,* pp. 144-160.
8. *Detroit Financial Projections 1977-1982,* p. 36.
9. *Ibid.*
10. *Ibid.,* p. 29.
11. *Ibid.,* p. 35.
12. *Ibid.,* p. 34.
13. Cf. *New York Times,* August 17, 1976, pp. 1, 13; August 18, 1976, pp. 1, 16; *Boston Globe,* August 26, 1976, p. 16.
14. Neal R. Peirce, *The Megastates of America* (New York: W. W. Norton & Company, Inc., 1972), p. 433.
15. *Detroit Free Press,* October 3, 1976, p. 16A.
16. *Detroit Financial Projections 1977-1982,* p. 23.
17. This section draws heavily on Peirce, chapter 7, and on Michael Barone *et al., The Almanac of American Politics 1978* (New York: E. P. Dutton, 1977), pp. 397-401.
18. Peirce, p. 407.
19. *Ibid.,* pp. 411-412.
20. Godfrey Hodgson, *America In Our Time* (New York: Doubleday, 1976), p. 436.
21. *Ibid.*
22. Peirce, p. 413.

EXHIBIT 7.1:   Metropolitan Detroit and Surrounding Area

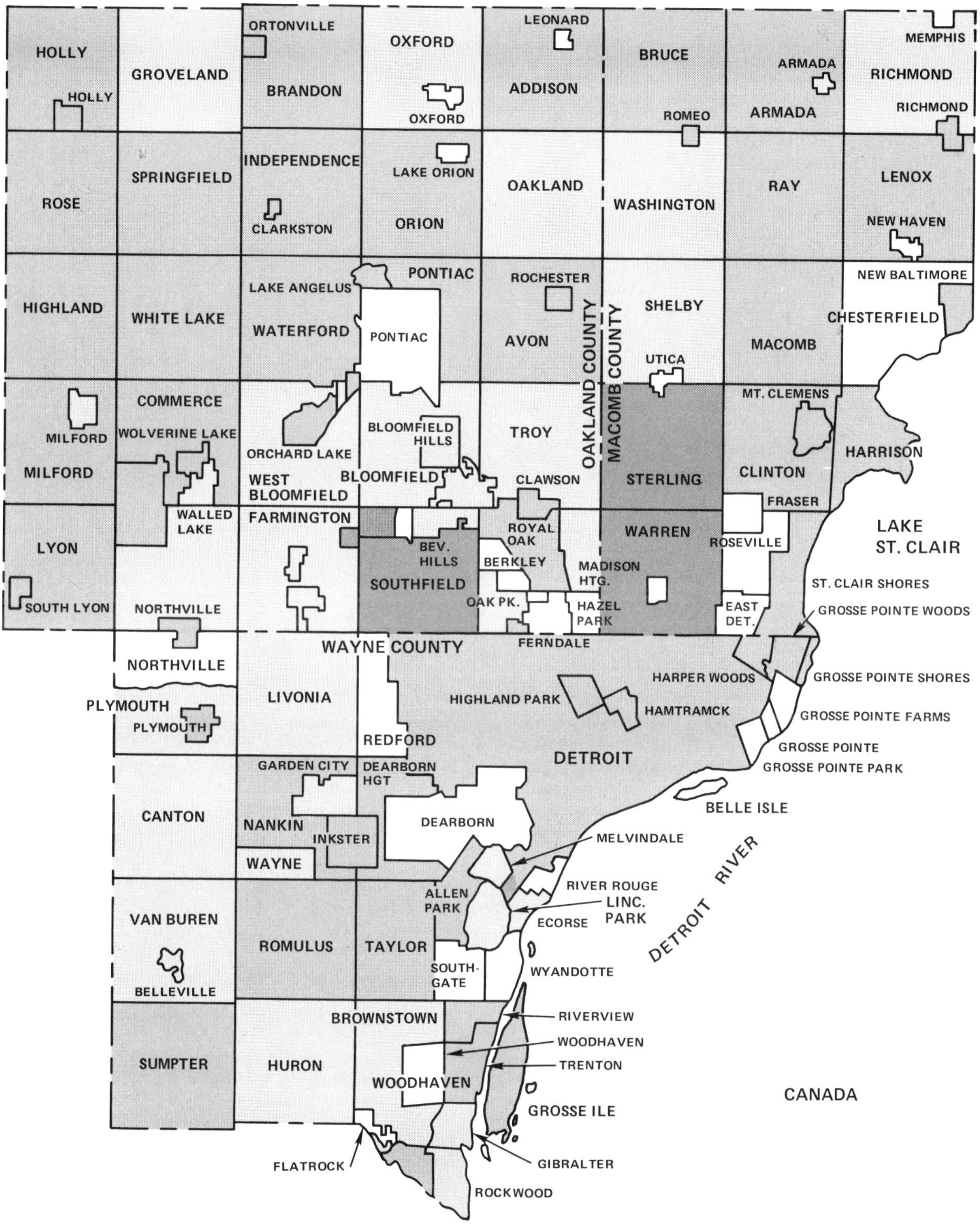

8

The Detroit
Fiscal Crisis (B)

In the mid-1970s, the city of Detroit faced fiscal problems of major proportions. For FY 1975-76, the city contemplated a total budget deficit in the amount of $43,300,000; and, assuming no significant changes in the then prevailing pattern of revenues and expenditures, the city projected that this deficit would grow to over half a billion dollars (almost half the projected city budget) by FY 1981-82. Long before that point, however, the city would have had to all but eliminate most city services or to declare bankruptcy, since the city charter requires the budget to be balanced, with projected revenues equal to projected expenditures.*

As of 1975-76, the city had already taken some steps toward a balanced budget, cutting net appropriations by $2.4 million (7-9% in real dollars) from 1974-75 to 1975-76; but such steps were clearly inadequate to forestall the disaster looming on the fiscal horizon.

As Mayor Coleman Young and the rest of the city administration saw the situation midway through the 1976-77 fiscal year, new revenue sources would have to be found and/or drastic service cuts instituted to save Detroit from the sort of near-bankruptcy that struck New York City in 1975. To add to the pressures, all of the major municipal union contracts were

---

*Actual revenues may differ from actual expenditures over the course of the fiscal year, resulting in a surplus or deficit; but to prevent the accumulation of past deficits, the charter requires that any deficit from the past fiscal year be fully included in the balanced budget submitted in the next fiscal year. This divergence between theoretical and actual budget balance allowed the city to maintain expenditures in years when economic conditions caused temporary and unprojected declines in revenues. It also led to occasions when the budget was technically in balance even when the city intended to

deficit spend if necessary. For instance, in the three fiscal years from 1958-59 to 1960-61, the budget failed to fund a portion of pension liabilities even though such funding was legally mandatory, and a large deficit was accumulated as a result. In fiscal 1975-76, to prevent even deeper cuts than took place and to make the point that the city should receive more revenue from the suburbs, the budget contained a $14 million revenue item from an increase in the city income tax on non-residents from ½% to 1%; the increase was never actually approved.

up for renegotiation in 1977, and pressure for wage and benefit increases could be expected. Finally, 1977 was an election year for the mayor and city council, and any substantial service cuts or tax hikes would not enhance their prospects for reelection.

BACKGROUND: EXPENDITURE/REVENUE TRENDS THROUGH 1976

Expenditures

During the debate over New York City's financial problems in 1975, many people argued that New York opened the doors to financial collapse because it attempted to do too many things for too many people, providing "frills" that the city could not afford, such as generous welfare benefits and a free city university. Similar arguments have been put forward to explain Detroit's fiscal distress, but with much less force: Detroit in fact provides a much lower aggregate level of services than do cities like New York. In part, the fact that Detroit is relatively small has lightened its load: Wayne County, not Detroit alone, pays for nearly all of the local share of welfare costs,* and the Wayne County property tax base includes some more well-to-do areas that have benefitted from suburban growth. New York City, on the other hand, is large enough to encompass five counties, so that it has no county government to fall back on. Also, Detroit turned the operation of Wayne State University over to the state in the late 1950s. (Before that time, it was—next to City College of New York—the largest municipal university in the country.) By a fortunate accident of timing (Detroit was having its first brush with financial trouble at the same time that the state wanted another university because of the Sputnik "technology gap" concern), Detroit was spared the problems of New York in the area of higher education.

Even after considering these differences, Detroit still maintained only a moderate level of city services before the recent recession. A 1974 survey of local government employment in the nation's 24 largest cities showed Detroit ranked sixteenth in number of local government employees per 10,000 residents and eighteenth in number of employees per 10,000 providing "basic city services"[1] (including fire fight-

ing, health, recreational and cultural activities—e.g., the art museum—and park maintenance).

Detroit has generally not gone into major debt to finance its services. Since the city charter requires that operating deficits be financed in the following year's budget and that budgets be at least technically in balance when enacted, it cannot go into debt beyond one or two years to finance current operations.

> In the fiscal year 1973–74, Detroit borrowed $42.7 million while paying $40.2 million on its capital and operating debts, for new borrowing of $2.5 million more than it repaid. In contrast, New York City in the same fiscal year borrowed $2,558 million and repaid $318 million for a net borrowing of $1,745 million.[2]

Despite Detroit's relative restraint in the provision of services, the city's expenditures have mounted alarmingly over the past several years. From 1962 through 1976 Detroit's net appropriations**—the amount of general revenue needed to finance city services—grew from about $191 million to over $465 million, or a growth of about 44% (about 35% in constant dollars adjusted according to the Detroit Consumer Price Index). Total appropriations for the city (which include both appropriations for capital projects and appropriations for revenue-generating city services), grew somewhat more slowly, but still substantially: from $296 million in 1962 to $666 million in 1976. (The amount the city spent on capital improvements decreased over this period by over 40% in constant dollars.)

Exhibit 8.1, which presents appropriations in recent years for all city departments spending more than 1% of non-capital appropriations, breaks down the areas of growth. As is apparent from the exhibit, appropriations for the police and fire departments rose rapidly both in absolute terms and as a percentage of the budget, particularly from 1969–70 to 1974–75. Non-capital appropriations for health and hospitals were roughly constant as a share of the budget, but net appropriations rose sharply in the early 1970s as state and county aid ear-marked for health was cut back and as medical costs rose faster

---

*The city of Detroit must pay approximately $3 million per year to Wayne County for welfare services. Detroit operated its own Welfare Department until 1965, when state legislation merged it with the county department.

**Throughout this case, appropriations will be used as a measure of city expenditures since final expenditure data is not available in great detail.

than reimbursement for patient care. Appropriations for sanitation dropped as a share of the total throughout the period, more because of attempts to increase productivity and because of lay-offs and subsequent rehirings under EEA and CETA (both federal employment programs) than because of services cuts. Public lighting appropriations followed the trend in energy prices, rising sharply with the oil embargo in fiscal 1973–74 and continuing at high levels thereafter. Higher charges for electric power sold to other governments after 1973–74 reduced net lighting appropriations from their peak percentages, although the department's share remained above pre-embargo levels. Overhead agencies such as the Budget and Finance Departments and the recreation and cultural departments saw their budget shares and real appropriations diminish generally over the entire period.

From 1971 to 1976, personnel costs (wages and fringe benefits) averaged about four-fifths of all non-capital appropriations. Since these costs comprise such a large share of the city's expenditures, and since the growth of these costs closely parallels the growth of municipal unions in the city, it is worth taking a brief look at the impact of the unions on wages and fringe benefits for city employees.

Before 1967, the only relatively large unions in Detroit were the Detroit Police Officers Association (DPOA), the Firefighters Union, and District 77 of the American Federation of State, County and Municipal Employees (AFSCME). Another dozen or two small labor organizations struggled along, but even the strongest unions at that time were hampered by small memberships, lack of exclusive representation, no grievance procedures (except for the individual appeal procedures under Civil Service regulations), and lack of funds.

Following the adoption of legislation by the state of Michigan giving unions the right to organize and negotiate contracts with local governments as the exclusive representatives of their bargaining units, municipal unions became influential in Detroit. The new law allowed for exclusive representation after elections, and the first contracts set up a grievance procedure and provided for a check-off of union dues, giving labor unions both more power and more

funds to carry out their programs.* The success of collective bargaining wage increases also caused employees not under AFSCME to join smaller unions (often representing only a single small group, such as the Governmental Analysts and Accountants Association with less than 100 members), so that by 1976–77 the city had to bargain with over 40 unions.

Since the institution of collective bargaining in 1967, the wages of municipal employees have risen rapidly. Comparing Detroit to eleven other large cities in 1970, the Bureau of Labor Statistics (BLS) found that wages in Detroit were high relative to wages in other large cities across the country, particularly for clerical employees.[3] Out of 12 clerical positions, for example, Detroit had higher wages than the other cities nine times and had the second-highest wage levels for the other three positions.) Comparing Detroit wages to a similar BLS study five years later, one finds a similar pattern with very high clerical wages in Detroit and wages above the average but not as high in other positions. Somewhat the same picture emerges when Detroit is compared to other cities in Michigan. The Citizens Research Council of Michigan compared City of Detroit salaries on January 1, 1976 with salaries of other Michigan municipalities, the State of Michigan, Wayne County, and private firms in the Detroit area. The study found that Detroit rates were higher than state of Michigan rates in all 16 categories. City salaries were found to range from 4% to 13% higher than the average of 15 Michigan municipalities for four positions, with the highest relative salaries in clerical positions. However, salaries were shown to be generally comparable to those paid by large firms in the Detroit area (firms that have—like the city—strong unions), though much higher than those of all firms.

In the area of fringe benefits, the city's policies appear to be generally comparable to those of other large cities. Vacation and sick leave policies for civilian, police, and fire employees were at roughly the median

---

*The city also agreed to the "agency shop," which provides that employees represented by AFSCME must either join the union, or pay "service fees" equal to membership dues (theoretically justified because the unions have the responsibility to represent all employees in their bargaining unit in the grievance and wage negotiation procedures, not just their members, under the law), or lose their jobs. However, as of 1977, litigation by a right-to-work organization has held up the institution of the "agency shop" for over five years.

of ten of the largest American cities, while the health insurance plan was slightly more generous than that of most cities. Also, Detroit's pension plans were somewhat more generous than other municipal plans for most categories of employees, and were considerably more generous for police and firemen. Until 1968, all employees hired in the Police and Fire Departments had the right to retire at half-pay, with pensions increasing in direct proportion to the wages of active employees. Thus, every time employees receive wage increases, retirees' pensions would go up by the same percentage. (Only one other city of the ten surveyed had this provision.) The city government realized that this provision was severely hindering the city's efforts to cope with its first brush with fiscal troubles in 1967 and 1968 and succeeded—against the opposition of the unions—in changing the city charter to provide for pensions.

Under the new system, pensions will only be raised 2% per year once new employees retire, saving the city an amount estimated at several hundred thousand dollars in the first year of the program and rising into the millions as the number of employees covered by the old pension plan decreases. (While savings are greatest in later years, immediate savings result because Detroit has a fully funded pension system. The city could therefore put away less money per employee for new employees' pensions than for those under the old system, starting with the first day in 1969 that employees covered by the new system were hired.) Thus, while the impact of the old pension plan would be felt for many years (employees will not be eligible to retire under the new plan until 1994), steps had been taken as of the late 1960s to lessen its burden on city finances.

Revenues

Revenues to finance the city's expenditures may be divided into six major categories: taxes, state aid, federal aid, user charges for services, miscellaneous revenues (licenses, fees, fines, charges to other governments for services, etc.), and revenue from bond and note sales. In the 1976-77 fiscal year, taxes were expected to finance about three-eighths of expenditures, state and federal aid about a sixth each, with about 30% coming from user charges and miscellaneous revenues. Bond sales, which finance only long-term capital improvements, averaged from $20 million to $35 million per year over the ten years from 1965-66 to 1975-76 or 3% to 5% of total revenues; note sales are used only to bridge seasonal gaps between expenditures (which occur all year round) and revenues (which are heavily concentrated when property taxes are due), and notes are repaid in the same year that they are issued. (See Exhibit 8.2 for a breakdown of FY 1976-77 revenues.) Because taxes constitute the largest single source of revenue for the city, and because this is the revenue source over which the city exercises the most independent control, the various components of the tax revenue are examined in somewhat more detail below.

Property Taxes.   Detroit's property tax rate appeared to be relatively stable, increasing from about 24-25 mills (dollars per thousand) in the 1970s.* However, the assessment practices were changed in the mid-1960s by increasing assessments to a level equal to State Equalized Valuation (SEV) or 50% of market value, from approximately 42% of market value, causing millage in terms of SEV to rise about 40% from 1962 to 1975. Despite this increase, Detroit's tax revenues failed to keep pace with inflation in the early 1970s. As Exhibit 8.3 indicates, budgeted tax revenues in 1976-77 were in real terms more than 50% above 1961-62 levels; but after 1970-71, total tax revenues dropped 11% in terms of the Consumer Price Index and 23% in terms of the Wholesale Price Index with the sharpest decline coinciding with the recession of 1974-75.

The main cause of this real decline in city revenues was the erosion of the property tax base, as documented by a 1977 study of the property tax base per capita in Detroit and in the rest of the SMSA. In 1962, the tax base per capita for Detroit was $3,156, above the SMSA median. By 1970, it had increased only 11.12% in current dollars to $3,507 (this small

---

*The city could not further increase property taxes because the Detroit City Charter limited municipal property taxes for general non-school purposes to 20 mills; additional taxes above this general constitutional limit were levied for special purposes such as library operations and debt service (repayment of bonds). The limit forced the city to seek new revenue through income and excise taxes as early as 1969-70, even though the full 20 mills for general non-school purposes was not levied until 1972-73. (An increase in property taxes from the 17.023 mills levied in 1969-70 to 20 mills would have only raised $16.6 million in new revenue, compared to the approximately $35-40 million raised by the income tax increase that year.)

increase largely resulted from the 150,000 decrease in city population during the 1960s), below the 25th percentile of the communities examined. In constant dollars, the tax base declined by 16.09%. (A decline in the real per capita tax base occurred in only seven of the other 50 communities: four very old industrial suburbs with the same problems as Detroit and three more prosperous newer suburbs.) Over the 15-year period from 1962-1977, the tax base declined by more than 40% in real terms.

Several factors caused the Detroit tax base to decline relative to that of the suburbs. First, assessments for personal (largely business) property in the city declined substantially in real terms over the 15 years from 1962-63 to 1976-77. During this period, personal property values increased only 5% in current dollars, declining 42-44% in real terms. Declines in the personal property portion of the city's tax base were greatest in the 1970s, reflecting the poor business conditions that created a 20% loss of jobs in the city from 1969 to 1973.

During this same period, however, the total assessed value of real estate in the city declined even more sharply, largely as a result of increases in the amount of tax-exempt property in the city. From 1962 to 1977, relative to suburban municipalities, the City of Detroit has large amounts of tax-exempt property (broken down to type in Exhibit 8.4). Exempt acreage for railroad property (particularly the 600 acres taken up by freight yards), private schools, state and federal facilities, hospitals, and even some city facilities (such as the Art Institute and Belle Isle Park) provided benefits to people living in the entire metropolitan area, and, at least partly in consequence, the proportion of these types of tax-exempt property was much lower in suburban areas. (A 1966 study estimated that suburbanites received annual benefits ranging from three to ten cents per capita from the tax exemption of Wayne State University, and that three of six suburbs studied benefitted from the tax exemption of Detroit hospitals.[4])

The expressway system, however, constitutes the greatest loss in tax base and also probably the greatest benefit to suburban residents. (The same 1966 study suggested that residents of six Detroit suburbs received per capita annual benefits ranging from 32 cents to $2.01 through not having to compensate Detroit in proportion to their freeway use for the loss of tax base from building limited-access highways.[5]) To build these expressways, 3,215 acres of taxable property were taken in the 15 years from 1956 to 1971, most in the early to middle 1960s, although additional construction has occurred since then. Two rough estimates of the impact of freeway construction on the city's tax base can be computed from different sets of data released by the City Assessor's Office. In 1971, the office noted, the total cost of land acquisition for freeways over the previous 15 years was $219 million. Assuming that the value of the property had not increased at all from its acquisition date to 1971, under assessment practices prevailing in 1971 the assessed value of the tax base was decreased by $83.2 million. With a 28 mill city tax rate, this estimate suggested a $2.3 million annual tax loss.[6]

A more refined assessment suggests that the loss was even greater. Of the 3,215 acres, 2,397 would not have been covered with city streets, if the proportion of streets on land acquired for freeways was the same as throughout the rest of the city. With a real estate tax base of about $4.2 billion in 1976–77, the tax base per acre of non-street property was approximately $63,000. If the freeways had the same proportion of tax-exempt property as the remainder of the city and the same average assessed value per acre, the decrease in tax base comes to $151 million and in taxes (at 28 mills) to $4.23 million.

In addition to the direct effects of destruction of tax base, freeway construction reduced the Detroit property tax base indirectly, by creating blighted zones within the city and by encouraging suburban migration. (The suburbs which experienced the most rapid growth in the 1960s and 1970s were those which relied most heavily on freeways, namely those located over fifteen miles from downtown and on or near expressways.) The decline of personal property values, freeway construction, suburban migration, all contributed significantly to the erosion of the city's tax base, but the major contribution to the decline in property values came from a federal home ownership program that left 10% of the city's housing abandoned and in the tax-exempt hands of the Department of Housing and Urban Development.

In the late 1960s, President Johnson proposed and Congress passed a home-ownership subsidy program, administered by the Federal Housing Authority (FHA) and the Department of Housing and Urban Development (HUD) to allow low-income people to buy houses. The program had a greater impact in Detroit than in any other city because Detroit had a smaller proportion of apartment buildings than most cities and a strong tradition of home ownership. (Detroit had the highest home ownership rate of any major American city.)

Before a house could be sold to someone under the program, FHA inspectors had to appraise it and also certify that it met building code standards. However, some real estate brokers bought substandard houses cheaply, made minor "cosmetic" repairs, and resold the houses at much higher prices, allegedly bribing appraisers. (Several dozen real estate brokers and HUD employees were eventually indicted and many convicted.) Poor people moved into the houses and were able to afford the payments, in spite of inflated prices, because of government subsidies. However, when major repairs became necessary because houses were not in as good condition as buyers had expected, many buyers—unable to afford the repairs—simply defaulted and moved out.

There are various other explanations for the high default rate. But the Mortgage Bankers Association of Michigan, for example, suggested that real estate speculators overpriced homes by 50% or more, so that savings from federal mortgage financing were not passed along to buyers. The Detroit Director of HUD, William Whitbeck, argued that high prices resulted more from FHA inexperience in central cities than from corruption. "The FHA mistakenly appraised old houses in the city core at the values of houses in better neighborhoods toward the city fringes." Whitbeck also observed that many of the "beneficiaries" of the program could not really afford home ownership even with federal subsidies:

> In 1970, the auto industry went into a slump and thousands of hard core unemployed who had been fired were laid off and many were never rehired.

Mr. Whitbeck maintains that "this was the main reason for the abandonment—the drying up of incomes—rather than the actions of real estate speculators."[7] William Knapp of the Assessors' Office of the City Finance Department agreed that people who purchased homes were not able to afford maintenance and were not experienced in home ownership. He also commented that the low down payments caused people to act as if they were renting rather than building up equity in a home, so that they would simply leave

if faced with major repairs. In testimony before a House subcommittee in 1972, then-Mayor Roman Gribbs argued that both fraud and inadequate income caused the massive abandonment. He claimed that HUD neither took actions to prevent fraud, nor informed subsidy recipients of the true costs of owning and maintaining a home, nor provided counseling and assistance.[8]

Whatever the reasons, by mid-1972, HUD was a major landowner in Detroit, holding 8,500 homes with more than 15,000 others under foreclosure proceedings. (In contrast, HUD owned in 1972 only 830 houses in Chicago and 1,700 in Philadelphia, both cities larger than Detroit.) In the end, approximately 30,000 pieces of property passed through HUD ownership, and in 1976, HUD still owned 8,000 to 10,000 substandard homes and 6,000 to 8,000 vacant lots where buildings had been razed. HUD attempted to deal with the problem by boarding up abandoned houses, destroying the most hazardous ones, selling vacant lots to neighbors at low prices, and attempting either to sell some houses to people who would be able to rehabilitate them or to rehabilitate and sell them itself. But these demolition and resale efforts went slowly and did not erase the program's negative impact on Detroit's tax base. Thirty thousand homes, worth $10,000 apiece and assessed at half their market value as required, would have added $150 million to the tax base. Had the program never been instituted, most of the $150 million in taxable property might have remained standing. Even more important than this direct loss of property value was the impact of vacant houses on neighborhood property values. As William Whitbeck of HUD put it, "One abandoned home on a block can do it. It just blows a hole in the block." Abandoned houses, stripped of their fixtures by thieves, addicts, and vandals, served as breeding grounds for crime; and children, vandals, and addicts "cooking" heroin in these houses increased the risks of fire.[9] William Knapp of the City Assessors' Office suggests that the effects of the HUD program were the major cause of the 5% annual decline in residential property values (in current dollars) that was recorded during the early 1970s. Moreover, beginning in 1973–74, HUD began to deed these abandoned or vacant properties to the city; since HUD had made payments in lieu of taxes, these transfers of title further reduced city revenues without enhancing the tax base.

The City Income Tax. Detroit levied a proportional income tax, first enacted in 1962 as a 1% tax on all income over an exemption level of $600 per person for both residents of Detroit and non-residents working in Detroit, but the non-resident tax rate was lowered to ½% by the state legislature effective in January 1965.* In October 1969, the legislature approved a raise in the rate to 2% for Detroit residents, but the rate remained at ½% for non-residents working in Detroit.

This differential tax treatment of residents and non-residents was a major point of contention between the city government and suburban interests in the legislature. In a November 1976 newspaper interview, Detroit Mayor Coleman Young reiterated something he had been saying for several years:

> We are the only state in the union that is required by state law to have a smaller assessment on non-residents than residents. That shows right now as one-half percent on non-residents and two on residents.
>
> If we could just bring non-residents up to the same two percent as residents, we would realize $42 million. That . . . would go a long way to help us balance our budget.[10]

Reflecting the mayor's position, the Budget Department's 1977–1982 revenue and expenditure forecast also emphasized the unfairness of the tax differential.

It is a fact that only a little over *one percent* of Detroit's budget is supported by non-resident income taxes. . . . It is only fair that those who work in the City and use its services, but live outside the City, thereby avoiding their fair share of costs of services should pay an equitable tax on the money they earn here. A tax rate that would be fair to residents and non-residents, as well as providing increased revenues for the City, would be one that charges residents and non-residents equally.[11]

If one corrects for the 1969 change in tax rates (and assumes constant rates), income tax revenues have not decreased in real terms nearly as much as property tax revenues, declining by approximately 2% to 4% from 1962–63 to 1966–67 and remaining constant from 1967–68 to 1971–72. They only began their steep decline with the combination of 12% inflation and economic recession in the auto industry in 1974, falling 12% in real terms from 1974–75 to 1975–76, and falling $6 million even before considering inflation.

Income in Detroit is much more volatile than in the Detroit suburbs or in the nation as a whole, because of the cyclical nature of the automobile industry. Unemployment in Detroit is consistently higher than in Michigan, and Michigan unemployment has been consistently higher than national unemployment; but, more importantly for the volatility of income tax collections, Detroit unemployment has been more variable. From the 1967 boom to the recession of 1970–71, unemployment rose by 4½% in Detroit, compared to 2% nationally. It fell approximately 2½% in Detroit from 1971–73, while national unemployment dropped less than 1%. The automobile-based 1974–76 recession had an even greater impact on Detroit incomes. Unemployment in Detroit rose from an average of about 8½% in 1973 to an average of nearly 18% in 1975 (peaking at 23%), while national unemployment rose from about 6% to the 9% range. High unemployment sharply reduced income tax collections even though workers were not losing much income (as is true in the auto industry with its supplemental unemployment benefit formula guaranteeing 95% of base take-home pay), because unemployment compensation benefits were not taxable. The cyclical nature of the local economy, combined with incentives to leave the city in good economic times, has caused income tax collections to lag.

---

*The imposition of suburban municipal income taxes was largely responsible for this change. In 1962, Detroit levied the only income tax in the state, but by 1965, some suburban residents working in Detroit were paying 1% to Detroit and 1% to the municipality where they lived. Over the opposition of the city government, but with strong suburban support, the state legislature passed a uniform municipal income tax law providing that people would pay 1% if they lived and worked in the same municipality or if they lived in a municipality with a local income tax and worked in one without a tax. However, people working in a municipality but resident elsewhere would only pay ½% to the city where they worked. Then, if their home municipality levied an income tax, it would be reduced from 1% to ½% for these people.

The Young administration suggested that increasing the non-resident income tax would have an effect on both the volatility problem and on incentives to leave the city. The Budget Department commented:

> The Municipal Income Tax is the second largest revenue item in the Budget. It serves to magnify the economic conditions in the City: when employment is high, tax collections are high, but when unemployment is high, tax collections drop dramatically. The volatility in the collection pattern is enhanced because of taxing rates on non-residents, who tend to be *less* affected by the business cycle.[12]

The report adds that lower taxes on non-residents "encourages the more affluent to leave the City."[13]

Several proposals have been made—increasingly frequently since Mayor Young took office—to increase the non-resident tax. In fiscal year 1975–76, the city budget included $14 million in prospective revenue from increasing the non-resident tax from ½% to 1%, but the proposal to increase Detroit's non-resident tax to restore the two-to-one tax ratio never even got out of committee in the state legislature. The 1977–1982 long-term budget projections asked for an increase in the city's taxing authority to allow a 3% tax on residents and a 1½% tax on non-residents, again restoring the two-to-one ratio, as a compromise if the legislature would not agree to raise the non-resident tax to equal the resident income tax.[14]

Utility Excise Tax. A 5% excise tax on utility bills "for public safety purposes"* became effective on October 1, 1970. Revenue from this tax decreased rapidly in real terms from 1970 to 1973 but began to increase after the "energy crisis," since energy prices were rising faster than the general price level. A utility excise tax is theoretically very income inelastic, as consumption of heat, electricity, and telephone service rises much more slowly than income rises. Thus, one would expect this tax to be less sensitive to change in income than either the average property tax or the personal income tax. Its strong performance as a revenue source in the Detroit budget resulted not from its lack of volatility in comparison to income (which caused it to decrease in real terms when prices were constant in the early 1970s), but because the price of energy was rising faster than that of other commodities, and the demand for energy remained fairly insensitive to price.

THE DIMENSIONS OF THE CRISIS

Exhibit 8.5 shows the surplus or deficit in the general fund for each fiscal year from 1961–62 through 1981–82. (The last six years are projections made as of January 1, 1976 by the city's Budget Department and assume no significant changes in the then-prevailing expenditure or revenue patterns.) Exhibit 8.6 outlines the expected changes in the various budget components that would contribute to the steadily increasing deficit. As is apparent from the exhibit, expenditures were expected to rise over one and a half times as fast as revenues; but the rates of increase vary dramatically among expenditure categories, with personal service costs—wages, pensions, and fringes—increasing at an average rate four times that of the slowest growing category, capital programs.

As noted above, the city government had already taken some steps as of fiscal 1975–76 to balance the city's budget; from 1974–75 to 1975–76, net appropriations fell by $2.4 million in current dollars. Decreases in net appropriations of over 35% were registered by the Public Lighting Department and Building and Safety Engineering, due to a combination of operating economies and higher user charges for services (power and building permits, respectively). Net appropriations for the Recreation Department fell by a third and those for public services such as the Fire Department and subsidies to Department of Transportation buses were cut by almost 10% in current dollars; even the Police Department experienced a cut of almost 3% in net appropriations (current dollars).

To effect these economies, the city had both discontinued some special services and made some general cuts in personnel. In 1970–71, for example, the city closed the Mayberry Sanitorium, a tuberculosis hospital, and sold the land and buildings for $3 million. Detroit also had been running the State Women's Prison on the grounds of the Detroit House

---

*This is a meaningless requirement since the Detroit Police Department budget far exceeds revenues from this tax. It was added by the legislature to prevent revenue from being spent on "frills" in future years, given then-Mayor Gribbs' argument that the tax was necessary to keep police services at existing levels.

of Correction, with reimbursements from the state. However, city officials claimed in 1973 that state payments were inadequate to provide for the cost of care for these prisoners. In 1974, after a two-year dispute with the state, the state finally agreed to purchase the buildings used for women prisoners for $1.5 million and took over the costs of operating the prison. The city also received $2.7 million from the sale of other excess land surrounding the House of Correction in 1974.

In the personnel area, the city began to leave unfilled positions vacant and to lay off employees, resulting in a major decrease in the number of city employees over the twenty years from 1954 to 1976. (Exhibit 8.7 details the decline.) (The employment increase recorded for 1972 is almost entirely attributable to federal Emergency Employment Act funding.) Many of the personnel reductions came from attrition and retirement, since hiring freezes were in effect for most of the period from 1970 to 1976 (except for some EEA- and CETA-hired employees and essential employees with a fairly high turnover rate such as nurses). However, 600 employees were laid off in 1970, and layoffs became more common as the 1974–76 recession deepened. In December 1975, the equivalent of 4,223 fewer employees were on the city payroll than in January 1975, a decrease of nearly 20% in one year. The equivalent of 641 police positions were lost in 1975 through unpaid days off, and 1,854 employees were laid off for thirty days and then rehired under CETA; some other positions were lost through attrition, but over 1,200 employees were permanently laid off. An additional 1,200 layoffs were set for April 1976, with 720 to be rehired under CETA and the remainder to be permanently furloughed.

The city's options in the area of layoffs, however, were limited somewhat by the municipal unions, although the unions have generally taken the position that layoffs are preferable to reductions in wages and fringe benefits. (In the 1975 fiscal crunch, only the building trades unions, the Emergency Medical Service technicians' union, and a small local of the Service Employee International Union negotiated lower pay increases or unpaid time off to preserve jobs; AFSCME, the Michigan Nurses Association, the Teamsters, DPOA, and the Firefighters—the largest city unions—all preferred layoffs.) Union contracts, however, called for strict adherence to a fairly complex seniority formula in layoffs and demotions (and

in subsequent rehirings and promotions); and this formula came into conflict with Mayor Young's affirmative action program, under which new (black and women) police officers had been hired with CETA funds. When, in May 1975, fiscal problems necessitated laying off some police officers, some of the women and blacks who had just been hired went into Federal Court to block their immediate layoffs on affirmative action grounds. District Judge Damon Keith issued a restraining order barring the layoff of anyone hired with federal funds (thus blocking the layoff of people hired under the mayor's affirmative action program).

The DPOA met this violation of seniority with a demonstration in front of the federal courthouse, during the course of which several off-duty police officers allegedly assaulted black bystanders. To calm the situation, the city and the union executive, under Judge Keith's direction, agreed to negotiate an alternative to layoffs. The DPOA executive and the city eventually agreed that each officer would have to take 24 unpaid days off over the following 18 months (saving the city approximately the amount it would have saved through the layoffs) and that there would be no layoffs for 12 months. This plan, however, was rejected by the union membership, who held out for layoffs based on seniority. The city, under prodding from the Police Chief Philip Tannian and in spite of very reluctant support from the Mayor and the Labor Relations Department (who were willing to implement Judge Keith's order after the membership rejected their compromise), finally agreed to reduce the number of unpaid days from 24 to 14 and to give ten additional paid days off to all officers to induce them to accept the plan. But this eventual solution, which the DPOA membership approved, did not reduce the police budget by as much as originally planned, and compensating cuts had to be made in other departments.

Finally, even though layoffs were the main method at the city's disposal to reduce expenditures, they did not reduce costs substantially in the short run. The city government is self-insured for purposes of unemployment compensation and must (under union contract) pay out an average of $136 per week for up to 39 weeks to most laid-off employees. (The average general city employee was receiving $18,370 in wages and fringe benefits as of 1977.) This amount is roughly 38½% of total compensation (wages and fringe benefits). Thus, to save the wages of three employees, five employees must be laid off in the short run.[15] If an employee is laid off on July 1 for an entire fiscal year and receives unemployment compensation for the maximum time, the city still pays out about 29% of the previous annual compensation in these benefits. If an employee is quickly rehired under CETA, the city may use $10,000 in federal money toward the employee's wages and fringe benefits. For the average employee, this means that the city is paying 45½% of previous compensation.

The Task Force on City Finances noted that layoffs could not close the projected $43 million budget deficit for fiscal 1975–76 in the four months remaining between the publication of its report and the end of the fiscal year. To save only $5 million, 1,300 workers would have to be laid off for the four-month period. Over 10,000 workers would have to be laid off to fill the budget gap, and the city had only 8,100 workers who could legally be laid off. (The remainder were in the Police Department and in smaller unions— where furloughs or wage cuts were negotiated in lieu of layoffs, were already hired under CETA, or were in non-general fund departments that would not affect tax-supported operations.) To reduce the budget by $5 million over an entire fiscal year would require the permanent layoff of 351 regular employees or the layoff of 396 employees later rehired under CETA.

FUTURE PROSPECTS

As of early 1976, a number of proposals had been made to reduce city expenditures and increase revenues. The remainder of this case briefly examines some of the more significant possibilities.

Withdrawal from Social Security

All employees of the city of Detroit except uniformed police officers and fire-fighters and certain part-time employees have been covered by Social Security since 1955, when state and municipal governments first became eligible to join the system. Even after local governments became eligible to join Social Security, however, the federal government could not constitutionally require them to join or to remain part of the system, as it could require private employers. Thus, local governments may or may not join the system, may provide benefits for some employees but not others, or may opt out of Social Security after giving two years' notice to the Social Security Administration.*

The Social Security tax is a proportional tax on all wages and salaries up to a limit (5.85% of income up to $16,500 in 1977) applied to employees and an equal tax on employers' payrolls. A withdrawal from the program by Detroit would save the city the employer's portion of Social Security taxes, which amounted to a savings of $17.0 million for the tax-supported budget at 1975–76 wage and tax rates. All workers would receive an increase in take-home pay of 3.85% of wages up to $16,500 (the 5.85% employee portion of the tax less an automatic 2% increase in city pension contributions which are tied to the Social Security contribution). While many younger workers not thinking of retirement (and knowing that there is a city pension plan or that they can eventually take a job covered by Social Security) might want the increased income, older employees would be very adversely affected by the withdrawal. Workers who had contributed for a long time but whose contributions stopped would face the possibility of dramatically reduced retirement benefits (or no benefits at all if they had not contributed for the required number of quarters). Thus, the unions could be expected to resist the termination of Social Security as a change in the terms and conditions of employment, and, at a minimum, they would probably demand higher pension benefits, which would eat into the city's potential savings from the termination.

Collective Bargaining Changes

In 1976 the Detroit city government called for the enactment by the state legislature of two bills that would change the collective bargaining and union contract system. The Budget Department commented:

Union demands which are excessive and irresponsible may require that a city no longer use employees to provide services to the residents, but that the city use the residents to provide for the

*Currently among the eleven largest cities, Dallas, Los Angeles, and Chicago do not participate in Social Security. New York City gave notice in 1976 that would permit it (the city) to leave the system in October 1978, but since municipal unions opposed such action, the city announced that it was only reserving its options, and had not reached any firm decision.

employees. Detroit is a union city. Unions have tremendous economic and political power. The wage and fringe packages which have been obtained for city employees attest to this. But they are forcing city costs up faster than the increase in revenue. The city has reached the point where any increase in workers' pay should be considered only when there is a demonstrated increase in productivity. Everyone hopes that salaries will keep pace with inflation, but Detroit cannot continue to give workers cost of living increases *and* percentage of base increases every year.[16]

The city asked first for legislation to change the negotiation process for police and fire unions. In 1969, prompted by concern about the possibility of strikes by public safety employees, the state legislature passed a law requiring binding arbitration of all outstanding disputes between municipalities and police and fire unions. Many labor economists, however, claim that binding arbitration limits the willingness of parties in collective bargaining to reach an agreement: unions and management have an incentive to emphasize, rather than minimize, their differences, on the assumption that arbitrators will split the differences between the two parties in some way.[17] Whatever the underlying reasons, binding arbitration appears to have hurt Detroit in its dealings with the unions. Contract bargaining begins in the spring for nearly all unions, but by the time the police and fire unions' cases come up for arbitration (assuming no prior agreement is reached, a likely assumption since no settlements have been made without arbitration since 1968, before the passage of the law), it is autumn and the city has already reached agreement with other unions. In good faith, the city offers the package agreed to with the other unions to police and fire unions as its final offer.* The police and fire unions refuse; the arbitrator splits the difference in some way; and these unions gain larger increases than other employees—and larger increases than the city really considered acceptable. Then, in the next round of talks, the other unions attempt to make up the gap between themselves and the police and fire unions, and the process repeats itself.

In addition to an end to binding arbitration, the city sought a legislative change—called a "circuit breaker provision"—that would allow local governments to reduce wages and benefits below contract levels (though not below the levels of the preceding year) to prevent major budget deficits. The city requested state legislation to allow wages to be reduced from contract levels if a projected budget deficit of more than ½% of State Equalized Valuation (approximately $27 million in Detroit) would result in any city if contracts were honored. The amount of the reduction which would be spread evenly among the city's unions, would be enough either to reduce wages and benefits to the past year's levels or to reduce the deficit to ½% of SEV, whichever was less. The city also asked for a legislative safeguard to provide for retroactive payment of the original negotiated wages[18] if the projected deficit did not materialize. Not surprisingly, however, unions voiced strong opposition to the plan, arguing that Detroit's problems were not caused by the unions, but rather by revenue shortages resulting from state and federal neglect.

Service Reimbursements

As of 1976, the city of Detroit was providing many services—particularly in police and health areas—that were provided by the state or by counties to nearly all other cities and villages. Detroit was the only municipality in Michigan that operated its own Police Crime Laboratory; the state police provided the service to all other governmental units. (The legislature passed a bill to reimburse the city for the $1.77 million cost of operating the Crime Laboratory, but Governor Milliken vetoed it in 1975.[19]) Detroit was also the only Michigan city for which the state police did not provide traffic enforcement on interstate freeways. Instead, the Detroit Police Department had been providing enforcement and assistance to motorists at an estimated cost of $1.7 million per year.[20] The Detroit Police Department also provided harbormaster services for the portion of the Detroit River bordering Detroit, although the municipal provision of this service is contrary to practice in other Michigan communities, where counties provide harbormaster service and are reimbursed for two-thirds of the cost by the state. Detroit received no state reimbursement toward its $1.4 million in harbormaster costs.

---

*If it offered less to police and fire than the other unions, it could be accused of bargaining in bad faith, and its lower offer would be discounted by arbitrators.

In the area of health and hospitals, Detroit also provided services not provided by other municipalities or with a lower rate of state reimbursement. In 1975–76, the state distributed 35 cents per capita to counties for the operation of their health departments. Detroit, by maintaining a full-time Health Department, reduced the burden on the Wayne County Health Department—but without compensation. Legislation was introduced in 1977 to increase the state grant for health services to 65 cents per capita and to treat Detroit as a separate county in the allocation of these funds. The bill would give Detroit $780,000 in revenue (extension of the 35 cents per capita grant to Detroit would provide about $420,000).[21]

Detroit was also engaged in a dispute with Wayne County over reimbursement for services provided by Detroit General Hospital. Three questions were at issue:

> Which level of government has the financial responsibility for the care of indigent or near-indigent patients who are not public charges; the per diem rate of reimbursement to be paid for those patients for whose care the county admits responsibility; and the financial responsibility for the care of any patients requiring less than 72 hours of hospitalization, which cases are categorically rejected by the County as ineligible for reimbursement.[22]

In 1963, the city and county agreed that the county would reimburse the city for "welfare clients" according to the costs per patient-day incurred in the city's prior fiscal year. However, the county's fiscal year begins December 1, and thus the reimbursements only cover the city's costs in the fiscal year ending June 30 of the preceding calendar year. A lag of 17 months results, during which rising costs are not reimbursed. The Task Force on City Finances estimated a loss of $9.3 million from 1970 to 1976 and an annual loss of over $1.8 million in both 1974–75 and 1975–76 due to this reimbursement method. Moreover, the county was required to pay the local share of payments for indigents on welfare or Medicaid, but it refused to pay for patients whose finances it could not completely investigate (including all those hospitalized for less than 72 hours), or patients who were indigents but not covered by private insurance or Medicaid. In 1975–76, the cost of these patients to the city amounted to $9.5 million, nearly 60% of the hospital's $17.2 million deficit.[23]

The Task Force suggested that while the county's actions may have been legal, they were not equitable because Detroit taxpayers were helping to pay for the deficit of a similar county hospital with few benefits to city residents, while county taxpayers outside Detroit paid nothing toward Detroit General Hospital.

> In the consideration of this whole problem, it is important to note that Wayne County General Hospital, located in western Wayne County, provides the same type of care and services for the same categories of patients as does Detroit General Hospital. The annual deficit arising from the operation of the County hospital is funded each year in the County's operating budget and, thus, a significant part of that deficit is paid for by City of Detroit taxpayers. The annual deficit of the Detroit General Hospital, which provides comparable services for its residents in eastern Wayne County, is met in its entirety by City of Detroit taxpayers.[24]

The operation of Belle Isle, a major city park covering a 700-acre island in the Detroit River and costing the city's taxpayers $2.5 million to operate in 1975–76, was another point of contention between the city and its suburbs. The Huron-Clinton Metropolitan Authority, which operates a dozen parks in the Detroit metropolitan area, is an intergovernmental agency representing five southeastern Michigan counties, including Wayne County, and financed by a 0.5 mill (50 cents per thousand) property tax levy throughout the five-county area. However, none of the parks operated by the Authority are within the Detroit city limits, even though city taxes provided approximately 30% of the Authority's operating budget. Detroit officials noted that 40% of Belle Isle users were not Detroit residents[25] and suggested that the size and cost of the operation of the Park was comparable to that of other Huron-Clinton parks. In the August 1974 primary election, a measure to increase Huron-Clinton Metropolitan Authority taxes by 0.25 mill (25 cents per thousand) to pay for operating costs of Belle Isle and improve operations and maintenance of other Authority parks was defeated by a 60-40 margin. City voters favored the small tax increase by about 2-1, but suburban voters overwhelmingly opposed it. The plan would have cost city taxpayers about $1.25 million in new taxes annually to save the $2.5 million cost of maintaining Belle Isle.

Detroit provided other services with regional benefits at its own expense, particularly recreational and cultural facilities. The Main Branch of the Detroit Public Library has the largest library collection in Michigan. The Detroit Institute of Arts, the Detroit Historical Museum, and the Detroit Zoological Park "all are more largely used by non-residents . . . than residents."[26] (Only 15% of visitors to the zoo, for example, are Detroiters; 75% live elsewhere in Michigan, and 10% come from outside the state.)[27]

In 1972, Detroit voters passed city charter amendments allowing the city to charge admission fees for the Art Institute, the Historical Museum, and the Zoo, in an attempt to recover some revenue from users—particularly non-resident users—of these facilities. Admission fees were instituted at the Zoo for adults and children (except for school children in groups) and the Art Institute and Historical Museum adopted a recommended fee of $1.00 for adults and 50 cents for children, but allowed anyone who made any contribution (even one cent) to enter. Although these fees may have had symbolic value, they did not have a major impact on the operations of these departments. (For example, admission fees raised $160,000 of a total Art Institute budget of $1,993,000 in 1973–74, and $50,000 of the Historical Commission's $1,052,000 budget for that year.)

As the fiscal situation worsened, the budgets of these cultural agencies were sliced, partly in an attempt to get the state to recognize the regional nature of these assets. Hours were cut at the Main Library in April 1976, and all branch libraries were closed for a two-week period and then reopened for very restricted hours with a staff paid for by CETA funds. Up to three-quarters of the Art Institute's galleries were closed at any one time after July 1, 1975, and the Fort Wayne Military Museum and Dossin Great Lakes Shipping Museum branches of the Historical Museum were also closed then. A temporary shutdown of the main Historical Museum occurred in April 1976, followed by its limited reopening with a much smaller staff.

These cuts prompted the state government to recognize some responsibility for the operation of the facilities. The Governor's Library Commission recommended in 1975 that the state provide substantial funding for the main library, and in late December 1975, the state provided $680,000 to reopen large portions of the Institute of Arts for the remainder of

the fiscal year.[28] Although the city requested more aid for these functions on a permanent basis, as of 1976 no permanent arrangement had been made.

Another regional service which Detroit provided to many suburbs was water supply, but for this service the suburbs had to pay full costs. The Detroit Metro Water Department was not a tax-supported department; it was required to be fully self-financing without tax aid (and even to reimburse the city general fund for staff services), but it was not allowed to make a profit for the city. However, suburban perceptions of the cost of water affected their willingness to grant other aid to Detroit. Water and sewer rates tripled over the six years from 1970 to 1976, and Edward Rago of the Detroit Budget Department commented, "We might go through another . . . [rate increase] that would make the last one look like a picnic." Suburban members of the legislature, responding to their constituents, began to complain that Detroit was profiting from them through its water rates. Some even introduced a bill to take the Water Department from city jurisdiction and place it under the State Public Service Commission.

Rago argued that the rate increases were justified and that the general fund had not made one penny from them. He noted that in the early seventies, the Water Department had undertaken several major capital projects, such as constructing pipelines and aqueducts from Lake Huron to expand the regional water supply (an expansion made necessary in part by suburban growth). In addition, federal sewage treatment requirements (under a treaty between the United States and Canada on Great Lakes pollution) increased Department costs, since the Department had to sell bonds to pay the local share of sewage treatment grants. Rago noted that city "ordinances require [the Department] to cover its debt service, its bonding," so that the rate increases were necessary. The increases were apportioned among all users, although rates rose somewhat more for beneficiaries of the Lake Huron project. But these assertions by the Budget Department notwithstanding, suburban residents faced with major rate increases authorized by an agency of Detroit city government felt—according to Rago and others—that Detroit was profiting at their expense; this perception reduced their willingness to vote in favor of increased aid to Detroit.

Raising City Taxes. Michigan law provides that the city councils of cities with less than 250,000 people may levy a property tax of up to 3 mills for garbage collection and disposal. (This tax is not included in their charter or constitutional tax limits.) The limitation on city size means that Detroit was the only city not allowed to levy such a tax in the state. While it was unclear whether Detroit's taxes, already four times the state average, should be raised, proponents of the garbage millage argued that leaving this source of revenue unavailable to Detroit was discriminatory, since the city could have raised up to $15.2 million with it.[29]

Late in 1975, Mayor Young also called for an increase in the city's income tax authority to 3% on residents and 1½% on non-residents. He stated that he did not actually want to impose the tax, but wanted the authority "only as a last resort if other alternatives fail."[30]

Additional State Aid. Aid from the state government, in the form of shared taxes, increased greatly during the 1960s and early 1970s, offsetting the decline in real city tax collections. From 1962-63 to 1976-77, state aid more than doubled in real terms (quadrupling in current dollars), largely through the enactment of new taxes and more generous local aid formulas by the state legislature. (Aid formulas were consistently revised to favor municipalities over counties.) By FY 1976-77, the state was contributing about $101 million to the city—an increase of about 116% in real terms since 1962.

The New Detroit Committee, a group of business, labor, community, and religious leaders formed after the 1967 riot, made a major proposal to increase state aid still further to Detroit and other Michigan municipalities in need. The Committee recommended that the state raise $102 million in new nuisance taxes* and give the money to municipalities based on the relative tax effort formula used to distribute income tax revenue sharing. Detroit would receive approximately $46 million of the $102 million, because its tax effort is so much greater than other municipalities. If the state would not raise these nuisance taxes or provide other aid, the Committee endorsed Mayor Young's request for increased income tax authority.

---

*Increasing the cigarette tax 5 cents per package to generate $62.5 million, the liquor tax from 9% to 14% of the retail price for $17.5 million, and increasing the tax on beer by 1 cent per bottle, raising $22.4 million.

The Task Force on City Finances solidly endorsed the nuisance tax package of state aid:

> We strongly urge the enactment of this package of State taxes and increased revenue sharing. The revenue could be raised quickly, and any citizen could avoid the tax burden by reducing consumption of the item taxed. We believe the nuisance tax approach is far preferable to the income tax approach because it avoids the risk of further deterioration of the city's economic future as individuals and businesses move out of Detroit to avoid paying higher taxes. As Mayor Young and the City Council have both said, Statewide taxation to meet the problems of all of Michigan's municipalities—if it can be achieved—is obviously "preferable" to a Detroit tax. This proposal should have the highest priority in the effort to find new revenue sources for the city in the coming weeks. In the event that necessary financial support for the city cannot be secured from any other sources, consideration should be given to seeking authority to increase income taxes, but only as a last resort to prevent financial disaster.[31]

Gambling. The Task Force on City Finances supported two bills in the legislature to legalize different forms of gambling: off-track betting and greyhound racing. It also supported the legalization of casino gambling under controlled conditions. The group suggested that most forms of gambling were "currently . . . being conducted illegitimately without any benefit to government in the form of revenue."[32] It estimated that $42 million in state revenue could be generated by off-track betting and $25 million from greyhound racing and asked that money be distributed not only to the states and counties, but that over a third go to the communities where the gambling takes place. While setting no estimate on revenue to Detroit from greyhound racing, it estimated a $10 million annual gain from off-track betting taxes.

In supporting the legalization of casino gambling, the Task Force noted that it could not provide immediate revenue. However, casino gambling, allowed only in central cities in a limited number of downtown hotels, could raise tax revenues, attract tourists, and play a major part in the development of downtown city resources.[33] Like all gambling bills, these proposals were controversial; but the casino gambling bill quickly aroused the most passion. The Detroit *Free Press* strongly editorialized against it and the Catholic Church came out in opposition, but several

Detroit legislators introduced a casino gambling bill in 1976 following the Task Force's recommendation.

Federal Aid

For fiscal year 1976–77, the city anticipated receiving about $200 million in federal grant revenues. The lion's share of this total (more than three-quarters) derived from three federal programs: the Comprehensive Employment and Training Act (CETA), Community Development Block Grants (CDBG) and revenue sharing. Because Detroit has generally experienced higher unemployment than the rest of the nation, the city's share of CETA funding has remained higher than most other cities'; but Detroit's allotment of CDBG and revenue sharing funds is expected to decline by 1980 because of the nature of the funding allocation formulas for these programs. (Detroit's portion of revenue sharing funds has in fact been declining steadily since the program's inception in 1972; and the portion of CDBG funding going to all central cities is—several studies contend—likely to decline with the phase-in of a new allocation formula.)

As of 1976, complaints about discrimination against central cities in federal funding allocation formulas had fallen on deaf congressional ears; and the federal government's response to New York City's financial crisis did not augur well for future federal aid to similarly afflicted cities. Nevertheless, many Detroit officials continued to view the federal government as the critical factor in Detroit's future. In 1976, the Budget Department called for a massive new program of federal capital investment in central cities, a "Marshall Plan for Cities."

> This plan must be multi-dimensional, addressing capital improvements, public safety, health care, environmental standards, education, commercial and industrial development, and residential rebuilding. Help must be massive enough to be visible, to assault the problems as the problems have assaulted the cities. As Mayor Coleman Young's "Moving Detroit Forward" plan stressed, massive financial commitments are the city's only hope.
>
> A composite need index . . . should be applied to the nation's fifty largest cities. Those that are judged needful should be guaranteed funds for capital redevelopment equal to 25% of their operating budget. The guarantee should be for at least 3 to 5 years initially. With this type of formula, both *need* and *effort* are considered . . .
>
> If the Federal Government provided monies equal to 25% of the annual operating budget of Detroit, each year, the downward trend of the city could be reversed in less than a decade.[34]

The Young Administration also argued that HUD policies had devastated Detroit much more than any other city and that the federal government, through HUD, should make reparations to Detroit.

> HUD is responsible for depleting our housing stock, blighting our neighborhoods, and cheating our residents. Criminal mismanagement has created thousands of abandoned houses, many vandalized and scavenged, providing refuge for vagrants, addicts, thieves, and rapists, threatening area residents, and ruining residential areas. The efforts of the "HUD tornado" is not just on those houses which were at one time or another part of the huge HUD inventory. The effect is on every house in the city. Every residential property was affected by what HUD did to this city. Every citizen was cheated by what HUD did to this city. That debt is still outstanding. *That debt must be paid*, both principal and interest to restore our neighborhoods . . .
>
> [HUD should therefore fund] neighborhood improvement projects that would assist local businesses, increase the value of homes, improve security, and rebuild healthy neighborhoods.[35]

By 1976 many in the city administration hoped that Gerald Ford would be replaced as President by Jimmy Carter (whom Mayor Young had supported early in the campaign). Under a Carter Administration, they thought Detroit could expect more countercyclical aid and perhaps some changes in the federal grant formulas for revenue sharing and community development. But this vague hope offered no immediate fiscal consolation and thus, for 1976-77 and the near future, city officials would have to find a solution to their fiscal problems somewhere close to home.

EXHIBIT 8.1: City of Detroit Appropriations ($000)

Department	1969–70	1970–71	1971–72	1972–73	1973–74	1974–75	1975–76	Net Change 1969–70 to 1975–76
Budget & Finance Depts.								
Non-capital Approp.*	9,053	9,928	9,149	9,201	10,608	13,353	11,197	+23.7%
Share	2.2%	2.2%	1.9%	1.7%	1.8%	2.1%	1.8%	
Net Approp.	8,591	9,447	8,742	8,926	10,253	12,592	10,380	+20.8%
Share	2.8%	2.7%	2.4%	2.2%	2.4%	2.7%	2.2%	
Building & Safety Engineering								
Non-capital Approp.	5,661	6,015	6,758	7,689	7,968	7,998	7,168	+26.6%
Share	1.4%	1.3%	1.4%	1.4%	1.4%	1.3%	1.1%	
Net Approp.	2,084	2,272	2,366	1,567	1,849	2,306	1,195	−42.7%
Share	0.7%	0.7%	0.6%	0.4%	0.4%	0.5%	0.3%	
Cultural**								
Non-capital Approp.	13,015	13,625	14,193	14,591	16,126	18,123	16,831	+29.3%
Share	3.1%	3.0%	2.9%	2.6%	2.8%	2.9%	2.7%	
Net Approp.	10,855	11,079	11,759	11,258	13,219	14,847	13,261	+22.2%
Share	3.6%	3.2%	3.2%	2.8%	3.1%	3.2%	2.8%	
Detroit General Hospital								
Non-capital Approp.	23,919	26,372	31,795	33,853	36,687	37,519	42,141	+76.2%
Share	5.8%	5.7%	6.4%	6.1%	6.3%	6.0%	6.7%	
Net Approp.	4,820	4,349	7,783	7,747	12,918	12,068	17,182	+256.5%
Share	1.6%	1.3%	2.1%	1.9%	3.0%	2.6%	3.7%	
Environmental Protection (public works)								
Non-capital Approp.	26,812	29,440	29,454	33,591	35,955	38,613	32,274	+20.4%
Share	6.5%	6.4%	6.0%	6.1%	6.2%	6.2%	5.1%	
Net Approp.	21,044	22,432	21,199	22,699	23,340	26,200	18,482	−12.2%
Share	6.9%	6.5%	5.7%	5.6%	5.4%	5.6%	4.0%	
Fire								
Non-capital Approp.	32,156	36,229	40,223	47,670	50,014	59,914	54,265	+68.8%
Share	7.8%	7.9%	8.1%	8.6%	8.6%	9.6%	8.6%	
Net Approp.	31,738	35,753	39,747	46,255	48,829	58,583	52,906	+66.7%
Share	10.4%	10.4%	10.7%	11.4%	11.3%	12.5%	11.4%	
Health								
Non-capital Approp.	13,870	15,302	16,029	14,207	16,336	17,683	15,903	+14.7%
Share	3.4%	3.3%	3.2%	2.6%	2.8%	2.8%	2.5%	
Net Approp.	4,233	6,617	6,998	10,651	12,982	14,811	13,073	+208.8%
Share	1.4%	1.9%	1.9%	2.6%	3.0%	3.2%	2.8%	
Parks & Recreation Dept.								
Non-capital Approp.	17,267	18,854	19,085	17,625	20,335	23,053	17,242	−0.1%
Share	4.2%	4.1%	3.9%	3.2%	3.5%	3.7%	2.7%	
Net Approp.	14,930	16,440	17,128	14,290	15,486	18,066	12,072	−19.1%
Share	4.9%	4.8%	4.6%	3.5%	3.6%	3.9%	2.6%	

*As noted in the text.

**Includes Arts, Historical Commission, Library and Zoological Park.

EXHIBIT 8.1 (continued)

Department	1969–70	1970–71	1971–72	1972–73	1973–74	1974–75	1975–76	Net Change 1969–70 to 1975–76
Police								
Non-capital Approp.	82,176	99,505	114,258	131,092	147,737	161,030	157,864	+92.1%
Share	19.9%	21.6%	23.1%	23.7%	25.4%	25.8%	25.1%	
Net Approp.	81,652	98,914	113,261	129,837	146,346	159,770	155,523	+90.5%
Share	26.9%	28.7%	30.6%	31.9%	33.9%	34.2%	33.4%	
Public Lighting								
Non-capital Approp.	12,419	15,070	17,111	17,747	22,102	28,089	25,725	+107.1%
Share	3.0%	3.3%	3.5%	3.2%	3.8%	4.5%	4.1%	
Net Approp.	4,701	6,462	6,869	6,313	9,918	13,364	8,168	+73.8%
Share	1.5%	1.9%	1.9%	1.5%	2.3%	2.9%	1.8%	
Solid Waste (garbage)*								
Non-capital Approp.	26,478	28,437	28,941	31,676	33,494	36,118	27,885	+5.3%
Share	6.4%	6.2%	5.9%	5.7%	5.8%	5.8%	4.4%	
Net Approp.	23,956	25,240	27,171	27,810	27,926	29,303	22,316	−6.8%
Share	7.9%	7.3%	7.3%	6.8%	6.5%	6.3%	4.8%	
Transportation								
Non-capital Approp.	46,263	49,060	54,014	60,527	62,281	61,918	63,681	+37.6%
Share	11.2%	10.7%	10.9%	10.9%	10.7%	9.9%	10.1%	
Net Approp.	2,340	7,487	7,685	6,792	6,128	8,969	8,110	+246.6%
Share	0.8%	2.2%	2.1%	1.7%	1.4%	1.9%	1.7%	
Other Departments								
Non-capital Approp.	23,077	25,563	31,286	42,672	45,312	57,833	81,330**	+252.4%
Share	5.6%	5.6%	6.3%	7.7%	7.8%	9.3%	12.9%	
Net Approp.	16,454	17,428	23,110	26,492	31,087	37,456	59,537**	+261.8%
Share	5.4%	5.1%	6.2%	6.5%	7.2%	8.0%	12.8%	
Non-departmental								
Non-capital Approp.	23,010	26,826	22,064	26,768	23,561	19,448	8,102	−64.8%
Share	5.6%	5.8%	4.5%	4.8%	4.1%	3.1%	1.3%	
Net Approp.	23,010	26,826	22,064	26,768	23,561	19,448	8,102	−64.8%
Share	7.6%	7.8%	6.0%	6.6%	5.5%	4.2%	1.7%	
Debt Service								
Non-capital Approp.	38,462	39,502	39,727	41,705	42,308	43,244	45,535	+18.4%
Share	9.3%	8.6%	8.0%	7.5%	7.3%	6.9%	7.2%	
Net Approp.	33,672	34,277	34,590	36,925	37,678	39,917	41,993	+24.7%
Share	11.1%	9.9%	9.3%	9.1%	8.7%	8.5%	9.0%	
Deficit								
Non-capital Approp.	20,000	20,000	20,000	23,000	10,000	—	23,000	+15.0%
Share	4.8%	4.4%	4.0%	4.2%	1.7%	—0—	3.6%	
Net Approp.	20,000	20,000	20,000	23,000	10,000	—	23,000	+15.0%
Share	6.6%	5.8%	5.4%	5.6%	2.3%	—0—	4.9%	

*Technically part of Environmental Protection.

**Includes $25,272 ($23,323 net) of city matching appropriations for federal employment programs.

**EXHIBIT 8.2:   Sources of Revenue—
Detroit Budget for FY 1976-77**

Source	Amount (current $ millions)	% of Total Tax-supported Budget****	% of Total Tax-supported**** Budget for Current Expenditures
Taxes			
Property*	187.36	22.0%	22.8%
Income	111.80	13.1	13.6
Utility excise	28.25	3.3	3.4
Total taxes*	327.41	38.4%	39.8%
State Aid			
State income tax	29.80	3.5%	3.6%
State sales tax	27.78	3.3	3.4
Intangibles & single business tax*	18.52	2.2	2.3
Gas & weight taxes**	24.70	2.9	3.0
Total state aid*	100.80	11.9%	12.3%
Federal Aid			
Revenue sharing	40.40	4.8%	4.9%
Community development	31.61	3.7	3.9
CETA#	71.29	8.4	8.7
Total federal aid	143.30	1€.	17.5%
User Charges***	119.71	14.1%	14.6%
Miscellaneous Revenue for Current Use	128.98	15.2%	15.7%
Total Revenue for Current Use	820.20	96.4%	100.0%
Sale of Bonds for Capital Improvement	30.28	3.6%	
Total revenue	850.48	100.0%	

Source: City of Detroit, Budget Department, Detroit, Financial Projections 1977–1982, December 27, 1976, p. 1.

*The State Single Business Tax Act, effective in early 1976, eliminated local property taxes on business inventories. The law required the state to furnish aid to municipalities to reimburse them for this diminution in local taxes. The $19.79 million paid to Detroit for this reason was included in local property tax collections and excluded from State Single Business Tax aid, to permit comparability with years prior to 1976–77.

**Gas and weight taxes are earmarked for street and highway-related improvements.

***Included in this category are fees charged by Detroit General Hospital, bus fares collected by the Department of Transportation, and money received for the sale of electric power by the Public Lighting Department to other units of government. Other minor user charges are included in "Miscellaneous Revenue for Current Use."

****The "tax-supported budget" is the budget for all city activities which are not supported fully by user charges and which do not earn a profit (e.g., water is excluded).

#Comprehensive Employment and Training Act, a public employment program.

EXHIBIT 8.3:   Tax Revenues Budgeted by the City of Detroit
Fiscal 1961–62 to Fiscal 1976–77 ($ millions)

Year	Current Dollars				1967 Dollars (WPI)*				1967 Dollars (CPI)*			
	Property	Income	Utility	Total	Property	Income	Utility	Total	Property	Income	Utility	Total
1961–62	119.42	—	—	119.42	126.37	—	—	126.37	134.63	—	—	134.63
1962–63	112.76	35.0	—	147.76	118.95	36.9	—	155.85	126.83	39.4	—	166.23
1963-64	110.08	39.5	—	149.58	116.49	41.8	—	158.29	122.58	44.0	—	166.58
1964-65	109.34	38.2	—	147.54	115.46	40.3	—	155.76	120.82	42.2	—	163.02
1965-66	105.45	43.3	—	148.75	109.16	44.8	—	153.96	113.88	48.4	—	162.28
1966-67	101.93	52.0	—	153.93	102.13	52.1	—	154.23	104.58	53.8	—	158.38
1967-68	112.17	48.5	—	160.67	112.17	48.5	—	160.67	112.17	48.5	—	160.67
1968-69	115.41	89.9	—	205.31	112.60	87.7	—	200.30	107.55	83.8	—	191.35
1969-70	121.99	92.8	—	214.79	114.54	87.1	—	201.64	110.30	83.9	—	194.20
1970-71	140.40	96.1	17.5	254.00	127.17	87.0	15.9	230.07	119.59	81.9	14.9	216.39
1971-72	148.39	96.1	17.5	261.99	130.28	84.4	15.4	230.08	121.93	79.0	14.4	215.33
1972-73	152.34	93.6	17.1	263.04	127.91	78.5	14.4	220.81	120.71	74.1	13.5	208.31
1973-74	152.72**	106.5	18.6	277.82**	113.38	79.1	13.8	206.28	113.55	79.2	13.8	206.55
1974-75	155.17	116.8	19.7	291.67	96.92	73.0	12.3	182.22	104.14	78.4	13.2	195.74
1975-76	161.43	110.8	24.3	296.53	92.30	63.3	13.9	169.50	100.83	69.2	15.2	185.23
1976-77	187.36***	111.8	28.25	327.41	101.67	60.7	15.3	177.67	110.73	66.1	16.7	193.53
Growth in tax revenue (%)												
1962-67	−9.60%	48.57%	—	4.18%	−14.14%	41.19%	—	−0.41%	−17.54%	36.55%	—	−4.72%
1967-72	45.58%	84.81%	—	70.20%	27.56%	62.00%	—	49.18%	16.59%	46.84%	—	35.96%
1972-77	26.18%	16.34%	61.14%	24.91%	−22.01%	−28.08%	−0.65%	−22.81%	−9.24%	−16.33%	15.97%	−10.16%
1962-77	66.05%	219.43%	—	121.47%	−14.59%	64.50%	—	14.69%	−12.75%	67.77%	—	16.38%

*WPI figures are deflated by the non-food Wholesale Price Index, CPI figures by the Consumer Price Index for Detroit.

**Excludes $18.69 million in current dollars ($13.87 million deflated by the WPI, $13.89 million deflated by the CPI) in property taxes imposed for one year only to pay for contributions withheld from the Department of Street Railways Pension Fund and ordered to be paid by Wayne County Circuit Court.

***Includes $19.79 million in state aid ($10.74 million deflated by the WPI, $11.69 million deflated by the CPI) provided by the State Single Business Tax Act to replace property taxes on business inventories that were eliminated on July 1, 1976 by the state law. The addition of this aid is necessary to make 1976–77 figures comparable to those of previous years when inventories were taxable.

EXHIBIT 8.4:   Acreage of Taxable and Exempt Property in Detroit by Type, 1968

	Acreage	Percentage of Total City Land Area Not Covered with Streets
City property (includes parks, Board of Education property)	9,777	14.70%
State and federal property (includes Wayne State University)	457	0.69%
Railroad property (tax-exempt under state law)	1,893	2.85%
Churches	706	1.06%
Private schools	1,044	1.57%
Hospitals	308	0.46%
Expressways	2,804	4.22%
Other	78	0.11%
Total Exempt Property	17,067	25.65%
Taxable Property	49,464	74.35%
Streets	22,700	
Total City Acreage	89,231	

EXHIBIT 8.5:   Surpluses and Deficits in City of Detroit General Fund 1961–62 to 1981–82 ($ millions, current)

Fiscal Year	Surplus (Deficit)	Cumulative Surplus (Deficit)
—	—	($ 8.984)
1961–62	($25.590)	(34.574)
1962–63	15.129	(19.445)
1963–64	10.999	(8.446)
1964–65	10.755	2.309
1965–66	3.149	5.458
1966–67	(16.402)	(10.944)
1967–68	(4.429)	(15.373)
1968–69	0.707	(14.666)
1969–70	(5.145)	(19.811)
1970–71	(0.648)	(20.459)
1971–72	(2.107)	(22.566)
1972–73	34.545	11.979
1973–74	2.467	14.446
1974–75	(30.798)	(16.352)
1975–76	(26.948)*	(43.300)
1976–77	(28.872)*	(72.172)
1977–78	(40.564)*	(112.736)
1978–79	(64.518)*	(177.254)
1979–80	(91.517)*	(268.771)
1980–81	(142.845)*	(411.616)
1981–82	(169.215)*	(580.831)

*Projections as of January 1, 1976, based on assumption of no major changes in appropriations or revenue patterns.

Source: City of Detroit Budget Department figures.

EXHIBIT 8.6:   Components of Projected Deficits

Item	Average Annual Increase 1976–77 through 1981–82	Total Increase 1976–77 to 1981–82
Revenues		
Utility excise tax	10.0%	60.7%
User charges	6.4	36.7
Property tax	4.8	25.7
Income tax	4.6	25.0
State aid	4.8	24.8
Federal aid	−1.1	−5.6
All other	2.4	12.6
Overall Revenues	3.7%	20.0%
Appropriations		
Wages, pensions, fringes	8.7%	51.5%
Hospital, library, transit	6.6	37.9
Supplies and services	6.0	33.9
Debt service	3.5	18.4
Capital programs	2.1	10.8
Overall Appropriations	6.2%	35.3%

Source: City of Detroit, Budget Department, Detroit Financial Projections, 1977–1982, *December, 1976, p. 1.*

EXHIBIT 8.7:   History of City Employment, 1954–1976

Year Ending June 30	General City	Police and Fire	Revenue Departments*	Total
1954	15,738	5,916	7,658	29,312
1956	14,641	6,129	7,078	27,848
1958	14,696	6,154	6,095	26,945
1960	13,948	5,984	5,409	25,341
1962	14,044	6,075	5,235	25,354
1964	13,259	6,175	5,501	24,935
1966	13,863	6,161	5,654	25,678
1968	13,333	6,264	5,663	25,260
1970	13,296	6,804	5,798	25,898
1972	14,100	7,337	5,272	26,709
1974	12,564	7,356	5,366	25,286
1976	11,054	6,680	5,029	22,763

The decline in the number of employees since 1954 is even more severe when one realizes that in 1954, virtually none of the 29,312 employees were funded by non-local, grant funds. In 1976, about 4,000 of the 22,763 are paid for by grant funds. That means that there are really about 10,549 fewer local tax-supported employees today than there were in 1954 —*a decrease of 36%.*

*Includes Housing, Water and Sewerage, and Street Railway Departments.

Source: City of Detroit, Budget Department, Detroit Financial Projections, 1977–1982, *December 27, 1976, p. 39. Annual Pension Valuation Report: General City figures include Municipal Parking Department and Aviation. Numbers are based on actual count of the last payroll paid in June.*

SEQUEL

The Detroit Fiscal Crisis

A patchwork set of provisions saved Detroit from financial disaster in fiscal 1976-77. The state legislature voted down the city government's proposed nuisance tax increase but gave Detroit the authority to levy the three-mill tax for garbage collection granted to other Michigan municipalities, and the city levied the tax. The state provided further "equity" aid to Detroit based on the theory of reimbursement for services; a $27.8 million aid package passed the legislature after a compromise with suburban Oakland County members that assured funding for the Pontiac football stadium built when the Detroit Lions moved away from the city. The package provided $9.7 million for cultural agencies: $5.5 million of the $6.3 million required to provide administrative services and operate the Main branch of the Detroit Public Library, $3.5 million of the $3.646 million operating budget for the Arts Department (with $100,000 of the remainder coming from admissions and contributions, leaving a cost to city taxpayers of only $45,000), and $700,000 of the $987,000 operating budget for the Historical Department.

With this money, all three of the Historical Department's museums, and all galleries in the Art Institute were opened, and the old schedule at the Public Library (before April, 1976 cuts) was restored. $1.05 million was also provided to pay for half of the City's original net appropriation for the Zoo, reducing it from $2.10 million to $1.05 million. Additional state aid was provided for the police crime lab ($1 million of its $1.7 million cost) and to pay the cost of Department of Transportation pensions ($9.072 million).* The dispute between Detroit and Wayne County over Detroit General Hospital was partially resolved as the state agreed to pay $8 million of the hospital's projected $21 million 1976-77 deficit. However, this aid package was passed with the understanding that it would be a temporary measure for 1976-77 only.

With the beginning of the 1976-77 fiscal year, additional city employees were laid off, including police officers (who had previously been exempt from layoffs), and the hiring freeze in place since July 1, 1975, was further extended. However, most of the laid-off police officers were returned to their jobs after an outbreak of gang violence in mid-August,** and the remaining officers were rehired in November, when city revenues showed an unprojected upturn due to improvements in the auto industry. In fact, the improving economy allowed the city to finance its entire $37 million accumulated deficit from 1975-76 in fiscal 1976-77 and to enter 1977-78 with a $6.8 million surplus. Mayor Young also hired new police officers with city funds to replace some of those who retired in the previous two years.

The fiscal 1977-78 budget contained no new taxes*** while providing for spending increases of $110 million over the previous year and restoring 2,088 of the 2,331 positions cut in 1976-77. Mayor Young suggested that these increases were made possible by Detroit's "unprecedented financial recovery" from the trough of the recession: "if we get sick sooner, we also get well faster." City income tax revenues for 1977-78 were projected to rise 11.7% to $124.9 million and utility tax revenues to rise 16.3% to $32.8 million. State tax-sharing aid rose 20.6% to $121.8 million (including a 37% increase in state income-tax sharing due to improvement in Michigan's economy and changes in the formula that gave municipalities 6% more revenue at the expense of counties). The state "equity" package was maintained at approximately the same level as in 1976-77. Federal grant revenue increased with the provision of $28.2 million in countercyclical aid to Detroit in 1977-78 and the extension of public employment under the Comprehensive Employment and Training Act. In

---

*This was treated as an "equity" issue, since the state subsidized the Southeastern Michigan Transportation Authority (SEMTA), but not Detroit's mass transit system. SEMTA currently operates suburban bus lines and has the authority to acquire the Detroit bus system once the problem of fully funding past pension liabilities is cleared up.

**The State Police also agreed to patrol Detroit freeways at that time, which effectively increased the strength of the Detroit Police Department elsewhere, clearing up that point of contention.

***Proposals to legalize and tax casino gambling were defeated in a non-binding referendum in 1976.

future years, Detroit would benefit from changes in the grant formula for community development block grants, passed by Congress in October, 1977, which included the inverse of a city's population growth and the percentage of a city's housing stock built before 1939 in the allocation formula.

Union contracts agreed to in September, 1977 (after brief strikes by the American Federation of State, County, and Municipal Employees (AFSCME) and the union of nurses at Detroit General Hospital) promised to have a moderating influence on the city's future rates of spending. The basic contract pattern provided for a 4.8% increase as of July 1, 1977, 4% increases on July 1, 1978 and 1979, and elimination of cost-of-living allowances. This contract was much less costly than the previous three-year contract which gave 4% in its first year and 4% in the second and third years plus cost-of-living allowances of one cent per hour per increase of 0.3 points in the Detroit Consumer Price Index (which allowances were then included in base rates of pay as of the following July 1). In addition, the contracts cut minimum rates of pay for clerical employees by 20% and froze minimum rates of most other job classifications over the three-year life of the contracts. (This provision affects the rates of pay at which new employees are hired; it does not affect raises paid to employees once they receive city jobs.) The contracts thus took steps that could cut the city's labor costs substantially.

Mayor Young won a landslide re-election victory in November, 1977; his opponent, black Councilman Ernest Browne, Jr., received the strong backing of the Detroit Police Officers Association and the city's white voters, but Young retained nearly all of the black vote to win 59% of the vote. Five black councillors—a majority—were elected. However, some of Young's policies—most notably affirmative action—were being challenged. In February, 1978, a Federal District Court held unconstitutional a plan proposed by Police Commissioner Philip Tannian and strongly supported by Mayor Young to use racial quotas to increase the number of blacks being promoted to Police Sergeant, prompting criticism of the court by Mayor Young and other black leaders.

Meanwhile, investment in Detroit's infrastructure was increasing. In October, 1976, after the federal government offered the Detroit metropolitan area $600 million for light-rail mass transportation, the legislature (including many suburban members who did not want to raise suburban taxes to help Detroit but did want the regional benefits of a large federal construction program) approved an increase in gasoline and motor vehicle taxes in Wayne, Oakland, and Macomb Counties to supply the required matching funds. Before it approved the $600 million, the Federal government required that $600 million in private investment in Detroit along the proposed transit lines be forthcoming, and by 1978 the investment commitments had been made (see below) and planning for the transit system was underway. Other major federally funded public works, including a Detroit riverfront stadium to replace the current hockey arena, were also approved.

As of January 31, 1977, 44 building projects costing more than $1 million each and having a combined value of $433 million were under construction. However, several earlier projects seemed to be having mixed impacts. The Renaissance Center's office space filled up rather slowly, and only Ford Motor Company, which rented an entire office tower in the complex, moved a large number of jobs in from the suburbs. A number of other firms chose to move to the Renaissance Center rather than to the suburbs from other downtown buildings; an older 20-story building was demolished, and other downtown buildings had difficulty finding tenants, partly due to the Center. The Detroit Plaza Hotel in the Center has been drawing large numbers of people to the downtown area from the suburbs and the rest of the city for its restaurants, entertainment, and shopping, and other Detroit hotels, including one built in 1966 three blocks from the Center, asked for tax abatements on grounds that the Renaissance Center was threatening them with bankruptcy. Although the state legislature passed a twelve-year property tax exemption on new multi-family units in January, 1977, as requested by developer Max Fisher and others, as of February, 1978, Fisher's plan for building middle- and upper-income downtown riverfront apartments had been all but scrapped because of difficulties in planning and obtaining government approval.

At the same time, the city's problems of a declining tax base, crime, and poor education remained. The true value of the city's property fell below $10 billion in 1978 for the first time since the 1950s, causing erosion of property tax revenues. The school system, 79% black in 1977 and dependent on property taxes for its sole revenues, was forced to eliminate athletic* and cultural programs and insti-

*However, a group of Detroit banks and other businesses contributed over $1 million to restore high school varsity athletics.

tute half-day sessions for many students after voters rejected an additional five-mill school tax in the 1976 election. After the millage increase was approved in 1977, the cuts were largely rescinded. Detroit's future, while not as grim as it appeared early in 1976, remained uncertain.

REFERENCES

1. U.S. Congress, Joint Economic Committee, *New York City's Financial Crisis* (94th Congress, 1st Session), November 3, 1975, p. 27.
2. City of Detroit, Mayor's Task Force on City Finances, "Report," February 24, 1976, p. 5.
3. Stephen A. Perloff, "Comparing Municipal, Industry, and Federal Pay," *Monthly Labor Review,* October 1971, pp. 46–50.
4. William B. Neenan, "Suburban-Central City Exploitation Thesis: One City's Tale," *National Tax Journal,* June 1970, p. 136.
5. *Ibid.*
6. City of Detroit, Board of Assessors, "Memorandum Re: Detroit Freeways, Assessed Valuation of Right of Way Acquisition," October 13, 1971.
7. *New York Times,* October 2, 1972, p. 73.
8. *New York Times,* December 6, 1972, p. 29.
9. *New York Times,* October 2, 1972, pp. 1 and 73.
10. "Mayor Young After Three Years," *Detroit Free Press,* November 23, 1976, p. 8A.
11. City of Detroit, Budget Department, *Detroit Financial Projections 1977–78,* December 27, 1976, p. 17.
12. *Ibid.*
13. *Ibid.*
14. *Ibid.*
15. Task Force Report, p. 10.
16. *Detroit Financial Projections,* p. 20.
17. Derek C. Bok and John T. Dunlop, *Labor and the American Community* (New York: Simon and Schuster, 1970), pp. 236–241.
18. *Detroit Financial Projections,* pp. 20–21.
19. Task Force Report, p. 17.
20. *Ibid.*
21. *Ibid.*
22. *Ibid.*
23. *Ibid.,* pp. 19–21.
24. *Ibid.,* p. 20.
25. *Detroit Financial Projections,* p. 16.
26. Task Force Report, p. 16.
27. *Detroit Financial Projections,* p. 16.
28. Task Force Report, p. 16.
29. *Ibid.,* p. 13.
30. New Detroit, Inc., "Recommendations and Proposals Regarding the State and City Budget and Tax Crises," Task Force Report, Exhibit 5.
31. Task Force Report, p. 12.
32. *Ibid.,* p. 22.
33. *Ibid.,* pp. 21–23.
34. *Detroit Financial Projections,* p. 9.
35. *Ibid.,* pp. 9–10.

9

Atlanta: A Statistical Profile

The *statistical profile* of metropolitan Atlanta comprises data on population, age distribution, and population migration patterns broken down by SMSA, Atlanta, and suburban areas; education, employment, and income, including income distribution; price indices; housing; crime; neighborhood satisfaction; business activity; government revenues and expenditures; and comparative national statistics. A map is included. Unless another source is given, all tables are constructed from census data, including the 1950, 1960, and 1970 censuses of population and the 1958, 1963, 1967, and 1972 censuses of business and of manufacturers. Other sources include Bureau of Labor Statistics data, the 1975 Annual Report of Atlanta's Commissioner of Finance, and Research Atlanta, Inc., *The Plan of Improvement: An Analysis of Services in the City of Atlanta and Fulton County* (Atlanta, 1974).

By analyzing these data you will be able to identify the major trends affecting the economy of the city.

TABLE OF CONTENTS

9.1   Population
9.2   Age distribution by race
9.3   Migration patterns

Education, Employment, and Income

9.4   Schooling of population over 25
9.5   Labor force participation and employment by sex and race—1960
9.6   Employment by industrial group
9.7   Location of jobs in the metropolitan area; place of work by place of residence
9.8   Family income distribution, median income, and income by race
9.9   Price indices

Housing

9.10 Housing statistics
9.11 Neighborhood satisfaction, 1975

Crime

9.12 Crime rate per 100,000 people

Business

9.13 Business statistics: retail trade, wholesale trade, selected services, manufacturing
9.14 Manufacturing by Standard Industrial Classification, 1967

Government

9.15 City of Atlanta, expenditures by function
9.16 City of Atlanta, revenues by source

9.17 City of Atlanta, property tax base, tax rate, and revenue
9.18 Population and general fund expenditures of municipalities in Fulton County—1973

Comparative Statistics

9.19 Comparative national statistics

Regional Map

9.20 Metropolitan Atlanta in 1975

EXHIBIT 9.1: Population (thousands)

	SMSA*	Atlanta**	Fulton County	DeKalb County	All Suburbs**	Fulton Suburbs*	DeKalb Suburbs	Clayton, Cobb & Gwinnett	State of Georgia
1950									
Total	727	331	474	136	396	180	99	117	3,445
White	554	210	329	122	344	152	89	103	2,381
Non-white	173	121	145	14	52	28	10	14	1,064
% non-white	23.8%	36.6%	30.6%	10.6%	13.1%	15.5%	10.6%	11.9%	30.9%
1960									
Total	1,016	487	555	256	529	110	215	204	3,943
White	785	300	362	234	484	97	200	188	2,817
Non-white	231	187	193	22	45	13	15	16	1,126
% non-white	22.7%	38.3%	34.7%	8.7%	8.5%	11.8%	7.0%	7.8%	28.6%
Growth 1950–60									
Total	39.9%	47.1%	17.3%	89.0%	33.6%	−38.9%	117.2%	74.4%	14.5%
White	41.7%	42.9%	10.0%	91.8%	40.7%	−36.2%	124.7%	80.8%	18.3%
Non-white	33.5%	54.5%	33.1%	57.1%	−13.5%	−53.6%	66.7%	14.3%	5.8%
1970									
Total	1,390	497	608	415	893	157	369	367	4,589
White	1,076	241	369	358	836	144	341	349	3,397
Non-white	314	256	239	57	57	13	28	18	1,192
% non-white	22.6%	51.5%	39.3%	13.7%	6.4%	8.3%	7.6%	4.9%	26.0%
Growth 1960–70									
Total	36.7%	2.0%	9.4%	61.5%	68.8%	42.7%	71.6%	79.9%	16.4%
White	37.1%	−19.7%	1.5%	53.0%	72.7%	49.5%	70.5%	85.6%	20.6%
Non-white	35.9%	36.9%	22.8%	159.1%	26.7%	0	86.6%	20.0%	5.9%
1973 Total***	1,487	459	595	453	1,028	176	412	440	4,831
1975 Total***	1,515	436	581	451	1,079	182	414	484	4,931
Growth 1970–75									
Total***	9.0%	−12.3%	−4.4%	8.7%	20.8%	15.9%	12.2%	31.2%	7.4%

*"SMSA" stands for Standard Metropolitan Statistical Area. The consistent definition of the Atlanta SMSA used in this set of materials includes Fulton, DeKalb, Cobb, Clayton, and Gwinnett Counties; the Census Bureau changed the definition of the SMSA in 1971, but all statistics after 1970 have been adjusted here to retain the old definition.

**1960 data for Atlanta, "all suburbs," and "Fulton suburbs" reflects the 1951 annexation of suburban land into Atlanta containing a population of 87,200 in 1950. The population of the annexed area grew to 171,500 by 1960, whille the population within the pre-1951 boundaries of Atlanta decreased by 15,000.

***1973 and 1975 data are not broken down by race. 1975 data are preliminary projections.

EXHIBIT 9.2: Age Distribution by Race

Age	SMSA			Atlanta			Suburbs		
	Total	White	Black	Total	White	Black	Total	White	Black
1960									
less than 5	12.05%	11.43%	14.13%	10.85%	9.00%	13.82%	13.15%	12.94%	15.41%
5-14	20.15%	19.63%	21.92%	18.12%	16.24%	21.14%	22.02%	21.73%	25.13%
15-19	7.10%	6.98%	7.50%	7.31%	7.37%	7.21%	6.90%	6.73%	8.69%
20-44	36.04%	36.74%	33.69%	34.70%	34.89%	34.38%	37.28%	37.89%	30.84%
45-64	18.13%	18.42%	17.15%	21.08%	23.13%	17.78%	15.41%	15.49%	14.55%
65 and over	6.53%	6.80%	5.60%	7.94%	9.36%	5.66%	5.23%	5.22%	5.39%
1970									
less than 5	9.23%	8.85%	10.58%	8.64%	6.70%	10.50%	9.56%	9.47%	10.94%
5-14	20.36%	19.44%	23.56%	18.21%	13.16%	23.03%	21.55%	21.26%	26.02%
15-19	8.98%	8.54%	10.53%	9.38%	8.35%	10.38%	8.78%	8.61%	11.24%
20-44	36.98%	37.90%	33.78%	35.14%	36.13%	34.19%	38.01%	38.41%	31.90%
45-64	17.94%	18.66%	15.44%	19.53%	23.59%	15.64%	17.06%	17.23%	14.52%
65 and over	6.50%	6.61%	6.10%	9.10%	12.07%	6.26%	5.05%	5.03%	5.38%

EXHIBIT 9.3: Migration Patterns

% of Population Aged 5 and Over by Residence 5 Years Previously

	Residence in Census Year					
	SMSA	Atlanta	All Suburbs	Fulton Suburbs	DeKalb Suburbs	Clayton, Cobb & Gwinnett
1960						
Population over 5	894,453	434,416	460,037	97,382	186,754	175,901
Same house as 1955	43.63%	46.64%	40.79%	44.05%	38.81%	41.09%
Different house:						
Atlanta	22.02%	33.03%	11.62%	10.34%	15.71%	7.99%
Atlanta suburbs	15.62%	3.96%	26.63%	26.85%	21.60%	31.86%
U.S. outside SMSA:	15.94%	12.68%	19.01%	16.71%	21.49%	17.65%
North & West	3.36%	2.53%	4.14%	4.44%	4.77%	3.31%
South	12.58%	10.17%	14.87%	12.27%	16.72%	14.34%
Abroad	0.71%	0.60%	0.82%	0.88%	0.74%	0.86%
Moved, 1955 location						
not reported	2.08%	3.09%	1.13%	1.17%	1.65%	0.54%
1970						
Population over 5	1,261,835	435,840	807,995	144,444	335,389	328,492
Same house as 1965	41.63%	44.39%	40.09%	41.58%	38.17%	41.37%
Different house:						
Atlanta	15.51%	27.21%	8.94%	11.81%	10.51%	6.07%
Atlanta suburbs	15.95%	5.48%	21.83%	20.61%	18.63%	25.62%
U.S. outside SMSA:	18.87%	13.86%	21.68%	18.21%	25.22%	19.59%
North & West	4.95%	3.06%	6.02%	5.49%	7.77%	4.46%
South	13.91%	10.80%	15.66%	12.72%	17.44%	15.13%
Abroad	1.01%	0.92%	1.05%	0.94%	1.02%	1.14%
Moved, 1965 location						
not reported	7.03%	8.14%	6.41%	6.85%	6.45%	6.21%

EXHIBIT 9.3 (continued)

	% of White Population Aged 5 and Over by Residence 5 Years Previously			% of Black Population Aged 5 and Over by Residence 5 Years Previously		
	Residence in Census Year			Residence in Census Year		
	SMSA	*Atlanta*	*Suburbs*	*SMSA*	*Atlanta*	*Suburbs*
1960						
Population over 5	695,369	273,715	421,654	199,084	160,701	38,383
Same house as 1955	41.16%	43.65%	39.56%	52.24%	51.73%	54.37%
Different house:						
Atlanta	18.95%	29.39%	12.17%	32.75%	39.24%	5.55%
Atlanta suburbs	18.00%	5.40%	26.17%	7.34%	1.51%	31.72%
U.S. outside SMSA	19.00%	17.26%	20.13%	5.23%	4.88%	6.68%
Abroad	0.86%	0.86%	0.86%	0.18%	0.14%	0.36%
Moved, 1955 location not reported	2.03%	3.44%	1.10%	2.27%	2.49%	1.31%
1970						
Population over 5	984,819	226,397	758,422	277,016	227,443	49,573
Same house as 1965	40.79%	43.80%	39.85%	44.61%	44.98%	42.94%
Different house:						
Atlanta	11.51%	21.93%	8.41%	29.72%	32.75%	17.05%
Atlanta suburbs	18.18%	6.59%	21.64%	8.00%	4.38%	24.61%
U.S. outside SMSA	21.84%	19.30%	22.60%	8.29%	8.43%	7.65%
North & West	5.94%	4.72%	6.31%	1.43%	1.39%	1.61%
South	15.90%	14.58%	16.29%	6.86%	7.04%	6.04%
Abroad	1.18%	1.52%	1.08%	0.37%	0.33%	0.58%
Moved, 1965 location not reported	6.50%	6.86%	6.38%	9.01%	9.13%	7.17%

EXHIBIT 9.4: Schooling of Population Over 25

	SMSA	*Atlanta*	*Fulton County*	*DeKalb County*	*All Suburbs*	*Fulton Suburbs*	*DeKalb Suburbs*	*Clayton, Cobb & Gwinnett*
1960								
8th grade or less	36.32%	40.11%	40.03%	24.76%	32.55%	36.58%	23.05%	40.83%
1–3 years high school	19.37%	19.43%	18.80%	18.64%	19.32%	17.71%	17.63%	22.11%
4 years high school	23.51%	20.98%	21.38%	27.71%	26.03%	25.00%	28.17%	24.23%
1–3 years college	11.04%	10.22%	10.44%	14.91%	11.87%	11.74%	15.74%	7.63%
4+ years college	9.75%	9.25%	9.35%	13.99%	10.24%	8.96%	15.41%	5.20%
1970								
8th grade or less	24.24%	30.92%	28.39%	16.54%	20.39%	22.47%	14.24%	25.84%
1–3 years high school	22.38%	22.63%	21.76%	19.68%	22.23%	20.25%	18.89%	26.65%
4 years high school	26.11%	22.56%	23.01%	28.32%	28.17%	24.67%	28.86%	29.07%
1–3 years college	12.97%	10.90%	12.34%	16.18%	14.17%	15.42%	17.27%	10.36%
4+ years college	14.29%	13.00%	14.50%	19.27%	15.04%	17.19%	20.74%	8.08%
% high school graduates	53.40%	46.40%	49.90%	63.80%	57.40%	57.60%	66.90%	47.40%

EXHIBIT 9.4 (continued)

Schooling of Population Over 25 by Race

	White			Black		
	SMSA	*Atlanta*	*Suburbs*	*SMSA*	*Atlanta*	*Suburbs*
1960						
8th grade or less	29.41%	29.92%	29.06%	62.44%	59.40%	76.85%
1–3 years high school	19.62%	19.35%	19.80%	18.46%	19.58%	13.18%
4 years high school	26.54%	25.15%	27.52%	12.06%	13.10%	7.10%
1–3 years college	13.00%	13.46%	12.67%	3.67%	4.07%	1.74%
4+ years college	11.43%	12.11%	10.96%	3.37%	3.84%	1.13%
1970						
8th grade or less	19.59%	22.55%	18.61%	43.18%	41.22%	52.93%
1–3 years high school	21.84%	20.97%	22.14%	24.58%	24.69%	24.03%
4 years high school	27.43%	23.42%	28.79%	20.75%	21.50%	17.03%
1–3 years college	14.82%	14.97%	14.77%	5.44%	5.88%	3.27%
4+ years college	16.31%	18.09%	15.71%	6.05%	6.72%	2.73%
% high school graduates	58.60%	56.40%	59.30%	32.20%	34.10%	22.60%

EXHIBIT 9.5:   Labor Force Participation and Employment by Sex and Race—1960

	SMSA		Atlanta		Suburbs	
	Male	*Female*	*Male*	*Female*	*Male*	*Female*
1960						
Population over 14	331,087	372,944	161,474	191,346	169,613	181,598
White	262,873	289,628	106,064	122,898	156,809	166,730
Non-white	68,214	83,316	55,410	68,848	12,804	14,868
Labor force participation	79.3%	40.5%	75.9%	43.9%	82.6%	37.0%
White	80.9%	38.5%	77.5%	42.3%	83.3%	35.7%
Non-white	73.0%	47.5%	72.8%	46.7%	74.0%	51.3%
Unemployment rate	3.1%	4.0%	3.6%	3.7%	2.8%	4.5%
White	2.8%	3.6%	3.4%	3.1%	2.6%	4.0%
Non-white	4.5%	5.2%	4.1%	4.9%	6.1%	7.7%
Number of people						
employed	250,180	145,010	111,516	80,811	133,664	64,199
White	202,797	107,506	77,935	50,343	124,862	57,163
Non-white	47,383	37,504	33,581	30,468	8,802	7,036

EXHIBIT 9.5 (continued)

% of People Employed by Occupation

	SMSA		Atlanta		Suburbs	
	Male	*Female*	*Male*	*Female*	*Male*	*Female*
Professional & technical	11.14%	11.37%	9.54%	10.64%	12.53%	12.30%
Managers, proprietors, etc.	13.74%	3.39%	11.91%	2.95%	15.32%	3.95%
Clerical	9.30%	34.69%	9.66%	30.37%	8.99%	40.14%
Sales	9.76%	7.01%	8.84%	6.18%	10.55%	8.06%
Craftsmen, foremen	18.27%	1.18%	14.34%	1.13%	21.69%	1.24%
Operatives	18.13%	11.73%	18.45%	11.23%	17.85%	12.36%
Laborers	6.79%	0.53%	8.19%	0.52%	5.57%	0.55%
Private household	0.31%	13.11%	0.54%	16.57%	0.10%	8.75%
Other services	7.34%	11.11%	10.84%	13.16%	4.27%	8.53%
Not reported	5.24%	5.87%	7.68%	7.27%	3.11%	4.12%

% of Whites Employed by Occupation

	SMSA		Atlanta		Suburbs	
	Male	*Female*	*Male*	*Female*	*Male*	*Female*
Professional & technical	13.09%	13.29%	12.70%	12.99%	13.32%	13.58%
Managers, proprietors, etc.	16.60%	4.34%	17.12%	4.36%	16.26%	4.33%
Clerical	10.09%	45.49%	11.07%	46.13%	9.48%	44.94%
Sales	11.74%	9.23%	12.52%	9.49%	11.24%	9.01%
Craftsmen, foremen	20.51%	1.39%	17.43%	1.43%	22.42%	1.36%
Operatives	16.29%	11.71%	14.55%	10.23%	17.38%	13.02%
Private household	0.05%	1.67%	0.02%	1.21%	0.06%	2.07%
Other services	3.47%	6.72%	4.10%	6.24%	3.06%	7.14%
Laborers	3.36%	0.32%	2.72%	0.15%	3.76%	0.48%
Not reported	4.82%	5.81%	7.73%	7.80%	2.99%	4.08%

% of Blacks Employed by Occupation

	SMSA		Atlanta		Suburbs	
	Male	*Female*	*Male*	*Female*	*Male*	*Female*
Professional & technical	2.80%	5.86%	3.15%	6.76%	1.26%	1.92%
Managers, proprietors, etc.	1.48%	0.67%	1.38%	0.62%	1.92%	0.88%
Clerical	5.91%	3.72%	6.79%	4.32%	2.01%	1.11%
Sales	1.29%	0.65%	1.41%	0.71%	0.75%	0.37%
Craftsmen, foremen	8.69%	0.57%	8.09%	0.64%	11.32%	0.27%
Operatives	25.99%	11.78%	26.32%	12.89%	24.53%	6.98%
Private household	1.43%	45.90%	1.59%	41.95%	0.73%	63.02%
Other services	23.90%	23.69%	24.46%	24.59%	21.47%	19.81%
Laborers	21.47%	1.13%	19.25%	1.12%	31.24%	1.15%
Not reported	7.05%	6.04%	7.57%	6.40%	4.77%	4.49%

EXHIBIT 9.5 (continued)

Employment and Labor Force Participation by Sex and Race—1970

	SMSA		Atlanta		Suburbs	
	Male	*Female*	*Male*	*Female*	*Male*	*Female*
1970						
Population over 16	445,444	505,322	160,110	193,530	285,334	311,772
White	357,826	395,701	88,056	101,965	269,770	293,716
Non-white	87,618	109,621	72,054	91,565	15,564	18,056
Labor force participation	81.8%	48.8%	75.3%	51.1%	85.4%	47.3%
White	83.5%	46.9%	75.5%	47.3%	86.0%	46.7%
Non-white	75.0%	55.7%	75.0%	55.3%	74.9%	57.5%
Unemployment rate	2.4%	4.0%	3.4%	4.7%	1.9%	3.5%
White	2.1%	3.4%	2.9%	3.3%	1.8%	3.4%
Non-white	3.8%	5.9%	4.0%	6.0%	3.0%	5.4%
Number of people employed	351,458	236,250	115,043	94,093	236,415	142,157
White	288,632	178,876	63,439	46,545	225,193	132,331
Non-white	62,826	57,374	51,604	47,548	11,222	9,826

% of People Employed by Occupation

	SMSA		Atlanta		Suburbs	
	Male	*Female*	*Male*	*Female*	*Male*	*Female*
Professional & technical	15.58%	16.00%	12.76%	14.71%	16.94%	16.84%
Managers, proprietors, etc.	14.50%	3.68%	10.56%	3.46%	16.42%	3.82%
Clerical	10.18%	41.99%	11.94%	34.22%	9.33%	47.14%
Sales	10.07%	7.49%	7.35%	5.91%	11.40%	8.54%
Operatives	16.00%	9.48%	20.55%	11.20%	13.79%	8.34%
Other blue collar	26.84%	2.92%	25.96%	3.28%	27.27%	2.68%
Private household	0.11%	5.42%	0.29%	10.03%	0.02%	2.37%
Other services	6.71%	13.02%	10.59%	17.19%	4.83%	10.26%

% of Whites Employed by Occupation

	SMSA		Atlanta		Suburbs	
	Male	*Female*	*Male*	*Female*	*Male*	*Female*
Professional & technical	17.86%	17.48%	18.55%	16.88%	17.60%	17.79%
Managers, proprietors, etc.	16.95%	4.44%	16.39%	5.60%	17.81%	4.03%
Clerical	9.84%	48.91%	11.50%	47.37%	8.69%	49.45%
Sales	11.83%	9.04%	11.59%	9.18%	11.96%	8.99%
Other blue collar	25.77%	2.59%	22.57%	2.60%	26.67%	2.51%
Operatives	13.15%	7.83%	13.46%	7.96%	13.05%	7.79%
Private household	0.01%	0.62%	0.03%	0.64%	—	0.62%
Other services	4.58%	9.09%	5.91%	9.76%	4.21%	8.85%

EXHIBIT 9.5 (continued)

	SMSA		Atlanta		Suburbs	
% of Blacks Employed by Occupation						
	Male	*Female*	*Male*	*Female*	*Male*	*Female*
Professional & technical	5.08%	11.37%	5.65%	12.59%	2.45%	5.51%
Managers, proprietors, etc.	3.26%	1.30%	3.40%	1.37%	2.63%	0.98%
Clerical	11.75%	20.43%	12.48%	21.36%	8.39%	15.97%
Sales	1.99%	2.65%	2.14%	2.70%	1.32%	2.45%
Operatives	29.08%	14.61%	29.26%	14.36%	28.26%	15.83%
Other blue collar	31.75%	3.95%	30.11%	3.95%	39.32%	3.98%
Private household	0.57%	20.39%	0.61%	19.22%	0.41%	26.07%
Other services	16.50%	25.27%	16.35%	24.46%	17.22%	29.22%

EXHIBIT 9.6:   Employment of SMSA, Atlanta, and Suburban Residents, by Industrial Group

	SMSA		Atlanta		Suburbs	
	1960	*1970*	*1960*	*1970*	*1960*	*1970*
Total number employed	395,190	587,708	197,327	209,136	197,863	378,572
Construction	26,469	37,824	11,200	11,964	15,269	25,860
Manufacturing:	87,355	115,882	35,319	34,994	52,036	80,888
Durables	43,030	64,872	11,978	16,333	31,052	48,539
Non-durables	44,325	51,010	23,341	18,661	20,984	32,349
Transportation	23,980	35,274	11,223	11,216	12,757	24,058
Communications, utilities, & sanitation	12,300	22,950	5,911	7,645	6,389	15,305
Wholesale trade	22,227	40,486	11,286	12,402	10,941	28,084
Retail trade	62,106	97,725	31,788	33,694	30,318	64,031
Health	6,991	25,765	4,182	10,769	2,809	14,996
Education	17,600	40,300	8,620	15,722	8,980	24,578
Other professional services	17,101	26,700	8,933	10,779	8,168	15,921
Public administration	21,710	35,874	10,585	13,118	11,125	22,756
Other	97,351	108,928	58,280	46,833	39,071	62,095

EXHIBIT 9.7:   Location of Jobs in the Metropolitan Area

Total Number of Jobs Held by Residents of SMSA by Place of Employment

Place of Employment	1960	1970	Growth 1960-1970
Total employed	391,156	580,960	48.52%
Atlanta	253,982	287,783*	13.31%
Fulton suburbs	27,906	55,693	99.57%
DeKalb suburbs	32,516	92,871	185.62%
Clayton, Cobb & Gwinnett	46,925	87,332	86.11%
Outside SMSA	9,825	13,350	35.88%
Not reported	20,002	43,931	119.63%

*52,243 employed in Central Business District; 235,540 in the rest of the city.

	Place of Residence					
Place of Work	SMSA	Atlanta	All Suburbs	Fulton Suburbs	DeKalb Suburbs	Clayton, Cobb & Gwinnett
1960						
Atlanta	64.93%	84.48%	45.45%	51.42%	55.72%	30.70%
Fulton suburbs	7.13%	2.89%	11.36%	36.65%	3.93%	5.42%
DeKalb suburbs	8.31%	2.30%	14.29%	2.05%	29.24%	4.55%
Clayton, Cobb & Gwinnett	12.00%	1.93%	22.05%	4.18%	2.54%	53.75%
Outside SMSA	2.51%	1.59%	3.43%	2.66%	4.10%	3.11%
Not reported	5.11%	6.81%	3.42%	3.03%	4.48%	2.46%
1970						
Atlanta	49.54%	68.85%	39.00%	44.60%	45.95%	29.34%
CBD*	8.99%	12.42%	7.12%	8.56%	9.36%	4.17%
Rest	40.54%	56.43%	31.87%	36.04%	36.59%	25.17%
Fulton suburbs	9.59%	7.25%	10.86%	33.93%	3.93%	8.11%
DeKalb suburbs	15.99%	7.14%	20.81%	5.71%	37.93%	9.52%
Clayton, Cobb & Gwinnett	15.03%	3.99%	21.06%	7.38%	4.13%	44.57%
Outside SMSA	2.30%	1.43%	2.77%	2.56%	2.64%	3.01%
Not reported	7.56%	11.34%	5.50%	5.82%	5.42%	5.45%

*Central business district.

EXHIBIT 9.8:   Family Income Distribution; Median Income

Income	SMSA	Atlanta	Fulton County	DeKalb County	All Suburbs	Fulton Suburbs	DeKalb Suburbs	Gwinnett, Cobb and Clayton Counties
1959								
less than $2,000	11.3%	14.3%	13.9%	6.8%	8.7%	10.0%	6.4%	10.4%
$2,000–2,999	9.4%	12.3%	11.7%	5.7%	6.9%	7.8%	5.1%	8.3%
$3,000–4,999	20.8%	23.1%	22.3%	16.3%	18.7%	19.5%	14.9%	22.4%
$5,000–6,999	21.2%	18.5%	18.7%	22.6%	23.6%	21.9%	22.4%	25.8%
$7,000–9,999	20.3%	16.1%	16.7%	27.2%	24.1%	20.9%	28.4%	21.2%
$10,000–14,999	11.5%	9.6%	10.2%	15.7%	13.1%	13.1%	16.7%	9.3%
$15,000 and over	5.5%	6.2%	6.5%	5.7%	4.9%	6.8%	6.1%	2.6%
Median income	$5,758	$5,032	$5,207	$6,873	$6,355	$6,122	$7,112	$5,689
1969								
less than $3,000	8.1%	13.7%	11.9%	4.9%	5.3%	6.7%	4.2%	5.7%
$3,000–4,999	8.1%	13.0%	11.0%	5.7%	5.6%	6.8%	4.6%	6.1%
$5,000–6,999	10.4%	13.4%	12.0%	8.2%	8.9%	8.8%	7.4%	10.2%
$7,000–8,999	12.7%	14.0%	12.9%	11.5%	12.0%	10.8%	10.9%	13.7%
$9,000–11,999	19.1%	16.2%	16.6%	18.9%	20.6%	18.3%	18.9%	23.2%
$12,000–14,999	15.5%	10.8%	11.9%	17.7%	17.9%	14.6%	18.6%	18.6%
$15,000–24,999	20.1%	13.1%	16.2%	26.4%	23.7%	23.4%	28.2%	19.4%
$25,000 and over	6.0%	5.8%	7.4%	6.7%	6.1%	10.6%	7.2%	3.0%
Median income	$10,695	$8,398	$9,359	$12,137	$11,856	$11,840	$12,652	$11,175
Growth in median income, 1959–1969	85.7%	66.9%	79.7%	76.6%	86.6%	93.4%	77.9%	96.4%

Family Income by Race

	SMSA		Atlanta		Suburbs	
	White	Black	White	Black	White	Black
1959						
less than $2,000	7.58%	26.67%	8.50%	25.47%	7.00%	32.10%
$2,000–2,999	6.21%	22.74%	7.07%	22.57%	5.67%	23.50%
$3,000–4,999	18.54%	29.91%	19.60%	29.86%	17.88%	30.12%
$4,000–6,999	23.35%	12.24%	21.37%	12.81%	24.60%	9.68%
$7,000–9,999	23.75%	6.20%	20.89%	6.74%	25.55%	3.75%
$10,000 and over	20.56%	2.25%	22.57%	2.55%	19.30%	0.85%
Median income	$6,558	$3,033	$6,226	$3,108	$6,767	$2,762
1969						
less than $3,000	5.28%	19.80%	7.92%	20.01%	4.56%	18.76%
$3,000–4,999	5.75%	17.83%	8.30%	18.12%	5.04%	16.36%
$5,000–6,999	8.87%	16.60%	11.02%	16.01%	8.27%	19.52%
$7,000–8,999	12.10%	15.30%	12.81%	15.37%	11.91%	14.97%
$9,000–9,999	6.41%	5.67%	6.35%	5.71%	4.21%	5.47%
$10,000 and over	61.57%	24.79%	53.60%	24.77%	66.00%	24.93%
Median income	$11,909	$6,462	$10,460	$6,451	$12,313	$6,524
Growth in median income, 1959–1969	81.6%	113.1%	68.0%	107.6%	82.0%	136.2%

EXHIBIT 9.9: Price Indices

Year	Consumer Price Index for Atlanta (1967 = 100)	National Non-food Wholesale Price Index (1967 = 100)
1956	83.0	90.8
1957	85.3	93.3
1958	87.5	93.6
1959	88.1	95.3
1960	89.3	95.3
1961	89.7	94.8
1962	90.5	94.8
1963	91.4	94.7
1964	92.8	95.2
1965	94.0	96.4
1966	97.0	98.5
1967	100.0	100.0
1968	104.0	102.5
1969	110.2	106.0
1970	116.3	110.0
1971	121.7	114.0
1972	125.8	117.9
1973	133.7	125.9
1974	148.5	153.8
1975	161.7	171.5

Source: Bureau of Labor Statistics

EXHIBIT 9.10:   Housing Statistics

	SMSA	Atlanta	Fulton County	DeKalb County	All Suburbs	Fulton Suburbs	DeKalb Suburbs	Gwinnett, Cobb & Clayton
1960								
Number of units	308,532	154,097	172,904	76,776	154,435	32,461	63,041	58,753
% vacant	5.56%	5.31%	5.45%	5.02%	5.82%	5.93%	5.05%	6.60%
Median number of rooms per housing unit	4.9	4.4	4.5	5.4	5.4	4.9	5.5	5.4
% of overcrowded units*	14.0%	16.2%	16.1%	8.6%	11.8%	13.0%	8.3%	16.0%
White	8.9%	8.0%	NA**	NA	9.8%	NA	NA	NA
Black	34.3%	32.7%	NA	NA	38.2%	NA	NA	NA
Median monthly rent (renter-occupied)	$67	$66	$65	$79	$70	$67	$83	$62
Median house value (owner-occupied)	$12,400	$12,100	$12,400	$13,500	$12,600	$12,800	$14,000	$10,900
% of owner occupants:								
All families	59.1%	45.6%	48.6%	72.7%	72.7%	67.5%	75.7%	72.3%
White	66.1%	53.7%	56.9%	75.5%	75.0%	71.1%	77.8%	74.0%
Black	31.2%	29.2%	29.6%	35.0%	40.7%	32.0%	41.0%	47.4%
1970								
Number of units	450,255	170,875	207,765	129,690	279,380	51,500	115,082	112,800
% vacant	4.64%	5.02%	4.91%	4.32%	4.44%	4.50%	4.27%	4.50%
Median number of rooms per housing unit	5.1	4.5	4.8	5.6	5.5	5.6	5.7	5.1
% of overcrowded units	7.6%	11.0%	9.4%	5.4%	5.6%	5.4%	4.2%	7.0%
White	4.5%	4.4%	NA	NA	4.5%	NA	NA	NA
Black	20.4%	19.4%	NA	NA	26.2%	NA	NA	NA
Median monthly rent	$98	$80	$83	$128	$118	$97	$136	$107
Median value	$19,800	$17,100	$19,200	$22,200	$20,800	$22,700	$23,100	$18,100
% of owner occupants:								
All families	54.8%	39.1%	43.4%	61.6%	67.4%	59.0%	66.2%	71.2%
White	61.9%	44.2%	50.9%	65.5%	68.3%	63.6%	66.6%	72.0%
Black	39.7%	37.3%	35.7%	55.9%	52.9%	38.5%	60.5%	48.6%

*Defined by the Bureau of the Census as having more than 1.00 persons per room.

**Data not available.

EXHIBIT 9.10 (continued)

	SMSA	*Atlanta*	*Suburbs*
1975			
Number of units	572,000	169,400	402,600
% vacant	11.49%	12.40%	11.10%
Median number of rooms			
per housing unit	5.2	4.6	NA*
% of overcrowded units	3.5%	6.1%	2.5%
White	1.9%	2.3%	1.8%
Black	9.4%	9.2%	10.0%
Percent of Units Built in			
Following Time Periods			
After 1970	26.01%	7.97%	33.10%
1965–70	19.32%	10.98%	22.83%
1960–65	14.62%	14.40%	14.70%
1950–59	17.69%	21.84%	15.95%
1940–49	9.20%	17.18%	5.84%
1939 and before	13.11%	27.69%	6.98%
% owner-occupants	58.4%	41.3%	63.7%
White	63.1%	45.4%	66.7%
Black	42.4%	38.5%	52.8%

*NA: Data not available.

Source: Bureau of the Census, Current Housing Reports, series H–170-75-21.

EXHIBIT 9.11: Neighborhood Satisfaction, 1975

	SMSA		Atlanta		Suburbs	
	White	Black	White	Black	White	Black
Number of households	393,100	111,300	66,700	80,600	316,400	30,700
Overall Neighborhood Rating						
Excellent	45.2%	17.5%	33.0%	16.0%	47.8%	21.6%
Good	41.4%	45.7%	42.4%	42.6%	41.1%	53.9%
Fair	11.4%	30.4%	20.4%	33.8%	9.5%	21.6%
Poor	1.7%	6.0%	3.6%	7.4%	1.3%	2.6%
Not reported	0.3%	0.3%	0.6%	0.2%	0.2%	0.3%
Undesirable Conditions in Neighborhood						
None	21.0%	26.9%	23.2%	28.7%	20.5%	22.1%
Some*	79.0%	73.1%	76.8%	71.3%	79.5%	77.9%
Airplane noise	29.6%	22.5%	20.8%	19.2%	31.5%	31.2%
Street noise	34.4%	30.3%	41.2%	32.6%	33.0%	24.3%
Heavy traffic	28.5%	27.0%	38.5%	29.2%	26.4%	21.1%
Streets need repair	14.7%	14.1%	6.4%	12.2%	16.4%	19.2%
Roads impassable	4.3%	9.7%	4.3%	9.8%	4.3%	9.4%
Poor street lighting	27.2%	17.1%	7.2%	12.3%	31.5%	29.9%
Crime	18.2%	22.1%	30.5%	24.7%	15.6%	15.3%
Litter	16.0%	23.8%	19.5%	25.3%	15.2%	19.8%
Abandoned buildings	6.7%	16.0%	13.2%	16.8%	5.3%	13.6%
Deteriorating housing	8.3%	13.6%	14.1%	14.3%	7.1%	12.0%
Commercial or industrial business	15.6%	10.5%	22.8%	10.6%	14.1%	10.4%
Odors	5.9%	7.2%	7.3%	7.2%	5.6%	7.1%
Adequacy of Public Services in Neighborhood						
Services adequate	60.2%	56.2%	67.0%	55.8%	58.9%	56.9%
Inadequate	39.8%	43.8%	33.0%	44.2%	41.1%	43.1%
*What is Inadequate?***						
Public transit	28.5%	14.1%	9.9%	9.3%	32.3%	27.0%
Schools	4.4%	3.3%	9.1%	3.3%	3.5%	3.3%
Shopping	7.0%	24.4%	12.4%	27.6%	5.9%	15.8%
Police protection	5.1%	11.4%	7.3%	13.5%	4.6%	5.9%
Fire protection	2.2%	3.8%	0.9%	3.9%	2.5%	3.3%
Health services	6.7%	11.2%	5.7%	10.9%	6.9%	12.2%

*Total of specific conditions does not sum to this number because some households listed more than one undesirable condition.

**Total does not sum to percentage claiming services are inadequate because some households listed more than one inadequate service.

EXHIBIT 9.11 (continued)

	SMSA		Atlanta		Suburbs	
	White	*Black*	*White*	*Black*	*White*	*Black*
% Wishing to Move From Current House	11.4%	20.6%	14.4%	20.7%	10.9%	20.1%
*% of Those Wishing to Move Citing Following Reasons**						
Airplane noise	21.8%	15.7%	12.5%	10.7%	24.3%	29.0%
Street noise	29.3%	26.5%	34.4%	29.2%	28.0%	19.4%
Heavy traffic	25.3%	21.7%	42.7%	16.1%	20.6%	37.1%
Street needs repair	12.7%	15.7%	7.2%	14.3%	14.1%	19.4%
Roads impassable	3.3%	11.3%	2.1%	11.3%	3.7%	11.3%
Poor street lighting	10.9%	16.1%	6.2%	13.1%	12.1%	24.2%
Crime	29.8%	39.1%	44.8%	43.5%	25.7%	27.4%
Litter	24.2%	40.9%	34.4%	44.0%	21.5%	32.3%
Abandoned buildings	7.3%	17.0%	13.5%	19.6%	5.6%	9.7%
Deteriorating housing	16.9%	29.1%	27.1%	31.0%	14.1%	24.2%
Commercial/industrial business	9.8%	7.0%	11.5%	7.1%	9.3%	6.5%
Odors	11.1%	13.5%	12.5%	16.1%	10.7%	6.5%
Poor public transportation	14.7%	18.3%	6.2%	12.5%	16.9%	33.9%
Poor schools	14.0%	7.0%	25.0%	6.5%	11.0%	8.0%
Poor shopping	8.6%	35.2%	15.6%	39.3%	6.8%	24.2%
Poor police protection	10.0%	20.0%	15.6%	25.0%	8.5%	6.5%
Poor fire protection	4.0%	7.0%	2.1%	8.9%	4.5%	1.6%
Poor health services	5.1%	12.7%	3.1%	13.7%	5.6%	9.7%

*Numbers do not sum to 100% because some households cited more than one reason.

Source: Bureau of the Census, Current Housing Reports, series H-170-75-21.

**EXHIBIT 9.12:   Crime Rate
per 100,000 People**

	Atlanta Central City	National
Murder	20.8	9.7
Rape	42.8	26.1
Robbery	345.0	209.0
Aggravated assault	298.0	214.0
Burglary	2,203.0	1,429.0
Larceny	2,304.0	2,473.0
Auto theft	554.0	461.0

*Crime Rates
(Compiled by Atlanta Police Department)*

Year	Total Serious Crimes*	Change
1960	17,259	
1961	19,384	12%
1962	20,389	5%
1963	21,205	4%
1964	24,682	16%
1965	21,697	−12%
1966	22,406	3%
1967	23,244	3%
1968	26,774	15%
1969	32,095	19%
1970	40,092	24%
1971	40,701	1%
1972	42,359	4%
1973	45,058	6%
1974	48,650	7%

*Includes the seven categories of serious crime: murder, rape, robbery, aggravated assault, burglary, larceny, auto theft.

Source: Atlanta Constitution, *March 23, 1975, p. 16A.*

EXHIBIT 9.13: Business Statistics

Retail Trade

	SMSA			*Atlanta*			*Atlanta as % of SMSA*		
	Sales	*Payroll*	*Employees*	*Sales*	*Payroll*	*Employees*	*Sales*	*Payroll*	*Employees*
1958									
Food	256.0	16.0	6,502	150.3	9.8	3,887	58.7%	61.2%	59.8%
Automotive	200.3	18.6	4,374	135.5	12.9	2,796	67.6%	69.3%	63.9%
Service stations	85.5	7.4	3,221	47.4	4.4	1,927	55.4%	59.5%	59.8%
Department stores	136.9	24.1	9,251	133.5	23.7	9,087	96.7%	98.2%	98.2%
Other retail trade	550.8	79.1	32,649	411.8	62.6	25,637	74.8%	79.1%	78.5%
Total	1,229.5	145.2	55,997	878.5	113.4	43,334	71.5%	78.1%	77.4%
1963									
Food	333	25.0	7,966	163	13.4	4,157	48.9%	53.6%	52.2%
Automotive	342	29.8	5,542	208	19.0	3,338	60.8%	63.8%	60.2%
Service stations	120	11.0	3,790	60	5.9	1,976	50.0%	53.6%	52.1%
Department stores	210	30.9	9,603	174	28.0	8,400	82.9%	90.6%	87.4%
Other retail trade	614	96.5	34,799	411	69.6	22,882	66.9%	72.1%	65.8%
Total	1,619	193.2	61,700	1,016	135.9	40,753	62.8%	70.3%	68.9%
1967									
Food	427	35.1	9,469	204	16.1	4,355	47.8%	45.9%	46.0%
Automotive	450	43.1	6,718	238	23.9	3,427	52.9%	55.5%	51.0%
Service stations	170	16.0	4,904	77	7.9	2,348	45.3%	49.4%	47.9%
Department stores	363	58.8	13,882	259	47.7	10,659	71.3%	81.1%	76.8%
Other retail trade	927	148.3	40,047	568	102.1	26,666	61.3%	68.8%	66.6%
Total	2,337	301.3	75,020	1,346	197.7	47,455	57.6%	65.6%	63.3%
1972									
Food	751	62.0	11,451	219	19.6	3,530	29.2%	31.6%	30.8%
Automotive	974	92.3	9,659	372	37.3	3,709	39.2%	40.4%	38.3%
Service stations	339	31.9	7,135	93	9.6	2,204	27.3%	30.1%	30.9%
Department stores	669	88.2	18,816	344	48.9	10,087	51.4%	55.4%	53.6%
Other retail trade	1,757	283.7	61,675	784	147.7	32,120	44.7%	52.1%	52.1%
Total	4,490	558.1	108,736	1,812	263.1	51,650	40.3%	47.1%	47.5%

Wholesale Trade

	Sales	*Payroll*	*Employees*	*Sales*	*Payroll*	*Employees*	*Sales*	*Payroll*	*Employees*
1958 total	3,999	170.7	34,283	3,314	149.8	29,601	82.9%	87.8%	86.3%
1963 total	5,733	257.7	41,825	4,366	207.1	33,074	76.2%	80.4%	79.1%
1967 total	8,498	378.2	52,409	5,847	269.0	36,908	68.8%	71.1%	70.4%
1972 total	14,687	638.8	63,139	8,054	360.2	34,968	54.8%	56.4%	55.3%

Sales and payroll in millions of dollars, number of employees in thousands.

EXHIBIT 9.13 (continued)

Selected Services

	SMSA			Atlanta			Atlanta as % of SMSA		
	Sales	Payroll	Employees	Sales	Payroll	Employees	Sales	Payroll	Employees
1958									
Hotels & tourist services	19.5	5.4	2,918	17.2	5.0	2,678	88.2%	92.6%	91.8%
Auto repair	34.7	8.0	2,481	27.5	6.6	1,986	79.3%	82.5%	80.0%
Business services	62.0	20.2	6,722	58.2	18.7	6,353	93.9%	92.6%	94.5%
Other	100.8	29.9	11,423	78.5	23.8	9,034	77.9%	79.6%	73.8%
Total	217.0	63.5	23,544	181.4	54.1	20,051	83.6%	85.2%	85.2%
1963									
Hotels, etc.	25.5	6.9	3,059	21.0	5.8	2,609	82.4%	84.1%	85.3%
Auto repair	51.8	11.8	2,950	40.0	9.2	2,259	77.2%	78.0%	76.6%
Business services	124.7	34.3	9.355	114.8	31.1	8,594	92.1%	90.7%	91.9%
Other	134.1	40.5	13,233	99.2	31.3	10,015	74.0%	77.3%	75.7%
Total	336.1	93.5	28,597	275.0	77.4	23,477	81.8%	82.8%	82.1%
1967									
Hotels, etc.	59.4	16.8	5,282	44.3	13.4	4,191	74.6%	79.8%	79.3%
Auto repair	77.6	16.3	3,499	55.2	11.3	2,443	71.1%	69.3%	69.8%
Business services	214.0	75.4	17,111	194.2	69.3	15,782	90.7%	91.9%	92.2%
Other	209.7	63.1	14,587	138.8	40.7	8,757	66.2%	64.5%	60.0%
Total	560.7	171.6	40,479	432.5	134.7	31,173	77.1%	78.5%	77.0%
1972									
Hotels, etc.	133.1	35.7	NA	97.5	26.1	6,294	73.3%	73.1%	NA
Auto repair	174.6	37.8	NA	102.7	21.7	3,129	58.8%	55.9%	NA
Business services	474.5	164.8	NA	348.5	125.8	23,934	73.4%	76.3%	NA
Other	328.5	111.9	NA	169.1	50.4	8,324	51.5%	45.0%	NA
Total	1,110.7	350.2	NA	717.8	224.0	41,681	64.6%	67.0%	NA

Sales and payroll in millions of dollars, number of employees in thousands.

Manufacturing

	SMSA			Atlanta			Atlanta as % of SMSA		
	Value Added	Payroll	Number of Employees	Value Added	Payroll	Number of Employees	Value Added	Payroll	Number of Employees
1958	711.9	371.1	82.5	411.1	200.3	48.7	59.3%	54.0%	57.8%
1963	1,153.2	538.6	95.7	612.5	275.3	52.4	53.1%	51.1%	54.8%
1967	1,604.0	809.6	117.2	693.3	338.2	54.0	43.2%	41.8%	46.0%
1972	2,254.2	1,089.5	115.4	973.4	426.1	47.8	43.2%	39.1%	41.4%

Value added and payroll in millions of dollars, number of employees in thousands.

EXHIBIT 9.14: Manufacturing in Atlanta SMSA by Industry—1967*

Industry Code & Description	Value of Shipments	Value Added in Manufacturing	Payroll	Number of Employees
20 Food and kindred products	504	191	64	11.2
21 Tobacco products		(NOT AVAILABLE)		
22 Textile mill products	101	49	30	6.6
23 Apparel, other textile products	212	72	39	9.0
24 Lumber and wood products	25	11	4	1.0
25 Furniture and fixtures	76	40	21	4.2
26 Paper and allied products	185	80	41	6.7
27 Printing and publishing	175	108	58	8.2
28 Chemicals and allied products	189	99	26	3.7
29 Petroleum and coal products		(NOT AVAILABLE)		
30 Rubber and plastics products	28	11	5	0.9
31 Leather and leather products	28	15	8	1.9
32 Stone, clay, and glass products	104	59	25	4.3
33 Primary metal industries	84	29	19	2.7
34 Fabricated metal products	145	57	33	5.3
35 Machinery, except electrical	91	51	30	4.4
36 Electrical equipment	83	44	19	2.9
37 Transportation equipment	2,006	657	325	35.4
38 Instruments and related products		(NOT AVAILABLE)		
39 Miscellaneous	43	27	14	2.8
Administration & auxiliary	—	—	48	5.5
Other (21, 29, 38)	16	4	1	0.5
Total	4,095	1,604	810	117.2

*1967 used as base year because definition of Atlanta SMSA changed in 1972 Census of Manufacturers.

EXHIBIT 9.15: City of Atlanta, Georgia: General Governmental Expenditures by Function, Last Ten Years

			Environmental and Streets		Parks, Libraries and Cultural Affairs		
Year	General Government	Public Safety*	Sanitation	Streets and Highways	Library and Aid to Education	Recreation	Total
1966	$ 5,871,990	$14,606,976	$ 6,047,928	$2,454,318	$1,143,187	$4,139,874	$34,264,273
1967	6,848,455	17,700,900	6,841,129	2,813,027	1,234,961	4,381,573	39,820,045
1968	7,957,406	19,322,635	8,293,060	2,872,421	1,388,053	5,613,402	45,446,977
1969	10,032,091	21,511,673	8,975,924	3,405,701	1,688,473	7,015,168	52,629,030
1970	11,515,124	24,928,598	9,411,644	4,624,386	2,504,528	7,490,333	60,474,613
1971	13,682,791	29,495,261	10,608,366	5,214,613	2,913,606	8,087,028	70,001,665
1972	14,451,744	32,291,287	9,328,620	6,826,126	3,023,517	7,651,102	73,572,396
1973	18,730,988	28,048,849**	9,426,364	7,409,671	3,568,011	8,688,619	75,872,502
1974	26,116,039	34,698,920	11,060,562	9,275,587	4,606,271	8,794,893	94,552,272
1975	31,678,656	37,656,420	15,126,634	8,910,187	4,927,930	8,657,747	106,957,574

*[Includes police, fire, and traffic engineering, Ed.]

**Fire Department salaries were paid with Revenue Sharing Funds during 1973 and 1974 [and do not appear in the budget, Ed.].

Source: City of Atlanta, Commissioner of Finance, Annual Report, 1975, p. 121.

**EXHIBIT 9.16:   City of Atlanta, Georgia: General Fund Revenues
by Source, Last Ten Years**

Year	Taxes	Licenses and Permits	Charges for Current Services	Fines, Forfeits & Penalties	Revenue from Use of Money and Property	Other Sales, Recoveries and Grants
1966	$20,340,627	$4,475,607	$ 5,215,207	$2,704,764	$ 648,079	$ 938,723
1967	22,850,656	6,243,216	8,912,806	2,803,942	721,977	1,043,735
1968	24,681,828	6,648,558	9,132,559	3,133,944	922,441	1,953,016
1969	30,513,480	8,499,825	9,673,292	3,727,022	1,215,101	1,787,426
1970	32,541,746	9,207,070	10,231,481	3,099,863	1,488,727	1,903,789
1971	40,771,083	9,175,281	11,197,174	3,229,023	1,172,694	4,122,753
1972	42,755,879	8,402,002	11,657,254	3,426,564	1,192,103	6,556,187
1973	46,316,005	9,955,316	14,221,893	2,866,764	1,473,118	9,775,350
1974	49,701,935	9,776,845	14,577,256	3,891,133	2,759,320	18,656,588
1975	56,398,975*	9,412,154	14,259,868	3,639,848	2,491,553	13,706,784

Year	Total Taxes	Property Taxes	Tax on Receipts of Public Utilities	Tax on Life Insurance Premiums	Alcoholic Beverages
1966	$20,340,627	$12,524,865	$2,718,394	$1,097,010	$4,000,358
1967	22,850,656	14,611,476	2,744,133	1,192,575	4,302,472
1968	24,681,828	15,809,484	2,779,590	1,353,228	4,739,526
1969	30,513,480	20,078,498	3,656,307	1,534,000	5,244,675
1970	32,541,746	21,558,825	3,719,324	1,627,337	5,636,260
1971	40,771,083	29,192,612	3,840,647	1,939,320	5,798,504
1972	42,755,880	30,041,539	4,718,747	2,042,257	5,953,337
1973	46,316,005	31,491,788	5,301,830	2,727,197	6,795,190
1974	49,701,935	31,978,541	6,619,532	2,762,206	8,341,656
1975	56,398,975	36,900,005	7,143,869	3,039,192	8,397,668

Source: City of Atlanta Commissioner of Finance, Annual Report, *1975, p. 122, 123.*

*Editor's note: This incorrect total appeared in the *Annual Report.*

EXHIBIT 9.17: City of Atlanta, Georgia: Property Tax Base, Tax Rate, and Tax Revenues

| Year | Assessed Value of Property | | Adjusted Assessed Value* | | Tax Rate | Adjusted Rate* | Revenue** |
	Real Estate	Other Business Property	Real Estate	Business			
1956	571.7	331.3	653.3	220.9	25.50	26.34	21.38
1957	586.8	351.4	670.6	234.3	25.00	25.91	22.54
1958	606.0	370.4	692.6	246.9	29.25	30.40	27.41
1959	627.8	383.6	717.5	255.7	29.25	30.40	28.45
1960	655.0	420.5	748.6	280.3	29.25	30.57	30.30
1961	681.1	435.6	778.4	290.4	29.25	30.56	31.50
1962	705.9	442.8	806.7	295.2	29.25	30.23	32.44
1963	741.4	462.1	847.3	308.1	32.00	33.33	37.31
1964	780.6	499.8	892.1	333.2	32.00	33.44	40.34
1965	811.9	503.6	927.9	335.7	32.00	33.31	42.19
1966	858.1	553.3	980.7	368.9	32.00	33.47	44.01
1967*	888.7	477.4	1,015.7	395.0	36.00	34.86	51.25
1968*	1,050.0	626.1***			36.03		59.29
1969	1,111.0	689.8			41.50		72.75
1970	1,164.4	754.4			44.75		84.06
1971	1,183.3	764.5			53.03		100.37
1972	1,541.0***	799.6			46.50		108.04
1973	1,780.3	932.0			41.85		112.72
1974	1,810.0	958.8			41.85		113.47
1975	1,864.6	992.6			48.79		127.10

All numbers in millions of dollars except tax rates in dollars per thousand.

*Until 1967, real estate was assessed at 35% of true value and business franchises and personal property were assessed at 60% of true value (except for 1967 only, when business property was assessed at 48.3% of true value). In 1968 and after, all property was assessed at 40% of true value. The "adjusted assessed value" column gives assessed value for all years prior to 1968 if 1968 procedures were followed, the "adjusted rate" column gives the tax rate necessary to generate the same amount of revenue as was actually received, if adjusted assessed values had been used.

**One cannot simply multiply the tax base by the rate to find revenue because taxes for city government operation (except debt service) are levied on total assessed value minus an exemption of $2,000 per owner-occupied home ($5,000 in 1975). The base multiplied by the rate overestimates revenue.

***Major reassessments took place in these years for these types of property.

Source: City of Atlanta, Commissioner of Finance, Annual Reports (various years).

**EXHIBIT 9.18:   Population and General Fund* Expenditures
of Municipalities in Fulton County—1973**

	Population Estimate	General Fund* Expenditures
Alpharetta	2,964	$ 380,000
Atlanta	459,291	73,572,396
Atlanta-in-Fulton	418,177	
Atlanta-in-DeKalb	41,114	
College Park	19,951	2,806,156
East Point	38,005	9,723,897
Fairburn	3,758	304,692
Hapeville	8,705	1,452,812
Mountain Park	249	(not available)
Palmetto	2,049	72,886
Roswell	13,261	512,416
Union City	2,994	286,034
Total of Incorporated Areas**	551,227	$ 89,111,289
Total of Incorporated Areas except Atlanta	91,936	$ 15,538,893
Unincorporated Fulton County	84,540	
Fulton County budget		$ 45,782,621
Total county and municipal budgets for Fulton County**	635,767	$134,893,910

*Excludes education, capital projects, and self-supporting utilities.

**Population and budget figures include the portion of Atlanta in DeKalb County.

Source: Population: Bureau of the Census, Current Population Reports *No. 709 (September, 1977). Budgets: Atlanta: City of Atlanta, Commissioner of Finance,* Annual Report, *1975, p. 121. Other municipalities: Research Atlanta, Inc.,* The Plan of Improvement: An Analysis of Services in the City of Atlanta and Fulton County *(Atlanta, 1974), p. 77. Fulton County: Ibid., p. 71, adding all grants and subtracting all capital projects listed on Ibid., pp. 72–73.*

EXHIBIT 9.19: Comparative National Statistics

Population (thousands)

	1950	1960	Growth 1950–60	1970	Growth 1960–70	1975	Growth 1970–75
Total	150,697	179,326	19.0%	203,210	13.4%	213,137	4.9%
White	133,217	158,832	19.2%	178,128	12.6%	195,198	4.0%
Non-white	17,480	20,491	17.2%	25,082	22.4%	27,940	11.4%
% non-white	11.6%	11.4%		12.3%		13.1%	

Age Distribution

	1960			1970		
	Total	White	Black	Total	White	Black
Under 5	11.3%	11.0%	14.1%	8.8%	8.3%	12.3%
5–13	18.4%	18.1%	21.5%	18.4%	17.5%	22.7%
14–19	8.9%	8.8%	10.0%	11.2%	10.9%	12.8%
20–44	32.0%	32.1%	31.3%	31.4%	31.5%	29.9%
45–64	20.3%	20.7%	17.0%	20.6%	20.9%	16.1%
65 and over	9.0%	9.4%	6.3%	9.7%	10.9%	6.2%
Median age	29.4	30.1	23.5	28.2	29.3	21.4

Schooling of Population over 25 in 1971

	Total	White	Black
8th grade or less	26.7%	25.2%	41.7%
1–3 years high school	16.8%	16.2%	23.5%
4 years high school	34.4%	35.5%	24.2%
1–3 years college	10.6%	11.1%	6.0%
4 years or more, college	11.4%	12.0%	4.5%
Median years completed	12.2	12.2	10.0

Family Income in 1969 Dollars

	1959			1969		
	Total	White	Black	Total	White	Black
less than $3,000	16.4%	14.0%	40.8%	9.3%	8.1%	21.4%
$3,000–4,999	14.0%	13.3%	21.8%	10.7%	9.6%	19.8%
$5,000–6,999	19.0%	19.2%	17.9%	12.3%	11.8%	17.4%
$7,000–9,999	23.6%	24.7%	12.2%	31.7%	21.9%	19.6%
$10,000–14,999	17.2%	19.3%	6.1%	26.7%	27.9%	14.7%
$15,000–24,999	6.7%	7.1%	1.2%	15.6%	16.6%	6.5%
$25,000 and over	2.2%	2.4%	0.1%	3.6%	4.0%	0.6%
U.S. median income	7,058	7,360	3,721	9,433	9,793	5,998
Median income in metropolitan areas	7,880	8,566	4,768	10,261	10,646	6,836

1970 Housing

% owner occupied:		% overcrowded:	
total	62.87%	total	7.96%
white	65.24%	white	6.91%
black	37.86%	black	19.06%

EXHIBIT 9.19 (continued)

Male Labor Force Participation and Type of Employment

	1960			1970		
	Total	White	Black	Total	White	Black
Population over 16 (thousands)	56,576	51,039	5,030	65,236	59,947	6,119
% in labor force	78.6%	79.1%	74.5%	76.2%	76.8%	72.4%
Unemployment rate	5.1%	4.7%	9.6%	4.1%	3.8%	6.8%
% of employed						
Professional and technical	10.9%	11.6%	3.3%	14.1%	14.8%	5.8%
Managerial	11.3%	12.2%	1.4%	14.4%	15.4%	4.1%
Clerical	7.6%	7.7%	6.1%	7.5%	7.4%	8.6%
Sales	7.0%	7.5%	1.6%	5.7%	6.1%	1.6%
Craftsmen	20.4%	21.3%	10.0%	19.9%	20.6%	14.2%
Operatives	20.9%	20.5%	27.0%	19.9%	18.9%	30.6%
Non-farm laborers	7.1%	5.6%	24.3%	6.8%	5.7%	18.9%
Service workers	6.3%	5.5%	15.6%	6.6%	6.0%	11.7%
Farmers and farm laborers	8.4%	8.1%	10.6%	5.1%	5.2%	4.5%

Female Labor Force Participation and Type of Employment

	1960			1970		
	Total	White	Black	Total	White	Black
Population over 16 (thousands)	64,961	58,087	5,925	73,852	65,421	7,317
% in labor force	34.5%	33.6%	43.0%	42.6%	41.9%	49.1%
Unemployment rate	5.3%	4.8%	9.6%	5.7%	4.9%	8.5%
% of employed						
Professional and technical	15.0%	14.6%	7.0%	13.8%	15.5%	10.0%
Managerial	4.4%	4.4%	0.7%	4.0%	4.7%	1.4%
Clerical	34.2%	34.9%	8.1%	31.9%	36.1%	18.9%
Sales	6.7%	8.8%	1.3%	7.9%	7.3%	2.5%
Craftsmen	1.1%	1.4%	0.9%	1.3%	1.1%	0.8%
Operatives	14.7%	16.7%	14.0%	16.5%	14.5%	16.8%
Non-farm laborers	0.4%	0.5%	0.8%	0.5%	0.4%	0.9%
Service workers*	22.1%	17.2%	63.7%	22.4%	18.8%	48.1%
Farmers and farm laborers	1.4%	1.5%	3.6%	1.5%	1.5%	0.5%

*Includes private household workers (1960: 8.0% of total, 4.0% of whites, 40.3% of blacks; 1970: 5.5% of total, 3.7% of whites, 19.1% of blacks).

EXHIBIT 9.19 (continued)

Retail and Wholesale Trade						
	1958			*1963*		
	Sales	*Payroll*	*Employees*	*Sales*	*Payroll*	*Employees*
Food	49,022	3,232	1,326	57,079	4,249	1,274
Automotive	31,807	3,030	721	45,376	4,111	794
Service stations	14,178	1,133	466	17,760	1,510	520
Department stores	13,359	2,218	808	20,537	2,942	970
Other	91,280	11,976	4,590	103,450	14,820	4,852
Total retail	199,646	21,589	7,911	244,202	27,632	8,410
Wholesale trade	284,970	13,199	2,797	358,385	18,101	3,089
	1967			*1972*		
	Sales	*Payroll*	*Employees*	*Sales*	*Payroll*	*Employees*
Food	70,251	5,543	1,444	100,719	8,820	1,722
Automotive	55,631	5,256	907	90,030	8,622	1,035
Service stations	22,709	1,898	575	33,655	2,974	748
Department stores	32,344	4,673	1,174	51,083	7,226	1,437
Other	129,279	18,805	5,281	183,353	27,730	6,269
Total retail	310,214	36,175	9,381	458,840	55,372	11,211
Wholesale trade	459,476	23,922	3,518	695,224	36,893	4,026

Sales and payrolls in millions of dollars; number of employees in thousands.

Selected Services						
	1958			*1963*		
	Sales	*Payroll*	*Employees*	*Sales*	*Payroll*	*Employees*
Hotels & tourist services	3,888	1,145	502	5,049	1,440	526
Auto repair	3,852	854	256	5,444	1,135	288
Business services	9,897	2,578	616	15,193	4,103	874
Other services	14,739	4,429	1,133	18,900	5,514	1,574
Total selected services	32,376	9,006	2,507	44,586	12,192	3,262
	1967			*1972*		
	Sales	*Payroll*	*Employees*	*Sales*	*Payroll*	*Employees*
Hotels & tourist services	7,039	1,990	617	10,638	2,971	726
Auto repair	7,028	1,468	316	12,081	2,553	392
Business services	22,595	6,699	1,212	37,802	12,250	1,759
Other services	23,880	7,367	1,696	33,350	9,758	1,838
Total selected services	60,542	17,524	3,841	93,871	27,532	4,715

Sales and payroll in millions of dollars; number of employees in thousands.

EXHIBIT 9.19 (continued)

Manufacturing	Manufacturing			
	Total Value of Shipments	Value Added in Manufacturing	Payroll	Number of Employees
1958	326,723	141,271	73,750	15,394
1963	420,973	192,083	99,899	16,958
1967	557,398	261,984	132,208	19,323
1972	756,467	353,973	174,187	19,026

Value of shipments, valued added, and payroll in millions of dollars; number of employees in thousands.

National Manufacturing by Industry, 1967				
Industry Code & Description	Total Value of Shipments	Value Added in Manufacturing	Payroll	Number of Employees
20 Food and kindred products	83,975	26,621	10,077	1,650
21 Tobacco products	4,903	2,032	377	75
22 Textile mill products	19,815	8,153	4,391	929
23 Apparel, other textile products	21,327	10,064	5,582	1,356
24 Lumber and wood products	11,206	4,973	2,799	554
25 Furniture and fixtures	7,750	4,170	2,258	425
26 Paper and allied products	20,970	9,756	4,436	639
27 Printing and publishing	21,738	14,355	7,152	1,031
28 Chemicals and allied products	42,148	23,550	6,443	841
29 Petroleum and coal products	22,043	5,426	1,216	142
30 Rubber and plastics products	12,759	6,800	3,286	517
31 Leather and leather products	5,169	2,626	1,459	329
32 Stone, clay, and glass products	14,449	8,333	3,826	590
33 Primary metal industries	46,731	19,978	9,851	1,281
34 Fabricated metal products	34,578	18,043	9,320	1,342
35 Machinery, except electrical	48,477	27,836	14,226	1,864
36 Electrical equipment	43,361	24,487	12,968	1,875
37 Transportation equipment	68,512	28,174	15,174	1,834
38 Instruments and related products	9,907	6,418	2,822	394
39 Miscellaneous	17,578	10,187	5,819	824
Administrative & auxiliary			8,728	830
Total	557,396	261,982	132,210	19,322

Value of shipments, value added, and payroll in millions of dollars; number of employees in thousands.

EXHIBIT 9.20:   Metropolitan Atlanta in 1975

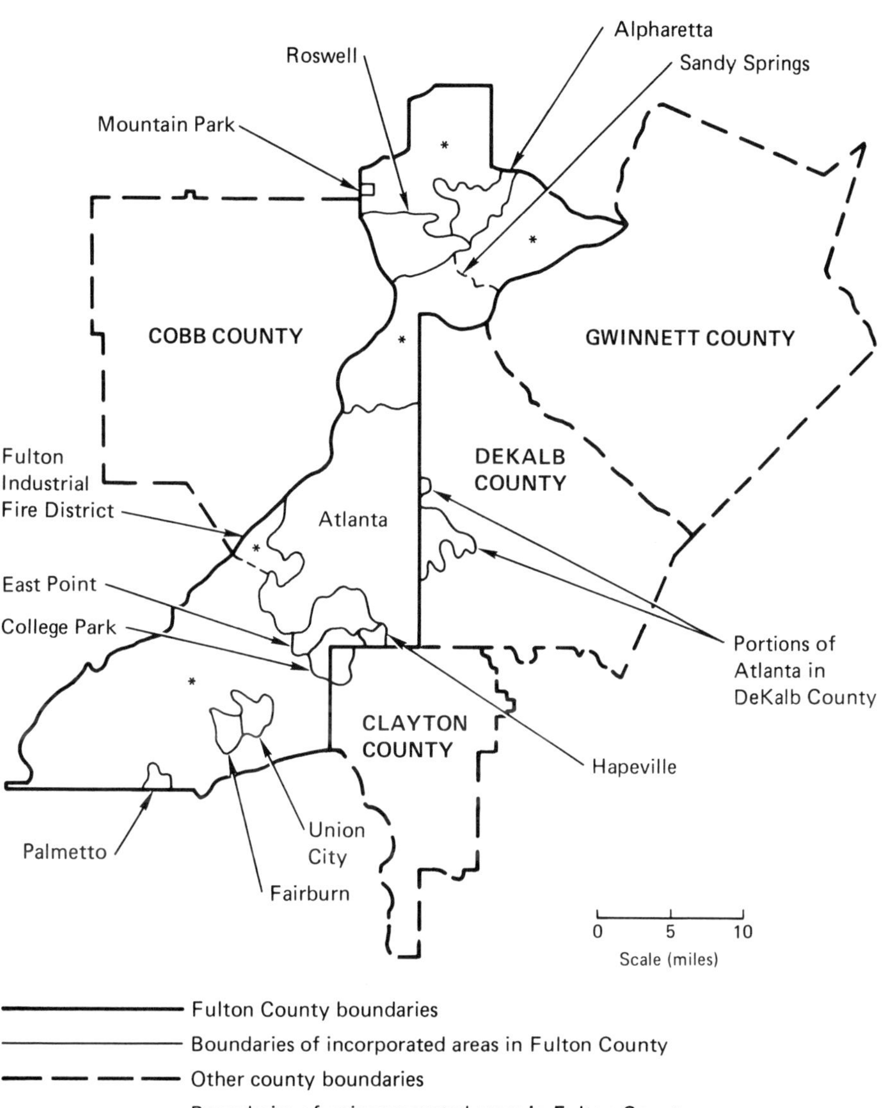

*Unincorporated area in Fulton County.

Source: Atlanta Regional Commission.

10

Expanding Atlanta's City Limits (A)

In 1975 and 1976, the Georgia General Assembly had under consideration several proposals to expand the city limits of Atlanta, the state's capital. These proposals, which sought to relieve the city's fiscal problems by enlarging its tax base, aroused strong opposition on both economic and racial grounds. Part A of this case, described in this chapter, provides background information on Atlanta, its form of government, and its political leaders at the time of the 1975-76 expansion debate; Part B, described in chapter 11, considers the expansion proposals in detail.

ATLANTA IN 1975[1]

In 1975, the Atlanta region had just completed its second decade of strong economic growth. From 1966 to 1975, the population of the Atlanta Standard Metropolitan Statistical Area (SMSA) increased 25.3% from 1,431,200 to 1,806,100, compared to a 9.0% population increase in the United States as a whole. From 1965 to 1975, non-agricultural employment in the Atlanta SMSA rose 53.8% from 477,000 to 733,000, compared to a more modest 26.6% in the United States as a whole. The region's strong economic growth was based largely on Atlanta's position as a regional transportation and communications center and on the growth of service industries. From 1965 to 1975, manufacturing employment increased only 6% in the region, and employment in the automotive industry—the largest component in the Atlanta region's manufacturing base—fell by over 30%. In contrast, transportation and communications employment increased 54%; retail and wholesale trade increased by 63%; employment in finance, insurance and real estate rose 67%; and services and government each employed about 90% more workers than a decade earlier.

This growth in employment led to growth in income as well. In 1960, the median family income for metropolitan Atlanta was $400 less than the national median for metropolitan areas; by 1970, it was $500 greater. Black family income in the SMSA increased by 113% over the decade, as compared to 86% nationally, although it remained lower than in many northern cities. Between 1960 and 1970, the number of poor families (defined as having a family income less than $3,000 in 1959, $4,000 in 1969) in the Atlanta SMSA declined by 21%, as against a 7% decline for all metropolitan areas.

However, the impact of economic growth was unequally distributed throughout the region. The SMSA's 37% population growth in the 1960s was composed of a 1.9% population increase in Atlanta and a 68.7% increase in the rest of the metropolitan area; suburban gains continued from 1970 to 1975, when Atlanta lost 25,000 people—5% of its population. Median family income in the suburbs was already 26% greater than in Atlanta in 1959, and over the 1960s, suburban income jumped 86.6% while Atlanta's median family income rose only 66.9%, creating a 41% gap by 1970 between suburban and city income—$11,856 as compared to $8,398. The percentage of the area's retail trade conducted in the central city fell from 72% in 1958 to 40% in 1972; department stores, virtually all of whose business was conducted inside Atlanta in 1958, drew half of their business from suburban shopping centers by 1972. Atlanta's position in wholesale trade declined from 83% of total sales in the SMSA to 55% over this 15-year period, and wholesale trade employment in Atlanta fell by almost 2,000 from 1967 to 1972, while 13,000 wholesale trade jobs were being added in the suburbs. Manufacturing employment fell from 54,000 in 1967 to 47,800 in 1972 in Atlanta, while rising from 63,200 to 67,600 in the suburbs. The overall strong growth of the service sector increased the number of jobs in both Atlanta and its suburbs, but Atlanta's share of this growing sector fell from 84% in 1958 to 65% in 1972.

Government finances were affected by the increasing inequality between city and suburb. City residents, generally poorer than those in the suburbs, demanded more government services than suburbanites but could ill afford the taxes to pay for them. By 1970, almost 10% of Atlanta residents were public housing tenants, while the suburbs steadfastly resisted any public housing construction in their areas.* In

1970, the per capita total expenditure of the city of Atlanta was $554, compared to $315 for the surrounding suburbs. State and federal aid did not close the gap: per capita aid to Atlanta was $97 in 1970 as compared to $95 for suburban regions. The inequality increased as Atlanta's property tax base grew more slowly than that of the suburbs and failed to keep up with inflation. From 1970 to 1974 the percentage of Fulton County's tax base within the city of Atlanta fell from 76% to 67%. (See Exhibit 10.1 for a map.)

Economic inequalities were accompanied by persistent or increasing racial segregation. While the racial composition of the SMSA held constant at approximately 23% black and 77% white, the city of Atlanta was 38% black in 1960, 51% black in 1970 and 56% black in 1975; some projections show a black majority in Fulton County by 1980 as whites leave for outlying suburbs in neighboring counties. Meanwhile, within the city, residential and school attendance patterns have become more segregated. The number of whites in Atlanta's public school system declined by 78.3% between 1968 and 1976, and the system as a whole lost 25.8% of its pupils as black enrollment gains failed to offset the massive white exodus. After a decade of attempts at school integration, over three-fourths of metropolitan Atlanta students attended schools with less than 10% of the minority race. In 1975, 37% of students in Fulton County were black; however, 84% of students in the Atlanta public school system were black while the suburban Fulton County system was only 13% black.

The recession of 1974-75 was the first to affect Atlanta since 1958. Although the city's sustained growth relative to the rest of the country had pulled it through the 1960-61 and 1970-71 recessions with almost no ill effects, by November 1974, unemployment had risen to 8.8% in predominantly black central Atlanta—the highest rate since the 1930s—and 6.2% in the city as a whole (compared with 4.9% for the SMSA). Several major real estate developments were bankrupted or nearly bankrupted by the lack of new demand for downtown office space; the earnings of Atlanta banks were adversely affected by "nonperforming" loans to real estate developers, and new housing starts fell by over 50% in the Atlanta region due to high interest rates.

---

*As of April, 1972, there were approximately 15,000 low-rent public housing units in Atlanta existing or under construction as compared to 3,140 in the remainder of the SMSA.[2]

The city government also suffered from the recession. Mayor Maynard Jackson had pledged that taxes would not be increased in 1974 and ran a small deficit in that year to fulfill the pledge. A further revenue gap of $4.7 million was seen, however, and Jackson asked department heads to come up with savings of $7.2 million to bridge the gap and fund a small pay increase of 4.5% for city employees. Although a property tax increase from $11.30 to $13.94 was enacted in 1974 for the 1975 budget, Georgia voters had increased the tax exemption on owner-occupied houses from $2,000 to $5,000 in a 1974 referendum, thus reducing actual tax collections by $2.1 million, or almost a third of the anticipated revenue from the tax increase.*

By early 1975, it became apparent that even with the property tax increase, the budget could not be balanced because all the savings requested by Jackson were not made and revenue was falling below projections. The one-step pay increase that Jackson had proposed was not paid; instead, a week's furlough without pay was enacted by the Council for all city employees. Mayor Jackson proposed that the state legislature increase the city's tax on the sale of beer, but legislative leaders vetoed the idea. Finally, halfway through fiscal 1975, the legislature passed a bill allowing Atlanta to levy a tax on hotel and motel bills with a revenue expectation of about $2 million annually. The new tax revenue, continuation of the economies in city expenditures begun in 1975, a continuation of the wage freeze for a second year (despite 16% inflation in the interim) and a failure to fully fund the city's pension plans, and a state-mandated 9% upward revaluation of property in Atlanta** allowed the City Council to lower Atlanta's property tax rate to $12.86 per thousand for 1976.

Despite this short-term decrease in Atlanta's property taxes, a permanent solution to Atlanta's fiscal problems had not been found. First, the tax cut for 1976 was predicated on a wage freeze and a failure to fully fund pension plans that could not be continued indefinitely without labor and other problems.

---

*This discussion of tax rates pertains only to Atlanta's general fund; the city also has special funds (e.g., for schools and debt service) supported by their own property taxes. See Appendix A for further information.

**The state claimed that Fulton County had under-assessed property in the county.

(Wages, fringe benefits and pensions account for roughly 83% of city expenditures: the range is from over 90% for police and fire to some 78% for streets and sanitation, 76% for parks and libraries, and 82% for general city departments.) Second, the fact that Atlanta's expenditures rose by 41% from 1973 to 1975, an increase greater than the inflation rate, while its property tax base rose by only 15% in that period, promised a serious revenue gap in the next ten years. (See Exhibits 10.2 and 10.3 for revenue and expenditure data for the period 1970–1975.)

THE ATLANTA CITY GOVERNMENT

Until 1973, Atlanta was governed under a "weak mayor" system, with a mayor, a vice mayor, and a board of 16 aldermen elected at large. Committees of the Board of Aldermen were responsible for most day-to-day operations of the government, and the heads of city departments were responsible to these committees. What power the mayor had came from his power to appoint these aldermanic committees. The city charter spelled out the structure and functions of the city government in great detail, and since state legislative approval was required for all amendments to the charter, the charter's specificity limited Atlanta's home rule authority. Early in 1973, a new city charter was adopted (based on studies by a charter commission begun in 1971) that was much less specific than the old charter, thus increasing the power of the city government to act without state approval. The new charter changed the name of the Board of Aldermen to the City Council and changed the composition of the council from 16 members elected at large to 18 members, 12 elected from districts and six at large. The office of vice mayor was abolished and replaced by the office of city council president, also elected by all city voters. The mayor lost power in appointing city council committees (this power went to the council president) but gained executive authority and the power to appoint city department heads. Other important changes made by the new charter included the merger of the police department, the fire department, and several minor departments into a single department of public safety, and new requirements for short, medium, and long-range city planning.[3]

The Budget Process

The city budget process, which remained essentially the same under the new charter, is in large part governed by 1937 state legislation designed to prevent a recurrence of Depression deficit spending in Atlanta. The budget process begins in August or September, when individual departments submit their estimates of expenditures to an appropriations committee consisting of the mayor, the chairman of the council's finance committee, three council members appointed by the mayor, and the director of finance. This group then submits an expenditure budget to the council after adjusting the departments' estimates. The committee then estimates the revenue side of the budget according to a means prescribed in the 1937 legislation. Total revenue from each tax or other revenue source (except property taxes) can at maximum be estimated as 99% of the revenue actually received from that source in the preceding year. The property tax base (the size of which is established by county assessments) must also be estimated for budget purposes as 99% of the base of the preceding year. The property tax rate is then set at least high enough to balance expenditures with revenues. A tentative budget under this formulation must be submitted to the council by December 16 for consideration and adoption by January 1.

The council has the right to change any expenditures (provided it adjusts the property tax rate upward if it increases expenditures above those in the budget). It also has the power to lower the tax rate and either decrease specific expenditures or resubmit the budget to the appropriations committee and require it to submit a plan of expenditure decreases to meet the lowered rate within ten days. The mayor has the power to veto any budgetary measure, with a two-thirds vote required to override a veto. If revenue exceeds the 99% estimates required by law, either through a growing economy or new grant revenue or taxing authority, the appropriations committee, with council approval, can allocate the additional money at any point during the year. The 1937 state law also prohibits borrowing for current expenses; expenditures can legally exceed tax and other revenues if the city can draw upon surpluses accumulated during previous years.

Atlanta's Relation to the State Government

The governmental powers of the city of Atlanta, like those of all other Georgia municipalities and counties, are rigidly circumscribed by the state constitution. The city's charter is granted by the state government and may theoretically be revoked or amended at any time by the General Assembly. (The legislature has seldom used this power to act unilaterally on a municipal charter, though legislative review and disapproval of municipally proposed amendments to local charters is fairly common.) Permission to levy or increase any tax other than the property tax must be granted by the Assembly; municipal and county debt ceilings are set in the state constitution; and the General Assembly has the power to set operating requirements for individual municipal governments.*

In spite of this extensive oversight of local affairs, the state provides comparatively little aid to local government, most of it in the form of categorical grants for road construction and other purposes. (Many Georgia legislators see local aid as expendable, to be eliminated when necessary to keep state taxes low.) Until 1971, the state had never appropriated money for general aid. When in that year it did so, it distributed the aid generally according to population, with no consideration of fiscal needs or tax rates levied by local governments. The city of Atlanta received approximately $1.3 million in general aid in 1971 and $2.6 million in each of the years from 1972 to 1975. In 1976, the state aid appropriation for Atlanta was cut to $1.9 million as part of a general austerity measure cutting over 20% of all grants to municipalities. Thus, while state aid constituted 3% of Atlanta's revenues in 1972, it constituted less than 2% by 1976.

Atlanta's Relation to the County Government

The division of responsibility for services between Georgia counties and municipalities varies. Most county governments are responsible for the provision

---

*Occasions of legislative intervention in Atlanta's municipal government include the 1937 legislation prescribing a method of estimating city revenue in the budget process; an attempt (vetoed by Governor Jimmy Carter) to block the imposition of a "residency" rule for city employees in early 1974; and a move by legislators, still pending as of 1977, to take control of the Atlanta airport away from the city.

of social services (welfare, hospitals, etc.) to the entire county, as well as for a county court system, certain public works functions, and school systems for smaller municipalities and for unincorporated areas. While unincorporated areas within a county theoretically enjoy lower taxes than municipalities at the price of greatly reduced municipal services, county governments usually provide at least a minimum level of municipal services (fire protection, police protection, provision of water and sometimes sewers, etc.) to these areas. A county may also contract to provide certain municipal services to incorporated towns and cities in the county. Taxpayers within the municipality pay for the services through municipal (not county) taxes, and the municipality reimburses the county for the full cost of the services.

The structure of county government, and particularly its provision of services to unincorporated areas, leads to the subsidization of unincorporated areas by municipalities. Services to unincorporated areas are generally provided by county taxes, with only a portion of the cost being directly recovered from the residents of unincorporated areas. The result is that residents of municipalities are paying twice for certain services—once for themselves on their municipal tax bill and again, to the extent that unincorporated areas do not pay for the full cost of services, on their county tax bills. This imbalance provides a disincentive for unincorporated areas to incorporate or to allow themselves to be annexed to existing municipalities, since joining a municipality would mean that they could no longer receive services financed by the county as a whole.

The formal division of services between Atlanta and Fulton County was defined by legislation passed in the early 1950s. Sponsors of the legislation had cited duplication of government efforts as a major factor increasing the cost of government in the Atlanta area, with Atlanta, Fulton County, and smaller municipalities providing the same service to different groups of people. As indicated in Table 10.1, the plan proposed a division of services that would leave only one level of government providing most services. The authors of the plan and its implementing legislation intended that the city of Atlanta provide many services, including police, fire, and sanitation, to all areas in unincorporated Fulton County receiving the services (not all areas in Fulton County receive all

TABLE 10.1: Service Allocations Under 1951 Legislation[4]

Continued by City	Shifted to City
water	police
sewer	fire
libraries	refuse collection
auditorium	inspections
traffic engineering	parks
airport	
	Shifted to County
Continued by County	public health
sheriff	
coroner	*Provided by both*
agriculture	*City and County*
almshouse	streets and roads
public welfare	schools
courts	planning and zoning

municipal services), and that the county government (or special taxing districts, of which there are currently two in Fulton County) reimburse the city for the cost of the services.

However, in the 20 years following the adoption of the plan, Fulton County became involved in the provision of many services originally reserved for provision by Atlanta under contract, including volunteer fire companies in several parts of the county, county libraries, and parks and recreation programs. The county began to provide fire protection, for example, because volunteer companies were cheaper than contracting with Atlanta, and other programs because Atlanta was unwilling to increase its service provision in the face of inadequate compensation from the county for the overhead costs.* Thus the original service distinctions in the Plan of Improvement have become blurred. (See Exhibit 10.4 for a chart detailing service provision in Atlanta, unincorporated Fulton County, and other Fulton municipalities as of the early 1970s.)

---

*Legislation establishing the service contracts between Atlanta and Fulton County provides that the county (or service district) shall pay the direct cost of providing the service plus 10% for "overhead" expenses of other city agencies. City studies suggest that actual "overhead" costs are 22% of direct costs for fire protection and 37% for libraries.

A 1974 study by Research Atlanta (a civic group composed chiefly of upper income voters from Atlanta's north side) estimated that Atlanta taxpayers paid from $5.5 million to $9.3 million more to Fulton County in taxes than they received in services.[5] (The lower figure represents an extra property tax payment of $2.12 per thousand dollars of assessed valuation, the higher figure a rate of $3.75 per thousand.) The study cited two sources for the subsidy: inadequate overhead in city contracts (which is eventually reflected on Atlanta residents' city tax bills because the city is paying for it) and provision of more services outside Atlanta than are being paid for by the county taxes of non-Atlanta residents.* To determine the subsidy amount, Research Atlanta divided county expenditures into four categories: non-Atlanta services from the county general fund, Fulton County school taxes paid by Atlantans, health and welfare expenditures, and general and administration services performed by the county. In 1973, the county provided $11.6 million in services exclusively to county residents outside Atlanta but county taxes and service charges raised only $4.75 million from residents outside Atlanta; the remaining $6.85 million was paid by Atlantans. The 0.8 mill (80 cents per thousand) county-wide school tax raised $2.8 million, $1.95 million of which was paid by Atlanta taxpayers even though Atlantans were forbidden to send their children to Fulton County Schools.

The county social services budget was used in the Research Atlanta study to offset the subsidy; Atlanta residents received $19.7 million of the county's $23.3 million budget for health and welfare, but Atlanta

revenues provided only $15.9 million, resulting in a subsidy to the city by the suburbs of $3.8 million. Remaining county expenditures accounted for $23.8 million, of which Atlanta received $18.5 million. To finance these services, Atlantans contributed $2.8 million in service charges and $16.2 million in other revenue, for a total of $19.0 million, leaving a $0.5 million subsidy to the rest of the county. Adding these figures, Research Atlanta concluded that in 1973 Atlantans paid $5.5 million more than they received in services. (See Exhibit 10.5 for Research Atlanta's subsidy estimates for 1970, 1973, and 1974.)

The Research Atlanta Study identified three factors tending to decrease the subsidy and one to increase it during the mid-seventies. First, development outside Atlanta decreased the Atlanta percentage of the county property tax base from 76% in 1970 to 67% in 1974. This shift in county wealth tended to reduce the subsidy by reducing Atlanta's share of Fulton County taxes. The subsidy is also gradually being reduced by the phased elimination of the county-wide tax for Fulton County schools: in the face of political pressure (including threats by Atlanta blacks to sue for the opening of Fulton County schools to city residents) in late 1971, after the publication of Research Atlanta's first study on Atlanta's subsidization of its suburbs, the Fulton County Commission voted to reduce the tax by 0.1 mill per year until it reaches zero in 1981. Third, the rapid rise in social service costs and the decrease in Atlanta's tax base has increased the county's health and welfare subsidy to Atlanta. But the contributions of all these factors to the reduction of Atlanta's subsidy have been nearly offset by the rapid increase in county services provided exclusively outside Atlanta; thus, as of 1975, the politically divisive subsidy issue had lost none of its capacity to trouble the political leaders of Atlanta and its suburbs.

POLITICAL LEADERSHIP IN ATLANTA

Since the Second World War, the city of Atlanta has emerged from its comparative southern obscurity to become a major metropolis, with a national reputation for racial progressiveness, political stability, and great potential for economic growth. Atlanta's political leaders have played a shifting role in this story.

---

*Fulton County officials argue that there really is no subsidy of the county by Atlanta; they attack the methodology of those who claim that the city pays more than it receives and assert that any "subsidy" is a matter of equity. Fulton County manager Harry West claimed that county expenditures cannot even be divided between Atlanta and non-Atlanta purposes. "You can't divide it up; it can't be allocated."[6] Jay Fountain, the Fulton County comptroller, told a public hearing that even if the county takes more revenue from Atlanta than it spends there, there is still no inequity because a large proportion of Atlanta property taxes come from business property.

> Commercial and industrial property located inside the city "must be considered as an asset of the entire metropolitan area and even the state."
> The county official said that once it is recognized that this money belongs to everyone "there can exist no clear definable inequity within the county."[7]

City politics were dominated from the late 1940s to the mid-1960s by a coalition of business leaders in the Chamber of Commerce, supported by blacks and upper income whites. Characterized by one study as a "ruling elite . . . bound by common values, and acting in concert,"[8] this group of businessmen was composed principally of the heads of regionally important, locally-owned corporations such as Coca Cola's Robert Woodruff and the officers of the Citizens & Southern National Bank. A study of the city in the 1960s contended that business influence in Atlanta resulted from the lack of competing groups such as Eastern and Southern European ethnic groups, political "machines," and labor unions (only 10 to 15% of the Atlanta work force was unionized in 1961, compared to almost 30% nationally). The same study argued that:

> Financial, real estate, construction, and retail firms have often acted with a unanimity rare in other communities. . . . One factor producing cohesion lies in institutional arrangements like the strong Chamber of Commerce and satellite organizations. . . . Cohesion is also based on personal ties, many of them stretching back over two or three generations. . . . Another source of cohesion is the role of a half-dozen or so economic firms as pace setters and opinion leaders for other members of the large business interests. Thanks to their resources [and their] relations with others, these opinion leaders help weld the business community into a united front.[9]

The administrations of Mayors William B. Hartsfield (1936–40, 1942–61) and Ivan Allen, Jr. (1961–69) were marked by racial moderation, fiscal conservatism designed to hold down the cost of government, and the development of capital projects promoting business expansion. Their mayoral campaign platforms emphasized the development of physical facilities such as the city auditorium and convention center, airport facilities, schools, and highways, all of which were subsequently funded by bond issues, support for which was organized jointly by business leaders and city officials.

Throughout these years, the political influence of the black community in Atlanta increased steadily. Following a 1944 U.S. Supreme Court decision abolish-

ing all-white Democratic primaries in several southern states, including Georgia,* Atlanta blacks registered in large numbers and became an important bloc (20% to 30% of Atlanta voters) in municipal elections. A 1963 article on Atlanta politics commented:

> In Atlanta, however, the adult Negro leaders do not form a monolithic bloc. . . . Although those leaders usually labeled conservative by the community, and frequently by themselves as well, now dominate most of the organizations which deal exclusively with elections and political issues, such as the Atlanta Negro Voters League and the Westside Voters League, several other groups have grown up in recent years which are not under their control, such as the local chapter of the Southern Christian Leadership Conference, a group of younger business and professional men called the Atlanta Committee for Cooperative Action, and a student organization called the Committee on an Appeal for Human Rights. Also, in the last two years, the local branch of the NAACP has shifted into relatively more militant hands.
>
> The conservative group is quite aware that its power is being challenged, and just as the students and the more militant adults manifest suspicion of the integrity of the conservative leaders, these men frequently question the motives and the honesty of the most militant group.[10]

Although blacks were not generally elected to office during Hartsfield's and Allen's administrations (there was only one black alderman out of 24 as late as 1965), blacks appeared to be better off in Atlanta than in many southern cities. In 1948, for example, only two years after blacks first voted in a primary election, Atlanta began to hire black police officers. To assure black support for bond issues, political leaders added projects directly benefiting the black community, such as street construction, to public works packages. The business establishment vocally supported moderate black organizations, refusing, for example, to remove the Urban League from its list of organizations receiving funds from its Community Chest fund-raising drives in 1956, in spite of pressure

---

*Curbs on black voting such as strict application of literacy tests and outright intimidation were less prevalent in the urban South than in rural areas. In many southern cities, blacks were allowed to vote, but the all-white primary made their votes so meaningless that few even registered.

from "states rights" Governor Marvin Griffith and other racial conservatives. Even relatively militant blacks were not treated as harshly as elsewhere. When, for example, students were arrested in 1960 for sit-ins and boycotts aimed at desegregating restaurants and other public facilities, Mayor Hartsfield negotiated with student leaders, ordered the release of the protestors, and the next year implemented a plan to desegregate public facilities.

White working-class voters, many of whom moved to the Atlanta area from more conservative rural areas in Georgia, tended to oppose Hartsfield's and Allen's coalition. Serious opposition to the administration, mainly by racial conservatives, appeared in the 1957 and 1961 elections: Hartsfield barely won a primary against a conservative Fulton County Commissioner in 1957, losing heavily in lower-income white precincts, and Lester Maddox emerged as a serious mayoral candidate in the 1957 general election, winning over a third of the vote in spite of being previously almost unknown. The 1961 election, after Hartsfield's retirement, was strongly contested among four candidates including Ivan Allen, Jr., President of the Chamber of Commerce and the choice of most of the city's business establishment, and Lester Maddox. Allen was the top vote-getter in the primary and handily won a run-off election against Maddox (though not by Hartsfield's 2-1 majority) with the old coalition of blacks and upper-income whites.

The Coalition Breaks Down

From 1960 to 1970 the proportion of blacks in Atlanta's population increased from 37.3% to 51.3%, and the proportion of blacks among the city's registered voters increased from 29% in 1960 to 41% in 1969, reflecting an increased rate of registration as well as the increase in black population. In 1969 the white business community found itself—for the first time in many years—on the losing side of a mayoral election. Four candidates were entered in the race, including Harold Tate, a black member of the Board of Education; Sam Massell, a Jewish white liberal who had been vice mayor under Allen; Everett Millican, a conservative Democratic alderman; and Rodney Cook, a moderate Republican with ties to city business leaders and the endorsements of the Chamber of Commerce and Mayor Allen (who had declined to run

again for reasons of health). Because of the split among voters in the October 7 primary, Massell finished first even though he trailed Tate among black voters and ran a poor third among whites. Cook won second place by winning an absolute majority in upper-income white precincts and running slightly behind Millican among working-class white voters while receiving virtually no black support. In the run-off election two weeks later, Massell combined 92% of the black vote with just over a quarter of the white vote to win 55% of the vote. Upper-income whites from the north side of Atlanta gave Massell a slightly smaller fraction of their vote than working-class whites. Massell's liberal positions on economic issues lost him upper-income support to the conservative Cook, but gained him more lower-income white votes than previous racially moderate, fiscally conservative candidates supported by business had received. Atlanta elected Maynard Jackson, a young black attorney with no previous experience in public office, vice-mayor; Jackson received nearly 60% of the vote on the first ballot against a member in good standing of the city's white political establishment, Alderman Milton Farris. Six blacks were elected aldermen, as opposed to only one in 1965, and black support elected liberal white candidates over more conservative incumbents in several cases.

After their election, Massell and Jackson argued that their victory indicated a specific liberal mandate from Atlanta voters; Jackson said that a new coalition of blacks and poor whites was emerging "centered on issues such as welfare, public housing, and treatment of domestic workers."[11] But although white support was necessary to the election of Massell and Jackson, many black voters thought that their concept of a biracial coalition missed the real point of the election—the expansion of black political power. The Southern Regional Council's Voter Education Project, "an organization assisting minority groups participating in the southern political process," issued a report in 1969 on the growing influence of black voters and their willingness to break with their former coalition partners:

> This year, black voters were not willing to support the choice of the white business elite. Rather than having only the usual choice between the favorite of northside whites and another candidate whose racial views made him anathema, black voters in 1969 had additional alternatives. For the first time there was a black candidate,

and also there was a white candidate whose reputation was more liberal than other white candidates, past or present. Both of these candidates
were more attractive to blacks than the candidate
supported by their former northside allies.[12]

Vernon Jordan, head of the Voter Education Project,
added his interpretation of the election, which the
Atlanta Constitution summarized as follows:

> The white moderate-to-liberal official can no
> longer make claim to an office controlled by 95%
> of the white vote because black political ambi-
> tion and the desire to serve will be a competing
> if not victorious force. . . .
>
> [Jordan said] "Members of the white busi-
> ness power structure are bad politicians. They
> have to grasp the new dynamic in the city's
> politics—black political power. They have failed
> to understand that blacks will no longer be junior
> partners in the old alliance."[13]

The Massell Administration

Mayor Sam Massell's administration was marked
by continued major business and public investment in
the central city, the development of a new regional
rapid transit system, and additional federal grants to
Atlanta; but it also saw fiscal stringency, a rise in
taxes, and the appearance of several racially divisive issues.

Economic Development.   In his first state of the
city address in 1970, Mayor Massell said his administration would be "more people oriented than brick
and mortar oriented."[14] Yet central city development
continued in the early 1970s. Several major private
downtown projects conceived late in Allen's second
term or early in Massell's term were completed while
Massell was mayor,* as were several public developments. For example, in 1971, a bond issue backed by
Massell was passed to build the Atlanta Coliseum, a
major new sports stadium. Massell also backed the
construction of I-485, a controversial freeway link

between the city center and the western suburbs, that
had the strong support of business interests favoring
development and the opposition of white working-
class voters whose neighborhoods would be disrupted
by construction.

The major developmental accomplishment of the
Massell administration, however, was expansion of
the Metropolitan Atlanta Rapid Transit Authority
(MARTA) from a planning agency to a mass transit
system. When Massell took office, the city bus system was privately owned and nearing bankruptcy,
and the city government expected to be forced to
buy the system and subsidize it through increased
property taxes. But the Massell administration proposed instead that MARTA take over and expand
Atlanta and suburban bus service by constructing busways and a rail transit system (with up to $1.6 billion
in federal aid and a $400 million local contribution)
in the late 1970s and early 1980s. The expansion
would be financed partly by fares and partly by a tax
increase in the affected counties. Lieutenant Governor Maddox opposed the plan as too expensive and as
promoting racial and social change in the suburbs and
attempted to block it in his role as president of the
State Senate. With Governor Jimmy Carter's support,
a transit plan was finally passed by the legislature,
subject to approval by a November 1971 referendum
in Fulton and DeKalb Counties. Under the plan, bus
service under MARTA would begin in January 1972.
Fares (40 cents under the old system) would be held
to 15 cents until 1979, and a 1% sales tax would be
levied in any county belonging to the MARTA system.

The referendum was hotly contested. Mayor
Massell, Vice Mayor Jackson, a large number of city
aldermen, all three Fulton County Commissioners,
and several prominent DeKalb County officials
backed MARTA. However, MARTA won only a narrow victory (less than 52% of the vote in both Fulton
and DeKalb Counties) and the vote demonstrated
major socioeconomic class differences in the Atlanta
region. Upper-income voters in both Atlanta and its
near suburbs voted heavily for MARTA; black voters
divided almost evenly on the issue with only a small
plurality for MARTA, in spite of the 15-cent fare and
strong support for the transit plan from many black

---

*The two most substantial privately developed projects were
Underground Atlanta, a network of narrow streets below
ground dating from before the Civil War, where shops and
restaurants were built in turn-of-the-century fashion to attract
tourists; and Peachtree Center, a major shopping center,
hotel, and office skyscraper. A third project, Colony Square,
called a "micropolis" by its builders and containing offices,
hotels, middle- and upper-income apartments, and a shopping
center, was started close to the center of the city.

political leaders*; and white working-class voters in south Atlanta and in newly developing suburban areas in North Fulton and South DeKalb voted heavily against mass transit.[15]

Fiscal Stringency. Under the Massell administration, Atlanta general fund expenditures (which excludes capital expenditures, debt service, and self-supporting city utilities and departments) rose from $60.5 million in 1970 to $75.9 million in 1973. Increased expenditures for police, pensions, and "general government" (overhead agencies like the Finance Department) accounted for much of the increase. To avoid still larger expenditure increases, the administration held down salary increases and placed limits on new hiring and purchasing. These measures kept the growth in expenditures at 5% between 1971 and 1972, compared with increases of over 15% per year in the last two years of the Allen administration and Massell's first year. Productivity increases kept sanitation expenses virtually constant over the four years of Massell's term (despite inflation), and reductions in park maintenance did the same for recreation expenditures.

To avert an illegal deficit, Massell and the Board of Aldermen increased the general fund property tax rate from $11.24 per thousand dollars of assessed valuation in 1970 to $16.02 in 1971.** That same year, however, Fulton County completed a reassessment of property, resulting in a 30% upward revaluation of real estate in the county and in the City of Atlanta. In response to pressure from angry homeowners, the Board of Aldermen cut the 1972 general fund tax rate by $3.02 per thousand, approximately $1.20 per thousand more than recommended by the city's Finance Director, who predicted major impacts on city operations. This additional $1.20 decrease cut total tax revenues by $2.66 million and prompted hiring freezes and layoffs. The city was spared further stringencies in 1973, Massell's last year, only by an increase of 15% in real estate values (reflecting economic growth in general and the completion of

Peachtree Center in particular) and $10.5 million in federal revenue sharing aid. The Board of Aldermen lowered general fund tax rates to $11.30 per thousand in 1973; without the federal aid, and assuming no further expenditure cuts, the 1973 general fund property tax rate would have risen to $15.24 per thousand.

The first appropriation of general state aid to municipalities was passed by the legislature in 1971, providing $1.3 million that year and $2.6 million per year thereafter. Finally, Mayor Massell sought authority from the legislature to levy a 1% income tax based on place of employment beginning in 1973. This tax was chosen in part because it would tax suburbanites working in the city and using city services but not paying other taxes; the burden of this new tax on city residents would be further reduced by a tax credit based on property taxes paid. However, legislative leaders stated that they would support only an income tax based on place of residence, and Massell's proposal was never even brought to a vote.

Racial Issues. Under Mayor Massell, black involvement in city government increased substantially. Of 782 new city jobs created between 1970 and 1972, 616 went to blacks; Massell also named three blacks as department heads, the first such appointments in Atlanta. Although only 13% of the city's managerial jobs and 19% of its professional jobs were filled by blacks in 1972, the proportion represented a marked increase over the ratio when Massell took office.[16] Nevertheless, despite praise from some groups in the black community, many felt that progress was not fast enough. Vice Mayor Jackson deplored the fact that blacks had not been appointed to all the committees of the Board of Aldermen (which contained ten whites and six blacks at the time) and announced that he would use his *ex officio* membership on Council committees to provide black representation on committees which Massell had left without black members.

School desegregation policies and action to alleviate "white flight" also stirred conflict during Massell's term in office. A federal District Court decision in early 1970 paved the way for a plan of school attendance by zones and the pairing of nearby schools

---

*Only one black alderman opposed MARTA, but several black groups opposed the plan as a subsidy to rich suburbanites and saw the low fares as a sop that would be taken away once the plan was approved.

**This discussion pertains only to the property tax that supports the general fund; Atlanta also has separate property taxes for special purposes, such as schools and debt service.

without busing.* After a 1971 Supreme Court ruling upholding the constitutionality of busing as a means of achieving integration, however, the NAACP asked the Fifth Circuit of Appeals to require further desegregation, noting that only 6.6% of black students in Atlanta attended schools that had white majorities.** Meanwhile, white families, particularly those with school-age children, continued to abandon the Atlanta school system for the suburbs as litigation on busing continued.

In late 1972 and early 1973, a movement to increase black economic power in Atlanta took shape under the leadership of Hosea Williams, a long-time activist in the Southern Christian Leadership Conference, who believed that existing black organizations were not doing enough to promote black economic gains. With picket lines around shops and plants, mass rallies and boycotts, Williams and his supporters moved against five of the largest and most powerful corporations in Atlanta, all major supporters of the moderate white establishment of the 1960s: Citizens and Southern Bank, Coca Cola, Rich's Department Stores, Mead, Inc., and Sears, Roebuck and Company. Demands included affirmative action in hiring and promotions but went beyond hiring into the more sensitive areas of relationships with suppliers, contractors, banks, and newspapers.*** Williams and his

---

*Although there was concern about possible violence in the first days of desegregation (since Governor Lester Maddox had asked citizens to disobey the order), schools were desegregated peacefully.

**Black leaders were not united on the desirability of further desegregation. Dr. Benjamin Mays, the first black president of the Atlanta Board of Education, claimed that more desegregation would only encourage more whites to move to the suburbs.

***For example, the agreement worked out with Sears, Roebuck, and Company (which agreed to the most extensive policy changes) included maintaining an average daily balance of $400,000 in black banks in Atlanta, publishing more advertisements in certain black newspapers, increased retailing of products of black manufacturers, and changing contracting policies so that 50% of Sears' contracts in the Atlanta area would be handled by minority contractors within several years, with a phase-in of increased minority participation.

group gained some concessions from all five companies, but in the process aroused considerable hostility among white business and political leaders. Mayor Massell strongly opposed the boycott as detrimental to Atlanta's economic health; Vice Mayor Jackson took no public stand on Williams' efforts.[17]

Mayor Massell and the Black Community. After the promising begining of his administration, Mayor Massell's relations with the black community turned generally cool, with two major actions creating black discontent. In April 1970, Atlanta's garbage workers struck the city for a wage increase. Massell's strong stand against a group of largely black strikers who were generally perceived to be earning low wages prompted criticism from Vice Mayor Jackson, who openly supported the strikers' demands, and from other black leaders who charged that the mayor had changed his attitude from election day, when he needed black support, to the time of the strike.

Massell further alienated many blacks by an October 1971 speech in which he argued that the black leadership in Atlanta was shortsighted, looked at issues solely in racial terms, and did not adequately support civic projects. The only solution to the city's economic problems, he said, was expansion of Atlanta to include its largely white suburbs; he attacked opponents of expansion for their "inferiority complex that suggests only blacks will politically support blacks."[18] Reaction to the speech was immediate and angry: Dr. Horace Tate, the 1969 black mayoral candidate, and Alderman Marvin Arrington expressed typical views. Said Tate:

> I think it was a political speech that was saying to the blacks, "You had better be good blacks, or else you won't have anything left but the shell of a city." The way blacks have been treated in the past, it may be better for them to be politically powerful in the shell of a city.[19]

And Arrington accused Massell of "shifting over to the white power structure," and added, "The very fact that he makes a black-white distinction tends to polarize the city."[20]

The 1973 Election

Because of the defeat of its preferred candidate, Republican Rodney Cook, in the 1969 election, the

Atlanta Chamber of Commerce declined to endorse any candidates for office in 1973, although it did issue a platform calling for further public works development and the expansion of Atlanta's city limits. However, many individual members of the business community lined up behind two candidates who opposed Mayor Massell. Charles Weltner, an attorney and a former liberal congressman who left office rather than sign a loyalty oath supporting Governor Lester Maddox, was endorsed by former Mayor Ivan Allen, Jr., and other business leaders. And in spite of his outspoken liberalism, Vice Mayor Maynard Jackson received strong backing from a segment of the business community who felt that Atlanta would benefit from the election of a black mayor.*

Mayor Massell had lost most of his earlier black support both because blacks now realized that they could elect their own mayor and because Massell's speeches and actions on issues such as expansion of Atlanta had alienated many black leaders. He therefore changed the tone of his campaign from 1969 to draw support from white working class voters, running a liberal campaign on economic issues and attacking the business establishment, but conducting a racially conservative campaign,

Maynard Jackson emerged with 46% of the primary vote—80% of the black vote and 10% to 15% of the white vote (mainly in upper-income areas). Mayor Massell barely defeated Charles Weltner for the second spot in the run-off election with 20% of the vote, winning working-class white areas and running second to Weltner in upper-income areas. Massell continued to appeal for conservative white votes in the run-off. He attempted to insure a large turnout of whites opposed to the militant black candidate for City Council President, Hosea Williams, and to gain their votes against Vice Mayor Jackson by speaking of a Jackson-Williams "ticket," calling Jackson a "racist" and

implying that Atlanta would be a "dead" city with the election of both black candidates.[22] However, this strategy failed: large numbers of whites who had supported Weltner turned to Jackson, who won as much as 40% of the vote in some upper-income north-side precincts and took 25% of the white vote in the city as a whole, along with 94% of the black vote, to win a 60–40 victory. Black militancy was also strongly rejected. Hosea Williams, whose candidacy was anathema to white business leaders after his actions against their firms, increased his share of the black vote to 70% in the run-off, but received less than 2% of the white vote, as white moderate Wyche Fowler won about 30% of black votes and 64% of the total vote cast. A City Council of nine whites and nine blacks was elected (Council President Fowler provided a tenth white vote in case of a tie), including several black candidates elected from majority white districts and one white candidate from a two-thirds black district.

The Jackson Administration

Maynard Jackson's performance in office was a disappointment to the business leaders who had supported him. Several business leaders, including John Portman, the builder-architect who had planned and constructed many of the large new buildings of downtown Atlanta, spoke of a new racial polarization in the city; while others, such as Richard Kattel, President of Citizens and Southern Bank and an early Jackson supporter, claimed that the new division of political and economic power in Atlanta created problems not experienced when the same group was in control of both aspects of the city's life.[23]

To some extent, these differences sprang from differences in style and rhetoric (and to that extent could in theory be smoothed over by conciliatory gestures and speeches). For example, Jackson stated on several occasions that he sought a "liberal coalition dedicated to social change":

> We have put poor people and black people and female people at the table for the first time. We want to create equal opportunity for people all over town, and it has alienated some people who do not want to see that happen. . . .
>
> If incidentally from doing what America says it stands for, a small group of people is alienated because of their elitist ideology or because of ideology based on race, I would regret that.[24]

---

*Jackson, who ran the most expensive mayoral campaign in Atlanta's history, received extensive business funding. Richard Kattel, head of Citizens and Southern National Bank, Atlanta's largest bank, assisted the Jackson campaign, and Citizens and Southern provided loans to Jackson's law firm. Over fifty of the senior executives of another important Atlanta bank, the Trust Company of Georgia, also reportedly contributed to the Jackson campaign.[21]

But in 1974 and early 1975, three substantive areas of disagreement between Jackson and business leaders emerged: development policy, affirmative action, and police and crime issues.

Development Policy. Mayor Jackson differed strongly with downtown business leaders on development. Before becoming mayor, Jackson strongly supported the efforts of a bi-racial group of aldermen to eliminate I–485, a planned link between Atlanta and its western suburbs that would cut through the white working-class Morningside area, in spite of heavy backing for the highway from Mayor Massell, Governor Carter and from what the *Atlanta Constitution* called the "downtown [business] groups that traditionally have been hearty advocates of all projects."[25] The Board of Aldermen withdrew their approval for the highway in 1973, but in 1974 business leaders and representatives of Atlanta's western suburbs forced the Atlanta Regional Commission (ARC) to reconsider the highway.* Mayor Jackson denounced the action of the Commission in support of the highway, and the project was narrowly defeated—but only after the leading gubernatorial candidate, George Busbee, stated that he would support the city of Atlanta and not fund the project in spite of the ARC's action.[26]

Jackson also angered business leaders by forcing the consideration of alternate sites to that preferred by the airlines for a second Atlanta airport, thus delaying the construction decision.** To the business leaders, Jackson's action was interference in the airlines' internal affairs. Joel Goldberg, President of Rich's Department Stores, a major Atlanta chain, commented at a September 1974 forum of business and government leaders sponsored by the Atlanta Realtors' Council, "The airlines are going to pay for it, and it ought to go where they want it to."[27] Nearly all of the business officials claimed that delay was extremely bad for Atlanta's economic health; in the words of former Governor Carl Sanders: "This airport should have been built several years ago; we can't wait any longer."[28]

Affirmative Action. The Jackson administration moved quickly after taking office to increase the number of blacks employed in city departments and doing business with the city. Very early in his term in office, Jackson announced his intention to seek "an ordinance requiring all new employees and all those receiving promotions to live in the city." (As of March 1974, 40% of all employees, 55% of police and 54% of fire employees lived outside Atlanta.) Supporters of the ordinance argued that it would insure that employees would have true commitment to the city and also claimed that it would indirectly encourage the hiring of blacks, as it would force whites to choose between city employment and suburban living. Opponents argued that it would dilute the merit system and would result in city services of lower quality and higher cost. Before the City Council could act, the General Assembly, under prodding of several white Atlanta members and with the support of many suburban and rural conservatives, passed a bill revoking the city's right to pass a residency requirement. However, Governor Carter vetoed the bill, and the veto was sustained. The City Council then passed a residency rule for police and fire employees with all nine blacks and two white liberals supporting the ordinance.

An even more controversial Jackson policy, one with wide economic ramifications, was a proposal to give minority firms at least a quarter of city work. Preference would be given to black contractors by encouraging "joint ventures" between white and black engineering, architectural, construction, and other firms***; joint ventures and minority firms would be accepted over lower bidders. The importance of this issue stemmed from the large volume of government

---

*The Atlanta Regional Commission is a 24-member body containing fourteen elected officials and ten citizens from the five-county area surrounding Atlanta. It is charged with developing a land use plan for Metropolitan Atlanta and with approving applications for and expenditures of federal grants in the metropolitan area.

**The airlines favored a site north of Atlanta, arguing that the initial cost of the northern airport would be less than that of the southern airport, and that the airport should be closer to their upper-income customers who generally lived on the northside of Atlanta and in its northern suburbs. Jackson suggested that another site south of Atlanta would promote more balanced regional economic growth and would also be up to $500 million cheaper to develop over the life of the airport.

***Joint ventures between firms are a commonly used means by which relatively small firms team up to bid for large government contracts. Two or more firms agree to bid on a contract and set up a new corporation (owned by the firms in proportion to their proposed participation in the contract) to bid on, and, if successful, carry out the contract. The process enables firms to work together on one specific project while remaining independent (or even competing) on others. The novelty of the Jackson administrations's idea was its use to encourage black participation on city contracts.

contracts to be let in the following several years for expansion of the old Atlanta airport, new airport construction, and construction of subways and busways under MARTA. These contracts would amount to several billion dollars, the largest set of government projects in the history of Atlanta. The share for black businesses, under Jackson's proposals, would be well over $500 million.

Many whites opposed the Jackson proposal (which had been adopted on a 14–5 vote by the city council, with all nine blacks voting for it), raising issues of equity and costs. Airline officials suggested that black involvement in construction at Newark Airport raised costs by 25%[29] and feared similar cost increases in Atlanta. (In August 1975, a contract for airport cleaning was awarded to a joint venture, the fourth-lowest bidder [of seven] at a cost of 5½% above the low bid.[30]) An unidentified white, active in contracting, told the *Atlanta Constitution*:

> The general impression that most . . . [contractors] have is that they don't like it because they're scratching like hell to get jobs. They resent it when they see a government job going to somebody for reasons other than price or performance.[31]

Some sections of the white community began to take action against this preferential treatment of blacks. (Business leaders had not been directly involved in the struggle against preferential joint venture contracts, although several council members most closely associated with the business community in earlier years were among its strongest opponents.) The first moves against the contracts came from rural Georgia legislators. Rep. Jim West (D-Jonesboro) had previously introduced a bill to place the Atlanta airport under state control. It was not taken seriously until House Speaker Tom Murphy threw his weight behind the bill as the preferential contracts issue heated up, promising House passage in the 1976 General Assembly.

Police and Crime Issues. Many of Jackson's former white supporters suggested that the mayor was inadequately concerned about the impact of crime on the social fabric of Atlanta and that his choices for high positions in the police department were not helping the crime problem. (Atlanta's crime rate had risen drastically since the mid-1960s, and its murder rate was the highest in the nation in 1973.) Central Atlanta Progress, a group of downtown businessmen

and developers, claimed that Jackson was paying inadequate attention to their needs for crime protection; only after they sent Jackson a 15-page letter outlining their complaints did the Public Safety Commissioner meet with them and agree to double the size of the downtown police force and increase foot patrols.[32] Others complained that the police department had no continuity in leadership when it was required to fight crime. For instance, there had been four intelligence (detective) chiefs in Jackson's first 18 months.

However, the main symbol of white and business frustration with the crime issue was the new black Public Safety Commissioner, A. F. Reginald Eaves, a college friend of the mayor. The previous Police Chief, John Inman (a white from a prominent Atlanta family), bitterly contested Eaves' appointment, and Jackson was forced to use all his political leverage to get Eaves confirmed by the racially split Atlanta City Council. Shortly after his confirmation, early in 1975, Eaves embarrassed the Jackson administration on several occasions; his actions were chronicled in the *Atlanta Constitution*:

> —On January 3, Eaves reversed a decision by Jackson's top aide and reinstated three firemen who had been fired or suspended for disciplinary reasons. . . .
>
> —On January 17, a city employee alleged that he was told to "fix" a $250,000 publicity grant for Eaves to insure that the grant would be awarded to a favored advertising agency.
>
> —On March 4, it was reported that Eaves' personal secretary, Daniel Louis Odum, who screened appointments for Eaves and had access to highly sensitive intelligence information, had been convicted of possession of heroin and carrying an illegal draft card. . . . Still another report revealed that Eaves had bent civil service rules to hand pick Odum as his secretary.[33]

Both business and working-class whites demanded that Eaves be dismissed. According to the *New York Times*:

> Atlanta's white business community, which has great economic power but limited political power now that the city is majority black, has been pressuring the Mayor to dismiss Mr. Eaves for many weeks.[34]

A coalition of black community groups threatened mass rallies and economic boycotts if further pressure were put on Eaves to resign, and both black and white community groups suggested that the Eaves matter was increasing racial tensions in the city. Thus, by 1975 Atlanta's political and economic leaders seemed increasingly divided as the Georgia General Assembly prepared to consider the expansion proposals described in Part B (chapter 11) of this case.

The 1974 results presented in Exhibit 10.5 are not directly comparable to those for 1970 and 1973. At the time the Research Atlanta report was issued, final 1974 budget figures were not available, and the analysis was based on appropriations data. A contingency fund of $2.7 million was established to cover unexpected costs exceeding appropriations. Research Atlanta notes that much of this fund will be spent on non-Atlanta appropriations:

> For example, as of May 31, 1974, slightly over $600,000 had been transferred from the contingency fund to specific expenditures areas. Of that amount, roughly $450,000 went into capital projects accounts, largely directed to non-Atlanta. Another $1.4 million of the contingency fund has been earmarked for salary increases to county employees. At least several hundred thousand dollars of this sum will be directed to employees engaged in the provision of services to non-Atlantans. Once these and other budgetary adjustments are finally made, non-Atlanta expenditures figures for 1974 will undoubtedly be higher than those listed in the appropriated amounts.

APPENDIX

The City of Atlanta's Non-General Fund Expenditures

As detailed in Exhibit 10.3, most of the expenditures normally associated with municipal government are paid for out of Atlanta's General Fund. However, Atlanta also has a number of special funds, which this appendix describes. Total 1975 expenditures from these funds were well in excess of $400 million.

By far the largest of these special funds is the Trust and Agency Fund. This fund was established to account for monies received by the city in the capacity of trustee, custodian or agent; perhaps the most important of such monies are federal revenue sharing grants. The Fund also accounts for the collection of delinquent property taxes and collects Atlanta's school tax. In 1975, the Trust and Agency Fund disbursed $72.5 million to the Board of Education, and $48 million to other funds with much of this amount going to the General Fund. In the same year the Fund purchased $76.7 million of short-term investments, repaid $48 million of Board of Education loans, and advanced $4.5 million to the Board. Total Fund disbursements for 1975 were thus about $250 million.

The Park Improvement Fund was created to account for revenues and expenditures for park improvement and construction of new parks. The fund was supported by a one-half mill property tax in 1975. The Sanitary Improvement Fund is used to account for revenues resulting from the sale of Sanitary Department Revenue Certificates and expenditures for the improvement of the city's incinerator system. In 1975 these Special Revenue Funds accounted for expenditures of $1.9 million: $1 million for parks and $0.9 million for sanitation.

Debt Service Funds are used by Atlanta to account for the payment of principal and interest on the city's long-term debt (except for self-supporting city operations, which are accounted for via Enterprise Funds). In 1975, total expenditures from these funds were $16.5 million.

Capital Project Funds are created from time to time to account for the receipt and disbursement of monies used for the acquisition of capital facilities, with certain exceptions (e.g., Enterprise Funds). These funds disbursed $5.8 million in 1975.

As noted above, Enterprise Funds have been created to account for the financial activities of self-supporting city operations such as the Atlanta airport and the water and sewerage system. In 1975, the Department of Aviation (airport) had operating revenues of some $30 million, the water and sewerage system some $31 million.

Atlanta has a Working Capital Fund to account for services rendered and commodities furnished to other city departments, e.g., automobiles, duplicating services, and office supplies. This fund had billings of $6.5 million in 1975.

The state Highway Expressway Fund was created to account for transactions in which the City of Atlanta acquires rights-of-ways for various expressway projects; these acquisition costs, which are reimbursed by the State Highway Department, accounted for only a few thousand dollars in 1975.

The Special Assessment Fund accounts for the cost of certain improvements such as residential streets, sidewalks, sewers and curbs. These costs, which are recovered from the affected property owners via special assessments, came to $1.5 million in 1975.

The Model Neighborhood Project Fund was created to account for financial transactions in connection with Atlanta's participation in programs under Title I of the Demonstration Cities and Metropolitan Development Act of 1966; 1975 expenditures from this fund were about $5 million. Similarly, the Comprehensive Employment and Training Act Fund accounts for transactions under the 1973 Comprehensive Employment and Training Act ($12.3 million expended in 1975), and the Community Development Fund serves the same purpose with regard to programs under Title I of the Housing and Community Development Act of 1974 ($547,000 expended in 1975).

REFERENCES

1. Material in this section is drawn from U.S. Department of Labor, Bureau of Labor Statistics, Southeastern Regional Office, "Atlanta 1965-1975: Another Decade of Growth," Regional Report 36 (Atlanta, 1976), pp. 1-7; Research Atlanta, Inc., *Which Way Atlanta?* (Atlanta, 1973); and census data.
2. U.S. Department of Housing and Urban Development, Federal Housing Administration, "Analysis of the Atlanta, Georgia Housing Market as of April 1, 1972," (Washington, D.C.: U.S. GPO, July, 1972), p. 4.
3. This description is based on a series of articles appearing in the *Atlanta Constitution* between August 12 and 17, 1973.
4. Research Atlanta, Inc., *The Plan of Improvement: An Analysis of Services in the City of Atlanta and Fulton County* (Atlanta, 1974), p. 3.
5. *Ibid.,* pp. 13–28.
6. *Atlanta Constitution,* November 17, 1971, p. 9C.
7. *Ibid.,* December 17, 1971, p. 4C.
8. Floyd Hunter, *Community Power Structure* (Chapel Hill, N.C.: University of North Carolina Press, 1953); M. Kent Jennings, *Community Influentials: The Elites of Atlanta* (New York: The Free Press of Glencoe, 1964), pp. 156–157.
9. Jennings, pp. 167–168.
10. Jack L. Walker, "Protest and Negotiation: A Case Study of Negro Leadership in Atlanta, Georgia," *Midwest Journal of Political Science, 7* (May, 1963), p. 105.
11. *Atlanta Constitution,* November 27, 1969, p. 8A.
12. Charles S. Rooks, The Voter Education Project, Inc., *The Atlanta Elections of 1969* (Atlanta, 1970), pp. 2–3.
13. *Atlanta Constitution,* January 29, 1970, p. 6A.
14. Fred Powledge, "A New Politics in Atlanta," *New Yorker,* December 31, 1973, p. 34.
15. *Atlanta Constitution,* November 10, 1971, p. 10A.
16. *Ibid.,* August 17, 1972, p. 9A.
17. *Ibid.,* March 26, 1975, p. 15A.
18. *Ibid.,* October 7, 1971, p. 20A.
19. *Ibid.,* p. 9B.
20. *Ibid.*
21. *Ibid.,* March 23, 1975, p. 16A.
22. *Ibid.,* October 6, 1973, p. 1A.
23. *Ibid.,* March 23, 1975, pp. 1A, 16A.
24. *Ibid.,* December 18, 1975, p. 14A.
25. *Ibid.,* September 22, 1974, p. 19A.
26. *Ibid.,* September 26, 1974, p. 5A.
27. *Ibid.,* p. 1A.
28. *Ibid.*
29. *Ibid.,* August 3, 1975, p. 11A.
30. *Ibid.,* August 5, 1975, p. 1A.
31. *Ibid.,*
32. *Ibid.,* September 26, 1974, p. 1A.
33. *Ibid.,* March 23, 1975, p. 16A.
34. *New York Times,* April 18, 1975, p. 17.

EXHIBIT 10.1:   Metropolitan Atlanta in 1975

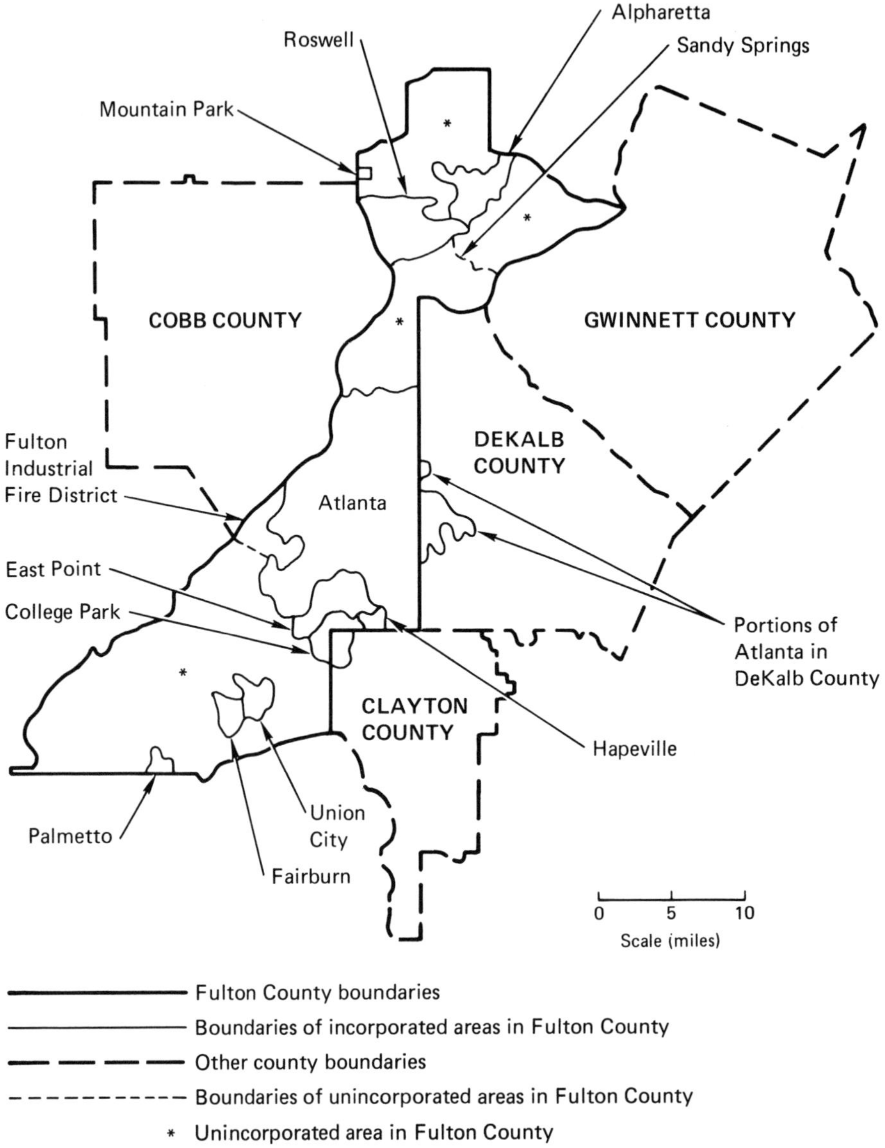

Source: Atlanta Regional Commission

**EXHIBIT 10.2:   City of Atlanta General Fund
Actual Revenues 1965 and 1970–1975 ($ thousands)**

Source	1965	1970	1971	1972	1973	1974	1975	% Increase 1965–1970	% Increase 1970–1975
Property tax	$11,878	$21,559	$29,193	$30,042	$31,492	$31,979	$36,900	82%	71%
%	30.5%	36.9%	41.9%	40.1%	37.2%	32.2%	36.6%		
Public utilities tax	2,124	3,719	3,841	4,719	5,302	6,620	7,144	75%	92%
%	5.4%	6.4%	5.5%	6.3%	6.3%	6.7%	7.1%		
Life insurance tax	1,379	1,627	1,939	2,042	2,727	2,762	3,039	18%	87%
%	3.5%	2.8%	2.8%	2.7%	3.2%	2.8%	3.0%		
Alcoholic beverage tax	3,119	5,636	5,799	5,953	6,795	8,342	8,398	81%	49%
%	8.0%	9.6%	8.3%	7.9%	8.0%	8.4%	8.3%		
License and permit fees	4,292	9,207	9,175	9,402	9,955	9,777	9,412	115%	2%
%	11.0%	15.7%	13.2%	12.5%	11.8%	9.8%	9.3%		
Sale of services	5,670	10,231	11,197	11,657	14,222	14,577	14,260	80%	39%
%	14.5%	17.5%	16.1%	15.5%	16.8%	14.7%	14.2%		
Fines, penalties, and forfeitures	2,939	3,100	3,229	3,427	2,867	3,891	3,640	5%	17%
%	7.5%	5.3%	4.6%	4.6%	3.4%	3.9%	3.6%		
State and federal aid*	—	772	2,823[#]	4,929	8,019	16,455[##]	10,992	—	1,324%
%	—	1.3%	4.1%	6.6%	9.5%	16.6%	10.9%		
Other revenues**	7,599***	2,621	2,461	2,819	3,229	4,961	6,922	−66%***	164%
%	19.5%	4.5%	3.5%	3.8%	3.8%	5.0%	6.9%		
Total (100%)	$39,000	$58,472	$69,657	$74,990	$84,608	$99,364	$100,707	50%	72%

*Does not include revenue sharing, which is accounted for under the Trust and Agency Fund.

**Includes interest on short-term investments, income from sale or rental of city property, miscellaneous revenues, and (for 1975 only) hotel and motel tax receipts of $918,242 or 0.9% of total general fund revenues.

***Until 1966, revenues from the sale of water accrued to the general fund; this accounted for $6,563,069 in 1965 or 16.8% of general fund revenues.

[#]State aid to Georgia municipalities began in 1971.

[##]Includes an $8.8 million EPA sewage treatment grant.

Source: City of Atlanta, Annual Reports of the City Comptroller (1965), Director of Finance (1970–1973), and Commissioner of Finance (1974–1975).

EXHIBIT 10.3: City of Atlanta General Fund
Actual Expenditures 1965 and 1970–1975 ($ thousands)

Purpose	1965	1970	1971	1972	1973	1974	1975	% Increase 1965–1970	% Increase 1970–1975
Police	$ 5,832	$11,188	$14,162	$16,196	$20,266	$25,319	$27,394	92%	145%
%	15.0%	18.5%	20.2%	22.0%	26.7%	26.8%	25.6%		
Fire	5,173	9,018	10,175	10,142	1,358*	5,085*	5,993*	74%	−34%*
%	13.3%	14.9%	14.5%	13.8%	1.8%	5.4%	5.6%		
Streets and Traffic	5,073	7,145	7,981	10,138	11,049	13,537	15,303	41%	114%
%	13.1%	11.8%	11.4%	13.8%	14.6%	14.3%	14.3%		
Sanitation	7,852	9,411	10,608	9,329	9,426	11,183	13,003	20%	38%
%	20.2%	15.6%	15.2%	12.7%	12.4%	11.8%	12.2%		
Parks and Recreation	2,562	7,490	8,087	7,651	8,689	9,801	9,832	192%	31%
%	6.6%	12.4%	11.6%	10.4%	11.5%	10.4%	9.2%		
Library and Cultural	1,066	2,505	2,914	3,024	3,568	3,601	3,754	135%	50%
%	2.7%	4.1%	4.2%	4.1%	4.7%	3.8%	3.5%		
Pensions	1,453	2,661	3,139	3,756	4,146	5,013**	5,264**	83%	98%
%	3.7%	4.4%	4.2%	5.1%	5.5%	5.3%	4.9%		
General Government	9,804	11,056	12,936	13,338	17,371	21,103	26,415***	13%	139%
%	25.3%	18.3%	18.5%	18.1%	22.9%	22.3%	24.7%		
Total (100%)	$38,815	$60,474	$70,002	$73,572	$75,873	$94,642	$106,958	56%	77%

*Beginning in 1973, firemen's salaries have been paid in major part out of the Trust and Agency Fund from general revenue sharing receipts; however, the actual amounts cannot be determined from that fund's financial statements.

**Atlanta underfunded its pension plans by an estimated $7.3 million in 1974 and $7.4 million in 1975.

***The principal components of the general government increase from 1974 to 1975 were expenditures under federal grants and spending for human services.

Source: City of Atlanta, Annual Reports of the City Comptroller (1965), Director of Finance (1970–1973), and Commissioner of Finance (1974–1975).

EXHIBIT 10.4:   Municipal Services in Fulton County

Service	Union City	Roswell	Palmetto	Mountain Park	Hapeville	Fulton County	Fairburn	East Point	College Park	Atlanta-DeKalb	Atlanta	Alpharetta
Airport							F				A	
Auditorium											A	
Fire	V	V	V	V	X	F&V	V	X	X	A	A	F(V)
Health						F				J		
Inspections				F		F				D	A	
Libraries	J	J	J		A	A	J	X	A	D	A	J
Parks & Recreation	F	X	F	X	X	F	F	X	X	D	A	X
Planning						F				A	A	
Police	A	X	A	X	A	A	X	X	A	A	A	X
Public Works	F	F	F	X	F	F	X		X	D	A	
Refuse Collection	1	X	X	1	X	1	X	X	X	A	A	X
Refuse Disposal	F	F		1	EP	F	F	X	F	A	A	X
Sewerage System	X	X	X		X	A	X	X	X	A	A	
Sewerage Treatment	F	F	X		F	A	F	J	F	A	A	F
Stadium						J					J	
Tax Assessors						J					J	
Tax Collection	F	F	F	F	F	F	F	F	F	F	F	F
Traffic Engineering						F				D	A	
Water Distribution	F	A	F		F	A	F	F	F	A	A	A
Water Supply	A	F	A	C	A	A	A	X	EP	A	A	F
Zoning	X	X	X		X	F	X	X	X	A	A	X

Code: A—Atlanta; C—Cobb; D—DeKalb; F—Fulton; J—Joint Atlanta-Fulton; V—Volunteer; EP—East Point; X—Municipality itself
1—Privately provided.

Source: Research Atlanta, The Plan of Improvement: An Analysis of Services in the City of Atlanta and Fulton County *(Atlanta, 1974), p. 76.*

**EXHIBIT 10.5:   Research Atlanta's Estimates of the Subsidy
from Atlanta to Non-Atlanta Portions of Fulton County**

Service Group	1970	1973	1974
Exclusively Non-Atlanta county services	6.1	11.6	10.8
Less service charges and taxes raised outside Atlanta for these services	2.7	4.75	4.4
BENEFIT TO NON-ATLANTANS	3.4	6.85	6.4
Fulton County school taxes levied on Atlanta residents	1.9	1.95	1.7
BENEFIT TO NON-ATLANTANS	1.9	1.95	1.7
County-wide and administrative services	15.6	23.8	28.2
Services provided to Atlanta	13.7	18.5	21.3
Less service charges and taxes paid by Atlanta for these services	15.1	19.0	21.5
BENEFIT TO NON-ATLANTANS	1.4	0.5	0.2
Total social services	19.3	23.3	29.2
Services to Atlanta	16.6	19.8	25.0
Less service charges and taxes paid by Atlanta for these services	14.8	16.0	19.6
BENEFIT TO NON-ATLANTANS	−1.8	−3.8	−5.4
TOTAL BENEFIT TO NON-ATLANTANS	4.9	5.5	2.9
TOTAL BENEFIT TO NON-ATLANTANS (excluding social services)	6.7	9.3	8.3

All numbers are in millions of dollars.

Source: Research Atlanta, The Plan of Improvement: An Analysis of Services in the City of Atlanta and Fulton County *(Atlanta, 1974), table, pp. 15, 20, and 23, description of 1974 expenditures, p. 17.*

11

Expanding Atlanta's
City Limits (B)

In 1975, the legal and fiscal relationship between the city of Atlanta and its suburbs became a major issue among residents of metropolitan Atlanta. Expansion of the city's boundaries to incorporate some of its suburbs was proposed by city officials as a solution to Atlanta's fiscal problems, and strong resistance developed throughout the metropolitan area. This case describes the debate on the expansion issue up to the time of the 1976 session of the Georgia Legislature.

THE EXPANSION DEBATE THROUGH 1974

Efforts to increase the size of Atlanta by annexing* suburban territory originated in the mid-1940s during the administration of Mayor William Hartsfield. In 1947, the city attempted to annex two heavily

---

*Annexation involves the addition of unincorporated territory to an existing municipality. In contrast, consolidation involves the merger of two or more existing municipalities into one. Consolidation requires a more complex legislative process including a number of constitutional amendments.

populated suburban areas, but the effort was defeated by referenda in the affected areas. (In most cases, Georgia law requires voter approval in a referendum for any area to be annexed by a municipality.) Interest in annexation, however, did not die. Proponents argued that expanding the city's size would not only increase the city property tax base and decrease the subsidy paid to other parts of Fulton County by city taxpayers, but would also avert stagnation. As one proponent put it:

> A city that cannot grow is destined to become a dead city. It loses many of its best citizens who move to the outskirts. It gets beaten in the competitive battle of attracting new industries. It loses its civic pride and it can become easy prey to political machines that thrive on the dissatisfaction that comes when civic pride disappears.[1]

In 1949, at the request of the city of Atlanta, the Georgia General Assembly passed an act establishing the Local Government Commission of Atlanta and Fulton County, a 12-member citizen panel convened to develop recommendations for the improvement of city/county government. The final report of the commission, titled "A Plan of Improvement for the Government of Atlanta and Fulton County," made four major recommendations. It first cited "the paralleling of service delivery between the city and county"[2] as the most important problem of government in the Atlanta-Fulton County area and a major cause of waste and inefficiency. Under the Plan of Improvement, many services provided by Atlanta to city residents and by Fulton County to county residents outside the city would become the exclusive responsibility of either the city or the county; Fulton County would reimburse the city of Atlanta for services which the city would be providing to other county residents. (See Part A (chapter 10) for details of the specific service divisions created by the plan.)

The commission also cited inequality in taxation as a serious problem, noting that residents of unincorporated areas did not pay the full cost of the services provided them by Fulton County because Atlanta residents paid city taxes to provide services to themselves and also county taxes to provide the same services to other county residents.

> Fulton County has dipped into the general fund to provide first one new municipal service and then another to persons residing in the unincorporated areas of the county....
>
> According to estimates for 1948, the residents and businesses of the City of Atlanta pay $1.62 to Fulton County for every $1.00 of services they get back. Though the county spends a great deal of money for the benefit of city people—through court, welfare, and hospital services, in particular—city payments to the county exceed county payments to the city by nearly $4,000,000.[3]

The commission recommended both a tax equalization program, which would increase the amounts paid by residents of unincorporated areas for services provided to them by Fulton County, and a complete reassessment of property, since Atlanta's property had previously been assessed at a higher percentage of real value than other county property, further increasing the tax burden on Atlanta residents.*

The Plan of Improvement further recommended that the Atlanta city limits be immediately extended to include 82 more square miles (including the two suburban areas which had rejected annexation in 1947) with a population of 87,000 and that a provision be enacted to allow the automatic annexation of contiguous areas outside the newly created city limits as they became sufficiently populated. This so-called "automatic annexation" provision would authorize the city to petition the Supreme Court of Fulton County for annexation of those unincorporated areas that have more than 40 occupied dwellings per land lot** or that exceed $200,000 per land lot in property value for tax purposes. Behind these recommendations lay the commission's conclusion that the traditional legislative and referendum methods of annexation, which required approval by the residents to be annexed, were unworkable in Atlanta because suburban residents could not be expected to vote for arrangements which they believed would lead to higher taxes. An analysis of the Plan of Improvement by Research Atlanta, a predominantly white upper-income civic group, commented on the reasoning leading to this recommendation:

> It is understandably difficult to extend a city's limits when the extension depends upon a vote of the people in the affected area. . . . In the short run, the immediate costs in these suburban incorporated areas are lower than in the city. But the reason is not that the county can render the services more cheaply than the city, but that the difference between the two is paid by city people through county taxes from which they get no returns.[4]

---

*Atlanta taxpayers also subsidized all of Fulton County—incorporated and unincorporated—through payment of Fulton County school taxes. Fulton County schools were supported by three sources: a county-wide school tax first approved in 1926; county-wide general fund revenues, some of which were first allocated to schools in 1943; and an additional school tax levied on property outside Atlanta (where residents attended Fulton County schools). The first two sources of revenue were provided in large part by Atlanta residents and businesses through property taxes, even though Atlantans were legally barred from using Fulton County schools. The Plan of Improvement made no changes in the school tax arrangements, although areas annexed to Atlanta under the Plan would join the Atlanta city school system.

**A land lot is generally a square piece of land (except where determined by municipal boundaries or natural barriers) with an area of about half a square mile.

Atlanta and Fulton County approved the whole plan by advisory referendum in June 1950, and five constitutional amendments implementing the plan's major recommendations were ratified in November 1950. During the 1950 Assembly session, both the automatic and immediate annexation provisions of the Plan of Improvement were approved. Several constitutional amendments implementing the Plan were ratified in November 1951, and implementing legislation provided for a division of services between Atlanta and Fulton County similar to that proposed in the plan.

In 1966, with the imminent emergence of a black majority in Atlanta, the issue of annexation acquired racial implications. In that year the Georgia General Assembly passed a bill to annex the predominantly white unincorporated area of Fulton County just north of Atlanta known as Sandy Springs (see Map 11.1) into the city of Atlanta upon approval by a majority of the voters. Black State Senator Leroy Johnson proposed an amendment to the bill to include the predominantly black area of Boulder Park in the annexation referendum, in order to help even the racial balance resulting from annexation. The amendment was accepted, with support from Atlanta delegation members, and in the election, Boulder Park residents approved annexation, while Sandy Springs residents soundly rejected it.

In 1968 the city petitioned to annex a portion of Sandy Springs (but not all of it as envisioned by the 1966 legislative action) under the automatic annexation provision of the 1951 legislation. However, residents of that unincorporated area sued the city to prevent the annexation, and after a year of litigation, the automatic annexation provision was ruled unconstitutional by the Georgia Supreme Court on the grounds that at the time the statute was passed (1951), it was unconstitutional to delegate essentially legislative power to either the city or the petitioners of a local area.[5]

In 1969, the legislature considered a bill to "abolish Atlanta" by providing that, in all counties of over 500,000 residents (Fulton County was the only one), the government of the county's largest city would "cease to exist" on January 1, 1972. The bill's provisions were deliberately left vague to attract support from legislators who might be less inclined to support any specific plan but favored the general concept of merging the Atlanta city government into Fulton County. Specific arrangements to consummate the

merger of Atlanta and Fulton County after the dissolution of Atlanta were to take place in the two to three year interim period after the bill became law. The bill's main backers were rural legislators—its main House sponsor came from Forsyth County, a rural county just north of Atlanta—and white suburbanites (particularly from DeKalb County), although a scattering of white Atlanta representatives supported it. Atlanta black legislators were infuriated by what they regarded as an attempt by the legislature to interfere on racial grounds in a local issue that would normally (under Georgia constitutional law and tradition) be left to the delegation of the area affected rather than to the whole General Assembly. (The rural legislators replied that any matter affecting the economic and political health of the state capital is a matter affecting the whole state.) The bill was defeated in the Senate on a 34-22 vote in January 1970, in part because Senator Leroy Johnson struck a deal with Senate President *pro tempore* Hugh Gillis, a conservative rural Democrat, whereby Johnson would support a bill to clarify the authority of Gillis's son, the State Highway Commissioner, in return for defeat of the "abolish Atlanta" bill.[6]

Also in 1969, Atlanta Mayor Ivan Allen, Jr. and the Atlanta City Council commissioned the Institute of Public Administration (IPA), a New York City research organization, to study the impact of consolidation of the Atlanta and Fulton County governments. The Institute's final report, issued late in November 1969 (after the mayoral election), contended that not only government efficiency and economy but also the economic viability of the entire Atlanta metropolitan area depended on consolidation. The report recommended a merger of city and county governments as well as school systems to achieve "social harmony," consolidate the tax base, and provide "unlimited opportunity to attract new industry."[7] To the argument that blacks would lose political power under consolidation, the report replied that Atlanta must take in its suburbs or fail economically, and that blacks would be most victimized by the problems stemming from a failure to act. The report stated:

> With its boundaries frozen, the city is threatened with problems associated with the out-movement of goods-handling and other jobs and middle-class

population. These include the confinement and disadvantage of minority groups by artificial jurisdictional barriers, while employment and other opportunities flow away; increased potential for racial polarization; transportation and development difficulties; and service demands rising faster than the city's tax base.[8]

The report proposed the consolidation of the Atlanta and Fulton County governments with representation in the governing body of the new consolidated government partly by district and partly at large—thus preserving some black representation in a 62% white municipality.

White racial moderates in Atlanta tended to support the recommendations and reasoning of the IPA report. For example, Alderman W.T. Knight said he supported consolidation "so county residents who share in services would share in costs."[9] Mayor Allen and the chairman of the Fulton County Board of Commissioners strongly backed consolidation as proposed by IPA.

While a poll taken by IPA suggested that 43% of blacks favored consolidation, with 22% against and 35% undecided,[10] most black leaders (and their white supporters, including Mayor-elect Sam Massell) opposed consolidation. For example, Reverend Sam Williams, former head of the Atlanta NAACP, said that the "merger could produce a 'reactionary' government without 'social considerations' because it would include those who have fled the city in recent years," and another black participant at an IPA meeting pointed to the "unresponsive" nature of Fulton County government to public housing needs to support this point. The Institute's formula for electing council members, some by district and some at large, was also contested, with some claiming that as few as two black members would ever be elected.[11] Fulton County whites outside Atlanta were also wary of the proposal.

Although many of Atlanta's business and political leaders supported the IPA plan, a few, most notably former Mayor William Hartsfield, opposed the type of consolidation being considered. He argued that consolidation should not be based strictly on governmental units but should consider regional growth patterns, and said that "a merged government of only Atlanta and Fulton could end up like St. Louis [where city-county consolidation had previously taken place] —stymied as far as any future growth is concerned."

Hartsfield contended that Atlanta's growth is mainly toward Sandy Springs and through [DeKalb County] and that the northernmost and southernmost points of Fulton aren't tied to Atlanta but to smaller municipalities farther out.

"I think it's a mistake to be oriented to the single obsession of merging Atlanta and Fulton. A city should do the natural and sensible thing of going where the people and taxable values are going. Atlanta should not move out of DeKalb when both citizens and taxable values are moving in."[12]

With the defeat of the "abolish Atlanta" approach to consolidation, the IPA report also became a dead issue.

Because he had viewed the "abolish Atlanta" bill as inspired by racism, Mayor Massell had initially opposed any annexation or consolidation attempts. However, by early 1971 the prospect of a major revenue shortfall had led him to state that he could support an annexation proposal for fiscal reasons. In an October 1971 speech, he endorsed some sort of consolidation plan that would "move the invisible corporate limits [of the city] to take on to our tax rolls those adjacent affluent whites already using all our city facilities and requiring basic urban services."[13] In November 1971, a study issued by Research Atlanta, Inc. further fueled the arguments of the annexationists by claiming that in 1970 Atlanta residents paid $4.7 million more to the Fulton County government in taxes than they received in services. (See Part A (chapter 10) for further information on the "subsidy" issue.)

Late in December 1971, at a Rotary Club luncheon before an audience made up predominantly of white businessmen, Massell unveiled an annexation plan to be presented to the 1972 legislative session. The plan called for the division of all unincorporated Fulton County into two separate cities: Atlanta would take in unincorporated North Fulton and one-fourth of the Fulton Industrial Fire District* (to support tax revenues), while the city of College Park would double in size through the annexation of all of South Fulton and the rest of the Fulton Industrial District. The

---

*The Fulton County Industrial Fire District is a small, sparsely populated area due west of Atlanta, where a large number of industrial firms, attracted by low county taxes, have located.

Atlanta and Fulton County school systems would both be financed through county-wide taxes (eliminating Atlanta's subsidy to Fulton County schools) but would otherwise remain separate. The plan would be implemented without a referendum.

Some observers suggested that Massell devised the plan to try to attain the two-thirds majority of the Fulton County legislative delegation necessary to make it "local" legislation (which would be considered only by the affected delegation, rather than by the entire General Assembly). These observers assumed that the plan would be backed by Atlanta's white representatives and by South Fulton legislators eager to incorporate South Fulton into a municipality, and opposed by North Fulton members and many black legislators. They suggested that Massell hoped to gain more black support than would have been possible under the complete Atlanta-Fulton consolidation proposed in the "abolish Atlanta" bill, because Massell's plan would leave Atlanta only 53% white, as opposed to Fulton County as a whole, which is 62% white.

Massell argued that his plan was not racially inspired and suggested that blacks could be elected in the consolidated municipality. He added,

> I think it most important to note that many affluent whites have moved north of the city, not to escape greater taxes or integration but simply because that's where the new living quarters are being developed. And we should realize that because of vast vacant lands, that is where residential areas will continue to be developed for many years in the future.[14]

Atlanta should, in effect, according to Massell, expand in the directions of growth in population and wealth.

The reaction from Massell's audience was enthusiastic. L. L. Gellerstedt, the president of the Atlanta Chamber of Commerce, said he offered his "wholehearted support" to the mayor and added, "It's time for us to get with him and make this an even greater city." Former Mayor Ivan Allen, Jr., said he was "delighted to see the mayor take this position" and would "heartily endorse the plan."[15]

However, both white northern suburbanites wary of higher taxes and inferior, integrated schools, and Atlanta blacks, fearing the dilution of their political power, immediately organized to oppose the plan. Rep. Earl Patton (R-Sandy Springs) called for a referendum on any annexation proposal, and a movement to incorporate Sandy Springs, preventing its annexation to Atlanta, was begun. Black leaders vigorously protested the timing of Massell's annexation proposal, calling it a blatant attempt to dilute their new black majority before the 1973 city elections. (Blacks became a majority of the Atlanta electorate in 1971, and 1973 would be their first opportunity to elect a black mayor and increase black city council representation.) One day after the mayor's speech, a meeting was called by a wide spectrum of black political leaders, including Vice Mayor Maynard Jackson, three of the five black aldermen, two state representatives, Reverend Andrew Young, and the heads of the Urban League and the NAACP. White legislators who had in the past received black support were invited to the meeting and given, as the *Atlanta Constitution* suggested, a clear message: "The black leaders told the white legislators that they had received black support in the past but would not get it again if they support Massell's plans."[16] Other blacks questioned the possibility of increased taxes for Atlantans under the plan (due to the extension of city services to the annexed areas) and the propriety of annexation without a referendum.

To gain legislative support, Massell proposed a compromise with his black and white critics, amending his proposal to delay annexation from 1973—before the municipal election—to 1975 and to include less area in the annexation. The bill proposing this "two-city" plan for Fulton County passed the House in late February 1972 but failed to receive a majority from the Fulton County House delegation. It was then killed by Lt. Governor Lester Maddox, who refused to bring it to a vote in the State Senate, partly because of the lack of Fulton County support in the House and partly because of his opposition to annexation without approval by (white) suburban voters.

1975: THE STATE GOVERNMENT TAKES ON EXPANSION

In early 1975 a number of Atlanta's business and political leaders held a meeting with Governor George Busbee to discuss "the future of the city in general and . . . generating a broad base of support for some kind of annexation" of Atlanta suburbs to the city.[17] Among the participants were Maynard Jackson, who had been elected as Atlanta's first black mayor in 1973; Ivan Allen III, president of the Chamber of Commerce; former Governor Carl Sanders; E. D. Smith, chairman of the board of the First National Bank; Richard H. Rich of the Rich's department store chain; Ed Rast, president of Southern Bell Telephone; and Jesse Hill, president of the Atlanta Life Insurance Company, the largest black-owned company in the U.S. Interest in the possibility of expansion had been growing through the preceding years; all the participants at the meeting, including Mayor Jackson spoke favorably of expansion as a means of alleviating Atlanta's fiscal problems. (However, Augustus H. Sterne of the Trust Company of Georgia noted that Jackson explicitly qualified his support of annexation with the proviso, "so long as it does not dilute black political power."[18]

Over the next several months, the expansion issue continued to grow in importance. Mayor Jackson assigned several staff members in the Atlanta Finance Department the task of preparing a full report on various expansion possibilities, commenting:

> Nobody has ever put the figures together. . . . If I'm going to sell a plan to the black community, I've got to be able to tell the people exactly what we're talking about.[19]

In late March the *Atlanta Constitution* carried a full-page article highlighting the expansion issue, and shortly thereafter, Ivan Allen III, gave a major speech to a predominantly black audience urging their acceptance of expansion. In early June, Mayor Jackson, who as vice mayor had opposed Massell's annexation plan, announced that he would "take a positive position this year on a plan to expand Atlanta's boundaries" though he indicated that any annexation plan must include the Fulton Industrial Fire District, because "if we're only talking about taking in housing, we're not talking about broadening our tax base."[20] Opponents of annexation also began to prepare for a fight on the issue. The executive director of the Southern Regional Council's Voter Education Project (an Atlanta-based black organization concerned with increasing Southern black political strength) strongly criticized annexation as an attempt to dilute black voting strength, and members of the suburban Fulton County legislative delegation held meetings to alert their constituents to the danger of Atlanta's expansion. The positions of the various interest groups concerned with expansion in 1974–75 are summarized below.

Business. Expansion had historically drawn support from white business leaders in Atlanta, who were actively backing it as the issue reappeared. Former Governor Carl Sanders, an attorney representing many large Atlanta corporations, told a September 1974 forum of business and political leaders that the governmental pattern in Atlanta was an inefficient crazy-quilt. "Right now we have 80 different governments and 65 municipalities and 15 counties in the Metro Atlanta area. No one could run a business that way."[21] However, business leaders' main arguments were economic. Ivan Allen III, son of the former mayor and a future president of the Chamber of Commerce, said at the same meeting that "as long as it is impossible for the city to expand its boundaries, we will continue to have these problems" of white flight and a tax base inadequate to support necessary services.[22]

In an August 1975 speech,[23] former Governor Carl Sanders spelled out the economic arguments for expansion in detail. He commented that the economic growth of the whole region depended on the central city and would not continue "unless the urban center can continue to attract new commercial and industrial concerns and provide jobs and a happy lifestyle for our people." He claimed that taxes twice as high as those in suburban counties and the threat of crime were causing businesses to relocate to the suburbs and suggested that the "flight to suburbia . . . adds fuel to the fiscal crisis facing the city. As the tax base erodes, the city must tax at a higher level those who remain—thus further compounding the tax incentive to leave the city." High Atlanta taxes were, in Sanders' opinion, a result of fiscal inequities: over half of the residents of the five metropolitan counties worked in Atlanta, and the city had to spend large sums of money to provide fire and police protection, street maintenance, and sanitation for these commuters who paid no taxes to support the services. Sanders added that a disproportionate amount of the region's tax-exempt property was located in the central city (because of state and federal government offices and non-profit organizations), so that Atlanta residents' tax base was decreased to provide services to the region as a whole. Finally, he noted that Atlanta had to deliver more social services to poor people than its suburbs and claimed that Atlanta residents should not be required to bear the whole burden of this expense. To relieve these inequities and the inefficient pattern of service duplication cited above, the former Governor strongly advocated expansion of Atlanta's city limits to include its suburbs.

Business leaders characterized opponents of expansion as representing narrow, rather than community, interests. Ivan Allen III commented:

> The white people in the suburbs will have to give up their prejudices and the blacks in the city will have to give up their selfishness about not wanting to dilute their political power in city government.[24]

Some business leaders, in particular former Governor Sanders, urged that political leaders attempt to persuade the people of the wisdom of metropolitan government, but added that if the people were not convinced, the legislature should impose a solution in any case:

> I don't think you'd get very far with a referendum [on expansion]. I think you've got to present it to the legislature. . . . I think you've got to get the rural boys to vote for it to override some of these boys up there in the city. Because I don't think these guys in the city are going to vote for anything.[25]

Rural Interest. Many rural conservatives were willing to vote for some type of expansion of Atlanta's city limits if it would undermine a black voting majority. They were highly dissatisfied with Mayor Jackson's performance in office: proposals were being made to place the city-run Atlanta airport under state control and to create special authorities for water and sewer functions, and even to make the state police responsible for Atlanta.* Some even proposed a direct

state takeover of the city or its removal from Jackson's hands by the annexation of enough suburban territory to create a strong white majority. In a September 1974 press conference, ultraconservative Republican gubernatorial candidate Ronnie Thompson, the mayor of Macon, stated that if elected, he would "ask the General Assembly to take control of the city of Atlanta if its government does not improve Atlanta's crime and race relations problems within six months after his inauguration." Thompson added that "there is rampant hate in Atlanta," claimed that the city was a "concrete and steel jungle that could end up as a high-rise ghetto" if it were not given better government, and accused Mayor Jackson of being "the most vicious racist mayor in the United States."[26]

Suburban Residents. A few politicians with suburban constituencies favored some realignment of governmental responsibilities in the Atlanta metropolitan area,** but almost no suburbanites favored expanding the city limits of Atlanta to include all or part of Fulton County. The chambers of commerce of both North and South Fulton, the South Fulton PTA, the teachers' union for the Fulton County schools, and many suburban legislators and municipal politicians strongly attacked Atlanta's expansion.

Suburban white opposition was based on three major arguments. First was a belief that taxes for all suburban residents, whether or not they were included in the area added to Atlanta, would rise if the city expanded: suburban residents included in Atlanta would pay higher taxes to support Atlanta's higher levels of expenditures, while excluded residents would pay more because the Fulton County tax base would decrease and because many plans would force residents of unincorporated areas to pay the full cost of services.

The second issue was the fate of the Fulton County school system. Many suburban residents did not want their children to become part of a school system, currently 87% black, which they viewed as

---

*In early 1974, conservative rural legislators had tried to limit Jackson's authority to require new city employees to live in the city (only to be thwarted by a veto by Governor Carter). The proposed airport and water and sewerage takeovers were a response to Jackson's delay in choosing a new airport site and his affirmative action contracting plans, while the proposal to replace city police with state police was a reaction to the controversial performance in office of Jackson's Commissioner of Public Safety, A. Reginald Eaves. See Part A (chapter 10) for further information on these issues.

**One suburban legislator, Rep. Virlyn Smith (R-Fairburn), proposed a new government incorporating portions of a five-county area with taxing powers to provide regional services, while existing municipalities remained responsible for other services. Milton Farris, a former Atlanta alderman and later a Fulton County commissioner elected with suburban support, proposed that Atlanta not be expanded but that all unincorporated parts of Fulton County be attached to existing or new municipalities and that all municipal residents be charged for county services on the basis of use. He suggested that Atlanta's subsidy to the suburbs had ceased and that suburbanites would gain $3 million per year, largely through reduced social service expenditures, through his proposal.

being of low quality. Eva Galambos, chairman of the Committee for Sandy Springs, Georgia (a group pressing for the incorporation of the Sandy Springs area just north of Atlanta into a separate municipality, and adamantly opposed to annexation), said:

> The major reason on everybody's mind for not wanting to be part of Atlanta is the schools.
>
> We don't think our going into the Atlanta school system will make them better. You know how the bad apples just keep on spreading. Neither do we think bigger is better, and we like our own schools.
>
> Besides, if we became a part of Atlanta, we'd lose a lot of people. The people with school children would move to Cobb [a neighboring county]. They're already doing it.[27]

The third strand running through suburban opposition to expansion was the simple emotional desire not be a part of the city of Atlanta. State Representative Dick Lane (R-East Point), an opponent of expansion, said of his constituents that

> They are not even going to consider [consolidation]. They say, "Our people fled Atlanta and we're certainly not going to become a part of it again.[28]

A Sandy Springs resident confirmed this description with his testimony at a public hearing on the expansion question:

> We owe Atlanta nothing. We don't exist to support Atlanta. Atlanta feeds on Georgia. We all want to be on a winning team, and winning teams don't have to annex.[29]

Many suburbanites believed that the push toward expansion of Atlanta's city limits was a false issue being fomented by downtown business leaders to restore their power. Senator James R. (Duck) Hamilton (D-College Park), a South Fulton opponent of expansion, said that members of the "downtown power structure" "were on every board in the city" prior to the Jackson administration. Now, "they're not on those boards and they're upset. That's a lot of the problem."[30] Eva Galambos of Sandy Springs agreed with this assessment, arguing that the issue was not fiscal but political: "property owners, the downtown owners, just don't have the control they once had"[31] and wanted to regain it. State Senator Haskew

Brantley (R-Fulton) charged that Atlanta whites were manipulating the race issue for political ends:

> Atlanta's white legislators want to improve the city's service delivery system and equalize the tax burden throughout Fulton County. But now they are using race as an issue to get what they want.
>
> You've got some white city legislators going to white rural legislators and saying, "you don't want niggers taking over our capital city, do you?" And the rural folks go right through the roof. It isn't right.[32]

The Atlanta Black Community. While in previous debates Atlanta blacks had lined up solidly against expansion, perceiving it as a threat to black voting strength, black legislators and city officials were divided in 1975. A number of black legislators stressed fiscal and economic reasons for expansion. State Representative Ben Brown, one of the earlier black expansion advocates, argued for expansion on the following grounds:

> While Atlanta has increased in importance to its citizens and the region as a whole, it has become less able to finance its costs. If the present trends continue unchanged, Atlanta will be forced to reduce or eliminate its services or impose exorbitant tax increases. In other words, instead of progress, we will have to regress. . . .
>
> Atlanta currently provides services which everyone in the metro area uses, but only Atlanta pays for. . . . While Atlanta has begun to develop and improve its city services for the benefit of the entire region, the taxable wealth had begun to trickle outside the city limits. . . . Commercial and industrial development, the mainstays of Atlanta's property tax revenues, has almost stopped inside the city.[33]

Brown also argued that any dilution of black political power in Fulton County would be only temporary, since Atlanta Regional Commission projections indicated that the whole of Fulton County would be 56% black by 1980.

Other blacks disagreed with Brown's interpretation. Representative Henrietta Canty (D-Atlanta) stated, "I feel that any annexation would be very detrimental to us in that it would dilute our voting strength, which is still very much in its infancy."[34] Representative Hosea Williams (D-Atlanta-in-DeKalb*), a black militant leader of the 1960s and early 1970s, objected most strongly to Brown's argument, charging that Brown's "advising blacks to give up political gains for economic gains is a betrayal of the black movement."[35]

Nearly all blacks in Atlanta, whether for or against expansion, agreed that white racism played a large part in the initial generation of the issue in 1974 and early 1975. State Representative Billy McKinney (D-Atlanta) said that black elected officials are "under attack by the media, the power structure, and whites in general. They are meeting and planning how they can take Atlanta back."[36] State Representative Julian Bond (D-Atlanta) told the *Constitution* that he "believes the whole question of annexation stems from displeasure across the state with black men exercising power,"[37] even though he said in the same interview that he could support certain annexation proposals. Hosea Williams suggested the existence of "a downtown super-rich clique" trying "to perpetrate an economic illusion on the voters of Atlanta that will in fact set black gains back 25 years."[38] Ben Brown agreed that racism was a major problem in the annexation debate but saw rural legislators as the main threat: "The crucial thing black folks have to understand is that once the legislature starts to move in a racist manner, there is nothing we can do."[39]

Legislative Action.   Governor Busbee took no official position on expansion, stating only that he would endorse any consensus reached by the Fulton County legislative delegation. His legislative floor leader, Representative E. Roy Lambert (D-Madison), however, expressed strong support for expansion: "I personally feel like it's got to happen—that some kind of consolidation has to be forthcoming."[40] In preparation for a major debate on the subject in the January 1976 legislative session, the Fulton County State Senate delegation in 1975 called upon all concerned parties to come forward with plans and suggestions for Atlanta expansion and later commissioned Georgia State University to complete a study on expansion alternatives by January 1, 1976, to help the senators draft legislation in the next session of the General Assembly. The President of the Georgia Senate, Lieu-

tenant Governor Zell Miller, appointed Senator Ed Garrard (D-Atlanta), a proponent of many of the earlier pieces of expansion legislation, to chair an Atlanta-Fulton Study Committee and chose four of Fulton County's remaining eight state senators to serve under Garrard. Senator James R. Hamilton (D-College Park), a member of the Senate committee who was adamantly opposed to expansion, attacked the whole committee structure:

> The fact that these committees were . . . appointed [by the Lieutenant Governor, not the Fulton County delegation] means that this legislation is going to be drawn up as general legislation. They [those in favor of annexation] are afraid that this will fail as local legislation. This way it will bypass the local delegation.**[41]

In the House, Speaker Tom Murphy named black State Representative Grace Hamilton (D-Atlanta) to chair an Atlanta-Fulton Study Committee. Of the 24 state representatives in the Fulton delegation, ten were selected by Speaker Murphy to serve on the committee under Representative Hamilton; according to Murphy, these ten were "a representative cross-section of the delegation."[42] (The Chairman of the House Judiciary Committee was named the eleventh committee member, even though he did not live in Fulton County.)

From August through mid-December 1975 the House and Senate Atlanta-Fulton study committees collected proposals and held a series of public hearings chaired by Senator Jack Stephens, chairman of the Fulton Senate delegation. Nearly all the proposals received by the committees came from advocates of expansion; only two—one to do nothing and one to create three cities in Atlanta—were received from suburbanites. The supporters and opponents of the remaining proposals cannot be really categorized: the

---

*Atlanta-in-DeKalb, a section of the city of Atlanta located in neighboring DeKalb County, had about 36,000 residents, three-quarters of whom were black in 1975.

**Georgia legislative practice recognizes two types of legislation—general and local. General legislation is considered and voted on by all Assembly members. But as to local legislation, the unwritten rule has developed that the Assembly will automatically give its assent if the affected delegations can reach a consensus. Thus, if the Fulton County House and Senate delegations failed to reach an agreement, the expansion of Atlanta might be reclassified as a general matter, in which case legislators from outside the metropolitan area—i.e., rural and small town legislators—could take part in the debate.

most far-reaching plan—to consolidate Atlanta and all of Fulton County—was prepared by black State Representative Ben Brown (D-Atlanta).

Mayor Jackson Speaks Out

In early September 1975, after various annexation plans had been presented to the House study committee, the Atlanta Finance Department issued a report on the impact of various expansion plans on Atlanta's fiscal health. The report, part of the research promised by Mayor Jackson before he committed himself to a particular expansion plan, claimed that the cost of municipal services to all of unincorporated Fulton County would exceed taxes to finance those services by over $17 million in 1980, $20 million in 1985, and $12.5 million in 1990. The report noted that only the Fulton Industrial Fire District would bring in more taxes than it paid out for municipal services. It also noted that if the school system were consolidated along with the municipal government structure, Atlanta taxpayers would gain from the annexation of both Sandy Springs and the Fulton Industrial Fire District, paying higher municipal taxes but much lower school taxes. Some of this gain would be erased by the annexation of other unincorporated parts of Fulton County, but even with full annexation, total municipal and school taxes would be two to three mills lower by 1990. More optimistically the report observed that if unincorporated suburban Fulton County were not annexed to Atlanta and instead included in a "special tax district" paying the full cost of services bought from the Atlanta and Fulton County governments, rather than receiving subsidies from the rest of the county, city taxpayers could gain a five to six mill reduction in combined city and county taxes.*[43]

With the presentation of this report, Mayor Jackson changed his position on the expansion issue. The report enabled him to argue that expansion was only one way to redress the fiscal imbalance between Atlanta and the suburbs (and in his view, not the preferred way of dealing with the problems because of

---

*City residents would gain more from "special tax districts" than from annexation because the unincorporated areas would receive only those municipal services they chose to receive rather than receiving all the services offered by the city of Atlanta to its residents. While suburban residents would pay higher taxes with the special districts than with no expansion, their taxes would not rise as much as if they were annexed to Atlanta.

its impact on black voting strength). Jackson told the *Atlanta Constitution*:

> . . . better fiscal arrangement in the area would eliminate the need for annexation. A tax-sharing set-up similar to what exists in Minneapolis–St. Paul where the various governments contribute money to a big pot, then parcel out tax revenues according to a previously worked out formula would solve the problem here.[44]

In an October 1, 1975 speech, Jackson strongly attacked expansion plans that would include large parts of Fulton County in Atlanta. He proposed instead the formation of a Committee on Fiscal and Annexation Matters (COFAM) to study the governmental and fiscal structure of the Atlanta-Fulton area and to issue a report within three years. He also asked that the state establish a Commission on Fiscal Relationships in the Atlanta Metropolitan Area to develop a plan of joint taxation and revenue sharing among the 15 counties in the Atlanta metropolitan area by 1977, giving particular attention to the financing of health and social services costs.[45]

Soon after this speech, Jackson offered a resolution to the City Council's Committee on the Executive (which is charged with considering legislation from the city's executive branch going to the General Assembly) urging the formation of a fiscal commission to study equitable taxation and revenue sharing. The resolution also called for a public referendum for all persons affected by annexation and asked the General Assembly to hold off any "drastic reorganization" of Atlanta's government from three to five years. On October 30, Jackson's resolution failed, 3-2, in the Committee on the Executive, whose three whites and two blacks voted along racial lines. However, Jackson offered a compromise proposal to the entire City Council two days later, and the council approved it 11-6, the six negative votes coming from white councilmen. The new resolution asked the General Assembly to create a Committee on Fiscal and Annexation Matters (COFAM) and to take no further action on expansion until the committee had studied the allocation of taxes and expenditures in Fulton County and made recommendations on intergovernmental tax- or revenue-sharing. However, the specific three- to five-year moratorium idea was dropped by Jackson at this point.[46]

The City Council's passage of the Jackson resolution was the city of Atlanta's last official action on expansion before the General Assembly convened in 1976, although the mayor's legislative liaison, Bill Alexander, often consulted with members of the House study committee.

The Focus Narrows

In November 1975 the House study committee began to consider specific plans for recommendation to the legislature. One of the first controversial issues to be considered was the future of Sandy Springs. Representative Dorothy Felton (R-Sandy Springs) proposed that, in any plan developed, Sandy Springs be incorporated as a separate municipality and not be annexed to Atlanta. The subcommittee deadlocked 5-5 on the issue. Felton was supported by the other two suburban members and by two white Atlantans, and opposed by Representative Sidney Marcus (D-Atlanta and head of the Fulton County House delegation) and the committee's four black members, all of whom favored some expansion of Atlanta's boundaries. Representative Ben Brown, whose plan for the full consolidation of all of Fulton County into a single government required the defeat of Felton's amendment, stated that thinking such as Felton's would leave Atlanta "a black island in a white sea," adding, "If you let Atlanta become 100% black you are not helping the Atlanta region. It needs people of both races to be viable."[47]

In early December, the House study committee decided to study two expansion proposals further and submit them both to the General Assembly in January 1976. The first would annex Sandy Springs to Atlanta, divide the unincorporated area of North Fulton County among the municipalities of Roswell, Alpharetta, and Mountain Park, and annex unincorporated South Fulton County to the city of East Point. The second would consolidate the city of Atlanta and unincorporated Fulton County, leaving other existing municipalities intact unless they opted to join the new government. (Observers felt that the proposals to annex the Fulton Industrial Fire District and Sandy Springs to the city, though not recommended by the study committee, had not been killed by the committee's action to recommend these other two broader plans.)

The first proposal would not merge the Atlanta and Fulton County schools and would deny South Fulton residents a separate referendum to determine their desire to be included in an expanded East Point. Instead, the committee proposed county-wide passage of a constitutional amendment to effect the annexation. Conversely, the second proposal would merge the two school systems and would require statewide passage of a constitutional amendment. Although Representative Hamilton attempted to force the committee to choose between the plans, its members voted to recommend both plans.

Meanwhile, the State Senate, whose own study committee had done little since its formation in June, was reviewing a recent study of Atlanta and Fulton County consolidation which it had commissioned Georgia State University to complete prior to the General Assembly session. The study assessed the potential impact of a city-county consolidation without making any specific recommendations. Senator Jack Stephens, chairman of the Fulton County Senate delegation, told the *Atlanta Constitution* that he didn't feel there was anything in the report which might cause the Senate to approve such a merger.

Thus, in the days immediately prior to the General Assembly, no effective deals had been struck and no coalition shaped behind any particular plan. However, House Speaker Murphy, Governor Busbee, and members of Atlanta's business power structure had all expressed an interest in working on expansion in the session after other legislation had been considered. Even Mayor Jackson changed his position as the legislative session was about to begin, stating in early January that "it may be a 'strategic necessity' for him and the City Council to devise a new annexation plan or endorse an existing one within a month."[48] Since the Georgia Constitution fixes the length of the General Assembly Session at ten weeks, the fate of the expansion issue seemed to depend on the Assembly's ability to reach expeditious agreement on the other legislation before it.

THE ASSEMBLY CONVENES

The regular 1976 session of the General Assembly was convened by Governor Busbee at 9:00 a.m. Monday, January 6, 1976. Georgia's legislators expected to settle the matter of governmental reorganization of the city of Atlanta and Fulton County by March 1. The legislature had before it information on the impacts of the following expansion alternatives: a plan (proposed by the House study committee) to annex Sandy Springs to Atlanta, divide the unincorporated area of North Fulton County among three municipalities, and annex unincorporated South Fulton County to the city of East Point; two plans, Plan I, which merged Atlanta and all of unincorporated Fulton County, and Plan II, which merged all governments in Fulton County into a single government; and three plans to annex the Fulton Industrial Fire District, or Sandy Springs, or both areas to the city of Atlanta. In evaluating the various plans, the legislature considered the following issues.

Legal Requirements for Consolidation and Annexation. Consolidation of several different units of local government is much more complex than the annexation of unincorporated land. The latter merely requires that the General Assembly exercise its authority to legislate alterations in city limits (which can be done with or without a public referendum).* In contrast, consolidation of Atlanta and Fulton County would require passage of "local" constitutional amendments to broaden the taxing authority of Fulton County to allow it to levy beer taxes, utility taxes, and hotel/motel taxes, all of which are currently levied by Atlanta, and to combine the bond debt ceilings of Atlanta and Fulton County (and other Fulton County municipalities under Research Atlanta's Plan II). (Consolidation would also require the General Assembly to enact a comprehensive governing structure for the newly merged governments after the passage of the local amendments.) The ratification of a local constitutional amendment is a complex process. Although two-thirds of the General Assembly must approve any amendment, whether of local or statewide impact, a "courtesy" rule has developed for local amendments whereby the General Assembly will automatically approve the amendment if the local legislative delegation supports it. The local amendment is then placed on the ballot in those political subdivisions affected by it. The votes cast in each political subdivision are counted separately, and a majority of the votes cast in every affected subdivision must approve the amendment for it to be ratified —the "concurrent majority" rule.

The "concurrent majority" rule would affect Research Atlanta's consolidation Plans I and II very differently. The constitutional amendments bringing about Plan I would have to be passed by concurrent majorities in only two areas: Atlanta and all of Fulton County (including Atlanta). Should Atlanta residents overwhelmingly favor consolidation Plan I, they would be able to determine its outcome in a county-wide election, since only a simple majority would be required and Atlantans comprise over two-thirds of the total population of Fulton County. Under Plan II, ratification of the amendments would require the concurrent majorities of all ten incorporated municipalities in Fulton County and a majority of the residents of unincorporated Fulton. (For a list of all municipalities in Fulton County and their populations, see chapter 9, "A Statistical Profile of Metropolitan Atlanta.") Thus, for example, concurrent majorities in all affected political subdivisions except for Mountain Park (population 295) might pass the amendment and the consolidation amendment would fail. However, such dilemmas could be prevented by passage of a general amendment to the Georgia Constitution removing the requirement of concurrent majorities, by passage of a general constitutional amendment authorizing the General Assembly to consolidate any county and its largest city, or by a federal constitutional challenge to abolish the concurrent majority requirement on the grounds that residents of independent governmental units are given voting power substantially in excess of that held by all the residents of the combined governments affected.

Neither Plan I nor Plan II would involve a consolidation of the section of the city of Atlanta located in neighboring DeKalb County. Any consolidation of this area with Fulton County would present special problems, since it would require either a two-county consolidation or an alteration of county boundaries. Since it is unlikely that DeKalb County would be willing to relinquish Atlanta-in-DeKalb to a Fulton County consolidation and since the Georgia Constitution mandates that both counties must separately approve the transfer of land, a general constitutional amendment (with a statewide vote and no concurrent majority requirement) would probably be necessary.

The Voting Rights Act and Black Political Strength. Under the Voting Rights Act extension ap-

---

*A municipality may pass an ordinance annexing contiguous land without state legislative intervention, but approval by a referendum in the area to be annexed is required. Only the legislature can annex land to a municipality without a referendum.

proved by the U.S. Congress in August 1975, the burden of proof that any consolidation or annexation plans do not "tend to deny or abridge the right to vote on account of race" is placed on local governments making the changes. As Exhibit 11.1 indicates, the only plan under consideration which would leave Atlanta with a black-majority electorate is the annexation of the Fulton Industrial District and no other territory. Nevertheless, consolidation or annexation would appear to be legal under the terms of the 1975 Supreme Court decision in *Richmond v. U.S.,* as long as two requirements are met:

(1) that the elections to the newly consolidated government's legislative body be through a ward system of voting that "fairly reflects the strength of the Negro community"—i.e., that it not be done on an at-large basis alone, and

(2) that some "objective, verifiable purpose" exist for the consolidation; that is, consolidation must not be specifically motivated by racial factors.[49]

The School Systems, Consolidation, and Annexation. A consolidation of Atlanta and Fulton County governments would not automatically join the Atlanta and Fulton school systems. It is possible, although unlikely, that the school systems might remain separate under a consolidation; the Atlanta Chamber of Commerce's original expansion plan would have left the two different school systems unconsolidated. However, there is no legal precedent for a single county operating two school systems in Georgia; a constitutional amendment would have to be passed in order to maintain the current Atlanta and Fulton County systems under a consolidation of city and county governments. The movement to pass such an amendment would undoubtedly invoke a new desegregation suit charging the newly consolidated Fulton County with operation of a dual school system in contravention of the equal protection clause of the Fourteenth Amendment to the U.S. Constitution.

The historically preferred method of consolidating school districts in Georgia has been by passage of a local constitutional amendment.* Following ratifi-

cation by concurrent majorities in each school district, the legislature is empowered to consolidate schools. Under annexation, the school consolidation issue would not arise: Georgia law provides that any school in an area of Fulton County which is annexed by Atlanta automatically becomes a part of the city system.

School Desegregation. Atlanta schools would still remain under federal court order to desegregate no matter which governmental reorganization plan was implemented. The Atlanta school system now reports its progress in desegregation to a court-appointed biracial committee on a semi-annual basis. So far this progress had been achieved without busing, but busing seemed a real possibility if the largely black Atlanta school system were consolidated with the largely white Fulton County system. If a school consolidation were effected and no students or teachers were transferred away from neighborhood schools, most Atlanta schools would be one-race schools—black in the former city limits and white near the county borders. Table 11.1 shows a racial breakdown of such a consolidated system based on 1974-75 enrollment figures.

Undoubtedly, any newly consolidated school system would be forced to integrate black and white pupils in order to avoid federal court action. One possible way to move from a dual school system to a unitary one without busing would be the "neighborhood" desegregation plan. In 1975 Federal District Court Judge Frank Johnson decided that a "neighborhood" plan which integrated nearby black and white schools and let others remain racially imbalanced, was an adequate remedy for the newly consolidated city-county school system in Montgomery, Alabama (despite the fact that one high school in a remote part of the county remained 90% black). Judge Johnson outlined the two requirements for a pure "neighborhood" system in his decision:

---

*There are two other means of consolidating school systems. The legislature could abolish the charter of the Atlanta system and force it to revert to the Fulton County system. However, a number of consequential constitutional amendments would be required, even though legislative action could theoretically create a single system. The Fulton County school board is now appointed by the Fulton County Grand Jury, not elected by the people, and a local amendment would be required to

institute popular elections. Also, present debt ceiling limitations, which are adequate for the Fulton County school system without Atlanta, would be too restrictive for a system that included Atlanta; a constitutional amendment would be needed to raise the ceiling. Finally, an amendment would be needed to change the terms of office of current Atlanta school board members. The second method, Georgia's uniform constitutional method of school consolidation, requires a referendum in each district affected, in which at least 51% of all registered voters must turn out. The average election turnout in Georgia is only around 30% of all registered voters, making the constitutional method of consolidation impractical.

TABLE 11.1:   Racial Composition of a Combined Fulton County School System

	Atlanta	Percent	Fulton County	Percent	Total	Percent
White Pupils	13,328	16	30,120	87	43,448	37
Black Pupils	70,584	84	4,621	13	75,204	63
Total	83,912	100	34,741	100	118,652	100

(1) the plan must ignore man-made and natural boundaries and consider only travel distance in assigning children to schools nearest their home, and

(2) the plan must establish a unitary school system.[50]

It is not clear how this decision would apply to Atlanta, considering the distances between center city schools (which are largely black) and remote suburban schools (which are mostly white). In 1972, a complicated city-suburban desegregation suit, *Emma Armour et al. v. State Board of Education et al.,* was filed in the Atlanta Federal District Court, and a panel of three federal judges will eventually determine whether Atlanta must use busing as a method to desegregate schools in the five-county metropolitan area. It is thus impossible to predict the future of desegregation in Atlanta and Fulton County schools, with or without a city-county consolidation.

The impact of annexation on the desegregation issue is similar to that of consolidation, though lesser in degree. There are four public high schools and nine public elementary schools in the Sandy Springs area and one public elementary school in the Fulton Industrial District. All these schools are predominantly white and their total student population is about 8,300. Because the school population is so small, the impact of annexation on the racial composition of Atlanta's school system would be minimal; but despite this minimal impact, Atlanta would remain under pressure to prove that it would not be operating a dual school system by maintaining the racial composition of Sandy Springs and FID schools.*

---

*Some cities, like Grand Rapids, Michigan, have sought to restrict school districts to their former area while the local government expanded its area outside the school district. A federal court suit recently contested the Grand Rapids expansion on the basis that such a move was intended to keep blacks in the urban core schools. However, the U.S. Sixth Circuit Court of Appeals upheld the district court's ruling that the real motivation for the law was not discriminatory, but was the concern of the suburban school districts that they would lose their tax base by piecemeal annexation under existing annexation procedures.[51]

Fiscal Considerations

In one study of the expansion question, Research Atlanta computed the tax rate for a consolidated Atlanta and Fulton County and for the annexation of Sandy Springs, the Fulton Industrial District and both of these areas. Exhibits 11.2 through 11.6 summarize the results, while Appendix A sets forth Research Atlanta's methodology and Appendix B presents a critique of the methodology.

Plan I. Under Plan I (the consolidation of Atlanta with unincorporated Fulton), a single government would provide municipal services to the consolidated area. Taxes for these services would be levied only in the consolidated area, so that residents of the remaining municipalities would no longer pay a portion of their county-wide taxes for municipal services in unincorporated areas, as is presently the case. The Research Atlanta analysis assumed that city and county schools would be consolidated; alternative assumptions were made regarding the inclusion of Atlanta-in-DeKalb in the consolidated area.

Exhibit 11.2 indicates that taxes for Fulton County residents outside Atlanta, in both incorporated and unincorporated areas, would increase sharply under Plan I while Atlanta would save tax dollars. Research Atlanta saw several reasons for these changes.

With regard to Atlantans, even if all service costs were equalized within one year, a consolidation with unincorporated Fulton County would save Atlantans tax dollars. Moreover, the difference between tax rates under consolidation and under the status quo would increase over time because of the more rapid tax digest growth of the presently unincorporated areas. Tax rates for general operating purposes would increase slightly under the consolidation due to the expense of providing municipal services over the consolidated area, but this increase would be more than offset by two other factors. First, Atlantans would no longer pay a portion of their county-wide tax for municipal services in the unincorporated areas (nearly 3.5 mills by 1979). The previously unincorporated areas would be paying a full share of the cost of the municipal services they receive as part of the consolidated government. Second, school tax rates under consolidation would show a significant decrease because Atlanta would be combined with an area whose digest is large, relative to its school population, and which is growing much faster than its school expenditure requirements.[52]

The effects on non-Atlantans would be largely the reverse:

> Taxes for Fulton County residents outside Atlanta, in both unincorporated and incorporated areas, would increase sharply under this plan. Those in the presently unincorporated areas would have to pay a full share of their municipal service costs after consolidation, since the cost of these services would no longer be subsidized by residents of the municipalities. In addition, government costs would increase. For example, Atlanta schools spend nearly one and a half times more per pupil than the Fulton County schools. After consolidation, expenditures in what is now the Fulton County school system would assume Atlanta's spending levels. Tax rates for residents of the other municipalities in Fulton County would also increase after consolidation, mainly because these areas would become a part of the more costly consolidated school system. Although the municipalities' general operating tax rates would not be affected at all and their countywide tax rate would drop due to the elimination of their subsidy of municipal services in the unincorporated areas, the large jump in school taxes would make this consolidation plan costly for the residents of Fulton's municipalities other than Atlanta.[53]

Plan II. As Exhibit 11.3 indicates, Plan II (consolidating all Fulton County governments into one government) would also be favorable to Atlanta taxpayers.

> Tax rates for schools and general operating purposes would increase due to the expense of providing services at Atlanta's expenditure level throughout the new jurisdiction. However, [as in Plan I] these increases would be more than offset by the elimination of the subsidy by Atlanta property owners to the Fulton County school system. Moreover, the new benefit to Atlanta property owners would increase over time, since the present unincorporated area's tax digest is growing much faster than its expenditures needs.[54]

As with Plan I, the effect outside Atlanta would be quite the opposite. As regards unincorporated Fulton,

> Tax rates for the residents of the previously unincorporated county, however, would increase sharply. Since their municipal services and public school system would no longer be subsidized, they would be paying the full cost of these services, which would rise even higher after consolidation to match Atlanta's costs. In addition, the cost of this plan for unincorporated Fulton property owners increases with time. Not only is the benefit of a rapidly increasing school tax digest diluted by its addition to a more slowly growing Atlanta digest, but also the municipal services subsidies, increasing in future years under present arrangements, would be lost.[55]

The situation with regard to the other nine incorporated Fulton County municipalities is not quite as clear, since tax rates for general operating purposes in the absence of a consolidation had to be estimated somewhat differently from those for Atlanta and unincorporated Fulton. Nonetheless, the same general picture emerges:

> Despite these qualifications, it is fairly certain that all of these municipalities would experience an increase in their tax rates. Although they would no longer be subsidizing the provision of municipal services to unincorporated areas through contributions to the county-wide general fund, they would pay considerably higher school taxes and, depending on the municipality, somewhat higher or much higher taxes for general operating purposes.[56]

Annexation of Sandy Springs. As Exhibit 11.4 shows, the annexation of Sandy Springs would have the effect of lowering tax rates for both Atlanta taxpayers and non-Atlanta Fulton County taxpayers. The annexation of Sandy Springs would significantly reduce the land area and population of unincorporated Fulton County and would thus decrease the amount of subsidy that Atlantans now pay in county-wide taxes for delivery of municipal services in unincorporated areas. This decrease is the primary reason why taxpayers in incorporated Fulton County would also save money as a result of a Sandy Springs annexation to Atlanta. Otherwise, changes in the school and general operating tax rates are offsetting.

Meanwhile, tax rates for Sandy Springs residents would jump for two reasons: first, municipal service delivery to Sandy Springs would no longer be subsidized by a county-wide levy; second, the higher cost of government delivery of services in Atlanta would add to the tax rate increase.

Annexation of the Fulton Industrial District. If the Fulton Industrial District were to become part of the city of Atlanta, Atlantans would benefit at the expense of all Fulton County taxpayers outside Atlanta (see Exhibit 11.5). The FID has a tax digest which is large compared to the small expenditures required for municipal services and schools, and Atlanta would benefit not only by the addition to its tax base but also by the reduction of the subsidy paid by Atlantans for municipal services in other parts of the county.

Fulton County taxpayers outside Atlanta would gain the small advantage of a decreased county-wide mill rate for municipal services delivered in unincorporated areas but would lose the significant tax contribution made by the FID to Fulton County schools, thus causing a large increase in the Fulton County school tax.

Annexation would also increase taxes for residents of the Fulton Industrial District. School taxes would increase because of higher spending levels in Atlanta city schools, and taxes for municipal services would increase because of Atlanta's higher spending levels and because payments for such services in the FID from a county-wide tax would be eliminated.

Annexation of Both Sandy Springs and the FID. Annexation of both areas to Atlanta would lower the tax rate for Atlantans more sharply than would annexation of either area by itself (see Exhibit 11.6). Tax rates for Fulton County taxpayers outside Atlanta would increase because the school tax increase resulting from the loss of the FID tax base would be greater than the decrease in the county-wide levy for municipal services in unincorporated areas.

In the areas of Sandy Springs and the FID, taxpayers would suffer from a dual annexation for the same reason they would suffer under an annexation of one area or the other, namely, Atlanta's higher spending levels for schools and municipal services and the elimination of the payment for municipal services in these areas from a county-wide tax.

APPENDIX A

Research Atlanta's Methodological Considerations

FINANCIAL ANALYSIS

The general purpose of each analysis was to determine the financial effects of each reorganization plan on every jurisdiction involved, and to compare those effects to those that would have been experienced during fiscal 1974 and beyond under the existing government structure. To do this, it was first necessary to divide local government operations into two categories: (1) general governmental operations and (2) public school operations.

General Governmental Operations

To estimate the financial impact on general governmental operations, it was first necessary to divide such operations into two types: (1) county-wide services, and (2) municipal services.

The costs of providing county-wide services (e.g., courts, health and welfare, elections, tax assessment and collection, etc.) were presumed not to change under reorganization. Because these services are already provided on a cross-jurisdictional basis, it was felt that their costs would remain constant.

Municipal service costs under a reorganized government were projected on the basis of the amount the City of Atlanta spent during fiscal 1974; that is, that the reorganized government would assume the spending levels of the City of Atlanta. Such projections were made on the assumption that the unit costs of municipal services within the city would re-

Source: Governmental Reorganization in Atlanta; *Research Atlanta; Atlanta, Ga. 1975, pp. 51–64. Tables have been renumbered.*

main constant when city limits and services were expanded. For most services, this unit cost was based on population, so it was assumed that the city's expenditures per capita would remain constant if its service district were expanded. For other services, different measures were used, all of which are listed in Table 11.2, along with the city's expenditures per unit of measure for fiscal 1974. Table 11.3 gives the values of the various units of measure for the different jurisdictions under consideration.

Although many studies have shown that such variables as income levels and population density are important factors in determining spending levels of governments, data on these variables for the several jurisdictions analyzed were not available. Thus, population was often employed in their place. As a result, the estimated expenditure requirements of each of the plans analyzed according to this methodology probably reflect the upper limitation of what actually could be expected. Experience in other reorganized cities, however, has shown that these estimates would not be too inflated.

The assumption that the unit cost of providing a given service will remain constant under reorganization implies the further assumption that economies of scale would not be realized. Although only a small number of studies have been made attempting to measure the relationship between the cost of providing governmental services and the size (or scale) of the government providing the service, some fairly clear conclusions can be drawn. Generally speaking, public services do not enjoy economies of scale comparable to those experienced in private industry. This is primarily due to two reasons. First, governmental operations are heavily labor intensive, as compared to private industrial operations which are heavily capital intensive. Thus, as a government expands its service area, additional service demands require additional

TABLE 11.2:   Basis on Which Expenditures Are Projected

Service	Unit of Measure	Atlanta Expenditure Per Unit
Municipal courts	population	$ 2.48
Ombudsman	population	.08
Planning	population	1.84
Buildings	housing units	9.82
Correctional services	population	2.57
Human services	population	1.12
Highways and streets	miles of road	5,892.56
Sanitary services	housing units	60.50
Traffic engineering	miles of road	2,869.26
Parks and recreation	population	17.52
Libraries	population	7.18
Cultural affairs	population	2.00
Police	population	44.04
Fire	population	24.13
Administration	in proportion to total increase in other services	25.98% of the total of the above

TABLE 11.3:   Background Data

	Atlanta	Unincorporated Fulton	Sandy Springs	Fulton Industrial District	Unincorporated DeKalb
Population	474,600	89,857	43,426	4,281	368,048
Miles of road	1,545	1,024	272	54	1,377
Housing units	184,849	33,184	16,028	1,593	132,190

labor inputs (policemen, firemen, and the equipment they use) at a fairly constant cost per unit of labor. As an industrial operation expands, however, additional demand would require only the more intensive use of existing capital equipment, at a decreasing cost per unit.

The second reason for the absence of significant scale economies in governmental operations is the political nature of those operations. As a jurisdiction expands its boundaries to absorb a larger, more diverse population, service demands will not only grow but will often conflict with each other. The political process will attempt to resolve these conflicting demands, often by attempting to satisfy each one. Thus, rather than becoming more economic, governmental operations will tend to become even more uneconomical as the scale of those operations increases.*

Once the projected expenditure levels for all municipal services were computed, that portion that would be financed from local property taxes was derived. In 1974, Atlanta used the property tax to finance approximately 30% of its general operating expenditures, with the remainder coming from other revenue sources such as licenses and permit fees, fines, sales, grants, etc. The effect of reorganization on each of these various revenue sources was taken into account. For the property tax, it was clear that revenues would increase in proportion to the amount of tax digest taken in. Other revenues, such as fines, forfeitures, and penalties were assumed to change in proportion to the amount of population taken in, while others, such as charges for services to other agencies and grants, were assumed not to change at all under reorganization. In this way, a separate figure representing the proportion of all expenditures paid for from the property tax was derived for each plan. Table 11.4 presents these figures.**

TABLE 11.4: Percentage of General Operating Expenditures Financed by Property Tax, 1974

Atlanta	29.21%
Atlanta-Fulton (Plan I)*	32.48
Atlanta-Fulton (Plan II)**	32.39
Atlanta-Sandy Springs	30.66
Atlanta-Fulton Industrial	30.27
Atlanta-Sandy Springs-Fulton Industrial	31.62
Fulton-DeKalb	34.50

*Without Atlanta-in-DeKalb, 32.77%
**Without Atlanta-in-Dekalb, 32.67%

After that portion of the projected expenditure levels to be financed from the property tax was determined using these figures, the resulting amount was then divided by the new tax digest resulting under reorganization. For the two consolidation plans, the highest existing regular and special homestead exemptions were assumed to apply throughout the newly reorganized government; for the three annexation plans, Atlanta's exemption levels were assumed to apply. (Because of the substantial increases in the city's and city schools' regular and special homestead exemptions between 1974 and 1975, all tax rate analyses will show a disproportionate jump in rates in that time frame.) The result of this computation was the tax rate necessary to finance the expanded jurisdiction's municipal service needs, assuming that all required expenditure increases would occur in the first year under reorganization (1974).

It is highly improbable, however, that all cost increases would be absorbed in the first year of reorganization. In fact, depending upon the particular reorganization plan, such increases (and the concomitant changes in tax rates to finance them) may take considerably longer to be fully incurred. Thus, for the

---

*Although the financial analysis also did not assume any "diseconomies" of scale, there is the distinct possibility that they would occur, particularly in the area of administrative costs.

**From this description, it can be seen that the mill rates calculated in this study are a result of the expenditure and digest figures used, and the estimate of the percentage of expenditures that would be paid for from the property tax for each plan. Using this method, the mill rate calculated for Atlanta in 1974 differed somewhat from the official mill rate levied in the year. It would be expected, therefore, that the actual mill rates levied after any reorganization would differ somewhat from what is projected here. The differences result be-

cause the calculated mill rates implicitly assume that the entire levy will be collected in the present year, whereas the official mill rates take into account the reality that some portion of the levy will be delinquent. Also, the expenditures used for the calculated mill rates and the projected expenditures used in determining the official mill rates may have differed somewhat. Nonetheless, the mill rates calculated here will serve for purposes of comparison from plan to plan and year to year.

two consolidation plans, tax rates changes were presented under the additional assumption that spending levels would increase over a five-year period.* For the three annexation plans, tax rate changes were presented over a two-year time frame, under the assumption that service cost equalization could take place in a much shorter period.

In each case, adjustments were made in governmental costs and tax digests to reflect normal increases in both. Cost increase factors were computed by adding an assumed 7% rate of inflation to the estimated annual changes in population (plus or minus) as a measure of demand. Tax digest growth was projected on the basis of trends established over the last two to three years. Although these growth rate estimates are admittedly crude and certainly will not hold up over long periods of time, it was felt that they were the best ones available given time and resource constraints. Table 11.5 shows the expenditure and tax digest growth rates used in this study.

TABLE 11.5:   Estimated Digest and Expenditure Growth Rates

Area	Digest	Expenditures
Atlanta	5.0%	7.0%
Atlanta-in-DeKalb	5.0	7.0
Fulton Industrial District	18.5	10.3
Sandy Springs	9.4	9.6
Unincorporated Fulton	11.7	11.2
Unincorporated DeKalb	12.9	10.7
Fulton County	7.0	7.5

Each of the reorganization plans analyzed in the study would also have an effect on that portion of county-wide tax rates used to finance the delivery of municipal services to unincorporated areas. This effect was calculated by subtracting the expenditures for municipal services in the area(s) affected by reorganization from the total expenditures for such services in all of the unincorporated areas. The property tax

---

*Although not considered in these analyses, it is legally possible to defer these cost increases, and therefore increased tax rates, in previously unincorporated areas by establishing them as special taxing districts in much the same way as Sandy Springs and the Fulton Industrial District are now set up as special fire districts. In such a way, a distinction could be made between those areas that require upgraded service levels and those that now enjoy services sufficient for their level of development. Ga. Code Ann. 2–7901a.

share of this remainder (72.3% in Fulton and 52.9% in DeKalb) was then divided by the appropriate county's digest to derive the county-wide mill rate for these services after reorganization.**

Public School Operations

The costs of public school operations were projected in much the same way as those for general governmental operations. Once again, Atlanta's school cost per unit was used as the basis of calculation, on the assumption that school costs would be upgraded to that of Atlanta. It was also assumed that Atlanta's school cost per unit would remain constant; that is, neither economies nor diseconomies of scale were considered in the calculation.

The unit of measure employed in these calculations was school population in average daily attendance (ADA). Table 11.6 shows the ADA for each of the areas under consideration.

TABLE 11.6:   Average Daily Attendance by Area, 1973–74

Atlanta	78,297
Fulton without Atlanta	31,406
Sandy Springs	7,694
Fulton Industrial District	816
DeKalb without Atlanta and Decatur	81,802
Decatur	3,481

Instead of calculating that portion of local revenues derived from the property tax in order to measure the effect of these expenditure increases on property tax rates, "computed local tax effort" was used at the outset in estimating those increases. Computed local tax effort is defined as total local tax revenues plus the local share of any beginning-of-year balance, minus its share of any end-of-year balance. Thus, if Atlanta were spending $931 per ADA in fiscal 1974 from locally raised property tax revenues, as defined in this way, and an additional 10,000 students were incorporated into city schools as a result of reorganization, an additional $9.31 million in local

---

**Of course, in the consolidation plans, since all unincorporated areas would be included in the reorganization, the county-wide tax for municipal services to these areas would be totally eliminated.

property taxes would have to be raised to provide them with educational services comparable to those now provided to Atlanta students.

Once school expenditure levels were estimated in this way, they were then divided by the new property tax digests resulting under reorganization to determine the tax rates necessary to finance the new spending levels. For the two consolidation plans, these tax rates were calculated for both a one- and a five-year phase-in period. For the annexation plans, estimations were made for a one- and two-year period. In both instances, adjustments were made both for expected cost increases (due to inflation and changes in demand measures) and tax digest growth over the time frames under consideration.* Table 11.7 shows the growth rates used in these adjustments.

TABLE 11.7: Estimated Digest and Expenditure Growth Rates

Area	Digest	Expenditures
Atlanta	5.0%	1.6%
Fulton outside Atlanta	11.3	4.5
Sandy Springs	9.4	3.0
Fulton Industrial District	18.5	7.0
DeKalb outside Atlanta and Decatur	12.9	11.7
Decatur	8.0	4.6

Most of the reorganization plans analyzed in this study would also have an effect on Fulton County's school tax rate to the extent that the digests and expenditure requirements of previously unincorporated areas would be removed from the county school system. These new tax rates were computed by dividing the expenditure requirements for the remaining students in. average daily attendance by the remaining

taxable digest. It was assumed that the current county-wide school tax levy would continue to be phased out by 0.1 mill a year.

It should be emphasized that the financial analyses presented in the following chapters depend heavily on the assumptions employed in this methodology. These analyses attempt to portray as accurate a financial picture of governmental reorganization as possible. However, to the extent that these assumptions differ from what actually would occur, the analyses will be somewhat distorted.

Governmental Finances Without Reorganization

The tax rates computed pursuant to this methodology were then compared over time with what tax rates would be for city and non-city taxpayers without reorganization in order to assess the net effect on both groups. Table 11.8 presents the projected tax rates for all jurisdictions considered in this analysis if present boundaries and governmental structures were to remain the same.

The tax rate trends shown in the table reflect the differences between the projected growth rates in expenditures and digests. A rising mill rate is simply the result of expenditures growing at a faster rate than the digest used to finance them. Conversely, a falling mill rate reflects a higher growth rate in the digest than in the expenditures.

Total tax rates for all jurisdictions are expected to decrease somewhat in future years. This is due to an anticipated drop in school tax rates resulting from declining school enrollments. In some jurisdictions, tax rates for municipal services will increase slightly, but these increases will be offset by larger decreases in school tax rates. In addition, the Fulton County school tax levied county-wide will be phased out, and will no longer exist after 1980.

---

*For the two consolidation plans, the highest existing regular and special homestead exemptions were assumed to apply throughout the newly reorganized school system; for the three annexation plans, Atlanta's exemption levels were assumed to apply, in order to estimate what the tax digest would be under reorganization.

TABLE 11.8:   Projected Mill Rates Without Reorganization

Jurisdiction	1974	1975	1976	1977	1978	1979
Atlanta						
General operating	10.25	11.44	11.67	11.89	12.12	12.35
Schools	25.64	28.40	27.48	26.59	25.73	24.75
County-wide for municipal services	2.69	2.86	2.97	3.08	3.20	3.33
Fulton County Schools (county-wide)	.70	.60	.50	.40	.30	.20
Total	39.28	43.30	42.62	41.96	41.35	40.63
Fulton County (outside Atlanta)						
County-wide for municipal services	2.69	2.86	2.97	3.08	3.20	3.33
Fulton County Schools	16.53	16.64	15.87	15.13	14.44	13.79
Fulton County Schools (county-wide)	.70	.60	.50	.40	.30	.20
Total	19.92	20.10	19.34	18.61	17.94	17.32
Sandy Springs						
Fire district tax	2.64	2.73	3.79			
County-wide for municipal services	2.69	2.86	2.97			
Fulton County Schools	16.53	16.64	15.87			
Fulton County Schools (county-wide)	.70	.60	.50			
Total	22.56	22.83	23.13			
Fulton Industrial District						
Fire district tax	2.71	2.59	2.41			
County-wide for municipal services	2.69	2.86	2.41			
Fulton County Schools	16.53	16.64	15.87			
Fulton County Schools (county-wide)	.70	.60	.50			
Total	22.63	22.69	21.19			
DeKalb County (outside Atlanta and Decatur)						
County-wide for municipal services	9.45	9.20	9.01	8.84	8.67	8.50
DeKalb County Schools	19.54	19.16	18.96	18.76	18.56	18.36
Total	28.99	28.36	27.97	27.60	27.23	26.86
Decatur*						
Schools**	25.00	25.84	25.02	24.24	23.48	22.74
County-wide for municipal services	9.45	9.20	9.01	8.84	8.67	8.50

*Since Decatur would not be included in the consolidation plan involving the DeKalb and Fulton Counties merger discussed in chapter 8, no changes in its tax rate for general operating purposes are expected as a result of consolidation. Presented in the table are only the two tax rates that would be affected by consolidation. Their total does not represent the total tax rate for municipal services and public school expenditures as is the case in the other jurisdictions.

**Adjustments have been made for the assessment ratio. The mill rates have been computed on the basis of a 40% assessment ratio for comparative purposes rather than the actual 50% for Decatur property.

APPENDIX B

A Critique of the Research Atlanta Study

The major shortcoming of the Research Atlanta study of the fiscal conditions of a reorganized municipality is its assumption that expenditures for all services would rise to current levels of Atlanta expenditures per capita. Research Atlanta recognizes that estimates based on current Atlanta expenditures could be biased upward because other variables are being ignored.* However, its study does not make even qualitative comments on the effects of omitted variables.

Traditional public finance literature recognizes several determinants of per capita expenditures on various municipal services, including fiscal capacity of the municipality (income, property tax base, etc.), grants-in-aid from other levels of government, and variables affecting the provision of services (whether physical—such as population density—or social—such as the percentage of blacks or unemployed people in a community).

Weicher[1] discusses these issues in detail and identifies some relationships which might be relevant to the Atlanta case. His study, a cross-sectional multiple regression analysis of police, fire, sanitation, and highway expenditures in 206 central cities in 1961, cannot provide quantitative material on Atlanta but does give instructive information.

Physical service conditions can cause changes in per capita expenditures on police, fire, and sanitation, according to this study. For instance, the percentage of the housing stock which is dilapidated is positively correlated with expenditures for fire protection. Similarly, per capita expenditures for police and sanitation increase with population density, while per capita highway expenditures decrease with increasing population density (indicating that the road-miles measure used in the Research Atlanta study for highways has some merit). These results suggest that the addition of more affluent, less dense suburbs could cause per capita expenditures on some services (except highways) to fall from current Atlanta levels after annexation, without a decrease in service levels.

Weicher's study shows that social factors are also involved. Per capita expenditures on police, fire, and sanitation, are significantly positively related to the percentage of non-whites in a city population, and other social class variables also show some significance. Both police and fire protection costs are negatively related to the percentage of the population with a college education and positively related to the unemployment rate. The addition of largely white, affluent suburbs could cause a decrease in per capita expenditures from Atlanta levels for these reasons as well.

On the other hand, the desire for increased public services may rise with the increased fiscal capacity of the new municipality, offsetting these physical and socioeconomic trends to some extent. Income and retail sales per capita both have significant positive coefficients in Weicher's regressions for police, fire, and highway expenditures. The percentage of the housing stock more than 30 years old (which is strongly negatively correlated with the property tax base—an omitted variable in Weicher's study) is negatively related to police, fire, and sanitation expenditures. Various studies relating to school finance (Feldstein,[2] Ladd[3]) suggest a strong positive correlation between school expenditures and fiscal capacity measures such as community wealth and income, as well as with socioeconomic factors such as the average education level of parents. Since the area being absorbed into Atlanta would raise the fiscal capacity of the new city (particularly if the Fulton Industrial District is

---

*The Research Atlanta study comments: "Although many studies have shown that such variables as income levels and population density are important factors in determining spending levels of governments, data on these variables for the several jurisdictions analyzed were not available. Thus, population was often employed in their place. As a result, the estimated expenditure requirements of each of the plans analyzed according to this methodology probably reflect the upper limitation of what actually could be expected."

Source: This material was prepared by William B. Marcus under the supervision of Professor Laurence E. Lynn, Jr. of the John Fitzgerald Kennedy School of Government, Harvard University. Copyright ©1976 by the President and Fellows of Harvard College.

included), somewhat higher expenditures per capita could be expected from this cause.

In a study of education financing in Metro Toronto before and after consolidation, Cook[4] concludes that consolidation increased education spending, all other factors held constant, due to the form the consolidation took. The article suggests that the retention of local school districts within Metro Toronto, along with a redistribution of taxes from richer to poorer parts of Metro and a common debt service fund, increased expenditures significantly. School districts receiving subsidies were estimated in a multiple regression study to increase spending by $1.75 for each dollar in subsidy; those paying the subsidies only decreased spending by $1.24 per dollar of subsidy, giving a net impact of an additional 50 cents in spending for each dollar in subsidy that was transferred. Centralization of debt service in the Metro government was also estimated to increase the willingness of local school boards to incur debt which would then be paid by all Metro taxpayers. While the form of the annexation that took place in Toronto is important in explaining the spending increases (because local school boards were retained but given the authority to spend money raised elsewhere in Metro), it shows that political and institutional factors can cause spending levels to change due to a consolidation of governments.

While the direction of per capita spending cannot be predicted from this additional information, it does provide indications that in any expanded city of Atlanta, service conditions would be conducive to spending decreases, but changes in income and property tax bases would encourage spending increases. However, the Cook study shows how the specific institutions created in a consolidation plan have an important impact on the cost of government afterward.

The Research Atlanta study also did not consider changing the regional tax structure to reduce reliance on the property tax, an issue that can be tied to the annexation controversy. In the absence of annexation, the imposition of an income tax on both residents and non-residents may be a way of redressing the fiscal imbalance resulting because the city provides more services to the suburbs than the suburbs pay for. In addition, an income tax could be considered as an alternative to exclusive reliance on the property tax in a new consolidated municipality. However, income taxes may have political problems in that they would impose even greater burdens on the more affluent citizens of the area to be annexed than the more regressive property taxes.

MAP 11.1:   Metropolitan Atlanta in 1975

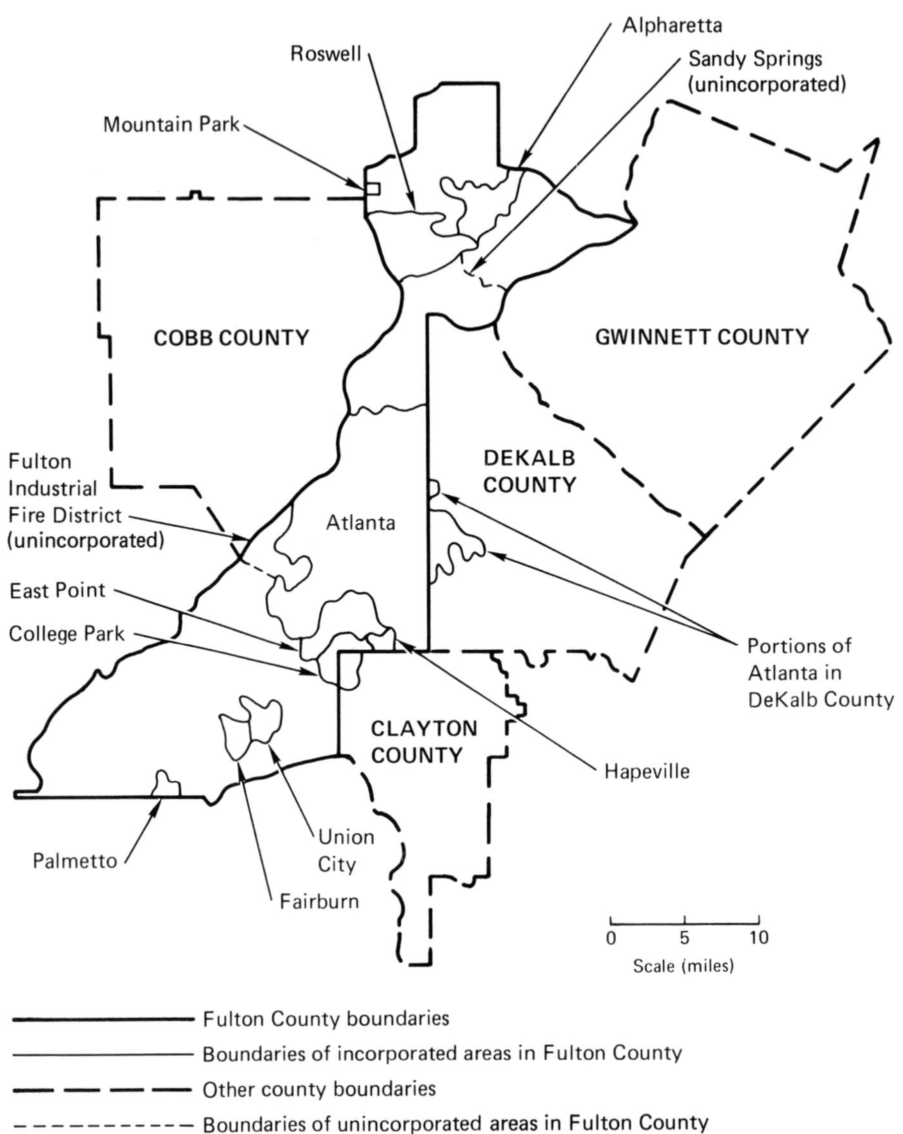

Source: Atlanta Regional Commission

EXHIBIT 11.1:   Impact of Expansion Plans on Racial Composition of the Electorate in 1975

	Number of Voters Registered			Percentage		
Situation	White	Black	Total	White	Black	Total
Present voter registration in Atlanta	91,800	97,115	188,915	48.6	51.4	100.0
Full consolidation of Atlanta and Fulton County (including Atlanta-in-DeKalb)	169,750	101,687	271,437	62.5	37.5	100.0
Full consolidation of Atlanta and Fulton County (not including Atlanta-in-DeKalb)	165,782	97,691	263,473	63.0	37.0	100.0
Annexation of Sandy Springs into Atlanta	117,532	97,222	214,754	55.0	45.0	100.0
Annexation of Fulton Industrial Fire District into Atlanta	92,532	97,702	190,234	49.0	51.0	100.0
Annexation of both Sandy Springs and Fulton Industrial Fire District into Atlanta	111,265	97,809	209,074	55.3	44.7	100.0

Source: Research Atlanta, Governmental Reorganization in Atlanta *(Atlanta, 1975), pp. 81, 119.*

EXHIBIT 11.2: Computed Tax Rates (Mills) for Atlanta-Fulton Consolidation (Plan I)

Jurisdiction	1974 (One year Implementation)	Five Year Phase-In Period						1979
		1974	1975	1976	1977	1978		1979
Atlanta-Fulton Consolidation (with Atlanta-in-DeKalb)								
General operating	11.28	10.48	11.95	12.31	12.70	13.11		13.25
Schools	26.09	24.69	26.78	25.99	25.23	24.48		23.40
County-wide for municipal services	0	0	0	0	0	0		0
Fulton County schools	0	0	0	0	0	0		0
Total	37.37	35.17	38.73	38.30	37.93	37.59		36.65
Atlanta-Fulton Consolidation (without Atlanta-in-DeKalb)								
General operating	10.90	10.07	11.43	11.81	12.20	12.61		12.75
Schools	24.95	23.52	25.44	24.72	24.02	23.39		22.31
County-wide for municipal services	0	0	0	0	0	0		0
Fulton County schools	0	0	0	0	0	0		0
Total	35.85	33.59	36.87	36.53	36.22	36.00		35.06
Atlanta (without consolidation)								
General operating	10.25	10.25	11.44	11.67	11.89	12.12		12.35
Schools	25.64	25.54	28.40	27.48	26.59	25.73		24.75
County-wide for municipal services	2.69	2.69	2.86	2.97	3.08	3.20		3.33
Fulton County schools	.70	.70	.60	.50	.40	.30		.20
Total	39.28	39.18	43.30	42.62	41.96	41.35		40.63
Fulton Outside Atlanta (without consolidation)								
County-wide for municipal services	2.69	2.69	2.86	2.97	3.08	3.20		3.33
Fulton County schools	16.53	16.53	16.64	15.87	15.13	14.44		13.79
Fulton County schools (county-wide)	.70	.70	.60	.50	.40	.30		.20
Total	19.92	19.92	20.10	19.34	18.61	17.94		17.32

Source: Research Atlanta, Governmental Reorganization in Atlanta *(Atlanta, 1975), p. 98.*

EXHIBIT 11.3: Computed Tax Rates (Mills) for Atlanta-Fulton Consolidation (Plan II)

Jurisdiction	1974 (One Year Implementation)	1975	1976	1977	1978
Atlanta-Fulton Consolidation					
(with Atlanta-in-DeKalb)					
General operating	11.56	12.72	12.78	12.85	12.92
Schools	26.09	27.92	26.74	25.59	24.47
County-wide for municipal services	0	0	0	0	0
Fulton-County School (county-wide)	0	0	0	0	0
Total	37.65	40.64	39.52	38.44	37.39
Atlanta-Fulton Consolidation					
(without Atlanta-in-DeKalb)					
General operating	11.23	12.30	12.36	12.42	12.47
Schools	24.95	26.57	25.47	24.38	23.39
County-wide for municipal services	0	0	0	0	0
Fulton County Schools (county-wide)	0	0	0	0	0
Total	36.18	38.87	37.83	36.80	35.86
Atlanta (without consolidation)					
General operating	10.25	11.44	11.67	11.89	12.12
Schools	25.64	28.40	27.48	26.59	25.73
County-wide for municipal services	2.69	2.86	2.97	3.08	3.20
Fulton County School (county-wide)	.70	.60	.50	.40	.30
Total	39.28	43.30	42.62	41.96	41.35
Unincorporated Fulton					
(without consolidation)					
County-wide for municipal services	2.69	2.86	2.97	3.08	3.20
Fulton County Schools	16.53	16.64	15.87	15.13	14.44
Fulton County Schools (county-wide)	.70	.60	.50	.40	.30
Total	19.92	20.10	19.34	18.61	17.94
Remaining Municipalities					
(without consolidation)					
Alpharetta					
General operating	12.52	12.52	NA	NA	NA
County-wide for municipal services	2.69	2.86			
Fulton County Schools	16.53	16.64			
Fulton County Schools (county-wide)	.70	.60			
Total	32.44	32.62			
College Park					
General operating	6.93	6.93	NA	NA	NA
County-wide for municipal services	2.69	2.86			
Fulton County Schools	16.53	16.64			
Fulton County Schools (county-wide)	.70	.60			
Total	26.85	27.03			

EXHIBIT 11.3 (continued)

Jurisdiction	1974 (One Year Implementation)	1975	1976	1977	1978
Remaining Municipalities (continued)					
East Point					
General operating	5.82	5.82	NA	NA	NA
County-wide for municipal services	2.69	2.86			
Fulton County Schools	16.53	16.64			
Fulton County Schools (county-wide)	.70	.60			
Total	25.74	25.92			
Fairburn					
General operating	7.00	8.00	NA	NA	NA
County-wide for municipal services	2.69	2.86			
Fulton County Schools	16.53	16.64			
Fulton County Schools (county-wide)	.70	.60			
Total	26.92	28.10			
Hapeville					
General operating	11.64	11.64	NA	NA	NA
County-wide for municipal services	2.69	2.86			
Fulton County Schools	16.53	16.64			
Fulton County Schools (county-wide)	.70	.60			
Total	31.56	31.74			
Palmetto					
General operating	10.00	10.00	NA	NA	NA
County-wide for municipal services	2.69	2.86			
Fulton County Schools	16.53	16.64			
Fulton County Schools (county-wide)	.70	.60			
Total	29.92	30.10			
Roswell					
General operating	10.28	11.28	NA	NA	NA
County-wide for municipal services	2.69	2.86			
Fulton County Schools	16.53	16.64			
Fulton County Schools (county-wide)	.70	.60			
Total	30.20	31.38			
Union City					
General operating	12.00	12.00	NA	NA	NA
County-wide for municipal services	2.69	2.86			
Fulton County Schools	16.53	16.64			
Fulton County Schools (county-wide)	.70	.60			
Total	31.92	32.10			

Source: Research Atlanta, Governmental Reorganization in Atlanta *(Atlanta, 1975), pp. 101–103.*

EXHIBIT 11.4:   Computed Tax Rates (Mills) for Annexation of Sandy Springs

Jurisdiction	1974 (One Year Implementation)	Phase-In Period		1976
		1974	1975	
Atlanta-Sandy Springs				
(after annexation)				
General operating	10.62	10.49	11.85	12.05
Schools	25.13	24.80	27.80	26.80
County-wide for municipal services	1.50	1.50	1.62	1.70
Fulton County Schools (county-wide)	.70	.70	.60	.50
Total	37.95	37.49	41.87	41.05
Atlanta (without annexation)				
General operating	10.25	10.25	11.44	11.67
Schools	25.64	25.64	28.40	27.48
County-wide for municipal services	2.69	2.69	2.86	2.97
Fulton County Schools (county-wide)	.70	.70	.60	.50
Total	39.28	39.28	43.30	42.62
Sandy Springs (without annexation)				
Fire district tax	2.64	2.64	2.73	2.74
County-wide for municipal services	2.69	2.69	2.86	2.97
Fulton County Schools	16.53	16.53	16.64	15.87
Fulton County Schools (county-wide)	.70	.70	.60	.50
Total	22.56	22.56	22.83	22.08
Fulton County Outside Atlanta				
(after annexation)				
County-wide for municipal services	1.50	1.50	1.62	1.70
Fulton County Schools	16.67	16.67	16.91	16.19
Fulton County Schools (county-wide)	.70	.70	.60	.50
Total	18.87	18.87	19.13	18.39
Fulton County Outside Atlanta				
(without annexation)				
County-wide for municipal services	2.69	2.69	2.86	2.97
Fulton County Schools	16.53	16.53	16.64	15.87
Fulton County Schools (county-wide)	.70	.70	.60	.50
Total	19.92	19.92	20.10	19.34

Source: Research Atlanta, Governmental Reorganization in Atlanta *(Atlanta, 1975), p. 124.*

EXHIBIT 11.5:   Computed Tax Rates (Mills) for Annexation of Fulton Industrial District

Jurisdiction	1974 (One Year Implementation)	Phase-In Period		1976
		1974	1975	
Atlanta-F.I.D. (after annexation)				
General operating	10.20	10.18	11.27	11.40
Schools	24.48	24.44	26.77	25.70
County-wide for municipal services	2.55	2.55	2.72	2.83
Fulton County Schools (county-wide)	.70	.70	.60	.50
Total	37.93	37.87	41.36	40.43
Atlanta (without annexation)				
General operating	10.25	10.25	11.44	11.67
Schools	25.64	25.64	28.40	27.48
County-wide for municipal services	2.69	2.69	2.86	2.97
Fulton County Schools (county-wide)	.70	.70	.60	.50
Total	39.28	39.28	43.30	42.62
F.I.D. (without annexation)				
Fire district tax	2.71	2.71	2.59	2.41
County-wide for municipal services	2.69	2.69	2.86	2.97
Fulton County Schools	16.53	16.53	16.64	15.87
Fulton County Schools (county-wide)	.70	.70	.60	.50
Total	22.63	22.63	22.69	21.75
Fulton County Outside Atlanta (after annexation)				
County-wide for municipal services	2.55	2.55	2.72	2.83
Fulton County Schools	18.49	18.49	18.83	18.15
Fulton County Schools (county-wide)	.70	.70	.60	.50
Total	21.74	21.74	22.15	21.48
Fulton County Outside Atlanta (without annexation)				
County-wide for municipal services	2.69	2.69	2.86	2.97
Fulton County Schools	16.53	16.53	16.64	15.87
Fulton County Schools (county-wide)	.70	.70	.60	.50
Total	19.92	19.92	20.10	19.34

Source: Research Atlanta, Governmental Reorganization in Atlanta *(Atlanta, 1975), p. 126.*

**EXHIBIT 11.6:   Computed Tax Rates (Mills) for Annexation of
Sandy Springs and Fulton Industrial District**

Jurisdiction	1974 (One Year Implementation)	Phase-In Period		1976
		1974	1975	
Atlanta-Sandy Springs-F.I.D.				
(after annexation)				
General operating	10.56	10.41	11.68	11.79
Schools	24.11	23.76	26.37	25.25
County-wide for municipal services	1.37	1.37	1.48	1.56
Fulton County Schools (county-wide)	.70	.70	.60	.50
Total	36.74	36.24	40.13	39.10
Atlanta (without annexation)				
General operating	10.25	10.25	11.44	11.67
Schools	25.64	25.64	28.40	27.48
County-wide for municipal services	2.69	2.69	2.86	2.97
Fulton County Schools (county-wide)	.70	.70	.60	.50
Total	39.28	39.28	43.30	42.62
Sandy Springs (without annexation)				
Fire District Tax	2.64	2.64	2.73	2.74
County-wide for municipal services	2.69	2.69	2.86	2.97
Fulton County Schools	16.53	16.53	16.64	15.87
Fulton County Schools (county-wide)	.70	.70	.60	.50
Total	22.56	22.56	22.83	22.08
F.I.D. (without annexation)				
Fire district tax	2.71	2.71	2.59	2.41
County-wide for municipal services	2.69	2.69	2.86	2.97
Fulton County Schools	16.53	16.53	16.64	15.87
Fulton County Schools (county-wide)	.70	.70	.60	.50
Total	22.63	22.63	22.69	21.75
Fulton County Outside Atlanta				
(after annexation)				
County-wide for municipal services	1.37	1.37	1.48	1.56
Fulton County Schools	19.50	19.50	20.19	19.62
Fulton County Schools (county-wide)	.70	.70	.60	.50
Total	21.57	21.57	22.27	21.68
Fulton County Outside Atlanta				
(without annexation)				
County-wide for municipal services	2.69	2.69	2.86	2.97
Fulton County Schools	16.53	16.53	16.64	15.87
Fulton County Schools (county-wide)	.70	.70	.60	.50
Total	19.92	19.92	20.10	19.34

Source: Research Atlanta, Governmental Reorganization in Atlanta *(Atlanta, 1975), pp. 128–129.*

SEQUEL

Expanding Atlanta's City Limits

No annexation or consolidation legislation for Fulton County and the City of Atlanta was introduced in the 1976 session of Georgia's General Assembly: the two month session was devoted almost exclusively to budgetary matters and other legislation. The Assembly did pass legislation implementing Mayor Maynard Jackson's request that a study committee be formed to examine the fiscal implications of regional tax-sharing and annexation; the committee's report was expected in 1978.

Sidney Marcus (D-Atlanta), Chairman of the Fulton County House delegation, offered a retrospective analysis:

The delegation was ready and we pretty much decided that whatever we did was going to be very time consuming and required a lot of effort. Unless we had some assurance that it was going to be successful on the Senate side, did we really want to waste our time?

There were those of us who thought we could better spend the limited time available dealing with other matters. We *did* meet, though; we met with the Governor, Lieutenant Governor, Mayor, and we were a hell of a lot further along on expansion than I suspect a lot of people felt, as far as the House is concerned.

The Senate, though, is such a different body. There are a number of metropolitan legislators who fear the spillover of the City of Atlanta. The non-metropolitan South Georgia legislator is in a quandary. He knows that something must be done in terms of the service delivery system in the metropolitan area, but by the same token he doesn't want to offend the suburban Atlanta legislator by muscling in and taking over . . . .

We're hearing a lot now about a revenue sharing plan much like the one which exists in Minneapolis-St. Paul, but for now I believe any attempts to expand Atlanta's city limits are doomed until we work out the problems of consolidating city and county schools.

In 1976, the Fulton County Commission eliminated the tax paid by Atlanta residents for Fulton County schools begining in 1977, thus eliminating the most visible portion of the alleged subsidy of the suburbs by the central city. The change reduced Atlanta residents' taxes by 0.5 mill.

Atlanta's regional economy experienced a quick recovery from the 1974-75 recession: unemployment fell to pre-recession levels by mid-1976. However, real estate over-development, particularly in downtown Atlanta, has left high vacancy rates for office space and condominiums despite the recovery, and Atlanta banks and real estate investment trusts were posting large losses from these projects as late as 1978. The vacancy rate in Atlanta's new developments, coupled with continuing declines in the central city population and the destruction of neighborhoods and small businesses by large apartment and office buildings, led some architects and planners to question Atlanta's mode of development.

In 1977, the city government held expenses down to keep pace with slow revenue growth by limiting municipal wage increases and resisting a two-week strike for higher wages by Atlanta garbage collectors. The property tax rate for general city operations was held at the 1976 level of 12.86 mills in both 1977 and 1978.

Mayor Jackson was re-elected in October 1977, winning 63% of the vote against three opponents, two white and one black. Jackson apparently managed to mend his political fences with the Atlanta business community prior to the election, as he won a large share of the vote in upper income white areas. However, Jackson's problems with white criticism of police operations continued. In February 1978, Public Safety Commissioner A. Reginald Eaves was accused of allegedly aiding black police officers in cheating on promotional examinations; whites demanded his resignation and blacks threatened mass action if he were forced out. Early in April, Jackson asked for and received Eaves' resignation.

In general, then, Atlanta in 1978 remained the central city of a region experiencing strong economic growth, but a central city of declining population and increasing racial and class segregation. Problems of fiscal equity between city and suburbs and racial issues appear likely to continue to dominate the political agenda of the city and region.

REFERENCES

1. Local Government Commission of Fulton County, *A Plan of Improvement for the Governments of Atlanta and Fulton County, Georgia* (Atlanta, 1949), p. 23.
2. *Ibid.,* p. 19.
3. *Ibid.,* pp. 20–21.
4. Kenneth M. Gregor, *A Study of Analysis of the Plan of Improvement of the Governments of Atlanta and Fulton County, Georgia,* p. 37 in Research Atlanta, Inc., *The Plan of Improvement: An Analysis of Services in the City of Atlanta and Fulton County* (Atlanta, 1974), p. 4.
5. *Jamison v. City of Atlanta,* 225 Georgia 41 (1969).
6. *Atlanta Constitution,* January 29, 1970, p. 1A.
7. *Ibid.,* October 1, 1969, p. 10A.
8. *Ibid.,* November 29, 1969, p. 11A.
9. *Ibid.,* October 1, 1969, p. 10A.
10. *Ibid.,* November 26, 1969, p. 16A.
11. *Ibid.*
12. *Ibid.,* November 29, 1969, p. 3A.
13. *Ibid.,* October 7, 1971, p. 20A.
14. *Ibid.,* December 28, 1971, p. 13A.
15. *Ibid.*
16. *Ibid.,* December 30, 1971, p. 10A.
17. *Ibid.,* February 28, 1975, p. 7A.
18. *Ibid.,* March 24, 1975, p. 1A.
19. *Ibid.*
20. *Ibid.,* June 6, 1975, p. 2A.
21. *Ibid.,* September 26, 1974, p. 22A.
22. *Ibid.*
23. Carl E. Sanders, "Address Regarding Government of the Atlanta Metropolitan Region," August 26, 1975. Quotations and general arguments given below are found on pp. 2–3.
24. *Atlanta Constitution,* September 26, 1974, p. 22A.
25. *Ibid.,* March 24, 1975, p. 14A.
26. *Ibid.,* September 27, 1974, p. 6A.
27. *Ibid.,* October 19, 1975, p. 20A.
28. *Ibid.,* July 2, 1975, p. 22A.
29. *Ibid.,* August 27, 1975, p. 1A.
30. *Ibid.,* September 11, 1975, p. 9A.
31. *Ibid.,* August 27, 1975, p. 11A.
32. *Ibid.,* June 29, 1975, p. 20A.
33. *Ibid.,* August 10, 1975.
34. *Ibid.,* July 2, 1975, p. 1A.
35. *Ibid.,* October 31, 1975.
36. *Ibid.,* May 4, 1975, p. 2A.
37. *Ibid.,* August 23, 1975, p. 4B.
38. *Ibid.,* October 31, 1975.
39. *Ibid.,* October 19, 1975, p. 20A.
40. *Ibid.,* July 1, 1975, p. 14A.
41. *Ibid.,* August 7, 1975, p. 11A.
42. *Ibid.,* June 29, 1975, p. 20A.
43. *Atlanta Constitution,* September 2, 1975, p. 1A; September 3, 1975, p. 1A.
44. *Ibid.,* October 19, 1975, p. 20A.
45. Maynard Jackson, "Speech to the Hungry Club, Atlanta, Georgia, October 1, 1975."
46. *Atlanta Journal,* November 3, 1975, p. 1A.
47. *Atlanta Constitution,* November 26, 1975, p. 1A.
48. *Ibid.,* January 7, 1976, p. 1A.
49. *Richmond v. U.S.,* 422 U.S. 358ff.
50. *Carr v. Montgomery Board of Education,* 377 F. Supp. 1123 (1974), affirmed 232 F. 2d. 705.
51. *Higgins v. Board of Education of the City of Grand Rapids,* 508 F. 2d 779ff. (1974).
52. Research Atlanta, Inc., *Governmental Reorganization in Atlanta* (Atlanta, 1975), p. 99.
53. *Ibid.,* pp. 99–100.
54. *Ibid.,* p. 104.
55. *Ibid.*
56. *Ibid.,* p. 105.

REFERENCES TO APPENDIX B

1. Weicher, John. "Determinants of Central City Expenditures: Some Overlooked Factors and Problems." *National Tax Journal, 23.* September, 1970, pp. 379–396.
2. Feldstein, Martin S. "Wealth Neutrality and Local Choice in Public Education." *American Economic Review, 65.* March, 1975, pp. 75–89.
3. Ladd, Helen F. "Local Education Expenditures, Fiscal Capacity, and the Composition of the Property Tax Base." *National Tax Journal, 28.* June, 1975, pp. 145–158.
4. Cook, Gail C. A. "Effect of Metropolitan Government on Resource Allocation: The Case of Education in Toronto." *National Tax Journal, 26.* December, 1973, pp. 585–591.

12

Public Policy for Day Care

In August of 1969, President Richard M. Nixon announced proposals for major reforms in federal welfare programs, including plans for expanded child care services to "make it possible for mothers to take jobs by which they can support themselves and their children." The President intended federally funded child care to be:

> . . . more than custodial. This Administration is committed to a new emphasis on child development in the first five years of life. The day care that would be part of this plan would be of a quality that will help in the development of the child and provide for its health and safety, and would break the poverty cycle for the new generation.[1]

The Nixon proposals elicited a flurry of legislative counterproposals, and a two-year debate ensued over the issues involved in creating a federally funded day care system.

Behind this debate lay several centuries of thought and action in the day care field. This case describes the historical development of the day care concept, and the arguments and proposals surrounding the issue in the early 1970s.

A BRIEF HISTORY OF DAY CARE: ENLIGHTENMENT TO GREAT SOCIETY

The history of the day care movement has been shaped by two competing perspectives. One holds that the primary function of day care should be to further the child's development. The other regards day care as primarily custodial. These theories have often been applied in a class-biased fashion, with education provided for children of the middle and upper classes and simple custodial care for working class children.

The developmental perspective can be traced to Enlightenment beliefs in the innocence of the newborn, the power of human reason, and the perfectibility of man and society. The first day nurseries in America reflected the optimism of European social reformers. For example, Robert Owen's utopian community at New Harmony, Indiana (established in 1825), included a nursery school for young children. Another example was Boston Infant School, founded in 1828 by a private charity. While both schools accommodated the needs of the poor by allowing mothers to work, they were also concerned with the happiness and education of the children.

By the mid-1800s the Enlightenment optimism had waned. Influenced by developments in medicine, the emphasis in the day nursery movement shifted to the child's physical well-being. In 1854, the Nursery for Children of Poor Women was established by the Child's Hospital of New York City. Its purpose was to provide physical care for the children of working mothers. In 1863, a similar day nursery opened in Philadelphia. These nurseries, patterned after the French crèche, became the models for day nurseries in this country. Besides providing child care for working mothers, they sought to reduce infant mortality and instruct mothers in the proper care of their infants.

Unlike the French crèches, which were subsidized and regulated by the French government, day nurseries in the United States did not receive government support. The nurseries were established mainly by philanthropic institutions such as hospitals, churches, settlement houses, or other volunteer social agencies. They existed to provide physical care for the children of poor mothers who had to work, and long hours of service were offered. (Some private charitable programs, however, tried to provide training in proper habits and manners, and the day nurseries often captured the attention of well-meaning, upper-class women who were concerned with the socialization, as well as the protection, of poor children.)

During the late 1800s, with industrialization, urbanization, and increasing immigration, day nurseries in the U.S. grew rapidly in popularity. In an effort to help the poor mother and her family, day nurseries began to offer child care, job placement assistance, and even training in domestic tasks; "preservation and restoration of the total family was the ultimate goal."[2] These nurseries had effects other than providing humanitarian benefits: while day care was a boon to the working mother, its availability helped to augment the supply of cheap labor.

By the turn of the century some 175 such centers had been organized in cities throughout the country, and in 1989, the National Federation of Day Nurseries was founded. The federation held conferences, published bulletins, and wrote reports in an effort to demonstrate the value of the day nurseries and to encourage high standards in the quality of day care. As a spokesman for the day nursery movement, the Federation adopted the stance that: (1) the day nurseries should be a form of charity; (2) their primary concern should be the preservation and maintenance of the home; (3) children should be better off in the nursery and thus, the nurseries should provide good examples for the mother; (4) the day nursery should be a positive experience which would prove instrumental in reducing the likelihood that these children would become relief problems.

Although the number of day nurseries increased steadily, the movement had its critics. Many felt that the wide availability of nurseries encouraged mothers to work, loosened family ties, and minimized parents' sense of responsibility toward their children. In 1909, the first White House Conference on the Care of Dependent Children issued a strong declaration in favor of home care for children, advocating nurseries be used as no more than a temporary expedient.

Critics of the nursery movement also noted that standards were very uneven and often nonexistent. Nurseries did not come under the educational system and received only sporadic medical oversight. Only a few states regulated nurseries through licensing and inspection. In short, the day nursery was far from being a commonly accepted agency of child care in this country. Day nurseries were considered "at best a custodial service, at worst, dens for the neglect and abuse of children."[3]

In response to these shortcomings (many of which were exposed in periodic day care scandals during World War I), efforts to formulate public policy towards day nurseries began. For example, in 1919 the Second White House Conference on Standards of Child Welfare reaffirmed that the child should be cared for at home whenever possible. However, the Conference recognized "the ultimate responsibility of the state in setting minimum standards for the protection of children in need of special care." Efforts at self-regulation also continued: many of the day nursery associations circulated information on nutrition, health and hygiene, training of nursemaids, relations with family and community, plumbing and fire protection—all designed to improve the quality of child care.

The need for women in the labor force during the war quieted some of the criticism of day care. But with the war's end, support for day care again weakened. Other factors also intervened. The imposition of America's first immigration quotas in 1924 dampened the demand by immigrant mothers for day care. The provision of pensions to war widows eased the economic pressures on many mothers. Adoption of the Nineteenth Amendment diffused much of the energy of the feminist movement.

At a time when the pressures for day care were abating, the movement was infiltrated by two new professional groups—educators and social workers. Influenced by the popular ideas of Frederick Froebel and Maria Montessori on the formative importance of the child's early years, teachers were effective in persuading some day nurseries to emphasize education to the exclusion of other aspects of care. The principal beneficiaries of this type of care, it turned out, were the children of families wealthy enough to pay for it.

The day nursery first became a regular topic of discussion for the National Conference of Social Work in 1919, as the professionalization of social work and a growing emphasis on social casework led to a rethinking of all aspects of charitable work. Strengthening the family remained a prime concern. But whereas philanthropists in the preceding century viewed the working mother as a victim of industrialization and a deserving beneficiary of societal assistance, social workers, steeped in the casework approach, saw the situation in terms of maladjusted families and incompetent mothers. The proposed remedy was therapeutic intervention by trained experts—the social workers—who were "unsympathetic to the notion that a mother should work and that a child should be cared for outside his home in a group setting."[4]

As a result of these converging forces—deep-rooted misgivings about the effect of day nurseries on the family, easing of the economic pressures for day care, and the unsympathetic perspective of the social workers—the day nursery during the post-war era assumed the role of a last-resort custodial service for the children of disadvantaged or "problem" families. Instead of being a normal service for all working mothers, day nurseries were available only upon referral by a social caseworker. Moreover, the philosophical divisions between educators and social workers ensured a separation in types of service: children of the well-to-do got enriched learning in a recreational environment (as long as their parents paid for it), while children of the poor got minimum custodial care, but only when the social worker recommended it. Philanthropic support for the day nursery dried up, and by 1931, even the National Federation of Day Nurseries had succumbed. In one of its last bulletins, the Federation stated that the mother, the relative, or the foster-home should always be chosen over the day nursery for the care of the child.

During the Depression, this picture changed again as a result of the Federal Economic Recovery Act and the Works Progress Administration (WPA). In 1933 federal funds became available to the states for the establishment of nursery schools for children of low-income parents. In an effort to increase employment, nursery school centers were set up throughout the country to provide jobs for teachers, nurses, nutritionists, cooks, janitors, and others. By 1938, the WPA had set up some 1,900 nurseries which served an estimated 200,000 children.

Because the state departments of education were often the disbursing agents for federal funds received under this program, the WPA nurseries (as they came to be called) were seen primarily as an educational service and were usually located in school buildings. These nursery school projects represented "the first official recognition by the federal and state governments that education and guidance of children from two to five years of age is a responsibility warranting the expenditure of public funds."[5]

As the 1940s approached, the Works Progress Administration was discontinued and the number of day care services again declined, but only temporarily. With the outbreak of World War II, women joined the labor force in large numbers. To meet the need for social services, the Community Facilities, or "Lanham," Act was passed in 1941. Under this act, federal funds were made available to the states on a 50% matching basis for the operation of day care centers. More than 1,100 centers were former WPA nurseries. The U.S. Office of Education was responsible for developing a nursery school program within local schools, and the Children's Bureau (which was created following the 1909 White House Conference on the Care of Dependent Children) was given the responsibility of developing day care centers outside the school systems. "The attitude of the Children's Bureau . . . was that mothers of preschool children should not be encouraged to work; but if they did indeed work, the community had an obligation to provide services to help parents care for their children, with state and local governments assuming the responsibility for supervising and maintaining adequate standards."[6]

By 1945 about $50 million of federal funds had been spent for the construction and operation of day care services. In July 1945, at the program's peak, 1.6 million children were enrolled in federally-funded nursery schools and day care centers. (In contrast, 25 years later only 1.3 million children were estimated to be enrolled in some type of day care arrangement, even though population had increased 40 percent.)[7] A 1945 report by the U.S. Federal Works Agency stated, "These nursery schools everywhere demonstrate their value as an efficient and beneficial mode of child care and have caused widespread hopes that nursery schools could be incorporated generally into the public school system for the benefit of all children."[8]

Although the program had gained wide acceptance, federal funds were discontinued when the war was over. The government took the position that assistance for child care under the Lanham Act had been based on the necessary employment of women in their own homes. In February 1946, Lanham Act funds were discontinued and 2,800 centers closed. Some communities, however, supported programs with local funds for varying lengths of time. State funds were made available in California, New York, Washington, the District of Columbia, and to a limited extent in Massachusetts. The Children's Bureau urged communities and states to set up planning groups to deal with the question of day care on a long range basis.

Despite cutbacks of support, the demand for day care did not decrease. On the contrary, both the number and the percentage of working mothers steadily increased from 1940, when one in eight mothers worked, to the end of the sixties, when two in five mothers worked. Deaths and family disruptions caused by the war left many women widowed, divorced, or deserted, or wives of incapacitated husbands. For some families the only way out of poverty was for both parents to work. For still others, the prosperous years following the war created an opportunity and an incentive for mothers to work.

During this period, working mothers and child advocacy groups became increasingly concerned over the need for adequate child care. In 1956, a spokesman for the Child Welfare League of America stated, "In our American culture today, day care is needed and will continue to be needed. Many parents cannot pay the full cost of good care. Good day care is not even available to those who pay. . . . It is a service which, by its very definition, needs help beyond what the family can give, whether the family can pay in dollars, or needs this help, too."[9]

Despite these concerns, there was little evidence of support for day care among the general public. During the 1950s, day care was again classified as a social welfare service and families with working mothers were again considered "social problems." The "ideal" mother, as portrayed by advertisers, the entertainment industry, and literature on child-rearing, remained in her home and cared for her children.

By the middle of the 1960s, attitudes toward day care became somewhat more favorable. Important factors were: (1) advancements in child development research; (2) new theories suggesting that the maternal deprivation syndrome is not a necessary consequence of mother-infant separation;[10] (3) awareness that women form an important segment of the labor force; (4) a growing interest in sexual equality; and (5) public desire to control the rising costs of welfare by freeing mothers to work.

Growing support for day care was reflected in a variety of legislative enactments in the Kennedy-Johnson years. In the absence of a clear consensus on the objectives of a national day care policy, however, a grab-bag of different laws was enacted rather than a comprehensive program. The most important enactments are summarized below.

The first federal funds specifically earmarked for child care in the 1960s came with the 1962 Social Security amendments. Congress appropriated day care funds (on a limited basis) for upgrading established centers. The amendments authorized federal grants-in-aid, on a three-to-one matching basis, to state welfare agencies for the development and support of licensed day care services. Among the conditions for receipt of federal funds were requirements for cooperative arrangements between day care centers and health and education agencies and safeguards to ensure that day care services were provided only when needed and wanted. Noteworthy, too, was "the recognition of day care as a means of enriching childhood and strengthening family life."[11]

In 1964, the Economic Opportunity Act authorized grants for the development, construction, and administration of day care projects within community action programs. The largest and most popular of these programs was Head Start. Designed to give disadvantaged preschool children an equal opportunity in their first years and so help break the school failure syndrome of later years, Head Start had a comprehensive program of educational, medical, and social services. Because of its apparent success,

> . . . Head Start rekindled government interest in financing preschool education; it directly connected child care with educational rather than custodial activities; it popularized the notion that early childhood education was appropriate for all children; and it helped turn the climate of opinion about proper child care for young children.[12]

In 1965, in the spirit of Head Start, Congress passed the Elementary and Secondary Education Act (ESEA). Since lack of education was seen by many as central to the poverty problem and since it was in poverty areas that educational services were seen to be the poorest, ESEA made funds available for day care programs for educationally-deprived children in areas with high concentrations of children from low-income families. Title I funds could be used to add educational components to established day care centers; and the educational centers authorized under Title II may be used as day care educational facilities.

A further increase in day care funds became available to states in 1967 under amendments to Titles IV(A) and IV(B) of the Social Security Act. These amendments were intended to facilitate reductions in the growing size of welfare caseloads by providing day care so that welfare mothers could work:

- Amendments to the Aid to Families with Dependent Children (AFDC) legislation enabled state welfare departments to provide day care benefits to every AFDC family and extended eligibility to include "past, current, and potential" welfare recipients. The federal government would provide funds on a three-to-one matching basis. States could provide day care services themselves, contract with private day care agencies, or provide direct assistance to individuals. In addition, under AFDC, states had to deduct child care as a work expense in determining income for welfare purposes.

- The Work Incentive Program (WIN) required states to try to place appropriate adult welfare recipients in jobs or in job training. The federal government would pay 75% of the cost of day care for children of WIN trainees: funds were distributed to state and local welfare agencies which could operate programs, contract for services, or give direct assistance to individuals.

- Child Welfare Services provided federal grants to state agencies for child welfare services, including day care. Funding varied according to child population and average per capita income. Services were available to all children, but priority was given to children from low-income families, and to geographical areas where the need for day care was the greatest.

Also in 1967, amendments to the Economic Opportunity Act and the Manpower Development and Training Act created the Concentrated Employment Program (CEP), which authorized day care funds in conjunction with a manpower training program for low-income people and the unemployed. Another amendment to the Economic Opportunity Act created an interagency Federal Panel on Early Childhood to help improve and coordinate the various day care programs now operating at the federal, state, and local levels.

DAY CARE 1969–1971: THE WELFARE REFORM DEBATE

By 1969, when President Nixon proposed his day care plan, approximately fifty legislative enactments governed day care programs; six different departments, eighteen federal agencies, and numerous state and local agencies with responsibilities for child care were involved. This legislation falls into four major categories: enabling legislation which authorizes day care programs and provides funds for them; legislation providing supportive services to day care programs; legislation, such as manpower training, promulgated for other purposes but which incorporates day care provisions; and legislation which is indirectly related to day care, such as the school hot-lunch program.[13] (See Exhibits 12.1–12.4 for statistics on day care utilization.)

Nixon's day care proposals were part of his Family Assistance Plan (FAP), which had as its principal goal the reform of much of the American welfare system. "Under this proposal," the President said, "every one who accepts benefits must also accept work or training providing suitable jobs are available either locally or at some distance if transportation is provided. . . . [B]enefits would be scaled in such a way that it would always pay to work."[14]

The Family Assistance Plan was intended to replace the current Aid to Families with Dependent Children (AFDC) program with a guaranteed minimum income for all families with children. In addition, FAP would replace the Work Incentive Program with a new system of training and employment opportunities. As a supportive service, "comprehensive day care services would be provided for all families that participated. Under this program HEW would make direct federal grants to day care operators, rather than going through the state welfare departments as was then required. Boards of education, community action agencies, business and labor organizations, as well as public and nonprofit day care agencies, would be eligible for federal money. HEW would pay 90% of the costs; the remaining local share could be paid in cash or in facilities or services. Funds could go for renovations and initial equipment but not for actual construction of new day care centers.

Under the bill, only those families receiving welfare who were either working or in training would be eligible for day care services. President Nixon estimated that 450,000 children should receive day care services the first year, and $386 million was allotted for this purpose. Of the total, 150,000 preschool children of welfare mothers would receive full day care at an estimated annual cost of $1,600 per child. An additional 300,000 school-age children would receive services after school and during the summer at an estimated cost of $400 per child.

During October and November 1969, the House Ways and Means Committee held hearings on the Nixon proposal, introduced as H.R. 14173. An Administration witness, HEW Secretary Robert Finch, told the Committee:

> The provisions for child care and supportive services under H.R. 14173 are an essential supporting element in our efforts to make it possible for welfare recipients to obtain training and employment. It is an established fact that inadequate care of the children of a trainee or employee can result in the early withdrawal of that person from the labor market, and the absence of child care can often mean no initial participation. . . .
>
> Beyond the value of the day care to the working parent, there are enormous benefits which accrue to the child who is enrolled in a comprehensive child development program. We now know that the child of poverty needs far more than custodial care if developmental deficits are to be overcome. It is this type of comprehensive child care, involving education, medical, dental, nutritional, and follow-up activities, that is contemplated by the President's recommendations. . . .[15]

Secretary of Labor George Schultz also praised the FAP child care provisions in his appearance before the Committee:

> It is an investment in the present generation in the sense that it frees the mother for training or employment. It is an investment in the next generation because it provides the child an early education, quality care, and attention to health and other needs. In looking at child care costs (and it is expensive), this double effect should be borne in mind, and we should not "charge" all these costs to helping welfare mothers get work. Much of the return will be in the kind of education we owe our young people anyway and in reduced welfare costs in the next generation. . . .
>
> If somebody asked me what is the most important thing in this whole plan, I would say it is the idea of quality child care![16]

Committee reaction to the Administration proposal was mixed. As he had two years earlier during hearings on the WIN program, the chairman of the committee, Wilbur Mills (D-Ark.), strongly supported work for welfare mothers, especially in the day care centers themselves. But Representative Al Ullman (D-Oregon) criticized the proposed federal role in child care, saying:

> You are opening up the Treasury of the United States. . . . I see here no rehabilitation . . . You have nothing here to stop any of that mushrooming cost in the AFDC program, but you have accelerated it. . . . You are also opening up the Treasury of the United States in a new sharing program that includes a 90% cost for State-instituted child care centers and all other administrative machinery you are recommending. . . . When we looked at this matter two years ago in the committee, we found that child care was one of the most expensive programs we could get into. But here is an open-ended recommendation that the states come in and the federal government pay 90%, the states only 10%.[17]

Making relatively minor changes, the House Ways and Means Committee endorsed the Administration's proposal, which was passed by the House on a 243–155 roll call vote in April 1970. In the Senate, however, it was another story. On November 20, following extensive hearings and bitter debate, the Senate Finance Committee voted 10–6 against the Family Assistance Plan.

The Brademas Bill

By the time of FAP's Senate defeat, the issue of federal involvement in day care had emancipated itself from welfare reform; and numerous other day care proposals had been (or were being) scrutinized by various congressional committees. In the House, the major proposal was introduced by Representative John Brademas (D-Ind.). Entitled the "Comprehensive Preschool Education and Child Day Care Act of 1969," this bill provided for federal grants to public and private agencies for preschool educational and day care programs to meet the needs of economically disadvantaged children, children aged three to five, and children of working mothers. Grants could be used for the planning of early childhood programs, for pilot programs, and for the establishment, maintenance, and operation of programs. Assistance would be provided for the construction or renovation of facilities if the Secretary of HEW found them necessary.

Authorizations under the Act of "such sums as Congress may deem necessary" would be allotted among states on the basis of 50% for the proportionate number of families with an annual income of less than $3,000 and the other 50% for the proportionate number of children aged three to five. The federal government would pay up to 80% of the cost of providing services.

Applications could be made by community action agencies, local educational agencies, or other public or nonprofit agencies with the approval of a community action agency in areas where one existed. The HEW Secretary would have been responsible for approving appropriations recommended by a State Commission and assigned priority according to a state plan. Some parent participation would be assured by having parents make up one-third of the membership in each state commission.

The bill also provided for the establishment of an Office of Child Development within the Department of Health, Education and Welfare as the principal agency for programs and activities relating to child development. The Secretary of HEW was to provide for research, demonstrations, and training programs, and was directed to "take all necessary steps" in establishing a common set of program standards and regulations and mechanisms for coordination at the state and local levels.

There were seventeen days of hearings and more than 1,000 pages of testimony on the Brademas bill (H.R. 13520), much of the testimony being devoted to the need for more day care services and the desirability of increased federal involvement in providing the services. As Representative John Dellenback (R-Ore.), a cosponsor of H.R. 13520, asserted:

> The United States is faced with a tremendous and still growing need for child development and child care services—for underprivileged children who need extra help in order to reach their full potential, and also for many of the more than 12 million children whose mothers work outside the home. . . .
>
> A large part of that need stems from growing numbers of wives and mothers, even those with small children, who seek employment outside the home. One-third of the wives in this country were employed outside the home in 1969 as compared with only one-fifth in 1952.
>
> There are now 5 million preschool children whose mothers work full or part time, as com-

pared with only 3.8 million in 1965—a 30% increase in just 5 years.

About one-fourth of the nation's mothers who live with their husbands and have preschool-age children are in the work force, and surveys indicate that many more would seek employment in order to help balance the family budget or to get off the welfare rolls, if only they could find suitable child-care services at prices they could afford. . . .

A second kind of need . . . [is that of] children from economically disadvantaged or otherwise deprived backgrounds who need extra educational, social, medical, nutritional and other services if they are to have a chance of receiving their full potential. . . . There are at least 3 million children aged 3 to 5 from disadvantaged families—Head Start's full year capacity is only a quarter of a million children; summer Head Start can accommodate just under that amount.[18]

Representative Shirley Chisholm (D-N.Y.) attributed what she called "the day care disaster . . . in the United States" to a "tradition of discrimination against women":

The prevailing attitude is—if women "choose" to work, then they shall just have to make "arrangements. . . . Poor, working poor, lower middle class, middle class—they are all in the same boat. . . . As for "arrangements," only 12 percent of [working mothers] use group day care facilities. The rest face a nightmare hodgepodge of "arrangements" with elderly relatives, a rapid turnover of sitters, and bleak custodial parking lots euphemistically called family-care centers.[19]

Chisholm's thinking was echoed by various women's groups, who urged that day care services be made much more widely available than the Nixon Administration had contemplated. Increased availability was also advocated by educators and psychologists, but on other philosophical grounds. As Dr. Jerome Bruner, Professor of Psychology at Harvard University, argued:

First, I do not believe that it is the best policy to single out the children of the economically disadvantaged for special day care services. Doing so has the effect of placing a stigma on such services and making the services seem like an adjustment

to get economically disadvantaged women to take employment of some kind in order to get off the public rolls, so to speak. With the number of women working for pay or as volunteers steadily rising each year, day care should be provided for all women who wish to work or carry out volunteer outside activities, with some of the cost to be borne by those mothers who can afford it. . . .

Second, limiting the program to the ages of 3 to 5 cuts off the possibility of help where it is more often needed. . . . Compensatory education for the very young has been found, in very important studies that are available, to be helpful in these early years. There seems no reason to cut off the possibility of care for the lower quarter of the 8 million children in the age range from 1 to 3. It would be a mistake, I think.[20]

Dr. Reginald Lourie, President of the Joint Committee on Mental Health of Children, expanded on Bruner's second argument:

There is increasing evidence that we must intervene in the earliest years if we are to truly deal with the roots of many of the problems facing this country and our cities such as violence, racism, respect for law, and poor educational preparation in significant segments of our disadvantaged inner city population.

Day care as outlined in H.R. 13520 offers an opportunity to have access to children in need of help to avoid distorted development in these early years. However, it should be strongly pointed out that the early years from this viewpoint includes the time when the brain is growing fastest and when the inputs are establishing foundation for later functions; that is, the first 2 years of life. This bill's major weakness is that it begins its programs at 3 years of age. . . .

However, echoing Dr. Bruner's concerns, he opposed any law which would require mothers of young children to work or accept job training:

We believe there is a great danger that forcing poor mothers to work could lead to inexpensive and damaging custodial arrangements, since the primary goal would not be to provide developmental and educational services for children, but to cut welfare costs.[21]

Not all psychologists agreed on the developmental benefits of day care for very young children. Dr. Sheldon White, Professor of Educational Psychology at Harvard, presented his perspective:

I am not as sure that early education should have as much priority as my colleagues are. . . . There are people who argue the younger child is the more open to environmental influence. That may be true. But it may be true that the younger the child is, the less accessible he is to a teacher or a stranger, someone not his mother, for various reasons having to do with child development. . . .

I think there is a terribly important amount of education that goes on before 6 years of age, but it is very closely tied to people that the child feels close to, and the child learns from his mother and father and it is hard to replace during those years.

I would like to see more attempts made to get outside of preschools and work with mothers, help parents, to give to the children what they need. I am not underestimating what the child learns in preschool years, but I am not sure that is the best way to do it. I would like to beef up the parents as teachers.[22]

Congressman John Dent (D-Pa.) expressed similar concerns, repeating a familiar refrain in the history of the day care movement:

I am wondering whether in trying to make it easier for the married woman who is working and has children, we may in fact be causing a breach of social relationship between the mother and the children that might be worse for us than giving the relief to the mother so that she need not go to work.

I think we had better do a lot more thinking about how many years . . . a kid is away from his mother. She comes home. She has to try and get something for dinner. Then by the time she gets things cleaned up, she gets the kids to bed right after their dinner. There really isn't any association between the parents and the children.[23]

And finally, witnesses for the Administration questioned whether existing day care technology really could offer a real alternative—much less a satisfactory or superior one—to home-based child care. As Howard Cohen, Deputy Assistant Secretary for welfare legislation, commented, "We don't have a day care technology, so what's the sense of going for $5 billion when we are unsure of the ground on which we tread?" And Jule Sugarman, Acting Director of the Office of Child Development,* warned that some of the studies on present federal day care programs are "not reassuring," and added, "Until we get a better fix on how to operate them, it is not considered advisable to expand them. . . . We are not prepared at this time to endorse legislation that would make these programs widely available."[24]

The Mondale Bill

While the Brademas bill was being discussed in the House, legislation introduced by Senator Walter Mondale (D-Minn.) dominated discussion in the Senate. S. 2060, the "Head Start Child Development Act," would have amended Title V of the Economic Opportunity Act to provide a comprehensive child development program which would: (1) assist children of preschool age from low-income families or from poverty areas to attain their full potential; (2) provide needed care to expectant or nursing mothers in low-income families; and (3) enhance the probability that families served by this program would become or remain self-sufficient. The Director of the Office of Economic Opportunity (OEO)** would be authorized to make grants to, or to contract with, public or private agencies or organizations to pay all or part of the costs of planning, developing, and carrying out child development projects; preference would be given to applications submitted by community action agencies. The federal share of the approved costs of such programs would be 90%. Financial assistance could also be provided to labor unions or business organizations where child care projects were financed in major part by the project sponsor.

Child development projects, both in homes and in centers, which were focused on preschool children from low-income families or from urban or rural areas with high concentrations of low-income persons, were authorized under the act. The OEO Director could permit persons who were not members of low-income families to receive services and could require payment in whole or in part.

---

*The Office of Child Development and several other child care related components of HEW were consolidated into the Administration for Children, Youth and Families in 1977.

**The Head Start, Economic Opportunity and Community Partnership Act of 1974 transferred all of OEO's responsibilities to a new Community Services Administration.

Projects were to provide "such comprehensive health, nutritional, education, social and other services as the Director finds will aid children to attain their full potential." Grants for the purchase of land and the purchase, construction, or renovation of physical facilities were also authorized. The act provided for direct participation by parents in the development, conduct, and overall direction of the program at the local level, and encouraged the use of nonprofessional and volunteer personnel as well. As Mondale subsequently observed.

> The heart of a healthy program is to be found in working with the parents and basing the thrust of the program from the beginning on the health of the family. That was far more important than what you might call the thrust of forcing the mother out of the house to work.[25]

Under S. 2060, the OEO Director and the Secretary of HEW were directed to "take all necessary steps" to coordinate programs and to establish a common set of program standards and regulations and mechanisms for coordination at the state and local levels. Authorizations of appropriations were set at $1.2 billion for the first year, ending June 30, 1970, increasing to $5 billion for the year ending June 30, 1974.

Despite the activity surrounding the proposed day care bills, no child care legislation was reported out of the House or Senate committees in 1970. The effort was renewed, however, the following year, and the conflict of opinions over the federal role in day care provision appeared increasingly irreconcilable.

The 1971 Debate

In 1971, President Nixon reaffirmed his commitment to welfare reform, including the child care provision contained in his earlier proposal, and on June 22, the House passed H.R. 1, the Administration-backed welfare bill. According to the House Report (92-231) on the bill:

> Child care for the preschool child should not be care of low quality, but should include educational, health, nutrition and other needed services whenever possible. However, the lack of child care of that level would not be good cause for failure to take training, if other adequate and acceptable care is available.

The provisions of H.R. 1 required employable members of welfare families to register for work and training under the Opportunities for Families Program, administered by the Secretary of Labor. Necessary child care for work-training registrants would be provided by the Secretary of Labor either directly or by using child care projects under the jurisdiction of HEW. The Secretary of Labor would be authorized funds to provide child care by grant or contract. Families receiving services could be required to pay all or part of the costs.

For unemployable families, a Family Assistance Program would be administered by the Secretary of HEW. Child care services would be provided by the Secretary if needed to enable family members to take advantage of vocational rehabilitation services.

Wherever feasible, facilities developed by HEW would be used for day care programs. Arrangements for after-school care would be made, insofar as possible, with local educational agencies. All day care would be subject to standards developed by the Secretary of HEW with the concurrence of the Secretary of Labor. Both Secretaries would have authority to make grants and contracts for payment up to 100% of the cost of care. The Secretary of HEW would have total responsibility for construction of facilities. Fifty million dollars would be authorized for construction and renovation for each fiscal year; $700 million would be authorized for the provision of child care services in the first fiscal year and such sums as Congress may appropriate in subsequent years.[26]

Critics of H.R. 1 felt that it raised serious problems with family rights and that it did not provide sufficient assurance of the quality of care children would be receiving. As in the previous year, a number of counterproposals were introduced, many of them aimed at creating a comprehensive child development program. Again, Brademas and Mondale sponsored major legislation, described below.

The Brademas bill, the Comprehensive Child Care Development Act (H.R. 6748), was basically similar to the legislation he had sponsored the previous year. It provided for HEW grants to prime sponsors for planning, development, operation, and maintenance of child development programs. Cities, counties, and local governments with populations of 100,000 or Indian reservations, states, or (under specific conditions) any public or private nonprofit agency could apply for sponsorship. To be eligible for grants, prime sponsors had to: (1) establish local policy councils whose members were elected by the parents of eligible children; (2) establish child development councils with half of the members appointed and half elected from the local policy councils; and (3) submit a comprehensive plan for approval by the HEW Secretary.

Under the provisions of the Brademas bill, the federal government would pay 80% of the cost of child care services and "such sums as may be necessary" would be authorized. After reserving funds for migrant, Indian, and handicapped children, appropriated funds would be allocated to the states and prime sponsors on the basis of this formula: 50% weight to the relative number of economically disadvantaged children under 14; 25% to the relative number of children under 5; and 25% to the relative number of working mothers and single parents. The bill also contained measures authorizing financial assistance for mortgages for child care facilities and for in-service training, as well as provisions for evaluation and technical assistance.[27]

In the Senate, Mondale sponsored the Economic Opportunity Amendments of 1971, S. 2007. These amendments called for a two-year extension of the Economic Opportunity Act as well as a $2 billion expenditure for child development programs for the next fiscal year. The Mondale and the Brademas bills were very similar. Both provided for a combination and extension of Head Start programs and new child development centers; both employed the prime sponsor system and the same fund distribution and allocation formulas. In both bills, priority was given to the economically disadvantaged, with free services provided for poor families. Both gave parents a prominent role in the policy councils; both provided for minimum standards, personnel training, and child development research.

While Congress worked on the Brademas and Mondale bills, the Administration was locked in an internal dispute over the appropriate role of a federally funded day care system. The OMB favored a limited program, as outlined in President Nixon's welfare reform legislation (H.R. 1). Under the provisions of that bill, child care assistance would be available only to welfare families whose parents were either working or in job training. As the *National Journal* reported:

One official, who leaned to OMB's viewpoint in the discussions, said in an interview that Nathan [Richard P. Nathan, a former OMB assistant director and then HEW's deputy under secretary for welfare reform planning] questioned whether the nation is ready financially to extend the public responsibility for education to the preschool years, as envisioned by the Mondale-Brademas proposals.

"These programs have customarily been paid for privately," the official said. "And whose role is it to make this decision? Such questions are usually matters of state and local government responsibility."

He said that OMB further questioned whether "in this period" an expensive new child development program is a priority item.

The OMB also pressed the argument that a close relationship should be maintained between child-care programs and public assistance.

In contrast, HEW, under Secretary Elliot Richardson, advocated a more comprehensive federal program, including a child care delivery system such as the Brademas and Mondale bills proposed.[28] Eventually, Richardson's view prevailed, and the Administration sent its own proposal for a comprehensive child care bill to Congress. The proposal called for the consolidation under one authority of the child care provisions of H.R. 1 and the existing federal child care programs (under Head Start, the Economic Opportunity Act, and the Social Security Act) but did not recommend federal funding beyond what was already authorized under those programs. To oversee the consolidated programs, the Administration proposed that state governments, municipal governments (serving populations of more than 500,000) and federally recognized Indian Reservations act as "prime sponsors" in the channelling of federal funds to local public and private day care agencies.[29] Each prime sponsor would be required to appoint a Child Development Council, with at least 25% of the membership composed of parents in the population to be served. The anticipated budget for this program, including funds which would be authorized if H.R. 1 passed the House and Senate, was set at $1.2 billion for fiscal year 1973.

As Stephen Kurzman, Assistant Secretary of HEW for Legislation, testified before the Senate Labor and Public Welfare Subcommittee:

First and foremost, [the Administration's goal] is to assure that there is consolidation and coordination of federal day care and child development programs. This, to us, is a major feature that should exist in any new proposal. . . .

Our second point is to assist in the development of a primary system for the delivery of day care and child care development services under those programs so that there is a principal mechanism under which various sorts of funding can be accommodated. These include the vendor payment funding through the H.R. 1 welfare reform system, which is, we hope, to be enacted shortly, the Title IV, Social Security Act system which has been in place for some years and the Head Start authority, which of course has also been in place for some time.

Our third purpose is to establish a targeted approach to the use of all of these federal funds, to pull them all together to reach the principal targets—the provision of day care services for children of low-income working families and the provision of child development services for children, regardless of the work status of their parents to the extent permitted by budgetary resources and with priority to economically disadvantaged children. . . .

Responsibility and accountability will reside in elected officials and consequently, a government program will be located where it can be monitored effectively. The role, then, of the federal government will be that of assuring that state plans are adequate, that proper guidelines are being employed and enforced, and that programs are administered equitably and in the best interests of children. . . .

Our proposal makes every effort to guarantee that those children who need child care and developmental services most do indeed receive them. We therefore propose that while all children between the ages of 0 and 14 may be served, priority should be given to economically disadvantaged preschool children.

The economically disadvantaged would be defined as those whose annual family income is below the H.R. 1 welfare reform break-even point—$4,320 for a family of four. Children from families above the H.R. 1 break-even point would be eligible to receive services on a fee basis, with the fees on a sliding scale related to income and size of family. . . .

If we are to provide more than minimal care for young children in federally supported programs, we must not expand services more rapidly than the system can accommodate.

The Administration proposals for child care arrived at Congress too late to have impact on the committees that were drawing up the legislation. The Mondale and Brademas bills were passed by their respective houses in September 1971, and Senate-House conferees began meeting in October to produce a compromise bill. The principal difference between the two bills was the cut-off figure for free child care services: under the terms of the Senate bill, a family of four with an annual income of less than $6,960 would be eligible for free child care, while the House bill gave the HEW secretary power to set the cut-off level (which would presumably end up at $4,320—the cut-off for eligibility under the Administration's welfare reform bill). After extensive negotiations and under threat of a veto, the conferees agreed on November 15 to accept the $4,320 as the level under which free services would be provided. Families with incomes above that figure would be charged for services on a sliding scale.[30]

As the *Washington Post* described the working out of House, Senate, and Administration differences:

> The conference has made some progress as Sen. Walter Mondale (D-Minn.) and Rep. Albert Quie (R-Minn.) worked out a scaled-down compromise measure.
>
> But the conferees have made no progress with President Nixon, who has threatened to veto any child day care plan that goes beyond the administration proposal. . . .
>
> Mondale, Quie, and other congressional proponents are strongly opposed to present quality day care programs which serve only the well-to-do and the very poor.
>
> "Some people in the administration," said Quie, "want to run a program only for welfare mothers. You have to have an economic mix. It's just as bad to segregate people by economic level as it is by race. I know that Elliot Richardson [the Secretary of Health, Education, and Welfare] agrees with us on this."
>
> The Nixon administration gave its philosophical support, if not its financial support, to comprehensive day care after a bruising intramural battle in which Secretary Richardson won out over the Office of Management and Budget.
>
> However, the administration is insistent that aid be limited to families with less than $4,300 income and that priority go to welfare mothers who can't be put to work.
>
> "We're talking about a major financial commitment," said a ranking HEW official, "doubling

spending on day care from $600 million to $1.2 billion. Some experts doubt that even that much money can be utilized effectively. But even if it could, there is just no more room in the budget.

"With limited dollars, we should concentrate that money on those who are employable, the poorest welfare recipients. If we had our way, it would be spent mostly on children over six, giving them part-time day care after school, until their mothers got off work. . . .

"Quie and I are taking heat from both the left and the right on this compromise," said Mondale. "If the administration tries to shave it further, that will be the end of the negotiations. A bipartisan majority of Congress favors providing day care for more than just the rich and the poor. If that's what the administration is going to insist upon, I guess we are going to have our collision."

If the administration turns down the compromise, Quie predicts that the Democratic Senate and House conferees will merely approve the original Senate bill, which the administration already has said President Nixon will veto.

"I expect that they'll turn it down," said Quie. "I think they'll find it too expensive for them. And they have a legitimate concern about the costs, and about not falsely raising people's expectations."

Several HEW officials said privately that they thought Secretary Richardson has little bargaining room left with the White House, and will reject the compromise plan rather than waging another fight in the administration. These officials said HEW would continue to insist on a plan that provided child care only to families with less than $4,300 annual income.

A White House source familiar with the situation said: "We want to stick at $4,300, but Richardson is calling the shots right now. If he is persuaded there should be a compromise he will discuss it further with the appropriate people at the White House and the Office of Management and Budget."

In early December, the conference committee's bill (now titled S. 2007, the Comprehensive Child Development Act, a new Title V of the Economic Opportunity Amendments of 1971) was adopted in the Senate by a 63-17 vote and in the House by a 210-187 margin. Considering the scope of the legislation and the threat of a Presidential veto, what Senator James Buckley (R-N.Y.) had termed "[possibly] one of the most deeply radical pieces of social legislation ever considered in the halls of Congress" generated surprisingly little public controversy. In an address before the New York State Associated Press Editors Association, Buckley observed:

> Now to many of you, the phrase "comprehensive child development" may seem innocuous enough. But I believe that even a cursory glance at the bill would disabuse you of that idea rather rapidly. For what is proposed here is not just a fancy federal baby-sitting service for children of the disadvantaged. As the name implies, it is truly comprehensive—both as to the number of people to be covered and as to the range of services sought to be provided. As to eligibility, the bill would cover, immediately, better than 32 percent of the population. And in the future, it proposed to include every child in the nation, without regard to income. . . .
>
> Let there be no mistake about it: a federal comprehensive child development program will establish the federal government as the most important, and ultimately the strongest arbiter of child-rearing practices in the United States. For those of you who may still be skeptical, I would ask you to listen to the words of Dr. Reginald Lourie, who testified in favor of the bill during the Senate hearings. Comprehensive child development, he said, should begin as early as possible because, in his words:
>
>> "In the first 18 months of life, the brain is growing faster than it ever will again. It is then also *more plastic and most available for appropriate experience and corrective interventions.*"

I have not pulled that statement out of George Orwell's *1984*, nor have I taken it out of context. Dr. Lourie means precisely what he said, and the implications of what he says, frankly scare the living daylights out of me.

EXHIBIT 12.1:   Labor Force Participation Rates of Mothers, Selected Years
(in percent)

	1950	1960	1964	1967	1970
All mothers	22%	30%	34%	38%	42%
Mothers with children under 6 years	14	20	25	29	32
Mothers with children 6 to 17 years only	33	43	46	49	52

Source: Department of Labor, Women's Bureau Bulletin 296, 1971, pp. 2–3.

EXHIBIT 12.2:   Child Care Arrangements: Number and Percent of Children
Whose Arrangements Were Reported Unsatisfactory, by Type of Arrangement
(numbers in thousands)

Arrangement	Total	Children for Whom Arrangements Were Reported Unsatisfactory	
		Number	*Percent of Total*
Care in own home by:			
Father	1,785	94	5.3%
Other relative	2,530	156	6.2
Under 16 years	556	66	11.9
16 years and over	1,974	90	4.6
Nonrelative	1,134	86	7.6
Total	5,449	336	6.2
Care in someone else's home by:			
Relative	943	72	7.6
Nonrelative	969	94	9.7
Total	1,912	166	8.7
Other arrangements:			
Care in group care center	255	21	8.2
Child looked after self	980	95	9.7
Mother looked after child while working	1,556	76	4.9
Other	63		
Total	2,854	192	6.7
TOTAL	10,215	774*	7.6%

*Includes some children for whom type of child care arrangement was not reported.

Source: Low & Spindler (1968)

**EXHIBIT 12.3:   Parental Satisfaction with Day Care Arrangement
(numbers in percent)**

| | *"Satisfaction"** | | | | | |
| | *Westinghouse-Westat* | | | | *Low and Spindler* | |
	Very Well Satisfied	*Pretty Well Satisfied*	*Not Very Satisfied*	*No Response*	*Satisfied*	*Dissatisfied*
In-home care by:						
Father	79.6%	3.6%	6.4%	10.4%	94.7%	5.3%
Sibling	58.0	22.6	7.4	12.0	NA	NA
Other relative	80.5	10.2	1.6	7.7	93.8	6.2
Nonrelative	72.6	10.0	10.3	7.1	92.4	7.6
Total	74.1	10.6	5.8	9.5	93.8	6.2
Other home care by:						
Relative	67.0	12.3	13.0	7.7	92.4	7.6
Nonrelative	74.6	11.1	11.1	3.2	NA	NA
Total	67.0	13.2	11.9	7.9	91.3	8.7
Day care—home	60.8	15.8	14.6	8.8	90.3	9.7**
Day care—center	78.1	10.1	3.8	8.0	91.8	8.2
Self-care	38.1	38.8	11.9	11.2	90.3	9.7
Mother at work	41.8	19.4	26.9	11.9	95.1	4.9

*Totals for in-home care satisfaction and other home care satisfaction are weighted averages.

**Low and Spindler do not distinguish between other home care by a nonrelative and a day care home.

Sources: Westinghouse-Westat, Table 4.37; Low and Spindler, Table A-54.

EXHIBIT 12.4:   Number and Capacity of Licensed or Approved Day Care Centers and Family Day Care Homes 1967–1969

	March 1967	March 1968	March 1969
Number of centers and homes:			
Day care centers	10,400	11,700	13,600
Family day care homes	24,300	27,400	32,700
Total	34,700	39,100	46,300
Capacity of centers and homes:			
Day care centers:			
Public	22,600	27,700	34,700
Voluntary	113,900	139,000	177,900
Independent	239,300	231,000	266,400
Auspices not reported	17,500	40,100	38,900
Subtotal	393,300	437,800	517,900
Family day care homes:			
Public	2,500	3,600	8,000
Voluntary	1,300	2,200	2,200
Independent	63,900	84,600	101,900
Auspices not reported	14,200	6,800	8,300
Subtotal	81,900	97,200	120,400
Total capacity	475,200	535,000	638,300

Source: Department of Health, Education, and Welfare, Social and Rehabilitation Service, Child Welfare Statistics 1967 *(table 13, p. 24);* 1968 *(NCSS Report CW-1, table 18, p. 27); and* 1969 *(NCSS Report CW-1, table 18, p. 28).*

SEQUEL

Public Policy for Day Care

In 1971 advocates of an expanded federal role in the provision of day care had their hopes fixed on two bills passed respectively in the House and Senate—the Comprehensive Child Care Development Act sponsored by Rep. John Brademas and the Economic Opportunity Amendments of 1971 sponsored by Senator Walter Mondale. Both bills provided for an extension of Head Start programs and new child development centers; both employed the prime sponsor system and the same fund distribution and allocation formulas. In both bills, priority was given to the economically disadvantaged, with free services provided for poor families. Both gave parents a prominent role in the policy councils; both provided for minimum standards, personnel training, and child development research. The two bills were incorporated as a new Comprehensive Child Care Development Act which would insert a new Title V in the Economic Opportunity Amendments. After lengthy negotiations in the House-Senate conference committee, a compromise was reached on the substantive provisions of the measure. Day care would be free to families with incomes of less than $4,320; families with incomes up to $5,916 would pay no more than 15% of their income for child care services; and only localities with a population of more than 4,000 would be eligible for prime sponsorship. Authorizations of $100 million for FY 72 and $2 billion for FY 73 were agreed to. Perhaps most significantly, the conferees agreed on a statement of objectives:

> It is the purpose of this title to provide every child with a fair and full opportunity to reach his full potential by establishing and expanding comprehensive child development programs, and services designed to assure the sound and coordinated development of these programs, to recognize and build upon the experience and success gained through the Head Start program and similar efforts, to furnish child development services for those children who need them most, with special emphasis on preschool programs for economically disadvantaged children, and for children of working mothers and single parent families, to provide that decisions on the nature and funding of such programs be made at the community level with the full involvement of parents and other individuals and organizations in the community interested in child development, and to establish the legislative framework for child development services.[1]

The Senate adopted the conference committee's report on December 2, 1971, by a 63–17 vote, and the House followed suit on December 7 by a 210–187 margin: on December 9th, however, President Nixon vetoed the bill, citing Title V as the "most deeply flawed provision of this legislation."[2] In his veto message, the President said that a comprehensive child development program, adopted as an amendment to the OEO legislation, went far beyond what the Administration had envisioned.

> Though Title V's stated purpose, to provide every child with a full and fair opportunity to reach his full potential is certainly laudable, the intent of Title V is overshadowed by the fiscal irresponsibility, administrative unworkability, and family-weakening implications of the system it envisions. . . . [F]or the Federal Government to plunge headlong financially into supporting child development would commit the vast moral authority of the National Government to the idea of communal approaches to child rearing over against the family-centered approach.[3]

(The Administration had originally hoped to deal with day care as a part of its larger design for reform of the welfare system, but the proposed reform—embodied in H.R. 1—never made it out of Congress.)

In 1972 and 1973, legislative activity concerning day care was inconsequential, and child care advocates spent most of their time lobbying unsuccessfully against the Administration's efforts to reduce social

Source: This case was revised by J. Bradley O'Connell from a draft prepared by Anngail Croswell, under the supervision of Professor Laurence E. Lynn, Jr. for use at the John F. Kennedy School of Government, Harvard University. Copyright © 1979 by the President and Fellows of Harvard College.

services spending.* During 1974, rewriting of federal social service standards was a major priority for HEW, social service (including day care) lobby groups, and state and local officials, but not until the final weeks of the congressional session was a compromise worked out among the interested parties. Whereas the previous year HEW had proposed regulations which would have significantly tightened federal oversight of state day care and other social service operations, the 1974 legislation represented a reversal of that department's position—one that was welcomed by the state and local governments. The new legislation gave the states broad flexibility in program operations, retaining for the federal government primarily regulatory and monitoring functions. These changes were intended to permit decategorization of programs and to facilitate more consistent planning and program development. Eligibility for free day care was expanded from past, present or potential welfare recipients to all families whose income was no more than 80% of the median income in their state; and families with incomes of less than 115% of the median were permitted to pay only a portion of the cost of services. The proportion of their total federal social services funds which states were required to spend on welfare recipients was reduced from 90% to 50%. Federal funds would be distributed on the basis of a matching system, with Washington providing 90% of the costs of family planning services and 75% for all other social services such as day care and aid to the aged, blind, handicapped and emotionally disturbed. Day care was not required to be employment related: states could provide child care for families with non-working mothers if, by providing the care, one of the five broad goals** stated in the social services legislation was met. The 1968 Federal Interagency Day Care Requirements were retained with some modification; the educational component would be recommended rather than compulsory, and staffing ratios for day care centers would be less strict (for children 6-9, 1:15 and for children 10-14, 1:20 instead of 1:10). If day care services were included in a state's social service plan, the state must

provide for the establishment of a state authority to be responsible for the establishment and maintenance of day care standards in line with recommended national standards.[4]

Also in 1974, independent of developments discussed above, Senator Mondale and Representative Brademas redrafted and reintroduced the Child and Family Services Act. This legislation was "designed to provide financial assistance necessary to help states and localities upgrade and expand their services for families and children."[5] Containing the same general principles outlined in the Comprehensive Child Development Act of 1971, the 1974 Act included the following:

(1) Programs would build upon and strengthen the role of the family by providing a wide variety of services from which parents could choose;
(2) Programs would give assurance of quality service;
(3) Services would be available to meet a broad range of family needs;
(4) There would be a one-year "phase-in" for planning and training to ensure an efficient program;
(5) There would be a heavy emphasis on training;
(6) Programs would be administered through a system of state and local prime sponsors (e.g., state and local agencies, educational institutions, and other public and private non-profit agencies).[6]

The bill differed from its 1971 predecessor in that the authorizations were smaller, Head Start was not included, and localities did not have to meet a minimum population requirement to become a prime sponsor. Otherwise, the bill would have authorized financial assistance, via prime sponsors, for planning, developing, and operating child and family service programs (i.e., medical diagnosis and treatment, prenatal care, help on food and nutrition, aid to the handicapped, minority group services, etc.); renting and mortgaging service facilities; training personnel; staffing and administering programs; and maintaining an information service. Apportionments would have emphasized preschool children, economically disadvantaged families, children with working mothers, and children of single parents. Programs would be voluntary, provide for a parent policy committee, have systematic dissemination of information to parents, and maintain regular parent consultation.

---

*In 1972 Congress placed a $2.5 billion annual ceiling on federal expenditures for all social services, with funds allocated among the states on the basis of population.

**These were: self support, self-sufficiency, protection for children and for adults unable to protect themselves, deinstitutionalization when appropriate, and institutional placement and services within some institutions when necessary.

These features of the bill were especially attractive to the child care lobby, who viewed the proposal as a major step toward comprehensive child care for all families in need. In a statement in joint hearings of the House Education and Labor and Senate Labor and Public Welfare Committees in August 1974, the American Parents Committee declared that they were "extremely impressed" with the legislation, cataloguing the following merits:

> The bill provides new money for additional, badly needed services for children and families.
>
> The standards will ensure that services are of good quality.
>
> There is specific funding for enforcement of those standards.
>
> Services to be provided will be free to many of those who need them most.
>
> Participation in all programs and services will be voluntary.
>
> An important role is mandated for parents.[7]

The bill was not enacted in 1974, nor again, in 1975, when it was re-introduced and additional hearings were held. It did, however, stimulate intense (and in part anonymous) hostile publicity and succeeded in getting itself denounced as a "Marxist plot to nationalize our children."

In February 1976 President Ford proposed that programs providing federal funds to states for day care and other social services for low income families and welfare recipients be consolidated into social services block grants, which would eliminate federal standards on eligibility, quality of care, fee-setting and reporting and thus would greatly increase the responsibility of the states for the administration of day care programs. The Ford bill would authorize $2.5 billion in federal funds for all social services—a slight increase; however, since it also eliminated matching requirements for states, day care advocates as well as other welfare and social service lobby groups opposed the measure, contending that its net impact would be the reduction of public spending on social services. The Ford bill went no further than the hearings stage in Congress.

Meanwhile, over the objections of several Republicans, Congress enacted its own day care funding bill, H.R. 9803, which mandated the implementation of controversial federal staffing standards for day care centers, beginning July 1, 1976. Ford vetoed the legislation in April 1976, declaring that the bill usurped the rights of states to set their own day care standards, and the Senate failed by three votes to override the veto. The Administration then offered to make available, through fiscal year 1980, an additional $800 million under the Ford bill (raising the ceiling to $3.3 billion) in exchange for eliminating a provision earmarking funds specifically for day care. An alternative was worked out between Senators Mondale and Packwood (a supporter and an opponent respectively of the federal staffing standards) and tacked on to a House-passed bill, H.R. 12455. In conference the House and Senate agreed to authorize $240 million for day care ($40 million for the transitional quarter and $200 million for fiscal 1977) but to eliminate state matching requirements and defer implementation of the staffing standards until completion of an HEW study of their appropriateness. President Ford signed the compromise measure into law on September 7, 1976.

At the beginning of 1977, the two principal congressional advocates of more comprehensive day care legislation withdrew from the fray. Senator Walter Mondale, Chairman of the Subcommittee on Children and Youth, was, of course, elected to the Vice Presidency; and Representative John Brademas requested that jurisdiction over preschool education and child development programs be transferred from his subcommittee on Select Education to Carl Perkins' Subcommittee on Elementary, Secondary and Vocational Education. One organ of the child care lobby, *Day Care and Early Education*, commented:

> The shift of preschool education programs to a new subcommittee was precipitated by the desires of Brademas, who is also Democratic Whip, for less jurisdictional responsibility. The controversial Child and Family Services bill brought undesirable and vicious publicity to Brademas. He also thought it would be best for the future of the bill —and his own political well-being—to have the bill associated with other members of Congress.[8]

In February 1977 Representative Donald Fraser introduced a bill—H.R. 3340—that would have provided "backdoor" assistance to day care through the tax system. Under the Tax Reform Act of 1976, Congress permitted taxpayers who used a portion of their homes exclusively for business purposes to claim deductions for maintenance expenses of that portion. H.R. 3340 would exempt from the "exclusive use" test individuals who used their homes to provide custodial care service on a regular basis for compensation; hence any homeowner providing services of this nature would be eligible for the deductions, regardless of whether or not that part of the home was used for other purposes as well. In April the bill was reported out favorably by the Ways and Means Committee, and on April 18 it was passed 320–1 by the House under suspension of the rules (i.e., no amendment permitted). It was then sent to the Senate and committed to the Finance Committee. Its fate is best summarized in the words of the committee itself, which reported it out July 13:

> The committee's amendment to H.R. 3340 strikes out the House-passed provisions (relating to day care ...) and substitutes an increase in the income tax credit for contribution for candidates to the United States Senate.[9]

The amended "day care" bill, incidentally, never received floor consideration.

With Mondale's accession to the Vice Presidency, many advocates of expanded federal involvement in day care expected to see a stronger executive initiative in the area than had materialized under Nixon and Ford. Like the Nixon Administration, however, the Carter Administration preferred to deal with day care as a parcel in a larger welfare reform package rather than as an issue in itself. The Program for Better Jobs and Income, unveiled by Carter on August 6, 1977, mandated that mothers of children between the ages of seven and fourteen accept full-time employment if day care services were available and part-time employment if they were not. To meet the anticipated increase in demand for such services, the program provided for 150,000 new public service jobs in the day care field, with employment priority given to lower income mothers. (The program would have created a total of $1.4 million worth of subsidized jobs, including the day care slots.) Also, working mothers receiving an income supplement would be permitted to deduct from their earnings up to $150 per month per child (for a maximum of two children) for day care services; in other words, working mothers using day care services were spotted up to an additional $300 which they could earn without causing reductions in their work incentive supplements.

Child care advocates were relieved by the fact that the Administration had made some allowance for day care in the welfare package, but were dissatisfied with the treatment of day care as a means to an end (facilitating welfare recipients taking jobs), rather than as something desirable in itself for all income classes. Also, as William Pierce, an official of the Child Welfare League observed, the allotment of $150 per month would "buy zilch" on the day care market.[10] Administration officials defended the adequacy of the amount, arguing that many welfare recipients would opt for non-institutional "babysitting" child care arrangements. This argument was not well received by representatives of the child care lobby, who pointed out the lack of any guarantee of quality care under such arrangements.[11] The child care lobby was also wary of staffing day care centers with 150,000 CETA employees, since they feared that children would receive custodial rather than professional attention. Finally, both day care advocates and welfare recipients objected to the work requirement for mothers of school age children, on the grounds that women were entitled to choose between working and caring for their children at home.

Ultimately, the question of whether or not the welfare package provided adequately for day care was never resolved. As a result of disagreements more wide-ranging than those over the day care features, the Program for Better Jobs and Income did not survive the second session of the 95th Congress. In January 1978 a special House Subcommittee on Welfare Reform, chaired by Representative James Corman, reported out a $20 billion version of the Carter plan. However, the bill ran into serious trouble in the full Ways and Means Committee, where Chairman Al Ullman refused to go along with a package so expensive. Time was also a constraint, since the committee was already saddled with two other number one priorities—the energy and tax cut bills. Efforts in the spring and early summer to design a compromise program costing no more than $10 billion were ultimately unsuccessful, and, in June, Speaker O'Neill essentially scuttled the program, having decided that there was not sufficient support for any compromise.

As of early 1979, the prospect for an expanded federal role in day care had not measurably improved. In what *Day Care and Early Education* termed the beginning of "the first dialogue on federal child care legislation since 1975,"[12] Senator Alan Cranston, the chairman of the Child and Human Development Subcommittee had declared in fall 1978 that the following year he would introduce major child care legislation embodying the following principles: federal minimum standards for day care centers, information and referral programs, support for working parents, good working conditions for center employees, and cost-effectiveness. But as of mid-1979, the anticipated "1979 debate" on child care has not commenced and no flurry of legislative activity has transpired.

REFERENCES

1. U.S. Congress, Senate Finance Committee, *Child Care Hearings, September 22, 23, and 24, 1971*. (Washington, D.C.: U.S. GPO), p. 92.
2. Gretta G. Fein and Alison Clarke-Stewart, *Day Care in Context* (New York: John Wiley and Sons, 1973), p. 17.
3. Margaret O'Brien Steinfels, *Who's Minding the Children?* (New York: Simon and Schuster, 1973), p. 57.
4. *Ibid.*, p. 59.
5. Lela B. Costin, *Child Welfare: Policies and Practices* (New York: McGraw-Hill, 1972), p. 192.
6. Anna Mayer, *Day Care as a Social Instrument* (New York: Columbia University Press, 1975), p. 27.
7. Edith H. Grotbert, editor, *Day Care: Resources for Decisions* (Washington, D.C.: Office of Planning, Research and Evaluation, Office of Economic Opportunity, June, 1971), p. 61.
8. U.S. Federal Works Agency, *Final Report on the WPA Program, 1935-1943* (Washington, D.C.: U.S. GPO, 1947), p. 61.
9. Judith Cauman, "What Is Happening in Day Care—New Concepts, Current Practice and Trends," *Child Welfare* 35 (1956), p. 22.
10. Lois Meek Stolz, "Effects of Maternal Employment on Children: Evidence from Research," *Child Development* 31 (December 1960), p. 779.
11. Costin, p. 194.
12. Steinfels, p. 85.
13. Day Care Policy Studies Group, Institute for Interdisciplinary Studies, Minneapolis, Minnesota, *Alternative Federal Day Care Strategies for the 1970's*. Minneapolis, March 1972, p. 3.
14. *Congressional Quarterly Almanac,* "Test of President Nixon's Speech on Welfare Reform," August 8, 1967, p. 76-A.
15. U.S. Congress, House Ways and Means Committee, *Social Security and Other Welfare Proposals* (Washington, D.C.: U.S. GPO, 1969) October-November, 1969, p. 124.
16. *Ibid.*, p. 260.
17. *Ibid.*, p. 161.
18. U.S. *Congressional Record*, February 9, 1970, p. 2789.
19. U.S. Congress, House Education and Labor Committee. *Comprehensive Preschool Education and Child Day Care Act of 1969.* (Washington, D.C.: U.S. GPO, 1969), November–December, 1969 and February–March, 1970, p. 792.
20. *Ibid.*, p. 817.
21. *Ibid.*, p. 592.
22. *Ibid.*, p. 54.
23. *Ibid.*, p. 708.
24. *Ibid.*, p. 93.
25. U.S. Congress, Senate Labor and Public Welfare Committee. *Comprehensive Child Development Act of 1971.* (Washington, D.C.: U.S. GPO, 1971), May-June, 1971, p. 719.
26. Erica Streuer, "Current Legislative Proposals and Public Policy Questions for Child Care," in *Child Care Who Cares?* Pamela Roby, ed. (New York: Basic Books, 1973), p. 51.
27. *Ibid.*, p. 56.
28. John K. Iglehart, "Welfare Report/Congress Presses Major Child-Care Program Despite White House Veto Threat," *National Journal* (October 23, 1971), p. 2126.
29. *Ibid.*, p. 2127.
30. John K. Iglehart, "Human Resources/Dems Term Richardson 'Administration Liberal,'" *National Journal* (November 20, 1971), p. 2321.

REFERENCES TO THE SEQUEL

1. Economic Opportunity Amendments of 1971, Senate Report No. 92-523, 92nd Congress 1st Session, 1971, p. 5.
2. Richard Nixon, "The President's Message to the Senate Returning S. 2007 Without His Approval, December 9, 1971," *Weekly Compilation of Presidential Documents VII,* 1971, p. 1634.
3. *Ibid.*
4. Joyce Goldman, "Washington Day Care," *Day Care and Early Education*, April 1975, pp. 19, 26, 35.
5. Joint Hearings, Senate Committee on Labor and Public Welfare, House Committee on Education and Labor, "Child and Family Services, October 1974," S. 3754, August 8 and 9, 1974, p. 66.
6. *Ibid.*
7. Joint Hearings, "Child and Family Services, October 1974," S. 3754, p. 221.
8. Joyce Lynn, "Washington Day Care," *Day Care and Early Education,* March/April 1977, p. 7.
9. Senate Finance Committee, Senate Report No. 95-342, July 13, 1977, p. 1.
10. Linda Demkovich, "A Job for Every Welfare Mother, But What About the Kids?" *National Journal*, March 4, 1978, pp. 341–344.
11. *Ibid.*
12. Joyce Lynn, "Child Care 1979," *Day Care and Early Education,* Fall 1978, p. 20.

13

Federal Financial Aid for Postsecondary Education

Before the nineteenth century, students were financed in their pursuit of higher education primarily by their parents, with scattered aid from private scholarships for those with extreme financial need or academic promise. The students attended private institutions, which were financed by private gifts and endowments, in addition to student tuitions. In the latter half of the nineteenth century, the taxpayer—through state and local government general purpose grants to public institutions—began to subsidize higher education. The low tuitions of the public schools were intended to induce more young people to attend college, since a college-educated population was thought beneficial to the state.

The federal government's contribution to the financing of higher education was small—confined virtually to limited grants to state governments for the establishment and support of land grant colleges in agriculture and mechanical arts (authorized under the Morrill Act of 1862). Although this authorization was increased under the Morrill Act of 1890 and the Bankhead-Jones Act of 1938 (a small amount of aid is still dispersed under this legislation), total federal contributions to higher education remained relatively insignificant until the second World War.

During the war, federal money for research purposes flowed to the universities in unprecedented amounts, and after the war, when research funds trickled out, the tuition assistance provided by the G.I. bill allowed large numbers of veterans to enroll in the nation's postsecondary schools. In the early fifties, universities again began to receive federal research money and by the mid-sixties the federal government had expanded its higher education contribution to include student aid, facility construction assistance, and numerous other categorical programs. By 1967-68, the nation's colleges and universities were spending $17.2 billion for higher education. Private sources contributed 52% of that total, while state and local government contributions accounted for 27% and federal government contributions, for 21%.* Unlike the state and local government contributions to higher education, however, the federal government spends its money for specific purposes: in 1967-68, 47% of the federal expenditures consisted of categorical grants for research and development in specific fields such as science, defense, and health; 17% of federal money went for the construction of facilities; and 18% consisted of student aid.

In 1970-71, this last category—student aid—became the topic of heated debate, both in the government and in educational circles across the country. The debate was prompted by the imminent (June 1971) expiration of the Higher Education Act of 1965, which had authorized four rather controversial student aid programs; in 1971, these four programs, administered by the Office of Education (OE), together affected some 1.9 million students and accounted for about $722 million in federal expenditures. The debate centered on specific proposals for extending, amending, or radically re-directing the federal efforts embodied in the four OE programs, but it also had implications for the entire future of federal support for higher education.

This case briefly recounts the history of federal involvement in student aid, with particular attention to the OE programs, and summarizes the issues confronting Congress in 1971 as it approached a decision on future federal student aid.

FEDERAL AID TO STUDENTS: BACKGROUND

Although the federal government distributes aid to higher education through a variety of programs and sources, the primary sources for student aid are the Veterans Administration (VA), the Social Security Administration (SSA), and the Office of Education (OE). Of these agencies, the Veterans Administration makes the most substantial contribution, accounting

for close to 40% of total federal student aid in 1970. The first major federal student aid program was the G.I. bill for veterans of World War II, which provided eligible veterans with grants for tuition, books, and other fees in the rationale that the veterans deserved a reward and could no longer depend on their parents for educational aid. Since the grants went directly to the student and not to the school for disbursement, the G.I. recipient could attend the school of his choice, constrained only by admissions policies. The schools were also compensated with cost of education grants for each G.I. enrolled.** The World War II G.I. bill cost $14.5 billion and benefitted approximately 7.8 million G.I.'s. A similar plan was adopted for Korean war veterans.

Presently, the Veterans Administration provides education funds for any veteran who served more than 180 days on active duty in the U.S. armed forces. For each month of active duty a veteran is entitled to one and one-half months of educational assistance for up to thirty-six months at a rate of $136 per month (for a full time student with no dependents). In 1970, the large number of Vietnam veterans accounted for a program cost of $1.4 billion.

Similarly, the Social Security Administration accounted for a sizeable chunk—$554 million—of federal student aid in 1970. Social Security benefits for undergraduate education depend on the extension of a child entitlement past age 18, when entitlement usually ends. Benefits are extended for persons who are under age 21, unmarried, and full-time students, dependent on a parent who receives either disability, survivor or retirement benefits. (The amount of the student's educational benefit is set in proportion to the parent's benefits.)

Although the VA and the SSA together spend the largest share of federal funds for student aid, the Office of Education is the federal government's principal agency for dealing with higher education prob-

---

*Institutional expenditures do not fully indicate the total cost of higher education, since they do not include a student's opportunity costs as well as his/her incidental expenditures. Moreover, the federal government's share of total expenditures is difficult to measure; construction loans, certain types of research contracts, and administrative costs are among the types of federal expenditures that are sometimes ignored. Depending on what is counted, total federal aid to higher education in 1967–68 has been estimated to range from $3.5 billion to $5.6 billion.

**A cost of education allowance is money paid to the institution for enrolling a student who receives federal aid. Since tuition only covers a portion of the total institutional cost of educating a student, a cost of education allowance helps reimburse the institutions for the additional cost they incur in furthering some national purpose. In 1958 a similar allowance accompanied graduate students who received National Defense fellowships.

lems. In spite of its central role, however, OE lacks real budgetary power and prestige in this area; only 10% of its budget is discretionary (the rest being distributed by formula), and consequently, its primary task has been simply to "get the money out." [Also, the agency has concentrated its (limited) policy-making resources more on elementary and secondary education than on higher education.] Almost three-quarters of OE's billion-dollar higher education budget is allocated among four student aid programs: the National Defense Student Loan Program (NDSLP), the College Work Study Program (CWSP), the Educational Opportunity Grants Program (EOGP) and the Guaranteed Student Loan Program (GSLP). These four programs, discussed below, served as the focus of congressional debate over federal aid to higher education in 1971.

National Defense Student Loan Program

The passage of the National Defense Education Act in 1958 constituted a major endorsement of a wide ranging federal contribution to higher education. The Act provided aid for student loans, graduate fellowships, equipment purchases, and construction toward the end of bolstering academic fields related to the national defense. For example, preference for undergraduate student loans went to students "with a superior capacity or preparation in science, mathematics, engineering, or a modern foreign language" and to those "with a superior background who express a desire to teach in elementary or secondary schools."

Under the program, a student could borrow up to $1,000 per year at 3% interest, but not more than $5,000 for five years. The interest was not compounded while the student was in school, and repayment (which could last as long as ten years) was deferred until nine months after graduation. The federal government provided 90% of the loan and the institution provided the remaining 10%. In addition, the program included a forgiveness provision by which the loan was cancelled if the student became an elementary or secondary school teacher.

The National Defense Education bill met strong opposition from members of the House, who feared that the bill marked the first step toward federal control of education and who had rejected previous Senate plans for increased federal contributions to higher education. House passage of the bill was largely

attributed to the Russian success in launching Sputnik and the fear that American manpower was lagging in scientific and technological fields. (The bill's proponents also exhibited considerable political acumen in combining national defense and education in the title of the bill. The combination was difficult to vote against.)

The NDEA's policy declaration clearly tied federal aid to higher education with the promotion of the national defense:

The Congress hereby finds and declares that the security of the Nation requires the fullest development of the mental resources and technical skills of its young men and women. The present emergency demands that additional and more adequate educational opportunities be made available. The defense of this Nation depends upon the mastery of modern techniques developed from complex scientific principles. It depends as well upon the discovery and development of new principles, new techniques and new knowledge. We must increase our efforts to identify and educate more of the talent of our Nation. This requires programs that will give assurance that no student of ability will be denied an opportunity for higher education because of financial need; will correct as rapidly as possible the existing imbalances in our educational programs which have led to an insufficient proportion of our population educated in science, mathematics and modern foreign languages and trained in technology.

The Congress reaffirms the principle and declares that the states and local communities have and must retain control over and primary responsibility for public education. The national interest requires, however, that the Federal Government give assistance to education for programs which are important to our defense.

To meet the present educational emergency requires additional effort at all levels of Government. It is therefore the purpose of this act to provide substantial assistance in various forms to individuals and to states and their subdivisions in order to insure trained manpower of sufficient quality and quantity to meet the national defense needs of the United States.

The administration of the loans set a precedent for the EOG and CWS programs. Largely in response to those congressmen who feared federal control of education, the bill specified that the colleges, and not the federal government, administer the student loans. Thus, to obtain a loan, the student applies to the institution for both admission and financial aid.

In order to grant loan funds to the student, the institution must have entered into an agreement with the Commissioner of Education. The agreement contains provisions relating to the use of funds, maintenance of records, maintenance of effort, methods for determining financial need, student eligibility requirements, and an administrative cost allowance. After assessing each student's need according to the criteria set out in the law or in OE guidelines, the financial aid officer applies to an OE regional review board for total institutional loan funds. OE then computes the institution's share of the loan funds allocated to each state. (Each state's allotment is based on its percentage of full-time enrolled college students.) Once supplied with loan funds, the financial aid officer decides on the size of the loan and makes an offer to the student. (Under the present system, the financial aid officer often "packages" an NDSL with an EOG or CWSP.)

The NDEA was extended and modified in 1961, 1964, and 1965. In 1964 and 1965, higher education programs other than those directly related to science, math, modern languages, or teaching were also made eligible for aid. For student loans, this meant the preference provisions were dropped and part-time students were made eligible. President Kennedy articulated one rationale for broadening aid to higher institutions when he argued for the Vocational Education Act of 1963 and the Higher Education Facilities Act of 1963:

> This nation is committed to greater investment in economic growth; and recent research has shown that one of the most beneficial of all such investments is education, accounting for some 40 percent of the nation's growth and productivity in recent years. It is an investment which yields a substantial return in the higher wages and purchasing power of trained workers, in the new products and techniques which come from skilled minds and in the constant expansion of this nation's storehouse of useful knowledge.

Senator Goldwater, on the other side, protested the expansion of the NDEA.

> The NDEA would be transformed into a program which approximates a species of general federal aid to education, and in which the provisions related to the nation's defense have become the less important portion of the legislation. . . . What we are witnessing is the slow but relentless advent of federal regulation of education carried out on the installment plan and seeking to remain undetected under the protective cloak of "national defense."

The NDSLP was again extended by the Higher Education Act of 1965. This time, however, many members of Congress expressed deep concern over the default rate on NDSLs, which (they claimed) had been estimated as high as 30%, in contrast to OE's figure of around 9%. The accurate figures were never found, but it was generally agreed that the colleges ought to tighten up their collection procedures. (Many students, apparently, were not even made aware that their loans were, in fact, loans. Moreover, many of the colleges had neither the manpower nor the inclination—for fear of alienating alumni—to press hard for repayment.) By 1970–71, the problem had not yet been solved, but except for some discussion of the high default rate of loans to proprietary school students, it received little attention from a Congress preoccupied with larger philosophical issues.

The Higher Education Act of 1965 not only extended the coverage of the NDSLP, but also shifted its focus significantly. Originally targeted to needy students with superior academic promise, the program became more exclusively focused on "need" as the primary criterion for aid. The NDSLP was incorporated into President Johnson's War on Poverty and became a tool for eliminating financial constraints on the poor and promoting equal opportunity.

In 1966, however, the NDSLP began to lose favor with the Administration. Disturbed by the program's increasingly large cost, President Johnson proposed that the private sector take over the government's loan burden. Noting that a large amount of the loan funds went to middle-income students, the Administration also urged that NDSL be limited to students from families with less than $7,500 annual income. Throughout the late sixties, the Administration continued to press Congress to cut appropriations for the program, but met with continued resistance. Executive unhappiness with NDSLP culminated in the Nixon Administration with a proposal that the program be shifted "off the budget" (the private sector then to provide the loan funds) and subsidies be limited to only the neediest students. (By 1970, 47% of NDSL's funds went to students from families earning less than $6,000 per year.) Congress responded to President Nixon's proposal by raising NDSL appropriations to $238 million, thus permitting an increase of about 100,000 in the number of loans, bringing the total to 560,000.

The College Work Study Program

Started in 1933 to enable already enrolled students to continue their education, work study is the oldest federal student aid program. The program was terminated soon after the New Deal, but was reauthorized as a small part of the Economic Opportunity Act of 1964. As part of the War on Poverty, the work study program was directed at students from low-income families and intended to give these students the opportunity to attend higher education institutions by working part time.

Like the NDSLP, the program is administered through the institutions to which the student applies for both admission and aid. The institution then applies to OE for funds, and OE allots institutional funds with reference to the allocations for the entire state. State funds are allocated as follows: one-third is based on the state's percentage of full-time college enrollees, one-third based on the state's percentage of high school graduates, and one-third based on the state's percentage of students under 18 whose families earn less than $3,000. Once equipped with CWSP funds, the financial aid officer often packages the aid with an NDSL or EOG and makes an offer to the student. Under the CWSP, the student can only work 15 hours per week in work found by the institution or provided by the institution itself. The federal government pays 80% of the student's wages, and the employer pays the remaining 20%.

In 1965, the CWSP was transferred from the Office of Economic Opportunity to the Office of Education. Another amendment removed the requirement that eligible students come from low-income families, but gave preference to such students. In fis-

cal 1971, the program aided 400,000 students and 57% of its funds went to students whose families earned less than $6,000 a year.

It is generally agreed that the CWSP has worked, and as a result, the program has remained non-controversial and relatively free of change. Some colleges, however, report difficulty in finding enough jobs for all who need them, and some small colleges acting as employers for their own students have urged that the matching requirement of 20% be dropped because it drains their funds.

Educational Opportunity Grants

The Educational Opportunity Grants program was established by the 1965 Higher Education Act. Strongly pushed by President Johnson, the program was targeted to students of exceptional financial need and academic or creative promise. Like the NDSLP and the CWSP, the EOGP is administered through the institutions. The student applies for aid to the institutions, the financial aid officer assesses financial need according to the specific criteria of the program, and OE allocates funds to the states by the NDSLP formula. Since EOGs are to be given to those of exceptional financial need, OE has provided detailed eligibility criteria. For example, the OE *Manual* suggests that no EOGs be granted to students whose family earns more than $9,000 a year or to students whose parent(s) can contribute more than $625 a year. The financial aid officer can award grants ranging from $200 to $1,000 per year. Moreover, the institution must match the amount of the EOG with another form of student aid—from another federal aid program, the institution's own funds, or state aid funds. As a result, EOGs are almost always awarded as part of a "package" of aid, and by 1970, 72% of EOG funds went to students from families earning less than $6,000 per year.

The EOG program—or rather, the issue of federal grants to undergraduates—has a long and controversial history. In 1958 the Senate included a program of federal scholarships to undergraduates in the NDEA bill, but the House rejected the provision. For the next seven years, Congress debated the issue from every possible aspect. In 1962, for example, Senators Lausche and Morse went round and round on the issue of student motivation. Senator Lausche asserted that students who really wanted to go to college could borrow the money and repudiated the idea that a highly intelligent student would not attend college unless he received a scholarship. Senator Morse replied that this argument was effective before an audience of self-made men and women, but that not everyone could be judged by those standards, lest "we be running the risk that some young men and women would not be willing to borrow the necessary amount to go to college, as we did, for example." Lausche replied: "A student who refuses to attend an institution of higher learning unless he is given an outright grant, instead of a loan, in all probability does not possess the moral fabric to justify making the grant to him."

Other aspects of the issue aroused other groups; land grant and state universities, for example, opposed federal scholarships because the G.I. bill had shown that scholarships which paid all the educational expenses of the student resulted in overwhelming numbers of students choosing private colleges over public colleges. The public schools feared enrollment depletions if a large federal scholarship program were established. Public school support, however, was won in 1965 by a proposal that the scholarships not pay the entire cost of education, but that they be a part of a financial aid package each student would have to accept in toto if he were to receive any aid at all. Such a program would leave the responsibility of attracting low-income students up to the college itself and would not necessarily shift attendance from one type of institution to another.

Although the Johnson Administration and, later, the Nixon Administration favored the EOGP because it targetted substantial aid to the poor, the program has been mired in confusion and controversy. Many members of Congress remained uncomfortable with the whole notion of grants, and particularly with the notion of grants awarded simply on the basis of income. Consequently, Congress incorporated a merit provision in the eligibility requirements for EOGP. However, in administering the program, OE focused the aid on low-income students, regardless of merit. For example, a 1969 OE memo to the financial aid officers describes the purpose of the program as the assistance of the "most needy" students and offers guidelines on how to determine the neediest students. This memo aroused the ire of Representative Edith Green (D-Ore.), Chairwoman of the House Special Subcommittee on Education and previously a strong supporter of the EOGP. Representative Green argued that the guidelines meant that if a financial aid officer were faced with four qualified students who were in need of relatively little aid and one student who needed a lot of aid, the financial aid officer must award the grant to the one student. This, she claimed, was contrary to congressional intent.

Other Congressmen were disturbed by disparities between the loan and grant policies. Citing instances of individual students receiving the same total amount of aid but in different loan/grant combinations, these Congressmen sought justification of the apparent preferential treatment of the students who received part loan and part grant, as opposed to students who received only loans.

The problem of inequitable distribution was not eased by Congress's reluctance to fund the program adequately. In fiscal 1971, EOGP appropriations amounted to \$168 million and aided 290,000 students, yet the College Entrance Examination Board estimated that EOGs were denied to 300,000 students recommended for the grants by their financial aid officers.

Guaranteed Student Loan Program

In 1965 President Johnson proposed the GSLP to head off the passage of a tax-credit-for-tuition bill that was narrowly defeated in the Senate the previous year by a vote of 48 to 45. (A proposed tax deduction for tuition was also defeated, 47–47.) The Administration strongly opposed the tax credit plan for several reasons. First, it would have meant a large federal revenue loss. Secondly, higher education institutions would probably have raised their tuitions and passed on the cost to the Treasury Department. Finally, the plan would have discriminated against lower-income groups who rarely pay taxes: higher-income groups would receive both a higher absolute subsidy and a higher marginal subsidy than a low-income family.

President Johnson argued that federal guarantee of student loans would be a "more effective, fairer, and far less costly way of providing assistance than the various tax credit devices which have been proposed." The GSLP, like the tax credit plans, was aimed at middle-income groups and was designed to enable and encourage middle-income students to obtain privately financed loans. (Previously, these students had found it difficult to obtain loans in the private market, since they generally had no security to offer the lender but their future earning expectations.) Thus, under GSLP, the government proposed to guarantee a student's loan against default, disability, or death for amounts of not less than $1,000 a year or more than $1,500 a year and at the prevailing interest rates (not to exceed 7%). A student could not borrow more than $7,500 altogether. Unlike the NDSLP, to obtain a loan the student applied directly to a lending institution. In deciding whether or not to grant the loan, the lending institution was required to disregard the student's family income. If, however, the student's family had an adjusted income of $15,000 or less, the federal government would subsidize the loan by paying the full amount of the interest while the student was in school. Students from families with an adjusted income of over $15,000/year were themselves required to pay the amount of interest while in school. (In both cases the payment on the principle was deferred until after graduation.)

The program was amended in 1969, when tight money and rising interest rates were found to be preventing thousands of students from obtaining loans on the private market. The amendment authorized the payment of a "special allowance" by the federal government of 3% over the previous maximum interest rate of 7%. The allowance was applicable to the subsidized loans only and continued through the life of the loan.

In spite of these efforts to encourage use of GSLP, the program was plagued by many problems. A 1970 House Committee report, entitled *Survey of Lender Practices Relating to the Guaranteed Student Loan Program,* outlined some of the difficulties. First, despite the special interest allowance the program still faced liquidity problems. In tight money markets the lending institutions are either reluctant to lend money to student borrowers because of the relative low profitability of student loans or they lack the money to lend. (Banking groups, led by the American Banking Association, supported the creation of a secondary market and/or a warehouse mechanism to provide constant liquidity.) Secondly, partly because of tight money, the survey found a remarkable lack of uniform administration of the loans by the lending institutions. Some banks required that the families of students do business with the bank before the bank would grant a student loan, thus often discriminating against lower-income families. Other banks, contrary to congressional intent, allocated their limited loan funds to students of the greatest financial need. Thirdly, financial aid officers, lenders, and the General Accounting Office all expressed concern over the lack of communication between the financial aid officers and the lending institutions. The financial aid officers did not recommend a loan size to the lending institutions, nor were they always aware if a student had received a subsidized loan. As a result, a student could wind up with more aid than he needed as well as with a large debt at graduation. Finally, many of the lending institutions complained about the excessive administrative costs of the program.

Nevertheless, GSLP had many proponents. It made aid available to the middle-income groups and provided a valuable back-up source of aid for those students who cannot receive any other kind of help. It was also a favorite among cost conscious federal officials, since the private sector provided the capital. (However, since the federal government's outlay in subsidy payments was open-ended—depending on the number of students who could obtain loans from the private sector—the rapidly rising costs of the GSLP had by 1971 become a topic of concern to the Administration.) Thus, despite many problems, the GSLP grew dramatically. By 1970 the program had provided over $3.3 billion in loans, and in that year alone aided close to a million students at a federal cost of about $160 million.

THE DEBATE

Controversy over the question of federal aid to higher education reached a peak during the two and a half years preceding the June 1971 expiration of the 1965 Higher Education Act. The debate, which engaged widespread elements in the educational community, both houses of Congress, and the Administration, took place against a backdrop of skyrocketing educational costs and widely publicized campus unrest.[1] Among the various topics exciting controversy, a few key questions recurred again and again:

Should the federal government embark on a new program of no-strings-attached institutional aid in order to solve the financial crises of colleges and universities, or should it concentrate its resources on student aid?

Despite the present student aid programs and relatively low tuitions at public schools, the poor do not buy much higher education. Should the federal government target its student aid only to the poor at the expense of (also financially constrained) middle-income students?

Should grants or loans be the principal means of student aid?

Is there a need for innovation and reform in higher education institutions, and should the federal government make an effort to stimulate reform?

Toward the end of resolving these and other related questions, the educational community, Congress and the executive branch produced innumerable studies and reports indicating widespread problems in the American system of higher education. Among the more widely quoted studies was a Carnegie Commission Report, authored by Earl R. Cheit, which found that 71% of his sample of colleges and universities were either in financial trouble or headed for it.[2] Cheit found that although costs and income for higher education institutions were both rising, costs were rising at a slowly growing rate while income was rising at a declining rate. According to Cheit, costs skyrocketed not only because of inflation, but because of the demands for additional—and more innovative—services that have been recently placed on postsecondary institutions. These increased demands have been met by a declining rate of income growth. For example, the growth of federal aid to higher education decreased from a 42% increase (1965 over 1964) to only a 2% increase (1968 over 1967 and every year after that until the time of the study). To be sure, tuitions have risen at a rate of 7.5% annually, but Cheit argued that this cannot continue without becoming prohibitive. To avert the impending crisis, Cheit urged that the federal government contribute significant amounts of no-strings-attached institutional aid to higher education institutions.

Similarly William R. Jelleman, in a survey of private schools done for the Association of American Colleges, concluded that "most colleges in the red are staying in the red, and many are getting redder, while colleges in the black are generally growing grayer."[3] In the area of student aid, the private school confronts a particularly vicious circle. As it extends scholarships, it must raise tuitions to help pay the cost of educating the aided students. The increased tuitions, however, mean that another group of students now need a subsidy to attend.

By the beginning of 1971, at least another dozen separate studies had documented the "new depression" in higher education and had underlined the pervasiveness of the financial crises in all regions of the nation and among both private and public institutions. However, a 1971 report, prepared by an HEW task force headed by Frank Newman, reached other conclusions.[4] Instead of finding that schools were in great need of funds, Newman found that the structure of higher education was in great need of fundamental reform. Newman saw "a growing rigidity and uniformity of structure that makes higher education reflect less and less the interests of society." The report noted that the present system of higher education, by relying too much on academic credentials and encouraging faculty and student isolation from the real world, particularly failed to meet the needs of low-income students. Newman recommended that higher education be viewed as appropriate for all ages and that the lockstep pattern of college attendance—the unbroken stream of high school/college/graduate school—be altered. The report called for the establishment of more flexible and diverse educational enterprises and urged more off-campus instruction. Finally, repudiating the conventional wisdom that more money would solve the problems, Newman contended that the higher education community must better assess its use of existing resources: cost and performance measurements, he maintained, could legitimately be applied to higher education. The Newman report received wide and favorable publicity as well as the strong endorsement of HEW Secretary Elliot Richardson. The higher education community, however, attacked the report as "distorted and misleading."

Other studies focused on the problem of the poor and higher education, revealing a direct correlation between low family income and low rates of college attendance.* The studies noted that the low tuitions of public institutions—which were originally intended to expand the higher education opportuni-

---

*Low rates of college attendance, however, have been attributed to a variety of complex factors in addition to poverty. For example, other studies of high school seniors who did not attend higher education institutions indicate that lack of ability, lack of interest, preference for a job or a lack of peer attendance are often more important reasons for nonattendance than the lack of money.

ties of low-income students—have rapidly risen beyond the reach of many poor students. More importantly, perhaps, the costs of a higher education—tuition, incidental expenses and lost opportunity costs—constitute a larger relative investment for the poor than for the rich. Moreover, poor students, with low expectations of their future earning power, often do not believe they will recoup their investment; and thus, according to many economists, they should be encouraged by subsidies to make this investment.[5]

In a report to the President, Alice Rivlin, Assistant Secretary of Planning and Evaluation in HEW, echoed the conclusion of a previous Carnegie Commission report that the primary goal of federal aid to higher education should be the promotion of equal opportunity.[6] Both reports contended that equal educational opportunities benefit not only the poor, but the entire nation. Since these benefits transcend state boundaries, the federal government should bear the primary burden of removing the financial barriers to higher education. Moreover, the reports observed, the traditional mode of state subsidy of higher education—low tuitions for all—does not efficiently target aid to those who need it most. Both Rivlin and the Commission called for the expenditure of substantial student aid funds. They argued that grants and low interest loans were the most appropriate form of aid for the disadvantaged, and urged the creation of a student loan bank to facilitate loans to middle-income students. Both reports also favored the notion of a cost of education grant, but rejected general institutional aid on the grounds that it would do little to promote equal opportunity. (Rivlin, for example, argued that institutional aid would merely subsidize all students by maintaining the present tuition levels and would not induce more lower-income students to attend college.)

The Rivlin and Carnegie reports also supported a proposal outlined in Jerrold R. Zacharia's report, *The Educational Opportunity Bank*, which recommended that the federal government establish a semipublic bank to provide money for student loans.[7] The bank would permit twenty-to-thirty-year repayment plans and would also make the amount of the loan repayment contingent upon future income. This alternative attracted a fair amount of congressional support since the bank would not only lower the risk to the student (particularly to low-income students), but might also encourage more students to borrow. (Some congressmen were particularly pleased with the loan bank idea because it seemed to solve what had been—for them—a very troublesome problem: the problem of the "negative dowry." These congressmen expressed profound concern over the marital prospects of women who were heavily in debt.) It also appeared that higher education financed by student loans would activate the market system for students, who would no longer have to shop around for the best financial deal from a college; instead, they could simply and freely choose the school they most wanted to attend. The dominant market power would thus rest with the students. In addition, since higher education would be financed by student loans, institutions (particularly private institutions) could allow their tuitions to rise to their proper level. Colleges would no longer need to worry about keeping their tuitions as low as possible and could use the infusion of additional funds to meet their financial squeeze. Finally, proponents of the student-loan bank suggested that the benefits, both financial and internal, that accrue to a graduate of a higher education institution are primarily private benefits, for which the student ought to bear the cost. With this premise, the loan bank appeared to be a useful vehicle for weaning the young away from a dependence on their parents and on society and making them responsible for their own education.

In 1970–71, opinions on the various federal and alternative issues coalesced among the four basic policy-making groups most intensely involved in determining the future shape of federal aid to higher education: the higher education lobby, the Administration, the House Special Subcommittee on Education, and the Senate Subcommittee on Education.

The Higher Education Lobby

The higher education lobby consists of close to 50 higher education associations, as well as numerous representatives of individual institutions. Most prominent among these associations is the American Council on Education (ACE), an umbrella group which often speaks for the associations and which is itself comprised of the Association of American Universities, the National Association of State Universities and Land Grant Colleges, the Association of American Colleges, the American Association of Junior Colleges, and the American Association of State Colleges and Universities.

The higher education lobby became identifiable as such during the early and mid-sixties, when the Washington-based higher education community expanded rapidly in response to the expansion of federal funds available for higher education. The leading associations, however, each serviced a different constituency and held widely differing views on the question of federal aid. For example, until 1963, the Association of American Colleges—which consists of private schools—voiced great fear of federal control over education and consequently, opposed any form of federal aid. While most of the other leading associations supported the concept of federal aid in general, they did not find it necessary, or even proper, to engage in heavy political lobbying for particular programs. The nation's colleges and universities did not face severe financial difficulties and the federal government often seemed willing to contribute aid if the institutions would help further federal goals. On the other hand, some members of the higher education community—particularly the specialized associations and the representatives from individual schools—were more concerned with grantsmanship than with developing a unified position on aid to higher education. As one observer noted, "Probably no other segment of American society has so many organizations and is yet so unorganized as higher education."[8]

By 1968, however, higher education institutions were faced with rapidly rising costs and the prospect of federal cutbacks in aid. The leading associations, pushed by the ACE, concurred on the necessity of communication and coordination among the various groups in order that they might advocate with one voice an increase in federal aid. Toward this end, they opened the National Center for Education in 1970. The building, located in Washington, now houses most of the higher education associations.

The attempt to unify the disparate voices of the higher education community has not been entirely successful, yet in 1970–71 most of the community presented a remarkably unified front. They supported the existing student aid programs, and particularly wished to maintain the institutional administration of the programs. They also urged that the programs be fully funded in the interest of satisfying the equal opportunity goals cited in the Rivlin and Carnegie reports.

Existing programs, however, were of lesser priority to the higher education community than were the prospects of obtaining some form of no-strings-attached institutional aid. The American Association of State Colleges and Universities and the National Association of State Universities and Land Grant Colleges argued:

> . . . the greatest unmet need in federal support of higher education in the country today is an institutional support program through which *flexible, predictable* funds can be made available to the colleges and universities on a *continuing* basis.

Similarly, the Association of American Colleges contended that "federal institutional grants for the support of basic instruction offer the best prospect for sustaining and improving American colleges and universities." The ACE added:

> It would be cruel indeed if the hopes of these people [federally aided students] were raised by promises which cannot be kept because institutional resources are not adequate to meet them. . . . Lack of money in the hands of the student is not the sole barrier to his going to college. There must be a place for him at an institution of higher education, and there must be teachers to instruct him, and books for him to read.

The higher education community claimed that federal aid was the only way to keep tuitions down, particularly when private groups and state and local governments were feeling the financial pinch. Most institutions indicated they would use noncategorical institutional grants to meet operating costs and thus try to keep tuitions at their present level. Since tuition only covers a portion of the costs of educating a student, education officials also argued that additional funds would be needed to upgrade quality. Moreover, to the extent that federal aid programs increase the enrollment of low-income students, the institutions fall victim to a form of "reverse revenue sharing," ending up absorbing alone the extra cost of educating these new students. (Since many low-income students come to college from educationally deprived backgrounds, the colleges must also provide, at their own expense, remedial instruction.) Cost of education grants, although acceptable to the lobby, were regarded as much less attractive than straight institutional aid. Finally, the lobby argued that the general institutional aid would give the institutions the flexibility and freedom they presently lacked because of the federal categorical grant programs, which often skew the true priorities of the institutions by inducing them to accept the goals of the federal government.

Unlike their positions on most other questions, the higher education community presented a unified front on the need for institutional aid. Beneath the surface, however, the question of how to distribute institutional aid remained divisive. The large universities favored a simple formula based on the number of students enrolled or on the number of degrees granted. Such a formula would favor those schools with large enrollments or those schools which could most readily expand their enrollment or churn out more degrees. (It should be noted that the large universities, both public and private, also win most of the federal government's special research grants.) Representatives from community colleges and black colleges argued, on the other hand, that they do the most to educate students from low-income families and thus deserve special help. Specifically, they urged that Congress adopt a program to aid developing institutions. And the small private colleges contended that they cannot compete with the low tuitions offered at public institutions, but since the education they offer is superior, they, too, need relatively more aid than other types of schools. Unlike the other types of institutions, the small private schools indicated that they would support some form of voucher system. They believed that if the student brings his own aid with him, as a veteran did under the G.I. bill, the student will choose to attend small private colleges over other types of institutions. Other groups within the lobby debated whether existing institutional differences in levels of non-federal funding should have an impact on future federal funding; i.e., should any proposed institutional grant vary according to the amount donated from other sources? If so, should the federal government reward institutional incentive in garnering aid from other sources or should it compensate institutions which find it difficult to obtain aid from other sources?

Although the ACE advocated basing institutional aid on total student enrollees, much to the chagrin of Representative Green, they were very slow to recommend a specific formula to Congress. Green strongly supported across-the-board institutional aid,

but during the lengthy discussions on a possible formula, she remarked, "I have been searching for one and found it impossible to devise one that is fair and have not had anybody else suggest one." In the end, most of the associations were willing to accept any type of institutional aid they could get. They did eventually propose a formula, but once Representative Green had modified it to her liking,* the associations simply sat back and watched the legislative struggle between the House and Senate. There was no real effort by the associations to provide data and information to other legislators to support their case, and observers noted that they relied too much on Representative Green to make their case for them. Senator Pell (Chairman of the Senate Subcommittee on Education), for example, complained, "I need help and I have not gotten a damn thing from the ACE."

As for the student loan bank proposals, the higher education community generally opposed them, despite the indications that institutions would receive additional funds from such a program. According to the ACE, higher education financed by student loans would overturn "the long established policy that views higher education as producing broad public benefits." An increase in student loans appeared to many to be the beginning of the end of large federal government subsidies to higher education. Also, though never explicitly stated, the higher education community feared the possibility of students gaining dominant market power.

The Administration

In the policy area of higher education, Nixon Administration concerns centered around the issues of the budget, targeting aid to the poor, and reform. Since its inception, the Nixon Administration had urged cuts in most OE budget items. Those concerned with the budget favored shifting the NDSLP "off the budget" and supported some form of a student loan bank to provide private money for student loans. Others in the Nixon Administration found the student loan bank proposals philosophically consistent with their view that students ought to pay their own way. Secondly, as with other welfare programs, the Nixon Administration favored restricting assistance to those with the greatest need. For this reason, the Administration had consistently urged Congress to expand the CWSP and the EOGP. In addition, many persons in

---

*See pages 293–294 for details.

OE, HEW's Office of the Secretary, and the Executive Office were convinced of the need for thorough-going reform of higher education. In a 1969 OE Subcommittee Report on "Easing Tensions in Education," these "innovationists" argued that OE should become the "advocate of change" in higher education and that "HEW should not support the educational establishment's desire to maintain current allocations of power with schools and universities."[9] The advocates of change saw rising student unrest as one symptom of the unresponsiveness of higher education institutions, in consequence of which they urged that the federal government disburse money directly to the students and not to the colleges, to strengthen the students' hand in bringing about change. (Many of those views were subsequently reflected in the Newman Report.)

In November 1969, the responsibility for devising a new Administration policy toward higher education fell to a twelve-member White House Working Group drawn from OE, HEW's Office of the Secretary, OMB, and the Council of Economic Advisors. The group met without outside consultation but under pressure, since in December 1969 Chairwoman Green began her hearings on higher education, and President Nixon (although in office more than a year) had yet to make any higher education proposal. To compound the problem, President Nixon had vetoed in December an HEW appropriation bill as inflationary. The vetoed bill was the culmination of the higher education community's unsuccessful effort to achieve fuller funding for education.

The Working Group did eventually draft a bill more or less embodying the Administration's position on higher education, but when the bill was introduced in Congress (in March 1970), it met with such vigorous opposition that the Administration—already troubled by campus unrest after the Cambodian invasion—agreed to postpone further action. In the summer of 1970, President Nixon appointed Elliot Richardson as Secretary of HEW (to succeed Robert Finch) and named Sidney Marland the Commissioner of Education (to succeed James Allen). Richardson and Marland consulted extensively with both the higher education community and with members of Congress in the preparation of new federal aid proposals, which were introduced in Congress in 1971.

Similar in basic approach to the abortive 1970 bill, the 1971 proposal embraced the promotion of equal opportunity as the goal of federal aid to higher education. On January 17, 1971, President Nixon repeated his March 19, 1970 message on higher education:

> No qualified student who wants to go to college should be barred by lack of money. That has long been a great American goal; I propose that we achieve it now.
>
> Something is basically unequal about opportunity for higher education when a young person whose family earns more than $15,000 a year is nine times more likely to attend college than a young person whose family earns less than $3,000.

In March 1971 the Administration presented its proposal to Congress. Richardson described the goals of the proposal:

> The primary thrust of our proposed student aid reforms can be stated quite simply—to give every qualified low-income student the same financial access to a post-secondary education as a student from a middle-class family . . . all students whose families can be expected to make the same contribution should have the same help available for the education from Federal sources.

The Administration argued that the existing programs did not go far enough in targetting aid to students from low-income families; Administration witnesses noted that only 45% of the students from families under $10,000 annual income received federal aid. In addition, the Administration criticized the existing programs on other, more specific grounds. First, they noted that the availability of NDSL, EOG, and CWSP funds to institutions is limited by complex state allocation formulas and institution-matching requirements. Secondly, they noted that the availability of NDSL loan funds in particular is further limited because the program requires such large capital outlays from the federal government. Moreover, in tight money markets, the chances of a student obtaining a loan in the private market through the GSLP are small. Third, they were troubled by the open-ended character of the federal commitment under the GSLP. Appropriations for the GSLP subsidies in 1971 were $160 million out of a total OE aid budget of $722 million. By 1975, the Administration estimated the cost would rise to $460 million. Thus, most student aid budget increases would have to be used to meet the GSLP subsidy; and since GSLP benefits students from middle-income families, student aid funds would be diverted from the neediest students to subsidize middle-income students. Fourth, the Administration observed that, because of the timing of the appropriations process, the variations among state allocation formulas, and the power of financial aid officers, the student could not predict whether or not he would receive aid when he went through the application process. This made it difficult for high school seniors to plan for college and perhaps discouraged low-income students from even applying for aid. As a corollary, there was no certainty that students of equal need were treated alike, and students often had to do a lot of comparison-shopping to come up with the best financial deal.

The Administration bill guaranteed each student $1,400 a year: $400 in the form of 3% loans, and $1,000 in the form of grants or work study, or a combination of both. The $1,400 was designed to put the student from a poor family on an equal footing with the student whose adjusted family income was $10,000 a year. (The Administration estimated that the $10,000-a-year family with two children—one of them in college—could contribute $1,400 toward the support of a college education.) Specifically, a student whose family earned less than $3,500 would receive the full $1,400, but as family income increased, the federal subsidy would decline. This national standard of aid was intended to insure that students of equal need were treated alike as well as to give students more consumer choice than they previously had. While the proposal would diminish the power of individual financial aid officers to award aid, it still provided for the administration of the aid through the institutions, and it left the determination of the family contribution in the hands of the financial aid officers, as long as they continued to use one of the four approved need-assessment formulas.

In addition, the student who qualified for the $1,400 in aid also qualified for a $1,500 cost of education loan at 3% interest. This loan provision would allow a low-income student to attend a high-cost institution and would prevent low-income students from swamping low-cost public institutions. Under the Administration's proposal, the HEW Secretary would publish a schedule every year showing the amount of funds available to each income level.

Many legislators criticized the Administration's claim of "guaranteeing" each needy student $1,400 in aid, because the exact amount of aid still depended on the amount appropriated for the program. In order to finance the expanded loan program, however, the Administration proposed shifting student loans to the private market.* This, in turn, would necessitate the creation of a National Student Loan Association (NSLA), which would raise money by selling its obligations and would serve as a secondary market for student loans by purchasing student loan paper from lending institutions. It would also lend money to other lending institutions for direct loans to students. Finally, the NSLA would provide loans at market interest rates for all those who failed to qualify for the grant, work study, and loan subsidies, i.e., middle-income students.

According to the Administration, the NSLA would solve the problems that plagued the existing loan programs. The Administration argued that by shifting loans "off the budget" to the private market, more total loan money would be available to students. The NSLA would also solve the liquidity problem which exists in tight money markets. And finally, unlike other lending institutions, which dislike extended repayment periods because the high service costs further reduce the already low profit margin of student loans, the NSLA could afford to be flexible in its repayment plans.

In comparing their proposal with existing programs, the Administration asserted that it would target more money to more students from low-income families; while $575 million would be available in grants and work study, and $1.2 billion in subsidized loans, only the very poor would receive grants or subsidized loans. Most students from middle-income families would have to rely on unsubsidized loans (made more available through the NSLA).

On the question of institutional aid, the Administration was divided and this type of aid was not included in the original proposal. (As Peter Muirhead, Deputy Commissioner of Education expressed it: "Very reluctantly it was decided that it was not possible at this time.") Secretary Richardson was more

---

*Financing NDSL through the private market and thus removing its cost from the budget was not a new idea. President Johnson proposed it in 1966 and it was part of the Administration's 1970 program.

emphatic: speaking for many in the Administration, he said:

> We are convinced that among the most inefficiently administered institutions in the United States, by and large, are our institutions of higher learning, and that before turning to means of providing help to them we ought to be clear about what help is needed.

To Richardson, it appeared that across the board institutional aid would simply perpetuate the status quo at a time when "there is urgent need to develop new and much more flexible forms of higher education."

The House

In the late fifties and early sixties, the House struggled long and bitterly before it even agreed to the principle of federal aid to higher education. The House mustered its greatest enthusiasm for federal aid to institutions and to low-income students in the mid-sixties, but has since cooled slightly. Student unrest dampened some of the enthusiasm, and Representative Edith Green, Chairwoman of the House Special Subcommittee on Education, dampened it some more. (In the late sixties, Green began to express considerable disillusionment with parts of the student aid program.)

Edith Green, in fact, proved a very influential figure throughout the long debate on student aid. Entering Congress as a Democrat from Oregon in 1954, she gained the chair of the House Special Subcommittee on Education in 1961. Originally reputed to be a "flaming liberal," according to various critics and to a Nader report, she became "intransigent in deepening conservatism." Her proponents characterized the shift of attitudes as a consistent response to new information and changing circumstances, while others felt that she was simply growing old. Nevertheless, she remained a strong proponent of most federal aid to higher education and a powerful force in policy-making.

Her approach to student aid, however, has shifted along with her general philosophical bias. In 1964 she enthusiastically supported the EOG and CWS programs targeted at low-income students, and opposed the (middle-income) GSLP because she saw "no need." In the late sixties she slowly reversed her position, coming to sympathize with the financial squeeze of middle-income families (these were her constituents) and working hard to protect the NDSLP and the GSLP, which aided those families. (She had also become convinced that disadvantaged and minority students fomented much of the unrest on the campuses.)

In addition, in 1969 she began detailed monitoring of OE, in the course of which her hostility toward that agency grew. She continually cited the 1969 OE memo (which claimed that EOGP was intended to aid the "most needy") as an example of OE disregard for congressional intent, as well as OE's abandonment of the needs of middle-income families. She also engaged in oversight of OE's extensive use of outside private consultants, and found poor procedures for the awarding of grants, inadequate monitoring of the grants (51 people monitor 50,000 ongoing contracts and grants), a massive waste of funds, and a flow of money into the "educational-industrial complex" at the expense of needy students and schools. In one article on the subject, she concluded that, "What we are finding is the simple absence of good management, or virtually any management at all, at OE." She also criticized OE for excessive delay in responding to her requests for information and consistently distrusted the information once it was presented to her. Her comments in the hearings indicate the extent of her skepticism:

> As I have looked very closely at the Office of Education I am absolutely persuaded that both Parkinson's law and the Peter Principle are at work. . . . I guess I have reached the point where I am in favor of just saying to the Office of Education, "You can't issue more guidelines on this. This is the law and our intent is clear." We have, in the past, given them much discretionary power, and it seems to me it has been greatly abused.

Green's attitudes substantially shaped the House subcommittee's reaction to the Administration bill. Chiefly disturbed by the targetting of aid to low-income students and by the lack of institutional aid, Green complained that the proposal showed a "blindness to the financial needs of the sons and daughters of middle-income families" and "a blindness to the great needs of private institutions." She also commented:

> If the administration has decided that it is necessary to use federal funds to rescue Penn Central from financial disaster and seems willing to use federal funds to save Lockheed from financial

disaster, why does it not propose some federal aid to save America's failing colleges and universities from financial disaster?

Referring to the Administration proposal for a $1,500 low-interest cost-of-education loan, she asked Secretary Richardson:

> Why is it the national interest to make it possible for the neediest student to go to the most expensive school? The middle-income student does not have that option.

Representative John Brademas added:

> I think it is most unfortunate that our subcommittee has been put in the posture of appearing to have to choose between poor and middle-income students. I am strongly in favor of helping both groups of students and I don't want to trade off poor kids for middle-income kids or vice versa, and if the Administration says we can't afford both, my attitude is that it is their problem. The Administration should go find the money someplace else.

Similarly, many members of the subcommittee criticized the proposals to terminate the GSLP and what they saw as the termination of the NDSLP, both of which aided many middle-income students. By shifting the NDSLP off the budget and eliminating the NDSL subsidy for most middle-income students, the Administration aroused the suspicion of the subcommittee. The Administration, on the other hand, argued that NDSL-type loans would still be available and in even greater supply—only the private market, instead of the government, would provide the funds ($1.2 billion compared to $369 million). This argument did not fall on sympathetic ears. As Representative Brademas expressed the subcommittee's skepticism:

> . . . the national student loan program requires capital outlays from the federal Government, and it is in essence there, it seems to me the reason you have gone through the trouble of this extraordinary, elaborate rearrangement to try to basically kill off what had been a very popular and successful program. . . . The Office of the Budget has said to the Office of Education, "Now why don't you fellows figure out a way you can save us a couple of hundred million dollars."

In response to the Administration bill, Green introduced her own bill, H.R. 7428, calling for the

extension of the existing programs at somewhat higher levels of funding. Her bill would have raised the EOG award limit from $1,000 to $1,500; increased the ceiling for GSLP to $2,500 annually and $10,000 aggregate; and expanded eligibility for EOGP and CWSP to include part-time students. She also proposed the establishment of a student loan market to facilitate student loans. Her bill would give even more authority to the financial aid officers for determining eligibility as well as the amount and mix of aid, and would also prevent the federal government from issuing regulations restricting the freedom of the officers to make these decisions.

Basically, then, Green was happy with the structure of existing programs, since these programs served the needs of students from a wide range of income groups. The committee report expressed her attitude:

> In practice, the programs have gradually evolved into a ladder of aid; starting with grants and moving up to work-study, NDEA loans, subsidized insured loans, and nonsubsidized insured loans. There is considerable overlap and flexibility with the general result that the financial aid officer has leeway to put together a "package" for the student in front of him.

Green bridled at the Pell* and Administration proposals to establish uniform national standards of aid based on income. Instead, she preferred treating each student individually by weighing his/her merit and need. Her bill, for example, broadened the definition of "need" to include factors other than simply income, since the income standard of need did not take into account various kinds of assistance available to lower-income families but not to middle-income ones (e.g., welfare payments, food stamps, housing subsidies, and no income tax). Her language changes included the removal of the $15,000 family income ceiling for those receiving the interest subsidy on GSLs and made need, as determined by the financial aid officer, the criterion for a subsidy. She also deleted the language which gave work-study preference to "students from low-income families" and restated the purpose of the program as aid to students "who are

---

*See page 295 for details of Pell's proposal.

in need." As a result of her changes, a middle-income student at a high cost institution could be considered needy. (She deliberately sought this result, since she feared that middle-income students were being squeezed out of high cost institutions.)

Most importantly, her bill proposed a formula for institutional aid based on the number of students enrolled in the institution. (Each school would receive $100 for each freshman and sophomore, and $150 for each junior and senior. The small private schools—in need of extra assistance—would receive an additional $300 for the first 200 students in the enrollment and $200 for the next 100 students.) Green argued the appropriateness of her formula on the grounds that it was simple and easy to administer and that all institutions needed help. The formula, however, also reflected mistrust of OE: if institutional aid were tied to student aid (as was proposed by HEW Secretary Richardson) OE could manipulate institutional aid by manipulating student aid, but under the enrollment formula, OE would have minimal influence. According to the committee report, noncategorical institutional aid marks the "federal acceptance of a responsibility for the financial well-being of the higher education community."

Green's formula was vigorously opposed by Secretary Richardson. Although the Administration had originally opposed any program for institutional aid, by mid-summer of 1971 it became clear that Congress was bent on providing some kind of aid to institutions. Rather than see Green's formula adopted, Richardson, with the approval of President Nixon, then developed a cost-of-education formula which would set institutional grants equal to a percentage of total federal dollars of student aid (student grants, subsidized loans and work-study payments) received at each school. Although not inflexibly committed to his own formula, Richardson remained adamant on the subject of Green's formula:

> It is hard to imagine a mode of financing less suited to alleviating an immediate, short-term crisis. . . . It is much too blunt an instrument for dealing with acute problems of particular institutions, for it would provide support to all institutions regardless of their needs without substantially affecting those which are in the greatest difficulty.

Despite the opposition of the committee Republicans who favored the Administration bill and the objections of Democrats Frank Thompson and John Brademas who disliked Green's institutional aid provisions and her tacit abandonment of low income students, the bill that eventually emerged from the House Education and Labor Committee overwhelmingly bore Green's imprint. The full committee, however, added emergency aid provisions for struggling institutions and adopted a compromise on institutional aid which provided that two-thirds of the aid would be awarded on the basis of Green's enrollment formula and one-third on the basis of the Administration's cost-of-education formula.

The Senate

Unlike the House, the Senate has a tradition of strong support for federal aid to higher education. This support became particularly marked in 1969, with the accession of Senator Claiborne Pell to the chairmanship of the Education and Public Welfare's Subcommittee on Education. As he consistently articulated it, Pell's primary goal in the field of higher education was to ensure that this education be considered a right, just like elementary and secondary education:

> I guess the difference in viewpoint that we have is that I am saying that the time will be coming soon, in my view, when college will be as much a matter of right as high school has become a matter of right, although it was never expected to be 80 years ago. . . . And what I am trying to do with my approach is to make sure that every youngster, as a matter of right, has the option of the post-secondary education that he can achieve, with no debts afterwards.

Towards this end, he proposed that the federal government provide direct grants to all needy students, thus establishing a floor of assistance. When he was largely ignored upon first proposing the plan in 1970, he rebuked his audience as follows:

> I would be wrong if, as chairman of the Education Subcommittee, I did not, in all fairness, consider all the different ideas and proposals that come to us. I have expressed great disappointment that the higher education community hasn't taken the trouble to reflect on and study our ideas which, we think, will help solve the problem.

For example, I read articles in the press and hear testimony along the same lines as my bill, yet witnesses are not familiar with it. If we have the courtesy and interest to familiarize ourselves with your thoughts and views, I think you, as specialists in this field, should have your opinions, pro or con, on our views up here on the Hill, because we have an active problem solving responsibility.

So, while it has been taken quite flippantly so far, it would seem to me that it might conceivably get into the final version of the bill.

Given the strength of his convictions, Senator Pell vehemently opposed the Administration's proposal to shift the burden of financing higher education to the students. For similar reasons, he dismissed the concept of a student loan bank; he opposed the ideas of students, particularly poor students, starting life after graduation with a loan hanging over their heads. He also feared the creation of a student loan bank would forestall the day of direct grants:

> Your [Richardson's] general testimony indicates that what the Administration is proposing is a long-range, perhaps a permanent, program of student assistance in which loans from the private sector would be the major form of assistance. . . . And if such a proposal becomes law, it is only natural to assume that college tuitions are going to continue to increase, with the result that higher education will be almost completely financed by tuition.
>
> To my mind, we should be seeking tuition-free higher education as a floor, but that does not seem to be a goal of the program the Administration offers. . . . . Do you really believe that we want to adopt a policy for the time being based on a philosophy of tuition-financed higher education, or do we want to go to this concept, eventually, of the floor?

Senator Pell incorporated his views in a Senate bill, S. 659, which was eventually co-sponsored by all the subcommittee members and, later, all seventeen members of the full committee. Pell's bill, like the Administration bill, advocated a program along the lines of a voucher system, but where the Administration relied primarily on loans, Pell relied primarily on grants. By providing a direct grant to the student, Pell hoped to produce a reasonably certain and well-understood source of funds for the student; direct grants, he believed, would encourage high school students to plan for college, and would also effectively target the funds to those who needed them most.

Pell initially proposed that each student would receive a direct grant of $1,200 minus the amount of income tax paid by the family. He later amended this to provide $1,400 minus the amount the family could contribute or one-half the cost of attendance, whichever is less (but in no case less than $200). (Pell's amendments were prompted by Administration criticism of the accuracy of an income tax return as a measure of need. Administration officials had pointed out that income tax returns do not take into account extraordinary expenditures such as other children in college, and that use of the returns might lead to parents emancipating their children so that the children could gain eligibility.)

As well as establishing his long-desired direct grant program, Senator Pell's bill provided for the continuance of existing student aid programs and for the establishment of a supplemental grant program, similar to the existing EOG program but targetted to students in high-cost institutions. The final Senate committee bill provided for yet another new program: a subsidy program to encourage states to undertake and expand state scholarship programs based on financial need. (Under this program, the federal government would pay 50% of the increased amount of state scholarship grants.)

Because the committee members believed in putting the "decision making in the hands of the consumer of educational services rather than in the 'conduits' of those services," the committee rejected noncategorical institutional aid. (Pell had also soured on institutional aid because of what he saw to be the unwillingness of the higher education community to look at new ideas, such as those put forth by the Newman Report.) The committee, however, did include a cost-of-education allowance, on the following rationale:

> To the extent that enrollments increase as a result of federal activities, the federal government is imposing a burden on institutions. If those institutions merely increase tuition, the purpose of student aid is defeated. The payments . . . are designed to reimburse the institutions for part of the federal burden incurred by them.

Under the Senate formula, an institution would receive aid for each student attending school on a basic federal grant, but the formula would be weighted so that small colleges would get the most help. The final committee bill provided $500 to the smallest colleges for each federal grant recipient, and only $100 to the largest universities. The committee bill also authorized $150 million in emergency aid for those institutions facing immediate bankruptcy. (According to one House Democrat, the institutional and student aid provisions of the Senate bill—which would subsidize both needy students and colleges enrolling needy students—reflect the Senate's "obsession with the disadvantaged.")

As finally drafted, the Senate committee bill was criticized by the Administration on several grounds, chief among which was its cost. The final committee bill authorized a total OE budget of $7 billion for one year—or seven times the existing OE budget. Approximately $4 billion of this budget was intended to cover the basic grant program, the cost-of-education allowance, and the existing student aid programs. (The Administration estimated the one-year costs of the basic grant program alone to range from $1 billion to $2 billion, depending on the choice of a family contribution schedule and the number of enrollees.) Although sympathetic to the intent of the bill, the Administration considered its costs not only excessive but unrealistic: in their view, the bill held out empty promises—never to be met by congressional appropriations.

Pell was not insensitive to these objections, but as one of his aides commented: "The idea was to pressure the Administration and the Appropriations Committees into providing a lot more money." Also, Pell did try to defuse some of this criticism with a ratable reduction formula that would reduce the amount of the basic grant in proportion to actual Congressional appropriations.

The Administration also heavily criticized the concept of OE providing direct grants to 2.3 million students—a concept which, to them, posed staggering administrative problems and would require the growth of a whole new bureaucracy. Apparently not having any strong sentiments about the administrative capacity of OE, however, Senator Pell remained unruffled by these objections.

* * * *

By the fall of 1971, the House and Senate committees had reached agreement on their respective bills. The Administration and higher education lobby, after testifying before the committees, also prepared to push their policy preferences before the full House and Senate. Before a decision could be reached, however, congressional interest in higher education issues was deflected by the busing controversy, and action on the bills was delayed until 1972.

SEQUEL

Federal Aid to Postsecondary Education in the Seventies

In the years to come, 1978 may be recognized as a pivotal moment in the development in federal aid to students in postsecondary education—one of those points at which crucial decisions were made affecting the course, form and focus of national policy in this area. While previous amendments to federal higher education programs had involved legislative or administrative tinkering with distribution formulas and incremental expansions of eligibility, each of the two rival aid concepts which competed for passage during the Ninety-Fifth Congress would have mandated broad changes in the federal role. The first of these, an amended version of President Carter's Middle Income Assistance Act, would represent the most significant expansion of the U.S. Office of Education (OE) since its enactment. Adoption of the alternative, a tuition tax credit, would be a still more fundamental departure from previous policy, a shift away from the grants-and-loans approach which has constituted the core of federal assistance to postsecondary students since the time of the G.I. Bill.

DEVELOPMENTS IN MIDSTREAM: 1972-77

Earlier in the decade important developments in the assistance programs administered by the OE fell roughly into four areas: The Education Amendments of 1972, the Amendments of 1976, the distribution of appropriations among the six aid programs, and the staggering default rates in the two loan programs.

The current six-program structure of OE assistance to higher education students is a result of the Education Amendments of 1972. The most important innovation of this legislation was the creation of Basic Educational Opportunity Grants (BEOG), under which the federal government would provide students with direct grants of up to $1,400. Eligibility was restricted to students from families with an income of less than $15,000 per year, and grants were not to exceed half the cost of attendance. BEOG differed significantly from another existing grant program, Educational Opportunity Grants (EOG, established in 1965 to provide aid to students of exceptional need and academic promise), in that Basic Grants were to be given directly to students rather than to the higher education institutions, which in turn awarded them to eligible students. This was, in part, a response to a criticism that the institution-based grant program, which distributed the funds unequally among the states according to a set formula, compelled students to choose a school less by personal preference than by the financial aid package it could offer.

Congress did not, however, abandon the institution-based program; it was re-authorized and renamed Supplemental Educational Opportunity Grants (SEOG). Three other existing programs were also re-authorized: the popular College Work-Study Program (CWSP), under which the federal government pays 80% of the wages of part-time student jobs either found or provided by the schools; the National Direct Student Loan Program (NDSL, formerly the National Defense Student Loan Program), in which the OE provides the capital for student loans administered by the educational institutions; and the Guaranteed Student Loan Program (GSLP), through which the U.S. guarantees loans made to students by private lending institutions. The 1972 Amendments did alter the GSLP criteria by which a student could qualify for federal interest subsidies while in school; a strict family income ceiling of $15,000 was replaced by a more flexible system in which need was determined by college financial aid officers. Finally, the 1972 legislation created the State Scholarship Incentive Grant Program (SSIG), which provided matching funds to states for setting up or maintaining their own scholarship programs.

The Higher Education Amendments of 1972 authorized these six programs—BEOG, SEOG, CWSP, NDSL, GSLP and SSIG—until June 30, 1976. In 1975, as the expiration date drew near, Senator Claiborne Pell, one of the principal architects of BEOG, declared that all that was necessary was a "simple re-authorization of the 1972 Amendments." However, there was a growing conviction in both government and educational circles that eligibility for the existing programs was too restrictive. For instance, a 1975 report of the Carnegie Council on Policy Studies in Higher Education recommended:

> The eligibility conditions for Basic Educational Opportunity Grants should gradually be liberalized, but only as appropriations increase sufficiently to permit such liberalization without penalizing students in the family income range in which students are currently eligible.[1]

More specifically, the Council urged elimination of the provision that restricted grants to no more than 50% of the cost of attendance. This change was suggested as part of a wider restructuring which would delineate the functions of the separate grant programs. Under this proposal, the BEOG program would be targeted to non-instructional costs only; this would particularly aid low-income students attending low or zero tuition public colleges. For students attending moderate and higher tuition colleges, assistance in meeting instructional costs would be provided through SEOG and SSIG funds. Finally, both the Carnegie Council report and a similar study undertaken by the Consortium on Financing Higher Education recommended increasing the maximum basic grant from $1,400 to $1,600.[2]

The Education Amendments of 1976 reflected awareness of many of the criticisms of the existing system, although they did not conform entirely to the specific proposals of the higher education lobby. Congress did eliminate the 50% coverage limitation on basic grants. On the other hand, no effort was made to resolve the confusion between the functions of the individual-oriented Basic Grants and the institutionally administered Supplemental Educational Opportunity Grants. As for the proposal to increase the maximum BEOG award from $1,400 to $1,600, Congress in a sense promised more and delivered less. As worked out in conference committee, the Education Amendments authorized a maximum award of $1,800, effective for the 1978–79 academic year; for the interim years, the maximum remained set at $1,400. (Proponents of the increase were thus able to obtain credit for it in press summaries both at the time of its enactment and at its effective date. A few years later, President Carter and other advocates would laud the fact that the maximum grant was to be raised to $1,800 under the Middle Income Student Assistance legislation of 1978.)

The final legislation contained two other important expansions of student aid. Eligibility for State Student Incentive Grants was extended to include all students attending non-profit institutions of higher education. This measure did not force each state to expand its SSIG program, but did free those states which had no constitutional or other restrictions on SSIG aid to apply their federal monies and their own matching funds to students in these schools. Finally, Congress raised from $15,000 to $25,000 the income level (for a family of four) below which a student could automatically qualify for federal interest subsidies under the Guaranteed Student Loan Program. (This change appeared as an early indication of a shift in the perception of need, by which progressively higher income groups were seen as the principal victims of the gap between college costs and the coverage and level of financial assistance.)

Senator Pell, once again a prominent figure in the legislative development of the bill, conceded that if the aid programs were not fully funded by Congress in the years to come, the expansion of eligibility to include more moderate income students might result in less assistance being available for low-income applicants. Budgetary issues also concerned Gerald Ford on October 12, 1976 when he signed the bill "with some reluctance because parts of the legislation are unwise and others contain authorization levels which we cannot realistically expect to meet." Specifically, Ford objected to the increased maximum BEOG award as a promise beyond the capacities of the federal budget. Whether springing from fear of scarce grants and loans due to an underfunded program or from fear of the budgetary impact of a fully funded

program, concerns over the bill's level of authorization were understandable; for Basic Educational Opportunity Grants, the single most expensive of the six core student aid programs, Congress provided no specific figure, only authorizing "such sums as are necessary."

The determination of "necessary sums"—i.e., the actual distribution of appropriations—reflects lack of Congressional/Administration consensus on higher education policy. BEOG had an especially difficult time establishing itself because of a stipulation in the authorizing legislation that no funds could be used for BEOG until the other programs were funded to at least a $653 million level and because the program was seen in part as a repudiation of the institution-based approach of the OE. Possibly BEOG's biggest liability in Congressional eyes was that the Nixon Administration pushed the program as a replacement for, rather than complement to, the congressionally popular SEOG. (The Administration's enthusiasm for BEOG was attributable to the fact that the program concentrated on the most needy students and eliminated the grant disparities among different states and different institutions, which marked SEOG and its loan counterpart NDSL.) As Table 13.1 reveals, the Nixon and Ford Administrations sought to budget no funds for SEOG and NDSL; these programs, however, enjoyed considerable support in Congress since they were the principal sources of middle class student assistance. Not only did Congress refuse to starve the institution-based programs, but it severely underfunded the Nixon favorite BEOG in the first years of its existence. Hence in 1973 the maximum grant the OE could award under BEOG was not $1,400 but $435.

The Ford Administration continued the Sisyphean effort to shift administration of grants and loans away from the campus-based SEOG and NDSL to the student-based BEOG and GSLP. Each year a few terse lines in the federal budget explained that the institutional programs merely duplicated BEOG and GSLP and required no funding. Although Congress continued to preserve SEOG and NDSL, the Republican Administration's campaign to establish the student-based approach as the core of federal assistance to higher education was not in vain. Congress gradually relented in its harshness toward BEOG, and after

**TABLE 13.1: Funding for Higher Education Programs
FY 1973–FY 1978
(in millions of dollars)**

	Fiscal 1973		Fiscal 1974		Fiscal 1975	
	Request	Appropriation	Request	Appropriation	Request	Appropriation
BEOG	622	122	1,300	650	1,300	660
SEOG	210	210	0	240	0	240
CWSP	270	270	250	300	250	NA*
GSLP	NA	NA	315	315	315	315
NDSL	24	269	6	347	0	NA
SSIG	NA	NA	0	19	0	NA
	Fiscal 1976		Fiscal 1977		Fiscal 1978	
BEOG	1,050	715	1,100	1,904	1,844	2,160
SEOG	0	240	0	250	0	270
CWSP	250	390	250	390	250	435
GSLP	452	452	400	357	281	281
NDSL	0	321	12**	310	15**	310
SSIG	44	44	44	60	44	63

*Figures not available.

**These requests were only for funds relating to the administration of past loans; no new capital funds were budgeted.

fiscal 1976, began to exceed Administration requests for this program. Similarly, only in fiscal 1977 did appropriations for GSLP fall below the budget request. More importantly, the philosophy behind these efforts to eliminate SEOG and NDSL—the conviction that these programs were inequitable since the OE distributed funds according to characteristics of states and of institutions rather than on a uniform basis of individual need—was revived in the Carter Administration in the decision to use BEOG and GSLP rather than their institutional counterparts as the vehicles for middle-income student assistance.

Finally, the two loan programs were the subject of growing concern as the frequency and extent of student defaults became apparent. Considerable legislative and administrative tinkering failed to narrow the gap between federal reimbursements on defaulted guaranteed loans and successful collections of these loans. Since evidence produced in congressional hearings had indicated that default rates were lower in states operating their own student guaranteed loan offices, several provisions of the Education Amendments of 1976 were designed to encourage states to set up such programs—for instance, the act mandated that a higher proportion of excess SSIG funds be targeted to states operating loan guarantee programs. Nonetheless, these provisions and efforts by the OE

to tighten up GSLP administration and monitoring produced few results. In 1977 a General Accounting Office report described the Office of Education collection system as a "clogged pipeline"[3] and summarized the dimensions of the problem:

> The Office of Education guaranteed four million student loans amounting to $4.5 billion through September 1976 and has paid out about $287 million to lending institutions because of student defaults.
>
> Through that date the office collected only $25 million; most of the defaulted loans still required collection. Collectors cannot handle their workloads, and the trend is toward even larger and less manageable workloads.[4]

The 95th Congress addressed one aspect of the problem in the Bankruptcy Revisions Act; this legislation would prohibit graduate-debtors from discharging their obligation by declaring bankruptcy for a period of five years after college completion. The bill (H.R. 8200) passed the House on February 1, 1978 but has not yet been considered by the Senate. It is unclear how many of the defaults will be affected by this provision. While some graduates have shielded themselves from loan collection, a larger number of the loans remain uncollected because of the difficulty of tracing hundreds of former students for whom the OE has no current addresses. Leo Kornfield, head of the OE's Bureau of Student Financial Assistance has said that the typical defaulter is not a classic "deadbeat" who has the money for repayment but is holding out:

> The defaulting student runs from the one who forgets he has a loan to be repaid to the one whose payments are so high compared to his income, that he has no choice but to default, to the one who has been induced to go to school, only to find out that he is ill-equipped and drops out, feeling cheated.[5]

In 1977 and 1978 the OE increased its efforts to trace defaulters. Some of its methods, such as cross-checking names of defaulters with federal payrolls, have produced positive results—in fact, 316 defaulters were discovered on the payroll of HEW itself. Nonetheless, the bad news continued to produce embarrassment. In February 1978 the OE revealed that NDSL, which many had thought relatively free from default violations compared to GSLP, actually had more than twice as many defaulters as the guaranteed loan program. NDSL defaults numbered 700,000 and amounted to $600 million compared with 300,000 GSLP defaults totaling $300 million.[6] Interestingly, the default issue has not resulted in an abandonment of the loan concept in federal aid. Although President Carter publicly castigated graduates who manufactured bankruptcies in order to avoid repayment, he gave GSLP a crucial role in his middle income assistance plan. Furthermore, advocates of tuition tax credits generally have not used the collection failures as ammunition in their attack on the Carter plan.

1978: MIDDLE INCOME ASSISTANCE AND THE FUTURE OF THE GRANTS AND LOAN METHOD

Events during the first several weeks of 1978 defined the contours of the higher education debate for the remainder of the 95th Congress and possibly for some time to come. In both houses, numerous bills were introduced which would provide tax credits of up to $500 for tuition at institutions of higher and vocational education and, in some of the proposals, for elementary and secondary school tuition as well.

Such proposals were by no means new. A higher education tax credit bill sponsored by Senator William Roth had passed the Senate on three previous occasions, only to be blocked in the House. In December 1977 a tax credit was struck from a larger tax bill in conference committee. In this session, however, there appeared to be more support for this approach than ever before. In January an amendment authored by Senators Moynihan and Packwood to H.R. 3946, a bill on the suspension of duties on wool, was considered to be the most viable of these proposals. (Moynihan and Packwood sought to bypass the House Ways and Means Committee, an obstacle to previous tax credit bills, by offering their proposal as an amendment to a House bill.) This plan would grant a credit for 50% of all tuition payments, up to $250, for higher and vocational education; two years later the maximum would rise to $500 and coverage would be extended to elementary and secondary school tuition.

On February 8 President Carter, a vehement opponent of tuition tax credits, countered with the Middle Income Student Assistance Act of 1978, a proposal to add $1.46 billion to the Administration's original FY 1979 budget request and to expand the existing student aid programs to include an estimated 263 million more recipients. Specifically, the proposal called for an additional $900 million for Basic Grants and raised the income ceiling from $15,000 to $25,000. The maximum grant would be set at $1,800; in the $16,000 to $25,000 range families would be eligible for a flat grant of $250. An additional $150 million was requested for the College Work Study Program and an additional $70 million for the Guaranteed Student Loan Program. Also, eligibility for federal interest subsidies was expanded to include families with incomes up to $40,000.

Both sides in the credit vs. aid controversy seem to share some new assumptions that reflect a shift in the public perception. More importantly, both sides feel that college costs are most burdensome and even prohibitive in the middle income category, and that the problem has become more serious in the past decade. On the other hand, there is a fair amount of satisfaction with the record of financial assistance to low income students. For instance, in introducing his proposal, President Carter remarked:

Our nation has long recognized our obligation to help lower income families in this educational area. Now we must increasingly take steps to help middle-income families as well.[7]

This attitude was echoed in the Senate Human Resources Committee report on the Carter proposal:

> In the past decade, the costs of sending a child to college have skyrocketed. Between 1967–76 the cost of sending a child to an average college has increased 77%. . . .
> It was the able children of the middle class who were unable to find any form of assistance except, possibly, loans to enable them to meet the staggering costs of college. Many promising careers were abandoned because of inability to seek further education.[8]

Similar statistics on increases in costs of both public and private institutions have been cited by advocates of tuition tax credits.

The severity of the problem faced by middle class families in meeting college costs is too complex a subject to address in these pages. However, income, college costs, and enrollment figures can indicate whether or not momentous changes have occurred in the middle income situation in the past ten years. The 77% increase in average college costs mentioned in the Senate Committee report is a misleading figure when stated alone: during the same period, average family income rose 88.6%.[9] Information from the Congressional Budget Office (Table 13.2) demonstrates that in absolute terms the financial situation of the middle class student has not changed appreciably over this period.

TABLE 13.2: Student Charges as a Percent of Median Family Income for Families with Dependents Aged 18–24

	1967	1975
Public school	12.9%	13.0%
Private school	26.8%	28.4%

Source: Congressional Budget Office, The Current Federal Role and Alternative Approaches *(Washington: GPO, February 1977), p. 58.*

Enrollment figures reveal a similar yet more disturbing story (Table 13.3).

TABLE 13.3: Enrollment by Family Income

Family Income (1975 dollars)	% of 18–24 Population Enrolled			
	Full-time		Part-time	
	1970	1975	1970	1975
Under $6,000	11.0%	12.5%	1.3%	2.7%
$6,000–8,999	13.4	11.5	2.5	3.2
$9,000–11,999	15.5	15.1	3.3	3.1
$12,000–14,999	20.8	19.7	4.6	4.7
$15,000–19,000	30.9	29.7	4.7	4.7
$20,000 or more	46.3	44.5	3.6	5.3

Source: Congressional Budget Office, The Current Federal Role and Alternative Approaches *(Washington: GPO, February 1977), p. 58.*

Not only has the rate of middle income enrollment not dropped significantly, but neither has the proportion of lower income youth matriculating increased during a period in which federal financial assistance for students has grown by billions of dollars.

There have always been two intended functions in federal higher education programs, as demonstrated by the different titles of the Carter proposal in the House and Senate—the Middle Income Student Assistance Act and the College Opportunity Act. These enrollment figures call into question the efficacy of the programs with respect to the latter goal—equalizing opportunity for higher education; there is no doubt that the programs have had impact on their concomitant function, easing the burden of college costs. Considering that enrollment rates for the families in the $15,000 to $40,000 range (the main beneficiaries of either the Carter or the tax credit plan) are already two to four times higher than for the lower income categories in this table, it would seem that the easing-the-burden function is also the primary thrust of these proposals. In fact, the tax credit plan is entirely independent of income-based need considerations. In any event, the adoption of the middle class as a principal target for college assistance, in whatever form, may be more indicative of a general change in perceptions than of any deterioration of that group's ability to meet educational costs.*

A second feature which cuts across the tax credit and middle income aid proposals is the absence of a strong institutional role. The tax credit, of course, would shift the process entirely away from the educational system; colleges would have no role whatsoever, and the Treasury Department rather than the OE would be the responsible federal agency. While Carter has not sought to eliminate SEOG and NDSL after the fashion of his predecessors, the great expansion of BEOG and GSLP will put the institutionally-based programs in a clearly secondary role. In short, BEOG has passed the trials of its shaky beginning in the 1972 legislation and the balance between the "basic" and "supplementary" programs may finally have been achieved. An indication of the current thought on the subject is the Senate Human Resources Committee's characterization of the aid system prior to the establishment of Basic Grants:

> . . . [T]he essential element in this process was that it was the institution, not the student, which was the focus of attention and decision-making. In too many cases, a student was forced to choose his college because funds were available, whereas, a preferred institution was unable to offer assistance.[10]

Whichever proposal is ultimately enacted, college financial aid offices will be less decisive in the overall picture of student aid.

Legislative Action

The Carter proposal was introduced in the Senate (S. 2539) by Claiborne Pell and in the House (H.R. 11274) by William Ford; the following day HEW officials testified in an unusual joint hearing of the Senate Human Resources Committee and the House Education and Labor Committee. In subsequent hearings the measure was also endorsed by several college presidents. The Carter package was reported out by the Senate committee on February 28 and by the

House committee March 14. The committees' products bore similar amendments. The Administration measure had not altered the BEOG formula by which the parental contribution is assessed as 20% of the first $5,000 of discretionary income (i.e., income above the poverty line) and 30% of any excess. Both committees proposed a flat 10.5% assessment rate for discretionary income. Under the Administration proposal, families of four in the $15,000 to $25,000 range would be eligible for flat $250 awards. As Table 13.4 demonstrates, the amended plan would allow

TABLE 13.4: Comparison of Presidential and Congressional Basic Grants Formulas

Income	S. 2539	President's Proposal
$6,000	$1,800	$1,800
$8,000	1,630	1,600
$10,000	1,450	1,270
$12,000	1,280	940
$15,000	1,020	250
$19,000	700	250
$21,000	540	250
$23,000	390	250
$24,000	310	250
$25,000	250	250
Total cost	$1.2 billion	$1 billion

grants to be graduated over that range. Table 13.5 compares the status quo with the program authorized by the Senate bill. Finally, rather than raise the ceiling on unsubsidized guaranteed loans to $40,000 per year, the committee bills would provide interest subsidies for all GSLP loans and remove the ceiling entirely.

Despite the speed with which the direct aid bill was cleared through the education committees, the legislation was by no means out of danger. Because of the popularity of both the tax credit and middle income assistance proposals, the crucial factor was time rather than votes. The competition between the two alternatives was a race rather than a debate. Most parties concurred that it was unthinkable that the nation could afford two "budget busters," yet it appeared unlikely that either proposal would be voted down on its own merits. Carter declared in a message

---

*Several years ago, various celebrated politicos bent to the mood of the times enough to include "obligatory sex scenes" in their novels. In this somewhat less interesting era, the "obligatory" item in political life is something called Proposition 13. (Another similarity between tax relief and sex is the popular belief that both originated in California.)

TABLE 13.5:   Basic Grants: Comparison of Congressional Program with Existing System

| | Existing Program | | | | |
| | Recipients | | Funds | | |
Income	Number (thousands)	Percent	Amount (millions)	Percent	Average Award
$0 to $5,300	464	21.1	$ 483	23.5	$1,041
$5,301 to $9,900	733	33.3	811	39.5	1,105
$9,901 to $15,900	745	33.8	624	30.4	838
$15,901 to $19,900	227	10.3	124	6.0	546
$19,901 to $26,500	35	1.6	12	0.6	343
$26,501 +	0	0.0	0	0.0	0
Total	2,204	100.0	$2,054	100.0	$ 934

| | Program Proposed by S. 2539 | | | | |
| | Recipients | | Funds | | |
Income	Number (thousands)	Percent	Amount (millions)	Percent	Average Award
$0 to $5,300	464	12.6	$ 483	14.9	$1,041
$5,301 to $9,900	735	20.0	837	25.8	1,139
$9,901 to $15,900	881	23.9	897	27.7	1,018
$15,901 to $19,900	627	17.0	505	15.6	805
$19,901 to $26,500	698	19.0	412	12.7	590
$26,501 +	276	7.5	106	3.3	384
Total	3,681	100.0	$3,240	100.0	$ 880

Source: Senate Human Resources Committee, "College Opportunity Act of 1978," Senate Report 95-643, February 2, 1978.

to Congress: "We cannot afford—and I will not accept —both a tuition tax credit and the increased student aid I have proposed."[11] Hence, which bill came up for consideration first became an immediate concern. On March 20, Representative Ford attempted to expedite passage of the amended Administration bill through a motion to "order a second"—that is, to suspend the rules and proceed to a vote on the bill. Ford's motion was defeated 218-156 and the bill was sent to the Rules Committee where Representative Delaney, an advocate of tuition tax credits, successfully resisted Ford's efforts to extricate the bill.

Meanwhile, tax credits gained momentum; the "frontrunner" among the credit bills proved to be a House bill, H.R. 12050, rather than the Moynihan-Packwood rider on the wool duty bill. During this time President Carter continued to seize opportunities to inveigh against the tax credit concept. His criticisms centered on three arguments: that it would fragment national education policy, that it would cost more than his own proposal, and most importantly that it

was not targeted toward those who needed it. The subject of cost was a confusing one in this context because the tax credit bill was constantly amended faster than Congressional Budget Office estimates could keep pace. However, attention was focused on the issue of the match between need and benefits. Carter characterized tax credits as "really a boon to the very affluent families."[12]

> It gives the credits to those who need them least and it makes the average parent, who is a working class person, pay for high tax benefits for families in a higher tax group who have their children in private schools.[13]

Carter and HEW officials contended that their bill would concentrate assistance on those in greatest need, such as families in $15,000 to $25,000 categories, who would be eligible for Basic Grants, while under the tax credit proposals relatively small awards, $250 or $500, would be dispensed to millions of families, including those in the highest income brackets. In addition, supporters of student aid in government and in the educational community expressed fears that adoption of tax credits this year might encourage cutbacks in funds for existing grant and loan programs in future years. Since the tax credit proposals were designed to be phased in over several years, their full impact on the federal budget was not anticipated until about fiscal 1981. Carter warned in March and April that he was likely to veto any tax credit bill that came across his desk.

The tax credit bills were encumbered by other political liabilities which to some seemed more serious than Presidential opposition. The middle income assistance was a fairly safe package in that it did not tend to excite debate on highly emotional issues other than government aid to education. In contrast, because in some of its stages of amendment H.R. 12050 applied to elementary and secondary schools as well as colleges and vocational institutions, religious and racial issues found their way to the stage just as they have in all the previous permutations of the debate over assistance to non-public schools and their students. More specifically, many supporters of the tax credit formula for higher education argued that its extension to elementary and secondary education would violate the establishment clause of the first amendment by helping pay tuition costs at schools operated by religious groups and would help subsidize resegregation by providing the means for whites to remove their children from public schools to segregated private ones. The House Ways and Means Committee struck the elementary and secondary education provisions of H.R. 12050 and on April 17 reported it out; the bill authorized a tax credit of 25% of the tuition up to $100 in fiscal 1978, $150 in 1979, and $250 in 1980. On June 1 the House reinserted elementary and secondary student aid by a vote of 209–194 and proceeded to pass the measure 237–158.

At this point the scenario of education legislation became even more confusing as a third crucial bill received consideration—the annual HEW appropriation bill. In the form that it reached the House floor, the bill set appropriations at the level that would be authorized by the Education and Labor Committee's version of the Middle Income Assistance Act, which remained tied up in the Rules Committee. During the debate on the bill, some tax credit advocates such as Representative Coughlin sought to turn Carter's "budget-busting" argument against him, holding that the nation could only afford one of the education assistance programs and that the House had already made its choice by its passage of tax credits earlier in June; yet these representatives did not move to cut the appropriations down to the level required by the OE programs in their current form. Nonetheless, an effort to slash some of the funds did materialize from an unexpected quarter—the Administration. Carter had criticized the House for exceeding his recommendations for BEOG funding, and on June 8 Representative Holland, apparently acting on the President's behalf, offered an amendment to slice $233 million from the appropriations. Representative Ford and others who had been carrying on the fight against tax credits and for middle income assistance saw this as a betrayal by the Carter Administration. As Representative Obey said:

> [If] the administration is supporting this amendment—and it is difficult to determine what they are supporting these days . . . that would in fact be a betrayal of every person in this House who, just a week ago, stuck with the President on the tuition tax credit proposal.[14]

The Holland amendment was defeated by a voice vote, and the House passed the appropriations bill. Table 13.6 is a comparison of 1978 higher education appropriations, the original FY 1979 budget request, the revisions made by the Administration for the Middle Income Assistance proposal, and the House product.

On August 4, two Senate committees acted on tax credit proposals. The Appropriations Committee issued a negative report on H.R. 3946, the rider on the wool duty bill, characterizing the tax credit concept as unsound and indicating support for Carter's direct aid plan: "The committee believes middle income students can best be assisted with their post-secondary education through the expansion of existing grant and loan programs in the Office of Education."[15] The bill was recommitted to the Finance Committee. Meanwhile, the Senate Finance Committee favorably reported out H.R. 12050, the bill which had passed the House, with several amendments. The tax credit formula was altered so that 50% rather than 24% of

TABLE 13.6:   Funds for Higher Education (millions of dollars)

	1978 Appropriations	Original 1979 Request	Revised Request	1979 House Appropriations
BEOG	$2,160	$2,140	$3,167	$3,400
SEOG	270	270	270	340
CWSP	435	450	600	520
GSLP	281	462	532	532
NDSL	310	304	304	311
SSIG	63	77	77	87

tuition was covered; the maximum credit was set at $250 for fiscal 1978 and $500 for fiscal 1980. The bill's most controversial feature, its extension to elementary and secondary school tuition, was left intact.

Late in August H.R. 12050 came up for consideration in the Senate. A very heated though ill-attended debate was carried on over three legislative days. Most of the time was consumed by consideration of an amendment by Senator Hollings to strike the elementary and secondary school aid. The proposal aroused intense emotions on both sides. Senator Hodges of Arkansas cited statistics on declining white public school enrollment in his state and characterized as immoral parents who abandoned the integrated public school system. Senator Moynihan defended the racial record of parochial schools and charged that much of the opposition to elementary and secondary tuition tax credits was fueled by anti-Catholic bigotry. On August 15 the Hollings amendment restricting tax credits to post-secondary education was adopted 56-41. Following the vote, the Senate rejected two amendments which would tilt the benefits away from upper income groups. Senator Metzenbaum, claiming that one billion dollars of the credit would go to families earning more than $40,000 per year, sought to begin reducing the credits at the $30,000 level and to eliminate them entirely at $40,000. Senator Long, arguing that "no one should be denied this tax credit because he is too poor" introduced a measure to give refunds to those whose incomes were too low to be taxed. Both amendments were voted down.

The remainder of the debate focused on the bill itself. There was considerable confusion even among the bill's proponents as to the expected distribution of benefits, presumably because the effects of removing the elementary and secondary tuition aid had not been assessed. Senator Roth stated that 78% of the benefits would go to families earning under $30,000 and 11% of those over $40,000. Cost estimates varied even more. Advocates of the Carter plan were in the uncomfortable position of recognizing that in the first year their plan would be more expensive than tax credits; however, since the level of tax credits was to be raised in subsequent years, the middle income assistance proposal was less of a budget drain in the long run. Senator Javits cited Congressional Budget Office estimates that S. 2539 (the Carter plan) would cost $1.464 billion in fiscal 1979 and $1.630 billion in fiscal 1983; the figures for H.R. 12050 would be $667 million in 1979 and $2.88 billion in 1983. Finally, there was confusion as to the public's preferences in the matter. A Roper Poll commissioned by H&R Block during the summer had shown that 54% favored direct aid to students or colleges while 23% favored a tuition tax credit. However, in the spring both a *New York Times*/CBS survey and a Gallop Poll had indicated just as strong a preference for tax credits. The Senate passed the tax credit bill by a not-quite veto proof margin of 65-27. The bill was then sent to conference committee to be reconciled with the House version which had a less generous tax credit formula and, of course, contained credits for elementary and secondary school tuition.

That the nation could not afford both education aid proposals had been one of the few points of concurrence from the beginning of this scenario in February. Nonetheless, in a less dramatic legislative session on August 26, the day after the adoption of the tax credits act, the Senate passed S. 2539, the "College Opportunity Act of 1978." Senator Pell lauded the income features of the bill, maintaining that 89% of the benefits would go to families earning less than $25,000, 64% to families in the $15,000 to $25,000 range. He also noted that the program's administration did not require the creation of any new bureaucracy, but only, as he termed it, a change in the computer formula at the OE.

As fall began the overall status of the middle income assistance plan was somewhat comical. The House had appropriated funds for the program but had not adopted it since it remained captive in the Rules Committee, while the Senate had authorized it but had not yet considered the HEW appropriations bill. Ultimately, the middle income aid bill was still the passive passenger on a seesaw with tuition tax credits. Despite the Senate's almost back-to-back passage of both bills, no one really wanted both to become law. When the Senate acted on the HEW appropriations bill on September 27, it hedged its bets by funding GSLP to the level necessary for lifting the income ceilings on eligibility and interest subsidies but appropriating only $2,627 million for BEOG. This would be more than enough for the program in its existing form but would permit only a fraction of the authorized assistance to go to middle income students during the first year. It was felt that this way there would be enough money in the federal budget in case both bills survived.

The debate over elementary and secondary tuition credits resurfaced in the efforts of conferees to reconcile the House and Senate versions. The conference committee reported out a bill limiting tax credits to postsecondary education. On October 12, in what was probably the single most damning action to tuition tax credits for this session, an obstinate House adopted by a vote of 207-185 a motion by Representative William Gradison to recommit the bill to conference committee with instructions that elementary and secondary aid be reinserted.

Like many of the other items of congressional business (e.g., the energy package, the tax cut) which had been subjects of prolific debate on and off the floor but little definitive action, the controversy over how to provide assistance to middle income students was resolved in marathon sessions in both houses beginning on the morning of Saturday, October 14 and adjourning Sunday night. Two last hopes for tuition tax credits were shattered. Moynihan and other conferees failed in an attempt to sell the Senate on a new compromise which would extend credits to high school but not elementary school costs; the bill was again recommitted to conference where, given the imminent adjournment of the session, it died. An effort was made to attach the Senate version of tax credits (i.e., for college education only) to the mammoth tax cut bill which was occupying much of Congress's and the public's attention; however, conferees decided not to jeopardize the tax cut legislation which Carter had already criticized for its largesse to the wealthy by including in it a proposal to which he was even more vehemently opposed.

Meanwhile late Saturday night the House version of the middle income assistance plan, which had been languishing for months in the Rules Committee, virtually galloped to ratification. A motion by Representative Dodd to permit consideration of H.R. 11274 was adopted 342-38. An amendment by Representative Erlenborn to restore the $40,000 cap on interest subsidies was voted down 301-86. After these hurdles were cleared, the House adopted the bill by a voice vote. This passage, however, was subsequently vacated in a complicated set of actions designed to avoid the necessity of a conference reconciliation of H.R. 11274 and S. 2539. Instead, S. 2539 was called up on the House floor and amended to conform to the House language; after this too was adopted by a voice vote, it was returned to the Senate where the House amendments were accepted, completing congressional action on the bill.

Senate-House differences on appropriations for the higher education programs were not quite so comfortably resolved from the perspective of middle income aid advocates. The product of the two-day session bore the mark of the Senate's Janus-like concern lest funds be required for both proposals. Table 13.7 summarizes the transformation of the OE programs during 1978. The authorizing legislation provides that funds may be applied to middle class grants only after the lower income portion of the program has been funded. Hence, unless a supplemental appropriations bill is passed early in 1979, few middle income students will benefit from BEOG, although all students, regardless of income, will now be eligible for GSLP loans and interest subsidies. Conceivably, as in the case of the original BEOG program, middle income assistance may have to fight for its survival for several years before it is fully funded.

**TABLE 13.7: Higher Education Funding
(millions of dollars)**

	FY 1978	Carter Request	FY 1979
BEOG	$2,160	$3,167	$2,627
SEOG	270	270	340
CWSP	435	600	550
GSLP	281	532	521
NDSL	310	304	311
SSIG	63	77	77

On the horizon for federal aid to higher education, there seems to be continued emphasis on the latter of the two functions noted earlier—equalizing opportunity and easing the burden. Considering that the 96th Congress will be born out of an election year in which Republicans and Democrats have climbed over one another in promising how little government will do, the idea of tuition tax credits is unlikely to die. The OE and the higher education community may have to fight to keep all the grant-loan programs on their feet. Meanwhile, Senator Kennedy has proposed that the existing system be replaced by a "tuition advance fund" which would possibly cover all college students. In the course of all this discussion, there is little agitation over the enrollment figures cited earlier. In light of the fact that the billions spent by the federal government in the past ten years on aid to low and moderate income students have not genuinely altered the class pattern of college enrollment, possibly it will eventually be decided that the goal (if it remains a goal) of erasing or mitigating the effects of income on educational attainment as well as success in later life must be pursued through some method other than financial aid. For the time being, however, the middle class is perceived as the nation's ailing child, and the decision has been made to preserve OE grants-and-loans as the instrument of redress.

REFERENCES

1. For other accounts see *National Journal*, May 22, 1971, p. 1085 and March 18, 1972, p. 472. See also Lawrence E. Gladieux and Thomas R. Wolanin, *Congress and the Colleges,* Lexington, Mass., 1976.
2. Cheit, Earl R. *The New Depression in Higher Education: A Study of the Financial Conditions in 41 Colleges and Universities,* Carnegie Commission on Higher Education, 1970.
3. Jellema, Earl W. *The Red and the Black,* Association of American Colleges, 1971.
4. Newman, Frank *et al., Report on Higher Education,* Department of HEW, Washington, D.C., 1971.
5. Joint Economic Committee, *A Compendium of Papers: The Economics and Financing of Higher Education in the United States,* Committee Print, 1969. See also David S. Mundel, *An Analysis of Federal Subsidies to Undergraduate Education*, Reprint Series, Harvard University, 1972.
6. U.S. Department of Health, Education, and Welfare, *Toward a Long-Range Plan for Federal Support for Higher Education*, Washington, D.C., 1969 and, *Quality and Equality: New Levels of Federal Responsibility for Higher Education,* Berkeley: The Carnegie Commission on Higher Education, 1968.
7. *Educational Opportunity Bank,* Washington, President's National Science Advisory Committee, 1967.
8. King, Lauriston R. *The Washington Lobbyists for Higher Education*, Lexington, Mass., 1975.
9. Excerpts in *Chronicle of Higher Education,* October 13, 1969. See also John P. Mallon, "Current Proposals for Federal Aid to Higher Education," American College Testing Program, 1970.

REFERENCES TO THE SEQUEL

1. Carnegie Council on Policy Studies in Higher Education, *The Federal Role in Post-Secondary Education: Unfinished Business, 1975–80* (Washington, D.C.: U.S. GPO, 1975), p. 25.
2. *Ibid.,* p. 27; *Federal Student Assistance: A Review of Title IV of the Higher Education Act* (Hanover, N.H., April 1975), p. 12.
3. U.S. Government Accounting Office, "Collection Efforts Not Keeping Pace with Growing Number of Defaulted Student Loans" (Washington, D.C.: U.S. GPO, August 11, 1977), p. 21.
4. *Ibid.,* Introduction.
5. Leo Kornfield quoted in Jean Conley, "HEW's Post-Graduate Problem," *National Journal*, December 31, 1977, pp. 2009–2011.
6. *Chronicle of Higher Education,* February 27, 1978.
7. President Jimmy Carter, White House briefing, February 8, 1978, *Compendium of Presidential Documents.*
8. Senate Human Resources Committee, "College Opportunity Act of 1978," Senate Report 95-643, February 28, 1978, p. 2.
9. U.S. Census Bureau information cited in Rochell Stanfield, "The Taxpayers' Revolt, Part II, Education Aid for Everybody?" *National Journal*, April 1, 1978, p. 510.
10. Senate Human Resources Committee, *op. cit.,* p. 3.
11. President Carter, Message to Congress, February 28, 1978, *Compendium of Presidential Documents.*
12. President Carter, Question and Answer Session with College Editors, March 4, 1978.
13. President Carter, press conference, April 11, 1978.
14. Rep. Obey, *Congressional Record,* June 8, 1978, p. H5169.
15. Senate Appropriations Committee, "Tuition Tax Credit Act," Senate Report 95-1065, August 4, 1978.

14

High Mountain Sheep Dam

The Hells Canyon reach of the Snake River is a series of unusual geological formations extending approximately 200 miles along the Oregon-Idaho border. It has been described as "one of the most scenic streams to be found anywhere and in an extraordinary natural environment." In a 1968 letter, Secretary of Agriculture Orville Freeman characterized the region as follows:

The Snake River, in its present free-flowing state, is an awesome stream consisting of a series of swift white-water rapids flowing into deep pools in one of the deepest canyons in the United States. The immediate shoreline is principally a series of sheer rock faces dropping almost vertically into the river or stretches lined with great boulders interspersed by occasional sand bars in back eddies. There is no doubt that this stretch of the Snake River represents one of the last of this country's great rivers that has been little changed by man and still challenges his best efforts to tame. It represents a scene of ruggedness probably not equalled anywhere in the United States today.

He later added:

The canyon of the Snake River is the locality in the United States having the greatest elevation difference between the canyon bottom and the tops of the immediately adjacent rim crags in the Seven Devils Area. There is no way that the some 76 miles which encompass the swift water portions of this canyon can be mitigated or replaced. While there is archaeological significance and recreational significance in the canyon area for recreation associated with the free-flowing river, the outstanding natural resource is the canyon itself with the free-flowing river in it. This cannot be replaced nor is it duplicated elsewhere, in the country.

However, in addition to its scenic value, the canyon also offers "perhaps the best remaining hydroelectric site in the coterminous United States." Because of the volume of water flowing in the reach, its narrowness, the steepness of the canyon sides, and the excellent foundation conditions, there are a number of attractive sites for the development of hydroelectric and related water storage facilities." Half of the canyon was flooded by three dams in the late 1950s (Hells Canyon, Brownlee, and Oxbow dams), and other dams are proposed by the Federal Government at Asotin and by the Pacific Northwest Power Company (later joined by the Washington Public Power Supply System) at High Mountain Sheep. (See Map 14.1.)

The preservation of the canyon as a wilderness area and its further development for hydroelectric power are clearly incompatible*; and the incompatibility has created a conflict involving electric power companies, environmental groups, Congress, the Federal Power Commission** (the agency with responsibility for approving such projects), and other federal agencies. This case examines some economic aspects of the conflict over the proposed High Mountain Sheep Dam project. The case includes a brief description of the Federal Power Commission, a short history of the project and the regional system of which it would be part, and a series of questions comparable to those that might have confronted FPC staff analyzing the project.

---

*Proponents of development contend that the scenic, recreational and other values of the canyon wilderness are overrated. The Pacific Northwest Power Company, for example, argued that: "There is the misconception that grows from generalized descriptions of Hells Canyon—the 'deepest' on the North American continent—'steep walls'—'wild and uncultivated'—'remote and lonely.' It is remote and wild, however, principally because it has little to offer. It is in no sense a spectacular gash like the Grand Canyon of Colorado.

**The Federal Power Commission was abolished in 1977 with the creation of the Department of Energy. Most of its functions were transferred to the Department's Federal Energy Regulatory Commission.

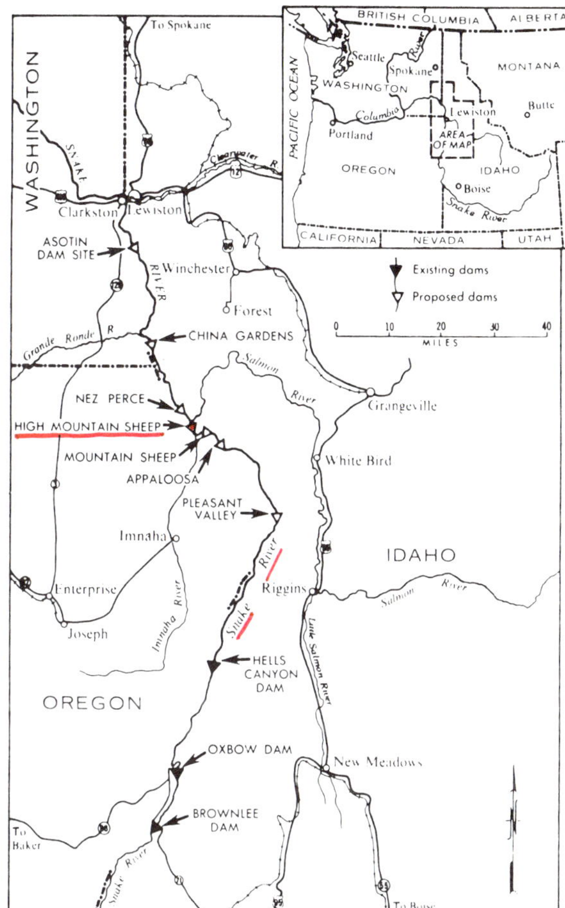

MAP 14.1:   Sites for Proposed Development of Hells Canyon

Source: Krutilla and Fisher, p. 93.

THE FEDERAL POWER COMMISSION: THE DECISION-MAKING STRUCTURE

The Federal Power Commission is an independent agency, similar in structure to the Federal Trade Commission and the Interstate Commerce Commission, with responsibility for setting rates on power sold in interstate commerce (in effect, most wholesale power sales), for regulating accounting practices of and securities issued by electric power companies, and for approving sites for nearly all hydroelectric power plants.

The FPC was originally established in 1920 as a progressive regulatory response "to deal with the ever expanding activities of the producers of electric current" and the technological developments that made hydroelectric power economically feasible. It was seen at that time as an alternative to public ownership. Through the 1920s, the Commission consisted of the Secretaries of War, Agriculture, and the Interior. Though it was powerful on paper, its close connections with the Administration limited its independence, particularly after the Republicans took office in 1921. In 1930, it was changed into an independent agency, as a partial response to sporadic demands for public power and regulatory reform throughout the 1920s, including Senator George Norris' (R-Nebraska) advocacy of public power on the Tennessee and Columbia Rivers and Governor Gifford Pinchot's (R-Pennsylvania) proposals for stiff new state regulation in 1928.

At present and as provided under the 1930 law, there are five Commissioners including the Chairman, all of whom are appointed by the President with the advice and consent of the Senate for staggered five-year terms. The Federal Power Act places certain limits on the President's power of appointment, providing:

> Not more than three of the commissioners shall be appointed from the same political party. No person in the employ of or holding any official relation to any licensee or to any person, firm, association, or corporation engaged in the generation, transmission, distribution, or sale of power, or owning stock or bonds thereof, or who is in any manner pecuniarily interested therein, shall enter upon the duties of or hold the office of commissioner. (16 U.S.C. 792)

To regulate the interstate sale of electric energy, the Federal Power Commission is empowered to divide the country into regional districts "for the voluntary interconnection and coordination of facilities for the generation, transmission, and sale of electric energy," with each district embracing "an area which . . . can economically be served by such interconnected and coordinated electric facilities." (16 U.S.C. 824a (a)) The FPC was also given the authority to require the interconnection of transmission facilities

for the sale or exchange of energy, provided that the interconnection did not cause the parties to expand generating capacity for this purpose alone. (16 U.S.C. 824a (b)) Rates for electric power in interstate commerce, in effect for wholesale electric power, are also under the jurisdiction of the FPC, which has the power to forbid rate discrimination between classes of consumers (16 U.S.C. 824d (b)) and to set "just and reasonable" rates for the sale of electric power in interstate commerce. (16 U.S.C. 824d (a) and 824d (e)) The FPC may also set standards for the issuing of securities by electric power companies operating where no state standards apply (16 U.S.C. 824c); may approve or disapprove mergers between electric power companies (16 U.S.C. 824b); and may set uniform accounting practices for capital depreciation by electric utilities. (16 U.S.C. 824g)

In addition, FPC approval is required for non-federal construction of hydroelectric facilities on nearly all U.S. waters. The FPC is empowered to issue preliminary permits and:

> To issue licenses to citizens of the United States, or to any association of such citizens or to any corporation organized under the laws of the United States or any State thereof, or to any State or municipality for the purpose of constructing, operating and maintaining dams, water conduits, reservoirs, power houses, transmission lines, or other project works necessary or convenient for the development and improvement of navigation and for the development, transmission, and utilization of power across, along, from or in any of the streams or other bodies of water over which Congress has jurisdiction under its authority to regulate commerce with foreign nations and among the several States (including the Territories), or for the purpose of utilizing the surplus water or water power from any government dam. (16 U.S.C. 797 (e))

The Federal Power Act provides that licenses issued for power development on special reservations of public land (e.g., military bases, Indian reservations) must also be approved by the Secretary of the relevant department as consistent with the specified use of the land. Furthermore, if power production involves effects (either positive or negative) on navigation, the approval of the Chief of Engineers of the

Army Corps of Engineers and the Secretary of the Army must be obtained. The Army Corps of Engineers may offer assistance and/or pay partial costs of private dam projects where navigation benefits would result from construction. The Act further requires the FPC to give "preference to applications . . . by states and municipalities provided the plans . . . are equally well adapted" to the site as those of a private applicant. (16 U.S.C. 800(a)) The FPC is also required to deny a license and to report to Congress if it believes that the project would be better developed by the federal government than by the applicant. (16 U.S.C. 800(b))

Before applying to the FPC for a license, the applicant may first obtain a three-year preliminary permit which authorizes the applicant to undertake studies of the project and which constitutes a kind of option on the site, precluding the licensing of any other applicant for the three-year period. When a final application for license is made to the FPC, it must include "such maps, plans, specifications, and estimates of cost as may be required for a full understanding of the proposed project." (16 U.S.C. 802(a))

The Federal Power Commission may approve, disapprove, or amend a proposal submitted by an applicant by a majority vote of the Commissioners. Most decisions of the Commission are in fact made the basis of staff reports, with only really major projects subject to an evidentiary hearing process. The legal criteria for approving a project are:

That the project adopted, including the maps, plans, and specifications, shall be such as in the judgment of the Commission will be best adapted to a comprehensive plan for improving or developing a waterway or waterways for the use or benefit of interstate or foreign commerce, for the improvement and utilization of water-power development, and for other beneficial public uses, including recreational purposes, and if necessary in order to secure such plan, the Commission shall have authority to require the modification of any project and of the plans and specifications of the project before approval. (16 U.S.C. 803(a))

The Regional Power System

Map 14.2 shows the FPC power supply areas and regions. High Mountain Sheep Dam, if constructed, would provide power to Region VII, and to a lesser extent, through interconnections, to Region VIII. The power supply in Region VII is already largely hydroelectric; as is apparent from Table 14.1, water power furnishes approximately 90% of the kilowatt hours (kwh)* of electricity produced by electric utilities in the five principal states comprising Region VII. By contrast, only about 15% of the power produced in the nation as a whole is hydroelectric.

TABLE 14.1: Power Production in 1972 by Means of Production

	Hydroelectric (thousands of kwh)	Fuels (thousands of kwh)
Montana	631,230	144,416
Utah	86,302	181,158
Idaho	850,368	4
Washington	7,063,361	781,596
Oregon	2,292,019	27,661
Total (5 states)	10,923,280	1,134,835

Also in contrast with most of the nation is the large role played by government power in the Region VII system. Development of power in the Pacific Northwest has been accompanied by a vigorous debate between public and private power advocates; the government's Grand Coulee and Bonneville dams, for example, were controversial installations when first built in the 1930s and 1940s. After bitter battles over licensing before the FPC, a mixed system has evolved with public and private power coexisting more or less peacefully. The principal power developer in the region has been the federal government, principally through the Army Corps of Engineers, the Bureau of Reclamation, and the Bonneville Power Administration (an independent agency responsible for the production and sale of power from Bonneville Dam and other Columbia River projects). Smaller developments are operated by other federal agencies (e.g., the National Park Service and the Bureau of Indian Affairs), by municipalities (the largest being Spokane and Tacoma, Washington, and Eugene, Oregon), and by Rural Electrification Administration (REA) cooperatives. In the late 1950s, REA cooperatives and municipalities in Washington joined to form the Washington Public Power Supply System, to share

---

*A kilowatt hour is a measure of electric energy equal to one kilowatt of power produced or consumed continuously for one hour.

MAP 14.2:   Electric Power Supply Areas

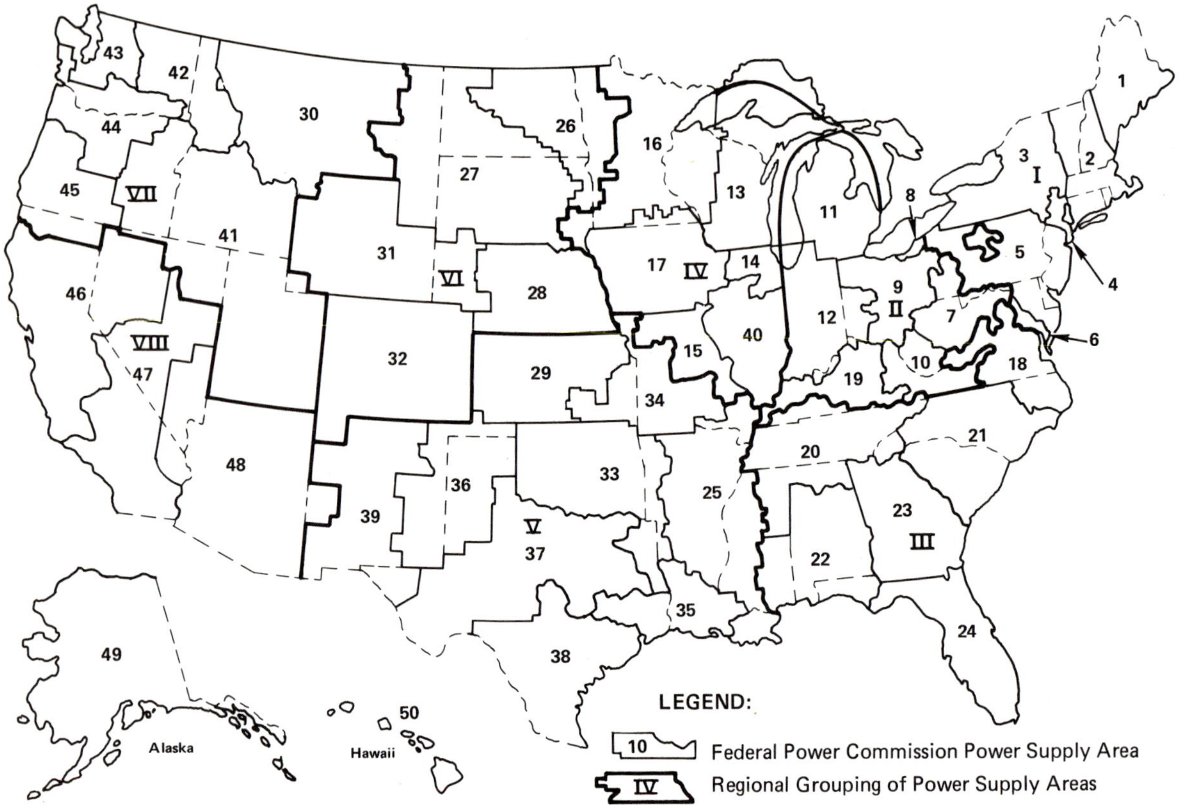

the burden of expensive new investment in hydroelectric facilities. Finally, there is a network of investor-owned utility companies. The three largest in the Pacific Northwest—Puget Sound Power and Light, Pacific Power and Light, and Portland General Electric—have joined with the Idaho Power Company in a consortium, the Pacific Northwest Power Company (PNPC), to build hydroelectric projects. PNPC is the main applicant for the license to construct High Mountain Sheep Dam.

In the early 1960s the Washington Public Power Supply System (WPPSS) contested PNPC's application for a license before the FPC, arguing that as a municipality, it—not a private company—should be granted the license under the Federal Power Act. In the mid-1960s, however, WPPSS agreed to a joint application and division of power with PNPC. Also, in the licensing hearings of the early 1960s, Secretary of the Interior Stuart Udall argued that, if High Mountain Sheep were to be developed at all, the federal government should develop it, to insure orderly regional marketing and to better protect migrating fish. Thus, in this case, the issue of private versus public power is still alive.

The High Mountain Sheep Dam Project

In the 1940s, the Army Corps of Engineers conducted a study of the Columbia River and its tributaries and recommended the eventual construction of several dam projects. Three in the upper reaches of Hells Canyon (Hells Canyon, Oxbow, and Brownlee dams) were completed in the middle and late 1950s and inundated approximately half the canyon. In its plans for later years, the Corps recommended construction of two more dams in the lower part of Hells Canyon, at Asotin and Nez Perce, respectively about 40 and 10 miles downstream from the High Mountain Sheep site. (The construction of Nez Perce would preclude building High Mountain Sheep and vice versa.) If these dams were constructed, the remainder of the canyon would become reservoirs.

The next step was taken by the Pacific Northwest Power Company, which applied to the Federal Power Commission on March 31, 1958, for a preliminary permit leading to a license* to construct one of two projects, either two dams at Mountain Sheep and Pleasant Valley, which together would supply 1,570 megawatts (MW) of capacity, increasing over time to 2,735 MW, or a single high dam at the High Mountain Sheep site, providing 1,400 MW of peak capacity and 600 MW of base load output. (This is a large capacity for a single station. The peak capacity could provide for 74% of the peak demand of the area served by Boston Edison in 1974, and the base load would provide approximately 51% of the total 1974 sales of electricity by Boston Edison.) By 1960, PNPC had eliminated Mountain Sheep–Pleasant Valley as uneconomical and was supporting the High Mountain Sheep site. At that time, High Mountain Sheep also had the reluctant support of some conservation groups, such as the Izaak Walton League, which considered it politically impossible to prevent dam construction in Hells Canyon and regarded High Mountain Sheep as a lesser environmental evil (presenting fewer impediments to migrating fish) than the Asotin site proposed by the Corps of Engineers.

Meanwhile, the hearing process for High Mountain Sheep Dam began. On October 21, 1959, the FPC asked for the comments of the Secretary of the Interior but received no response until March 15, 1961, when Secretary Udall wrote stating that a license should not be issued until the problem of damage to anadromous fish (salmon and steelhead) could be corrected. In November, 1961, he further wrote of wildlife losses:

Several thousand acres of mule deer range would be inundated and there would be a moderate reduction in the number of deer as a result of loss of range. There would be losses of upland game, fur animals, and waterfowl. Reservoir margins would be barren and unattractive to all wildlife groups. Waterfowl use of the reservoir would be insignificant. There does not appear to be any feasible means of mitigating wildlife losses.

On June 28, 1962, the hearing record was closed, but was reopened shortly thereafter to permit Secretary Udall to submit material suggesting that the project should be built federally if at all. Udall claimed that the power from High Mountain Sheep Dam would not be needed by the regional system until 1972–73 and that its sale by private corporations before that time would adversely affect the Bonneville Power Administration. A secondary argument considered environmental issues, stating that "federal development would provide greater flexibility and protection in the management of fish resources." On October 8, 1962, however, the hearing examiner issued a decision licensing PNPC to construct High Mountain Sheep Dam. Secretary Udall asked the full Commission for leave to intervene and file exceptions to the hearing examiner's decision, but after hearing Udall's evidence, the FPC sustained the examiner and issued the license on February 5, 1964.

Secretary Udall appealed the decision to the courts and in 1967, the Supreme Court ruled 6–2 that the FPC had violated Sections 7 and 10 of the Federal Power Act (16 U.S.C. 800 and 803) by not closely examining both Secretary Udall's claim that power should be provided federally if at all and the various environmental issues, particularly the value of non-development. The decision provided that the FPC must rehear the case to consider these issues. (*Udall v. Federal Power Commission et al.*, 387 U.S. 428ff) Justice Douglas, writing the majority opinion, castigated the FPC for not adequately dealing with the issue of federal power development, and, more importantly, for ignoring "the question whether any dam should be constructed."

The issues of whether deferral of construction would be more in the public interest than immediate construction and whether preservation of the reaches of the river affected would be more

---

*High Mountain Sheep Dam comes under FPC jurisdiction because: (1) a portion of the Snake River is navigable, from its confluence with the Columbia River to Lewiston, Idaho; (2) the dam would be constructed across a state boundary between Oregon and Idaho; and (3) much of the land of the proposed site is in a national forest.

desirable and in the public interest than the proposed development are largely unexplored in the record.

The ruling noted that Sec. 10(a) of the Federal Power Act (16 U.S.C. 803(a)) requires the FPC to consider those projects "best adapted to a comprehensive plan of improving or developing a waterway . . . and for other beneficial public uses including recreational purposes" and said:

> The objective of protecting "recreational purposes" means more than that the reservoir created by the dam will be the best one possible or practical from a recreational viewpoint. There are already eight lower dams on this Columbia River system and a ninth one authorized, and if the Secretary is right in fearing that this additional dam would destroy the waterway as a spawning ground for anadromous fish or seriously impair that function, the project is put in an entirely different light. The importance of salmon and steelhead in our outdoor life as well as in commerce is so great that there certainly comes a time when their destruction might necessitate a halt in so-called "improvement" or "development" of waterways. The destruction of anadromous fish in our western waters is so notorious that we cannot believe Congress through the present Act authorized their ultimate demise.

The opinion also noted congressional efforts to pass the Anadromous Fish Act of 1965 and the Wild and Scenic Rivers Act of 1967 as expressing congressional intent that the FPC must consider non-developmental issues rather than assume that "the Federal Power Act commands the immediate construction of as many projects as possible."

On the urgency of the project, Justice Douglas' opinion examined the need for power and took issue with the Commission's conclusions that " '[o]f more significance . . . than the regional power situation are the load and resources of the [Pacific Northwest Power Company] companies themselves,' which could use the power in the near future." The opinion then summarized the court's position as follows:

> The question whether the proponents of a project "will be able to use" the power supplied is relevant to the issue of the public interest. So too is the regional need for the additional power. But the inquiry should not stop there. A license under the Act empowers the licensee to construct, for its own use and benefit, hydroelectric projects utilizing the flow of navigable waters and thus, in effect, to appropriate water resources from the public domain. The grant of authority to the Commission to alienate federal water resources does not, of course, turn simply on whether the project will be beneficial to the licensee. Nor is the test solely whether the region will be able to use the additional power. The test is whether the project will be in the public interest. And that determination can be made only after an exploration of all issues relevant to the public interest, including future power demand and supply, alternate sources of power, the public interest in preserving reaches of wild rivers and wilderness areas, the preservation of anadromous fish for commercial and recreational purposes, and the protection of wildlife. The need to destroy the river as a waterway, the desirability of its demise, the choices available to satisfy future demands for energy—these are all relevant to a decision under §7 and §10 but they were largely untouched by the Commission.

In compliance with the Court's directive, the FPC then reheard the case, amassing a voluminous record of conflicting opinion over a period of almost four years, from 1968 to 1971.

EXERCISE*

You are an FPC staff member who has commissioned consultants to search the hearing record, visit the site, speak to officials of PNPC and to federal and state officials concerned with administering non-developmental (largely recreational) uses of Hells Canyon, and to construct suitable data for a cost-benefit analysis of the High Mountain Sheep Dam project.

The analysts assume that a power plant of equivalent capacity to High Mountain Sheep will be necessary in the near future and will be built. They therefore do not attempt to measure the total benefit of the electric power since that power will be furnished

*Much of the material on which the exercises are based is drawn from John V. Krutilla and Anthony C. Fisher, *The Economics of Natural Environments: Studies in the Valuation of Commodity and Amenity Resources,* published for Resources for the Future, Inc., by the Johns Hopkins University Press (Baltimore, 1975).

whether High Mountain Sheep is built or not. They also assume that there will be no significant change in electric rates if either High Mountain Sheep or an alternative is built.

Your aim is to decide whether the project should be constructed, using their evidence as a starting point. You will first undertake a cost-benefit analysis of the project. The consultants' report to you raises five analytical issues. These issues are reflected in the five questions that follow. You should first prepare a work sheet containing the answers to these questions with *brief* (several sentences at most) answers to the essay questions. This worksheet will be submitted to assist the hearing examiner and the commissioners in their decision.

Then, you should prepare a concise (no more than five pages) lucid memo to the hearing examiner and the commissioners supporting or opposing construction of the project. This memorandum requires no additional research and should use information gathered in your worksheet. However, you need not feel constrained by the information or methodological approach used in your cost-benefit analysis. In particular, to defend your position on substantive issues, your memorandum should indicate the extent to which you believe cost-benefit analysis is appropriate in this situation and should briefly discuss any methodological issues which you feel limit its usefulness. (For example, most studies of this type do not introduce technological change. Do you think it was handled well here?)

(1) The analysts have supplied data on costs and benefits for five different discount rates, including the estimates in Table 14.2 for average annual costs of the project. *What is the present value of the cost of the project, given a 50-year life span and assuming 1976 as year zero? Justify your choice of a discount rate.* Tables for finding present values given various discount rates are attached as Appendix A. (All costs and benefits given in this exercise are expressed in thousands of dollars.)

(2) The benefit from building a hydroelectric plant rather than a thermal plant* is the amount of resources saved in generating a given quantity of electricity by hydroelectric means as compared to the least-cost thermal alternative. It is thus a measure of cost savings.

Electric power production is characterized in general by two forms of cost: capacity, or fixed cost (the amortized cost of the power station plus other fixed items like insurance and taxes), which varies with plant size but not with the rate of plant utilization; and fuel costs, which vary directly with the number of kilowatt hours of electricity produced (except for nuclear plants where the relationship is more complex). The cost savings—i.e., benefits—attributable to High Mountain Sheep Dam are thus the difference between the capacity and fuel costs of the regional electric system with High Mountain Sheep Dam and with a thermal alternative of equal capacity.

(a) The annual capacity cost (i.e., annual fixed cost) of the High Mountain Sheep Dam varies with discount rates. The Pacific Northwest Power Company has also supplied estimates of the annual fixed cost of

---

*A thermal power plant produces electricity by using either fossil fuels or nuclear energy to convert water into steam. The steam then drives turbines which produce electricity, in effect, converting heat energy into mechanical energy and then into electric energy. Hydroelectric plants directly use mechanical energy of swiftly flowing rivers to drive turbines and produce electricity without fuel costs.

TABLE 14.2

Interest Rate	3%	6%	8%	10%	12%
Annual fixed costs (amortization over 50 years, insurance, state and local taxes)	$13,443	$20,445	$25,979	$32,109	$38,601
Operation, maintenance and administration	2,328	2,328	2,328	2,328	2,328
Transmission of power	4,529	6,398	7,644	8,894	10,136
Total	$20,300	$29,171	$35,951	$43,331	$51,065

constructing a nuclear plant with the same capacity as High Mountain Sheep Dam at the present time. (The nuclear plant has a project life of approximately 30 years but the figures below reflect estimates for capacity replacement through 50 years. See pages 318 and 319 for an explanation of these estimates.)

Interest Rate	Capacity Cost of Nuclear Plant
3%	$14,899
6%	$22,283
8%	$27,683
10%	$33,506
12%	$38,305

(i) *Therefore, assuming no future change in the cost of building nuclear plants, what would be the annual capacity benefit for the High Mountain Sheep Dam project?*

(ii) However, technological change improving the efficiency of electric power generation is expected to occur over the 50-year life of the High Mountain Sheep Dam. This change will most likely involve improvements in capital equipment which would cause the real cost per watt of new capacity to decrease. Any plant built to replace the thermal alternative at the end of its 30-year life would be equipped with this technology. *How would expectations of technological change affect present projections of future capacity benefits?*

(b) Since hydroelectric plants use no fuel, they offer obvious fuel cost benefits over other types of power plants. The fuel savings benefits of a hydroelectric project depend upon both the demand for power and the capacities and varying fuel utilization efficiencies of different thermal plants in the entire electric power system. To understand the fuel savings benefit, one must understand the difference between peak and off-peak demand. The peak demand for an electric power system is the highest rate of demand (usually described over a period of a year) for power sold by that system. The annual peak for most power systems occurs in a very hot summer week. At this time, the system is using virtually all of its power-generating capacity and is buying power from other regional systems not experiencing peak conditions. There is a lesser peak in the winter* and also smaller daily fluctuations with system peaks around 4 to 8 PM

in the winter and earlier in the day in the summer. Off-peak demand is defined as demand at other than peak conditions.

The mathematical expression of the fuel cost of an electric power system—as opposed to a single plant—is discrete rather than continuous. The fuel cost function of an individual power plant is a fixed fuel cost per kwh up to capacity levels, where fuel costs become infinite (no more power can be produced by the plant). Different plants in use in the system, however, have different efficiencies and hence different fuel costs. At peak demand times, more capacity is in use than at off-peak hours. As the electric company does not want to waste money and fuel, it generally uses older power plants, which produce less electricity from a given amount of fuel, at peak times only and leaves them idle at off-peak hours. In many systems, a few of the oldest plants are used only at annual system peak periods.

(i) *Represent the marginal fuel cost function of an electric power system graphically, assuming that the system has plants of five different efficiency levels. Show where hypothetical peak annual and peak daily demand curves might fall.* (Assume that the price elasticity of demand is constant over time, and choose a day which is not the day of the annual peak demand.)

(ii) To find the fuel savings benefits of High Mountain Sheep Dam, one must compare the fuel cost structure of the Pacific Northwest power system in two cases: first, if High Mountain Sheep Dam is built in 1975; and second, if the thermal alternative is built in 1975. The first case is represented by the graphs in questions (ii) through (v).

The addition of plants which are more efficient (in terms of electricity per unit of fuel) would therefore cause relatively inefficient plants to be left idle at off-peak (and possibly even peak) hours, resulting in a fuel savings benefit. That is, at off-peak hours, there is at least one plant not operating.

Since hydroelectric projects have no fuel costs at all, off-peak energy savings benefits would ordinarily be quite large. However, in this case, the regional power system which High Mountain Sheep would serve consists exclusively of hydroelectric power at present. This situation is represented graphically in Figure 14.1.** *What would this information suggest*

---

*The Pacific Northwest (Region VII) is the only FPC region with a winter annual peak.

**In Figures 14.1 through 14.4, heavy lines represent cost functions; thin lines represent peak demand curves. D peak means peak demand.

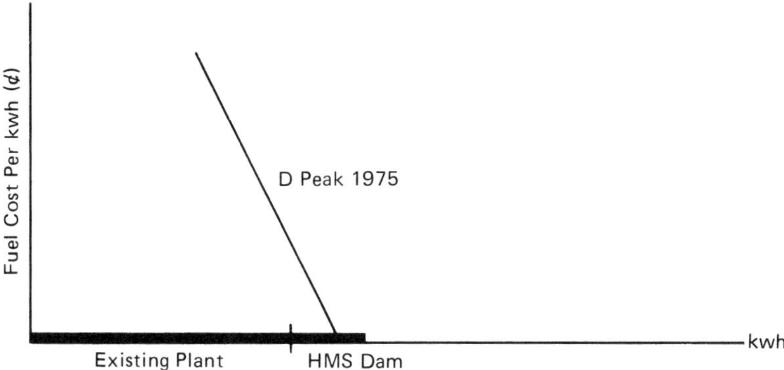

FIGURE 14.1

about present projections of off-peak fuel savings benefits in the short run?

(iii) At the same time, the analysts note that High Mountain Sheep represents "the last potentially economic hydroelectric energy" project in the power region. Therefore, new capacity built to meet demand shifts in the 1980s and beyond would be thermal. The situation after the first thermal plants were built is shown graphically in Figure 14.2. *If you expect thermal plants to be built in the 1980s, how, if at all, would present projections of off-peak fuel savings benefits in the 1980s differ from benefits of the late 1970s?*

(iv) Demand for electricity is projected to increase rapidly in the late 20th and early 21st centuries. New plants must be built if this new peak and off-peak demand is to be accommodated without severe price rises. Since technical progress is occur-ring to make new power plants more fuel efficient, the new plants would have lower fuel costs than those built in the 1980s. This can be represented graphically as shown in Figure 14.3. *What effect would this information have on your present projections of off-peak fuel savings benefits from the 1990s to 2010 assuming the 1980s thermal plants are still in use under peak conditions?* Assume that capacity is constructed to meet but not exceed demand.

(v) However, thermal power plants have a shorter life span than this project. Therefore, before the end of the High Mountain Sheep Dam project life in 2024, all of the 1980s thermal plants will have been replaced by plants using energy more efficiently. *How would replacement of the 1980s plants affect projections of off-peak fuel savings benefits near the end of the life of the project?* (See Figure 14.4.)

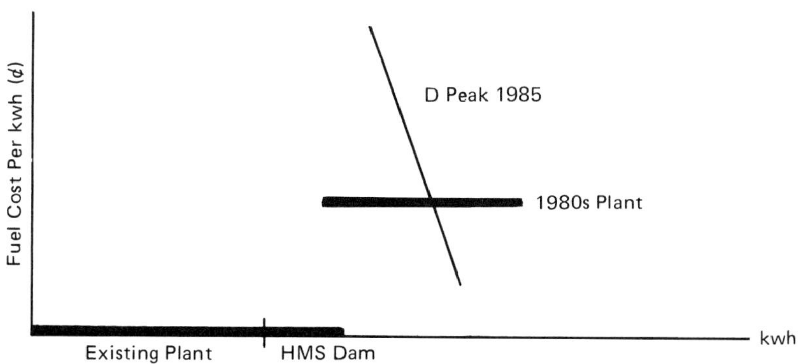

FIGURE 14.2

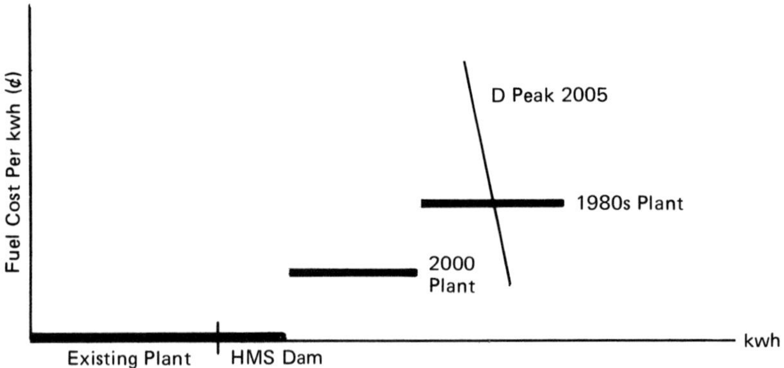

FIGURE 14.3

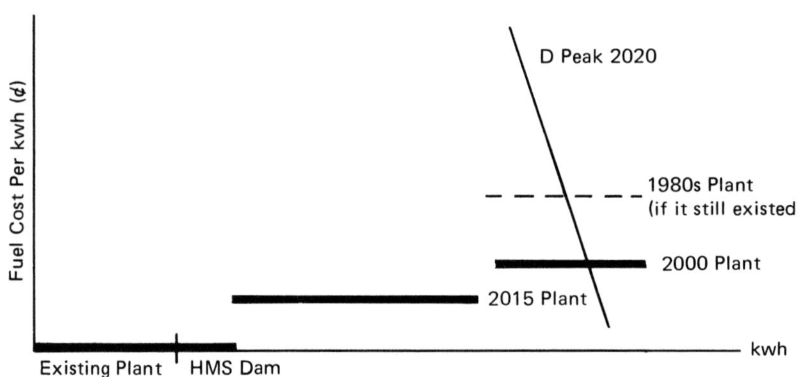

FIGURE 14.4

(3)   The analysts then supplied data on power benefits of the hydroelectric project. They valued the power produced by High Mountain Sheep Dam as equal to the cost of producing the same amount of power from the least-cost alternative thermal plant. In finding the cost of the thermal alternative, they converted the discrete cost functions discussed above into a continuous approximation. They assumed that a thermal power plant would depreciate at 3% per year. It was assumed that capacity would be replaced as it depreciated, with immediate reductions in fuel costs, and thus the whole plant would be replaced by less costly new facilities at the end of 30 years, which then, in turn, would be depreciated and replaced. Capacity costs were assumed to diminish at the rate of technological progress in the industry—taken as 4% per year in this exercise—and fuel savings from the new plant were assumed to increase at the same rate. (Sensitivity analyses using rates of technological change of 3% and 5% are given in Appendix B for some discount rates.) In addition, the analysts included increases in energy prices (relative to other prices) of about 25% in 1980 and a further 5% in 1990. Thus, thermal power costs reflect increasing energy prices to a certain extent.*

(a) Although the effects of technological change cause each year's annual thermal power cost to be different, the analysts aggregated these costs into three periods by finding the annual dollar stream with the same present value as that of the unequal costs for

---

*These calculations are based on assumptions and an algorithm developed in Krutilla and Fisher, pp. 108–110.

each of the three periods. The analysts also found that the dam specifications permitted the realization of a small amount of flood control benefits, but they noted that benefits from "flat-water" recreation on the reservoir formed by the dam would be less than the separable cost of providing recreation facilities. Benefit and cost streams in thousands of dollars are given in Table 14.3. *Find the present value of net benefits of this project.* Assume that 1976 is year zero and that annual benefits are constant within each time period. *Is the project justified on strictly economic grounds, neglecting environmental costs?* Explain very briefly (in a couple of sentences).

(4) If the project is not built, there would be benefits from preserving the area in a wilderness state. (Alternatively, there are economic costs of destroying the wilderness in addition to economic costs of building the project.) If the present value of the preservation benefits exceeds the present value of the dam project, then, strictly on grounds of comparing measurable benefits and costs, one would argue for the preservation of the area.

Since wilderness area is irreplaceable, the cost of wilderness destruction is not limited to the life of the project but is a perpetuity equal to the value of demand for the wilderness in all future years discounted to a present value. Also, because of the irreversibility of destruction, the value of "option demand" must be counted among the project's costs. ("Option demand" is the value of preserving their own and their descendants' options to use the wilderness in the future.)* Further, some economists argue that future generations, having more wealth than we, would in all probability be willing to compensate us for not destroying wilderness land; and that, therefore, reliance on the present market to establish a value for wilderness preservation would produce inefficient decisions. To correct for this inefficiency, some of these economists advocate that, for all irreversible development decisions, we set the discount rate at or near zero for preservation benefits while retaining an ordinary opportunity cost of capital rate for development.

---

*More background on this subject can be found in Krutilla and Fisher, pp. 67–69 (and earlier for a mathematical derivation) and in Kenneth Arrow and Anthony C. Fisher, "Environmental Preservation, Uncertainty, and Irreversibility," *Quarterly Journal of Economics,* May 1974.

TABLE 14.3

	3%			6%		
	1976–1980	*1981–1990*	*1991–2025*	*1976–1980*	*1981–1990*	*1991–2025*
Flood control	$ 245	$ 245	$ 245	$ 245	$ 245	$ 245
Annual thermal power cost	24,066	24,108	19,078	33,308	33,202	27,025
Annual hydro power cost	20,300	20,300	20,300	29,171	29,171	29,171
	8%			10%		
Flood control	$ 245	$ 245	$ 245	$ 245	$ 245	$ 245
Annual thermal power cost	39,903	39,311	32,635	47,200	46,414	39,485
Annual hydro power cost	35,951	35,951	35,951	43,331	43,331	43,331
	12%					
Flood control	$ 245	$ 245	$ 245			
Annual thermal power cost	53,938	53,899	46,507			
Annual hydro power cost	51,065	51,065	51,065			

(a) *What are the implications of a zero discount rate on preservation benefits and a positive discount rate on development benefits?* (Answer briefly.)

(b) Others argue that intertemporal inefficiency can best be overcome not by changing the discount rate but by estimating future demand for preserved wilderness over time, knowing that the demand will rise with rising income and that the supply can only decrease.

Briefly evaluate the two alternatives, bearing in mind your answer to part (a). Could you see some use for both approaches depending on the uniqueness of the particular wilderness site?

(5) The value of wilderness services is extremely difficult to estimate and changes over time. There are two factors that would cause these changes:

1. changes in the price of wilderness services relative to prices of other goods, and
2. shifts in the demand curve for wilderness services.

Shifts in the demand curve are equivalent to changes in demand at zero price due to demographic, income, and similar changes. These shifts can be roughly estimated by looking at current trends of growth in demand, since there presently is a zero price for the use of the Hells Canyon area. Studies by the FPC staff have shown that demand for wilderness recreation in the Hells Canyon area is increasing at 15-20% per year, while in the Pacific Northwest as a whole, the growth in the use of undeveloped land has been estimated at about 10% per year by the U.S. Forest Service.

The analysts suggest that demand for wilderness areas like Hells Canyon will continue to increase rapidly for a period of time because most users of wilderness areas begin with "easy access" camping before going on to wilderness use, and a larger percentage of children have been exposed to "easy access" camping than adults. However, there are two constraints on a growth rate of zero-price demand of 10% per year. First, demand for wilderness cannot continually grow faster than the population; second, wilderness areas will reach their carrying capacity, resulting in a diminution of the solitude valued by wilderness users as well as in government-imposed charges and other deterrents to assure that the wilderness remains wilderness. Therefore, for the purposes of this exercise, the analysts assume a shift of wilderness demand of 10%

per year until the 20th year, when capacity is reached. Growth in demand is then assumed to decrease until it reaches the level of population growth, taken as 1% in this exercise, after 50 years. A sensitivity analysis of these parameters is presented in Appendix C, using 7½% growth for 25 years decreasing after 50 years to 1% and 12½% growth for 15 years decreasing to 1% after 50 years.

To set relative prices of wilderness services is even more difficult due to the absence of markets. The analysts note that demand for wilderness services is income elastic and has no satisfactory substitutes and that wilderness land is irreplaceable once destroyed. Demand is therefore influenced by the growth of national income and hence by the rate of technological change in the economy as a whole; sensitivity analysis for lower and higher rates are also presented in Appendix C.

But even with rough estimates of the growth rate of demand for recreation, assigning an initial value to recreation benefits would be difficult. To avoid the problem of having to value all demand for Hells Canyon as a wilderness, the analysts first calculated the present value of a benefit stream starting with $1.00 in the first year and growing according to the rates of relative price change and demand shifts in succeeding years, giving results shown as Alternative A.* This benefit stream can be compared to the present value of $1.00 per year in perpetuity with no growth due to other forces (Alternative B).

Alternative	3%	6%	8%	10%	12%
A	∞	$428.20	$162.64	$86.55	$53.81
B	$33.33	$ 16.67	$ 12.50	$10.00	$ 8.33

The analysts next provide information projecting use of the lower Hells Canyon area of the Snake River (near the High Mountain Sheep Dam site) for stream-based recreation and for hunting (Table 14.4).

These valuations of stream-based recreation and hunting are somewhat arbitrary but still conservative, considering costs to users of getting to the area (since the only Standard Metropolitan Statistical Area within

---

*These calculations are based on those prepared in Krutilla and Fisher, pp. 147-150.

TABLE 14.4: Opportunity Costs of Altering Free-Flowing River and Related Canyon Environment by Development of High Mountain Sheep

(1) Quantified Losses	(2) Recreation Days 1969[a]	(3) Visitor Days 1969[b]	(4) Visitor Days 1976
Stream-based recreation[c]			
Total of boat counter survey	18,755	28,132	51,000
Upstream of Salmon-Snake confluence	9,622	14,439	26,000
Nonboat access			
Imnaha–Dug bar	9,678	14,517	26,000
Pittsburgh Landing	9,643	14,464	26,000
Hells Canyon downstream			
Boat anglers	2,472	1,000	1,800
Bank anglers	9,559	2,333	4,000
Total stream use above Salmon River	40,974 plus[d]	46,753 plus[d]	84,00 at $5/day = $420,000
Hunting Canyon area[e]			
Big game	7,050	7,050	7,000 at $25/day = $175,000
Upland birds	1,110	1,110	1,000 at $10/day = $ 10,000
Diminished value of hunting experience[f]	18,000	18,000	29,000 at $10/day = $290,000
Total quantified losses		$895,000 ± 25%	

Unevaluated losses

  A Unmitigated anadromous fish losses outside impact area

  B Unmitigated resident fish losses:

      (1) Stream fishing downstream from High Mountain Sheep

  C Option value of rare geomorphological-biological-ecological phenomena

  D Others

a) "Recreation days" corresponds to definition as per *Supplement No. 1, Senate Document No. 97*; namely, an individual engaging in recreation for any "reasonable portion of a day." In this particular study, time involved must be a minimum of 1 hour, as per letter from Monte Richards, coordinator, Basin Investigations, Idaho Fish and Game Department.

b) "Visitor days" corresponds to the President's Recreational Advisory Council (now, Council on Environmental Quality) *Coordination Bulletin No. 6* definition of a visitor day as a 12-hour day. Operationally, the total number of hours, divided by twelve, will give the appropriate "visitor day" estimate.

c) Source: "An Evaluation of Recreational Use on the Snake River in the High Mountain Sheep Impact Area." Survey by Oregon State Game Commission and Idaho State Fish and Game Department in cooperation with U.S. Forest Service, Report dated January 1970; and memorandum, W. B. Hall, liaison officer, Wallowa-Whitman National Forest, dated January 20, 1970.

d) Not included in the survey were scenic flights, nor trail use via Saddle Creek and Battle Creek trails. Thus, estimates given represent an under-reporting of an unevaluated amount.

e) "Middle Snake River Study, Idaho, Oregon and Washington," Joint Report of the Bureau of Commercial Fisheries and Bureau of Sports Fisheries and Wildlife in *Department of the Interior Resource Study of the Middle Snake*, tables 10 and 11.

f) The figure 18,000 hunter days is based on witness Pitney's estimate of 15,000 big game hunter days on the Oregon side, and estimated 10,000 hunter days on the Idaho side (provided in a letter from Monte Richards, coordinator, Idaho Basin Investigations, Idaho Fish and Game Department, dated February 13, 1970), for a total of 25,000 hunter days (excluding small game, i.e., principally upland birds) in the canyon area, less estimated losses of 7,000 hunter days. This provides the estimated 18,000 hunter days, 1969 total, which, growing at estimated 5 percent per year for deer hunting and 9 percent per year for elk hunting, would total 29,000 hunter days by 1976.

Source: Krutilla and Fisher, pp. 136–137.

100 miles is Lewiston, Idaho/Clarkston, Washington) and considering fees imposed upon private hunters in many parts of the world; they suggest that first year benefits from stream-based recreation and hunting alone are on the order of $900,000.

Given that this $900,000 initial-year benefit represents only a portion of the benefits obtainable from the wilderness, and using cost-benefit analysis as the sole criterion, recommend whether the dam should be built, the wilderness preserved, as more information is obtained under each of the following conditions:

(a) *a zero discount rate*
(b) *the discount rate used for evaluating electric power benefits and*
   (i) *Alternative A, incorporating growth in the value of wilderness services,*
   (ii) *Alternative B, no growth in value of wilderness services.*

APPENDIX A

Present Value Calculations

To find the present value of a stream of benefits or costs over the lifetime of a project, the following general formula is used:

$$PV(M) = M_0 + M_1/(1 + d) + M_2/(1 + d)^2 + \ldots + M_t/(1 + d)^T,$$

where M_t is the amount of the benefit or cost in the tth year, d is the discount rate and T is the number of years being evaluated. This formula may be truncated at either end to measure benefits for limited numbers of years within the project life. For example, the present value at time zero of benefits B received from the 5th to the 14th year of a project can be expressed as follows:

$$PV(B) = B_5/(1 + d)^5 + B_6/(1 + d)^6 + \ldots + B_{14}/(1 + d)^{14}.$$

Table 14.5, giving summations useful for calculation, assumes a constant annual stream of $1 per year for each of the years included.

TABLE 14.5

PV at Time Zero of an Annual Stream of $1 Per Year in Years	3%	6%	8%	10%	12%
0–4	4.7171	4.4651	4.3121	4.1699	4.0374
5–14	7.5790	5.8299	4.9321	4.1968	3.5908
15–49	14.2056	6.4126	3.9680	2.5396	1.6728
0–49	26.5017	16.7076	13.2122	10.9063	9.3010

APPENDIX B

Analysis of Sensitivity of Thermal Power Costs to Technological Change Parameter

Material showing the changes resulting from the use of a rate of technological change in the electric power industry of 3%, 4%, and 5% is provided in Table 14.6. It indicates that for all of the selected discount rates a change in capacity costs of 1% over the first five years, 1-2% over the next 10 years, and 7-9% over the last 35 years occurs. Total thermal power costs are reduced by somewhat less. The large effect of this coefficient in the later life of the project results from the assumption that the original thermal plant will be replaced in the 30th year. In addition, changes in the parameter have slightly less effect at higher discount rates.

TABLE 14.6

Technology Parameter	1976–1980 Cost	3% Discount Rate	
		1981–1990 Cost	1991–2025 Cost
3%	$24,077	$24,225	$19,382
4%	24,066	24,108	19,078
5%	24,053	23,996	18,811
		8% Discount Rate	
3%	39,919	39,449	33,586
4%	39,903	39,311	32,635
5%	39,888	39,192	31,727
		12% Discount Rate	
3%	53,952	53,929	48,115
4%	53,938	53,899	46,507
5%	53,923	53,743	44,832

APPENDIX C

Analysis of Sensitivity of Wilderness Value Estimates to Demand Shift and Technological Change Parameters

One finds that wilderness value estimates are quite sensitive to changes in the parameters, particularly at relatively low discount rates, where the growth rate caused by the parameter is close to or exceeds the rate at which the benefit stream is being discounted. However, even with a 12% discount rate, a 1% change in the technology (income growth) parameter causes a 25% change in the value of wilderness benefits estimated. The estimate is somewhat less sensitive to demand growth, but even changes in this parameter cause large changes, particularly between the 7.5% and 10% demand growth rates. Six percent and higher discount rates are shown in Table 14.7. (The benefit sum is infinite for all choices using a 3% discount rate.)

TABLE 14.7

Technology (income) Parameter	Demand Growth (original)					
	7.5%	10%	12.5%	7.5%	10%	12.5%
	6% Discount Rate			8% Discount Rate		
3%	$197.39	$243.58	$238.44	$ 89.76	$113.90	$117.42
4%	355.66	428.20	405.29	129.68	162.64	163.53
5%	∞	∞	∞	203.25	250.29	244.57
	10% Discount Rate			12% Discount Rate		
3%	$ 51.56	$ 66.18	$ 70.91	$ 33.79	$ 43.37	$ 47.79
4%	67.72	86.55	90.98	41.88	53.81	58.46
5%	92.57	117.37	120.74	53.26	68.33	73.04

SEQUEL

High Mountain Sheep Dam

On February 23, 1971, the Federal Power Commission rendered a decision on High Mountain Sheep Dam, issuing a license to Pacific Northwest Power Company (PNPC) and Washington Public Power Supply System (WPPSS) for the construction of one of three alternative projects on the Middle Snake River, including High Mountain Sheep. The license left the actual choice of project to the utilities, but specified that construction could not take place until after September 11, 1975, in order to provide "time for the Congress to consider making the Middle Snake River a component of the National Wild and Scenic Rivers System."

Construction was never commenced. Because the decision was made after passage of the National Environmental Policy Act, environmental impact statements were required from both the applicants and the FPC staff. The FPC staff draft EIS was filed on June 8, 1971, while the electric utilities filed theirs on July 23, 1971. The filing of environmental impact statements was expected to bring the FPC into compliance with NEPA so that the license could then be issued as originally specified. However, the Second Circuit Court of Appeals ruled on an unrelated case in 1972 that the FPC must admit environmental impact statements into evidence and hold hearings on them, allowing intervening parties to conduct cross-examination. (*Green County Planning Board v. FPC*, 455 F.2d 412 (1972)) The FPC scheduled another (third) set of hearings on High Mountain Sheep Dam, and the license was rescinded. These hearings were expected to extend into 1976.

The FPC actions took place in a context of mounting congressional concern over the preservation of the Snake River. In 1970 and 1971, the Senate passed a bill requiring an eight-year moratorium on FPC licensing in the Hells Canyon region, during which time the merits of preserving the Middle Snake River could be studied. However, committee hearings were never held on these bills in the House, and they never reached the House floor. After the 1972 defeat of Representative Wayne Aspinall (D-Colo.), the pro-development Chairman of the House Interior and Insular Affairs Committee, and the retirement of Senator Len Jordan (R-Idaho), who had opposed plans to preserve Hells Canyon, stronger legislation was considered. The Senate Interior Committee held extensive hearings, both in Washington, D.C. and in the affected region of Idaho and Oregon, on legislation (sponsored by all four Senators from Oregon and

Idaho) to create a Hells Canyon National Recreation Area. The Senate passed the legislation in 1974, in spite of opposition from the Corps of Engineers (which opposed immediate deauthorization* of Asotin Dam and proposed instead to restudy its benefits and costs) and from the FPC, which claimed that existing legislation was sufficient to allow for the protection of the Middle Snake. (The FPC ironically cited the 1967 High Mountain Sheep Dam case before the Supreme Court as a legal guarantee that preservation interests would be considered.) However, since the Senate bill was passed late in the session, it never reached the House floor, despite strong support from the House Committee on Interior and Insular Affairs.

Finally, in 1975, legislation was passed which prevents development of Hells Canyon for electric power and preserves it in its wilderness state. The bill passed in the Senate on a voice vote with no debate on June 2, and in the House on a 342–53 vote on November 18, in spite of the opposition of both Representatives from Idaho. The final version of the bill, which President Ford signed on December 31, establishes a Hells Canyon National Recreation Area of over 600,000 acres.** Sixty-eight miles of the Middle Snake River, including the Asotin and High Mountain Sheep Dam sites, are included in the Wild and Scenic Rivers system, while the inclusion of the remaining thirty-three miles is under study. The law deauthorizes Asotin Dam and prohibits the FPC from licensing any power development in the entire 101-mile stretch of the river. It provides that the canyon walls be left as wilderness area and limits use of remaining partially developed non-wilderness areas (currently in national forests but included in the recreation area) to existing levels of non-recreational uses, permitting selective timber cutting (but not clear-cutting)*** and grazing. Thus, the law now recognizes and preserves the wilderness value of the Hells Canyon reach of the Snake River.

Development of thermal power has proceeded in the Pacific Northwest; in 1976, WPPSS issued revenue bonds to finance construction of a new nuclear power plant. With no new hydroelectric sites available and with the impending expiration (in the 1980s) of the long-term contracts governing the sale of power by the Bonneville Power Authority, new disputes are emerging between large industries (including the aluminum industry, which is heavily dependent on electric power and moved to the Pacific Northwest because of low electric rates), municipal power authorities, and investor-owned utilities over the question of which groups will receive cheap federally-produced hydroelectric power in the future and which will be required to develop the more expensive thermal sources.

---

*Federal water resources projects must be authorized by Congress before funds for their construction can be appropriated; deauthorization thus puts an end to a project.

**A "National Recreation Area" is a region of public land where various land uses are permitted, but where recreation is the primary use. The term is thus quite broad. In order of restrictiveness, the remaining land designations of portions of the Hells Canyon site are as follows: 1) wild rivers and wilderness areas, areas untouched by man, in which no development is permitted; 2) scenic rivers, which are not wilderness but have reverted to a wild state and where no development is permitted; and 3) national forest, a government-owned tract of land where multiple uses, including timber cutting, grazing, mining, and recreation, are permitted.

***Clear cutting means cutting all the trees in a designated area; selective cutting means cutting only selected trees in the area, usually in such a manner that the forest still contains young, growing trees, thereby assuring its preservation as a forest.

15

Automobile Emissions Control: The Sulfates Problem (A)

In December 1970, Congress enacted the Clean Air Act Amendments containing new, explicit, and strict standards for the control of atmospheric pollutants in automobile exhaust. The enactment of these standards reflected both growing public concern over air pollution and growing congressional concern over the apparent recalcitrance of the automobile industry in dealing with this problem. The deadline for compliance with the new standards was set for 1975 and the task of enforcement was assigned to the newly created Environmental Protection Agency (EPA), then under the direction of William Ruckelshaus.

EPA's task, however, was complicated from the start by technological uncertainties, by a less than enthusiastic auto industry, and by confusion and conflict within the agency itself. In 1973, a new complication arose with the discovery of potentially dangerous amounts of sulfuric acid in the exhaust emissions of automobiles equipped with catalytic converters—the technology adopted by the auto industry for purposes of meeting the emission standards.

In 1975, the automakers petitioned Russell Train (who had replaced Ruckelshaus as EPA Administrator in 1973) for an extension of the deadline for compliance. One extension had already been granted by Ruckelshaus in April 1973, and interim standards had been created for 1975 and 1976. Were Train to grant another extension, the original Clean Air Act statutory standards might not go into effect until the late 1970s.

This case—divided into two parts—examines the evidence facing Train as he prepared to make his decision. Part A (this chapter) provides background information on the automobile pollution issue and on the political and administrative handling of the sulfates* problem. Part B (chapter 16) summarizes the technical information available to Train on the extent and severity of the problem.

---

*Sulfuric acid is one of a class of compounds called sulfates, several of which are found in automobile exhaust. The problem of automobile emission of sulfuric acid and other sulfates is usually called the sulfates problem, although in this context sulfuric acid is the most dangerous of the sulfates.

BACKGROUND: AUTOMOBILE
EMISSIONS CONTROL*

Although doctors first recognized the dangers of automobile emissions in the early 1920s, the issue did not arouse much public concern until the early 1950s. At that time, the people of California became concerned about "smog" in the Los Angeles Basin, which had just become visible. After eliminating other possible causes, investigators identified auto emissions and sunlight as the components of a photochemical reaction which produced oxidants—irritating and potentially dangerous components of smog—in the Basin.

In 1959, California adopted legislation calling for the installation of pollution control devices as soon as the major auto manufacturers or any of the independent manufacturers could develop them. In response to this legislation, the automakers asserted that the technology to reduce emissions did not exist. Their assertion was effectively invalidated in 1964, when California's newly created Air Resources Board certified that three independent manufacturers had developed workable add-on emission control devices. Subsequently, the state established auto pollution control standards and enacted a legal requirement that new autos comply with California's standards beginning with the 1966 model year**—whether or not the automakers had developed any control devices. Immediately, the major auto manufacturers announced that add-on control devices were unnecessary and that they could clean up their cars with technology they had already developed. For Ford and General Motors, this technology meant a simple air pump, while for Chrysler, it entailed a more complicated "clean air package." But the purpose of both the pump and the "package" was essentially the same: to increase oxygen supply in the exhaust, which would

---

*See Appendix A for a chronology of events. Background on automobile emissions control is largely taken from *The Impact of Auto Emission Standards,* a staff report of the Subcommittee on Air and Water Pollution of the Senate Committee on Public Works, Serial No. 93-11, October 1973, hereafter cited as the Senate Subcommittee Report.

**A "model year" begins in September or October of the preceding calendar year; thus, the 1966 model cars appeared on the market in the fall of 1965.

more completely transform hydrocarbons and carbon monoxide into harmless water and carbon dioxide.

California's pioneering efforts received national attention and prompted the introduction in 1964 of federal motor vehicle pollution control legislation. This legislation, enacted in 1965 as the Motor Vehicle Air Pollution Control Act (Title II of the Clean Air Act of 1963, P.L. 89-272), provided in Sec. 202(a):

> The Secretary [of Health, Education and Welfare] shall by regulation, giving appropriate consideration to technological feasibility and economic costs, prescribe as soon as practicable standards, applicable to the emission of any kind of substance, from any class or classes of new motor vehicles or new motor vehicle engines, which in his judgment cause or contribute to, or are likely to cause or contribute to, air pollution which endangers the health or welfare of any persons. . . .

The standards adopted by HEW in 1966 for implementation on 1968 model cars were the same as the standards effective in California in 1966.

During this time, automakers became increasingly concerned over a number of proposals by states to adopt differing auto emission control requirements. Thus in 1967, citing the adverse impact on commerce of differing state standards for national auto manufacturing companies, the auto industry called on Congress to preempt state emission control laws. Congress responded favorably, amending the Clean Air Act so that state authority to regulate emissions was preempted, although California's unique position was maintained. Preemption was based on the condition that the federal standards would be sufficiently tough to assure protection of the public health and welfare in parts of the U.S. with the most severe auto-caused pollution problems; federal emission controls sufficiently stringent to improve air quality in those "worst case" areas would necessarily be strict enough to maintain or improve air quality in less polluted areas.

By 1969, however, the 1965 Act had not produced the results that Congress had intended, because the magnitude of the technological problem had proved greater (and in the view of some observers, the auto industry's interest in solving it, less) than had been expected. Little progress was made by the auto industry in the development of a clean conventional engine or a viable alternative. Control systems on cars in actual use tested by an independent laboratory did not perform to the level of emission reduction for which the prototype models had been certified by HEW.* Partially in response to growing public pressure over the automobile pollution issue, and also in response to studies prepared by the Public Health Service which documented health hazards from auto emissions, the Nixon Administration called the auto and oil industries to a White House meeting in late 1969. The auto industry agreed to stiffer emission standards for 1975 and a 90% reduction in auto emissions for 1980, and the oil industry agreed to change fuel composition to remove substances that might interfere with the operation of emission control devices.

Congress, however, decided to act independently. On the basis of testimony by the U.S. Public Health Service before the Senate Public Works Committee's Subcommittee on Air and Water Pollution in March of 1970, Congress decided that the timetable agreed to by the auto industry and the President was too slow; the used car problem (a car's average life span is a decade and each one-year delay in implementing standards meant 10 million new cars on the road) and the evident failure of existing controls produced congressional concern that the automobile danger to public health would continue to 1990. Congress decided to force the automakers' technological hand by amending the Clean Air Act to make the 1980 emission standards applicable to 1975 and 1976 model cars.

The 1970 Clean Air Act Amendments

This decision marked a shift in the national attitude toward auto pollution. Throughout the 1970 debate over the Clean Air Act Amendments, the timetable for achievement of the clean air goal—not the validity of the goal itself or the health data that supported it—was the prime point of disagreement with the auto industry. Though the health standards were later questioned, they were subjected only to limited criticism in 1970. As a Ford spokesman explained, "We don't even try to argue the need any more for incremental reduction of emissions. We're going to get it all out, whether it really has to be or not."

Title II of the Clean Air Act Amendments of 1970 required the EPA Administrator to promulgate auto emission standards that would lead to at least a 90% reduction (from 1970 levels) in emissions of hydrocarbons (HC) and carbon monoxide (CO) effective for 1975 model cars and at least a 90% reduction (from 1971 levels) in emissions of nitrogen oxides (NO_x) effective on 1976 models. (The extra year was allotted for NO_x control in recognition of the probability that these emissions would prove harder to control than CO or HC.) A one-year extension for each of these deadlines could be granted by the EPA Administrator, in accordance with criteria spelled out in the Act. Also, the EPA Administrator was authorized (among other actions) to conduct pertinent research; test for compliance (both in the factory and on the road); and impose a fine of up to $10,000 per vehicle on vehicles failing to meet the standards. The National Academy of Sciences (NAS) was directed to commence a study of the technical issues raised by both the emission standards themselves and the deadlines for meeting them.

Table 15.1 compares the emission standards established by EPA in conformity with the 1970 Clean Air Act with uncontrolled emissions and with emission standards imposed administratively by HEW and EPA.**

Although the Amendments, as finally passed, were generally acknowledged to be "tough," many segments of the population had advocated that they be even tougher. The *Christian Science Monitor,* for example, reported that 62% of Americans polled said that they favored outlawing the conventional piston ICE (internal combustion engine) to force automakers to develop clean power sources. (The *Monitor* did not, however, ask respondents how much they would be willing to pay for this changeover.) The United Auto Workers and environmental groups formed a coalition and asked Congress to set standards "so tough they would banish the piston ICE from autos by 1975."

---

*The 1965 Act provided that if a prototype of a given model car were certified as meeting emission standards, then all production units of that model would be covered by the certification. However, prototype models are often built and maintained with greater care than actual production units; some studies showed that over half the cars of certain models on the road failed to meet emission standards after only a year or two of use.

**As noted earlier, the 1965 Motor Vehicle Air Pollution Control Act authorized HEW to set automobile emissions standards, which it did for the 1968–1971 model years. The 1970 Amendments continued the authorization for the 1972–1974 model years; in December 1970, EPA assumed HEW's air pollution control duties.

TABLE 15.1:   Automobile Emission Standards
(in grams per mile)

	HC	CO	NO_x	Percent Reduction***		
				HC	CO	NO_x
Uncontrolled cars						
(pre-1968 model year)*	8.7	87.0	3.5	—	—	—
1968 and 1969 model year						
HEW standards	6.2	52.0	—**	29%	40%	0%
1970 and 1971 model year						
HEW standards	4.1	34.0	—**	53%	61%	0%
1972, 1973, and 1974 model						
year EPA standards	3.0	29.0	3.1	66%	67%	11%
1975 Clean Air Act standards	.41	3.4	3.1	95%	96%	11%
1976 Clean Air Act standards	.41	3.4	0.4	95%	96%	89%

*On the basis of 1975 test procedures.

**No NO_x standard was set for these model years.

***From uncontrolled levels.

However, the Senate Public Works Committee had recommended (and Congress had agreed) that the auto industry should remain free to solve the problem in its own way. Thus, the law specified the emission reductions to be achieved, but did not dictate a technological solution.

Behind the Senate Committee's recommendation, however, lay the conviction of Senator Edmund Muskie (D-Maine), chairman of the Subcommittee on Air and Water Pollution and a principal author of the Clean Air Act, that the conventional piston ICE, even with add-on devices, could never be made clean enough to meet the emissions standards and that a new power source for the automobile had to be developed. While Muskie and his Senate colleagues were aware that the development of alternative technologies would not be possible before 1975, their intent was first to create a statutory timetable. Then, if the industry failed to comply with the statutory standards using an add-on approach, Congress could grant extensions which would be contingent upon the development of alternative technologies. In other words, the Subcommittee felt that it was necessary to make the industry get serious about the problem and to make the auto manufacturers demonstrate "good faith" in progressing toward clean air goals. After that, it was hoped, a reliable alternative technology would be developed.

Industry's Answer: The Catalyst*

The technology chosen by the auto industry for the purpose of meeting the Clean Air Act emission standards was the catalytic converter, also known as the catalyst or oxidation catalyst. The catalyst is installed between a car's exhaust manifold and its tailpipe and is intended to oxidize the hydrocarbons (HC) and carbon monoxide (CO) normally found in the exhaust of internal combustion engines into carbon dioxide and water. While such oxidation catalysts effectively control HC and CO emissions, control of nitrogen oxide (NO_x) emissions requires other types of catalysts, which are incorporated in "dual-bed" and "three-way" systems.

The total increase in cost of standard-size 1974 catalyst cars over non-catalyst 1974 models was estimated to be from $130 to $225: $60 to $100 for the catalyst itself, and the rest for improved chokes, carburetors and ignitions. While some catalyst systems have been designed to require catalyst replacement after about 24,000 miles of use, most cars have been designed not to require any catalyst change for 50,000 miles. Replacement costs vary between $40 and $100 depending on the manufacturer.

All catalyst-equipped 1975 models, and some non-catalyst 1975 models, were designed to use only

---

*This section is largely based on EPA Environmental Fact Sheet FS-29, "Oxidation Catalysts for Automotive Emission Control."

unleaded gas and were equipped with an apparatus which prevents refueling except with the smaller nozzles on pumps that dispense unleaded gas. (Lead prevents catalysts from functioning properly. However, if a catalyst were to be "poisoned" by lead or fail due to "heat shock" [overheating], no change in automobile performance would result, except for an increase in HC and CO emissions, which would probably still remain well below the emission levels of uncontrolled cars.) While unleaded gas costs more than leaded regular, these costs were expected by General Motors (GM) to be more than offset by the lower average operating costs of catalyst-equipped cars using unleaded gasoline as compared with current cars using leaded gasoline. The lower operating costs were attributed to the improved fuel economy of many catalyst-equipped cars and the longer life of such components as spark plugs and exhaust pipes, which deteriorate less rapidly with unleaded gas. Ford and Chrysler, however, predicted no gains in fuel economy.

Although California gave catalysts tentative approval in the early 1970s, automakers found it possible to meet early emission standards by making adjustments on the engine itself, thus avoiding the need for sophisticated add-on mechanisms like the catalyst. Catalysts were also thought by some to be impractical because lead-free gas was generally unavailable at that time. Non-catalyst techniques were used by the automakers to meet administratively-imposed emission standards for the 1969 through the 1974 model years. However, throughout this period the automakers made no serious efforts to alter engine technology substantially enough to meet the more stringent 1975 standards: rather, they placed their reliance on the catalyst. Thus it happened that up to 85% of all 1975 model cars sold in America (almost 100% in California) were equipped with one of these devices.

Although there have been allegations that the emission standards set forth by the Clean Air Act of December 31, 1970 forced the auto industry to concentrate on catalyst control technology at the expense of other systems, the industry's commitment to the converter in fact appears to have been made in 1969 and 1970, before passage of the Act. In 1967 Ford and Mobil Oil Company formed the Inter-Industry Emissions Control (IIEC) program, which (according to a Mobil Oil report) was to conduct research upon "the basic premise . . . that the conventional gas-powered ICE will be the automotive power plant for some years to come." Also, GM furnished the Senate Subcommittee on Air and Water Pollution with internal documents which revealed that the decision to continue emphasis on the current engine was made because GM favored the ICE, not because the Clean Air Act had eliminated other possible control options. GM's catalyst development program began at its automotive parts subsidiary in late 1969.

Testimony at public hearings before both the House Commerce Committee's Subcommittee on Public Health and Environment and the Senate Subcommittee on Air and Water Pollution in 1969 and 1970 also reveals that the auto industry was at that time committed to catalysts and the ICE. A principal point of industry testimony before both subcommittees was the necessity of removing lead from gasoline in order to permit implementation of catalyst systems for purposes of emission control on ICEs.

Implementation Problems: 1972 Senate Subcommittee Hearings

Though the provisions of the 1970 Clean Air Act Amendments were not to apply until almost six years later, it was evident as early as 1972 that there was growing doubt about the effectiveness of auto emission controls on 1972 and 1973 model cars. Expressions of concern were voiced by two different camps: those who lamented that, despite six years of federal emission controls and eight years of California emission controls, auto-related air pollution had not decreased greatly, and those who questioned whether cleaner air was worth the price of deterioration in both fuel economy and performance attributed by some to control systems such as the catalyst.

In the spring of 1972, the Senate Subcommittee on Air and Water Pollution, chaired by Senator Muskie, held five days of hearings on auto emission standards. Further hearings were held in the summer and fall of that year. The hearings revealed increasing national concern that Clean Air Act goals were not being met, that emission control strategies adopted by the auto industry were inappropriate, and that the industry's technical choices might prove excessively costly to consumers, since the $1 billion spent in developing catalyst technology would likely be passed on to car buyers. Eventually congressional and public concern led to an investigation of auto emission standards that began in October 1972 and culminated with 12 days of hearings by the Muskie Subcommittee in April, May, and June of 1973, at which representatives of EPA, NAS, manufacturers of catalytic converters, the oil industry and the major auto manufacturers appeared. Subcommittee staff investigators visited EPA research locations in Detroit and Durham, North Carolina; questioned Engelhard Mining and Manufacturing Company officials (experts in catalyst metals); and met with several doctors, scientists, and state officials in California and Massachusetts. The investigation led the Subcommittee to the following conclusions.*

Quality Control. Certification procedures were recognized as not representative of actual driving conditions and not indicative of the performance of emission control systems in customer use.** Catalyst-equipped cars were tested by continuous driving on a flat track with few stops, which precluded testing for the impact of such phenomena as "thermal shock" (the rapid acceleration of cold engines). The only available test to check the performance of motor vehicles in customer use required more than 12 hours to complete and thus could not be performed at motor vehicle inspection stations. Consequently, the warranty requirements specified in the Clean Air Act*** were effectively unenforceable, which meant that automakers could safely risk the use of catalysts without the prospect of future financial burdens arising from massive failure of control systems under warranty.

---

*See pp. 29–32 of the Senate Subcommittee Report.

**Before manufacturers are permitted to introduce and sell their various models of cars, each model prototype must be tested over 50,000 miles to demonstrate compliance with federal emission standards. In addition to this testing, many of the manufacturers have carried out independent tests of catalyst-equipped fleets over extended mileage to assure themselves that, with appropriate maintenance, the emission control system will function properly over the 50,000-mile lifetime required by the Clean Air Act. EPA regulations limit the maintenance during compliance testing to items likely to be done by owners; e.g., tuneups may not be performed more often than every 12,500 miles, and only one servicing of the catalyst is permitted during the 50,000 miles. (Even the single servicing is permitted only if the driver is warned by the appropriate warning light.)

***Manufacturers must warrant that new cars meet applicable emission standards.

Quality control procedures were of particular concern, since the fragility of catalyst systems was widely acknowledged. In a statement to EPA on March 27, 1973, Chrysler highlighted the catalyst system's faults, including failure in a high percentage of systems as a result of repeated periods of prolonged acceleration, heavy engine loads, malfunctions in ignition systems, or use with only one tankful of leaded gas. Also in 1972, the National Academy of Sciences' Annual Report warned against "mass production of what are presently deemed to be relatively fragile, catalyst-dependent systems, of unproved reliability in actual service which may engender an episode of considerable national turmoil." Basically, the NAS agreed with Chrysler that the ICE-with-catalyst system was the most expensive (up to $625 more over five years of operation than non-catalyst cars primarily due to fuel penalty and maintenance problems), least dependable, and least fuel efficient of possible control technologies.

Health Standards and Emission Control Requirements. Current evidence indicated that the ambient air quality standards from which auto emission reduction levels were derived were valid, i.e., that they would result in air quality levels sufficient to minimize adverse health effects on sensitive groups.

Emission Control and Energy. The best information available indicated that emission control strategies in use from 1968 to 1973 reduced fuel economy 7–15%. However, there was a dispute over whether those fuel penalties would continue with the emission control technology of the catalyst system: GM predicted fuel economy gains of 20% with catalysts; Ford, Chrysler, and Mobil predicted no change; Texaco and the NAS predicted heavy losses. (As this suggests, the major automobile manufacturers were divided over the merits of catalysts: GM, the primary developer of catalyst technology, favored them, while Ford and Chrysler did not.) Assessment of probable fuel penalties from catalysts was further complicated by the fact that fuel economy was heavily influenced by variables other than emission controls; i.e., longer and faster trips generally require less fuel per mile, increased car size and weight require more fuel per mile, and convenience accessories may increase fuel consumption.

Emission Control Technology. There was no dispute that alternative engine systems—diesel, rotary, and stratified charge—could meet the HC and CO standards without add-on devices like the converters. (See Appendix B for a brief discussion of these alternatives.) There was little dispute that ICEs with a catalyst would be able to meet the standards, although the reliability of the converter and the possibility of unregulated emissions were matters of uncertainty. There was a question about whether diesel engines could meet the NO_x standards.

Nitrogen Oxide Measurement Problems. Several difficulties, including measurement technique problems, were apparent in EPA's method of determining ambient air concentrations of NO_x. Also, it appeared that the present EPA system of measurement had been selected because it cost less than more accurate alternatives; this raised the question of the extent to which perceptions of cost and technical simplicity had affected considerations of public health.

Leadtime. The Muskie Subcommittee rejected the suggestion that the Clean Air Act Amendments of December 31, 1970 foreclosed development of alternative engines because of the limited leadtime. As previously noted, the primary decisions with regard to adoption of the catalyst approach and maintenance of the ICE system were apparently made in 1969. Also, the fact that other new engines were developed after 1970 for reasons unrelated to pollution control suggested to the subcommittee that the auto manufacturers had the ability to make engines with superior emission control characteristics had they so desired. As an example of the industry's versatility, the subcommittee cited the history of GM's development of the Chevrolet Corvair which involved a radical new engine design for American manufacturers—rear-mounted, air-cooled with opposed cylinders:

> September 1956—Drafting room work on the Corvair began
> April 1957—Plans for V–8 dropped
> August 1957—Proposed engine displacement increased to 140 cubic inches
> January 1958—Engine completely redesigned
> January 1959—First road test
> July 1959—Mass production begins

GM had displayed similar versatility in the development of its Opel. As one EPA document noted:

> GM's position that alternative technology is not available to allow achievement of the 1975 standards is somewhat puzzling considering the fact that a GM owned company (Opel) is currently mass producing a Diesel powered automobile

which has been tested by EPA and has achieved emission levels below federal 1975 standards with less than 1.5 grams per mile of NO_x.

Ford had also demonstrated its flexibility by introducing, for example, a radical new V–6 spark ignition engine on the 1974 Mustang. Finally, in mid-1973, the NAS provided estimates regarding leadtime and created a timetable demonstrating that diesel and/or stratified charge engines could be mass produced by late 1975 for Detroit's 1976 model cars.

The examples cited by the Muskie Subcommittee were, however, somewhat misleading in the view of some analysts, who argued that the rear-mounted air-cooled engine (Corvair), the diesel engine, and the V–6 represented not new or radical innovations but rather extensions of existing technology; the more innovative Opel was a limited-production item. In contrast, a mass-produced engine able to meet the 1976 statutory standards without using a catalyst would have been a major breakthrough.

The Muskie Subcommittee concluded nevertheless that with design of alternative engines already advanced, all that appeared needed to get them into mass production was the will to do so. (The subcommittee did not mention that retooling automobile production facilities to mass produce alternative engines could cost billions of dollars and take many years—an investment the industry was reluctant to make without demonstrated widespread consumer demand.) The subcommittee was unable to determine why those firms which believed the catalyst was unacceptable and involved great risks did not take a few chances and begin producing one of the available alternative systems. Ruckelshaus had testified before the subcommittee that, during EPA's March 1973 hearings, the automakers showed little interest in changing direction even if given more time to do so:

> At the hearings I asked each of the automotive companies what they were willing to do in the event I were to grant them an extension to develop alternative power sources. They almost universally testified that they would proceed with attempts to perfect the technology they were now trying to perfect during that period of time.

Extending the Deadlines

At about the same time that the Senate Subcommittee was evaluating progress under the existing emission control standards, the automakers were expressing skepticism about their ability to meet the more stringent standards scheduled for 1976. In February 1972, the major corporations had requested an extension of the deadlines on the grounds that catalytic technology was not yet developed to the point of successful application to mass-produced vehicles. After hearings were held, EPA Administrator Ruckelshaus denied their request, but the automakers appealed his decision to the U.S. Court of Appeals, which eventually ordered Ruckelshaus to review his decision and re-hear the case.

In April 1973, after re-hearings on the requests for a delay in the deadline in meeting Clean Air Act standards, Ruckelshaus relented. In his decision granting the delay, he noted that 93% of GM cars and 55% of Ford cars could have met the HC and CO standards without an extension. However, the extensions were granted to GM and to Ford because, as the decision pointed out, the 66% of total industry production that could meet the standards was not enough to satisfy consumer demand for new cars.* On the question of whether the automakers had made "good faith" efforts to meet the standards (raised in particular in connection with the Chrysler Corporation), Ruckelshaus also observed:

> If Congress had provided me with some sanctions short of the nuclear deterrent of, in effect, closing down that major corporation, my finding on good faith may have been otherwise.

According to the agency's view of "feasible" compliance on a reasonable timetable, Ruckelshaus created Interim Standards for 1975 and 1976 models to replace the newly-suspended statutory requirements. Table 15.2 compares the Interim Standards with statutory standards.

---

*At hearings in March 1973, GM had claimed that "if GM is forced to introduce catalytic converter systems across the board on 1975 models, the prospect of an unreasonable risk of business catastrophe and massive difficulties with these vehicles in the hands of the public must be faced. It is conceivable that complete stoppage of the entire production could occur, with the obvious tremendous loss to the company, shareholders, employees, suppliers, and communities. Short of that ultimate risk, there is a distinct possibility of varying degrees of interruption, with sizable dislocations."

THE SULFATES PROBLEM

Even as Ruckelshaus was considering the auto manufacturer's 1972 request to delay the effective date of the Clean Air Act auto emissions standards, EPA began examining the technology that the industry proposed to use to meet the standards. After "it became clear that catalytic converters were going to be used on cars," Eric Stork, head of EPA's Office of Mobile Source Air Pollution Control (see Exhibit 15.1) asked his staff to test the converters "as a matter of ordinary technical prudence." Dow Chemical Company, which did the testing under contract with EPA, found a "somewhat higher [level of] particulates" emissions in a Ford prototype converter than had been expected, and Ford requested the sample for analysis. On February 5, 1973, the following letter was sent to EPA by H.L. Misch, vice-president of the Ford Motor Company for environmental and safety engineering:

Mr. Robert L. Sansom
Assistant Administrator, Air and Water Programs
Environmental Protection Agency
Washington, D.C.

Dear Mr. Sansom:

Our Scientific Laboratory has reported to us work done by the Dow Chemical people under contract to the EPA in which they find an increase in the emissions of particulate matter from an engine running on lead-free fuel when an exhaust oxidizing platinum catalyst is used. Dow provided our Laboratory with samples for analysis, and we found the excess particulate matter to consist mainly of hydrated sulfuric acid droplets.

We hypothesize that the sulfuric acid is produced by the oxidation of organic sulfur compounds in the gasoline and likely proceeds from SO_2 formed in the combustion chamber to SO_3 formed in the catalyst. The SO_3 then reacts with water vapor in the exhaust stream to form sulfuric acid.

If our data are correct, it must be concluded that catalyst equipped vehicles will be emitting a potentially serious pollutant into the atmosphere. The amount and the residence time of the acid in the air are not presently known to us.

We are planning a program to provide further definition to this phenomenon and would like to meet with you at an early date so that whatever knowledge you have of this matter can be considered in planning our work. Would you inform me as to when such a meeting would be convenient.

Sincerely,

/s/

H. L. Misch

TABLE 15.2:   Automobile Emission Standards
(in grams per mile)

	HC	CO	NO_x	Percent Reduction**		
				HC	CO	NO_x
1975 Interim Standards*						
Federal 49-State Standards	1.5	15.0	3.1	83%	83%	11%
California Standards	0.9	9.0	2.0	90%	90%	43%
1975 Clean Air Act Statutory Standards	.41	3.4	3.1	95%	96%	11%
1976 Interim Standards*	.41	3.4	2.0	95%	96%	43%
1976 Statutory Standards	.41	3.4	0.4	95%	96%	89%

*Imposed by EPA as interim standards after suspension of statutory standards, except for California's HC and NO_x standards, which were set by the state. (Under the 1970 Clean Air Act, California may set emission standards that are lower than those applicable to cars sold in the other forty-nine states.)

**From uncontrolled levels.

This discovery caused some concern at EPA. Since EPA's monitoring of nationwide medical and air quality data had shown "adverse health effects . . . associated with . . . finely-divided, suspended particulate sulfates," EPA, in an internal document of March 1973 (entitled "Gasoline Composition and Gasoline Additives: Effect on Emission Products and Impact on EPA Mobile Source Emissions Control Strategy") recognized the need to research the problem and pledged to undertake such a study. If the study uncovered serious problems EPA could—under the authority of the Clean Air Act—publish regulations within 30 days to prevent any danger to public health.

The discovery of the problem, however, was not publicized. Sansom was concerned but believed that Ford's tentative data required confirmation. He notified Stork and Dr. Stanley Greenfield, EPA's Assistant Administrator for Research and Development, of the results and, in turn, they asked Dr. John Moran of EPA's research facility in Durham, North Carolina, to initiate a study of sulfate emissions from catalyst-equipped cars. Moran began a $2 million effort to test cars and devise sulfuric acid measurement techniques.

Moran's investigation was undertaken in the context of a certain amount of organizational confusion and conflict. As described in a National Academy of Sciences report, the administrative and scientific staffs at EPA were at that time somewhat at odds, to the agency's detriment. Some EPA scientists felt that they were not consulted on critical decisions, while some EPA administrators felt they were not receiving the scientific information necessary for making the decisions. Relations between these factions were exacerbated in May 1973, when funds for the investigation of sulfate emissions were cut during EPA's preliminary budget review. The budget cut appears to have been more a product of bureaucratic confusion than a firm policy decision, but nevertheless the preliminary cut of the sulfates program (to whch EPA scientists had given top priority) was sufficiently controversial to cause a leak to the press, which focused widespread attention on the problem. Moran, seeking to save his program, called Senator John Tunney of California and notified him of the potential gravity of the situation. In turn, Tunney told CBS News, and the problem gained national exposure. The Muskie Subcommittee subsequently restored the $2 million program.

Thus, by the time Russell Train became EPA Administrator in September 1973,* the sulfates problem had become a public issue. That fall, hearings on the problem were held by the Senate Subcommittee on Air and Water Pollution and the House Subcommittee on Public Health and Environment. Train, who had been briefed on the sulfates problem soon after taking office, admitted to the subcommittees that EPA's scientists had

> . . . concluded that, in the absence of a mechanism to control sulfate emissions from catalyst

---

*On April 27, William Ruckelshaus was named Acting Director of the FBI, and on July 26, President Nixon nominated Train, then chairman of the Council on Environmental Quality, to succeed him.

cars, more than one model year of cars equipped with catalysts could result in ambient levels of sulfates reaching levels at which recent studies suggest there will be adverse health effects.

However, Train emphasized that the data were preliminary and that he did not have a high degree of confidence in any of the quantitative estimates of the problem's dimensions:

> [The findings on sulfates are] not sufficient at this time to state that this is any more than a normal risk that one might expect with new technology and not one which would warrant certainly at this time an abandonment of the current timetable [for achieving the Clean Air Act standards].

Train said that he had considered reducing the 1975 standards and prohibiting the use of catalysts, but decided to do neither because such steps would have meant a loss of momentum in the air pollution control effort and would have required the introduction of other pollution control devices that were not ready for mass production. He also promised that research on the sulfates problem would continue and noted that "there are alternatives to deal with sulfate emissions if further studies indicate such action is necessary to protect public health." (He specifically cited desulfurization of gasoline as one such alternative.)

The automakers also testified at the 1973 hearings, urging a delay in the deadlines for achievement of the Clean Air Act standards, principally on the ground that emissions control devices cause an unacceptable decline in fuel economy. The three leading manufacturers differed in their treatment of the sulfates problem: Ford cited it as a reason for delaying the standards, but admitted that the problem was not then quantifiable; Chrysler said nothing on the issue; and GM President Edward N. Cole testified:

> In sum, we believe that there is insufficient existing health effects information and air monitoring data on ambient levels of suspended sulfates and sulfuric acid aerosols* to indicate that these pollutants are present at levels [sufficient to] adversely affect public health.

GM spokesmen argued that oxidation of sulfur dioxide to sulfur trioxide, which combines with water vapor to form sulfuric acid, occurs even without catalysts and that the converter only speeds up the process. GM also claimed that resulting atmospheric sulfate levels would remain harmless unless the sulfur content of gasoline increased and that, in any case, 99.4% of atmospheric sulfates comes from non-automotive sources such as coal-burning power plants.

By the end of 1973, the sulfates problem had been eclipsed in the public eye by the Arab oil boycott and consequent "energy crises." In the late fall, emergency energy bills containing extensions of the Clean Air Act deadlines were moving through Congress. The White House supported extending the deadlines, and since Train did not, the White House did not consult with EPA in lobbying for an extension. By the year's end, both the House and the Senate had passed emergency bills containing extensions, but the bills died when differences on other points could not be resolved by the end of the session. Reintroduced in 1974, they eventually became the Energy Supply and Environmental Coordination Act (ESECA), passed by Congress and signed by President Nixon in June of that year. For mobile sources, ESECA extended the 1975 model HC and CO interim standards through the 1976 model year and also authorized the EPA Administrator to grant a further one-year delay, prescribing interim standards for the 1977 model year; the delay request could be made at any time after January 1, 1975. The law forbade any further suspension of the NO_x standard.

On January 2, 1975, the Ford Motor Company and Chrysler and, about a week later, General Motors, requested another extension of the deadline for meeting the Clean Air Act's final emission standards on the grounds that they could not meet both the emission standards and the nation's energy conservation goals with existing technology. By their requests, the auto manufacturers were asking EPA Administrator Train to employ his newly granted authority and prescribe interim standards for 1977 model cars. If Train granted these requests for an extension of the emission control deadline, the Clean Air Act statutory standards would not go into effect until the 1978 model year, three years after Congress had originally

---

*"Suspended sulfates" refers to tiny particles of sulfate compounds floating in the air, "sulfuric acid aerosols" to sulfuric acid in the form of a fine mist.

intended. If he did not, he might be responsible for a potentially hazardous increase in the level of atmospheric sulfates, since the stricter emission standards would require wider use of catalytic converters because no other reliable emission control technology was then available for mass production.*

THE CONTEXT FOR TRAIN'S DECISION

The extension requests were made in the context of a number of economic, political, administrative and scientific factors that might enter, in some degree, into Train's analysis of the requests.

The Economic Picture

By the beginning of 1975, the United States was at the height of its most serious economic slump since the Great Depression. Nationally, unemployment stood at over 8%; the rate in Michigan was even worse —roughly 13%—as auto manufacturers closed plants and laid off hundreds of thousands of workers. (December 1974 auto production was off 18.3% from the December 1973 output.) Meanwhile, inflation was still running at around 10% annually, due in large part to the nation's increasing consumption of costly imported oil.

The "Big Three" automakers (GM, Ford and Chrysler) were the first, third and fifth largest industrial corporations in the United States in 1970, making the automotive industry the largest manufacturing industry in the country; and the production and maintenance of the automobile accounted for 10-15% of the country's gross national product. In this situation, any move that adversely affected the already ailing auto industry was certain to draw heavy criticism. Failure to extend the emission reduction deadlines would mean that a sizeable proportion of the 1977 model cars might not comply with auto emission standards, leaving the industry the choice of either halting production or else shipping the noncomplying cars and running the risk of a fine of $10,000 per car.

The Auto Industry

As the above discussion suggests, the auto industry carries a great deal of economic—and political—

power and has proven very difficult to regulate. The 1973 Senate Subcommittee Report cited the following incidents as examples of this power:

(1) In the fall of 1971, Ford unlawfully shipped 200,000 cars to dealers before EPA had certified compliance with federal emission standards. EPA subsequently fined Ford a nickel a car, or a total of $10,000,** hardly a discouragement against future violations. (It might have cost Ford more to store the cars while awaiting certification.)

(2) In May 1972, Ford revealed that unauthorized maintenance had been done on prototype vehicles submitted for 1973 certification tests, thus invalidating certification. Under the Clean Air Act, uncertified vehicles cannot be shipped to dealers; and EPA could have closed the company down by preventing the shipment of all 1973 model cars. Instead, the agency permitted Ford to ship the uncertified cars to dealers—the same violation as in 1971—but collected a fine of $7 million from Ford in February 1973.

(3) In March 1972, EPA sent a letter to all auto manufacturers stating that the clear intent of the Clean Air Act was to define a model "year" as 365 days. Three months later, EPA revealed that despite its definition, almost the entire industry planned to produce models under 1972 controls for more than 365 days—another example of noncompliance due to inconvenience. Again, EPA backed down, choosing not to enforce any penalties.

(4) In July 1972, EPA announced that automakers were installing devices on 1973 cars which would shut off emission controls immediately under certain normal driving conditions. None of these "defeat devices" were discovered during regular EPA testing because the manufacturers had constructed prototype cars so that shut-off devices would not be discovered in the EPA tests. Such devices were ordered unlawful by EPA.

In conclusion, the subcommittee staff reported that "the operation of competitive forces in the auto

---

*Emission standards are based ultimately on calculations of aggregate emissions from all cars; the higher the standard, the more cars must be equipped with control devices to reduce aggregate emissions.

**Although the Clean Air Act authorized fines of "up to" $10,000 per car, at that time (1971) EPA interpreted this to mean that the maximum fine did not have to be imposed. A few years later, EPA changed its views and began interpreting the law to require the full amount.

industry provides insufficient incentives to meet the nation's environmental objectives. It may be that penalty provisions, either in the form of limits on production relative to degree of control or in the form of emission charges on non-complying vehicles or yet other mechanisms will be needed to assure that the goals of the act are met."

In defense of their poor record in emission control, the automakers have repeatedly pointed to market pressures—i.e., the need to produce a sufficient number of vehicles to meet "basic demand"—which inhibit their flexibility to adopt new technology. The automakers say "basic demand" means producing 10 to 12 million cars a year in a wide range of models to satisfy the public's various requirements. "Basic demand" also has implications for jobs in the industry and among suppliers. Other groups, including the National Academy of Sciences, have argued that the "basic demand" concept is of "dubious validity." The assumption of "basic demand," however, was reflected in the 1973 decision of the U.S. Appeals Court to remand to the EPA Administrator for further consideration of EPA's denial of the auto companies' 1972 request for an extension of the 1975 model statutory standards. The decision observed that:

> A significant decrease in auto production will have a major economic impact on labor and suppliers to the company. We have no reason to believe that effective technology did not comport within its meaning sufficient technology to meet a basic level of consumer demand.

Nonetheless, many continued to question whether the automakers were in fact making the "good faith" effort to reduce emissions that the Clean Air Act required as a precondition of an extension.

The White House and Energy

The automakers were not without allies in the political arena in their quest for a second extension of Clean Air Act deadlines; as Train later recalled, "We had an awful lot of controversy [in the Administration] in the late fall of 1974 . . . a lot of pulling and hauling over the auto emission standards. . . ." On December 12, 1974, President Ford met with the heads of the major automakers (GM, Ford, Chrysler and American Motors) and United Auto Workers

President Leonard Woodcock to discuss measures to aid the auto industry. The requests made to the President included a five-year delay (until 1982) of the Clean Air Act standards and a freeze of the interim standards at the existing (1975 interim) levels. President Ford met several times in 1974 and early 1975 with Train, energy adviser Frank Zarb, economic adviser L. William Seidman, Transportation Secretary Claude Brinegar, and others to discuss the industry proposals; Train recalls that there was "lots of sympathy" in the Administration for a freeze on emission standards or even a rollback to higher emission level standards.

The main reason that the industry requests received such a sympathetic hearing in the Administration were the economic ill health of America's leading industry (see above) and the fuel economy issue. Although opinion was divided, some of the major automakers believed that the emission control devices, needed to attain the Clean Air Act standards, would substantially reduce fuel economy. Train himself admitted the importance of this issue in a January 2, 1975 announcement in the *Federal Register* regarding criteria that would govern the suspension hearings:

> The Administrator has determined that the impact of emission standards on fuel economy shall be an issue relevant to the suspension proceedings, both as an element of the public interest criteria, and as one factor bearing on the question of whether the technology to meet the statutory emission standards in 1977 is in fact available.

Knowing that the automakers were about to request a one-year delay in standards under ESECA, Train had argued in December that the President should remain silent on the issue in his 1975 State of the Union message; but in his address on January 15, 1975, President Ford listed energy independence as a top national priority and said he would ask Congress to delay final auto emission standards until 1982 in return for a commitment by the auto industry to improve fuel economy by 40% on 1974 to 1980 models. The Administration's Energy Independence Act, sent to Congress on January 31, 1975, also proposed stricter interim standards for model years 1977–1981. In effect, then, the President was endorsing the auto industry's request for a delay in the effective date of the final standards. Train called the President's proposals "reasonable"; but as he later recalled, "whatever [the President] said, [it] couldn't govern what the outcome of the suspension decision [would be]. . . . It was important to protect the integrity of that suspension process [and] the quasi-judicial function of the Administrator."

Congress and the Environmentalists

It was unclear how Congress would react to another delay in the standards. The post-Watergate election of 1974 had produced a heavily Democratic majority that was united on the need to do something about energy and the economy but divided on what it should be. The prospects were for a partisan struggle over President Ford's energy and economic proposals.

At the same time, key legislators who were strongly pro-environment had returned to the congressional committees charged with oversight of EPA—Muskie's Senate Subcommittee on Air and Water Pollution, and the House Subcommittee on Public Health and Environment, chaired by Representative Paul Rogers (D-Fla.). Muskie, the main author of the 1970 Clean Air Act, was known to be very skeptical regarding the auto industry's statements as to what was technologically possible; moreover, Muskie had called the 1974 congressional delay of the standards in ESECA "special legislation to deal with a specific situation . . . not intended to set precedents" and had expressed his opposition to a further extension. Train had earned the respect of Muskie and other legislators for his commitment to the environment, but Roger Strelow, EPA's Assistant Administrator for Air and Waste Management and a close Train advisor, recalled that "there was just no question—we knew we [would] take a beating from the people up on the Hill [if we granted the suspension requests] . . . . EPA has always been an agency at the heart of controversy and . . . would be in great trouble were it not for the strong congressional support it has had."

Finally, environmental groups, who could probably be expected to be sensitive to the nation's need to conserve energy, had already expressed their belief that "the auto companies had the technology to meet existing emissions deadlines and improve fuel economy at the same time." They insisted that new evidence about the effects of air pollution on human health made strict enforcement of the law more important than ever. If environmental groups found the sulfates problem a credible one, they were more likely to press for desulfurization of gasoline than delay of hydrocarbon and carbon monoxide standards as an

answer. (Ralph Nader, for example, took this position in his testimony at the suspension hearings.) Desulfurization, however, was certain to be opposed by the oil companies as a costly undertaking.

Technical Information and the Public

Before the extension hearings were scheduled to begin in late January, Senator Tunney, seeking an update on the sulfates problem, called John Moran on a weekend to find out the results of the latest sulfate analysis. Moran, who had recently completed a study of the public health impact of catalysts, was unsure about releasing any information; he called his boss, Jack Finklea, the supervisor of EPA's Durham research center, and asked his advice. Finklea called a low-ranking official in the public affairs office of EPA for approval, and was given permission to release the study to Tunney. By Monday evening, CBS News had the story.

The object of this interest—an EPA report entitled "Issue Paper—Estimated Public Health Impact as a Result of Equipping Light-Duty Motor Vehicles with Oxidation Catalysts"—was a complex scientific analysis that had not been reviewed by anyone in Washington prior to its release to Tunney by the Durham people. Train was thus placed in a difficult spot; his response to the press was a tentative endorsement of the report but also indicated that he could not be sure that the sulfate problem existed. However, his disclaimer was not emphasized by the media and soon large numbers of the public believed that a serious health problem was posed by catalyst-equipped automobiles. The Issue Paper was released on January 30, 1975. It summarized the technical information (which did not greatly differ from what was learned during the 1973 congressional hearings) upon which Train would base his decision on the extension requests as follows:

> . . . Vehicles [currently] being built to meet the National Interim Emissions Standards [the standards then in effect] have lower sulfuric acid emissions than do those designed to meet either the California Interim Standards or the Statutory HC/CO Emissions Standards [which Train was being asked to suspend], for which comparable sulfuric acid emission rates are expected.

Physical model exposure estimates suggest that on and near major arterial thoroughfares in major urban cities the incremental sulfuric acid exposures will exceed the health effects threshold a few days of the year after two model years of vehicles are equipped with catalysts in Southern California and after three to four model years are so equipped nationally. . . .

Three basic control approaches are available to limit sulfuric acid emissions: increased use of noncatalyst technology, modifications to catalyst systems to reduce sulfate formation or trap sulfates before they are emitted, and reduction in gasoline sulfur levels. Gasoline desulfurization cannot be expected to have much impact before 1980 although as an interim measure gasoline sulfur reductions through blending and allocation procedures (probably on a selective geographic basis) may be possible. Control of vehicle sulfate emissions through an emission standard would likely have no impact before the 1979 model year. At 49-State or California Interim Standard levels, or at Statutory Standard levels, manufacturers are unlikely to eliminate catalyst usage on a major proportion of their production before the 1979 model year.

A public health benefit/risk analysis which weights the benefits associated with decreased carbon monoxide and oxidant exposures against the risks due to increased sulfuric acid exposures suggests that on a national basis health risks exceed the benefits after four model years are equipped with catalysts. It should be noted, however, that this conclusion is based upon assumptions about dose responses and human exposure about which there still remain uncertainties. . . .

The March 4 Meeting

In January and February, EPA conducted hearings on the requests to extend the deadline for achieving the Clean Air Act statutory standards from 1977 to 1978. At the hearings, the automakers' testimony focused on the availability of technology to meet the standards, the economic impact of requiring further emission reductions, and the incompatibility of the statutory standards with improved fuel economy, while environmentalists decried the loss of momentum in the pollution control effort that would result from a further suspension of the standards. Witnesses who addressed the sulfates question called it a "speculative" problem.

Train had to make a decision within 60 days of the manufacturers' initial request—in this case, by

March 5. During February, he met more and more frequently with his close advisors to discuss the suspension question, and as the deadline for a decision approached, this became almost the only subject of discussion for the Administrator. On the evening of March 4, Train chose to meet with six men for a final discussion: Roger Strelow, Assistant Administrator for Air and Waste Management; Dr. Wilson K. Talley, Assistant Administrator for Research and Development*; Robert L. Baum, Deputy Assistant Administrator for General Mobile Source Air Pollution Control; Dr. Kenneth L. Bridbord, a medical officer at EPA's Durham laboratory; and William Pedersen, a staff attorney in the Air Division of the General Counsel's office. (See Exhibit 15.1 for an EPA organization chart.) (Dr. Alvin Alm, EPA's Assistant Administrator for Planning and Management, was out of town at the time of the meeting. The Office of Planning and Management is responsible for the overall planning activities of the agency. It develops, initiates, and monitors new and redirected agency goals and programs, and administers a planning-programming-budgeting system for the entire agency. Because of Train's desire for privacy in the decision-making process, Alm was not represented by a stand-in.)

At the meeting Strelow, Train's closest advisor, recommended that Train relax the statutory timetable to allow the 1975 Interim Standards set for California to become effective nationwide in 1978 and to postpone the effective date of the 1976 Clean Air Act statutory standards until 1979. Strelow later recalled his position:

> I very grudgingly and with no inconsiderable frustration supported a position that said some extension probably was needed because of this [sulfates] risk factor, even though if somebody had said "do you believe the data, do you really think this is going to be a problem," my reaction [would have been] no, I don't believe it, I don't think it's going to be a problem, but I have to admit that unless we can thoroughly . . . dismiss any risk, then . . . we're sort of caught. . . .
>
> . . . The one thing that really tipped the balance for [me] was that discounting all you want for the flakiness of the [technical data], nobody really knew . . . I mean, there was a potential

---

*Talley replaced Dr. Stanley Greenfield in this position late in 1974.

here, at least a theoretical potential, for this kind of build-up [of sulfate emissions]. And in the absence of further information, if you took the course that said, "well we don't believe it, let's just go ahead," you ran the risk of having an *affirmative* government action . . . possibly causing an increase in an unhealthy pollutant. . . .

Strelow noted that EPA studies had shown that both the actual health effects of delaying the HC and CO standards for a year and the actual health benefits from not delaying them would be relatively small.

On the other hand, Baum, who in conjunction with Stork and John Dekaney (head of EPA's Ann Arbor laboratory) had chaired the suspension hearings, argued that the suspension request should be denied because the technology was available to meet the standards; he felt that the potential sulfates problem did not outweigh that fact. Stork agreed that the final HC/CO standards were technologically feasible. He did not believe the sulfuric acid problem was as severe as EPA medical personnel claimed, and feared that converters might eventually be eliminated entirely, which, in the absence of other methods of control, would mean a serious setback in efforts at emission control.

Talley emphasized that denying the request and adhering to the stricter standards would produce incremental benefits from reduced emissions of HC and CO but would also add to the environment a new pollutant (sulfuric acid) in undetermined quantities and with undetermined effects. However, since quantification of the problem was impossible, a good risk-benefit analysis could not be done and therefore, in Talley's view, the ultimate decision would have to be a "judgment call by Train." Pedersen, who acted as the meeting's "scribe," felt that, given the unknown dimensions of the sulfates risk, it would be easier to justify granting the extension than to defend moving forward to stricter standards and presumably greater sulfate emissions.

Bridbord argued vehemently against any continued catalyst use and told Train to grant the extension requests, claiming that the risks of continued exposure to the potential dangers of sulfuric acid greatly outweighed those risks involved in exposure to present HC and CO levels. He claimed that sulfuric acid was a "serious threat" and that "EPA's doctors could not be responsible for introducing another dangerous pollutant into the air." As Train later recalled,

I look back sort of surprised at the strength and virulence of the health scientists' feeling about the catalyst and about increasing the standard—tightening the standard—if that meant widespread use of catalysts. . . . This was presented to me as an ethical, ideological increase in health impacts [from higher sulfate emissions]; it wasn't a matter of weighing that risk against other possible benefits of keeping the industry on track and pushing the development of new technology (which presumably would follow from moving ahead with the schedule), but that *any* increase that we ourselves generated by EPA action was per se unacceptable—unconscionable and unacceptable and *outrageous.*

Later that evening, Train sat in his Waterside Mall office and considered the alternatives. The next day, his 60 days would be up. Before him lay a copy of the Clean Air Act Amendments of 1970. Section 202(5)(D) of the law reads:

The Administrator shall grant such suspension only if he determines that (i) such suspension is essential to the public interest or the public health and welfare of the United States, (ii) all good faith efforts have been made to meet the standards established by this subsection, (iii) the applicant has established that effective control technology, processes, operating methods, or other alternatives are not available or have not been available for a sufficient period of time to achieve compliance prior to the effective date of such standards, and (iv) the study and investigation of the National Academy of Sciences conducted pursuant to subsection (C) and other information available to him has not indicated that technology, processes, or other alternatives are available to meet such standards. . . .

(E) Nothing in this paragraph shall extend the effective date of any emission standard required to be prescribed under this subsection for more than one year.

Sitting alone in his office, he contemplated the pros and cons of another postponement of the statutory standards. If he did not postpone them, would he be able to enforce them without the cooperation of the auto industry? Were the health effects data conclusive enough to justify the risk of getting farther behind on the HC and CO timetables? Could he justify putting still another dangerous pollutant into the air at unknown levels? Could alternative technology be implemented before long-range health risks would outweigh benefits?

President Ford's earlier endorsement of the delay placed tremendous pressure on Train. Throughout his career as an environmentalist, and particularly during his stints at the Council on Environmental Quality and now at EPA, Russell Train had earned the reputation of being his "own man." He had bucked the Nixon Administration on many occasions when he felt environmental concerns had been unjustly subordinated. Now, however, he was faced with economic and energy problems which had greater impact than ever before on environmental policy decisions. While he was not bound by the President's endorsement, Train could not avoid considering the repercussions that a rejection of Mr. Ford's recommendation might hold.

These and many other questions were factors in his decision-making. His closest advisors had been unable to agree upon either the gravity of the problem or a timetable to achieve the original clean air goals set forth in the 1970 statute. He reread the suspension criteria within the Clean Air Act and reviewed the dilemma from historical and scientific viewpoints. Late that evening he made up his mind.

APPENDIX A

Chronology of Events: The Sulfates Problem

Year	Event
1920s	Doctors recognize automobile exhaust as a potential health threat.
1950s	Research links automobile exhaust to Los Angeles smog.
1959	California legislation calls for installation of pollution control devices as soon as technology becomes available.
1963	Clean Air Act passed.
1964	California Air Resources Board certifies development of add-on control devices; the state legislates emission standards for 1966 models.
1965	Clean Air Act Amendments passed, authorizing HEW to set emission standards for 1969 models.
1967	Auto industry asks federal pre-emption of state emission control laws; Congress agrees, but exempts California. Ford and Mobil form Inter-Industry Emissions Control (IIEC) program.
1969	HEW-imposed emission standards effective. At White House meeting, automakers agree to stiff interim standards for 1975 and 90% emissions reduction for 1980, and oil companies agree to changes in gasoline. GM starts catalyst development program.
1970	Clean Air Act Amendments (CAA) passed, pushing 1980 standards up to 1975–76. EPA created; imposes interim standards for '72–'74 models.
1972	Automakers request extension of CAA deadlines. EPA Administrator Ruckelshaus denies the request, but U.S. Court of Appeals orders reconsideration. EPA begins to get data on health effects of sulfates, and under EPA contract, Dow Chemical Company begins analyzing emissions from converter-equipped cars.
1972–73	Senate Public Works Committee's Subcommittee on Air and Water Pollution (the Muskie Subcommittee) investigates implementation of CAA.
1973	
February	H. L. Misch of Ford Motor Company notifies EPA of discovery of sulfuric acid in exhaust of converter-equipped cars (the "sulfates" problem).
March	EPA study recommends study of the sulfates problem.
April	Ruckelshaus grants extension of CAA deadlines.
May	EPA sulfates research budget cut; restored by the Muskie Subcommittee.

September	GM testifies before House Commerce Committee's Subcommittee on Public Health and Environment that the formation of sulfuric acid from auto exhaust is not a serious problem. Russell Train named EPA Administrator; promises major investigation of sulfates problem. Train testifies in September and again in November that the sulfates problem does not warrant freeze or postponement of CAA standards.
December	President Nixon asks Congress to delay the deadline for meeting CAA emission standards from 1975 to 1977.
1974	
June	Congress delays CAA deadlines until 1977; authorizes EPA Administrator to grant further one-year delay.
November	EPA report on sulfates research released.
December	President Ford meets with automakers, who say they need 5-year delay in CAA standards to develop fuel-efficient non-polluting cars.
1975	
January	Automakers request one-year EPA delay of final emission standards. President Ford asks 5-year congressional delay in CAA final standards, with stiffer interim standards. EPA Issue Paper on sulfates leaked, then released.
February	Hearings on Ford Motor Company's delay request.
March	Train meets with advisors on March 4; decision on extension request due March 5.

APPENDIX B*

Alternative Engine Systems

Diesel, stratified charge, and rotary engines are alternative power systems which demonstrate great promise of meeting statutory emission standards without the use of catalysts. Each has been developed to the point where it can be mass-produced.

DIESEL ENGINES

The diesel engine was introduced in 1923 by Peugeot and is now mass-produced successfully by GM, Peugeot, Mercedes Benz and Austin of England. At present, only Mercedes and Peugeot market diesel passenger cars in the United States.

The Mercedes and GM diesels have been found to meet the statutory HC and CO standards and come much closer to the NO_x levels specified in the law than the present internal combustion engine. Also, EPA states that a diesel-powered auto gets as much as 75% better fuel economy than comparable 1973 ICE cars and there is evidence that diesels are considerably more durable than gasoline engines.

However, diesel cars are relatively slow at acceleration, and U.S. automakers say that unacceptable performance is a tradeoff which the American public will not accept. Other drawbacks include low horsepower, limited fuel availability, noise, smoke, odor, high initial cost, and cold starting.

Today, GM mass-produces, in Germany, a car with a base price around $4,000. This car, the Opel, meets the HC and CO statutory standards, and because it already exists, it avoids any risks which might be entailed in starting up a new production line for an automobile. A test of the diesel engine could be achieved simply by adding the required safety devices to the Opel diesel and shipping them to this country in place of or in addition to some of the other cars GM now imports.

STRATIFIED CHARGE ENGINES

The stratified charge is the most publicized alternative engine system. Currently, Honda manufactures a car with a stratified charge engine which meets 1975 statutory standards without any add-on devices.

---

*This appendix is largely based on pages 85–94 of the Senate Subcommittee Report and does not take into account developments subsequent to the events described in this case.

Also, the Honda type engine achieves NO_x emission levels far superior to anything that has been admitted as technologically feasible with other ICEs.

Other advantages of the stratified charge engine are better fuel economy and the prospect that the American public could save $53 billion over two years compared to the conventional piston ICE with catalysts and other add-on devices necessary to meet HC and CO standards. The NAS indicates that each stratified charge engine would save its owner $700 compared to a single catalyst car to meet HC and CO standards and $1,000 compared to a dual catalyst car to meet NO_x standards.

However, the advantages of the stratified charge engine have thus far been demonstrated only on models smaller in size than the typical American car. Since the engine is fairly heavy to begin with, enlarging it to suit American size and horsepower standards may create severe problems with fuel economy, as well as other—yet unknown—difficulties.

ROTARY ENGINES

While the rotary engines are not inherently cleaner, their small size permits the addition of thermal reactors and other control devices to clean up emissions. In addition to size advantages and its apparent potential to meet HC and CO standards, the rotary engine has faster acceleration than other engines of similar size.

One drawback is that the rotary engine has never met NO_x standards. Others include a 30% fuel economy penalty, a high degree of oil-burning (one quart for 500–1,000 miles), and durability problems (almost half of the rotary engines in existence have had warranty work done on them). The *Wall Street Journal* reported that a survey indicated that 20% of rotary engine cars that had gone over 30,000 miles had had a major engine failure. Detroit has indicated that any more than a 3% failure rate in the first 50,000 miles for any equipment is regarded as unacceptable.

General Motors has led the auto industry in the attempt to develop the rotary engine. In 1970, GM entered into contracts with five other automotive firms to begin production tooling for rotary engine vehicles. For the last five years, and at a cost estimated by GM to be over $100 million, GM has proceeded with rotary development. In late 1975, however, GM concluded that in order to sufficiently control HC emissions, rotary engines must pay an exorbitant fuel penalty. As a result, GM has halted its plans to develop the rotary engines, and its enormous investment may be a total waste of time.

344

EXHIBIT 15.1: Environmental Protection Agency

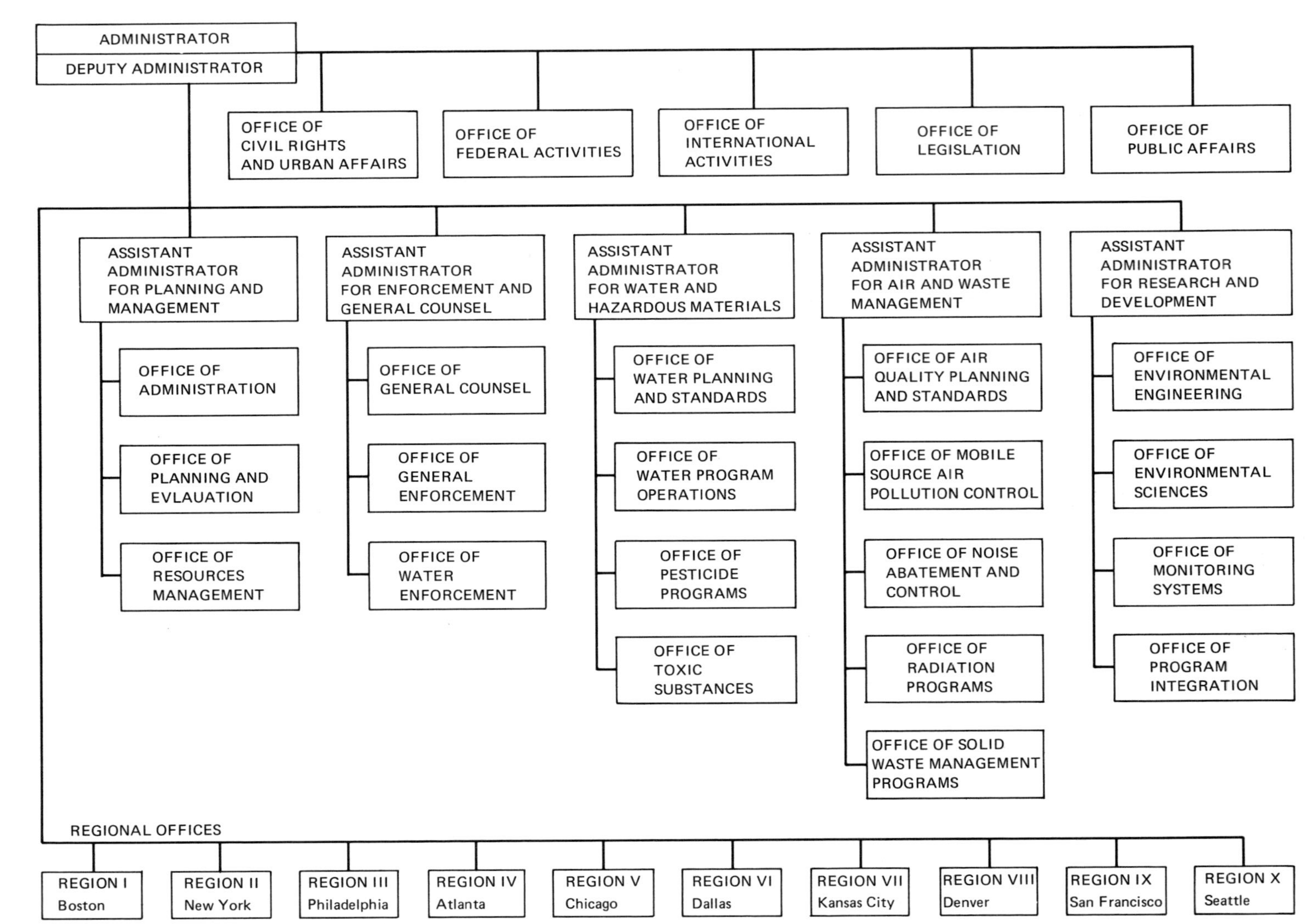

Note: Prior to 1974, Air and Water programs were combined under one assistant administrator and Pesticide, Noise, Radiation and Solid Waste programs under another, and there was no separate office for Toxic Substances.

16

Automobile Emissions Control: The Sulfates Problem (B)

By March 5, 1975, EPA Administrator Russell Train had to decide whether to grant an auto industry request that he delay for one year the effective date of the Clean Air Act's final auto emission standards. As Part A (chapter 15) of this case noted, much of the technical data available to Train was summarized in a January 30, 1975 EPA Issue Paper entitled "Estimated Public Health Impact as a Result of Equipping Light-Duty Motor Vehicles with Oxidation Catalysts." Part B of this case (this chapter) examines in detail the evidence for and against the conclusions of that paper.

DIMENSIONS OF THE PROBLEM

Atmospheric sulfates, which are particulate compounds containing the sulfate (SO_4) ion, usually exist in the atmosphere dissolved in water droplets. They are produced by reactions involving sulfur dioxide (SO_2), oxygen (O_2), and sunlight. Although these reactions are not clearly understood, other pollutants —ammonia, metallic aerosols, and smog components— apparently act as catalysts; that is, the other pollutants increase the rate at which sulfur dioxide is converted into sulfate compounds without themselves being consumed by the reaction.

On a global basis, natural (e.g., volcanic) and man-made sulfur dioxide emission sources each account for about half of the atmosphere's sulfur dioxide (and thus sulfates) content. (Very few atmospheric sulfates are the result of direct emissions of sulfate compounds; most are produced by reactions involving sulfur dioxide.) In industrial areas, man-made SO_2 emissions dominate. (Exhibit 16.1 shows the average sulfate concentrations in the contiguous United States for the period 1963–1970; increments from industrial activity or increased automotive sulfate emissions would be added to these levels.) Coal combustion* in power plants and other industrial facilities is the big-

---

*All fossil fuels—coal, oil, gasoline, etc.—contain sulfur; when the fuel is burned, i.e., combined with oxygen, sulfur dioxide is formed.

gest source of man-made SO_2 emissions; on the average, automobiles account for less than one percent of total man-made sulfur dioxide emissions, although the percentage is higher in heavily urbanized areas.

Sulfuric acid is the most dangerous atmospheric sulfate, although adverse health effects can result from breathing other sulfates. (Sulfuric acid is thought to comprise a major portion of the atmosphere's sulfates content in some areas, while in other areas it is a minor constituent.) As Part A (chapter 16) of this case discussed, studies in 1973 by the Ford Motor Company showed that the use of catalytic converters to reduce automobile emissions of harmful pollutants such as carbon monoxide (CO) and hydrocarbons (HC) would result in increased emission of sulfuric acid aerosols (i.e., sulfuric acid in the form of a fine mist or spray). Sulfuric acid is also present in the exhaust of non-catalyst cars, but only in trace quantities.

Automotive sulfate emissions originate primarily in sulfur-containing impurities which occur naturally in petroleum. Most of these impurities are removed during the refining process but a small percentage ends up in gasoline after refining (300 parts per million on the national average). Also, some gasoline contains sulfur compound additives. During combustion, the sulfur is oxidized to form sulfur dioxide which is then further oxidized to sulfur trioxide (SO_3). The oxidation catalysts used in catalytic converters speed up both of these processes. The SO_3 then reacts with water vapor (H_2O) in the exhaust stream to form sulfuric acid (H_2SO_4). The potential for health problems would arise from exposure to heavy concentrations of sulfuric acid from catalyst-equipped vehicles before significant dilution of the sulfates could occur in the air.

Both the exact amount of sulfuric acid emitted from catalyst-equipped vehicles (the sulfate emission factor) and concentrations of the acid in the air resulting from automobile emissions (the sulfate exposure level) have yet to be definitively determined. Also, although it is generally agreed that sulfuric acid (and other particulate sulfates) can be potent respiratory irritants, the exact threshold of danger to human health remains controversial. The remaining sections of this case summarize information regarding six issues discussed in EPA's January 30, 1975 Issue Paper: the emission of sulfuric acid by catalyst-equipped cars; models for predicting human exposure to those emissions; probable health effects of various levels of exposure; possible emissions of other pollutants from catalyst-equipped cars; analysis of benefits and risks associated with catalyst use; and strategies for controlling the sulfates problem.

EMISSION FACTORS

In attempting to project emission factors, the EPA study tested prototype catalyst-equipped vehicles using the Federal Test Procedure (FTP) (which involves both hot and cold starts) as well as the EPA Highway Fuel Economy Test (HFET). The report noted that emissions of sulfuric acid varied with levels of fuel sulfur (the report assumed a U.S. average of 0.03% and a California average of 0.05–0.07%), HC/CO control levels (Federal interim, California interim, or Clean Air Act standards), fuel economy (since sulfates production is proportional to fuel consumed), catalyst pre-conditioning (referring to the fact that catalysts may store sulfates and later release them) and catalyst age (no one knew at the time how catalyst effectiveness changed with time and use, but it was assumed that sulfate production would change proportionately). Exhibit 16.2 summarizes the results. In describing these results, the Issue Paper concluded:

> Vehicles being built to meet the National Interim Emissions Standards have lower sulfuric acid emissions than do those designed to meet either the California Interim Standards or the Statutory HC/CO Emissions Standards. . . .

Shortly after EPA released the January 30, 1975 Issue Paper, the Manufacturers of Emissions Controls Association (MECA) commissioned Energy and Environmental Analysis, Inc. (EEA), a consulting firm, to study emissions factors. The EEA findings are summarized in Exhibit 16.3.

In testimony before the EPA hearing panel in February 1975, Dr. Robert Sansom of EEA, formerly EPA Assistant Administrator for Air and Water programs, called attention to yet another set of emission factor test results (see Exhibit 16.4); Sansom pointed out that the Ann Arbor laboratory's results were generally substantially lower than the Durham laboratory's results cited in the Issue Paper.*

---

*In a later interview, Sansom suggested that EPA scientists had differing views on catalysts and allowed those views to influence their reports. (He also noted that most data on emission factors are based on tests of prototype cars, which are known for a higher degree of control over HC and CO emissions than assembly-line cars; this in turn would create higher sulfate emission factors on the prototypes.)

As the data presented thus far suggest, sulfate emission factors are influenced by the type of catalyst used and the sulfur content of the gasoline. Sulfate readings obtained under the HFET and FTP with the two main types of catalysts are shown in Exhibit 16.5. Exhibit 16.6 shows data from a study by the National Academy of Sciences using "cold start" test procedures on a variety of catalyst types, with varying fuel sulfur levels.

It was apparent at the time all of these calculations were made that sulfate emission factors—however measured—were unlikely to remain constant. Some of those concerned with the problem suggested that calibration changes on production cars appeared to lower sulfate emissions substantially (perhaps as much as 50%) compared to the levels measured for the prototype cars in the Durham study (Exhibit 16.2). Also, it appeared possible that reformulation of catalysts might reduce acid emissions. Finally, changes in fuel composition and changes in catalyst systems necessitated by future (stiffer) emission standards would be reflected in changes in sulfuric acid emission levels. At the time of Train's decision, only the state of California was operating under stiffer emission standards, but no tests had then been performed on California prototypes or production cars. However, two 1974 studies (one by the Bureau of Mines) and a February 1975 EPA study entitled "Tradeoffs Associated with Possible Auto Emissions Standards" concluded that gasoline sulfur levels were lower than had been thought, particularly in California, and that even with stricter auto emission standards, fuel sulfur content both nationally and in California could be expected to remain in the 200–250 ppm (parts per million) range. Since EPA's Issue Paper had used estimated fuel sulfur levels of 300 ppm nationally and 500–700 ppm in California, the emission factors reported in the Issue Paper were potentially overstated by a factor of 2.0 to 2.5.

EXPOSURE ESTIMATES

Emission factors quantify how much sulfuric acid will be released by automobiles; how much acid people will inhale is a separate question. At present, no technique exists for measuring ambient air concentrations of H_2SO_4 directly; consequently, indirect techniques—models—must be employed. This section discusses both the models used in the EPA Issue Paper and others that were available at the time.

Physical Activity Models*

EPA researchers employed what has been termed "the CO dispersion/physical activity computer model" to generate H_2SO_4 exposure estimates. A CO dispersion model assumes that sulfuric acid aerosols disperse like a stable gas (i.e., CO). The physical activity model used in the EPA study assumed, for its 24-hour exposure estimates, that a commuter spends two hours daily on an expressway, one hour in a street canyon, thirteen hours at home, and eight hours at work. For its peak hourly exposure estimates, EPA assumed a person traveling the ten-lane expressway under the conditions described in Exhibit 16.7. Using this model, the EPA report broke down exposure estimates for differing years and meteorological conditions, with the results shown in Exhibit 16.7.

Exhibit 16.8 reports exposure estimates for a variety of circumstances and locations. For the *major throughway* a heavily traveled ten-lane expressway was assumed, with a daily flow of 233,000 vehicles and a peak flow of 20,000 vehicles per hour. (JFK Expressway in Chicago carries 267,000 vehicles per day and the Santa Monica Freeway in Los Angeles carries 226,000. It has been estimated that these "worst case" conditions exist on only 16 miles of freeway in the country.) The *intersecting freeways* were assumed to be eight lanes, each with 2,000 vehicles per hour for four lanes each and 1,000 vehicles per hour for each of the other four lanes. Adverse meteorological conditions—"E" stability (slightly stable), and wind velocity at one meter per second— were assumed. The *expressway street canyon* was an eight-lane expressway with 2,000 vehicles/lane/hour in four lanes and 1,000 vehicles/lane/hour in the other four lanes. Vertical-walled, flat-topped buildings with a two-meter-per-second wind at 90° were assumed. The *sporting event* used to project a complex source exposure assumed a parking area and sport center 600 meters by 700 meters adjacent to two intersecting four-lane streets. The parking lot was assumed to contain 3,000 vehicles which exit via three exit roads onto the two four-lane streets in one hour. These vehicles were imposed upon a flow of 100 vehicles/ lane/hour on the two four-lane streets. Light wind

---

*Much of the material in this section has been drawn from the EPA Issue Paper, January 30, 1975.

(one meter/second), neutral (D) stability, and a 1,000 meter mixing height were assumed.*

Because southern California gasoline contains more sulfur than the national average gasoline, California vehicles emit greater amounts of sulfuric acid. Resultant exposures are, therefore, higher. Were California gasolines to be reduced in sulfur content to national averages, the emission factors for the 1975–76 California Interim Standards would be the same as the National Statutory Standards emission factors.

Surrogate Models

Relying exclusively on the CO dispersion/physical activity model, the January Issue Paper concluded that exposure levels would exceed the threshold for health effects—which was estimated at a 24-hour level of roughly 10 ug/m^3—"after two model years of vehicles [were] equipped with catalysts in Southern California and after three to four model years [were] so equipped nationally." However, numerous other models were available at the time of Train's decision and were, in fact, employed in subsequent studies of the problem; most of those models yielded lower exposure levels. Termed "surrogate" models, they basically assume that sulfate concentration will resemble the concentration of other substances believed to be similar to sulfates in dispersion pattern and chemical reactivity. The remainder of this section examines three of the more prominent surrogates: lead particulates, carbon monoxide, and carboxyhemoglobin levels in the bloodstream.

Lead Surrogate Models

Lead surrogate models have been used in many predictions of sulfate levels and have been justified as surrogates on the grounds that lead emission at the roadside is primarily auto-related and that lead and sulfate particles are released in relatively similar fashion under similar driving conditions. However, human exposure to lead particles differs from exposure to sulfuric acid aerosol particles in that a significant portion of the former are too large to be respirable (more

than about two microns in diameter). The best estimate is that about half of lead emissions are of respirable size. Also, not all of the lead contained in gasoline is emitted as lead particulate; a good estimate is about 70%. A further complication in lead surrogate models is the fact that roadside dust containing already emitted particles may be kicked up by passing automobiles.

The following three examples of lead surrogate models represent independent efforts at predicting sulfate exposure.

California Air Resources Board. In the course of deciding to adopt more stringent HC and CO emissions limits than those recommended by EPA, the California Air Resources Board (CARB) employed a lead surrogate model to estimate 24-hour sulfate exposures for people residing within 150 feet of major freeways after ten years of catalyst cars. CARB analysis produced the following results:

H_2SO_4 Emissions Factor (g/mi)	Maximum 24-Hour Average Exposure
.015	3.8 ug/m^3
.03	7.5 ug/m^3
.05	12.8 ug/m^3

The calculations used in preparing the above table are presented in Exhibit 16.9.

General Motors. GM has also used a lead surrogate model to develop exposure predictions, making two estimates of sulfate exposure based on lead monitoring near busy roadways. Monitoring data were collected on a highway with a daily traffic level of 168,000 cars (JFK Expressway in Chicago is the nation's busiest, carrying 267,000 vehicles per day), and at a four-lane interchange in Los Angeles. The results were as follows:

H_2SO_4 Emissions Factor (g/mi)	Maximum 24-Hour Exposure
.015	1.7–5.6 ug/m^3
.03	3.3–11.2 ug/m^3
.05	5.5–18.7 ug/m^3

For the upper estimates, the lead level was measured at the shoulder of the road, average hourly traffic was overestimated by up to 50% (i.e., the estimated 1985 levels), and the adverse meteorology was assumed to

---

*It has been estimated that on average, these adverse meteorological conditions occur only 9–15 hours per year. Neutral (D) or slightly stable (E) air coupled with low wind velocity discourages, or at the least does not encourage, dispersion of pollutants in the atmosphere. A mixing height of 1,000 meters means that a thermal barrier at that altitude prevents further upward dispersion of pollutants.

hold for all 24 hours. In 1973, GM developed 24-hour average exposure estimates of 0.20–4.56 ug/m^3 (depending on distance from roadside) based on an emission factor of .009 g/mi; 216,000 vehicles/day; catalyst usage on 25% of the cars; and adverse meteorology. GM also estimated 24-hour average concentrations in a street canyon to be 2.10 ug/m^3 one meter from the street and 1.07 ug/m^3 at a distance of ten meters.

Ford. Ford has also projected worst case sulfate exposures based on recorded lead monitoring data from a busy freeway. Assuming a commuter spends one full hour daily in traffic, the Ford projection predicted the following exposure levels after ten years of catalyst cars.

H_2SO_4 Emissions Factor (g/mi)	Peak Hourly Exposure	24-Hour Average
.015	49 ug/m^3	4.6 ug/m^3
.03	98 ug/m^3	9.3 ug/m^3
.05	163 ug/m^3	15.8 ug/m^3

These projections are based on the highest ambient lead concentrations ever recorded (taken in a vehicle moving in LA freeway traffic).

Carbon Monoxide Surrogate Models

Carbon monoxide (CO) can also be used as a surrogate for projecting potential sulfate exposure levels. A CO surrogate approach has been advocated by many because there is a great deal of CO monitoring data, because CO is primarily auto-related, and because the minute size of the sulfate aerosol droplets emitted by cars lead to the conclusion that they should disperse like CO, which is a gas.

Because the health effects of CO are more immediate than those of lead, almost all CO monitoring is for one-hour to eight-hour intervals rather than the 24-hour intervals used for lead. Also, CO monitoring devices measure CO emitted from stationary sources and trucks as well as cars. CO and sulfate emissions generally vary oppositely with vehicle speed, with CO dropping and sulfates rising as speeds increase—both because of the relevant reaction chemistry and the preconditioning phenomenon discussed earlier (i.e., catalysts may store sulfates and release them later). While CO surrogate modelling relates CO emissions to sulfate emissions in much the same manner as the lead surrogate model in Exhibit 16.9, these speed and storage factors make the actual relationship exceedingly complex.

Three CO surrogate estimates have been developed using New York City, California Department of Transportation, and EPA data.

New York City. General Electric monitored hourly CO levels at a number of roadside locations in New York City in 1970. Some mechanical receptors were placed at the road, and the others were placed between six and 100 feet away. Vehicle speed and volume were also monitored. Exhibit 16.10 shows the resulting projected maximum one-hour sulfate concentrations (based on the highest CO level at each site) after all cars are equipped with catalysts. While GE did not estimate 24-hour levels, the ratio of 1-hour:24-hour CO concentrations is roughly 10:1 according to most estimates.

California Department of Transportation. In 1972 the California DOT monitored hourly CO concentrations at five sites on the Santa Monica, San Diego, and Harbor Freeways in Los Angeles. The highest CO reading was monitored on a probe four feet above the median strip of the San Diego Freeway during the morning rush hour of 15,000 cars with wind speeds about 5.5 mph and wind angle approximately 10° from the road under stable atmospheric conditions. The following shows the one-hour sulfate concentrations derived from a CO surrogate model using this peak CO level reading.

H_2SO_4 Emissions Factor (g/mi)	Peak 1-Hour Sulfates (ug/m^3)
.015	30.0
.03	60.0
.05	100.0

The above estimates are based on the highest roadside CO concentrations found in over 4,000 one-hour samples on Los Angeles freeways and the peak CO value does not reflect the relatively small difference found between readings at upwind and downwind locations.

EPA National CO Data. A CO surrogate model can also be derived by utilizing the highest recorded one-hour and eight-hour CO levels found in 1972–73 EPA reports on air quality trends. This estimate might tend to yield results on the high side since it is based on the highest values obtained in some 2.4 million samples over a two-year period. There is no compensation for non-automobile CO sources, i.e., trucks and stationary sources. The following summarizes the EPA findings.

H_2SO_4 Emissions Factor (g/mi)	1-Hour Exposure (ug/m^3)
.015	15–21
.03	30–40
.05	50–67

Carboxyhemoglobin (COHb) Surrogate Model

The carboxyhemoglobin surrogate model uses the measured COHb (CO combined with hemoglobin in the blood) concentrations of "normal" blood donors throughout the U.S. to estimate CO exposures, which are then related to sulfate exposures in the same complex manner as in a CO surrogate model.

Exhibit 16.11 shows estimated 24-hour effects after ten model years of cars are equipped with catalysts: the COHb data are from Los Angeles, where nearly all CO emissions are from mobile sources. For example, if one assumes an emission factor of .03 grams/mile, then 70% of the test population was exposed to sulfate concentrations of (roughly) 6.25 ug/m^3 or less in the average day, based on levels of COHb in their blood. Percentiles above the 95th should be disregarded, since they are extreme values which are caused by factors like occupational exposure or unusual personal physiology.

HEALTH EFFECTS*

Sulfuric acid can be a health hazard at relatively low concentrations compared to some other pollutants. A number of studies have been carried out in which human volunteers were exposed to H_2SO_4 aerosols and many others have been conducted using laboratory animals. In addition, the EPA Community Health and Environmental Surveillance System (CHESS) has been conducting major epidemiological studies in several urban areas. The health parameters used in the CHESS studies reported are chronic respiratory disease, lower respiratory disease, pulmonary

malfunction, acute respiratory disease, irritation of asthmatics, and aggravation of symptoms reported by the general population during an acute air pollution episode.

All of these studies indicate that particulate sulfates (including H_2SO_4) can be potent respiratory irritants. Effects on the respiratory system in animals have been observed at sulfuric acid concentrations of 30 micrograms per cubic meter. Healthy human volunteers exhibited rapid increases in breathing rates when exposed for even short duration (15 minutes) to sulfuric acid aerosol concentrations of 350 to 500 micrograms/cubic meter and immediate irritation of the throat and nose at 1,100 micrograms/cubic meter.

SO_2, from which sulfuric acid aerosols and particulate sulfates are formed, is a much less potent irritant by itself. It will not cause symptoms in most humans even at concentrations exceeding 10,000 micrograms/cubic meter.

In addition, these studies also suggest that the concentration of sulfates is an insufficient basis upon which to predict irritant potency: particulate size, chemical composition, and temperature all determine the toxic potential of particulate sulfates.

"From these and other studies," according to the January 30th EPA Issue Paper on the public health impact of catalyst use, "the . . . best judgment threshold concentrations [shown in Exhibit 16.12] for selected adverse health effects due to suspended sulfate particulate exposures are projected."

The exposure level required to detect respiratory effects in healthy people is quite high compared to the levels which appear to adversely affect individuals with preexisting heart or respiratory diseases. While there are difficulties in establishing a precise exposure level which constitutes an adverse health effect's *threshold*, the above data suggest that at a level of about 6–10 micrograms/cubic meter (24-hour average) the most susceptible segment of the population will experience measurable adverse health effects such as increased frequency and severity of asthmatic attacks. In its statement of conclusions, the Issue Paper gave 10 ug/m^3 (24-hour average) as the threshold.

The EEA study argued that the threshold danger levels of sulfuric acid exposure was ten times higher. As proof that EPA's estimate of dangerous health effects was too cautious, the EEA study noted that

---

*The summary of research done on health effects of sulfates is largely drawn from the EPA Issue Paper of January 30, 1975.

the occupational standard for sulfuric acid is 1,000 micrograms per cubic meter for an eight-hour day and that only a small fraction of all sulfates measured in ambient air is H_2SO_4 (others include ammonium, zinc, and metallic sulfates). Assuming the occupational standard to be correct for healthy workers, it translates to about 250 micrograms for a 24-hour day. For people with heart and lung diseases, EEA suggested the standards might be lowered to 50–100 micrograms per cubic meter.

In testimony criticizing the Issue Paper's methodology, Dr. Robert Sansom of EEA stated:

> . . . *no* mortality studies on sulfates have been done by EPA. EPA, in order to develop a mortality "threshold," attempted to relate SO_2 to sulfate levels found in three separate studies to SO_2 mortality data found in three other studies done at different times in different places. When the statistical techniques proved inadequate, EPA applied "best judgment" to define a "threshold" which was used in benefit/risk analysis. It is difficult to accept EPA's continual use of "best judgment" when the basis and criteria of EPA "best judgment" are not explicitly made public. Time will tell if EPA's "best judgment" can be backed up by sound scientific data.

The CHESS studies on which these "best judgments" were based have been criticized by two highly respected epidemiologists. Drs. Ian Higgins and Benjamin G. Ferris, Jr., from the National Academy of Sciences Panel on Sulfur Oxides and Particles reached the following conclusion on the CHESS study:

> The sample studies, the response rates in certain categories, the methods and procedures which have been used and the analysis of the results can all be criticized. It is particularly disquieting, in view of these deficiencies, that there has been a rather marked tendency to over-interpret the data and in particular to select findings which point to an effect of pollution on health and ignore those which do not.*

OTHER NON-REGULATED EMISSIONS**

The Issue Paper pointed out that sulfuric acid was not the only dangerous pollutant associated with catalysts; emissions of platinum, palladium, alumina, carbon di-sulfide, hydrogen sulfide, phosphine, and carbonyl sulfide from various catalyst systems had been reported or strongly suspected.

Platinum, palladium and alumina (catalyst support material) were discovered by a few laboratories in exhaust particulate samples from earlier prototype catalysts. While EPA did not believe that platinum or palladium posed a general health risk, the longer term potential risks associated with large-scale introduction of these metals into general use could not be assessed. The future effects of alumina were also unknown, but slight increases were seen with current catalyst systems.

Hydrogen sulfide and phosphine are apparently formed when insufficient oxygen is present in the exhaust passing the catalyst. While the principal concern has been hydrogen sulfide emissions, which give off a disagreeable odor, research has suggested that the odor is not uniquely hydrogen sulfide, but also carbon di-sulfide and/or carbonyl sulfide.

Fortunately, most of these compounds can be detected by their odor at concentrations well below dangerous levels. In sufficient concentrations, however, all are highly toxic. Reported emission rates of hydrogen sulfide (40 parts per million maximum) and phosphine (1 ppm maximum) were low enough that exposure to levels sufficient to produce bad health effects appeared unlikely except, potentially, in highly confined spaces, in which case CO would also be a health threat. Research regarding all these unregulated pollutants was underway by 1975.

Substantial decreases in the emissions of polynuclear aromatic hydrocarbons, phenols and aldehydes, and lead were also expected from the use of catalysts. Except for lead, none of these were being regulated in auto exhaust but all were undesirable from a health standpoint, and their reduction would thus constitute a health benefit from the use of catalysts.

Since lead and phosphorus were known to poison catalysts and render them ineffective, EPA in 1974 had legally required the availability of unleaded fuel grade for all catalyst-equipped cars. As a result, lead emissions decreased substantially. However, if the engine performance of cars with catalysts were to prove unsatisfactory, substitute anti-knock compounds

---

*Proceedings of the Conference on Health Effects of Air Pollutants, Assembly of Life Sciences NAS-NRC, October 3–5, 1973, U.S. Senate Report 93-15, November 1973.

**Most of the data in this section is taken from the EPA Issue Paper of January 30, 1975.

might be used.* If these compounds were metal-containing, yet another unregulated emission could be created.

BENEFIT-RISK ANALYSIS

The January 30 Issue Paper analyzed the benefits and risks associated with catalyst use and concluded as follows:

> A public health benefit/risk analysis which weighs the benefits associated with decreased carbon monoxide and [hydrocarbon] exposures against the risks due to increased sulfuric acid exposures suggests that on a national basis health risks exceed the benefits after four model years are equipped with catalysts. It should be noted, however, that this conclusion is based upon assumptions about dose responses and human exposure about which there still remain uncertainties.

The detailed benefit-risk analysis is quoted in the following paragraphs.

Mortality

"One expects that reducing carbon monoxide exposures will reduce premature deaths from myocardial infarctions and that increasing particulate sulfate-sulfuric acid exposures will increase the risk of premature death in elderly persons already afflicted with chronic heart and lung disorders. A benefit/risk comparison suggests that the use of oxidation catalysts should, after ten model years, prevent a modest number of premature deaths. Initially, *benefits* can be expected in large cities in both the eastern and western United States. Later, one can maintain net *benefits* in large western cities but a net *risk* for excess mortality will be created in the east. Most of the *benefits* attributable to catalysts occur in the first four to six years when uncontrolled vehicles are replaced with new catalyst equipped vehicles, while the *risk* associated with catalysts increases linearly over time."

---

*The octane in gasoline works to prevent engine knock, and lead added to the gas acts as an octane booster. If the octane in unleaded gas were to prove insufficient to stop engine knock, a non-lead, substitute "booster" might be added to improve engine performance.

Aggravation of Asthma

"Photochemical oxidants** and particulate sulfate-sulfuric acid can aggravate asthma. This benefit-risk analysis indicates that any reduction in the aggravation of asthma attributed to reduced oxidants will be overwhelmed in all geographic areas by an increased *risk* attributable to catalyst-generated particulate sulfate-sulfuric acid. Statistically, one would expect increased risk for asthma to begin rather promptly with measurable adverse effects seen in cities of over 100,000 population in the second to fourth catalyst model year."

Aggravation of Heart and Lung Disease

"Elevated ambient levels of oxidants and particulate sulfate-sulfuric acid are thought to aggravate the symptoms experienced by elderly persons with chronic heart and lung disorders. The benefit-risk approximation indicates a net increase in the aggravation of heart and lung disorders when all vehicles are equipped with catalysts. However, one would expect most of the *benefits* in the far west and most of the increased *risk* in the eastern United States. Net *benefits* are expected for four to six model years in Southern California while only net *risks* are projected elsewhere at any time."

Acute Lower Respiratory Disease in Children

"While particulate sulfate-sulfuric acid exposures are thought to increase the frequency of acute lower respiratory disease in children, the existing epidemiological studies have not yet been able to disentangle such oxidant effects. EPA scientists, however, feel that measurable benefits would follow the reduction of peak oxidant exposures in Southern California. The analysis projects little or no catalyst-associated *risk* among children in Southern California, but substantial *risks* for children in the eastern United States.

Chronic Respiratory Disease Symptoms

"At the present time there is not a substantial body of laboratory or epidemiologic evidence suggesting that either oxidants or carbon monoxide consti-

---

**Hydrocarbons emitted in the burning of fossil fuels are transformed in the atmosphere into photochemical oxidants; it is these compounds rather than the hydrocarbons themselves that pose the greater health hazard.

tutes a risk factor for chronic respiratory disease. Such is not the case for particulate sulfate-sulfuric acid. The analysis suggests that the use of catalysts will result in a substantial increased *risk* for chronic respiratory disease. Again, almost all of the projected *risk* occurs in the eastern United States and will begin to occur only after the expected exposures projected for two to four model years of catalyst-equipped vehicles are maintained for several additional years."

Prevalence of Irritation Symptoms Among Otherwise Healthy Adults

"Eye irritation, transient cough, ill defined chest discomfort, and headache are considered. Increases in the frequency of such symptoms after exposures to elevated levels of oxidants are well documented. While no dose-response function* is available for exposures to particulate sulfate-sulfuric acid, increases in irritation symptoms are hypothesized. The use of oxidation catalysts thus provides a net benefit insofar as irritation symptoms are concerned, particularly in Southern California."

* * * *

The Issue Paper summarized this discussion as follows: "While there are a number of important caveats repeated in this benefit/risk analysis paper, the conclusions are:

1. The introduction and continued sales of light duty motor vehicles equipped with oxidation catalysts will probably result in a net public health *risk* if no control measures are instituted.
2. A large portion of the *benefits* projected will occur in Southern California.
3. A large portion of the *risks* will be concentrated in, but not limited to, the eastern United States.
4. *Benefits* will be greater for the first few model years as uncontrolled vehicles are replaced by stringently controlled vehicles.
5. On balance, public health *risks* will exceed *benefits* in all areas of the country after four model years are equipped with catalysts."

---

*A dose-response function is a model that relates the amount of exposure to a pollutant to the resulting health effects.

Exhibit 16.12 indicates EPA estimates of health threshold levels of three major automotive pollutants after various exposure durations.

This benefit/risk analysis was severely criticized at the time of its release. For example, Dr. Sansom of EEA stated in his testimony in February 1975:

The EPA risk/benefit analysis appears both arbitrary and incomplete. It is the most severe test of how much scientific gibberish the public can stand. For example, mortality effects for CO are estimated, whereas acknowledged health damages short of death are not. On the other hand, the study is not at all timid in estimating a variety of health damages due to sulfates even though the agency is not prepared to put out a health-related standard.

Another problem is the form of the damage functions. The document lists damage functions for all effects of sulfates even though the epidemiological data (in EPA's words) show that . . . "no pattern of response emerged in terms of relating symptoms to increases in any pollutant." It is also interesting that *all* damage functions are perfectly linear, even though no data are given to support any function, and no statistics are shown to allow its reliability to be validated.

The backup documents and reports point out that many benefits are attributable to the use of catalysts, which were *not* part of the benefit/ risk analysis. These benefits include all of those due to decreased CO (except death) and all benefits attributable to reduction of phenols and PNAs [polynuclear aromatic hydrocarbons] (some of which are carcinogenic). Due to this and other factors, EPA admits that benefits may be underestimated by at least a factor of three. . . .

As Dr. Sansom noted, however, the news media accounts of the Issue Paper focused only on the conclusion that the risks from continued catalyst usage would exceed the benefits after two to four model years.

OPTIONS FOR CONTROLLING SULFATE EMISSIONS

The Issue Paper concluded that

Three basic control approaches are available to limit sulfuric acid emissions: increased use of non-catalyst technology, modifications to catalyst systems to reduce sulfate formation or trap sulfates before they are emitted, and reductions in gasoline sulfur levels. Gasoline desulfurization cannot be expected to have much impact before 1980 although as an interim measure gasoline sulfur reductions through blending and allocation procedures—probably on a selective geographic basis—may be possible. Control of vehicle sulfate emissions through an emission standard would likely have no impact before the 1979 model year. At 49 State or California Interim Standard levels, or at Statutory levels, manufacturers are unlikely to eliminate catalyst usage on a major proportion of their production before the 1979 model year.

The next sections discuss these three options in more detail, as well as another possibility not considered in the Paper.

Non-Catalyst Technology

As noted in Appendix A to Part A (chapter 15), there are several alternatives to the conventional piston-type internal combustion engine (ICE). The Issue Paper analyzed these alternatives and found that most had clearly lower sulfate emission factors (less than .001 g/mi) and at the same time could meet the standards for HC and CO. The Paper noted that implementation of non-catalyst technology to satisfy either the 1965 California Interim Standards or the 1977 Statutory Standards was not likely before 1979. However, it also pointed out that "non-catalyst technology need not be applied to all cars in order to avoid sulfate concentration problems."

Modifications to Catalyst Systems

EPA could impose an emission standard for sulfates, analogous to the HC, CO and NO_x standards, if it found that they posed a health hazard. If auto manufacturers were unwilling or unable to meet the standard by switching to an alternative engine technology, they would presumably have to modify their catalyst systems or introduce another add-on device. As to the former option, the Issue Paper concluded that most presently feasible catalyst modifications would be unable to effect a major reduction in sulfate emissions while still meeting HC and CO standards; other modifications were still in the experimental stages. The Issue Paper did point out that improvements in fuel economy would reduce sulfate emissions independent of catalyst system design, since less gasoline would be burned per mile.

A more promising approach was the sulfate trap, an add-on device installed in the tailpipe that absorbs sulfuric acid through chemical reaction with a solid trapping material.* A prototype trap was tested over 25,000 miles of use and showed consistent reductions in sulfate emissions of 90% or more during all types of driving. Also, particulate emissions resulting from disintegration of the absorbent material were found to be minimal.

The prototype trap had one major flaw: excessive pressure drop which increased with use of the trap. Although tests were being conducted to screen other possible trap materials and investigate ways of reducing the pressure drop while maintaining high trapping efficiency, reports from the automakers indicated that no effort to develop sulfate traps was being made by the industry.

Even if the manufacturers were to initiate a major effort to develop sulfate traps, it was unlikely that they could be available for installation before the 1979 model year. The cost of a trap would be about an additional $50 to $100 per catalyst-equipped vehicle, exclusive of possible replacement costs.

Reduction of Fuel Sulfur Content

Section 211 (c) of the Clean Air Act authorizes the EPA Administrator to regulate the composition of any fuel and fuel additive for use in motor vehicles:

> (A) if any emission products of such fuel or fuel additive will endanger the public health or welfare, or (B) if emission products of such fuel or fuel additive will impair to a significant degree the performance of any emission control device or system . . . which the administrator finds has been developed to a point where in a reasonable time it would be in general use were such regulation to be promulgated.

(This authority was used by the Administrator to regulate the amount of lead and phosphorous in "unleaded" gasoline.)

One way to reduce sulfate emissions from catalyst cars would be to reduce the sulfur level of the gasoline they use. Since the sulfur content of some of

---

*Information on the sulfate trap is taken from the January 30, 1975 Issue Paper.

the materials used in producing gasoline can vary widely, refiners could blend their (limited) stocks of low sulfur materials into unleaded gas to create a no-lead, low sulfur gasoline. However, the Issue Paper saw problems in this approach:

Practically, the refiner is limited in the extent to which he can carry out this process. First, the components that are low in sulfur are high in octane. These high octane components must be used to some extent in the leaded gasolines to provide satisfactory octane quality. In fact, the institution of the lead phase-down regulations would increase the need for these low sulfur components in leaded grades. This is further compounded by the fact that high sulfur components do not achieve as large an octane boost from adding lead as do low sulfur materials. Thus, there is an incentive to the refiner to use the low sulfur components in the leaded, rather than unleaded, grades. Finally, the refiner is limited in the extent to which he could reduce unleaded gasoline sulfur levels through blending by the relative demand for unleaded and leaded gasolines. As more and more cars on the road demand unleaded gasoline and fewer leaded, the refiner must begin to use more of the higher sulfur materials in the unleaded grade in order to produce the needed amount of that product.

Reduction in sulfate emissions could also be accomplished by desulfurization of all gasoline. While the Paper conceded the existence of the necessary technology, it foresaw a lengthy regulatory process and possible litigation before the oil industry would agree to invest the necessary capital; the Paper estimated that desulfurization would have little impact until the 1980s.

Others, however, saw the matter differently. In 1975, Clarence Ditlow, an attorney for the National Clean Air Coalition (NCAC), stated:

Only by regulating the sulfur content of fuel can the Environmental Protection Agency reduce sulfuric acid emissions from catalyst-equipped cars on the road now. With a moderate 0.01% sulfur gasoline blending and desulfurization option, total sulfuric acid emission from catalyst-equipped cars, while meeting the statutory standards on schedule, would be only 2.3 billion grams after 5 model years or about 25% of the acid emissions from heavy duty diesels.

While it was not certain how much gasoline could immediately be made low sulfur and lead-free, the Clean Air Coalition estimated that 50% of all gasoline feedstocks could be quickly desulfurized, while EPA estimates ranged from 20% to 30%. At the suspension hearings for Ford Motor Company in February 1975, Exxon Corporation officials testified that it could distribute 15% to 17% of its gasoline as low sulfur and leadless. According to NCAC, this would be sufficient fuel for two model years of catalyst-equipped cars and would require essentially no capital investment. Exxon indicated that it could phase in desulfurization equipment at its five refineries over 1976–77, achieving full desulfurization by 1978.

However, according to an article in the April 12, 1975 issue of *National Journal*, one Exxon executive felt that the 1978 goal of desulfurization could be met only if there were no other priorities. He estimated that cutting the sulfur content of gas to 100 parts per million within three years would cost Exxon about $270 million, the petroleum industry $3 billion, and the consumer one to two cents per gallon; he added that before Exxon would commit "a capital investment of that magnitude, we have to be sure that there is a hazard from sulfuric acid and that it's worth the money."

Other desulfurization cost estimates varied. Shell estimated its costs to desulfurize to 400 ppm at $200 million and the industry cost at $2.4 billion. The Kellogg Company, EPA's consultant on low sulfur fuel, estimated $2.3 billion for the industry to desulfurize to 600 ppm. A study done for EPA by Arthur D. Little showed the industry's cost range to be from $1.7 to $3.9 billion, depending upon the degree of desulfurization.

According to *National Journal*, Roger Strelow, EPA's Assistant Administrator for Air and Waste Management and one of Train's closest advisers, was reluctant to support desulfurization. Recognizing that EPA's decisionmaking on the sulfates problem would be based on incomplete information and, in his words, "speculative analysis," Strelow stressed the need for new data:

Once we get more information from 1975 catalyst cars, the problem might not be as serious as we expected. If we find then that we don't need desulfurization and we've already required it, then EPA and the whole environmental movement would take a beating.

However, Ditlow of NCAC summed up the feelings of many environmentalists on the subject of desulfurization:

> By refusing to blend and desulfurize gasoline, the Environmental Protection Agency admits the special relationship that exists between the oil industry and the Ford Administration. It is all right to raise gasoline prices 20 cents a gallon and create windfall profits but it's not all right to raise gasoline prices a penny a gallon to protect public health.

Pollutant Interreaction

The Issue Paper failed to consider evidence which linked a reduction in HC, NO_x, and ozone (O_3) levels with a reduction in the conversion of SO_2 into sulfates. Enviro Control, Inc., an environmental consulting firm, used data collected at Continuous Air Monitoring Program (CAMP) sites to analyze empirically the interrelationships between the standard photochemical smog constituents and atmospheric sulfates. This analysis was presented in a June 1973 report.

Enviro Control classified daily pollutant levels into high and low ozone and high and low nitrogen dioxide (NO_2) categories, and then plotted the ambient air concentrations of SO_2 to those of sulfates for all the days falling into each O_3/NO_2 category. Data from CAMP stations in Chicago which monitored 24-hour sulfate levels at a frequency of three to four times per week for three years were used. The summers of 1966–1968 were selected as a time frame.

Results indicated that at high NO_2 and O_3 levels, there was a striking lack of response of sulfates to SO_2 levels. Reducing only O_3 levels yielded some improvement in sulfates. Alternatively, reducing only NO_2 levels achieved a very large reduction in sulfates, as large as the reduction due to a simultaneous decrease in NO_2 and O_3. Equally interesting was the fact that only *after* reductions in NO_2 did the sulfate level respond strongly to decreases in SO_2.

Enviro Control repeated the analysis using total hydrocarbons (THC) and NO_2 instead of O_3 and NO_2, with similar results: reductions in NO_2 yielded the strongest reductions in sulfates and increased the sulfate response to SO_2 reductions. Enviro Control offered the following summary:

> It appears that, in Chicago, sulfate levels are closely controlled by the photochemical process and that SO_2 concentrations have significant effects on sulfate levels only on days of low photochemical activity.
>
> . . . To confirm these insights, this type of analysis needs to be repeated in other CAMP cities and should be expanded to include the available NO measurements as well as meteorological effects such as isolation, precipitation and humidity.

These interrelationships among pollutants offered a basis for proceeding with HC and NO_x controls even with the resulting increase in sulfate emissions caused by catalyst use, since it was possible that decreasing the emission of hydrocarbons and nitrogen oxide would lower the amount of sulfates converted from SO_2.

EXHIBIT 16.1:   Nationwide Distribution of Average Sulfate Concentrations, 1963–1970
Annual Average ug/m³ *

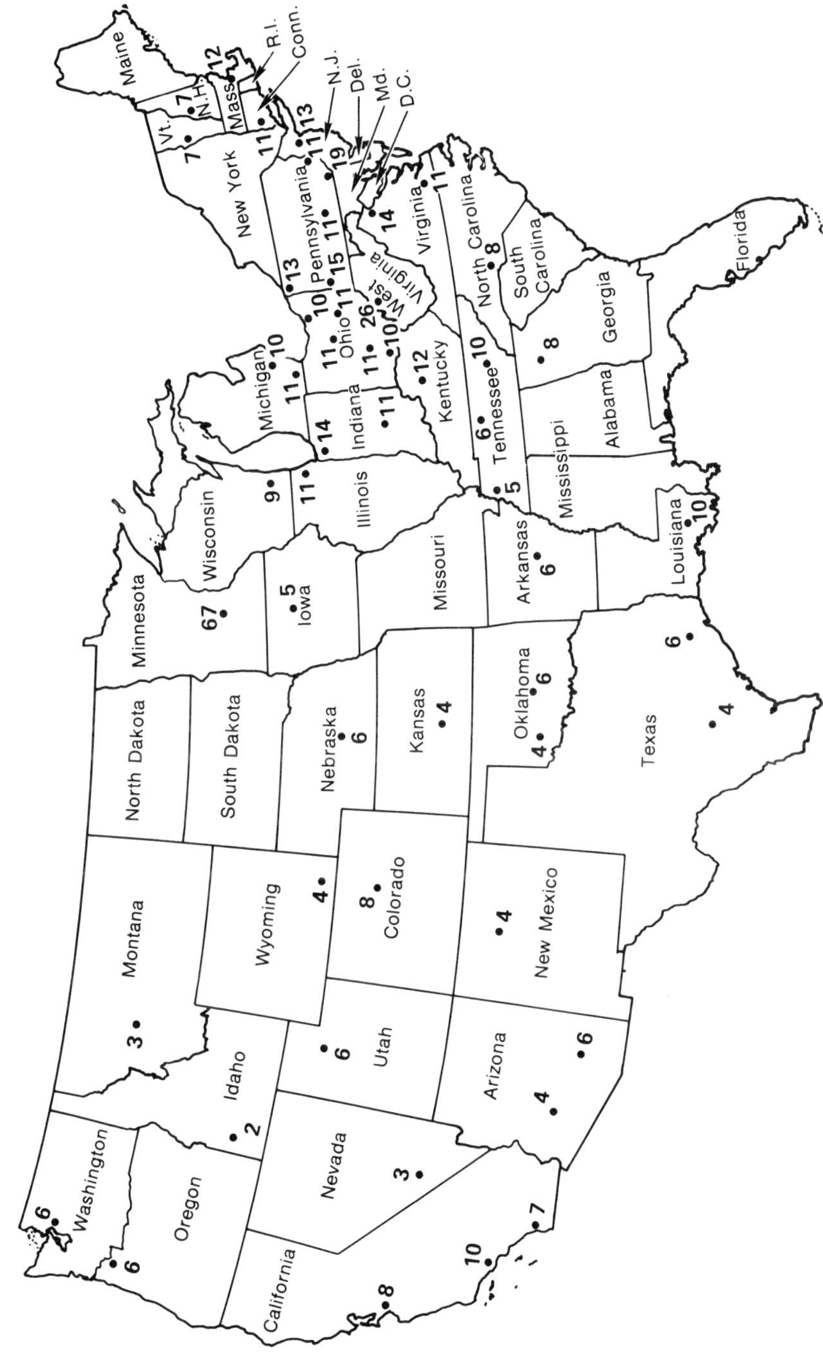

(All numbers above are integers. Dots represent major population centers.)

*ug/m³ —micrograms per cubic meter is the standard measurement for the concentration of air pollutants; the 24-hour maximum concentration is roughly five times the annual average concentration for the area.

Source: Energy and Environmental Analysis, Inc., An Analysis of the Automotive Sulfate Question, April 1975, p. 12. The map is based on 1974 data.

EXHIBIT 16.2: Sulfuric Acid Emissions Factors for 1975 and Subsequent Model Year Light-Duty Motor Vehicles (assumes 100% catalyst usage in California 1975–76 and nationally 1977–86)

| Vehicle Model Year | Fuel Sulfur | HC/CO Emission Standard | H_2SO_4 Emission Factor (gms/mile)[a] | | | | |
| | | | | | Cruise (mph)[d] | | |
			FTP[b]	HFET[c]	30	40	60
1975/76	0.03%	Federal Interim[e] (49-state)	.01	.03	.03	.03	.04
1975/76	0.05%	California Interim[e]	.025	.08	.12	.11	.09
1977–1986[f]	0.03%	Statutory (all 50 states)[e]	.02	.05	.07	.07	.06

[a]Emissions factors are measured in grams of pollutant emitted per mile travelled.

[b]Federal Test Procedure.

[c]EPA Highway Fuel Economy Test.

[d]Emissions are measured while the automobile is travelling at the indicated speed in miles per hour.

[e]California Interim and Statutory Emission Standard Catalyst-Equipped vehicles are assumed to use air injection to maximize oxidation of CO and HC.

[f]The 1975 National Interim Standards average fuel economy was applied in predicting emissions factors for future model years.

Source: EPA Issue Paper, January 30, 1975, page 12.

EXHIBIT 16.3: Illustrative Sulfate Emission Factors*

Vehicle Type	Sulfates (grams/ mile)
Oxidation catalyst (platinum or platinum/palladium)	
—without excess air (interim)	.025
—with excess air (statutory)	.040
Oxidation catalyst (platinum/rhodium)	
—without excess air (interim)	.013
—with excess air (statutory)	.020
Non-catalyst conventional engine (including lean burn system)	.003
Stratified charge engine	.004
Diesel engine**	.010
Three-way catalyst system	.001
Dual catalyst system	.006

*Based on prototype vehicle emissions; not accounting for catalyst aging or post-1975 fuel economy improvements. Fifty-fifty composite of urban and expressway conditions, and all operated on lead-free fuel on 300 ppm sulfur.

Example of variability:

Oxidation catalyst:

without air	Urban (.001 to .01), cruise (.03 to .05)
with air	Urban (.008 to .03), cruise (.03 to .07)

**Sulfur content of diesel fuel, $\approx$ 3,500 ppm.

Source: EEA, An Analysis of the Automotive Sulfate Question, *page 9. Although this study was not released until April 1975, the figures in Exhibit 16.3 were based on previously published data that would have been available to EPA before March 5, 1975.*

EXHIBIT 16.4: Average Sulfuric Acid Emission Levels (grams/mile) as Measured by EPA's Ann Arbor Laboratory (0.033% fuel sulfur)

Vehicle and Emission Control System	1975 FTP	1972 FTP Hot-Start	Highway Economy	60 mph Cruise
1975 GM prototype-pelleted catalyst	.001	.001	.005	.023
1975 Ford light duty truck prototype-monolith catalyst	.024	.030	.047	.030
Datsun with Gould reduction catalyst and monolith oxidation catalyst (25,000 miles)	.012	.004	.005	.006
Chevrolet equipped with sonic flow Dresser carburetor	.007	.002	.002	.004

Source: Appendix A–1, "Annual Catalyst Research Program Report," EPA, written October 1974.

EXHIBIT 16.5: Effect of Fuel Sulfur Level on Sulfuric Acid Emissions from Oxidation Catalyst-Equipped Vehicles

Fuel Sulfur Wt %	Cycle	Catalyst Type	H_2SO_4 grams/mile
.019	40 mph	Monolithic	0.010
	Cruise	Pelleted	0.002
.091	40 mph	Monolithic	0.123
	Cruise	Pelleted	0.126
.110	40 mph	Monolithic	0.163
	Cruise	Pelleted	0.168
.019	FTP	Monolithic	0.009
.032	FTP	Monolithic	0.014
.057	FTP	Monolithic	0.019
.082	FTP	Monolithic	0.023
.107	FTP	Monolithic	0.029

Source: EPA Issue Paper, January 30, 1975, p. 9.

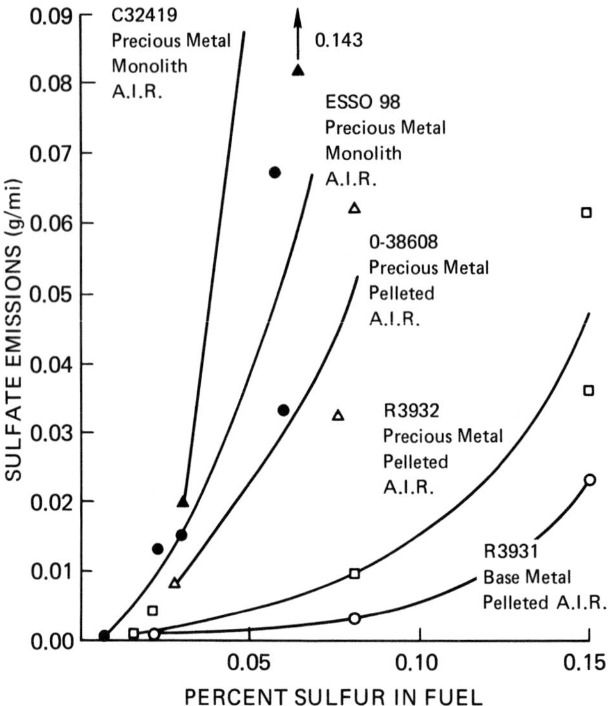

EXHIBIT 16.6: Effect of Catalyst Type on Sulfuric Acid Emissions
SULFATE EMISSIONS (g/mi)
PERCENT SULFUR IN FUEL
C32419 Precious Metal Monolith A.I.R.
0.143
ESSO 98 Precious Metal Monolith A.I.R.
0-38608 Precious Metal Pelleted A.I.R.
R3932 Precious Metal Pelleted A.I.R.
R3931 Base Metal Pelleted A.I.R.
0.09
0.08
0.07
0.06
0.05
0.04
0.03
0.02
0.01
0.00
0.05
0.10
0.15

EXHIBIT 16.7:   Incremental Sulfuric Acid Peak Hourly Exposures for a Pedestrian Near a Major Arterial Thoroughfare and 24-Hour Average Exposures for a Commuter Living Near and Away from the Expressway

Assumptions: CO dispersion model from a 10-lane expressway with 20,000 vehicles per hour at 30 mph average speed

Hydrocarbon/CO Emission Control Scenario	E.F.*	Peak Hourly Incremental Exposure to H_2SO_4 (ug/m^3) After				Incremental 24-hour Exposure for Commuter Living Near Expressway**				Incremental 24-hour Exposure for Commuter Living Away from Expressway			
		2 yrs.	4 yrs.	7 yrs.	10 yrs.	2 yrs.	4 yrs.	7 yrs.	10 yrs.	2 yrs.	4 yrs.	7 yrs.	10 yrs.
Continue 49–State Interim Standards for 10 years.	.03												
Adverse meteorology		52	104	156	208	5	10	15	20	4	8	12	16
Normal meteorology		3	6	9	12	.8	1.6	2.4	3.2	.6	1.2	1.8	2.4
Implement California Interim Standards or Statutory Standards nationally in 1977.	.05												
Adverse meteorology		52	140	227	315	5	13.8	22.6	31.4	4	10.7	17.4	24
Normal meteorology		3	8	13	18	.8	2.1	3.4	4.7	.6	1.6	2.6	3.6
California Interim or Statutory Standards in California only.	.08												
Adverse meteorology		140	280	420	560	13	26	40	54	10.7	21	32	43
Normal meteorology		8	16	24	32	2	4.3	6.4	8.5	1.6	3	4.8	7

*Emissions factor in grams/mile.

**Assumes a commuter living within 150 feet of expressway.

Source: EPA Issue Paper, January 30, 1975, pages 2 and 18.

EXHIBIT 16.8:   Dispersion Model Projected Incremental Peak Hourly Exposures to Catalyst Generated Sulfuric Acid for Specified Vehicular Sources, Sulfuric Acid Emission Factors, and Receptor after 2, 4, 7, and 10 Model Years

Source	Sulfuric Acid Emission Factor (HC/CO) Emission Standard[1]	Peak Hourly Incremental Exposure H_2SO_4 in ugm/m³ after:[2]				Receptor[5]
		2 yrs.	4 yrs.	7 yrs.	10 yrs.	
10-lane expressway[3]	.03 (49 State)	52	104	156	208	Pedestrian near
Adverse meteorology:	.08 (Calif.)[4]	140	280	420	560	expressway
worst wind angle	.05 (Stat)	52	140	227	315	
10-lane expressway	.03 (49 State)	3	6	9	12	Same
	.08 (Calif.)	8	16	24	32	
Normal meteorology	.05 (Stat)	3	8	13	18	
Intersecting 8-lane	.03 (49 State)	25	50	75	100	Pedestrian near
expressways	.08 (Calif.)	66	132	198	265	expressway
Adverse meteorology:	.05 (Stat)	25	66	107	148	500 meters
worst wind angle						downwind of
(40 mph)						intersection
Same	Same	5.5	11	16.5	22	Resident 100
		14	29	44	58	meters from
		5.5	14	23	32	each express-way downwind
Expressway Street	.03 (49 State)	7	14	21	28	Pedestrian next
Canyon	.08 (Calif.)	19	38	57	76	to expressway
	.05 (Stat)	7	20	33	46	
Sporting Event	.01 (49 State)	6.4	12.8	19.2	25.6	Parking lot, *no*
(one hour)	.025 (Calif.)	16	32	48	64	perimeter
	.02 (Stat)	6.4	19.2	32	44.8	streets contribution
	above for lot area *plus*					
	.03 (49 State)	6.6	13.2	19.8	26.4	Edge of parking lot *with*
	.08 (Calif.)	16.5	33	49.5	66	perimeter
	.05 (Stat)	6.6	19.7	32.8	45.9	streets contribution
	(perimeter streets)					

[1] 49 State—1975/76 National Interim Standards
Calif.—1975/76 California Interim Standards
Stat—Statutory HC/CO Standards
1977 on *assumes 49 State for 1975–76*

[2] 2, 4, 7 and 10 years represent approximately 25, 50, 75 and 100% vehicle miles traveled by vehicle age.

[3] 24-hour average exposures at this specified receptor would be approximately 0.125 of the peak hourly values.

[4] California emission factors are approximately the same for Interim California and Statutory Standards.

[5] See Exhibit 1 for descriptive maps, each case.

Source: EPA Issue Paper, January 30, 1975, p. 16.

EXHIBIT 16.9:   CARB Exposure Calculations

1. Lead content of gasolines used in the South Coast Air Basin in 1973:

Gasoline Grade	Lead, g/gal.	Sales Split (%)
Premium	2.6	50
Regular	2.0	50

2. Average fuel economy on the freeway: **19** miles per gallon.

3. Lead emitted from vehicle exhaust: 70% of lead in gasoline.

4. Fraction of lead emitted that is fine **particle size less than 2 microns: 46%.**

5. Maximum measured 24-hour average ambient lead concentration: 10 ug/m^3.

6. Fine particle lead emission rate:

$$\frac{(2.3 \text{ g lead/gal.})(0.7 \text{ emitted})(0.46 \text{ fine particle})}{19 \text{ miles/gal.}} = 0.039 \text{ g lead/mile.}$$

7. Ratio of maximum 24-hour ambient concentration of lead to average emissions of fine particle lead:

$$\frac{10 \text{ ug/m}^3}{0.039 \text{ g/mile}} = 256 \text{ ug/m}^3 \text{ for each gram per mile of lead emission.}$$

In other words, the estimated maximum 24-hour sulfate concentration caused by emissions from this vehicle (termed the

Average Sulfate Emission Rate) $= 256 \dfrac{\text{ug/m}^3}{\text{g/mile}}$

Example:

For a sulfate emission rate of 0.01 g/mile the estimated increment in the maximum 24-hour sulfate concentration is:

$$(256)(0.01) = 2.56 \text{ ug/m}^3$$

EXHIBIT 16.10:   Projected Peak Hourly Sulfate Levels in New York City Using a CO Surrogate Model

Road	Average Daily Traffic	Average Peak Hour Speed	E.F. = .015 g/mi		E.F. = .03 g/mi		E.F. = .05 g/mi	
			Nearest Receptor	Roadside	Nearest Receptor	Roadside	Nearest Receptor	Roadside
Cross Bronx Express.	118,000	42 mph	5	41	9	81	15	135
B–Q Express.	107,000	33	6	63	12	127	20	212
Canal Street	28,000	10	4	16	8	31	13	52
Bruckner Express.	54,000	43	5	20	10	39	17	65
B–Q Express.	107,000	33	3	14	6	28	10	47
Grand Central Parkway	110,000	39	8	23	16	46	27	77
Trans-Man. Express.	174,000	32	8	45	16	90	27	150

The table's Peak Hourly Sulfates ug/m^3 spans the six value columns.

**EXHIBIT 16.11:   COHb Concentrations
vs. Sulfate Exposure**

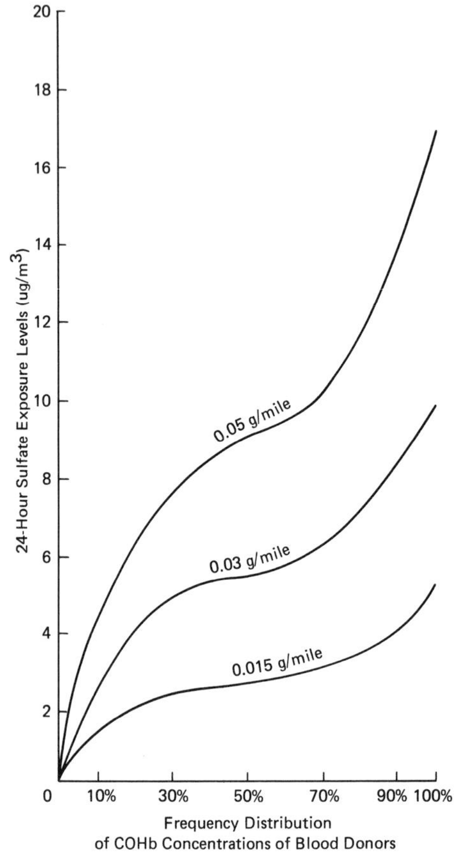

Source: Compiled from 1973 EPA data.

**EXHIBIT 16.12:   Threshold Concentrations of Suspended Sulfate Particulate
Exposure for Selected Adverse Health Effects (best judgment)**

Adverse Health Effect	*Threshold Concentration of Suspended Sulfates and Exposure Duration*
Increased daily mortality	25 ug/m³ for 24 hours or longer
Aggravation of heart and lung disease in the elderly	9 ug/m³ for 24 hours or longer
Aggravation of asthma	6–10 ug/m³ for 24 hours or longer
Excess acute lower respiratory disease in children	13 ug/m³ for several hours
Excess risk for chronic bronchitis (non-smokers)	10 ug/m³ for up to 10 years

Source: EPA Issue Paper, January 30, 1975, p. 23.

SEQUEL

Later Research on Sulfates

In the wake of the controversy described in the April 12, 1975 *National Journal* article, entitled "EPA Study May Bring Reprieve for Catalytic Converter," researchers conducted numerous experiments to provide more definite data on sulfate emissions. The results of two major studies are summarized as follows.

THE GM EXPERIMENT

In October 1975, General Motors and the Environmental Protection Agency jointly conducted a sulfate dispersion experiment at the General Motors testing ground in Milford, Michigan. The experiment was conducted as a cooperative effort by scientists from GM, EPA and other organizations to obtain data on sulfates during controlled operation of a fleet of catalyst-equipped vehicles.

GM ran a fleet of 352 low-mileage 1975 and 1976 cars equipped with catalysts and/or air pumps at its Michigan proving ground for experimental two-hour runs daily over a four-week period. Cars were driven over a ten-kilometer four-lane highway under simulated freeway traffic conditions (speed 80 km/hour; traffic density 5,460 vehicles/hour). EPA and GM scientists measured the concentrations of sulfates, sulfur dioxide, sulfuric acid, and other emissions. Analysis of data led to several principal conclusions:

1. The catalysts did not oxidize as much of the fuel sulfur as had been thought, thus producing lower acid emissions. The difference in results was attributed to different testing procedures (constant cruising speeds in the EPA tests vs. the more realistic fast/slow driving in the GM test).
2. The sulfuric acid was formed as very small aerosols, making it behave like a gas. This meant that it would disperse more quickly than had been thought (preventing build-ups); on the other hand, it would penetrate more deeply into the lungs if inhaled.
3. "The [dispersion] model used by EPA did not accurately represent real conditions," because "turbulence from cars tends to lift pollutants up and away from the roadway, even when there is no wind." EPA's model thus overestimated sulfate build-ups along roadways by a factor of two to three when there is wind and a factor of as much as 20 when there is no wind.
4. Exposure levels were also lower than previous tests had indicated. Acid inside the passenger compartments of test vehicles existed at concentrations of 1.2 to 3.3 ugm/m^3; concentrations along the roadway ranged from three to seven ugm/m^3 (although the figures might be about four times that amount on a densely travelled road). Most of these exposure levels are below the Issue Paper's health effects threshold.

In short, although the experiment was not free from methodological problems,* it led most analysts to conclude that "sulfuric acid is probably not a problem."

LOS ANGELES CATALYST STUDY (LACS)

EPA's LACS study was designed in 1974 to monitor emissions along a real highway—the San Diego Freeway: EPA established monitoring stations along the freeway to measure meteorological conditions and auto emissions over a period of years. The results showed sulfates exposure levels from auto emissions of less than one ugm/m^3, well below EPA's most conservative health effects thresholds. Emissions of platinum and palladium from the catalyst material were found to be negligible. The results also indicated 25% reductions (from 1974 to 1977) in CO, particulates, and lead—reductions attributable in large part to the use of catalysts and unleaded gasoline. However, NO$_x$ emissions increased by 50% during the same period, confirming its status as possibly the most difficult auto-emitted pollutant to control.

---

*See *Science*, Vol. 198, October 21, 1977, pp. 280–284 for a fuller discussion of the experiment.

17

The C-5A (A)

On March 2, 1968 the first C-5A Galaxy was "rolled out" of its hangar in Marietta, Georgia. To the hundreds of military and government VIPs present for the ceremony, the C-5A represented more than just another military cargo aircraft; it signaled the opening of a new era in American power. "For the first time," said Lyndon Johnson in his dedicatory speech, "our fighting men will be able to travel with their equipment to any spot on the globe where we might be forced to stand—rapidly and more efficiently than ever.... We are observing a long leap forward in the effective military might of America.... The aircraft that we roll out here today is the signal that we shall not abandon the road of responsibility. We shall march it proudly."

Designed for the mission of rapidly transporting troops and heavy support equipment, the C-5A was an aircraft of monumental proportions. Nearly as long as a football field, it boasted a cargo hold large enough to accommodate fourteen jet fighters. Carrying a maximum load of 265,000 pounds, the plane was to cover 2,500 nautical miles without refueling; its maximum range carrying a load of 112,000 pounds was to be 5,500 nautical miles. The C-5A was equipped with a newly developed "high flotation landing gear" which would enable it to land and discharge its cargo at unimproved support airfields (very close to the front lines). Turn-around time for landing, unloading, and takeoff was to be a maximum of one hour—without the aid of ground support. While technically a state-of-the-art* aircraft, the C-5A represented a dramatic increase in U.S. airlift capability. Only twelve of the giant planes could have handled the entire Berlin airlift (which required 224 planes in 1948), and a fleet of one hundred C-5As could move 13,000 troops with all their

---

*It was believed that all the technology needed to build the C-5A was already well in hand at the time the contract was let.

supporting equipment to Europe in under twenty-four hours.

The origins of the C–5A can be traced back to 1962, to the Office of Systems Analysis (later renamed Systems Analysis and Evaluation Office) within the Department of Defense (DOD). The efforts of Systems Analysis (SA) to address mobility problems in a comprehensive fashion reflected the impact of the "management revolution" wrought by Robert S. McNamara, who became John Kennedy's Secretary of Defense in January of 1961. Under McNamara's Program Planning and Budgeting System, mobility problems were for the first time studied as a whole: airlift, sealift, and prepositioning of stocks and supplies in overseas bases were drawn together as a major Defense Department program; specific responsibility for the analysis of this program was assigned to a group of analysts within the Systems Analysis Office. The idea for a large cargo aircraft that could carry military troops and equipment relatively cheaply was almost entirely a product of SA's airlift/sealift group. Considered one of the major success stories of the McNamara era, the C–5A represented nearly five years of work directed towards estimating deployment requirements and evaluating various mobility systems. By 1965 the SA group had produced analytical justification for the C–5A sufficiently convincing to merit McNamara's authorization of the program—despite the fact that the decision was by no means unanimously endorsed.

This case, the first of two dealing with the C–5A, summarizes the management techniques adopted by McNamara in order to rationalize DOD decision-making and examines the C–5A as a product of that process. The case deals specifically with the role of Systems Analysis in developing the C–5A concept and in bringing it to fruition. Part B will examine the procurement of the C–5A by the Air Force.

DEFENSE MANAGEMENT

One of John Kennedy's major campaign issues had been the adequacy of the U.S. defense posture. Specifically, Kennedy was concerned with the U.S. capability for limited war, a capability which had been consistently down-graded under the Eisenhower-Dulles policy of massive retaliation,* with its emphasis on the nuclear deterent at the expense of conventional forces. As Kennedy saw it, the U.S. had limited itself to the nuclear option and was unprepared to respond in kind to more limited threats. The choice was that of general war or surrender. As Kennedy stated the problem:

> The periphery of the free world will be slowly nibbled away. . . . Each Soviet move will weaken the West, but none will seem sufficiently significant by itself to justify our initiating a nuclear war which might destroy the U.S.

Discontent with the massive retaliation strategy had been building during the late fifties, and by 1960, many in the military, such as General Maxwell Taylor, army Chief of Staff, were advocating a conventional build-up that would enable the United States to respond to situations requiring non-nuclear force. Suggesting that the U.S. was prepared to fight the one war it wanted least and was least likely to initiate, Kennedy, in his campaign, decried the policies which had led to American inflexibility:

> We have steadily cut the numbers and strength of our ground forces—our Army and Marines. We have steadily failed to provide our conventional

---

*Massive retaliation, or the "New Look" as it was known, was in part an attempt to deal with the economic strain associated with high levels of conventional preparedness and growth of the military. As Eisenhower formulated the rationale, "The foundation of military strength is economic strength. A bankrupt America is more a Soviet goal than an America defeated on the field of battle." Thus, the Administration proposed that the future security of the United States would have to rest primarily on nuclear weapons, since a nuclear war capability is less expensive than the capability to wage a major conventional war. This proposal was adopted by the National Security Council and embodied in its chief planning document, the Basic National Security Policy (BNSP). However, as defense expert William Kaufmann has pointed out, the "New Look" policy was ambiguous: the BNSP, which characterized the "New Look" as constituting "main but not sole reliance on nuclear weapons," was very broadly worded and subject to various interpretations. Former Army Chief of Staff General Maxwell Taylor recalls that by 1958, "a clear split, right down the middle of the Joint Chiefs of Staff" existed over massive retaliation versus a flexible response capability (i.e., over whether America's response to a Soviet provocation should be limited to an all-out nuclear strike or whether other options—a limited nuclear attack, a conventional response, etc.—should be available).

forces with modern conventional weapons, with effective, versatile fire power, and we have particularly failed to provide the airlift-sealift capability necessary to give these forces the swift mobility they need to protect our commitments around the world.

Almost immediately upon his inauguration, therefore, Kennedy instructed his new Secretary of Defense, Robert McNamara, to thoroughly review strategies and programs with a view towards achieving the capability for a flexible military response to various forms and degrees of aggression. The new defense posture was to encompass capabilities ranging from limited brushfire engagements to general nuclear war.

Further instructions from Kennedy to McNamara concerned the implementation of the new policy. McNamara was to analyze and develop the force structure necessary to our military requirements without regard to budget ceilings and then to procure these forces at the lowest possible cost. McNamara soon concluded however, that existing defense planning procedures were unresponsive to such objectives. The three branches of the armed forces, which had maintained long traditions of jealously guarded independence in the areas of program planning and resource development, had thwarted previous attempts to institute central planning. (See the Appendix for a brief history of past DOD/military relations.) Several of Kennedy's advisors had therefore recommended reorganization in order to enhance the Secretary's control over the Department. However, McNamara saw issues other than organizational ones as critical. In his book *Essence of Security* he wrote:

> From the beginning in January 1961, it seemed to me that the principal problem in efficient management of the Department's resources was not the lack of management authority. The National Security Act provides the Secretary of Defense a full measure of power. The problem was rather the absence of essential management tools needed to make sound decisions on the really crucial issues of national security.

Planning Pre-McNamara: The Problems Identified

Under the previous Administration, defense planning began with a National Security Council document known as "Basic National Security Policy" (BNSP), which presented the general strategic guidelines within which forces and contingency plans were to be formulated. However, the BNSP was widely regarded as a very unhelpful and imprecise document. According to General Maxwell Taylor:

> The end product . . . has thus far been a document so broad in language as to provide limited guidance in practical application. In the course of its development, the sharp issues in national defense which confront our leaders have been blurred in conference and negotiation. The final text thus permits many different interpretations.

Theoretically, on the basis of BNSP the Joint Chiefs, aided by the military departments and the 400-man JCS staff, were to prepare the Joint Strategic Objectives Plan (JSOP), giving force requirements (over a period of four or five years) and the contingencies for which these forces were to be used. The Secretary would then determine the annual defense budget based on various compromises between force levels determined by the Chiefs and the general level of defense spending determined appropriate by the President and his economic advisors.

Although in theory this system appeared reasonable enough, in practice a number of problems had been observed. First, each service tended to plan unilaterally. The JSOP thus became less a comprehensive estimate of overall military needs than a pasting together of individually-developed service plans. For example, in planning for its bomber and missile programs, the Air Force failed to take into account the Navy's plans for the Polaris system—which was designed to fulfill the same mission. Similarly, the Army's plans for its force structure and readiness were designed without consideration of Air Force or Navy plans for the airlift and sealift necessary to transport troops to combat areas. These problems resulted because interservice rivalry led each branch to vie for the most sophisticated weapons or prestigious missions, and in JCS review the service chiefs tended to support each other's requests in order to forge a united front. Even within the services some missions were preferred to others as Charles Hitch (DOD Comptroller in the early sixties) describes:

> The Air Force, for example, gave overriding priority to the strategic retaliatory bombers and missiles, starving the tactical air units needed to support the army ground operations, and the

airlift units needed to move our limited war forces quickly to far off trouble spots. The Navy gave overriding priority to its own nuclear task force, notably the aircraft carriers—while its anti-submarine warfare capability was relatively neglected and its escort capability atrophied.

A second problem with the JSOP arose because it was developed on the basis of "purely military" considerations, without regard to costs. Because there was no mechanism to force the Chiefs to consider in detail the costs of their requests, they regularly asked for more than the budget would support. Top decision-makers such as the Secretary, lacking coherent information about the relationships among forces, cost and resulting military capabilities, had no systematic way of reducing requests or choosing between alternative requests. For the most part, the Chiefs' requests were reconciled with resources by means of a budget ceiling. The total defense budget, which ranged between 9% and 10% of the G.N.P. during the Eisenhower administration, was allocated among the three services according to ceilings set by the Secretary. Each service would prepare a budget submission within its ceiling* and attach additional requests on an addendum or "B" list for consideration. As Charles Hitch, McNamara's first Comptroller, explains it, the consequences

> . . . were precisely what could have been predicted. Each service tended to exercise its own priorities, favoring its own unique missions to the detriment of joint missions, striving to lay the groundwork for an increased share of the budget in future years by concentrating on alluring new weapons systems, and protecting the overall size of its forces even at the cost of readiness.

The budget itself was another problem. First, the budget was presented in terms of inputs—military personnel, procurement, etc.—while forces were planned according to mission. The difficulties of translating one into the other left the Secretary without reliable data as to the amount spent on any particular mission—the cost of Continental Air Defense, for example. Second, the fact that budgets focused on one year at a time obscured the much larger lifetime costs (and benefits) of defense weapons systems; this let the services get a foot in the door on expensive projects

for which the real cost implications would not be known for several years. Third, the budget was not based on systematic analysis: cost estimates and the underlying analytical studies of military requirements were rarely based on careful analysis of the various elements of the country's defense posture and their interrelationships.

Defense Planning Under McNamara

For McNamara, efficient management was based on two principles; first, that all decisions must be made on an informed, impartial, and rational basis; and, second, that all defense decisions were economic decisions. Since resources used for defense were resources unavailable for other uses, strategy, technology, and economy were not three independent considerations; rather, they were interdependent elements of the single problem of the efficient use of resources. In the light of these principles, McNamara set about the task of instituting an entirely new method of planning and decision-making within the Department of Defense.

First, he instituted a Planning, Programming and Budgeting System (PPBS), developed by his Comptroller Charles Hitch and operable in time for the preparation of the FY 1963 budget. PPBS was designed to bridge both the gap between military planning and civilian fiscal control and that between the two crucial defense department activities—planning and budgeting. Under this system, all the various programs and activities of the Defense Department were grouped into meaningful program elements, that is, into "integrated combinations of men, equipment, and installations whose effectiveness could be related to National Security objectives." For example, a B-52 bomber force, together with all its supplies, weapons and manpower constituted a program element. In the programming stage of PPBS, program elements were related to the basic missions of the Defense Department. As described by Hitch, programming assembled "related groups of program elements, that, for decision purposes, should be considered together either because they supported each other or because they were close substitutes. The unifying principle underlying each major program is a common mission

---

*During the Eisenhower years each service received a relatively constant cut of the budget: Army 22%; Navy 29%; and Air Force 47%.

or set of purposes for the elements involved."* Nine major programs were designated, encompassing over 1,000 program elements:

1. *The Strategic Retaliatory Forces* consisted of the triad of strategic nuclear weapons: the manned bomber force, the sea-based ballistic missiles, and the land-based inter-continental ballistic missiles. These forces, along with headquarters and command support activities, comprised the offensive capabilities of the United States in a general war situation.
2. Related to offensive forces in their focus on general war were the damage-limiting capabilities of *Continental Defense Forces.* These included the North American surveillance, warning and control network (consisting of land-based, sea-based, and airborne radars and control centers), the manned interceptors, surface-to-air missiles, ballistic missile warning systems, and the civil defense program.
3. The *General Purpose Forces* were designed to fight local or limited wars or to engage in theatre operations in a general war. These forces included all Marine Forces; the Army General Purpose Forces, with command and combat support elements; and the Navy General Purpose Forces, which included all combatant ships and support vessels (except strategic missile-firing submarines, radar, transport) and all Navy planes.
4. The *Airlift and Sealift* program constituted the fourth major program of the Defense Department. This included the troop carrier wings of the Air Force, the Military Air Transportation Service (MATS), and the Military Sea Transportation Service (MSTS).
5. The fifth major program was composed of the *Reserve and National Guard Forces* arranged by service and by major missions.
6. The sixth major program, *Research and Development,* included a range of activities. Research denoted very basic efforts to expand knowledge without explicit regard for military application.

The phase of Exploratory Development focused on exploring application of emerging technology to military problems. The Advanced Development phase was concerned with the development of experimental hardware, the identification of each project with its military application, and the examination of potential operational benefit versus the cost of development, production and deployment. During the Engineering Development stage, a particular weapon system was engineered for service use, although it had not yet been approved for production or deployment. (Since this stage involved a large commitment of resources, the operational requirements and cost-effectiveness of the system had to be confirmed at this point.) The Research and Development program also included continued development and improvement of systems already operational.

7. The seventh major program was *General Support,* which included training, education, intelligence collection, and medical services. This miscellaneous category totaled 30% of the Defense budget.
8. *Retired Pay* was listed as a separate category because it represented costs beyond the control of the Department, as terms of retirement and rates of pay were fixed by law.
9. The last major program was that for *Military Assistance*—the equipment and training provided to some 59 foreign countries.

All of the program data, together with a description of forces, tasks, and missions, procurement lists and facilities lists, were combined into a single document for the use of the Secretary—the Five-Year Defense Plan (FYDP), which contained an eight-year projection of forces and a five-year projection of costs displayed in mission-oriented programs. Thus the FYDP combined both benefits and costs, forces and financial planning. FYDP costs reflected expenditures over the lifetime of the program element and included all support activities necessary to the program.

FYDP provided an official set of planning assumptions—an authoritative record of what the Secretary had approved for forces and financial planning. It was designed to enable planners to balance the requirements of each service with those of the others, to improve estimates of the total costs of existing and proposed programs, and to effect program changes in orderly fashion.

---

*Charles Hitch, *Decision-Making for Defense* (Berkeley: University of California Press, 1967), p. 33. The following description of the major programs is based on pp. 35–38 of *Decision-Making for Defense.*

After the development of the FYDP, the annual "Basic National Security Policy" was dropped completely.* The annual Planning, Programming and Budgeting cycle, then, began directly with the JSOP, which was to be submitted by the Chiefs to the Secretary for review by February. By mid-May the Secretary was to have completed his review and prepared his proposed revisions to the JSOP in the form of a Tentative Force Guidance which served as a basis for the preparation of Program Change Proposals (PCPs) to the official five-year program. The PCP was the mechanism by which new programs were incorporated into the FYDP. The value of this formal change procedure, as summarized by Hitch, is:

1. that there is only one channel for major decision-making;
2. that proposed changes receive a rapid but complete review by all parties concerned;
3. that program decisions are made on the basis of the best information available, including a validation of long-range cost implications;
4. that all major changes are made only after approval of the Secretary of Defense; and
5. that there is always available an up-to-date, approved Five-Year Program for U.S. defense activities;

In making his program decisions, McNamara relied heavily on one of the most controversial components of PPBS: Systems Analysis. The newly established Office of Systems Analysis, comprising teams of analysts concentrating on particular mission areas, was part of the Office of the Secretary of Defense (OSD) and was responsible solely to the Secretary and not to any one of the military branches. The office worked closely with the staffs of the military departments and Joint Chiefs on questions of major

weapon systems procurement and force planning in a combined effort not only to evaluate existing proposals, but to generate alternatives. The cost-effectiveness studies produced by the office gave McNamara the type of information he desired for the purposes of choosing between alternative strategies or weapons.

As Alain Enthoven, McNamara's Assistant Secretary for Systems Analysis, described it:

> The Systems Analysis approach we have developed in the Department of Defense emphasizes the basic economic concepts. The interesting question is not whether more of a particular capability would be nice to have; the significant question is whether the alternatives foregone in order to obtain it are of greater or less value. Of particular interest to the systems analyst are marginal comparisons. Rather than viewing the problem of military requirements determination as one of the calculation of the forces required to achieve an arbitrarily selected objective, it is often sensible to reduce the problem to one of judging at what point an increase in effectiveness is no longer worth the associated increase in cost. Many requirements issues have been resolved by observing that, at some point, more forces would put us "out on the flat of the curve"; that is, they would put us in the position of paying large sums of money for small increases in effectiveness.
>
> Another crucial part of this approach is explicit treatment of uncertainty. Rather than conceal uncertainties, a good analysis will bring them out and clarify them for the decision maker. This is important. A best guess is not the same as certain knowledge. Whether it is a question of uncertainty about quantitative matters such as operational factors, or uncertainty about enemy strategies, it is desirable to analyze explicitly the implications of the full range of likely possibilities. We often carry through our analyses three estimates—a high, a low, and a most likely—of those parameters to which the outcome is sensitive.

By October, under PPBS, the Joint Chiefs had basically completed their part in the preparation of the following fiscal year's budget and had begun work on the next budget. The Secretary and the services then prepared a final review of the budget for submission to the President. The budget itself, expressed in traditional appropriations categories as well as missions, represented a detailed analysis of the financial requirements of the first annual increment of the approved Five-Year Defense Plan.

---

*According to Alain Enthoven, McNamara's Assistant Secretary for Systems Analysis (see p. 8), ". . . its absence is not missed. The annual Basic National Security Policy simply impeded recognition of the interdependence of our objectives, strategy, forces, weapons systems, and budgets, and caused increasingly sterile debates about strategic concepts. It diverted attention from the real task of systematically examining the allocation of resources among alternative uses according to their relative utility at the margin."

The rationale for the program decisions reflected in the budget was provided by another McNamara innovation: the Draft Presidential Memorandum (DPM). As McNamara recalled the origins of the DPMs:

> I wanted a vehicle—and President Kennedy was very interested in a vehicle—to acquaint him with the background of the military decisions. But the more I thought about it, the more it seemed like a good device to get the views of appropriate decisions for my own review. By passing [the DPMs] back and forth [between me, the services and the JCS] we were able to force the divergent views to the surface. I insisted that each party of interest comment.

DPMs covered broad functional areas, such as NATO Strategy, General Purpose Forces, Tactical Air Forces, etc. Prepared during the spring and summer of each year by the Systems Analysis office under the direct supervision of the Secretary, these drafts were to spell out precisely the assumptions, rationale and supporting analysis for the Secretary's tentative recommendations in each area. Even in the early stages, each draft incorporated a great deal of the analysis and judgment of the military and JCS. After publication, they were routed to the services and all interested departments for review, thus initiating a process of debate and interaction—formal comment, special studies, and additional memoranda— which lasted most of the year. As the debate proceeded, areas of agreement and disagreement were identified, key assumptions isolated, uncertainty examined. As a result of this process, the Secretary considered that he could better identify alternatives and make more reasonable choices among them. The DPMs provided the Secretary with an overview of the major areas of military concern, while also serving as the principal means by which the Secretary submitted recommendations to the President and, on approval, the means by which he made his decisions and policies known throughout DOD.

As Charles Hitch summarized the achievement of the new management system in *Decision-Making for Defense:*

> ...We have provided for the Secretary of Defense and his principal military and civilian advisors a system which brings together at one place and at one time all the relevant information that they need to make sound decisions on the forward program* and to control the execution of that program. And we have provided the necessary flexibility in the form of a program change control system. Now, for the first time, the largest business in the world has a comprehensive Defense Department-wide plan that extends more than one year into the future. And it is a realistic and responsible one—programming not only the forces, but also the men, equipment, supplies, installations, and budget dollars required to support them.
>
> Budgets are in balance with programs, programs with force requirements, force requirements with military missions and military missions with national security objectives. And the total budget dollars required by the plan for future years do not exceed the Secretary's responsible opinion of what is necessary and feasible.... From a small beginning, systems analysis has now become a vital and integral part of the Defense Department decision-making process. . . . Systems analysis provides the analytical foundation for the making of sound objective choices among the alternative means of carrying out these missions. Thus, the Secretary of Defense now has two tools he needs to take the initiative in the planning and direction of the entire defense effort on a truly unified basis.

While the new system satisfied McNamara's overall objective—that of consolidating the control of the Secretary over the department—the objective itself was not uncontroversial. The effect was the centralization of management, with McNamara himself making force decisions in minute detail. Unlike his predecessors, who acted largely as referees in military decision-making, McNamara saw his role

> . . . as being that of a leader, not a judge. I'm here to originate and stimulate new ideas and programs, not just to referee arguments and harmonize interests. Using deliberate analysis to force alternative programs to the surface, and then making explicit choices among them is fundamental.

McNamara's philosophy of "management at the top" was bound to be provocative, particularly in view of

---

*I.e., the Five-Year Defense Plan (see page 370).

traditional service attitudes. Thus, although McNamara eliminated budget ceilings and actually raised overall defense spending substantially, the military objected strongly to the Secretary's increased controls.

In particular, the services objected vigorously to the Office of Systems Analysis, which over the years became the focus of most of the criticism directed at the Defense Department. While a great deal of the criticism appeared to be of the "sour grapes" variety, several of the issues raised seriously challenged the wisdom of McNamara's management arrangement. Among the most telling was the complaint that military judgment was consistently downgraded under the new system, and that the Systems Analysis Office was capable of "capturing the debate" by controlling all communications with the Secretary. According to L. Mendel Rivers, Chairman of the House Armed Services Committee (who repeatedly sought to have the office abolished), numerous examples existed of "proposals in the field of military strategy and tactics that had their origins in the Systems Analysis Office and proceeded to a decision unchanged, in the face of the most carefully considered professional military judgment that they were unsound." Critics contended that SA options were not subjected to as exacting an analysis as were other options. The line between analysis and advocacy was allegedly crossed in several cases—not the least significant of which was the C-5A.

The debate over McNamara's use of systems analysis was, and continues to be, heated. Despite the controversy, however, McNamara remained unwavering in his support, and the SA office grew in both size and importance during the McNamara era. Whatever its abuses, supporters contended, SA provided an independent source of information and analysis that was crucial to any Secretary who chose to be an active leader rather than a passive arbiter or judge.

AIRLIFT AND SEALIFT

In the spring of 1961, McNamara set a team of systems analysts to work on one of the most critical components in the development of a flexible response capability: the military transport system or specifically, airlift/sealift. The effectiveness and credibility of the U.S. conventional forces, which were then being augmented, would be substantially enhanced by the capability for transporting ground forces and supporting equipment rapidly to trouble spots as the need arose. At that time, three deployment systems were in existence: airlift provided by the Military Air Transportation Services (MATS); sealift, mainly troopships and cargo haulers operated by the Military Sea Transport Service (MSTS); and the prepositioning of supplies and equipment in European and Southeast Asian bases. McNamara asked his team of analysts to evaluate these various systems toward the ultimate end of determining the optimal mix (in terms of both numbers and capabilities) at the least possible cost. Under the mission-oriented PPB System, airlift, sealift, and prepositioning were, for the first time, considered together as a single program. However, the initial analyses conducted by the group reflected relatively primitive and unstructured investigations into the mobility problem: early studies focused on what type of aircraft to buy for short-term build-up of airlift capability because McNamara felt that the deficiency in this area was so great that a quick build-up was needed.

Background: The Role of Airlift

Although airlift clearly provided the most rapid form of transport, it had never really been considered for the mission of deploying fully-equipped troops or supplies. Despite successful demonstrations of aircraft cargo-carrying capabilities (such as flying the Hump in World War II, the 1948–49 Berlin airlift, and the 1958 intervention in Lebanon), both military and airline men had a fixed idea that airplanes carried primarily passengers or high-value cargo and that their operating costs prohibited any other uses except in emergencies. In fact, until after the second World War, the capability of military airlift was considered so limited that responsibility for providing airlift was disbursed in a haphazard manner among several military agencies.

In 1948, strategic (i.e., long-distance) airlift was partially unified with the creation of the Military Air Transportation Service (MATS) within the Air Force. As viewed at that time, MATS was a general-purpose operation servicing the three branches of the Armed Forces:

> The Military Air Transport Service will maintain, in being, the Military Air Transport Forces, service forces, enroute bases and air routes to the approved wartime requirements of the Depart-

ment of Defense as approved by the JCS. Further, MATS will train to maintain this readiness and while training, MATS will airlift cargo, personnel, patients, and mail according to DOD directives.

During the fifties, and under the Eisenhower-Dulles concept of massive retaliation, military planners directed the majority of their attention to planning for general nuclear war, in which the bombers of the Strategic Air Command (SAC) were expected to play an overwhelming role. At that time, SAC consisted mostly of short-range bombers which would be deployed to overseas bases before being launched. Since MATS was needed to airlift SAC's supporting equipment and personnel to these bases, SAC's war plans determined both the number of MATS transports necessary and their utilization rates during an emergency. Even as SAC acquired longer-range bombers, MATS still played a supporting role to SAC; MATS aircraft were intended to rendezvous with returning SAC bombers at "post strike" bases in order to prepare them for another mission.

During this period, MATS was not generally regarded as an Army supporting force. The Army itself had been reduced in size in the fifties in consequence of the "New Look" strategy with its emphasis on nuclear weapons, and the principal air support for Army operations was provided by the Tactical Air Command (TAC), which performed tactical (i.e., short-range) transport and parachute missions.* Thus, MATS occupied a rather low-glamour, low-budget position within the Air Force. Also, MATS' functions were to some extent duplicated outside the Air Force by the Navy's Military Sea Transportation Service (MSTS). Troops and military equipment had traditionally been moved by ship, and the Army had, for the most part, accommodated itself to this mode of transportation (so much so that, in the early fifties, they agreed to pay the Navy for troop ships whether they used them or not).

For all these reasons, airlift played a relatively minor role in the scheme of military transportation throughout the 1950s. In the late fifties, however, the strategic potential of airlift began to attract increasing attention—largely as a result of growing dissatisfaction with the Eisenhower-Dulles policy of reliance on massive retaliation. Dissidents to this policy began to urge that the role of the conventional forces be reexamined. As early as 1955, for example, Army Chief of Staff General Matthew B. Ridgeway had argued for the strengthening of the strategic reserve, whose mission it was to augment deployed forces or conduct operations in areas where no U.S. forces were stationed. Ridgeway emphasized the importance of a "mobile ready force" available to counter threats "growing out of the Soviet ability to concentrate at will." A year later Ridgeway's successor, Maxwell Taylor, argued that the nation's strategic airlift was markedly deficient for deploying troops to trouble spots around the globe; he advocated the modernization and augmentation of MATS airlift capability.

The possibility of expanding MATS' role as an Army support force was enthusiastically picked up by a small handful of MATS, Army, and Air Force staff, but was rejected by Secretary of Defense Charles E. Wilson, who perceived no need for more airlift:

> There has been a great deal of discussion and consideration given to the requirements for the airlift of tactical units and supplies. The current composition of the Air Force structure has been carefully examined, and it appears that it presently provides adequate airborne lift, in the light of currently approved strategic concepts.

Expansion of MATS was also opposed by the civil air carriers, who had long complained that MATS' peacetime activities threatened to undermine the commercial transportation industry. (To maintain readiness during peacetime, MATS carried military personnel and cargo that would otherwise have been transported by international carriers.)** The complaints of the commercial carriers found sympathetic ears in Congress, which eventually allocated funds specifically for procurement of commercial transport for military personnel and cargo.

---

*The formal distinction between tactical and strategic missions is the difference between intra-theater and inter-theater operations, respectively: MATS was responsible for strategic airlift, while TAC's authority was limited to intra-theater operations. However, there was a great deal of confusion and competition over these responsibilities, compounded by each service's use of aircraft which could perform either mission.

**The controversy over peacetime utilization rates (URs) raged throughout the fifties and sixties with the MATS advocating a five-hour UR per plane per day and airline representatives seeking something closer to one hour per day. As MATS increased its participation in airlift exercises, the airlines were able to acquire a greater portion of routine military traffic.

Congress then, like DOD, was unenthusiastic about any expansion of military airlift capability. When, in 1960, the Air Force asked for the new jet cargo aircraft for MATS, Congress refused the request, indicating that it viewed the requested appropriation as unnecessary:

Adequate transport capacity for this portion of MATS' mission exists in private commercial aircraft during the present cold war situation and in the Civil Reserve Air Fleet (CRAF) in the event of mobilization.

To airlift advocates this solution—reliance on CRAF—seemed particularly unacceptable. Although the CRAF (about 200 commercial aircraft that the airlines had committed to military use if needed) was obligated to respond in the event of general war, the President's authority over the fleet did not extend to situations other than general war or national emergency. The Army was reluctant to count on CRAF's ability and motivation to respond, and was also concerned that, in the event of general mobilization, the CRAF airfleet would be needed to handle augmented air traffic within the U.S.

Finally, in 1960, the various issues surrounding the airlift question came into a sharper focus with the appointment of a special subcommittee of the House Armed Services Committee charged with investigating the role of airlift in national defense. The hearings were precipitated by remarks made by Secretary of the Army Wilbur Brucker and General Lyman Lemnitzer, the Army Chief of Staff, in connection with the FY 1961 budget. Both men expressed their misgivings about the adequacy of current airlift capability, thus reflecting a growing interest in strategic airlift.

Two events immediately preceding the hearings were to have a great impact on the subcommittee's thinking. The first was a joint Army-MATS exercise called "Big Slam Puerto Pine," in which MATS effected the strategic deployment to Puerto Rico and return to the U.S. of 21,000 troops and 11,000 tons of equipment. Throughout the exercise, the Army and MATS maintained a direct relationship and engaged in joint planning. The exercise both dramatized the potential role of airlift and attracted attention to MATS. The second event of greater interest to the subcommittee was also an act of joint planning: an unprecedented agreement between Army Chief of Staff Lemnitzer and Air Force Chief of Staff General

Thomas D. White on quantitative Army airlift requirements. The agreement was the product of several months of negotiations at the staff level following a discussion initiated by General White, who believed that Army–Air Force planning for limited war deployment would be greatly facilitated if a joint agreement on Army requirements could be reached. The Lem/White agreement, as it was known, specified that the Army should be provided with sufficient transportation to:

1. Fly one or two reinforced battle groups* (with essential equipment) to any trouble spot in the world. These units would commence their departure within one hour of the time that the order to move was given.
2. Within a matter of days increase the size of the force to one division with adequate supplies, equipment, and supporting force to conduct sustained operations against the aggressor.
3. Continue augmentation of the fighting force to a two division force within two to four weeks.
4. Continue reinforcement supply as required.

The subcommitte convened in March under the chairmanship of L. Mendel Rivers and immediately addressed the issue of the adequacy of current airlift capacity to meet Army requirements as specified in the Lem/White agreement. The subcommittee was briefed on three JCS studies initiated in 1959 to evaluate airlift requirements under three war contingencies: two involving general war (with and without prior mobilization), the third, a resumption of limited hostilities in Korea. The committee rejected the first study (which included a 60-day mobilization period) as unrealistic and urged JCS to concentrate future planning on limited war. Review of the other two studies revealed that existing airlift capacity would prove inadequate for both troops and cargo during the first 20 days of general war and for cargo alone during the first 20 days of a limited war in Korea. General Lemnitzer told the subcommittee that deficiencies would be even greater if troops and equipment had to be moved to the Middle East or South East Asia, where

---

*A reinforced battle group comprises 4,067 men and 2,570 short tons of equipment.

no U.S. forces were deployed and supply facilities were inadequate. A one or two division force, for example, would not be airlifted to Vietnam within the time limit required by the Lem/White agreement.

Alarmed by these deficiencies, the subcommittee recommended expansion and modernization of the airlift fleet. At the time of the hearing, the Air Force had requested $50 million to initiate development of a new strategic transport and $70.4 million to procure 25 new tactical transports. The subcommittee recommended these expenditures and urged the immediate procurement of 100 off-the-shelf aircraft (50 C-130s and 50 C-135s) as an interim measure.* The import of these various recommendations was to underline the potential of airlift—MATS in particular—as an Army supporting force. Significantly, the subcommittee also recommended that MATS' name be changed to MAC—Military Airlift Command—to reflect its new importance.**

The subcommittee's report and recommendations, published in May of 1960, were approved unanimously by the full House committee. Congress subsequently approved for FY 1961 the Air Force's original request for $50 million to initiate the development of the new strategic transport and $70.4 million for 25 new tactical transports. In addition, $200 million was appropriated for the purchase of the 100 interim aircraft for use until the new planes were available.

Expansion of Airlift Capability: Systems Analysis

Almost immediately upon assuming office, McNamara addressed himself to the airlift issue—which had figured as a minor campaign issue in the 1960 election. His initial response had been to approve both the purchase of interim aircraft and the development of the new jet transport—the C-141—designed by the Lockheed Georgia Company. Although the C-141 was the first American jet designed primarily for cargo, its adequacy for carrying heavier items of

military equipment appeared—from a very early date—open to question. Physically, the C-141 was an elongated jet version of the C-131 (also produced by Lockheed); its specifications had been heavily influenced by the deployment concepts of the late fifties, in that it was designed to transport the lightly-equipped airborne troops as called for by the 1960 Lem/White agreement. Furthermore, the C-141 reflected a MATS staff bias for an aircraft that would be economical in peacetime, airline-type operations. Although the plane offered impressive economies in cost-per-ton mile (the cost of transporting a one-ton cargo one mile), it was not suitable for carrying unusually bulky military cargoes such as mobile bridges or tanks. Thus, when the Systems Analysis airlift/sealift team began to address the problem of an optimal aircraft fleet mix in spring, 1961, the cargo capacity of the C-141 constituted one of the principal topics of concern. McNamara had put the following questions before the team:

> Should we modify C-141 for increased capacity?
>
> Should we buy swing-tail 707s as a substitute for C-141? [Swing-tail 707s were commercial jets produced by Boeing which had larger cargo capacity than the C-141s but which required major modifications for military use.]
>
> Should we abandon MSTS (troop ships) in view of their high costs?
>
> Should we buy additional C-141s to increase overall airlift capability?

The airlift/sealift team worked on these questions under the direction of William Niskanen until August 1969, when Niskanen left to complete his PhD thesis at the RAND Corporation and John Keller arrived at SA to assume responsibility for the group. The analysis completed up to that point had been predicated on a phase-out of troop ships and the transfer of all military cargo to MATS. In his analysis Niskanen, a Chicago school (i.e., free market-oriented) economist, had highlighted the waste of manpower involved in time-consuming sealift and had demonstrated that MATS could perform the transport mission at lower unit costs. While Keller, a five-year veteran of the DOD Comptroller's office with a background in engineering and philosophy, agreed with this analysis, the JCS and the Navy were markedly reluctant to do away with the ships; and, although MATS was unof-

---

*The subcommittee also examined the responsiveness and availability of CRAF and recommended that the military purchase aircraft from CRAF members only, that CRAF be required to upgrade equipment, and that the President's authority over CRAF be expanded.

**The name change was not made until 1967, however.

ficially in favor, the rest of the Air Force was only lukewarm, being generally unimpressed by the importance of the transport mission. Despite the Army's growing interest in airlift, the Army supported the Navy's position on this issue.

With respect to the C-141, Niskanen's analysis found the aircraft deficient in loadable floor space and incapable of carrying much of the Army's bulky equipment. He had therefore recommended reducing the purchase of C-141s and substituting cargo-adapted swing-tail Boeing 707s. Keller, however, was much more favorably disposed to the C-141. His own analysis indicated that with certain modifications (such as moving the crew rest compartment off the main deck to a position under the flight deck and carrying partial payloads on the rear ramp), the C-141 would be more cost-effective in cost-per-ton-mile than either of two possible alternatives—the swing-tail 707 or the C-141 enlongated by a 20-foot plug in the fuselage. Keller further emphasized that an adapted commercial transport like the 707 would lack the flexibility and desirable military characteristics of the C-141, such as short take-off and landing distances, easy cargo loading, and airdrop and jettison capability. Based on these observations, he recommended an increase in the production rate of the C-141 from four aircraft to seven per month and an increase in planned procurement from seven squadrons to thirteen squadrons.

In the course of working out these analyses, the SA team came to the realization that although the Lem/White agreement had been the first attempt at specifying quantitative troop-lift requirements, the accord was not a well thought-out rapid deployment plan. Keller's examination of Niskanen's working papers revealed that Niskanen had implicitly rejected the Lem/White force requirements as logistically unrealistic. The lightly-equipped show-of-force troops specified in the agreement appeared more like an "anemic airborne division" than a viable combat organization. Niskanen's pessimistic conclusions about the C-141 were based on his use of a still slim but, in his view, more realistic force, which became known as the 22 September force. Recognition of the disparity of force estimates prompted Keller to initiate a series of studies toward the end of developing "credible" airlift requirements based on much heavier Army forces. Keller studied estimates of the size and sequence of various deployments, reviewed Army force structure estimates and asked the JCS Special Studies Group to develop some definitive estimates on deployment requirements.

In December of 1961, Keller was joined in his efforts by Jack Stockfisch, an "extremely bright" (Keller's description) economist, who had come to the SA office as official director for airlift/sealift. Keller, who was now convinced that combat-viable forces would actually weigh considerably more than even the 22 September force, began to explore—with various industry representatives—the feasibility of a new transport to succeed C-141. Boeing initially proposed an "advanced" version of their C-135 (basically a C-135 with a longer fuselage), but Keller and Stockfisch found numerous inadequacies in this design. As they explained it, a new transport would have to incorporate a large cross section for handling heavy deployment, all-weather capability, forward primitive airstrip use, and ALOC* to be an adequate answer to the rapid deployment problem. Although similar discussions were conducted with other interested aircraft manufacturers, those with Boeing proved most productive. According to Keller:

> Without saying anything to us, the Boeing folks went home and really went to work—both in terms of systems analysis and aircraft design.

From that point on, the design that Boeing was developing, called the CX-4, became the basis for analyzing the role of a large jet transport with respect to cost and performance.

In 1962, the CX-4 idea was propelled into the spotlight by an Air Force request for a replacement for the C-133, a Douglas transport that had been used to carry outsized equipment (such as radar vans, rocket engines, ICBMs and Army vehicles). The C-133 had a long and troubled history of mysterious crashes, major vibration, and maintenance problems, in consequence of which the Air Force proposed that the CX-4 be developed to replace the C-133 in the outsized transport mission. The Systems Analysis team, however, could not support such a limited purpose for the CX-4, since they were principally concerned at that point with the more general problem of moving heavy regular forces by air. Thus, they explored alternative and less expensive methods for solving the outsized transport problem. Keller, for example, directed the Army to conduct a special study of the feasibility of

---

*Air Line of Communication (ALOC)—continuous airlift from the starting point through to the battle area, thus eliminating the need for secondary in-ground transport.

disassembling regular division equipment (e.g., M-60 tanks, M-88 tank recovery vehicles, M-113 armored personnel carriers, artillery, bulldozers) for transport in the C-141 (which could not otherwise accommodate such equipment). The study indicated the impracticality of disassembly, and the SA team continued to search for alternatives, including various modifications to existing aircraft proposed by Lockheed and Douglas. Preliminary analysis, however, indicated that these alternatives were less cost effective than development of a new aircraft.

Thus, the concept of a new aircraft with outsized cargo capability and capable of moving heavy regular forces came to seem increasingly attractive to the Systems Analysis office. The concept was enthusiastically supported by MATS as a means of expanding its Army support role, but the Army itself viewed the idea with growing apprehension. Despite its interest in airlift capability, the Army had never really considered moving a full regular division, with support equipment, by air. As the CX-4 idea began to emerge and develop, the Army staff realized that it might preempt a large chunk of funding which was theoretically available for PEMA (Procurement, Equipment and Missiles, Army), the Army's main hardware budget category. The Army, then began to withdraw its previous support for airlift and attempted, for example, to prove that the entire combat-ready army was transportable in the 13-squadron C-141 forces. As Keller, however, noted in a critique of the Army's study, this "transportability" was achieved at considerable sacrifice; combat units, for example, were stripped of much of their supporting equipment; long lapses were accepted between arrival of troops and arrival of support; and in-theater travel and force positioning problems were ignored entirely.

In late spring, 1962, Boeing publicly announced its CX-4 design.* Boeing offered credible evidence that its CX-4 would be markedly more cost effective than the C-141 even for handling regular cargo and would have outsized capability as an additional feature. Boeing therefore urged that C-141 funds be diverted to the development of the CX-4. Although the SA was favorably disposed toward the CX-4, it concluded that the analytical basis for such a shift was still inadequate and that curtailment of C-141 for

CX-4 development at that time would create an unacceptable hiatus in the growth of airlift capability.

The CX-4/C-5A in Context

While Boeing was working on design specifications for the CX-4, the Systems Analysis Office was working on the broader question of the role of airlift *vis à vis* sealift and prepositioning in attaining rapid development capability. The possibilities of prepositioning and sealift had come to seem increasingly attractive with the development of two new ideas: the Forward Floating Depot (FFD) concept and various improvements to the MSTS Comet Ro/Ro Ship (roll on/roll off ship for transporting and quickly unloading vehicular cargo).

The FFD concept arose out of Jack Stockfisch's early work on sea-based prepositioning. Until the 1960s, the Army had been maintaining prepositioned stocks of supplies and heavy equipment in European and Southeast Asian bases, but these bases were both expensive to maintain and vulnerable. Stockfisch proposed to eliminate these problems by prepositioning the stocks on refitted Victory ships, which would be ready for rapid deployment to any trouble spot. The possibilities of this Forward Floating Depot concept were noted in the 1961 DPM, but no decision was made on development at that time. At the same time, construction of one large, high speed Ro/Ro ship was decided upon, although doubts remained about the ship's role *vis a vis* the FFD.

By the summer of 1962, SA's analysis (while still primarily directed toward the airlift build-up) had identified many of the key issues in the mobility problem. The notion of having least-cost aircraft fleet mixes in some kind of optimal balance with ships and land- and sea-based (FFD) prepositioning was generally accepted. However, the ship and prepositioning components were not yet well-defined, and there was no generalized model for integrating the contributions of airlift, sealift and prepositioning. The 1962 DPM reflected this situation. As summarized by Keller:

1.   Some idea of force requirements and weights for various contingencies in different theaters had emerged from the Army's General Purpose Forces studies. These indicated the

---

*As the concept developed, the CX-4 became the CX-HLS, the CX-X, and ultimately the C-5A.

need for a deployment capability far greater than previously contemplated. Thus the Lem/White requirements had been completely discredited and full ROAD* divisions were being used in airlift capability calculations.

2. In view of the increased requirements (based on ROAD divisions plus support units), the already much improved airlift capability seemed insufficient and therefore prepositioning appeared to be the more feasible course.

3. The FFD concept was an accepted element in the program.

4. The development of higher-speed Ro/Ro with over-the-beach capability was advocated.

5. The potentials of the CX–4 concept, and the aircraft's apparent cost-effectiveness advantage over other aircraft were noted, though mainly as an afterthought.

6. Questions concerning the value of rapid deployment capability *per se* were raised. At the time the military value of a forward strategy** was asserted, supported only by intuitive belief and qualitative argument.

During 1963, Keller (virtually alone in his work now that Stockfisch had moved to the Treasury Department) continued to address the mobility problem, conducting a study of mission support aircraft*** which later proved valuable as an exercise in model building. The study required the development of a computer-based model for evaluation of the competing mission support aircraft (new and inherited) in order to choose a least-cost fleet mix. At this point Keller noted among other things that the C-135s in MATS service were forecast to run out of useful life shortly and that the maintenance problems on the C-133s (outsized carriers) had assumed major dimensions.

It was during this period that Keller's high regard for MATS became apparent. Unlike MSTS officials (who Keller felt to be locked into the past, not analytically oriented, and not particularly conscious of cost-effectiveness—or even cost) the MATS staff welcomed a warm and unofficial liaison with Keller and OSD (SA). MATS had, by this time, unambiguously assumed the role of an Army supporting force. Further-

more, its prestige relative to TAC had been greatly increased as a result of the Cuban crisis, during which MATS had assumed responsibility for planning the proposed airdrop landing.****

While Keller's interest in airlift expansion increased, there were other elements within the Defense Department—particularly the Office of the Assistant Secretary of Defense for Installations and Logistics, OASD (IL)—that consistently opposed airlift augmentation, and, in Keller's view, diverted attention from the most profitable analysis. OASD (IL), whose responsibility for the purchase of commercial shipping services had led to close ties with commercial shipping interests, argued that existing airlift capability was adequate to meet deployment needs for existing force levels.***** The services were, likewise, only lukewarm on transport augmentation since they believed it would divert funds from other, more glamorous projects.

SA enthusiasm for sealift development proved similarly uninfectious, despite a major technological breakthrough in Ro/Ro design in 1963. Over the preceding year, Systems Analysis had been advocating development of a new, faster Ro/Ro with some over-the-beach capability. In 1963, Hudson Waterways proposed to lease MSTS an improved Ro/Ro ship designed for them by a maverick firm of naval architects, John McMullen and Associates. The ship, which used gas turbine engines and was built for easy unloading, was large, very fast, and could be operated by a much smaller crew than older Ro/Ro ships. Furthermore, it appeared that the ship would be relatively cheap to build and operate. SA advocated the development of at least one of these ships so that its features could

---

*Reorganized Army Division, or 40,000-50,000 short tons.

**A strategy that calls for the ability to bring troops into combat quickly.

***Aircraft not flying combat missions.

****It was generally agreed that TAC was insufficiently analytical in its approach to transport and completely preoccupied with exotic jetfighter missions.

*****OASD (IL) comments on the 1962 DPM argued that airlift was adequate to meet deployment needs and that planned additions to the C-141 fleet were excessive. The reason for this conclusion was that OASD (IL) calculations were based on annual transportation studies by the JCS, which in turn were based on transportation requirements developed by theater commanders, e.g., CINCPAC (Commander-in-Chief, Pacific). Since the CINC contingency requirements were always to be "implementable" they were tailored to existing forces and current deployment capabilities. The analysis was circular, though it projected an aura of "true military requirements." Each year OASD (IL) revived the argument.

be tested and evaluated. However, MSTS and the Navy found the design too radical and resisted its development.

The 1963 DPM again reflected the year's activities:

1. The Hudson Waterways ship, while unnamed, was advocated for point-to-point service.
2. The need for testing the FFD in operation was noted.
3. The question of the value of rapid development was raised again. For the first time, the notion that the airlift component of a rapid deployment capability was dependent on how rapid the deployment has to be was advanced. As in 1962, arguments for a forward strategy were neither explicit nor quantitative.
4. The phase out of C–135s and C–133s was commenced. The Secretary's recognition of a minimum additional airlift need of 25% led to a program for adding seven more squadrons to the C–141 force.

More significantly, however, the first draft of the 1963 DPM (written by Keller and annotated by McNamara) had recommended approval of a three-squadron force of the original 2,300 square foot, six-engine Boeing version of the CX–4. Keller, in order to disassociate the aircraft from the Boeing design, had at this point redesignated the aircraft CX–HLS (Heavy Logistics System). The argument for CX–HLS was based on an analysis performed by Keller of the three competing aircraft: C–130, C–141, and CX–HLS. The analysis revealed that in no case was the C–130 more cost effective than the C–141 and that the CX–HLS would be less expensive than the C–141 even for carrying lighter loads. Since the results rested directly on Keller's cost and performance estimates, McNamara eventually rejected the CX–HLS option in favor of further studies designed to examine CX–HLS cost and performance. He therefore approved a $10 million appropriation for 1964 for more detailed feasibility studies of the CX–HLS by interested airframe and engine manufacturers.

Another study, ordered by McNamara for 1964, was to have great significance for the airlift/sealift picture. This was a study by the Chairman's Special Studies Group of the Joint Chiefs of Staff (CJCS-SSG) on the potential payoffs of rapid deployment—the first attempt to answer quantitatively the question

which had been raised in successive DPMs. The specific task was to determine the cost and advantages of various time phasings of forces required to implement alternative military strategies for limited war situations. Three strategies were examined: a forward strategy calling for rapid deployment capability; a less demanding median strategy; and a minimum defense strategy. In each case, the strategy was divided into a containment phase, in which the enemy advance was halted, and a counter-attack phase, in which the status quo ante was restored. The result was a quantitative assessment of the effectiveness of each strategy and the conclusion that a forward strategy could mean shorter wars, fewer casualties to the U.S. and its allies, much less destruction of the attacked country, and a smaller total force requirement. The military value of a rapid deployment capability was confirmed.

The release of the CJCS-SSG report gave new impetus to the CX–HLS concept, this time, however, in the form of a new entry into the Heavy Logistics field, the CX–X. Proposed by the Air Force Systems Command (AFSC), the CX–X took the notion of a very large cargo transport one step further, with a plane that could fly anywhere in the world and return without refueling. Toward this end the CX–X would require

> exotic things like laminar flow wings, boron filament construction, wild bypass ratios on the engine—and GNP's worth of dollars and years of extra development time

Keller, with the help of Boeing, studied the proposal and concluded that even if ground refueling bases were to become unavailable (as the AFSC contended), it would still be cheaper to procure CX–HLS (which would be designed for in-flight refueling from a tanker plane) than to buy the CX–X. One result of the AFSC proposal, however, was a decision to develop CX–HLS in a more advanced version than the 2,300 square foot, six-engine aircraft recommended in the 1963 DPM. The Air Force opted for a larger 2,900 square foot edition equipped with four new and more powerful (40,000 lbs. thrust) engines. SA analyses indicated that these changes enhanced the cost-effectiveness of the plane. In December, 1964, the various airframe and engine manufacturers studying CX–HLS filed reports indicating that the aircraft could indeed be built economically. According to Keller, the Boeing design was again technically superior and was much improved in cost effectiveness over the earlier versions.

A C–5A Decision

As 1964 came to a close, a decision to proceed with the preparation of contract specifications for the CX-HLS was impending. There was strong support for this program within Systems Analysis, and analysis seemed to justify going ahead. Of particular relevance to the CX-HLS decision were the CJCS-SSG study and studies performed by the airframe and engine manufacturers which had, among other things, shown the feasibility of economically developing "high flotation" landing gear (which would permit the plane to land on relatively unimproved airstrips) and the more powerful engines. Keller had recommended that the Air Force proceed with the CX-HLS and concurrently cut back on C-141 production. However, a late entry into the mobility game–the Fast Deployment Logistics Ship (FDL)–appeared just in time to challenge airlift expansion.

The FDL idea had originated some months earlier, during an evaluation of sea-based prepositioning (FFD) and Ro/Ro costs. One analyst had suggested that a Hudson Waterways type Ro/Ro, operated as a FFD would provide a very attractive sealift system. Though of little consequence at the time, the idea reappeared near the end of the year, supported strongly by the Navy, in the form of a Center for Naval Analysis (CNA) proposal.

In Keller's view the CNA proposal came as a reaction to a paragraph in the 1963 DPM which had said that a hypothetical force of fifteen CX-4 squadrons could carry all of MSTS' peacetime traffic or support all of our forces in Europe during a land war. As Keller said, "It's hard to justify a Navy when there are no sea lanes to protect–and they surely rose to the challenge." The first inkling of a riposte was a memo from Secretary of the Navy Paul Nitze in September 1964, when the DPM was in its drafting stages. Nitze argued that CX-HLS was not the best solution to the rapid deployment problem and that no decision on it should be made that year since he would shortly have the results of a study that would prove the advantages of rapid sealift over CX-HLS. While Keller characterized this "Sealog" program as a "last ditch gambit," those within CNA responsible for its development held a strikingly different view.

The essence of the Sealog proposal was abandoning the peacetime employment of ships as cargo haulers and instead using them as a readiness force whose cost could be viewed as the price of a rapid deployment capability. As envisioned at the time, Sealog ships would be preloaded with equipment and deployed forward (i.e., close to possible theaters of operations) to provide early deliveries. Army troops would be airlifted to the area for "marry up" with their equipment. Although there was some controversy over design details on the ships, the CNA proposal outlined what would later be known as the FDL Program. According to then-Captain Thomas Davies of CNA, an officer with a maverick reputation who had been involved in previous Navy-Air Force disputes, the proposal reflected the intuitive realization that although aircraft were suitable for carrying light cargos rapidly, ships could carry heavier and larger cargos at a slower rate, and the disadvantages of ships could be easily overcome by stationing them closer to the area in which they would be needed. CNA's FDL calculations were all carried out by hand, and loading and unloading simulations were conducted with scale models of the ship and tiny versions of their Army cargos. "Because we didn't use any computers," observed Davies, "the SA office regarded us as rather crooked."

The FDL concept, in the view of CNA analysts, offered several advantages over the airlift approach advocated by Keller. However, they worried about Keller's receptiveness to the new idea, especially at such a late date. As one CNA staff member said, "there is a point at which the analyst changes roles and becomes a proponent of a system merely because at some point something has to be implemented." Keller was felt by CNA to have moved into this second role in his advocacy of CX-HLS; he himself admitted that he was intellectually and emotionally committed to the CX-HLS ("I had become a believer"). While the CNA proposal was routed through Dan Rathbun, an SA analyst, primarily because he was responsible for all Navy proposals, other considerations appear to have played a role in this maneuver–several CNA members felt that they could not get a "fair hearing" from Keller. This fear appears to have been justified: when the CNA team was called over to present the proposal to Keller and his staff, they found the meeting packed with C-5A advocates. As Davies recalled, "We were presenting our proposal to a fairly hostile audience." (Keller claims that he was still interested in possible uses of Ro/Ro vessels in a rapid deployment system, but he had greater confidence in what he viewed as the more thoroughly tested airlift concept.) The result was a debate which was to last through the end of 1964 and into 1965 with Rathbun and the CNA supporting the FDL, and Keller and the Air Force advocating the CX-HLS.

The CNA proposal had advocated an extreme position: no CX-HLS, little prepositioning, reductions in the C-141 force, and 45 FDLs. Keller found the proposal to be "so highly selective in its assumptions as to make a predetermined answer come out." (For example, the CNA calculations were based on the assumption that deployment ended when troops were landed at a port—even if the actual fighting was some distance inland.) However, CNA believed the same of Keller's assumptions—the vulnerability question was one example. The CX-HLS was to be fitted with high flotation landing gear, thus enabling it to land and unload its cargo at the forward edge of the battle area (FEBA). This capability made it theoretically superior to any form of sealift, which was necessarily limited in its approach to the battle area and would require trucking or secondary airlift to get its equipment to the front lines. However, the SA work assumed an administrative landing—that is, one without opposition. Under real battle conditions, CNA doubted that such an expensive aircraft would really be operated within distance of the shooting.

CNA's critique of the CX-HLS program was buttressed by a more general critique by the Military Aircraft Panel (MAP) of the President's Science Advisory Committee (PSAC).* Charged with providing the president with advice on matters of science and technology, PSAC's military panels—composed of prominent civilian and industrial scientists—had routinely studied scientific questions raised by the Draft Presidential Memoranda; in this way, the MAP had begun to study the fast deployment question in mid-1964. As MAP Chairman, Richard L. Garwin, a physicist with varied consulting experience in defense matters, stated, "Our concern was to obtain the greatest military capability per dollar, with due attention to balancing of technological risk, delay, utility, and the like."

Early on, MAP began to conclude that SA's CX-HLS program had not adequately addressed a number of issues.

1. MAP calculations showed that more intensive use of the existing C-141 fleet could achieve many of the performance capabilities of the proposed CX-HLS fleet.

2. Much of the anticipated benefit of the CX-HLS derived from its ability to land on unimproved airstrips, e.g., muddy fields, by using "high flotation" landing gear. MAP studies showed that the C-141 could be fitted with an equivalent of such gear at a cost of $40,000 per plane.

3. SA's calculations of the required size of the fast deployment air fleet were based on a utilization rate of three hours per plane per day. MAP felt that since ordinary commercial airlines were achieving UR's of 12-15 hours/plane/day, the three-hour figure was unreasonably low and thus overstated the need for new aircraft.

4. The cargo-carrying capacity of existing aircraft such as the C-141 was limited by the amount of weight the plane could carry. MAP suggested that the Army could develop lighter weight equipment (e.g., aluminum tanks) far more cheaply than the Air Force could develop the new CX-HLS.

5. Finally and most seriously, MAP felt that the FDL option had not been adequately explored by SA. As Garwin put it, "By this time SA had become such an advocate of the [CX-HLS] that they were unwilling to give us the benefit of their experience by estimating the relative costs of this FDL option and the [CX-HLS] option." MAP estimated that by taking advantage of advances in ship design such as operating the engines directly from the bridge (instead of through an engine room crew), Ro/Ro ships that could land at unimproved "ports," and high-speed engines, the FDL could be developed into a relatively inexpensive but militarily satisfactory alternative to the CX-HLS.

Garwin embodied these conclusions in an October 20, 1964 memo to Donald Hornig, the President's Science Advisor, recommending that the CX-HLS program be deferred for further studies of the optimal mix of fast deployment systems. Hornig was sufficiently impressed by the report to set up a meeting between MAP and DOD officials.

But despite the critiques offered by CNA and PSAC, Secretary McNamara approved the CX-HLS in December 1964. Redesignated the C-5A, the program moved into the Contract Definition Phase, during

---

*The President's Science Advisory Committee was abolished in 1973.

which the exact terms of the procurement contract (e.g., performance specifications) were developed. Three airframe manufacturers (Boeing, Douglas, and Lockheed) and two engine manufacturers (General Electric and Pratt & Witney) entered into competition for the contract award, which would be announced late in 1965. C-141 production would be curtailed and the C-5A developed in its place. At the same time, the merits of the FDL concept were noted, and plans to move ahead with further studies of the ship were laid.

Apparently several factors influenced these decisions. The breakeven analysis performed by Keller in 1964 provided the rationale for curtailing C-141 production and focusing on the C-5A as a replacement. McNamara was reputed to have high regard for Keller's work, and as time went on the Secretary had become steadily more impressed by the apparent advantages of extremely rapid deployment of American forces via airlift. (McNamara may also have felt that work on the C-5A had to move into the Contract Definition Phase to preserve Air Force interest in the rapid deployment mission.) Finally, none of the analysis performed during 1964 had systematically examined the composition of the least-cost fleet mix in order to justify the C-5A decision. Although cost had become an issue as advocates of the CX-HLS and the FDL had searched for arguments to prove the superiority of their alternative, the analytic techniques available in 1964 were not sufficiently refined to permit precise specification of the least-cost fleet mix.

The Linear Programming Model

Keller's 1963 study of mission support aircraft had employed a linear programming model to calculate the numbers and types of aircraft that could provide a designated level of capability—for example, in terms of the number of flying hours needed for different routes and missions—for the lowest cost. At about the same time defense analysts in civilian research organizations began experimenting with the use of linear programming models to calculate least-cost forces of aircraft that could meet specified strategic airlift requirements. Keller began working with an experienced group of these analysts at the Research Analysis Corporation, a research organization in nearby Northern Virginia that did studies primarily for the Army, to develop a linear programming model of the airlift/sealift problem. Because the problem had come to be viewed within DOD as one of determining

the mix of aircraft, ships, and prepositioned equipment, that could meet strategic mobility requirements for the lowest cost, a linear programming model seemed like an appropriate analytic tool to use.

In simple terms, a linear programming model involves an *objective,* a set of *activities* that can contribute to achieving the objective, and *constraints* on the extent to which the activities can actually be used. In the airlift/sealift problem, the objective is to be able to deliver forces and supplies at specified times to designated locations around the world where the forces may be needed. The activities are the different aircraft, ships, and configurations of prepositioned equipment. The constraints include such factors as the capacity of seaports and airfields. The model was "linear" in the sense that it assumed that the amount by which an activity contributed to meeting the objective was proportional to the amount of the activity used; doubling the number of aircraft of a particular type would double the volume of material that could be moved by these aircraft. (This seems reasonable, but you see how the assumption might be violated: twice as many aircraft might cause traffic congestion and unloading bottlenecks that would slow everything down.)

Using the model, analysts could calculate the numbers and types of aircraft and ships that would move the specific combat forces on the required schedules for the lowest cost, reckoned as the total cost of buying and operating the forces over a ten-year period. The analysts could also do "sensitivity analysis," i.e., change any assumption—the speed at which the forces had to be moved, the costs of different aircraft and ships—and see how the change affected the answer.

By 1965, the model had been developed to the point that it could be used to determine what mix of C-5As, FDLs, FFDs, and C-141s would be most economical in providing the levels of movement capability that were associated with the now popular rapid deployment strategies. Repeated uses of the model with widely varying assumptions convinced Keller, Enthoven, and McNamara that DOD should maintain a balanced posture of six C-5A squadrons; 14 C-141 squadrons; 30 FDLs; equipment prepositional in both Europe and the Pacific; and, as back-up, a Civil Reserve Air Fleet and several hundred commercial cargo ships. Moreover, sensitivity analysis convinced them that the costs of the C-5A would be double current estimates and it would still be economical to buy it; if costs were lower than estimated, perhaps a dozen squadrons would be needed.

The model became the center of attention as the year wore on. Keller and his associates in the Air Force regarded it as a boon to their cause. The reaction of Sealift advocates, on the other hand, ranged from skepticism to outrage. Many were convinced that the model was rigged to favor the C-5A. As one of them noted, if you assume that a scissors bridge, air transportable only in the C-5A, has to arrive in the battle area by the third day, naturally the C-5A is indispensable no matter what it cost. Indeed, calculations showed that when deliveries very early in a war were not required, the C-5A became dispensable. Such findings brought scorn from the airlift advocates. If you assume World War II, they said, sure you can do it with just ships; but the whole idea is *rapid* deployment, and ships simply cannot move combat forces to a battle area rapidly.

A major area of unresolved controversy was the cost estimate for the C-5A. Although the model had suggested that the least-cost fleet mix was relatively insensitive to variations in individual systems cost, CNA nevertheless felt that the estimates used for the C-5A were wholly unrealistic. While both the Systems Analysis and Air Force estimates priced the C-5A program at approximately $3 billion for six squadrons, 1964 estimates for the CX-HLS (the original 2,300 square feet, six engine version) when extrapolated for increased capability approached $5 billion. Don Weir, CNA's economist, priced the C-5A very close to the latter figure. While this estimate purportedly infuriated Keller, the figure was confirmed by a SA cost expert who unofficially priced the C-5A at approximately $5 billion. He was subsequently told that his estimate might endanger a favorable decision on the program. When the aircraft went on contract the official estimates were used as the basis for program funding.

APPENDIX

Historical Role of the Secretary

The original War Department, as established by Congress, was headed by a Secretary who was a member of the President's cabinet. This small military establishment (which in its first year consisted of an army of 46 officers and 672 men) was considered adequate to meet the limited national goals of the young country. Principal reliance for meeting national emergencies was placed on the states' milita, which was to be supported by the states without cost to the federal government. It was not until 1798 that the ground forces under the War Department were supplemented by naval forces under the Department of the Navy. As national security objectives expanded, together with the growth in size and power of the military establishment, so too did the problems of management in the War Department. In the War Department, military commanders were possessed of absolute authority in the field, while fiscal responsibility was lodged in the General Staff under the civilian Secretary of War. This disjunction between resources and operations led to a problem of dual control which was not resolved until Secretary of War Root proposed a straightforward solution: the Secretary of War should be the undisputed head of the Army under the President. Root felt that in no other way could the original concept of civilian supremacy over the military be maintained. In 1903 Congress adopted this recommendation by abolishing the position of Commanding General, and creating a Chief of Staff who would be the advisor and executive agent of his civilian superior, the Secretary. The Navy followed suit in 1915. However, the problem of civilian v. military input in defense decision-making was to persist for many, many years.

Lack of coordination between the War Department and the Department of the Navy also caused

---

Source: This account is based on Charles Hitch, Decision-Making for Defense *(Berkeley: University of California Press, 1965), pp. 5–18.*

considerable apprehension. It was not until World War II, in which combined land, sea, and air operations played a vital role, that coordination of the services with respect to planning was achieved. During that war, a Joint Chiefs of Staff was created and unified commands were established. The Army Air Corps was represented on the JCS as a virtual equal with the Army and the Navy. In 1945, therefore, President Harry Truman sent to Congress specific legislation which would formalize these wartime arrangements. Truman proposed a single Department of National Defense to be headed by a Secretary of cabinet rank.

The Department was to comprise three coordinate branches (Army, Navy, and Air Forces) each under an Assistant Secretary. Each branch was to have a military commander; they together with the Chief of Staff of the Department of National Defense were to constitute an advisory body to the Secretary and President. President Truman wanted a unified, centralized common service organization and he stressed the principle that "strategy, program, and budget are all aspects of the same basic decisions." Though the Army had become amenable to the notion of unified command, the Navy was opposed. The law which emerged, the National Security Act of 1947, provided for a confederation of services rather than for the unification of them. The Act created a military establishment headed by the Secretary of Defense and comprised of three separately organized and administered executive departments (Army, Navy and Air Force). Provision was made for a Joint Chiefs of Staff. The role of the Secretary under the 1947 Act was to establish "general" policies and exercise general "direction, authority and control."

Under the stewardship of first Secretary James V. Forrestal, the National Security Act was amended to increase the control of the Secretary. The 1949 amendments abolished the executive department status of the services, and placed them under three assistant secretaries to the Secretary of Defense. A chairman was appointed for the Office of the Joint Chiefs of Staff. Thus the primacy of the Secretary of Defense as the principal assistant to the President on defense matters was firmly established. The amendments also provided for the Office of Assistant Secretary of Defense, Comptroller, and unified budget and fiscal procedures.

Top management at DOD was again reorganized in 1953. Old agencies were abolished and the number of Assistant Secretaries was increased to nine. In transmitting the reorganization plan, the President made it clear that "*no* function was to be carried out independently of the Secretary of Defense and that Secretaries of military departments were to be operating managers' of the Secretary."

Partly in response to Sputnik, 1958 saw the authority of the Secretary increased once more . . . especially in the area of Research and Development. The Joint Staff was strengthened, and the new lines of authority ran from the President, to Secretary of Defense, through the Joint Chiefs to the unified commands. Military departments were no longer "separately administered," but "separately organized." President Eisenhower said at the time:

> . . . complete unity in our strategic planning and basic operational direction [is a vital necessity]. It is therefore mandatory that the initiative for this planning and direction rest not with the separate services but directly with the Secretary of Defense and his operational advisors, the Joint Chiefs of Staff, assisted by such staff organizations as they deem necessary.

When President Kennedy took office, he began to seek further changes at DOD which would make the Department more responsive to national security objectives and changes in technology. Stuart Symington and his committee on the Defense establishment, as well as advisors Thomas Finletter, Roswell Gilpatrick, and Mark Leva, proposed to replace the Service Secretaries with Undersecretaries of Defense, thus vesting in the Secretary of Defense the administration of the Service; the Chiefs would have become solely heads of their respective services. However, McNamara proposed to achieve these goals without further reorganization of the Department.

18

The C-5A (B)

In December of 1964 Secretary of Defense Robert S. McNamara gave the "go ahead" for the development of the C-5A, a large cargo aircraft which would provide the United States with a dramatic increase in its military airlift capability. As conceived by the Defense Department's Systems Analysis office (which was largely responsible for the idea—see Part A (chapter 17)), the C-5A would be capable of deploying troops and supporting equipment to trouble spots around the globe with unprecedented speed and efficiency. Although the estimated cost for the development and production of 120 aircraft was about $2 billion, the C-5A was considered well worth the expense in view of its military value and relatively low operating costs. This case, the second of a two-part study, will trace the procurement of the C-5A by the Air Force.

THE PRE-CONTRACT PHASE

In November of 1963, more than a year before the Secretary approved the C-5A program,* the organizational groundwork was laid with the establishment of a special unit within the Aeronautical Systems Division of the Air Force Systems Command (AFSC) at Wright-Patterson Air Force Base in Ohio. This unit, the C-5A System Program Office (SPO), was charged with several responsibilities concerning the development of the aircraft. The SPO would be responsible for the refinement of specifications and, assuming the program was approved, the choice of contractors. Ultimately, the SPO would oversee the development and production of the plane until it was turned over to the Military Air Transport Service (MATS) for use.

---

*The aircraft was designated C-5A in December 1964. Prior to that time it was known as CX-HLS (Heavy Logistics System) and, still earlier, as CX-4.

By March of 1964, the concept of the C-5A had been sufficiently well developed to enable the SPO to issue a "Specific Operational Requirement" (SOR) for a heavy logistics aircraft. The 12-page SOR defined general design characteristics, operational performance requirements, and system operation and maintenance specifications for the proposed aircraft. In April, Requests for Proposals (RFPs) for feasibility studies were released to all interested airframe and engine manufacturers.* Five airframe manufacturers (Boeing, Lockheed, Douglas, General Dynamics and Martin-Marietta) and three engine manufacturers (Pratt & Witney, General Electric, and Curtiss-Wright) responded with proposals for studies. From these, Boeing, Lockheed, and Douglas were awarded three-month system study contracts and G.E. and Pratt & Whitney received similar contracts for engine studies.

The pre-program study contracts elicited elaborate responses from the competitors. Lockheed, for example, built a wooden simulator to determine cargo area dimensions and loading techniques. Tons of military equipment that had never been airlifted before (e.g., the Army's M-60 battle tank) were driven into the simulator, chained down, and unloaded all within specific time limits. This and other such studies established the feasibility of the proposed aircraft and refined certain design requirements: drive-through loading, larger cargo compartment dimensions, special provisions for carrying troops to operate the airlifted vehicles, and high flotation landing gear (for use on unimproved airstrips) were all shown to be essential to the aircraft's operation and were incorporated by the Air Force into a revised SOR. The studies were so favorable that, by October of 1964, the Air Force had recommended to the Secretary that the program be funded and that it move directly into the Contract Definition Phase.** This recommendation was re-

flected in the Secretary's December 1964 decision authorizing the commencement of contract definition and designating the program—for the first time— "C-5A."

The pre-program technical development of the C-5A coincided with the development of a new procurement policy designed to hold down costs and maintain performance standards on Air Force systems. The new policy, which was to have a substantial impact on the history of the C-5A, was intended to reverse the pattern of cost overruns characteristic of military procurement in the 1950's. During this period, most military contracts were let on an "emergency basis," resulting in the rapid development of many untried systems and also in large cost overruns. (A 1962 study of 12 major weapons systems, for example, found that their final costs averaged 220% above the original bids.) The size and frequency of the overruns could be traced to two primary problems with the existing procurement system: the contractors' practice of "buying in" and the military practice of issuing Cost Plus Fixed Fee (CPFF) contracts. Contractors who "bought in" submitted an unrealistically low bid in order to win a contract, and then made up their losses or "got well" by increasing the price tag later through costly engineering changes permitted by the contracting system. Although this practice would appear risky for the contractor, the CPFF contract (which guaranteed full reimbursement for allowable costs plus a fixed fee as profit) in fact placed most of the risk on the government.

In McNamara's view, CPFF contracts were justified only when no meaningful performance measures could be established in advance. Since this was not the case for most weapon systems, McNamara proposed to use incentive contracts for most procurement. Unlike CPFF contracts, incentive contracts offered the contractor increased profit for reducing costs below estimates, for shortening time schedules, and for exceeding reliability specifications. Further, McNamara encouraged a shift from non-competitive to competitive bidding, the introduction of a Program Confirmation Phase (later termed Contract Definition Phase) into the acquisition process, and the use of the Program Evaluation and Review Technique (PERT). The Program Confirmation Phase was a time period specifically set aside during which the government and the contractors would establish "what is wanted, how it is to be designed and built, how it will be used, what it will cost, and how the development and production program will be managed." The PERT system

---

*As used here, airframe refers to all of the plane except for the propulsion system and certain Air Force-supplied navigational equipment and weapons. Airframe and engine manufacture require different technological capabilities, and the two are usually contracted for separately. The studies to be undertaken served several purposes: confirming the feasibility of the overall aircraft design; allowing the Air Force to assess the capabilities of the various manufacturers; and formally involving the contractors in designing the aircraft.

**In the Contract Definition Phase of military procurement, detailed specifications for the item to be purchased are defined.

then identified the key activities necessary to maintaining the production schedule and provided for periodic reviews of the procurement activities to reduce administrative lead times and standardize operations.

Total Package Procurement

Further efforts to forestall overruns were contributed by Robert Charles, who came to DOD (the Department of Defense) in 1963 from an executive position in the McDonnell Aircraft Corporation. As Assistant Secretary of the Air Force for Installations and Logistics, his responsibilities included supervision of supply, maintenance, transportation, communication and procurement. Charles accepted the post, he said, because

> I was convinced that we were spending more than we needed to on our national defense, that defense equipment was costing far too much due to procurement methods which imposed little discipline on either industry or government, and that I could do something about it.

Before Charles' arrival at DOD, the risks associated with the procurement of "off the drawing board" weapon systems* had been considered so great that a preliminary contract was let for the research and development of a system and a second contract was later concluded for actual production of the system. While the R & D contract was usually awarded on a competitive basis, the value of this initial contract only ran to about 20% of the total costs. Non-competitive negotiation with the development contractor on the production contract was inevitable if the system was to be introduced on a timely basis and without duplication of much of the development effort. The government then was virtually forced to accept the company's bid for the follow-on production contract (80% of the total costs) or cancel the program.

This procedure, which Charles characterized as "iceberg procurement," did offer some advantages (such as reduced technical risk and more realistic cost estimates at the time of the production contract award), but it also encouraged buying in and, consequently, unforeseen costs to the government. Charles' answer to this problem was the Total Package Pro-

---

*I.e., weapon systems for which no prototypes had been built.

curement System (TPPS). The idea behind TPPS (or the Charles Plan, as it was known) was that at the outset all anticipated development, production, and support** should be procured as one total package and incorporated into one contract containing price and performance commitments. Since a complete and firm program price (for both development and production) would be negotiated in a single contract, TPPS would encourage industry to be more precise in their estimates of performance, cost, and schedules and discourage overly optimistic bidding by not allowing the contractor to "get well" under a non-competitive production contract. The contract would include incentives for improving performance and cost specifications, stiff penalties for schedule delays, and severe restrictions on engineering changes. The advantages of TPPS contracting were seen as follows:

1. The system requires a tightening of design and configuration discipline, both in the proposal stage and in the actual work under the contract.
2. It largely eliminates unrealistic salesmanship, including underestimation of cost and overestimates of performance which are encouraged when bidders are required to make firm commitments on only a small portion of the total sales.
3. The contractor, committed to cost and performance figures before the detail design work begins, will have a "strong motive" for economical production, product reliability, and simplicity of maintenance.
4. The selected company, under pressure to meet its contract guarantees will obtain supplies and services from the most efficient sources.
5. It permits the government to make a choice between contractors based not on mere estimates but on binding commitments concerning the performance and price of what is really required—operational equipment.

As thus envisioned, the Total Package Procurement System could be realistically applied only to "low risk" systems—that is, to systems that required no large steps beyond the technical knowledge of the aircraft industry and systems for which estimates of production costs could be made without extensive prior development. As defined in the SOR, the C-5A was to be just such a system: a state-of-the-art aircraft.

**"Support" refers to the maintenance of a weapon system throughout its anticipated lifetime.

The Air Force, therefore, requested that the C-5A be developed under Total Package Procurement, and, in anticipation of approval for their request, began to incorporate the concept into the RFPs. Since TPPS was still under consideration by DOD at that time, Dr. Harold Brown, Director of Defense Research and Engineering, advised the Air Force that:

> If . . . for some reason it might be determined that contracts for the Total Package Concept cannot be awarded, the Government would have the option to retreat to the conventional procedures of a development contract followed by a production contract. The possibility of the Government using this alternative should not be made known to the contractors in order to strengthen the Government's negotiating position.

By December 1964, both the C-5A program and the use of TPPS were approved. Near the end of the month, the C-5A SPO released the RPF for contract definition (the setting of detailed specifications, including a firm price commitment) to the three airframe manufacturers and two engine manufacturers who had participated in the earlier studies. The RFP contained over 1,500 pages of specifications and requirements, covering the total development and production of 58 aircraft. The engines were to be contracted for separately and furnished by the government to the airframe contractors.

THE CONTRACT COMPETITION

The release of the RFP marked the official beginning of the competition for the C-5A. However, the RFP was by no means a static document. During the five months of the Contract Definition Phase, the SPO authorized nearly three hundred changes and issued approximately 1,600 pages of clarifications and revisions. Over the same period, the manufacturers, who were unfamiliar with the new contracting procedures, addressed to the SPO a total of 783 specific written questions, chiefly concerning three areas: systems analysis, TPPS, and the preparation of cost proposals. The C-5A competition was quite beyond the scope of anything they had previously experienced. In addition to the technical work associated with the design of the aircraft, the manufacturers were required to prepare complicated data submis-

sions on all aspects of the program. The task was so monumental that each was forced to institute program controls of the sort normally applied to major development programs. At Boeing the C-5A "team" comprised over 1,300 people, while Douglas and Lockheed each assigned over 1,700 personnel to the project. Although each contractor received approximately $6 million for this work, the project was considered so important because of its size, the possible commercial applications, and the prospects for further military business that success with the new TPP System might bring, that Boeing and Douglas spent about $20 million and Lockheed about $16 million of their own funds during this phase.

Although competition for large military contracts is always intense, the battle for the C-5A was, according to *Business Week*, "the most strenuous in aerospace history." The stakes were appreciably greater than the $2 billion contract itself, since each competitor hoped to capture the commercial market for large transport aircraft. Although the airlines remained non-committal about commercial prospects, all of the competitors were optimistic about C-5A's sales potential. Still fresh in their minds was the example of the Boeing 707, the technology for which had been developed under military contract for the KC-135 aerial tanker. Successful commercial application of this technology had allowed Boeing to get a big jump on its rivals at the beginning of the jet age. Although Douglas later bought into the commercial jet market (spending $300 million on the development of the DC-8), it was believed that the winner of the C-5A contract would be able to dominate the market for at least a dozen years, since no other company could be expected to finance the development on its own. Commercial applications aside, the C-5A had significant military sales potential (with the Air Force contemplating a purchase of over 200 aircraft) not only in its cargo form, but also adapted to serve as an aerial tanker, giant airborne hospital, or flying command center. Moreover, the C-5A program—like other large military programs—would serve as an overhead "absorber" for concurrent commercial ventures.*

At the time of the C-5A competition, Boeing was in the most favorable overall economic position with the biggest backlog of commercial orders in its history (445 jetliners worth $2.4 billion). However, its

---

*That is, research and development activities related to commercial ventures could be charged to C-5A R & D.

military sales were coming to an end with the production of the last few KC-135 tankers. Boeing's last transport, the C-135, had been regarded as a successful aircraft, and Boeing's reputation with the military was generally good. Also, Boeing had a reputation for superior engineering and technical capability and had worked closely with the Systems Analysis office of DOD in bringing the C-5A concept to maturity.

Douglas, on the other hand, was the least financially stable of the three competitors. Douglas was producing no military aircraft at the time, and the future of their current DC-9 program rested on their success or failure in the C-5A competition. Douglas' standing with the military was relatively poor, as their last transport, the C-133, was generally regarded as a technical disaster. (The C-133's turbulent history included a number of unexplained crashes and overwhelming maintenance problems.) Furthermore, the company was deemed to have rather "primitive" analytical capability. An agreement between Douglas and North American Aviation on joint participation in the competition, however, appeared to improve the company's prospects considerably.

Lockheed's position at this time was somewhat unique. Lockheed had dominated the military transport area since the development of the successful C-130 Hercules in 1955. While the Hercules was relatively unsuccessful commercially, military sales approached 1,000—making it the standard military cargo aircraft. In 1960, Lockheed had won the contract to produce the C-141. Again they produced an excellent aircraft, but lost out in the commercial market as Douglas and Boeing produced successful cargo versions of their biggest jets. Thus, although Lockheed's relations with the military were at their peak, their poor showing in commercial aircraft left them in an uncomfortable economic position: at the time of the C-5A competition, Lockheed was almost 90% dependent on government contracts. Since the C-141 was to be cut back in order to make room for the C-5A, losing the contract would put Lockheed out of production for the military by 1968, thus causing the company severe financial distress. Weighing in Lockheed's favor during the C-5A competition was the sheer volume of its transport business, which promised economies in production and might enable it to submit the lowest bid.

Source Selection

In April of 1965 the Contract Definition Phase ended with the delivery of over 35 tons of proposals and supporting data to the SPO. (A single copy of each contractor's technical/management proposal averaged over 50,000 pages.) The period April 27-30 was devoted to oral presentations from the contractors, and at the end of the month the last phase of the competition—source selection and the negotiation of firm contracts—was ready to begin.

In preparation for source selection, a Source Selection Board, consisting of two Air Force Major Generals and two Brigadier Generals, had been established in November of 1964. Although ultimate authority for selection would rest with the Secretary of Defense, the Source Selection Board performed an important advisory role. By March 1965, a 400-man evaluation group had been selected and divided into teams to cover specific items within the proposals. Each team was responsible for developing precise standards against which the competitors' proposals would be evaluated. Technical proposals were to be evaluated only against these written standards, and not against each other. Cost proposals were to be evaluated against an independent government estimate which had been prepared on the basis of historical costs on the C-130, C-133, and C-141 programs. Concurrent with the preparation of item standards, the Source Selection Board decided on the weights which would later be applied to each item. (These weights were not revealed to members of the evaluation group.)

Nearly five months elapsed before the evaluation group was able to complete its review of the contractors' technical and cost data and rate their work. Throughout this period, the contractors were advised of deficiencies or discrepancies in their proposals.

By August the Source Selection Board had concluded its review and forwarded its recommendation to the Air Council (consisting of the Vice Chief of Staff and seven 3-star generals); concurrently, the commanders of MATS, AFSC and AFLC (Air Force Logistics Command) sent separate letters of recommendation. The Source Selection Board, supported by the AFLC commander, recommended Boeing, but the commanders of MATS and AFSC recommended Lockheed. (Douglas was at this point considered to have lost the competition.) The Boeing design was cited by its supporters primarily for its overall superior technological sophistication and for its greater speed and lift. Although the Boeing bid was $330 million above Lockheed's, the Source Selection Board felt that the performance advantages inherent in the Boeing design were worth the additional cost. Lockheed's design was deficient in precisely those areas in which Boeing's excelled—speed and lift—and there was some controversy over Lockheed's ability to meet RFP specifications for short takeoffs and landings.* However, the Lockheed design offered advantages in ton-mile operating costs and also in loading characteristics: while Boeing had built around the minimum RFP cargo area width of 17.5 ft., Lockheed's cargo area width measured 19 ft. This added width was seen as a significant advantage in view of potential loading accidents. (Air Force officials feared such possibilities as a GI driving a tank through the side of a fuselage.)

These considerations evidently played a part in the decision by Secretary of the Air Force Eugene Zuckert to offer each contractor a final opportunity to revise its proposal, and on September 1, 1965, each contractor was given a critique of its proposal. Zuckert indicated that he found sufficient merit in the Lockheed design to warrant further study. Although the Source Selection Board's ruling was never intended to be final, it would not be overruled lightly: the last time McNamara had overruled a source selection board was on the ill-starred TFX jet fighter. (Conceived as a high-performance all-service fighter, the TFX developed severe problems of excess drag and low approach speed and had to be terminated. McNamara's choice of General Dynamics over Boeing for the airframe contract—against the recommendation of both the Navy and the Air Force—was attacked

by some in Congress as politically motivated.) Therefore Zuckert formed a special review group of senior officers to reevaluate source selection.

At this point Lockheed revised its proposal by increasing the wing area from 5,600 sq. ft. to 6,200 sq. ft. to improve takeoff and landing performance. However, this increased the plane's gross weight from 700,000 to 728,000 pounds, requiring the addition of leading edge slats over the entire length of each wing for additional low-speed lift. (As one Lockheed official said, "We thought they were trying to tell us something.") Douglas and Boeing revised their bids downward, but the Lockheed bid remained the lowest of the three. The revised designs were then referred to the Air Council, the commanders of AFSC, MATS, and AFLC, the three Air Force Assistant Secretaries, and, finally, to the Air Force Chief of Staff. Although additional cost and schedule risks associated with Lockheed's revisions moved several officers on the Air Council to vote for Boeing, a three-fourths majority of the Air Staff recommended Lockheed. Consequently, on September 23, 1965, Secretary Zuckert and the Air Force Chief of Staff recommended Lockheed as the prime contractor to the Secretary of Defense. Zuckert's recommendation emphasized Lockheed's low bid as the determining factor of the competition:

> Given the design proposal which is evaluated to meet the essential elements of the RFP with minimum risk, the cost must become a major element . . . based on the contractors' proposals, the target price quoted by Boeing is $330 million higher than that quoted by Lockheed. At the Air Force's most probable cost for each contractor, the difference in cost to the Government of the Boeing proposal over that of Lockheed falls between $241 and $290 million. . . . It is important to note that at the ceiling price of the proposal the Government has, in effect, a fixed price contract at only $13 million above Boeing's target price.

Seven days later (on September 30, 1965) McNamara announced the award of the C-5A contract to Lockheed. While the announcement was greeted with considerable joy at the company's Marietta, Georgia plant,** the decision was by no means unanimously endorsed. The overruling of the Source Selection Board was criticized by some

---

*Much of the controversy centered on Lockheed's wing design, which had been regarded with some suspicion since the competition began; one observer later speculated that Lockheed had forgotten to alter its wing design after a 1964 decision to build the C-5A with four large engines instead of six lighter ones. (See Part A (chapter 17).) The wing problem was especially worrisome in light of the plane's weight. The pre-contract feasibility studies had indicated that the plane's gross weight should be between 645,000 and 681,000 pounds; however, all three airframe competitors had recommended design changes that would bring C-5A's gross weight to 700,000 pounds, and the C-5A SPO had approved the proposed changes. Increased weight means longer takeoff and landing distances, lower takeoff speeds, etc.

**The C-5A would be developed and produced by Lockheed-Georgia, a division of the Lockheed Aircraft Corporation.

observers, as was the Air Force's emphasis on cost as the deciding factor. Many of those concerned with the decision agreed with the Source Selection Board that Boeing's design promised superior performance well worth its higher price.

Speculation soon arose concerning the role, if any, played in the reversal by political considerations, since intervention in the award of DOD contracts by senators or congressmen whose constituencies would be affected is not unheard of. One account of the C-5A source selection, for example, has it that after a visit from Marietta's mayor, Senator Richard Russell of Georgia (Chairman of the Senate Armed Services Committee) went to plead Lockheed's case to President Johnson. Such claims, however, are difficult to substantiate, and Air Force officials involved in the source selection have maintained that they were unaware of any political pressure.

Possible economic considerations involved in the decision provoked similar speculation. A December 1965 article in *Fortune Magazine*, for example, noted that, while the loss of the C-5A would not seriously damage Boeing's financial future, it would imperil the future of Lockheed's Georgia division. Loss of the contract would mean layoffs approaching 10,000 workers and—possibly—the closing down of the Marietta plant (probably the world's biggest aircraft production facility under one roof). According to this argument the decision reflected a government desire to maintain Lockheed-Georgia's defense production capability—over and above the specific considerations of the C-5A competition.

One final area of controversy concerned the realism of Lockheed's bid and the Air Force estimate against which it was evaluated. The charge was essentially that of "buying in" on the part of Lockheed and an understating of costs on the part of the Air Force. Lockheed's bid and the Air Force estimate are shown in Table 18.1.

TABLE 18.1: Estimated Cost to Government for 120 Aircraft (in millions of dollars)

Lockheed Proposal		Air Force Estimate	
Target cost	1,768	Actual cost	1,860
Target profit	+177	Profit	+149
Target price	1,945	Price to Gov.	2,009
Ceiling price	2,299	Ceiling price	2,299

However, these estimates covered only the Lockheed airframe contract; Lockheed estimated that the total program—including 120 aircraft, the General Electric engine contract, and Air Force adds*—would have an initial cost (exclusive of maintenance) of $2.985 billion. This price was $131 million lower than an October 1964 Air Force estimate of $3.116 billion for a lower-performance aircraft (the original CX-HLS). When the October 1964 estimate is extrapolated for the C-5A, the resulting figure is $481 million above Lockheed's estimate of total initial program cost. The controversy over C-5A cost estimates had been building since late 1964. Proponents of a rival rapid deployment system, the Fast Deployment Logistics Ship (see Part A (chapter 17)) were convinced that the C-5A would cost far more than the Systems Analysis Office (SA) had estimated. Both their estimate and an unofficial Systems Analysis estimate had priced the total program at close to $5 billion. While these estimates should have suggested that the Lockheed bid was too low, the Air Force nevertheless went ahead and used the Lockheed figures for program funding. Some sources have claimed that the Air Force believed all three contractor bids to be somewhat "optimistic" and that Lockheed had deliberately underbid in the expectation of recouping its losses through commercial applications of C-5A technology. In any case the Air Force handled the problem with relative unconcern in view of the TPPS contract under which Lockheed was committed to a firm ceiling price, costs above which were the sole responsibility of the contractor.

The Contract

According to Guy Townsend, Director of the C-5A System Program Office, "When the C-5A went on contract, it was by far the best defined weapon system that we ever had." Specifications and requirements had been fully worked out, and management responsibilities and production schedules had been tentatively established. The contract covered:

Research and development

Production, testing and evaluation of five experimental aircraft

---

*An add is an addition to the procurement cost as a result of government action such as the changing by the government of a specification; included is equipment supplied by the government for use in the aircraft.

Production of 53 aircraft

Production of an additional 57 aircraft at the Air Force's option

Production of a final 85 aircraft at the Air Force's option*

Flight and ground test programs

Crew and maintenance programs for six squadrons (120 planes)

Ground support equipment

Spare parts

Lockheed was to assume responsibility for the delivery of the total system by late 1969. The engines, which were covered by a separate contract between General Electric and the Air Force, were to be furnished to Lockheed and, once accepted, to become the company's responsibility. The contract provided for penalties of $12,000 per aircraft per day on the first 16 aircraft delivered late. It also stipulated that the contractor would correct any design deficiencies at his own expense and that he would earn no profit on design changes.

Fourteen single-spaced pages of the contract were devoted to performance guarantees. For example:

> During flight tests the C-5A was to demonstrate 85% reliability for the total system, allowing for no more than 15% subsystem failures on 3 aircraft during 1,080 hours of flight. Should the C-5A fail this test the Air Force could reject the aircraft and return it to the contractor for modification or replacement of the subsystems at no increase in price.

> Two years after the C-5A becomes operational, 90% of all aircraft on a ten-hour mission must reach the destination without a major subsystem failure. An additional 8% must not abort because of a failure or be delayed more than 15 minutes for mechanical reasons.

Lockheed was offered performance incentives of $1.5 million for each 1% improvement in overall performance up to 15%.

---

*The exercise of both options would mean Air Force procurement of 200 planes (5 + 53 + 57 + 85 = 200); however, all plans involving the C-5A were based on a force of six squadrons or 120 planes.

With regard to cost commitments, Lockheed's target price of $1,945.3 million for 120 aircraft was allocated as shown in Table 18.2. As noted on page 392, the target price reflected a target cost of $1,768 million plus a 10% profit of $177 million. (The higher per-plane costs for the RDT&E and Run A aircraft reflected the large initial development costs.) The government would share cost overruns (and underruns) with Lockheed on a 70/30 basis up to a ceiling of 130% of the target cost; if costs were to rise above the ceiling, they would become the sole responsibility of the contractor. (The operation of this formula is illustrated in Appendix A.)

TABLE 18.2
(in millions of dollars)

Research, Development, Testing and Evaluation (RDT&E) (5 aircraft)	$ 514.1
First production run (Run A) (53 aircraft)	$ 892.4
Optional second run (Run B) + 5 Run C aircraft (Total 62 aircraft)	$ 538.8
Lockheed Target Price	$1,945.3

However, it was realized quite early on that the TTPS contract placed unprecedented risk on the contractor. In discussions during the contract competition with Assistant Air Force Secretary Charles, industry representatives had suggested some sort of safeguard which would prevent catastrophic losses in the unlikely event something should go wrong, and $150 million was agreed upon as a maximum acceptable loss. Charles then instructed an attorney from the Air Force General Counsel's office to incorporate into the C-5A contract a repricing formula designed to limit contractor losses to $150 million. The repricing formula would operate as follows: if the combined RDT&E and Run A costs should rise above their 130% ceiling, then the price of Run B aircraft would be increased by a percentage equal to 1.5 times the actual over-ceiling percentage; if overruns were to reach 140.5% the factor would be increased to two. (The operation of this formula is illustrated in Appendix A.)

As development of the C-5A continued, cost estimates continued to be revised and made more inclusive. The total C-5A program cost for six squadrons or 120 planes, including Lockheed and G.E. contracts, Air Force adds, and initial spare parts, was estimated as $3.388 billion in the Air Force's Program

Change Request (PCR)* of October 11, 1965; this estimate was based on (1) negotiated contracts, (2) evaluation of the source selection review team, and (3) revisions in Lockheed's production schedule.

DEVELOPMENT AND CONSTRUCTION

As development of the C-5A proceeded, in late 1965 and early 1966, an atmosphere of extraordinary enthusiasm surrounded the project. SA's analytical work, which had provided the justification for the program, was widely acclaimed as "a major success story," and the C-5A's TPPS contract, the first of its kind, was highly touted as the toughest contract in military history and "a major breakthrough in contracting techniques."

In keeping with the spirit of the contract, Lockheed was to be allowed maximum independence in carrying out the program. Government monitoring activities were divided between the Air Force Plant Representatives Office (AFPRO), responsible for on-site monitoring and reporting, and the Systems Program Office, which had charge of routine administration (adjusting funding to program needs, progress reporting, etc.), provision of government services and supplies, and definition and negotiation of any new work requirements arising in the course of production. The AFPRO, in its daily monitoring role, was not to tell the contractor what to do or how to do it; rather if a serious problem was perceived, the AFPRO was simply to notify the SPO and, if appropriate, suggest possible solutions for Lockheed's evaluation. The key word in Air Force-contractor relations was to be "disengagement."

For Lockheed's part, the company had set up an elaborate system of management controls. A separate division, headed by a corporate vice president, was established within the company and nine assistant program managers were designated for critical contract responsibilities. The Lockheed program management team was supported by a computerized system—known as "Sentinel"—for integrated program planning, control, and reporting. As a Lockheed brochure described the advantages of the Sentinel system:

The problem with management systems of the past is that they did not measure true progress since it was quite easy to be on budget and seemingly on schedule but really lagging in progress because performance goals were not being met. By integrating technical performance time and cost, Lockheed will be able to properly manage progress and arrive at better decisions.

Both the government and Lockheed expressed great confidence in these arrangements and in the TPPS contract. However, quite early on a number of unexpected problems began to surface.

1966–1967: Technical Problems

On July 1, 1966, the Air Force submitted a revised PCR on the C-5A program, requesting an increase in the program's funding. The price increase was explained as follows:

(1) Wage rates, overhead, and general and administrative expenses were higher than expected.
(2) Subcontracts were negotiated at higher rates than expected.
(3) Engineer recruitment problems developed, necessitating overtime
(4) Design changes were dictated by early wind tunnel tests.

In part the increased costs for these items reflected the general inflation in the economy, but in part they sprang from a boom in the commercial aircraft industry and from the steadily increasing demand for defense production for the war in Vietnam—two demands that competed with the C-5A and other programs for scarce manpower and material.

The effect of the cost increases was to reduce Lockheed's expected profit from 10% to 4.6%. At this time, General Electric was not expected to have any cost overrun, and therefore the Air Force estimated that G.E. would realize its 10% profit. When the Lockheed overruns were added to AFLC investment for spare parts, RDT&E, and Military Construction Programs,** the estimated total C-5A program costs were shown in Table 18.3

---

*A PCR is the mechanism through which a new program is incorporated into the approved Five-Year Defense Plan (see Part A).

**I.e., construction of facilities to accommodate the C-5A force.

TABLE 18.3
(in millions of dollars)

RDT&E (5 planes)	$ 934
Aircraft Procurement (115 planes)	2,163
Initial Spares.	468
Subtotal	$3,565
Military Construction.	59
Total C–5A Program Cost	$3,624

While these early increases remained relatively minor as military projects go,* by the fall of 1966 it was becoming increasingly clear that cost escalation was an indicator of developing technical problems. Wind tunnel tests on models of the Lockheed design had indicated too much drag for short takeoffs, correction of which would necessitate redesign of the wing and nose. Furthermore, the weight of the aircraft—a problem which had already been acknowledged during the contract competition (see page 391)— was becoming increasingly worrisome, since weight affected such critical factors as takeoff and landing distances. As noted on page 391, the SPO had approved several weight-related design changes during the contract competition, but by 1966—with the aircraft in mid-development—the SPO was reluctant to authorize further changes. One official has reported that Lockheed requested an increase in the weight specification and recommended higher thrust engines to compensate for the increase,** but the SPO refused this request in an effort to stick to the original contract requirements.

By early 1967, the Air Force had become sufficiently concerned about Lockheed's apparent inability to meet certain performance specifications that it issued an almost unheard of "cure notice" to Lockheed on February 1, 1967. This notice outlined deficiencies in the following areas:

(1) the empty weight was too high;
(2) the takeoff distances were too long;
(3) the initial cruise altitude was too low; and

---

*One study of 12 major weapon systems developed during the 1950s showed cost overruns of 220% and only one overrun less than 100%.

**The same official reported that Boeing, which applied technology acquired during the C–5A competition to its successful 747 program, also experienced weight increases during development and eventually opted for more powerful engines.

(4) the range/payload characteristics (i.e., how much the plane could carry and how far) were deficient.

The "cure notice" concluded:

> Unless such condition is cured or a satisfactory plan for curing this unsatisfactory condition is furnished to the procuring contracting office within 30 days following the receipt of this notice, the government may terminate subject contract for default . . .

The cure notice was no mere slap on the wrist; this was the first time one had been issued on a major contract. During 1967, Lockheed set to work on correcting the deficiencies—which caused substantial cost increases. As one observer wrote:

> The emphasis in this letter was clear, and Lockheed took the necessary steps to meet and in some cases even exceed the required specifications. However, during this time period, there does not seem to have been any concern about the cost implications of "holding Lockheed's feet to the fire" on performance. The large cost increases that became apparent in the C–5A program in 1968 may, in part, have been the price we paid for deciding to meet all the performance specifications outlined in the "cure letter."

As of July, Lockheed had proposed 110 design changes; the SPO had approved 31, rejected 17, and was in the process of considering 62 others. As a hedge against further weight problems, Lockheed developed a "weight bank" of 80 items which, if necessary, could be replaced with lighter but more expensive materials. These design changes and modifications were reflected in a January 1967 request for $79 million in additional funding—a 57% increase over the initial request for that year.

As noted above, the financial problems caused by the design changes were compounded by the boom in the aircraft industry as a result of U.S. involvement in Southeast Asia and a concurrent expansion of the commercial aircraft market. These phenomena combined to leave Lockheed short of both required items and trained engineering personnel, thus forcing the company to pay its own engineers a good deal of overtime, to hire new personnel at higher wages, and to farm out some of its work to engineering firms in England. (Assistant Air Force Secretary Charles estimated that these factors accounted for nearly 25% of the increases in C-5A costs.) Although Lockheed requested relaxation of performance specifications and delivery schedules, the SPO held to the original contract requirements despite the resultant increase in price.

1968: Overrun in the Making

In February 1968 Lockheed submitted its year-end report, which showed no serious cost problems. This conclusion, however, was challenged by two 1968 Air Force estimates, one in April, the other in October. These estimates (Table 18.4) indicated major overruns in the C-5A program.

Some idea of the source of these increases can be obtained by comparing itemized cost estimates for the five RDT&E aircraft and Run A prepared by Lockheed in December 1967 with the Air Force's October 1968 estimates (Table 18.5).*

By late 1968 Lockheed's financial condition had deteriorated to the point where it appeared probable that the company would be unable to complete Run A unless the government exercised the Run B option (the deadline for which was January 31, 1969). Since the Air Force now anticipated that Lockheed would overrun its RDT&E and Run A ceiling by $671 million (well over the net worth of the company) failure to exercise the Run B option would force Lockheed into bankruptcy and leave the Air Force with 58 aircraft "in bits and pieces."

However, if the Air Force exercised its Run B option, Lockheed (and G.E.) could recover some of

---

*Over the same time period, General Electric's estimated cost for engines for RDT&E plus Run A increased by $88.8 million or 18%.

TABLE 18.4:　Total C-5A Program Cost to Completion (120 Aircraft)
(in millions of dollars)

	FYDP Approved Funds as of January 1968	April 1968	October 1968	Increase over Approved
RDT&E	1,030.2	1,002.7	1,002.7	−27.5
Aircraft procurement	2,259.3	2,823.1	3,359.4	1,100.1
Initial spares	330.3	450.0	550.6	220.3
Total	3,619.8	4,275.8	4,912.7	1,292.9

TABLE 18.5:　Cost for RDT&E + Run A (in millions of dollars)

	December 1967 Lockheed	October 1968 Air Force	Amount of Increase	Percent Increase
Engineering	$　234.9	$　305.6	$　70.7	30%
Tooling	96.1	149.3	53.2	55%
Manufacturing	176.5	438.7	262.2	149%
Quality Assurance	25.3	47.9	22.6	89%
Materials	289.7	460.1	170.4	59%
Subcontracts	293.7	447.2	153.5	52%
General/Administrative/ Other	419.4	587.0	167.6	40%
Total	$1,535.6	$2,435.8	$900.2	59%

TABLE 18.6
(in millions of dollars)

A/C Procured	Cumulative Cost to Government	Cumulative Lockheed Profits	Cumulative G.E. Profits
RDT&E +			
3 squadrons (= Run A)	2,558	−671	−23
4 squadrons	3,378	−463	− 9
5 squadrons	3,990	−292	− 8
6 squadrons	4,437	−169	− 7

its losses, because the large cost overruns on Run A had voided the ceiling price and established a new Run B ceiling based on the actual contractor cost for Run A, the price revision formula, and the number of additional aircraft ordered.* The effect of Run B orders on the contractors' losses is shown in Table 18.6. Based on these estimates, the contractors would recoup the amounts shown in Table 18.7 against previous losses.

TABLE 18.7
(in millions of dollars)

A/C Procured	Lockheed	G.E.
4 squadrons	208	14
5 squadrons	379	15
6 squadrons	502	16

However, it began to occur to some Air Force officials late in 1968 that the very price revision formula designed to protect contractors against "catastrophic" losses contained a built-in disincentive for controlling costs. Lockheed's actual costs for RDT&E plus Run A had already exceeded 140.5%, triggering large increases in the Run B ceiling, and each dollar of further increase in Run A cost would result in more than a dollar's increase in the price for Run B aircraft. (See Appendix A for illustrative calculations.) Although Air Force officials had for some time been aware that this was a technical possibility, they had not been greatly concerned by it, since no one had expected that costs would run anywhere near 140.5%. (Air Force officials believed that there was little chance of the contractor purposefully inflating Run A

prices in order to take advantage of the loophole: such a strategy would involve exceedingly high risks, based solely on the expectation that the Air Force would indeed order the Run B planes.)

In view of Lockheed's substantial overruns, and the "reverse incentive" contained in the contract, officials were faced with two critical decisions at the end of 1968: (1) a decision on the ultimate size of the C-5A force and (2) a decision on whether to change the C-5A contract.

THE FOURTH SQUADRON

The Air Force favored the purchase of additional C-5As, arguing that the plane was meeting or exceeding performance specifications as a result of Lockheed's cure efforts. The Air Force proposed to address the "reverse incentive" problem by negotiating with Lockheed a "most probable cost" for Run A and then using this figure for whatever Run B aircraft were procured.

This Air Force position was opposed by the Office of Systems Analysis (SA), which recommended that C-5A procurement be terminated after Run A and that the force level be reduced to three squadrons; and that reserve associate airlift units be attached to each of the 14 C-141 and three C-5A squadrons to increase their wartime capability to 15 flying hours per day. (An active squadron is equipped to a ten-hour daily wartime utilization rate.) In a reversal of its original support for the plane, SA was in effect calling for increased productivity from existing aircraft instead of further C-5A procurement. New analysts at SA, less committed to the C-5A than their predecessors, had reassessed the case for the plane in light of its increasing costs and possible technical

---

*The ceiling price was actually a per plane ceiling, so that the effect of Run B ceiling changes on contractor profits depended on the number of aircraft ordered.

problems and concluded that deployment of the full six squadrons was no longer warranted.

At the same time as defense officials were beginning to face the issue of cost overruns, the Subcommittee on Economy in Government of the Joint Economic Committee, chaired by Senator William Proxmire (D-Wis.), began to hold hearings on the C-5A program. Rumors of a $2 billion overrun in the making led Proxmire to invite several officials to testify before the subcommittee in November, 1968. Air Force officials were reluctant to admit that there was a problem,* but sufficient information was made available to the subcommittee to prompt Proxmire to ask the General Accounting Office (GAO) to begin an investigation. Proxmire also wrote Defense Secretary Clark Clifford,** urging him to postpone the decision on further C-5A procurement pending the completion of the GAO investigation.

On November 18, 1968, Deputy Secretary of Defense Paul Nitze called a meeting to discuss the C-5A program.*** The meeting was dominated by Air Force Secretary Harold Brown, who countered the SA position by arguing that a 15-hour utilization rate was only achievable under ideal conditions (and hence was not a useful figure for planning force sizes) and that although six C-5A squadrons might not be necessary, more than three certainly were needed to achieve rapid deployment objectives. Brown also opined that Lockheed's financial position was not as bad as the Air Force had estimated in October and could thus be left out of account for the time being. Brown recognized the existence of the reverse incentive, but argued that if the Air Force negotiated a new price for Run B, planes could be procured at $25 million per aircraft (based on a contractor cost of $22 million plus 10% profit).

Based on Brown's assurances, Deputy Secretary Nitze decided at the meeting to retain six C-5A squadrons in the FYDP for planning purposes and to purchase 23 Run B aircraft in Fiscal Year 1970 to complete a four-squadron force. The Air Force was to begin negotiations with Lockheed to modify the existing contract and obtain a price for additional aircraft. If negotiations proved unproductive, Nitze would review the force level decision. The contract negotiations with Lockheed were commenced under the supervision of Assistant Air Force Secretary Charles.

For Charles and other Air Force officials, the purchase of additional planes was never an issue, only the contract conditions under which the planes would be bought. Air Force officials thought that the C-5A, as a result of Lockheed's 1967 corrective actions, would now meet or exceed performance specifications, and Air Force attention began to focus on Lockheed's parlous financial situation, which if unremedied could force the company into bankruptcy with consequences—unfinished planes and the destruction of a major defense contractor—that the Air Force found undesirable.**** Although Nitze had directed the Air Force to negotiate new contract prices with Lockheed (in the November 27, 1968 memorandum), by the end of December it had become increasingly clear that the Air Force did not intend to change the contract. Two December 1968 memoranda from Undersecretary of the Air Force Townsend Hoopes to Nitze indicated that the Air Force accepted the October 1968 overrun estimate of $671 million; was concerned about Lockheed's losses; and felt that in order to maintain the integrity of the government as a buyer and to be equitable to Lockheed, the terms of the original contract should be adhered to, particularly the application of the price revision formula.

The Air Force planned, then, to negotiate a most probable cost for Run A and apply the revision formula to calculate a new overall ceiling. This proposal was again opposed by the Systems Analysis Office, which was at that time drafting a proposal to reduce the C-5A force level objective and, concurrently, preparing an independent cost estimate so that—should a "more probable cost" be negotiated with Lockheed—Nitze would have another estimate on which to base his decision.

The SA Office embodied their recommendations in a draft memo presented for discussion at a December 20, 1968 meeting of Assistant Secretaries Robert

---

*During the hearings, allegations surfaced that the Air Force was attempting to cover up the information on cost overruns. See Appendix B for a brief account of this controversy.

**Clifford replaced McNamara as Defense Secretary in 1968.

***Given Secretary Clifford's almost total preoccupation with the Vietnam war, authority over the C-5A program had devolved to Nitze for all practical purposes.

****The Air Force officials involved in the negotiations with Lockheed did not share Secretary Brown's personal belief that Lockheed's financial problems had been overstated.

Moot (Comptroller) and Thomas Morris (Installations and Logistics), Assistant Air Force Secretary Charles, and Deputy Assistant Defense Secretary (Economic and Resource Analysis) Laurence Lynn. At the meeting, Charles requested that, in consideration of inaccuracies in the draft (misinterpretation of the cost estimates and Air Force plans), he be given more time to examine the draft and be allowed to reconvene the group during the first week of January.

Charles, however, did not keep his promise; rather, on January 11, 1969, Air Force Secretary Brown delivered a memorandum to Nitze containing the Air Force procurement plan for the C-5A and the Air Force's rationale for exercising its Run B option:

(1) Many of the assumptions on which the Systems Analysis [Office] had based its recommendations were unrealistic.
(2) The failure to purchase additional planes would force Lockheed to terminate the contract in order to avoid bankruptcy leaving the Air Force with 58 planes in various stages of completion.
(3) The plan was still needed and was exceeding performance specifications.
(4) A reverse incentive would only begin to function with the purchase of more than 33 Run B planes and that, by exercising its option for only 23 additional planes, it could review the situation again at a later date.

Later that same afternoon, in a meeting between Nitze, Moot, Morris, and Brown, the following actions were approved:

(1) exercise the Run B option for all 57 aircraft;
(2) procure 23 aircraft in FY 1970;
(3) leave the contract unchanged.

These recommendations were hastily conveyed to Secretary Clifford who on January 16, 1969, announced that the Run B option would be exercised and that 23 aircraft (the fourth squadron) would be procured in FY 1970.

Congressional Reaction

During 1969, the C-5A became the topic of considerable interest to a number of congressional subcommittees besides Proxmire's. The Proxmire hearings themselves, which reconvened concurrent with the release of Secretary Clifford's decision, uncovered no new information on the C-5A: the GAO investigation commissioned by Proxmire finally supplied the committee with the official Air Force cost figures, as did the additional Air Force witnesses. Robert Charles, for example, praised the plane's performance characteristics, noting that "actual performance exceeds both the contractor's proposed performance and his contractual commitments by nearly 1% (both of which exceed Air Force expectations by 7%) and in no single characteristic is there a deficiency." He noted that the Air Force was disappointed with regard to cost, but assured Proxmire that increases were not due to inefficiency or a "corporate plot," but rather resulted from normal development problems compounded by abnormal escalation in the economy and the disruption of the aircraft market as a result of the Vietnam War. He suggested that the repricing formula was desirable in view of the risks involved, that incentives were as they should be, and that actual cost overruns were substantially less than had been suggested.

The Senate Armed Services Committee, under Chairman John Stennis, conducted special inquiries into the C-5A on April 4, 1969, hearing testimony primarily from Air Force and Lockheed officials. While these witnesses did not agree on the exact extent of Lockheed's overrun, they did agree on two principal points: that a substantial portion of the overrun was attributable to inflation and that the C-5A was meeting—and in some cases exceeding—its performance guarantees. Hearings conducted by the House Armed Services Committee, under Chairman L. Mendel Rivers, provided equally sanguine testimony about the C-5A. Appreciation of the need for the C-5A and Lockheed's fine job in producing the plane were duly expressed by the chairman; and former Assistant Secretary Charles testified that current tests had indicated that the C-5A would perform at 101% of its contractual requirements and that the program's cost history compared favorably with that of other major weapons systems, many of which had exceeded original estimates by several hundred percent.

During the fall of 1969, the debate over the C-5A moved into the spotlight with the presentation of annual military budget requests to Congress. (The Air Force C-5A requested $533 million for the controversial fourth squadron.) Although all C-5A funding had thus far passed routinely, primarily on the strength of recommendations from the Armed Services Committees, this time amendments were entered in the House by Representative Otis Pike and in the Senate by Proxmire calling for deletion of 4th squadron funds pending the GAO investigation. During the budget debates, several allegations surfaced concerning the C-5A's technical performance, including several references to contract changes and a downgrading of performance requirements. Representative Pike, for example, noted that on July 13, 1969, a C-5A had suffered a cracked wing during grouud tests at 128% of its design load limit. While the crack had occurred at 28% above the plane's maximum load, the contract had called for the C-5A to demonstrate an ability to fly at 150% of its maximum normal load. Lockheed proposed to correct this problem by means of aluminum bracings built into all new planes and retrofitted to aircraft already produced. Two months later, however, the wing fix failed at only 83% of the normal load. Nevertheless, Air Force officials staunchly denied that there were any major design deficiencies in the aircraft or engines and affirmed that "there is a high probability that all range, payload, takeoff, and landing performance requirements will be met."

During the budget debates, Proxmire also referred to two Systems Analysis studies that had indicated further purchases of the C-5A might not be justified. However, this attack was countered with a letter from Secretary Laird urging approval of the fourth squadron and noting that:

> The job of the Systems Analysis staff is to make critical appraisals of defense programs. In their review and evaluation they examine both sides of an issue, but especially the critical side, since others will emphasize the positive aspects of an issue. This is an essential function of significant assistance to me. But critical studies are not the only basis on which decisions are made. They are part of the wide variety of information I need to draw conclusions and make judgments on defense programs. . . . If internal critical studies prepared by the Systems Analysis staff continue to be given public expression and used as the source for attacking DOD programs their valuable contribution to the defense decision-making process will be significantly reduced.

Laird went on to say that he "firmly recommended the fourth squadron purchase," deeming it "essential to the national defense." In response to similar arguments emphasizing the strategic necessity of the plane, Proxmire alone offered the challenge:

> The Air Force study calls these plans a major instrument of national policy. This Senator asks, "What national policy?" "Where are they to be used?" "In what circumstances are the troops and weapons they carry to be deployed?"

In spite of Proxmire's efforts, the Senate eventually defeated his amendment and approved fourth squadron funding on September 9, by a 64–33 vote. The House similarly defeated the Pike amendment on September 26, by a vote of 136–60.

1969 AND THEREAFTER: THE END OF OPTIMISM

On November 14, 1969 the Air Force announced that it had reduced the C-5A force from a planned six squadrons to the four already programmed. The reduction, it was announced, was prompted by a July 1969 review of the program which had estimated total program costs at $5.3 billion.

While the C-5A debate had until this time centered primarily on the plane's cost problems, by late 1969 the performance issue began to move center stage. On December 15, 1969, Representative William Moorhead (D-Pa.) revealed that the first shipment of C-5As due for delivery were sadly deficient. According to a GAO report:

1. As a result of the wing failure the plane's load limit had been reduced to 100,000 pounds—less than half its maximum capacity.
2. Because of failures in the engine mounts the plane could not take off from unimproved runways.
3. Its maximum speed had been severely restricted due to design problems with the ailerons.
4. Landing gear problems were preventing the plane from making cross-wind landings and from "kneeling" to load cargo.
5. The radar, altimeter, and automatic pilot were not functioning properly.

Moorhead urged that the Air Force refuse delivery of the defective planes, saying:

> We were told it could do all sorts of marvelous things. How many of these marvelous things can C-5A do now? As of now, it cannot do one of them. As of right now, the C-5A has been so severely restricted that it cannot land or take off from a rough field at all. So the remote presence [of American military power] that was so highly touted to us in Congress a few months ago is more remote than we were led to believe.

While at first Air Force officials continued to maintain that there were no "major" technical problems with the C-5A, it seems that even they had misjudged the plane's technical qualities and the difficulties involved in bringing it up to standard. Eventually they conceded that the C-5A was considerably less than they had bargained for.*

The Lockheed Loan

While the Air Force was attempting to come to grips with the C-5A's performance problems, Lockheed was experiencing a financial crisis. The Air Force's decision to eliminate squadrons five and six had reduced Lockheed's chances of recouping some of its Run A losses (which were apparently about to be compounded by the necessary wing fixes for all Run A aircraft). On January 17, 1970 Lockheed filed a complaint with the Armed Services Board of Contract Appeals, charging that the Air Force had breached the C-5A contract by ordering only 23 planes of the second run. Soon thereafter Lockheed's Board Chairman Daniel Haughton wrote a letter to Deputy Secretary of Defense David Packard,** requesting an additional $500 million for the C-5A to remedy a severe cash flow problem.*** Lockheed's financial

condition appeared so perilous at this point that many feared the company would be forced into bankruptcy, signalling an aircraft industry disaster and the loss of thousands of jobs.

The prospect of a Lockheed bankruptcy was clearly unacceptable to the Air Force and DOD in general since the preservation of Lockheed's defense production capability was deemed essential to national security. Therefore, on May 31, 1971 the Air Force restructured Lockheed's C-5A contract. The new contract was, in effect, a cost *minus* fixed fee arrangement: Lockheed would agree to accept a $200 million loss and the Air Force would absorb other costs including wing fixes and repairs. Despite the restructuring, however, Lockheed's losses were still considerable. The $200 million represented more than half of the company's net worth. (The controversial repricing formula had been based on an acceptable loss of $150 million.) That month Treasury Secretary John Connally announced that the Nixon Administration would seek approval of a $250 million federal loan for Lockheed "to keep it from going broke."****

Opponents of this bill, including Senator Proxmire and Representative Moorhead, claimed that the guarantee effectively rewarded Lockheed for its poor management. Furthermore, they noted that the guarantee would subsidize one company at the expense of the taxpayers, including Lockheed's competitors, and set a precedent for large scale federal interference in private enterprise. However, the loan was defended as a means of protecting the more than 25,000 jobs that would be lost should Lockheed declare bankruptcy and as a means of preserving Lockheed's defense production capability—the same considerations which had played a part in the restructuring of Lockheed's C-5A contract. The House, after a spirited fight, finally approved the loan bill by 192-189, and on August 2, 1971, the Senate followed suit 49-48.

---

*The Air Force defense of the C-5A was based in large part on its satisfactory (or better) performance with respect to variables such as speed, takeoff and landing distance, and payload. The problems that surfaced related to structural problems with features such as the wings and landing gear—problems that did impact on speed, payload, etc. but whose major impact was to drastically reduce the plane's useful life.

**Packard replaced Nitze as Deputy Defense Secretary in 1969.

***Outside evaluation of the cash flow problem, however, revealed that Lockheed needed the money not for the C-5A, but for the L-1011 tri-jet air bus, a commercial venture built on C-5A technology that had been pinpointed by the Systems Analysis office as a developing disaster.

****The loan bill was precipitated by other problems in addition to the C-5A overruns. Lockheed has sustained losses on various military contracts totalling about $500 million (including the C-5A overrun). Also, Lockheed's partner on the L-1011—Rolls Royce Ltd.—had declared bankruptcy on February 4, 1971, and completion of the Rolls Royce contract by the British government was made contingent upon "assurance of Lockheed's financial viability through the U.S. Guaranteed Loan."

Although Lockheed now had a guaranteed loan of $250 million on its commercial ventures and a restructured contract on its military one, the company continued to generate controversy. On September 29, 1971, a middle level manager from the Georgia plant, Henry Durham, testified that Lockheed was guilty of "gross mismanagement, and falsification of records to facilitate progress payments." He offered a huge collection of documentation and examples of overpriced items of common hardware. A GAO report, delivered March 8, 1972, confirmed Durham's charges. The C-5A, too, continued on its ill-starred course. On September 29, 1971, for example, while a C-5A was preparing for takeoff at Altus Air Force Base, one of its engines took off without the plane, rising high in the air before finally skidding to a stop in flames well down the runway. Soon, fatigue cracks began showing up in the wings at 2,000 hours and failures at 8,000 hours of simulated flying. With patching, it appeared that the aircraft might last one-half of its originally estimated airframe life. Although many C-5As did eventually become operational and flew missions both during the 1973 Yom Kippur war and the evacuation of Vietnam, the aircraft continued to experience technical problems; as late as fall, 1975, for example, the GAO estimated that the funds required to strengthen the wings and repair the plane's faulty rear cargo doors would amount to over $1.5 billion.

As a direct result of the C-5A, TPPS was repudiated after only one try and became the standard scapegoat for the whole affair. The Air Force announced that it was returning to its old two-step contract policies and hoped, as far as possible, to "fly before we buy" in the future. However, the C-5A and its contract were not quite the "boondoggle" portrayed in popular accounts. As both Alain Enthoven and Robert Charles point out, the C-5A's cost history compares favorably with those of other military projects, very few of which experience overruns of less than 100%. The real tragedy of the C-5A, one observer has contended, was not related to cost but rather to effectiveness: The C-5A could not perform as required.

POSTSCRIPT

By 1978, it had become apparent that the wings on the C-5A would have to be replaced if the plane was to remain in use for anywhere near its originally expected life.* Although the C-5A is supposed to have a flying life of 30,000 hours, it had been calculated that the wings have a safe life of only 8,000 hours—and by January 31, 1978, the planes had already flown over 4,000 hours. The Air Force decided to request funds from Congress to replace the wings on all 77 C-5As;** the repair bill was set at $1.3 billion. Because of its work in building the plane, Lockheed was considered the leading contender for the repair contract, which sparked opposition by Senator Proxmire to the funding request. Nonetheless, the Air Force expects installation of the new wings to begin in 1982. Lockheed continues to deny that it "botched" the original contract, and the Air Force's commitment to the plane remains strong: as one Air Force officer said, "The C-5[A] does everything it is supposed to except fly a long time."

---

*This postscript is based on Kenneth H. Bacon, "C5 Woes Again Vex Air Force: Wings are Weak, and Replacement Bill is Estimated at $1.3 billion," *The Wall Street Journal,* May 16, 1978, p. 44.

**Of the 81 planes eventually purchased by the Air Force, four had crashed or burned due to various defects.

APPENDIX A

Operation of the Cost Overrun and Repricing Formulae

The Lockheed contract provided that the government would assume 30% of cost overruns up to 130% of the target cost. If the target cost were $1 million, the target profit would be

$100,000 (10% × $1 million),

and the target price for the government would be

$1 million + $100,000 = $1.1 million.

If the actual cost proved to be $900,000 (an underrun), then Lockheed's profit would be

$100,000 + 30% × ($1 million − $900,000)
= $100,000 + $30,000 = $130,000.

If the actual cost proved to be $1.1 million (an overrun), then Lockheed's profit would be

$100,000 − 30% × ($1.1 million − $1 million)
= $100,000 − $30,000 = $70,000.

If the actual cost of the plane proved to be $1.310 million, then Lockheed's profit would be zero, since Lockheed would assume 30% of the overrun up to $1.3 million (130% × $1 million) and 100% of everything over that:

Profit = $100,000 − 30% × ($1.3 million
− $1 million) − 100% × ($1.310 million
−$1.3 million) = $100,000 − $90,000
−$10,000 = 0.

If the actual cost exceeded $1.310 million, Lockheed would lose money.

The repricing formula was designed to limit the amount of money Lockheed would lose. Assume a target price for Run A of $831.9 million but an actual price of $1,425.9 million, such that Lockheed is losing $419.3 million on Run A. However, the 130% cost ceiling for Run A has been exceeded, triggering the repricing formula. Assume a Run B target cost of $489.9 million.

1) $\dfrac{\text{Actual Cost Run A}}{\text{Target Cost Run A}}$ − Run A Ceiling %

$$= \% \text{ Variance}$$

or $\dfrac{\$1,425.9 \text{ million}}{\$831.9 \text{ million}}$ − 130% = % Variance

and % Variance = 41.4%

2) (% Variance × 2) + 100%
= Target Cost Adjustment Factor (TCAF)
TCAF = (41.4% × 2) + 100%
= 182.8%

3) TCAF × Run B Target Cost
= New Run B Target Cost
182.8% × $489.9 million = $895.5 million

4) New Run B Target Cost × 130%
= New Run B Ceiling
$895.5 million × 130% = $1,164.2 million

This Run B price increase will help offset some of Lockheed's Run A losses (although Lockheed probably will still not make a profit on the contract). Moreover, a further $100 million increase in Run A's actual cost—to $1,525.9 million—will push the new Run B target price to $1,013.1 million—an increase of $117.6 million. (The Run B ceiling will increase to $1,317 million.)

APPENDIX B

The Cover-Up Controversy

One of those Senator Proxmire asked to testify at the November 1968 hearings was A. Ernest Fitzgerald, a cost expert from the Air Force's Office of Financial Management. As early as 1966, Fitzgerald had begun to argue to his superiors that large overruns were in the making. Proxmire asked Fitzgerald to prepare a written statement for the subcommittee, but according to Fitzgerald,* his superiors refused to allow him to do so and sent him to the hearings as a back-up witness. Proxmire ignored this attempted arrangement, and under questioning Fitzgerald effectively confirmed the rumored estimate of a $2 billion overrun on the C-5A program. He later prepared written calculations, but these were altered by other Air Force officials to reduce the apparent magnitude of the overrun; the Air Force claimed that Fitzgerald's calculations did not accurately depict the true situation. Fitzgerald subsequently provided Proxmire with his original calculations; later he was unofficially relieved of many of his duties and his career tenure was revoked. The Air Force denied that these actions represented reprisals against Fitzgerald.

The effect of all this was to make it appear that the Air Force was deliberately attempting to conceal the magnitude of the C-5A overruns; that impression received fresh support from further hearings by the Proxmire subcommittee in April 1968, when an Air Force officer admitted that overrun data had been deleted from Air Force reports in 1966-1968. Assistant Secretary Charles, at whose behest the information had been deleted, claimed however that the data had in fact been transmitted to the appropriate authorities and that public disclosure would have unfairly jeopardized Lockheed's delicate financial situation. (Charles did not believe that the overruns were Lockheed's fault, and in common with other Air Force officials he was concerned about the spectre of a Lockheed bankruptcy.)

The various congressional hearings never led to any legal charges of official or corporate wrong-doing: allegations such as Fitzgerald's were obscured in the debate over Air Force procedures, the proper way of computing program cost estimates, the propriety of disclosing corporate financial information, and the actual performance of the C-5A.

---

*Fitzgerald's account is contained in his book *The High Priests of Waste* (New York: W. W. Norton and Company, 1972).

19

The Connecticut Enforcement Project (A)

On May 23, 1973, the Connecticut State Legislature passed Senate Bill 1973, an act authorizing the state's Department of Environmental Protection (DEP) to assess civil penalties against violators of the state's various pollution control laws. This case, the first in a series of three, examines the events leading up to the passage of the act. In particular, the case briefly summarizes background information on previous pollution control efforts in the state; discusses the creation of DEP as the state's response to mounting environmental concerns; and examines the DEP's handling of the enforcement problem, culminating in the drafting and passage of the Enforcement Act.

HISTORICAL BACKGROUND

Connecticut was one of the first states in the country to make conservation a focus of governmental concern. In the 1860s, the state established a Board of Fisheries and Game, followed by the Parks and Forests Commission in 1913. Water pollution legislation was approved in 1925 and a State Water Commission established to enforce it. These early boards and commissions followed a very common pattern of governmental organization in Connecticut. Consisting of part-time, often unpaid, lay members appointed by the Governor, the boards provided broad general direction to an executive secretary appointed by the board and a staff of civil servants who ran the day-to-day operations of the agency. Members of the boards tended to have strong interests in the narrow areas covered by their particular board's mandate, and discoveries of new problem areas more often prompted proliferation of boards than expansion of existing ones. Thus, by 1955, for instance, responsibilities for water resources were dispersed among the State Water Commission, the New England Interstate Water Pollution Control Commission, the Connecticut River

Valley Flood Control Compact Commission, and the Flood Control and Water Policy Commission.*

In 1959, the Democratic legislature enacted a proposal by Governor Abraham Ribicoff to attempt to increase the accountability of the boards and commissions involved in natural resources and conservation. The Parks and Forest Commission, Board of Fisheries and Game, State Water Commission, and 13 smaller boards and commissions were placed under the administrative control of a reorganized Department of Agriculture and Natural Resources (DANR); Agriculture Commissioner Joseph Gill, a Democrat, continued as head of DANR. Since the board structure was retained, little change in departmental operations and policy resulted. As new environmental concerns developed in the 1960s, responsibilities for air pollution, radiation control, and solid waste disposal were distributed through a similar structure of boards and commissions, loosely affiliated with the Department of Health and its ongoing activities in sanitation and public health hazards.

Not surprisingly, given this history of decentralized responsibility for environmental affairs, the State of Connecticut's approach to environmental problems appeared to vary greatly from agency to agency. The Water Commission, for example, considered itself primarily a service organization, assisting industries in complying with requirements and preferring persuasion to legal force. (The Commission issued only 31 orders in the 42 years prior to 1967.) Nevertheless, the Water Commission staff was viewed by many observers as a group of competent engineers under the competent direction of John Curry, a Yale engineering graduate who had joined the Commission in the Depression and worked his way up over the years.

The Air Pollution Commission, on the other hand, was much less well regarded. Established by the legislature in 1969 and affiliated with the Health Department, the commission consisted of seven members, including representatives of the oil, brass, and electric power industries. In the few years of its existence, this Commission had received an inordinate amount of criticism. An engineer for the Health Department suggested that "the word was out to take it easy on major industrial polluters, to avoid rocking the boat. Municipal incinerator operations were never

questioned; violation notices were directed primarily at apartment house and store incinerators."[1] Rita Kaunitz, a member of the Commission, was deeply critical of her fellow commissioners (with the exception of a progressive minority of three members). She alleged potential conflicts of interest and noted several cases in which Commission members had apparently "tipped off" industry representatives about pollution control inspections, so that they might temporarily shut down polluting operations. She cited one case, in Stamford, where word of a town air pollution inspection was apparently passed to the industry involved, and inspectors were allegedly prevented from working by plant employees. In short, because of industrial representation, she suggested that "one could check the enforcement and it was just about nil."

The Air Pollution Commission's enforcement efforts were also apparently impeded by a poor relationship with the Attorney General's office, which under state law represented the Commission (and all other state agencies) in court. Assistant Attorney General James Grady and two other assistant attorney generals represented DANR and several other state agencies. Kaunitz suggested that "the Attorney General's office wouldn't touch anything." A more dispassionate observer, Russell Brenneman, a Democratic environmental lawyer and a member of a Task Force on Environmental Quality appointed by Democratic Governor John Dempsey in 1970, noted "a lot of pulling and hauling" between the Commission and the Attorney General's office and suggested that "personalities were such that there was not even a chance that anyone would get along with anyone else" in the enforcement effort.

According to various observers, the smaller units working on issues such as radiation and pesticides were principally hampered by a lack of coordination. Brenneman suggested, for example, that the pesticide unit in the Department of Agriculture had little access to environmental health information (in the Health Department) during the DDT controversy. And a representative of Northeast Utilities, Connecticut's leading electric utility, once pointed out that regulations on radiation emission into water from nuclear power plants were enforced by two separate agencies, the State Water Commission and an agency specifically

---

*This duplication was not quite as bad as it appears on the surface, since all of these commissions used the same staff as the Water Commission.

established to monitor radiation hazards in the Health Department. In addition to coordination problems, a report to the Governor concluded that, as a result of their structure, the smaller boards and commissions were "resistant to central administration and political responsibility,"[2] and were controlled by interests of industries they were supposedly regulating.

During the 1960s, the rather haphazard method of environmental regulation outlined above was severely strained by burgeoning environmental legislation. Although the sixties saw a number of significant environmental measures enacted in such areas as land acquisition, air pollution control, and tidal wetlands management, by far the most sweeping piece of legislation was the Water Pollution Control Act of 1967, which went well beyond the federal standards in effect at the time.

This act, produced by Assistant Attorney General Grady and his staff in cooperation with John Curry, director of the Water Commission, and strongly backed by Governor John Dempsey and DANR Commissioner Joseph Gill, contained three principal provisions. A total of $160 million was authorized for the construction of municipal sewage treatment plants. Tax credits were granted to industries building pollution control facilities; and as the stick to go along with the carrot, the bill provided for increased enforcement powers, contrary to the Water Commission's previous policy of relying on voluntary compliance. The bill increased the Commission's enforcement powers by limiting the Commission's discretion not to issue orders, by requiring sources to obtain permits, by mandating increased detection efforts, and by imposing greater penalties. The bill "prohibits the discharging of any water, substance or material into the water of the state, after the effective date of the act, without a permit or in violation of an issued permit."[3] It allowed the Commission to issue orders, as in the past, but set more stringent standards on which to base them.

> The present standard that . . . has traditionally been used in Connecticut is a standard of economic feasibility. The distinction between the present standard and the standard suggested in the bill is that the standard that we are currently operating under allows for broad exceptions and exemptions from the meaningful effect of orders of the water resources commission. . . . The proposed standard is one of technological reasonableness and possibility.[4]

The bill also required that the Commission include "a time schedule of steps the course of which must be adhered to to accomplish the goal of the abatement" in all future permits and orders. With this requirement, the Commission could legally monitor the source under order, and the violation of any step in the schedule could be a cause for action by the Commission. (Previously, only a failure to comply by the final date of the order could be a cause for action.) The legislation increased the Commission's detection powers, requiring it "to investigate sources of discharge operating pursuant to existing permits" and allowing it to "search out potential sources of pollution."[5] Finally, the act provided for the imposition of penalties of up to $1,000 per day through civil actions initiated by the Attorney General's office— a provision that substantially raised the penalty limits set under the 1925 legislation and changed them from criminal to civil. The provision was designed to facilitate Commission enforcement action, since civil procedures were slightly less cumbersome than criminal ones, and also less "drastic." As Senator William Stanley (D-Norwich) suggested:

> Now I think that while we must be diligent and we must be firm in trying to eliminate pollution, we also must be fair. Let us not enact legislation ever that will manufacture criminals.[6]

Between the passage of the 1967 Water Pollution Control Act and the 1970 gubernatorial election, the constituency for environmental issues grew remarkably in Connecticut, as it did nationwide. Both the Democrats and the Republicans emphasized environmental issues in their 1970 campaigns, producing an environmentally conscious and narrowly Democratic legislature (99–78 in the House, 19–17 in the Senate). A Democrat, Robert Killian, was elected Attorney General, but the Republicans captured most other state offices, including the governorship, which was won by Thomas Meskill. When the new legislature convened, over half of the members requested seats on the Joint Environment Committee, a committee that proved extremely active in the 1971 legislative session. Under the strong chairmanship of Senator Stanley Pac (D-New Britain) the committee reported out 150 bills (all but five of which became law),[7] including a law giving citizens and municipalities standing to sue alleged polluters, as well as the reorganization legislation establishing the Department of Environmental Protection.

The citizen suit bill, which was the first major environmental bill to clear the legislature in 1971, provided "a right of action for declaratory and equitable relief for protection of air, water and other natural resources of Connecticut. The thrust of this bill is to give anyone, including the state or its subdivisions and any person or other legal entity a course of action in court of law against anyone else . . . who unreasonably pollutes the environment."[8] Patterned after earlier legislation in Michigan and other states, the bill placed the burden on the plaintiff to prove that pollution has occurred or is about to occur and that it is unreasonable. If the court in fact finds unreasonable pollution, it may: enjoin the source from further pollution; deny an injunction "but impose whatever terms and conditions the court deems necessary and proper to bring the pollution and the condition that is complained of to as speedy and satisfactory an end as is possible"; or refer the case to a state administrative agency for action, while retaining jurisdiction over the case, "so that if it is simply put to one side and forgotten or not given the attention that it properly deserves, the plaintiff without incurring additional costs simply must bring this matter to the attention of the court and the court can then prod the agency and impose whatever orders it deems necessary."[9] If the court did grant a temporary injunction to any plaintiff (except a state agency), the court was mandated (except in extraordinary circumstances) to impose a bond on the plaintiff adequate "to answer all damages" that might accrue to the defendant while awaiting a hearing on the permanent injunction. (If the permanent injunction were denied, the plaintiff would forfeit the bond.)[10]

The bill was seen by many legislators as a response to problems of enforcing environmental legislation. As Senator Pac of the Environment Committee summed it up:

> Now whatever environmental legislation we pass, its success is really dependent on its enforcement and its right to legal redress. To me this is the whole guts of the conservation movement. I am convinced that our ability to clean up the air in our environment rests not so much on . . . legislation but rather, in the courts of this land. And though we have the basis for legal redress and

succor in tort law, with this bill we give the courts and we give the aggrieved, I think, a helping hand.[11]

Both parties generally supported the bill, although the Republicans attributed the need for it to poor enforcement under the previous Democratic administration. The Minority Leader in the House, Francis Collins (R-Brookfield Center), specifically singled out the Attorney General's office (still held by a Democrat after the 1970 elections) for criticism. He noted:

> In 1967, we passed a rather extensive and significant water pollution bill. We did the same thing with the clean air bill in 1969. If those bills and the programs implementing those bills had been properly and thoroughly carried out by the state agencies and the Attorney General's office charged with their administration, it might just be that a bill of this nature would not be necessary.[12]

The bill's major opponent in the House, Representative Robert King (R-West Willington), took issue with the bill squarely over the need for additional enforcement powers, claiming that existing agencies had adequate authority and that the bill in effect was a declaration of a lack of confidence in them.

> There is no action within its [the bill's] purview which cannot or should not be handled by existing departments of our state government, including the Water Resources Commission, the Clean Air Commission, the Department of Health, the Department of Natural Resources, the Attorney General's office and perhaps others. We should be concentrating our efforts on improving and strengthening these branches of government rather than surrendering their functions to individuals or groups who may not be responsible, who may or may not have a valid view, or who may or may not have harassment as their main objective.[13]

In the end, the arguments on behalf of the bill proved persuasive. The bill passed both houses of the legislature easily, with the support of both parties and the strong endorsement of the Republican Governor and the Democratic Speaker of the House.

ESTABLISHMENT OF THE DEPARTMENT OF ENVIRONMENTAL PROTECTION

In Connecticut, as elsewhere in the country, the growth of concern for the environment in the late 1960s prompted talk of governmental reorganization to centralize environmental responsibilities. In their 1970 election platforms, both the Democrats and the Republicans endorsed the creation of a Council on Environmental Quality "to conduct studies and to monitor state programs relating to the environment, to propose germane legislation, and to evaluate and take action on citizen complaints."[14] After Republican Thomas Meskill was elected Governor in November, Connecticut Action Now, a New Haven-based environmental organization started by Daniel Lufkin, offered its assistance "in drafting the necessary act and in 'formulating, creating and/or staffing' the Council, which the [Republican] platform demanded."[15] This offer, however, was not taken up.

In 1971, the vacuum of leadership in the area of environmental reorganization was quietly filled by the activist Joint Environment Committee. Democratic Senator Stanley Pac, chairman of the Committee, introduced a bill to consolidate all environmental functions into a single Department of Environmental Protection, giving the Commissioner broad powers to set standards and issue regulations. With the tacit support of Democratic legislative leaders,* Senator Pac pursued a very low-keyed strategy. Russell Brenneman commented that he was "literally keeping [the bill] . . . in his pocket during the entire session." The Environment Committee first held hearings on bills to establish a council with advisory powers. These hearings revealed little enthusiasm for the creation of an integrated, powerful department. With the deadline for reporting bills from committee on April 6, Senator Pac set a hearing on a bill to establish the Department for April 5 and requested an extension of the deadline for committee study of the bill.[16]

Opponents of the bill—principally sportsmen's and agricultural groups and existing boards that would be consolidated into the new Department—were well represented at the hearing. They contended that the new department, under the direction of a commis-

sioner appointed by the Governor, would be more susceptible to political pressure than the existing boards (and hence, less professional), would lodge excessive power in one position, and would—because of the sheer size of the department—prove more bureaucratic and wasteful than the individual boards and commissions. Theodore Bampton, Director of the Board of Fisheries and Game, summed up these views:

> Now the last reorganization of the Board of Fisheries and Game occurred in 1954, which gave us the organization we have today: a five-man citizen board and professionally staffed department. . . . Now to implement the proposal under consideration would remove what we believe is a proven concept of state government, one where the citizen can participate. . . . We also believe that a citizen board . . . provides a buffer between a professional administrator and the pressure groups which do exist. . . .
>
> [Furthermore,] many of these [existing] agencies have a quasi-judicial function. Certainly Fish and Game does, Public Utilities does, the Water Resources Commission does. If I read the bill properly, the existing boards and commissions are . . . removed. If this is so, then we find ourselves with a single individual making all these quasi-judicial decisions.[17]

This negative view of the impact of reorganization was challenged by Richard Bowers, an active conservationist and member of the Republican Platform Committee in 1966, who argued that a new department could effectively coordinate environmental interests and would bring political responsibility into the process. He stated that the 1959 reorganization did not provide enough political input into the process and claimed that the 1959 reorganization, in placing the boards and commissions under the Commissioner of Agriculture, was intended from the beginning to isolate the Governor from the decision-making process.

Other supporters of the proposed new agency, mainly from environmental interest groups, enumerated the benefits to be derived from coordination. David Beizer of Connecticut Action Now, for example, contended that

> 1. [The bill] would establish uniformity and coordination of the actions and efforts of various state departments. Right now the various state

---

*Observers were later to theorize that this support was more partisan than real; i.e., that Democratic leaders supported Pac because his idea went beyond the Governor's platform and could possibly draw a veto that would make the Governor look like an anti-environmentalist.

departments are each going off on its own tangent, sometimes together, sometimes at odds with one another. 2. It would avoid a lot of duplications. Approval of plans would now be governed by a single authority that would be under one man, and that one man could move things along rapidly and avoid a lot of delays that now exist. 3. A new statutory set-up would provide greater incentive to abate deleterious conditions. In particular, I know that this bill provides for a special deputy attorney general who is responsible in this area . . .* 4. This particular bill would initiate a change of values. Right now we have the environment . . . playing second fiddle to development. This bill would focus our attention statewide on a set of values that we have shunted to the background. 5. This bill would provide for long-range planning, something that we haven't done.[18]

Beizer's view of the lack of coordination among existing state agencies was supported by the secretary of one town conservation commission, who noted that "the infighting that goes on between the various agencies in the state is incredible" and could be resolved by the creation of a unified department.

The need for an independent "legal arm" was reiterated by several speakers, including Ritz Kaunitz, a member of the Clean Air Commission (and the only member of an existing commission who supported the bill in the hearings). Kaunitz observed that:

> One of the lacks . . . of the Clean Air Commission is the lack of any legal advice. It's hard to believe at this important time that a commission with the regulatory powers of the air agency really can't avail itself of adequate legal advice. This is, in my opinion, one of the reasons we are not very forceful in the clean air program.[19]

When the controversial bill was finally reported to the legislature in early June,** it was apparent that the arguments of DEP proponents had prevailed. The bill abolished virtually all of the boards and commissions and established a Department of Environmental Protection, under the direction of a powerful commissioner.*** (The legislation effectively separated agriculture from natural resources so that agricultural programs would now receive concentrated attention in their own department, rather than have to compete for attention with rapidly expanding environmental programs.) The bill required that the new Environmental Protection Department be divided broadly into two sections, Environmental Quality and Conservation and Preservation (responsible for parks, fish and game, etc.) each under a Deputy Commissioner; but otherwise, the Commissioner was also given complete discretion over organization and staffing. The Commissioner was also given more power than most Connecticut department heads to seek outside assistance: i.e., "to hire consultants and such personnel for rendering legal and financial advice as he sees fit."[20]**** Substantively, the Commissioner would have the power to issue pollution abatement orders to alleged polluters. Under ordinary circumstances, an order could be issued only after a hearing; but hearings could be waived in rare cases where irreversible damage was threatened, although a hearing would then be required within ten days of the issuance of the order.

Legislative debate was perfunctory and pervaded by a spirit of conciliation. The bill passed both houses easily. Governor Meskill apparently had doubts about the bill, but—according to Senator Pac—was convinced to sign it by Republican Senators George Gunther (R-Stratford) and Roger Eddy (R-Newington), members of the Environment Committee and strong supporters of the legislation.[21]

Russell Brenneman subsequently suggested that "the bill's passage was a personal vote of confidence in Senator Pac"; he claimed that it passed because Pac held onto it throughout the session while "doing such an excellent job" as Committee Chairman. Despite Pac's influence, however, many observers detected hard feelings below the harmonious surface. The Democrat Pac had in fact engineered a serious assault on the power of the Old Guard of the Democratic Party, since this legislation swept away (in Brenneman's words) "25 plus boards and commissions . . .

---

*The provision for a special deputy attorney general was dropped by the time the bill was reported out of committee.

**The legislative session was constitutionally mandated to adjourn on June 10.

***The bill also established the advisory Council on Environmental Quality.

****This clause was later seen by some as an attack on the Attorney General's office, as it was used by DEP's first commissioner to establish an in-house legal staff (see below).

loaded with Democrats" and replaced them with a Commissioner and two Deputies appointed by a Republican Governor. Also, criticism of the old system by supporters of the new Department rankled with many of the long-term employees—particularly those in the Attorney General's office, where the criticism was seen partly as a Republican attack on a Democratic incumbent.

ORGANIZING THE NEW DEPARTMENT

Daniel Lufkin, a 35-year-old graduate of Harvard Business School, was appointed by Governor Meskill to be the first commissioner of the DEP, to take office on October 1, 1971, when the Department was to begin operations. Lufkin had co-founded the investment banking firm of Donaldson, Lufkin, and Jenrette and, acting on his belief that private businesses should assume more public responsibility, had taken up political action in Connecticut as a progressive Republican. He founded Connecticut Action Now (CAN), a New Haven-based community organization originally active in environmental, drug, and housing issues, though later concerned exclusively with environmental issues.

Under the direction of a full-time paid executive director and with a reputation for good environmental research, CAN had contributed valuable support toward the establishment of an integrated Department of Environmental Protection, so the appointment of Lufkin—rather than some "insider" in state government—was regarded by many as a sign of Governor Meskill's commitment to the new department. However, others noted that Lufkin had been the principal fund-raiser for Meskill's campaign and saw his appointment, at least in part, as the repayment of that political debt. Lufkin himself later stated that he twice refused the job and took it at Meskill's request only after they had failed to find an acceptable candidate who would serve at the low Connecticut state salary scale ($30,000 for the Commissioner).

Russell Brenneman, who acted as Lufkin's counsel during the early days of the Department's organization, commented that Lufkin immediately "acted to make it clear that the old rules were over." Specifically, within days of his appointment "all the old files were open" to citizens (except for legally protected material). In Brenneman's words, "The

result of that style was instant credibility." Douglas Costle, Deputy Commissioner for Environmental Quality, noted that the work environment within the new Department was stimulating and productive, but very informal, often chaotic, with Lufkin and most of his close staff working in one large room.

Lufkin's first year as commissioner was a chaotic one. As he put it, "There weren't any priorities.* The place was a mess—it was a matter of keeping the wolf away from the door each day." Many of Lufkin's most pressing problems were administrative in nature:

> Seventeen or eighteen agencies . . . were amalgamated by the legislature into something called the Department of Environmental Protection. It had all of the attendent problems with civil service and job descriptions. . . . You also had all of the problems associated with budget and the individual pieces of programs that came from these various entities. . . . The [department] was way underfunded, . . . and the place was way understaffed.

Lufkin immediately set out to find funds and staff for the Department. Using his business connections, he convinced McKinsey and Company, a prominent New York management consulting firm, to donate their services to develop a departmental structure. He also began a strenuous effort to increase the department's funding. With federal environmental legislation and citizen concern increasing the demand for DEP services, and with Governor Meskill pushing fiscal austerity, funding loomed as a major problem; as Costle put it, more, not less, money was required for "assimilating the tremendous flood of new legislation both federal and state." Some of the needed funds were obtained from the federal government, since Costle had discovered, in the course of preparing the budget, that Connecticut was only taking advantage of 60% of the federal funds to which it was entitled. Lufkin and Costle also used their political influence and that of the environmental movement in

---

*Lufkin states that he had no particular orders from Governor Meskill:

> Meskill basically said, be sensitive to the political problems that obviously will arise. Be sure that you keep me informed of how you see those political problems . . . impacting on my administration. But within reason, anything that you want to get done, that you feel is important to get done, I'll back you one hundred percent. . . .

Connecticut to gain more state funds in spite of the austerity administration. Their efforts produced "a 40% increase in resources for about two consecutive years" in combined state and federal funds.

In developing a new staff, Commissioner Lufkin embarked on what Douglas Costle called a "national talent search" for a Deputy Commissioner of Environmental Quality and for upper and middle-level people to staff a new solid waste unit and a completely reorganized air quality unit. For new positions, the Department appointed relatively young people, many from prestigious universities, with an aggressive interest in environmental issues. Douglas Costle, a San Francisco lawyer and leading Ash Council staff member,* was recruited for an advisory role after his return from a Woodrow Wilson Fellowship and became Deputy Commissioner for Environmental Quality. For Director of the Air Compliance Unit, Lufkin chose Eckhardt C. (Chris) Beck, the young director of an aggressive town air pollution control program in Stamford that was often at odds with the State Clean Air Commission. Henry Beal, a Yale Law School graduate, was assigned as an Audubon summer intern with DEP in the Air Unit and became Beck's assistant. In the Water Compliance unit, Jack Curry, the Director of the old State Water Commission and a 30-year civil servant, retired (some say involuntarily) but was retained as a consultant by Lufkin; Robert Taylor, a middle-level engineer with the Water Commission, was appointed to head the unit. In addition to these top-level people, the Department also recruited young lawyers and engineers who were committed to environmental quality and willing to work at low Connecticut state salaries.

The DEP Legal Staff

Of all of Lufkin's staffing initiatives, the most controversial were those directed at building a strong general counsel's office with a "first-rate young lawyer" assigned to each program area (such as air, water, etc.). Lufkin explained his reasons for wanting an in-house legal staff as follows:

> We had an authority problem, which was really a structural problem. . . . And that was that the Attorney General's office was the legal arm for

all state bodies. We had two . . . Assistant Attorney Generals assigned to us, and all legal action had to flow through those two Assistant Attorney Generals to the Attorney General's office . . . and from thence into the courts. [That office was] a zoo, staffed by political hacks. [It was] ridiculous.

Costle also defended the need for the office by noting that federal law and the state's Administrative Procedures Act passed in 1971 created more stringent legal requirements for conducting hearings. He observed that "the business of adjudication in the Department was getting more complex" and that the previous practice of using engineers as hearing examiners without legal advice could more easily lead to reversals in court on points of law after the Administrative Procedures Act. Because the Attorney General's office had to approve the Department's regulations and decide whether to proceed in court on cases after hearings, it took the position (correctly, in Costle's view) that "it was not proper for them to be involved in internal hearing procedures in the Department. . . . They couldn't come down and give us legal advice in the process of building a case."

Some observers felt that the development of a substantial legal capability in DEP was prompted by partisan interests and that it produced some friction between DEP and the Attorney General's office. Alan Kosloff, formerly a lawyer for DEP and currently an Assistant Attorney General working with DEP, claimed the existence of "a degree of partisan tension. . . . It was felt that since the Attorney General's office was Democratic, reliance could not be placed on that office"; Kosloff added that many felt that there was "antagonism between attorneys serving the Commissioner and attorneys serving the State of Connecticut." The new DEP leaders felt that James Grady, the Assistant Attorney General responsible for DEP, was strongly opposed to the plan to set up a legal staff in the Department and took it as a personal affront; as Costle stated, "I think it always bothered Jim Grady that we did that." However, Costle disagreed with the assertion that a legal staff was built up in DEP for partisan reasons:

> I never detected a single instance where the Attorney General acted in a political fashion. The two Assistant Attorney Generals assigned

---

*Established by President Nixon in 1969 to study government reorganization, the Ash Council had recommended among other things the creation of the federal Environmental Protection Agency.

to us were both professionals. Neither would tolerate the idea of politics entering their decisions.... Without question, we disagreed with them on occasion, but they were legitimate disagreements on the merits of issues.

For his part, Grady later stated that "it's no secret that I do not advocate a double legal staff." In Grady's view, DEP had no need for its own legal staff:

In my judgment [the Attorney General's] office has had many very well qualified and dedicated people who have done a tremendous job.... I think we've enforced [environmental laws] uniformly regardless of politics, money or anything else.

For the Department's general counsel's office, Lufkin immediately hired Russell Brenneman, a well respected Democratic lawyer, as an interim consultant to assist in interpreting the legislation and establishing the Department in its critical first stages, with the understanding that a permanent appointment would later be made. David Tundermann, another young Yale Law School graduate, was hired in mid-1972 as Assistant Commissioner for Legal and Governmental Affairs, in effect to be general counsel; Tundermann recruited eight recent law school graduates for the DEP legal staff. However, since under Connecticut law only the Attorney General or his assistants could represent a state agency in court, and since some of the new DEP lawyers were not members of the Connecticut bar, as far as litigation was concerned the legal staff was limited in function to drawing up the legal documents for a case and submitting them to the Attorney General's office. That work, serving as hearing officers, and rendering unofficial legal advice became the main duties of the new legal staff.

In addition to making new appointments, the new Department leaders also demoted (or removed from positions of influence through lateral transfers) several people with long service in the existing agencies who were close advisors to DANR Commissioner Joseph Gill. Although civil service regulations prevented their outright dismissal, the regulations did allow transfer of employees to other positions when a governmental unit was being reorganized. The various demotions were at least partly intended to signal a shift in emphasis; staff who had been committed to the old structure, which was felt to have a strong emphasis on natural resources, were exchanged for staff more

attuned to the environmental movement and the new emphasis on pollution control. But competence was an issue, as well as "emphasis." For instance, Doug Costle called those who had been previously running the air pollution program "clock watchers" and noted that Dan Lufkin "had very low tolerance of bureaucrats who talked and acted like bureaucrats or thought they were politicians." Henry Beal of the Air Compliance unit commented that in 1972, "The impression given to new people was that [their predecessors] ... weren't too competent and weren't too active" even though he acknowledges that it was "an unfair perception" by and large. Though Costle admitted in retrospect that some of the personnel judgments were a "little too harsh," he recalled a consensus among core staff members on the need for a thorough housecleaning at the DEP. However, Gill later stated that Lufkin fired people without regard to merit and that this "hurt the merit system more than anything I know."

THE ENFORCEMENT PICTURE

Although the first year of operations in the new department was largely devoted to ironing out organizational, budgetary and personnel problems, the new commissioner also had a heavy substantive agenda. As Lufkin put it,

There were a series of legislative requirements ... that really had fallen between the cracks. There was defined legislation established and funding to some extent—not often—provided. A definite law was in action that was not being adhered to. Coastal wetlands is the primary example.... We also had the priority established by federal legislation—the Clean Air Act [Amendments of 1970] —we were moving inadequately under the federal legislation.* Waste management was nuts—16 incinerators in the state, 15 didn't comply with our own regulations. There were about 300 and some odd ... so-called sanitary landfills, and 50 percent were polluting ground water and underground water, and 90 percent were not in compliance with all regulations that were there, which

---

*The Clean Air Act Amendments of 1970 required the states to develop "state implementation plans" for achieving specified air quality standards or face federal pre-emption in the area of air pollution control.

weren't much. [Attempting to deal with these problems] is essentially what we were doing during the first [year].

The conviction that enforcement posed a serious problem grew during late summer of 1972, when work on the legislative package for the 1973 session was beginning. David Tundermann noted that the directors of the various enforcement units (air, water, etc.) were constantly bringing enforcement problems to his and Costle's attention. And, in Costle's view, action on enforcement just "seemed to us the logical next step [after having] faced the immediate pressing needs of getting something moving."

In an October 1972 report on its first year of operations, DEP noted that only about 58% of the orders issued by the State Water Commission or the Water Compliance Unit since 1967 had been complied with by 1972. Lufkin and Costle felt that the Air Compliance Unit confronted similar enforcement problems. With the issuance in 1972 of regulations mandated by the federal Clean Air Act,* enforcement attempts became more vigorous and enforcement problems and delays more apparent. The Air Unit issued 231 violation notices and 100 orders in its first year of operation, in the process resurrecting many cases which had been dormant for years under Health Department jurisdiction. A massive source registrations program, initiated under the 1972 regulations, required approximately 12,000 air pollution sources to register, but only about 4,000 did so, and the cost of prosecuting the other 8,000 sources appeared prohibitive.[23] For substantive violations, the legislation authorizing the 1972 clean air regulations directed the Commissioner or his representative "to endeavor by conference, conciliation, and persuasion to eliminate any source of air pollution"; only after

such steps had been taken could the Commissioner issue an order.[24] Thus, recalcitrant sources could hold long drawn-out negotiations with no intention of settling the issue. The litigation process was also very complex:

> The polluter was given thirty days in which to request a hearing, which was to be held as soon as "practicable." Modification or revocation of the order might follow. The polluter had another thirty days in which to appeal the final order to the Superior Court; the appeal acted as a stay of the order. The judgment of the Superior Court could be appealed to the Supreme Court. Should the order be affirmed, and the violater continue the offending activity, the Department's only recourse was to request the Attorney General to begin court proceedings, seeking a civil fine or an injunction.[25]

Although the Department and its predecessors had the power to seek fines, not once in six years had a Connecticut court either levied a fine or held anyone in contempt in an air (or water) pollution case. The three cases outlined below (taken from the Department's records) exemplify the sorts of problems confronting the air unit:

> A manufacturer makes a product whose fabrication creates ferocious odors. The company was issued an order in 1969, which it did not appeal. After the company ignored the order for over a year, the case was referred to the Attorney General in 1970. The company still did little to comply with the order. In 1972, a new injunction was issued requiring that four specific abatement actions be taken by late summer, 1972. The company began missing initial deadlines provided in the injunction but never enough to incur a contempt citation. To date [May 1973], the four steps have not been completed.

In May 1972, the Department issued an order to a company requiring it to provide a schedule by which the polluting emissions from three company plants would be brought under control. The company offered a schedule which was formally approved by the Department. Since then each deadline has been missed by substantial margins. Complaints from citizens in the vicinity of the plants continue to flow in. The company is in present violation of numerous air

---

*The regulations set emission standards for individual stationary sources for particulate matter, carbon monoxide, sulfur dioxide, oxides of nitrogen, and hydrocarbons. Compliance deadlines for the emissions standards were also set for various industries. To enforce the standards, the regulations required that existing sources register with DEP and that all new sources obtain permits. The regulations established procedures for the issuance of orders to control air pollution, allowed pollution abatement orders to be issued with compliance in several stages (similar to orders authorized in the 1967 water pollution control legislation), and established monitoring and progress report requirements. However, enforcement of orders and report requirements still rested with the Attorney General's office and the courts.[22]

standards. A court action against the company is as likely to delay the date of final compliance as to advance it. The difficulty is not the failure by the company to act but failure to act in a timely fashion. Court action may cause them to suspend abatement activity altogether.

A Hartford department store operates an incinerator which reportedly has been in violation of regulations regarding permissible emissions of particulates and odors since January 7, 1971. On March 10, 1972, an order was issued requiring the store to remedy the situation. It was ignored. "As clear as the violation is," reported Department officials, "it is one of hundreds of similar offenses." Each is too time-consuming and too insignificant to refer to the Attorney General. The prospect of prosecution is not considered to deter non-compliance of this kind, for the offender realizes that the likely penalty would consist of no more than a court order to install abatement equipment.[26]

In the first instance, a company ignored an order and appeared to delay compliance deliberately. In the second, cumbersome court procedures were seen by officials as unlikely to speed compliance by a company with apparent willingness to comply, but to do so more slowly than DEP had ordered. In the third case, the cost to initiate court proceedings could not be justified by the trivial nature of the offense, and the prosecution would not act as a deterrent in any event, since there would likely be no economic penalty. As Chris Beck, Director of Air Compliance, indicated: "Legislators had just not realized what a litigious person could do with the prescribed procedures."[27] And as Costle saw it, the situation could only get worse:

We got the 1970 [Clean Air Act] Amendments and the requirements for state implementation plans, and all of a sudden it became much clearer . . . the magnitude of the job the state was going to be up against, and if in fact the experience we had in the early cases . . . was any [basis for a] forecast, and we were suddenly dealing with thousands more polluters, the whole thing would just bog down. . . . For [environmental enforcement] to work, you need a very high voluntary compliance rate. . . . You're dealing with twelve thousand air pollution sources in Connecticut [and] if you had to go out and litigate [against] each one of them, you'd never get the job done.

Lufkin and Costle attempted to deal with these problems by such means as creating an in-house legal staff and by a public relations campaign against polluters, but in their judgment these efforts had only limited success. Dissatisfied with the enforcement tools available under existing legislation, by October 1972, Lufkin, Costle and Tundermann had become convinced of the need to increase DEP's enforcement powers, even though they had no precise solutions in mind.* Lufkin decided to give "primary legislative attention" to two issues for the 1973 session of the General Assembly—solid waste recovery and enforcement.

DESIGNING THE ENFORCEMENT ACT

Early in December 1972, Lufkin began assembling a task force of volunteer lawyers and consultants to draft legislation strengthening DEP's enforcement powers. Lufkin called upon many of his old business connections, including Davis, Polk and Wardwell, a prestigious Wall Street law firm; McKinsey and Company, a consulting firm that had helped him in organizing DEP; and the investment banking firm—Donaldson, Lufkin, and Jenrette—that Lufkin himself had co-founded. Lufkin also requested help from Wiggin and Dana, a major New Haven law firm, to provide advice on matters of Connecticut law and to avert charges that any legislation emerging from the task force was solely the product of out-of-state Wall Street lawyers. To head the task force, Lufkin designated William Drayton of McKinsey and Company. Drayton, a graduate of Harvard College and Yale Law School, had heard about the project through Henry Beal, an assistant to Air Compliance Director Chris Beck and a former classmate of Drayton's at Yale; Drayton asked to join the task force out of an

---

*Other observers suggested that political or personal motivations—rather than the simple perception of an enforcement problem—lay behind the DEP staff's interest in expanding their regulatory powers. Although Russell Brenneman, for example, cited delays in enforcement as the principal factor in building support for new enforcement tools, he stated that Lufkin "was loath to rely on the Attorney General and the local prosecutors to enforce his program." Brenneman also noted that having a Democratic Attorney General in a Republican administration was "a recipe for difficulties."

interest in environmental affairs and a desire to develop professional expertise in regulatory alternatives such as Lufkin was proposing. Lufkin had had business dealings with Drayton and held him in high regard.

Lufkin explained his decision to use outsiders rather than in-house staff as follows:

> I really feel very strongly about that: there are great talents . . . who earn well into the six figures in their normal pursuits who would be delighted to devote, on a pro bono or largely pro bono basis, their talents to the welfare of the city or community or state in which they live. So I was biased towards bringing in outsiders. . . . Also, you have more, much more that you can do [with outsiders]. We [at DEP] were understaffed, underpaid.

Deputy Commissioner Costle identified another reason for using outside volunteers to draft the Enforcement Act: he and Lufkin wanted to build as broad a base of political support for the act as possible to help ensure passage by the Democratic legislature.

The full task force was not assembled until just before Christmas 1972, and did not really start its work until early in January of 1973. Because in Connecticut the deadline for filing any legislation to be considered in a session is during the first week in February, the group had less than a month to draft a bill for Lufkin's consideration. Lufkin, Costle and Tundermann all considered it important that the bill be submitted for the 1973 session: all three felt that support for the environmental movement was waning in Connecticut (and nationally) and that a bill expanding DEP's enforcement authority might not pass if delayed until 1974 or later. As Costle put it, "We struck at exactly the right time; a year later I doubt we could have gotten [the act] through."

Because of this time pressure and the complexities associated with designing a new enforcement scheme, the task force members conceived their assignment to involve the development of relatively general legislation that could eventually be implemented by detailed regulations based on a much more complete analysis than was possible in the few weeks allotted for drafting the bill. As Drayton put it:

> Although we did our best in the analysis to try and get a clear idea of the type of program we thought we wanted ultimately, thinking through the implications of whatever we attempted to create, the time and resource constraints that confined our work made it relatively clear that we should design the legislation as enabling legislation leading up to subsequent careful design work [on implementing regulations].

And Robert Lovejoy of Davis Polk agreed that the shortness of time was the "overwhelming consideration" from his standpoint.

Once Lufkin had outlined his general goal of strengthening DEP's enforcement powers to reduce the delays in the enforcement process, he left the day-to-day direction of the task force's efforts to others. Drayton supervised the analysis of the existing enforcement process to see how it could be improved. Tundermann provided liaison with the various law firms involved, and Costle supplied insights on the Commissioner's thinking.

Although Drayton was a law school graduate, he had never practiced law; his work since law school had consisted of graduate study in economics and management consulting for McKinsey. In his work on the task force, he focused on the managerial and economic aspects of enforcement: what were the disincentives for compliance with pollution control laws; how could a system be designed that would give DEP effective leverage on polluters' behavior; and similar questions. The Davis Polk lawyers, on the other hand, were principally (although not exclusively) concerned with drafting a bill that could survive legal challenges; to this task they brought the lawyer's skills in analyzing precedents and drafting precisely worded legal documents.

These differing perspectives had some effect on the workings of the task force. In Drayton's view, the lawyers were unable to suspend the usual lawyerly thought processes to understand his economic/managerial analysis of the problems with the enforcement process (see below), while, according to Robert Lovejoy of Davis Polk, Drayton (and Tundermann) were thinking in "relatively conceptual terms, at a rather theoretical level," whereas with some three weeks to draft a bill, the need was to be extremely concrete very quickly. Drayton felt that "given the difference in our objectives and perspectives and [our] lack of personal relationship . . . , it was excruciatingly difficult to work with [the Davis Polk team] on drafting."

Thus, the task force worked most of the time as two separate groups, one focusing on economic issues and the other on legal matters. The next sections examine these two factors.

THE ECONOMICS OF ENFORCEMENT

Although Lufkin had set for the task force the general goal of finding ways to reduce the delays in the enforcement process, he had not yet settled on specific proposals for achieving this; the task force therefore began its work with a wide range of possibilities open to it. Drayton, Tundermann, Costle, and Deputy Air Compliance Director Henry Beal began their work in mid-December with a theoretical analysis of the enforcement process to determine the points at which bottlenecks could arise. They divided enforcement into seven stages (detection, negotiation, prosecution, adjudication, sentencing, review, and execution) and into the various types of pollution (air, water, solid waste, etc.), so that differences between types of control technologies would be considered. Rough information on the amount of time necessary for each stage of the existing enforcement process was developed by interviewing the heads of the various enforcement staffs.* According to Drayton,

> Throughout my involvement at this phase of the project, I clung [to] and forced everyone else to spend a good deal of time working with a [model of the] flow of the steps in the enforcement process. One of the major [pieces of] analysis we did with this flow was an analysis of what the incentives facing every actor in each step in the process were. Not surprisingly, we discovered that many of the incentives were stacked in such a way as to lead to exactly the sorts of problems we were facing.

As a result of their analysis, the Drayton-Tundermann group identified the following principal problems as underlying the gap between enforcement caseload and existing enforcement capacity.

> There is no simplified process for the mass of small cases.

> Process regulations [such as registration requirements] . . . can be ignored with impunity.

Bottlenecks reinforce one another.

> Violators often find it profitable to delay abatement expenses by litigating.

> Both issues and remedies can be highly technical, but few courts or prosecutors have such training.

> There is only a limited body of precedents and codes.[28]

The group then identified three basic approaches to alleviating the problems. First, they considered the possibility of increasing the capacity of the system by continuing present legal practices but increasing the manpower and money spent on enforcement and/or giving environmental suits precedence on crowded court dockets.** Alternatively, they considered the possibility of increasing capacity by increasing the efficiency of the system. As they saw it, more enforcement per state employee could be achieved by: (1) use of private attorneys for enforcement on a contingent fee basis (to be paid by the pollution source if the state's case were successful); or (2) requiring pollution sources to post bonds that would be forfeited for failure to comply with a DEP order (thus obviating the need for court injunctions); or (3) establishing a specialized environmental court to expedite cases. Finally, they considered lessening the workload on the system by both simplifying procedures for small cases (to allow for almost automatic small fines for minor violations, as in a traffic court system) and by providing disincentives for foot-dragging in the form of escrow requirements for fines that would accrue during an appeal process.

By January 9, 1973, the Drayton group had refined these basic approaches into six specific recommendations, contained in a 35-page internal document entitled "Strengthening Environmental Law Enforcement in Connecticut." First, they recommended that pollution sources be required:

> . . . to file periodic reports describing their emissions, their equipment, their progress in complying with any orders, . . . and such other matters

---

*Each program area—air, water, etc.— has its own enforcement staff.

**Lufkin and Costle, however, decided that the sort of budget and staff increases needed, for example, to monitor and if necessary litigate against Connecticut's 12,000 air pollution sources could not be obtained in addition to the increases Lufkin had already secured; nor did they think it likely that the resources allocated to environmental enforcement by the Attorney General's office would be substantially increased.

as DEP required. Independent reports from a list of consulting engineers approved, possibly trained, and licensed by DEP could be required at the source's expense. DEP would be given power to impose fines for non-cooperation with the registration and certification process which, though appealable, would in fact not be appealed in almost all instances just as very few traffic court tickets are contested.[29]

This requirement, introduced by the New York City Environmental Protection Administration, was expected to greatly reduce the bottleneck at the detection and negotiation stages of the enforcement process. With small but readily enforceable penalties for violations of this provision, it seemed likely that the problem of thousands of unregistered sources could be eliminated. Also, if information on the certificates and progress reports were admissible as evidence in court, "the number of issues likely to be litigated would drop,"[30] decreasing the workload in the prosecution and adjudication stages. Violation of DEP orders could also be detected more readily through self-certification. If inspectors could verify certified information over the phone and reduce their reliance on time-consuming physical inspections, their capacity could be increased.

The second recommendation would empower the DEP

> . . . to engage private attorneys to undertake the litigation required for the Department to enforce its orders if the Attorney General's staff were unble to handle the load. These attorneys would be paid on a "reasonable, contingent fee" basis analogous to SEC derivative suits) by the defendant if proven guilty of the alleged violation.[31]

This recommendation was not only intended to expand the capacity of the enforcement system at no expense to the state, but also to provide an inducement to pollution sources to settle out of court. In addition, the contingent fee system was thought to provide a check against DEPs bringing "frivolous cases," since private attorneys would not accept cases without a reasonable chance of success. The Drayton group saw this system as the most realistic alternative for expanding litigation capacity:

> While an increase in the Attorney General's staff is unlikely because of budget constraints, and while the only other means of closing the crucial

litigation gap, increasing DEP's legal staff and giving them the power to litigate, is constrained both by budget stringency and the Attorney General's opposition to such a delegation [and by the statutory requirements that the Attorney General represent all state agencies in court], the use of private, contingent fee litigators would have no impact on the budget and might be justified as a temporary measure to deal with a pressing temporary bulge of environmental litigation.[32]

The Drayton group's third recommendation was aimed at eliminating the profitability of dilatory appeals of DEP orders. In the early stages of their analysis, the group had identified a disincentive for prompt compliance with DEP orders: if a source does not appeal a case, it incurs the cost of an immediate investment in pollution control equipment, but if it appeals, it retains the use of the money to be spent on the pollution control equipment until the period of delay—even if it loses the appeal. Further, because of this profitability problem, it seemed likely that any attempt to strengthen the enforcement system prior to the appeal stages would simply produce a massive increase in the number of appeals, unless a strong disincentive to appeal were supplied. The most obvious disincentive—waiver of fines for unappealed cases—proved on closer examination problematic, since analysis indicated that even with a waiver of fines, appeal would generally be unprofitable only if fines were very large, investments very small, or the delay between appeal and settlement very short.*

To counteract this problem, the subgroup recommended that the fines be allowed to accumulate throughout the time of appeal (but be refundable with interest if the appeal were successful). Two alternatives were proposed: either "a user charge levied according to a set schedule varying with the amount

---

*The costs of an appeal are the legal expenses of the appeal and the eventual cost of the fine payment. If these costs are less than the benefit from deferring the investment, it is profitable for the source to appeal even if it is sure to lose the case. To determine the "present value" of appeals, the task force prepared a simple computer model using several different assumptions for all the major parameters affecting the decision to appeal: size of legal fees, amount of fine, cost of investment, amount of delay until the appeal is disposed of, and the discount rate (cost of capital) facing the source. Application of this model produced the conclusion cited above.

and type of discharge or emission, and/or an escrow requirement equivalent to daily/monthly/yearly cost of operating the completed facility."[33] (Under either option, the charge would have to be greater than the cost of the new investment, amortized over the proper period, to provide an incentive to settle the case.) The first alternative constitutes an effluent tax proposal, and Costle and the others decided, after a review of the literature on effluent fees and of the experience with a modified fee system in Germany, that effluent fees or charges require for their success an ability to continuously monitor emissions from polluters and a knowledge of the economics of the polluting firm that simply did not exist. That option was therefore discarded. The second alternative, an economic means of enforcing a set standard, was favored by the subgroup although they noted that "such remedies may be challenged as unconstitutional because they inhibit the right to appeal."[34]

The subgroup's fourth recommendation was designed to expedite the processing of violations. As they described it:

> Small clearly defined violations (of standards or process requirements) would be removed to a much simplified process which would minimize litigation. They would be treated much like traffic violations.
>
> Convictions would entail no serious stigma.
>
> Very few defendants would find it worth their while to litigate, though the right would be preserved.
>
> Offenses and penalties would be narrowly defined.
>
> A large number of officials (and deputies) would be charged with ticketing violators—e.g., DEP staff, local police and health officials.
>
> Initial trials would take place outside the court system—e.g., at regional DEP tribunals, before Justices of the Peace, at existing traffic courts.[35]

This practice would allow de facto administrative fines, thus effectively de-criminalizing small violations. (Under many state constitutions, the levying of fines for a "criminal" offense is a "judicial" function which cannot be performed by an "administrative" agency.) The subgroup's January 9 report noted that large and small violations were eventually treated identically, so that "small violations [are] now de facto beyond the reach of the law" since the Department could not afford to prosecute small violators.

The report suggested that although the new procedures would increase enforcement costs because previously ignored offenses would now receive attention, the actual burden of prosecuting and adjudicating the minor cases would be small because of "the overwhelming resort to the guilty plea."[36] The report also noted that non-payment of fines might pose a problem, but it observed that "applying a lien for the fine plus costs to [violators'] property might solve [it]."[37]

In evaluating the adjudication phase of the enforcement process, the subgroup concluded that lack of judicial expertise in environmental problems—as well as crowded court dockets—constituted a major source of delay in settling cases. Accordingly, they recommended the establishment of an environmental court, presided over by specially trained judges, along the lines of the Environmental Control Board set up in New York City in 1972. They noted, however, that budgetary restraints and the novelty of the court concept could pose serious implementation problems.

To ensure compliance with either court or unappealed DEP orders, the Drayton group's final recommendation was that a bonding requirement be adopted:

> Violators under either unappealed Departmental orders or final court orders to abate a violation according to an implementation schedule requiring more than 30 days to complete would be required to be bonded to ensure prompt execution much as construction companies must be bonded to undertake major construction projects.[38]

Since the bond would be automatically forfeited if an order were not complied with on time, no further prosecution would be necessary to penalize delays. However, since a bond or escrow fund represents loss of income to the source,* it also creates an incentive to appeal DEP orders. Although the group recognized that interim measures would be needed to offset this incentive, they did not consider the problem serious enough to negate the merits of the bonding provision.

---

*A bond or an escrow account would carry a lower rate of interest than an ordinary investment of corporate funds, creating an after-tax income loss of 2% to 8% of the bond amount per year.

LEGAL AND POLITICAL CONSIDERATIONS

While Drayton, Tundermann, Costle and Beal were analyzing the enforcement process from an economic/managerial viewpoint to determine what enforcement system would be theoretically most effective in securing widespread voluntary compliance with DEP pollution control orders, lawyers from Davis Polk and Wiggin Dana were independently examining the legal literature on environmental enforcement to ascertain what could and could not be done from a legal standpoint, i.e., what enforcement tools were supported by statutory or case law precedents. The Davis Polk team of six attorneys was first briefed on DEP's enforcement needs on December 21, 1972; over the next few weeks, while Drayton *et al.* went through the analysis summarized above, the lawyers, according to Robert Lovejoy of Davis Polk, undertook three tasks: ascertaining what could and could not be done under the Connecticut and federal constitutions; pulling together information on statutes and regulations in other states; and reviewing the literature on ecology and environmental law enforcement. The attorneys also had to compile the existing Connecticut environmental statutes after it was discovered that no such compilation existed.

On January 8, the Davis Polk team was briefed over the telephone on the six enforcement options developed by Drayton and his associates and asked to prepare a draft bill over the next three weeks. Although preliminary research indicated no insuperable legal problems with any of the six options, Lovejoy and the other Davis Polk lawyers were concerned that the short time frame precluded drafting a very complex statute: the Davis Polk draft would have to be scrutinized by the other task force members, by Lufkin, and by the Connecticut lawyers, the comments of these groups incorporated, and a final draft prepared for submission to the General Assembly by the first week of February.

On January 18, Lufkin met with the members of this task force and with Deputy Commissioner Costle, Assistant Commissioner Tundermann, Rita Bowlby (Lufkin's legislative advisor) and Russell Brenneman (now a DEP consultant) to review the recommendations of the task force. In conversations with Costle, Tundermann and Drayton, Lufkin had refined his analysis of DEP's enforcement needs; he saw the primary problem as the existence of substantial incentives for polluters to delay in their compliance with DEP orders:

> There was built [into the existing enforcement scheme] . . . an economic bias to the polluter to continue polluting even if he knew he was wrong. Because if he delayed through court action, he could measure categorically the expenses of delay—the legal expenses—and he could measure categorically the expenses of compliance—which are equipment, service and personnel expenses—and he could see, in large measure, that [the latter] far outweighed [the former]. . . . So why not cloud the issue and delay?

Lufkin had been an investment banker before coming to DEP, and in his analysis of the enforcement problem he emphasized the need to consider how businessmen react to environmental laws:

> Businessmen make decisions on economic considerations, primarily. . . . They're good citizens . . . by and large, but they have enormous numbers of conflicting pressures upon them, [so] you want to weave in good citizenship with economic considerations. You [have to] . . . make sure that there is no untoward economic consideration that throws good judgment out the window, that puts them competitively at a disadvantage. . . . They don't necessarily not want to comply, but if their competitors aren't complying, or some crook down the street isn't, they've got a real problem.

For Lufkin, then, the key to successful enforcement was the deterrence of egregious non-compliance:

> There are two things about enforcement. . . . One is the actual enforcement procedure, and the other is the threat of enforcement. . . . There were cases, specific cases, which were overwhelming in their avoidance of the law—there was just a [thumbing] their nose at the law—which although few in number, were very severe in their impact on the rest of the [business] community. [So I needed] not only the enforcement procedure *per se* but the threat of enforcement.

Thus, Lufkin's analysis of the economics of enforcement largely paralleled that of the task force. However, Lufkin and Bowlby had also been sounding out individual legislators on the political acceptability of various proposals, and Lufkin now applied his political judgment to the economic and legal arguments of the task force members.

Lufkin approved of penalties for failure to register or file progress reports, administratively imposed fines tied to the cost of compliance, and rejected the ideas of contingent fees for private attorneys and the creation of a new environmental court. The former would have required the amendment of Connecticut's citizen suit law (see p. 408) to authorize the payment of fees to private attorneys, and Lufkin feared that if the legislature were to reconsider the citizen suit law, it might be weakened or repealed. The statute had faced considerable opposition from Connecticut's business community in 1971, and Lufkin, Costle, and other DEP officials felt that the climate for environmental causes had worsened since then. Lufkin also felt that a move to provide contingent fees for private attorneys would be seen as an attack on the Attorney General's office; for the same reason, he vetoed a suggestion that the enforcement bill seek to repeal the requirement that the Attorney General's office represent all state agencies in court.

As to the environmental court option, Lufkin felt that it was simply too radical and costly to win legislative support. Finally, the lawyers pointed out that the "traffic court" idea of an expedited process for small cases essentially created a new class of minor criminal offenses or misdemeanors and would therefore presumably have to be enforced by local police and prosecutors; Lufkin and Costle were wary of a scheme that required cooperation from officials untrained in environmental matters and preoccupied with major criminal offenses, but he left the option open if a way could be found to place enforcement in DEP's hands.

With this guidance from Lufkin, the lawyers prepared a draft bill which authorized the Commissioner or his delegate to levy civil penalties against violators of departmental orders, to promulgate "procedural regulations" which could be enforced in the same manner as substantive orders, and to require performance bonds of violators under a departmental order. No separate procedure was set forth for small cases, but according to Robert Lovejoy of Davis Polk, neither did the bill commit DEP to use the same hearing procedures for all cases; in his view, this left open the possibility of using an expedited procedure for minor

cases. In David Tundermann's view, though, the bill's silence on this issue had the effect of guaranteeing small violators the same procedural protections as large ones, thereby defeating his and Drayton's desire for a speedier process for small cases; as he put it, the lawyer's efforts ended by providing "a complete panoply of procedural protection for all violations." However, the extent to which the bill could have created the desire expedited process was limited by constitutional requirements of due process and by statutory requirements governing hearing procedures in administrative agencies.

In drafting the bill, the Davis Polk team had three principal concerns, according to Lovejoy: to make sure that the bill got drafted in time for submission to the 1973 session of the legislature; to ensure that it was broad enough to permit DEP to do what it needed to do; and to produce a bill that would stand up to legal, constitutional and political challenges. The bill's central and most innovative concept—an administrative fine that would be tied to the cost of compliance and would accrue during any appeal—raised the most constitutional questions and received the most attention from the lawyers.

The two main issues raised in connection with the administrative fine were the constitutionality of delegating to an administrative agency the power to set fines and the constitutionality of allowing the fine to accumulate while the polluter appealed the departmental order. Under Connecticut constitutional law, the setting of fines is a legislative and judicial function: the legislature prescribes a schedule of fines for various classes of offenses and the court applies that schedule to particular cases. What the DEP enforcement bill was proposing was a delegation of these functions to an administrative agency; and in Connecticut, the courts require that a statute authorizing such a delegation must

> . . . declare a legislative policy, establish primary standards for carrying it out, or lay down an intelligible principle to which the administrative officer or body must conform, with a proper regard for the protection of the public interests and with such degree of certainty as the nature of the case permits, and enjoin a procedure under which, by appeal or otherwise, both public interests and private rights shall have due consideration.
>
> If the Legislature fails to prescribe with reasonable clarity the limits of the power delegated or if those limits are too broad, its attempt to

delegate is a nullity. *State v. Stoddard,* 126 Conn. 623, 13A. 2d 586 (1940); *Adams v. Rabinow,* 157 Conn. 150, 251 A. 2d 49 (1968).

The Davis Polk team was thus faced with the problem of drafting, within a few weeks, a statute that would give DEP the broadest possible authority to set civil penalties while still passing constitutional muster. The solution arrived at was to establish maximum penalties for various classes of violation and to authorize the Commissioner to promulgate penalty schedules within those maxima; in adopting those schedules, the Commissioner was required to take into account the amount needed to

> insure immediate and continued compliance, and the character and degree of injury or impairment to, or interference with, (i) public health, safety or welfare, (ii) the public trust in the air, water, land, and other natural resources of the state, and (iii) reasonable use of property which is caused or is likely to be caused by [the polluting activity].

And in setting the penalty in an individual case, the Commissioner was required to consider seven other factors, including the amount needed to ensure compliance, the character of the violation, the past history of the violator, including prior violations, the violator's financial condition, and the violation's impact on public and competing private interests.

By thus hedging the Commissioner's discretion to some extent, the Davis Polk team hoped to construct a statute that would survive constitutional challenge. Drayton, however, would have preferred an even broader grant of authority:

> The draft also included some language singularly ill-suited to the end purpose which we thought probable which, while allowing us to do what we wanted, may well cause us trouble on subsequent court cases if the court so wishes. For example, the long list of seven factors other than [the amount needed to ensure] "prompt and effective compliance" that the Commissioner must consider in settling an assessment represents a major millstone.

Drayton wanted to design an enforcement system that would be maximally effective in securing widespread voluntary compliance with DEP pollution control orders; given what he perceived as the complexity of that task and the very short time available for drafting more detailed regulations later. Davis Polk, while also concerned with enforcement effectiveness, feared that an over-broad bill would not have sufficient support in statutory and case law precedents to withstand legal challenge. The differences over this issue thus exemplified the different perspectives brought to the drafting process by Drayton and the lawyers.

The other major constitutional issue involved the accumulation of fines during the course of an appeal. The Drayton subgroup of the task force had proposed that a polluter be required to pay the accumulating fine into an escrow fund while he was appealing a DEP order; but as the lawyers saw it, this might unconstitutionally burden the defendant's exercise of his due process right to appeal. Instead, the David Polk draft provided that a fine would begin accruing as soon as DEP issued a final order, that it would continue to accrue during an appeal, and that an unappealed final order or an order upheld on appeal could be enforced by action of local law enforcement officers in the same manner as any other court order. The provision for a hearing before a final order was issued also buttressed the constitutionality of the accrual provision, as well as the delegation of fine-setting authority to the Commissioner.

THE POLITICS OF PASSAGE

The Davis Polk draft, with minor modifications, was submitted to the legislature in the first week of February 1973, and hearings were held in March. At the March 8, 1973 hearing before the Joint Environment Committee, response to the bill was almost completely favorable. Commissioner Lufkin testified on the merits of the legislation and the necessity for it.

> What the bill does: The bill authorizes the Commissioner to assess civil fines after very careful and considered public hearings as to the regulatory procedure to set up that fine schedule and after conforming with a range of considerations that the Commissioner must take into account....
>
> The bill provides full protections for the rights of persons subject to these civil fines . . . all protections and rights under the Administrative Procedures Act are guaranteed and of course this includes a right of an appeal. . . .

The bill carefully structures that Commissioner's discretion, as I mentioned a moment ago. When we adopt a schedule, that is subject to careful and clear public hearing, and when we assess a civil penalty, that civil penalty must be in conformance with provisions of the Act which are quite clearly spelled out.

The bill relieves the courts of part or all of their [environmental] trial load and places the courts in the position, as I mentioned before, of [an appellate] tribunal. The bill decriminalizes environmental violations.[39]

He noted that cumbersome procedures for environmental enforcement created a backlog in the Attorney General's office, but made it clear that he was not criticizing the Attorney General or his staff personally:

The bulk . . . of the problem . . . is because of the backlog in the Attorney General's office. Because of the inability to move forward rapidly with the abatement orders as issued, we simply don't refer problem areas to the Attorney General's office because there is no action there.

It is not totally the Attorney General's fault, I might add, both from the point of view of operating with limited personnel, but also from the point of view of the cumbersome structure of the law which gives him only one option and that is to issue an order or do nothing, similar to our department. . . . He is a victim of the mechanics prescribed for him as well as a thin organization.[40]

Lufkin also emphasized the benefits that the bill offered to law-abiding industries:

These breakdowns [of the present enforcement system] work to the benefit of the relatively few who fail to comply and at the expense of the vast majority of Connecticut industry which complies willingly. The Enforcement Bill provides a flexible tool to encourage compliance by tailoring remedies to fit violations, and it provides a full range of procedural protections to guard against abuse. It adds a necessary tool to the Department without which enforcement would be inadequate and is now inadequate. Fundamentally, it insures environmental concerns equal protection under the law.[41]

Lufkin's testimony was supported by a number of conservation and other groups, such as the Sierra Club, the League of Women Voters, the United Auto Workers, the Connecticut Citizens Action Group, and the Conservation and Environmental Quality Section of the State Bar Association (the latter supporting the bill in principle but asking for further procedural safeguards of polluters' due process rights which were later incorporated into the bill). The bill also benefitted from the management of Senator Philip Costello, the Republican chairman of the Joint Environmental Committee and a lawyer who understood and strongly supported the civil penalties concept and defended it ably.

Nonetheless, serious opposition to the bill developed among Senate Democrats, who thought that it unconstitutionally violated due process by giving an administrative agency the power to levy what were essentially fines, and House Republicans, who saw the bill as an unnecessary burden on business.* DEP was forced to lobby heavily for the bill, but the effort was successful: the bill passed the Senate on May 16 by a vote of 21-14; all of the 21 favorable votes were cast by Republicans (who at that time held a 23-13 majority in the Senate), while 12 of the negative votes were cast by Democrats. On May 23 the bill passed the House 119-21, with Republicans voting 68-17 in favor, and Democrats, unlike their Senate colleagues, supporting the bill overwhelmingly, 51-4.** The next step for the Department, to be discussed in Part B of this case (chapter 20), was to draft detailed implementing regulations.

---

*Although DEP officials, after meeting with representatives of the Connecticut Business and Industry Association (CBIA), had agreed to certain mildly weakening amendments, such as a provision that a company acting within the terms of a DEP permit or order could not be subjected to a civil penalty, CBIA remained critical of the bill's alleged violation of industry's due process rights, though the Association did not lobby heavily against it.

**Observers have suggested that the House caucuses are more loosely disciplined than those in the Senate, and feelings toward Commissioner Lufkin seem to have been less negative among House than Senate Democrats, allowing Lufkin's lobbying efforts to succeed more easily in the lower chamber.

REFERENCES

(Unless otherwise noted, all quotations in the case are from interviews with the person quoted.)

1. Janis Rogers Latham, *Environmental Enforcement in Connecticut: An Administrative Approach to the Formulation of Legislation* (Trinity College, unpublished thesis, 1974), p. 75.
2. Latham, p. 77.
3. Connecticut General Assembly, *House Proceedings,* April 11, 1967, p. 925.
4. *Ibid.,* p. 926.
5. *Ibid.,* p. 927.
6. Connecticut General Assembly, *Senate Proceedings,* April 20, 1967, p. 668.
7. Latham, p. 78.
8. *House Proceedings,* March 16, 1971, pp. 736–737.
9. *Ibid.,* pp. 742–743.
10. *Ibid.,* p. 740.
11. *Senate Proceedings,* April 15, 1971, p. 1090.
12. *House Proceedings,* March 16, 1971, p. 745.
13. *Ibid.,* p. 748.
14. Latham, p. 76.
15. *Ibid.,* p. 80.
16. William Keifer, "Environment Agency Proposal Debated," *Hartford Courant,* April 6, 1971, p. 10.
17. Joint Environment Committee, *Hearings,* April 5, 1971, p. 652.
18. *Ibid.,* p. 650.
19. *Ibid.,* p. 654.
20. *Senate Proceedings,* June 9, 1971, p. 3397.
21. Latham, p. 83.
22. Connecticut, Administrative Regulations, 19–508.
23. Connecticut Department of Environmental Protection, "Why the Enforcement Bill Is Necessary," May 1973, p. 4.
24. Latham, p. 104.
25. *Ibid.*
26. "Why the Enforcement Bill Is Necessary," pp. 1–3 for the first two cases; Connecticut Department of Environmental Protection, "Case Histories of Enforcement Problems," January 1973, pp. 1–2, in Latham, p. 108, for the third case.
27. Latham, p. 104.
28. "Strengthening Environmental Law Enforcement in Connecticut" (internal memorandum from Task Force to various officials of the Department of Environmental Protection, January 9, 1973), p. 6.
29. *Ibid.,* p. 13.
30. *Ibid.,* p. 13a.
31. *Ibid.,* p. 16.
32. *Ibid.,* p. 18.
33. *Ibid.,* p. 20.
34. *Ibid.,* p. 23.
35. *Ibid.,* p. 24.
36. *Ibid.,* p. 26.
37. *Ibid.*
38. *Ibid.,* p. 31.
39. Joint Environment Committee, Hearings on the Enforcement Act, March 8, 1973, pp. 266–267.
40. *Ibid.,* p. 270.
41. *Ibid.,* p. 267.

20

The Connecticut Enforcement Project (B)

In May 1973, the Connecticut General Assembly passed the Enforcement Act of 1973, authorizing the Commissioner of the state's Department of Environmental Protection (DEP) to assess civil penalties against violators of Connecticut's pollution control laws. This legislation, very broad in its mandate, had been drafted during the preceding December and January by a group of consultants assembled by the DEP; the drafting of regulations implementing the Act, however, was to prove a much more complex and time-consuming activity. In anticipation of the time and expense involved, the DEP had filed a grant application with the Federal Environmental Protection Agency, to design an enforcement program that could serve as a national prototype. Soon after this grant application was filed, Daniel Lufkin resigned as DEP Commissioner to return to his business interests; he was succeeded by Deputy Commissioner Douglas Costle,* who had close ties to several top officials at

EPA. (Costle was succeeded as Deputy Commissioner for Environmental Quality by Eckhardt (Chris) Beck, who was succeeded as Air Compliance Director by his deputy, Henry Beal.) Shortly after Costle's appointment, DEP received a $120,000 grant from EPA to design the enforcement program, the grant to begin on June 1, 1974.

With the money in hand, Costle then appointed Bill Drayton, a consultant from McKinsey and Company, to head the Connecticut Enforcement Project (CEP)—the title given to the small group of consultants and department employees charged with drafting the enforcement regulations. Drayton, a Harvard College and Yale Law School graduate, had been a volunteer member of the task force that had drafted the Enforcement Act. Working as a consultant with Drayton on CEP was Don Gogel, then a student at Harvard Law School. Drayton and Gogel had the part-time assistance of David Tundermann and had a staff of summer interns, law students, and consultants that ranged in size up to a peak of about 25. With the

---

*Costle was originally an out-of-stater and a Democrat, and Lufkin had to persuade the Republican administration to accept him, both as Deputy Commissioner and as Commissioner.

staff thus assembled, CEP began to study the DEP's existing enforcement procedures.

THE ENFORCEMENT PROCESS

Like many other agencies with enforcement responsibilities, the Department initiated its enforcement efforts with a pre-inspection questionnaire, followed by an on-site inspection. When an inspector detected a violation of an environmental standard, he would issue a notice of violation requesting that the violation be corrected within 30 days. In most cases the enforcement process ended here, since sources generally corrected their violations without further Department action. However, when a source refused to comply within the 30 days, the Department instituted a more formal "department order" process. The order usually required a source to meet a series of scheduled deadlines, each deadline bringing the source closer to final compliance. Generally, the Department was able to obtain a source's consent to an "order," but if consent were not obtained, the Commissioner could unilaterally impose the order on the source. The source could then request a hearing on the order and, if dissatisfied with the results of the hearing, could appeal the order in court.

Responsibility for the day-to-day work involved in this process was assigned to enforcement staffs attached to each of the Department's sub-units (Air, Water, Water Resources*) and consisting for the most part of young engineers. The Air enforcement staff under Gerry Brodsky, for example, consisted of some 38 people (including a few clerical employees), of these, roughly 90% were recent college graduates trained in biology, chemistry, mechanical engineering or chemical engineering; the remaining ten percent were middle-aged men who had been with state government (or, in Brodsky's case, private industry) for some time. According to Brodsky, his young employees were "very environmentally conscious and gung ho" and were far more motivated than the "typical government worker." In age and motivation, then, CEP and enforcement staffers were quite similar.

The differences between the two groups related to their organizational roles. Enforcement staff personnel generally intended to make a career in state government; their orientation was towards the requirements of their job, which was pollution control—i.e.,

the achieving of relatively visible, relatively quick improvements in environmental quality.** CEP staff members, on the other hand, had been retained as temporary or part-time consultants for little pay and did not expect to make careers with the Department. Drayton, who headed CEP and strongly influenced all of its members, saw the project as an opportunity to try out an innovative approach to environmental enforcement—an approach that might have national applicability. He was particularly concerned not to jeopardize the experiment by taking controversial enforcement positions that might arouse a "political" backlash, whereas Brodsky was (in his own words) "purposely insensitive" to politics.***

Some friction between the two groups surfaced almost immediately, in the course of a CEP survey of the Department's past and present enforcement experience. CEP wanted to obtain a quantitative picture of the time and costs involved in the key steps of the enforcement process, and toward this end, the CEP staff had to expend a certain amount of both time and good will. The data collection effort took several weeks and required that CEP staff go through Air Unit enforcement records on a randomized case-by-case basis. CEP staff members felt that this sifting of records produced a considerable amount of ill-feeling among some enforcement personnel, both because of the disruption to their files and because of an (occasionally voiced) feeling that CEP was trying "to get something on" the Department staff.

Brodsky also raised substantive objections to the survey's methodology. Brodsky had become head of the air enforcement staff in 1973, and in his view the situation he found was "anarchy," with each member of the enforcement staff doing everything (e.g., everyone did inspections) and with no system to ensure that orders were written and followed up on. Brodsky instituted a number of management reforms, such as dividing the staff into a group of thirty Field Inspectors and Supervisors; a four-member Stack Testing

---

*DEP's Water Compliance unit deals with water pollution problems, amd the Water Resources unit deals with preservation of wetlands.

**As Brodsky put it, he had "the strange idea that [he] was responsible for the enforcement of Connecticut's air quality regulations."

***Brodsky says that he took this stance in order to be the "operational protagonist," i.e., to make sure that all the "technical" arguments in any situation were aired; he assumed that his superiors would take "political" factors into account of their own accord.

Group; and an Enforcement Control Center made up of himself, Jim Vickery (his chief deputy) and two others who instructed the inspectors which facilities to visit, wrote violation notices, negotiated compliance orders, and followed up on them. In Brodsky's view, these simple reforms paid large dividends by reducing delays and increasing compliance rates. But CEP's enforcement survey went back to 1971, well before these changes, and thus—in Brodsky's view—tended to overstate his unit's enforcement problems. Moreover, cooperation with CEP required a good deal of Brodsky's and Vickery's time; although Brodsky maintains that he willingly cooperated with the survey, Costle states that at times he had to "knock heads" to obtain that cooperation. Drayton felt that such tensions had created "unpleasant" working relations and urged CEP staff members to "take an engineer to lunch" to open up lines of communication.

Notwithstanding these differences in outlook, CEP staff felt that their methodology was sound and would produce useful information; Commissioner Costle concurred in this view. Since subsequent regulation design efforts were based largely on the CEP survey, the following pages describe in detail the kinds of data collected by CEP and the conclusions drawn from that data.

Between October 1971 and May 1974, approximately 4,000 field inspections were conducted by the Air Pollution Control Unit. Forty-nine percent of these inspections were annual pre-announced inspections of major sources; 20% were to assure compliance by sources already under order to meet standards; 18% were the result of citizen complaints; and 13% were spot checks and "special source" inspections, where particular types of facilities are singled out to be checked. A large majority—63%—of the sources inspected were in compliance with standards or orders, while 37% were in violation. Of the violations detected, 49% were either procedural or involved mobile source (motor vehicle) emissions; these complaints were usually handled without recourse to the order process. Two-thirds of the remaining 51%—the stationary source emissions violations—involved particulate emissions, one-tenth involved noxious odors, and the rest involved violations of standards for hydrocarbons, oxides of nitrogen, and sulfur oxides.

Sources found in violation by an inspector were sent notices of violation. After receiving a notice, a source had 30 days to bring itself into compliance, unless it informed DEP that it could not comply

within the time specified. In the 30 days, 78% of the notices of violation were settled. Nearly all motor vehicle and procedural cases were dealt with in this time period, so that the remaining 22% (323 cases) were almost entirely stationary source emissions violations.* If the source did not comply with a notice of violation, the Air Unit issued an order that it take specific steps to come into compliance by a certain date. Approximately 112 days were required on the average between the detection of the violation and the issuance of an order:

1. After the 30-day grace period for compliance with the notice of violation, an average of 26 days were spent assigning the case to an Air Unit engineer, notifying higher authorities in DEP, and preparing a "package" setting for the necessary information for the engineer in charge of the case;

2. A conference was arranged between DEP and the source, since no order can be issued without a hearing; it took an average of 16 days to arrange the conference, with six additional days between the time it was arranged and the time of the conference;

3. After the conference, the order was drafted, reviewed by the DEP General Counsel's office, the Assistant Director and Director of Air Compliance, and the Commissioner** of the Department, and sent—all of which took 34 days for the average case.

The survey showed that an order could be processed in an average of 3.2 months for cases in which compliance was achieved on schedule. The average time to process an order for cases with delays in compliance was 4.2 months, while the 8% of cases with the greatest delays in complying with orders required an average of 5.9 months between detection of a violation and issuance of an order. Moreover, sources had some discretion in arranging a conference time, and the worst 8% of cases took an average of 3.6 months to arrange a conference—175% more time

---

*No pattern in size of company or type of industry was apparent among order recipients.

**Under the law establishing DEP, only the Commissioner or his designated deputy can issue an order.

than in cases where there were no later delays in complying with an order.

Once an order was issued, it could be challenged in a further administrative hearing. As of November 1974, only nine of the 1469 air standards violators had challenged their abatement orders, and five of the challenges were settled before a formal hearing. CEP attributed the lack of challenges to two factors:

That so few orders are challenged could be because the Department's orders are generally accepted as reasonable and/or regulatees are reluctant to undertake the expensive, time-consuming [litigative] fight, especially as long as they feel they can ignore the order or at least its compliance deadlines with relative impunity. The second of these factors has unquestionably been important. But the exceptionally low contest rate seems also to reflect the first factor significantly. In interviews the Air Compliance Enforcement Unit staff uniformly stated that their objective was to establish a reasonable compliance schedule with the source—and then to try to hold the source to this schedule. The Unit in fact expends considerable effort trying to get the source to propose its own schedule and to negotiate the order directly with the source based on the source's proposal. Until recently the Water Compliance Unit did not negotiate with the source prior to issuing its orders; and, although the engineers there also tried to establish reasonable orders, that Unit experienced a 14% request-for-hearing rate in its initial years and 5% rate over the last several years. However, now that the Water Compliance staff negotiates with its sources, its rate of actual hearings has dropped to roughly the same level as that of the Air Unit.[1]

The average order allowed 6.3 months for compliance, while the average order requiring installation of equipment allowed 11 months for implementation: five months prior to ordering equipment for engineering studies and letting bids, four months between ordering equipment and its delivery, and two months for installation and testing. However, in spite of these long time periods, 56% of sources under order overran their compliance deadlines, though only 23% of them overran deadlines by more than a month.* The average

overrun of all cases with delay was 5.1 months; for cases where the order required that equipment be installed, cases with delays had overruns averaging nine months. (Of sources under order to install equipment, 65% gave delays by equipment suppliers as the reason for their own delays.) The majority of cases with delays experienced overruns of less than a month; of the remaining cases with delays (23% of all major notices of violation) 7% had compliance overruns longer than 15 months.

The attractiveness of non-compliance to this minority of sources was enhanced by the low risk of prosecution. Between October 1971 and November 1974, only 16 of the 323 Air Unit cases not settled within DEP were referred to the Attorney General's office for prosecution.** CEP commented:

The low rate of referrals to the Attorney General is explained by (1) the usually good records of Air Compliance regulatees and (2) the perceptions of the Air Compliance staff that the utility of referral is low. The members of the Air Compliance Section refer cases only when they feel all benefit from negotiations has ended and that legal action is the only available recourse. This procedure has not led to results satisfactory to the Air Compliance staff: court proceedings are slow, cumbersome, and uncertain.[2]

Of the 16 cases referred, six were still pending in November 1974. Negotiated settlements were reached by the Attorney General's office in two cases and by the Air Unit in one under the threat of court action; the federal Environmental Protection Agency took over enforcement proceedings in three cases; DEP and the Attorney General's Office lost one case in court; and three injunctions were issued against violators. In no cases were fines or other penalties collected. In the Water Compliance Unit, the average pollution source overran its compliance deadline by 100%. Sixteen percent of the Water Unit's cases were referred to the

---

*The problem is much more serious in other units of DEP than in Air Compliance. Only 23% of Water Compliance orders were completed on time, and 42% were completed over a year behind schedule.

**As noted above, of the 1469 violation notices issued between October 1971 and May 1974, 323 were not followed by compliance within 30 days. In all of these 323 cases the order process was commenced and a formal DEP order was issued; only 9 of those orders were challenged administratively. However, some sources who did not challenge their orders administratively did not comply with them either, producing the 16 referrals mentioned here.

Attorney General; of those, 70% took over six months after referral to resolve, 54% took over a year, 38% over a year and a half, and 25% took over two years. In the period 1971-1974, one injunction was issued and no fines were imposed.

In addition to the costs to the environment, CEP felt that delays by a few sources were costly to the Department, both financially and in terms of morale. CEP estimated that Gerry Brodsky, the head of air enforcement, and three of his assistants spent 41% of their time attempting to reduce delay by negotiating and amending orders and notices of violation and checking progress reports. However, Brodsky noted that this finding amounted to no more than saying that the head of enforcement and his chief deputies spent much of their time with the hardest cases, which in Brodsky's view was hardly surprising and scarcely constituted a major drain on DEP resources. CEP also noted that the costs of compliance overruns were substantial: it estimated that the average case where a source complied with an order without delay cost the Department $335, while an average case which overran its deadlines cost $583. The very worst 7% of cases, with delays averaging over 15 months, cost the Department $842 on average, 137% more than in cases without delay. CEP also concluded that the failure to make headway against sources not only diverted staff attention from other enforcement efforts but also lowered the morale of some staff members. (Brodsky, head of the air enforcement staff, demurred from this conclusion.

SETTING PRIORITIES
FOR RULEMAKING

As a result of its enforcement survey, CEP concluded that two stages of the enforcement process were responsible for most of the Department's problems. The first was the stage of negotiating a Department order. Even when the Department detected a clear violation, a violator did not have to agree to a Department order to correct it. Instead, a violator could refuse to cooperate and wait for the Commissioner to unilaterally impose an order. Then a violator could delay the final effective date of the order by exercising his rights to a hearing and subsequent appeals to the Department and the courts. The possibility of tying up the Department for literally years in an appeals process had, in CEP's view, two major deleterious effects on Departmental enforcement.

One was the inconvenience, delay, and continuing environmental damage caused by the few polluters who chose to be uncooperative. The other was the weakening of the Department's negotiating position generally: since sources knew the Department was anxious to avoid hearings and appeals, they could, theoretically, exert considerable leverage to obtain a favorable order that allowed them a long period to bring their polluting facilities into compliance with environmental regulations. No evidence was offered, however, that sources had actually exercised this leverage.

The second major problem CEP saw in the order process was enforcement of the order timetable. Orders generally included a schedule of dates by which a source agreed to complete certain steps on the way to final compliance. The Department tried to carefully monitor the on-time performance of each step to assure that final compliance would be achieved as scheduled. Sources however, invariably fell behind schedule: in fact, more than half of all the Department orders were completed beyond the originally scheduled compliance date. Despite a lot of jaw-boning and thinly veiled threats of referral to the Attorney General, most sources knew that even weak excuses would serve to delay their order timetable and thus postpone the costs of pollution control that they would have to bear.

As a remedy for these perceived problems, CEP staff envisioned three related sets of regulations defining civil penalties for different stages of the order process. (In deciding to focus the first drafting efforts on civil penalties regulations, Costle and CEP were selecting for initial emphasis one of several options available under the Enforcement Act; Appendix A discusses one alternative that was not pursued in as great detail.) One part of the regulations would be addressed to the underlying emission standard violation and would assess civil penalties against polluters who had received notice of their violation but who had not cooperated in developing a compliance schedule. A second part would aim at enforcing timely performance with steps in the order timetable. The third part would create a sanction for violation of the Department's requirement that sources under order submit regular progress reports about the status of their performance of steps in the order.

However, the young technically-trained people who comprised DEP's various enforcement staffs (Air, Water, etc.) disagreed with CEP staff members on whether the first new regulations should deal with substantive standards or with the enforcement process itself. Thus, for example, Gerry Brodsky wanted CEP to work first on designing civil penalties to enforce the regulations which prohibited open burning, e.g., the burning of leaves or similar refuse. Since Brodsky had experienced a great deal of frustration over the Department's vacillating attitude toward enforcement of this unpopular regulation, he wanted to finally get the Department behind the regulation. Brodsky felt that civil penalties should be tested first on a relatively simple problem like open burning before they were employed to attack what he regarded as a more complex problem of industrial air pollution.

In the view of CEP staff, however, it would have been a colossal political debacle if the open-burning regulation had been chosen for the first drafting efforts. Open-burning was an "enforcement difficulty" because there was no consensus that the regulations should have existed, let alone that they should have been enforced. According to Bill Drayton, it ultimately required an "emotion-charged" meeting between Chris Beck, Henry Beal, and Gerry Brodsky to make a final decision against beginning with the open-burning regulations; Chris Beck finally just said "No." Yet this all seemed very difficult to the CEP staff, which found itself in an apparently catalytic role that seemed likely to embroil it in controversy and engender long-term ill-will.

Eventually, based on the results of the recently completed profile of enforcement in the Air Compliance unit, Costle and CEP made the decision to give first priority to developing regulations dealing with the overall process of issuing and enforcing Department orders, rather than to developing any one substantive regulation. Cutting across many substantive regulations, the order process was the Department's most common enforcement response to violators who failed to install pollution control equipment. (About 85% of all the Air Unit's enforcement cases, for example, involved the order process.) Since the order process was already established, CEP would be able to work with a basic pattern of enforcement with which the Department was familiar. Also, because variants of the order process were used by all units in the Department, the work performed in designing regulations for one unit could be easily applied to other units. Finally, since the enforcement profile seemed to indicate that a small minority of violators under order were able to impose a disproportionate administrative burden on the Department, a regulation expediting the order process held promise of benefitting DEP's other administrative activities.

Costle and CEP were also faced with the question of how best to allocate CEP's scarce staff resources among the Department's various pollution control programs. For a number of reasons, air and water pollution control seemed logical candidates for the initial regulatory design efforts. These were the Department's chief programs, and CEP's federal grant required some work on regulations in both areas. CEP also thought it desirable, though, to do some work on drafting regulations for Water Resources so as to involve both halves of the department in the new enforcement effort.* But to attempt to simultaneously develop complex enforcement regulations in all three areas would have stretched CEP's limited staff resources too thin.

Very quickly, CEP, with Costle's approval, decided to focus its initial efforts on air pollution control. Costle and CEP staff made this choice in part because they expected a great deal of help from Henry Beal, the director of the Air Compliance Unit and a member of the task force which had drafted the Enforcement Act. Conversely, they anticipated that work with the Water Compliance Unit would be more difficult since the director of that unit, Robert Taylor, had not been an enthusiastic supporter of the Enforcement Act. They also regarded the air pollution unit as likely to pose fewer administrative and technological uncertainties. Bill Drayton of CEP further explained the selection of Air Compliance as follows:

> Solid Waste was ruled out because we could not imagine our beginning with such a program, especially in the face of the change in administrations that could be envisioned easily at that point,

---

*DEP is divided into an Environmental Quality unit (headed at the time by Deputy Commissioner, Eckhardt C. (Chris) Beck) that encompasses air and water pollution problems and a Conservation and Preservation unit (headed by Deputy Commissioner Theodore Bampton) that covers a wide range of conservation programs from fisheries and wildlife to coastal and inland wetlands (Water Resources).

by instituting a program of state fining of munici-palities.* Pesticides was ruled out because entirely new legislation was just being introduced and no enforcement system could be designed until it was put in place.

As noted above, Water Resources was another conceivable candidate for initial emphasis, but it too was ruled out because Costle and CEP considered the subject of water quality much more complex than air pollution control and felt that regulating local govern-ments (which controlled many of the wetlands and related pollution sources) was too difficult politi-cally.** Moreover, they regarded the Water Resources unit as understaffed and lacking in data on its enforce-ment needs.

As the above suggests, political considerations were a "major factor" in Costle's thinking as he set all of these priorities.

> We needed to get the [Legislative] Regulations Review Committee [which must approve all administrative regulations in Connecticut] in the habit of expecting regulations coming through. ... We wanted to maximize our opportunities to get political consent to that first set of regula-tions, so we chose them fairly carefully as regulations that would allow us to deal with fairly incontrovertible situations where every-body would understand the logic of what we were doing and [that] would be relatively uncontroversial. ... We also knew that the first regulations would yield the first cases [and] some of them would be appealed ultimately, and we wanted to maximize the opportunities that the first cases going up would be fairly strong cases. ...

*Democrats were expected to sweep the 1974 state elec-tions, and CEP considered the Democratic Party very respon-sive to the concerns of local officials. Since municipalities collect most solid waste and dispose of it through landfill or incineration, the control of such waste could require the fining of municipalities.

**According to Costle, strict environmental enforcement "clearly got controversial the minute we began cracking down on municipalities. I suspect I got into the most trouble not for going after a big industry or anything like that but for going after some town that was running an open dump that was polluting a waterway."

Thus, considerations of enforcement effectiveness and political acceptability combined in Costle's mind to produce his top priority for the drafting of regula-tions to implement the Enforcement Act: regulations focusing on the enforcement of DEP orders requiring the installation of air pollution control equipment. With this priority set, work could begin on drafting a schedule of civil penalties for violations of such orders.

REGULATION DESIGN: ECONOMIC CONSIDERATIONS

CEP now began to attempt to calculate penalty amounts that would exactly equal the benefits that a polluter derived from not correcting his violation. While CEP staff realized that few companies carried out a sophisticated cash flow analysis in deciding whether or not to correct pollution control viola-tions, they also understood that setting penalties too low would not provide adequate incentives to comply with the law, and setting penalties too high would increase the risk that the entire scheme would be voided by the courts as a "punitive penalty" that must be levied judicially rather than administratively. By going through the detailed calculations, CEP hoped to enable DEP to convince polluters that penalties were high enough to remove the benefits of noncompliance and the courts that they were not so high as to be punitive in nature. As CEP staff described the eco-nomics underlying their thinking about civil penalties:

> Economic remedies must be just large enough to make compliance economically attractive: They must take away the entire benefit of non-compliance—including whatever return the non-complying regulatee may be able to earn on the use of the money it has not spent on pollution control for however long the delay continues. Such economic assessments will ensure voluntary compliance because they simultaneously remove the incentive to delay and guarantee those who do comply a commercially attractive "return" on their abatement investment—not having to pay the assessment. This "return" will be sufficiently attractive to make citizens feel that the compli-ance "pays" because it is calculated at the cost of capital rate appropriate for each source, i.e., because it is as large as the returns the source is obtaining on investments it has recently chosen to make.
>
> An economic assessment is defined to be that payment which would, if made at the end of

each month throughout a specified assessment period, have the same net economic impact on a company as the expenditures necessary for compliance with Department requirements throughout that assessment period. In other words, the present value of the stream of assessment payments made over the assessment period would equal the present value of the net flow of compliance costs over the same period.

Economic assessments are based on a simple economic calculus that is commonly used by businessmen in evaluating investment alternatives. This calculus requires four main steps:

(1) Identify the gross cash flow of all expenditures necessary for the source to comply with the law during each year of the assessment period and adjust for anticipated inflation (deflation). Both initial and replacement installed capital costs and operating and maintenance expenses must be considered.

(2) Obtain net cash flow by adjusting the figures in (1) for the effect of tax deductions and credits, chiefly for depreciation of capital equipment and for operating and maintenance expenses.

(3) Discount this net cash flow to a present value (using a cost of capital rate if the source is a business).

(4) Calculate the final civil assessment as that amount which would, if paid monthly over the assessment period, create a stream of payments whose present value (using the same discount rate as in (3)) would equal the present value of the cost of compliance.[3]

Although the CEP staff were confident of the theoretical validity of this economic approach to calculating penalties, they became increasingly concerned about the availability of data to actually carry out the calculations. They anticipated that data on capital, operating and maintenance costs required for pollution control installations would prove most difficult to obtain. To get a rough estimate of the time required to amass this data, CEP carried out a telephone survey of professional environmental cost engineers in the Connecticut area and also designed a mock costing calculation for several Department engineers to perform. Both the survey and the exercise indicated that the time required—several hours—would be unacceptable for the enforcement program, which was expected to make frequent use of assessment calculations. (CEP anticipated that assessments would have to be calculated for almost every negotiating session, but would not be imposed in most cases.)

Over several months, the Project staff tried to find ways to routinize the costing operation. Eventually, they located a number of graphs, developed for the Environmental Protection Agency, which related both capital and operating and maintenance costs for various forms of pollution control equipment to the volume of polluted air to be "cleaned." CEP matched these federally-produced costing graphs against actual Connecticut cost experience for completed pollution control installations and decided that the curves were reasonably accurate. For the relatively few cases where no federal cost information was available, Department staff were able to plot Connecticut data and create Connecticut cost curves.* In other cases, the federal cost curves were adapted for local Connecticut conditions, e.g., the local cost of power. Department staff brought both sets of data up to date with current price indexes.

In addition to the costing information, penalty calculations required data on inflation, cost of capital, and a host of tax provisions. To provide ready access to this information, CEP put together a set of indexes compiled by both the Government and private industry. Thus, for example, CEP pegged the inflation rate to a three-year floating average of percentage changes in the Bureau of Labor Statistics' Wholesale Price Index. Similarly, CEP calculated costs of capital for industrial firms based on the debt-equity ratios published by the Federal Trade Commission and on bond ratings contained in *Moody's Industrials.*** Since the actual assessment calculations were quite time-consuming, even with all the variables supplied, CEP programmed its assessment formula into a small desktop calculator so as to require the input of only five variables (equipment cost, operating and maintenance costs, rate of inflation, cost of capital, and depreciable life of the pollution control equipment). Given access to the tables and charts developed by CEP, assessments could be calculated in less than an hour for a typical case.

---

*The number of data points on which these and the EPA curves were based varied widely: some were based on as few as five data points, others on as many as 40.

**Since each individual firm has its own cost of capital, calculations on a firm-by-firm basis would have been prohibitively expensive. However, a CEP research project (as well as discussions with business school professors) demonstrated that industry-wide averages were accurate to within 1% in almost all cases.

REGULATION DESIGN: LEGAL CONSIDERATIONS

Even as CEP staff were gaining confidence in their economic assessment analysis, they were beginning to worry that their economics did not fit easily into the statutory language of the Enforcement Act, which set forth different factors to be considered in setting penalty amounts but did not assign weights to them. The statute thus provided that in adopting the schedule or schedules of civil penalties, the Department was to consider the amounts, or ranges of amounts

> necessary to assure immediate and continued compliance, and the character and degree of injury or impairment to or interference with, (1) public health, safety or welfare, (2) the public trust in air, water, land and other natural resources of the state, and (3) reasonable use of property which is to be caused by the type of activity described in such schedule or schedules.

In addition, the statute listed seven factors to be considered by the Department in assessing a penalty in any individual case.

> (i)   The amount of the assessment necessary to insure immediate and continued compliance;
>
> (ii) The character and degree of impact the unabated activity has on the public trust in the air, water, and land and on the natural resources of the state, especially any rare or unique natural phenomena;
>
> (iii) The character and degree of injury to, or interference with, public health, safety or welfare which is caused or threatened to be caused by the unabated activity;
>
> (iv) The conduct of the person incurring the civil penalty in taking all feasible steps or procedures necessary or appropriate to comply or to correct the unabated activity;
>
> (v)   Any prior violations by such person of statutes, regulations, orders or permits administered, adopted or issued by the Commissioner;
>
> (vi) The economic and financial conditions of such person;
>
> (vii) The character and degree of injury to, or interference with reasonable use of property which is caused or threatened to be caused by such unabated activity.[4]

To CEP staff, this language seemed problematic.* First, it apparently required the Department to consider an unmanageable number of factors (some of which were unquantifiable). Although Project members were certain that assessments that assured "immediate and continued compliance" would, by implication, satisfy the other statutory standards, the assessments were not designed as a direct function of interference with "public health, . . . the public trust in air . . . [or] the reasonable use of property." The CEP staff tried to measure the correlation between their proposed penalty amounts and the statutory factors, but since many of the factors were unquantifiable, the exercise could only determine that correlation would be as hard to rule out as to establish.

Eventually, CEP addressed these statutory difficulties by drafting the regulation with a schedule listing the maximum assessments for any given level of capital and operating and maintenance costs that should have been expended. CEP derived the maxima by calculating assessments with the most disadvantageous set of variables realistically possible, e.g., a high rate of inflation, a period of rapid depreciation causing higher costs, etc. The regulation provided that no assessment could be higher than the maxima listed in the schedule; but the Department would consider all the additional factors mentioned in the statute in deciding upon an individual assessment. In addition, CEP drafted a special "mitigation" provision which provided that the "Commissioner may mitigate any civil penalty upon such terms as he in his discretion deems proper or necessary upon consideration of the factors set forth in Sections 2(b) and 2(c) of Public Act 73-665."[5] This provision seemed potentially controversial because of the high degree of discretion it gave the Commissioner, but CEP believed that the regulations would withstand judicial challenge on this point.

Another major legal concern arose from the statutory language authorizing a schedule of penalty "amounts." CEP's analysis clearly indicated that penalties would have to be related to the period of delay as well as to the magnitude of the violation, but the statutory "amount" language did not seem broad enough on its face to support a schedule of rates to be paid for a given period of violation. Some members

---

*As related in Part A (chapter 19), Drayton had objected to the inclusion of these provisions in that Act, but Davis Polk lawyers had written them in to prevent certain constitutional challenges to the Act.

of the Department believed that the distinction between a rate and an "amount" was a minor one. Yet CEP staff were uneasy about the problem since they anticipated that even such a fine point of form could provide the legal basis of a judicial challenge to the regulatory scheme. (CEP had been advised by a group of lawyer-consultants that the Connecticut Supreme Court tended to strict construction of statutes.)

CEP was not able to definitely resolve this issue. Since the substance of the proposed enforcement scheme demanded that assessments be tied to the time period of delay, there was no way to avoid a schedule of "rates." Even so, CEP spent several weeks of legal research looking for support in the ambiguous and often inconsistent legislative history of the Enforcement Act. Finally, CEP found language in the floor debate on the Act which suggested an intent to match the assessment amounts to the period of delay. Given this language and the overriding intent to assure immediate and continued compliance, the "rate" approach seemed relatively secure and CEP drafted it into the schedule of assessments.

In addition to the problems posed by the statutory language, the CEP staff was forced to confront constitutional questions. Under the separation of powers doctrine, the power to impose penalties has traditionally been restricted to the judiciary. A narrow line of cases, however, supports administrative imposition of penalties for clearly "civil," as opposed to "criminal," violations. Courts have generally found statutes and regulations "civil" in nature if they were "regulatory" or "remedial" in purpose rather than "punitive." Similarly, the courts were likely to find that the legislature intended a scheme of "civil penalties" if the statute provided for compensation of the public or the state, rather than merely exacting a penalty from the violator.

The possibility of a successful constitutional challenge to the regulations on these grounds greatly concerned Costle, and accordingly CEP attempted to stress the "remedial" and thus "civil" nature of the entire scheme by excising the word "penalty" from the regulations and replacing it with the less punitive, more remedial-sounding "assessment." Thereafter, all CEP staff members referred to the "civil assessment regulations." Also, the draft regulations deemphasized assessments for past violations—which might seem "punitive" in nature—and focused on encouraging immediate and continuing compliance in the future—which seemed more "remedial." (See discussion in next section on how this was accomplished.) Further, the Project was persuaded by the Connecticut Business and Industry Association to limit the application of the backward-looking portion of its incentive program to regulatees who had received actual notice of their obligation to comply with the law, and, in most cases, of their potential liability for failing to do so. Thus, Project members believed that even the backward-looking portion of the incentive program could be quite logically defended as being remedial in its impact.

These legal issues were only the preliminary ones which surfaced during the initial design efforts. Other legal problems related to the schedule of penalties (e.g., whether it was permissible to use government-related cost indexes to find variables for the assessment calculations) continued to arise throughout the design effort. During most of the summer and fall of 1974, at least one CEP staff member was involved in legal research, and CEP staff conferred frequently with a number of Connecticut lawyers and law professors. Costle also met frequently with the CEP staff, either at their instigation or his, to monitor the drafting process and to decide among alternative courses of action.

Although the legal research and economic analysis did much to reassure the CEP staff about the general acceptability of the civil assessments approach to enforcement, they also took some specific steps to underline the equity of the regulations. Most visibly, CEP created a "correction-of-right" provision, which allowed a source subject to a civil assessment to obtain a hearing on the accuracy of the Department's estimate of the costs of compliance. Upon presentation of adequate evidence of actual cost, the Department would automatically reduce the amount of the assessment and refund any overcharges with interest at the "cost of capital" rate. Although this provision was principally intended to ensure equity, it also reduced the chances that sources would appeal on the basis of the assessment amount alone, since the amount could be contested in a separate proceeding. As noted above, the draft regulations also contained a mitigation procedure whereby the Commissioner could consider special circumstances in imposing assessments. The results of all major mitigation procedures, however, were to be made public as a means of assuring that the Commissioner was not giving "special consideration" for political reasons.

EMISSIONS ASSESSMENTS OR ORDER ASSESSMENTS?

After several months of analyzing the economic and legal issues outlined above, CEP had arrived at two draft civil assessment regulations—the first to cover past and continuing emissions violations and the second to cover delay in meeting compliance deadlines after an order had been signed.* However, as Costle, other members of the Department, and the CEP staff began to explore the implications of these two proposed regulations, they uncovered a number of problems, chief among which concerned the assessment of penalties for past violations. The mere fact of current violation seemed an inadequate basis for presumption of past violation, and the amount of proof necessary to establish past violation seemed prohibitive. Because of these problems in proving past violations, it appeared that polluters under assessment for past violations would find the prospects for appeal very attractive. Moreover, CEP staff had lingering fears that the seemingly "punitive" character of penalties for past behavior would undercut the "remedial" nature of the scheme and thus subject it to legal attack as a constitutionally impermissible "criminal sanction."

During this same period, Commissioner Costle, Deputy Commissioner Chris Beck, and Drayton felt increasing concern over the political feasibility of assessing penalties for past violations. Although no penalty could be assessed for violations before the effective date of the regulations (that would be *ex post facto* lawmaking), Costle, Beck and Drayton were sensitive to the anticipated claims of "innocent" polluters caught some years in the future who would have built up huge civil penalty liabilities: this issue was explicitly raised in meetings with the Connecticut Business and Industry Association. While the CBIA agreed that they would not oppose the regulations in public hearings, they insisted that there be no

---

*CEP had also drafted regulations imposing fines of $50 to $100 on polluters who failed to file required clean-up progress reports, but these were relatively simple and did not raise the sorts of issues discussed here.

liability for past violations in cases where an individual source was unaware of its potential liability under the assessment regulations.

To address these various problems, CEP designed a regulation that would deemphasize penalties for past violations while using the threat of these penalties as a "plea-bargaining" incentive to get sources to agree to DEP orders. Section 602(g) (4) of the regulations provided, in effect, that sources which quickly signed a Department order (or who quickly came into compliance) would be forgiven their past liability for the underlying emission violation. This single provision gave the Department a valuable negotiating tool (DEP engineers could threaten an assessment if a source did not quickly agree to an order) and took pressure off a legally vulnerable section of the regulations (since the assessment for past violations would be seldom imposed, the Department would rarely have to face the problem of proving continuous past violations). On its face, however, this provision seemed to take the teeth out of the emissions violation civil penalty. In cases where a "guilty" polluter was detected, he could avoid the imposition of the penalty for the emission violation by signing a Department consent order. While that source would thereafter be liable for any delays in meeting his compliance schedules, his escape from liability for past misdeeds would be complete.

The drafting of this mitigation provision was another instance of tension between CEP and the Air enforcement staff under Gerry Brodsky. Brodsky had opposed the provision in early discussions because he thought it forfeited a valuable "club"—the threat of liability for past violations—in return for something which Brodsky felt he could already obtain easily—consent orders. He saw the emissions assessment regulations as a powerful deterrent which might not be used much but which would help make companies "self-regulating," since management would have to constantly determine whether they were running the risk of potentially large liabilities, instead of doing nothing until they were forced to sign a consent order.

The manner in which the mitigation provision was actually adopted caused some ill-feeling between Brodsky and Drayton. Rightly or wrongly, Drayton felt that the political situation (discussed below) made it imperative to get the regulations drafted and approved as soon as possible and accordingly did not consult much with Brodsky in drafting the mitigation clause. However, from Brodksy's point of view, the lack of consultation was part of Drayton's generally "one-way" method of operation:

> We [Brodsky and his deputy Jim Vickery] did lots of work for CEP. . . . We turned the place upside down for them. . . . But they just interrogated us and never reacted to our views: they sought information but never gave it. They never consulted with us, never heard our opinions [with regard to the mitigation provision].

Although Brodsky continued to feel that civil penalties were a "boon" to the enforcement staff and could have "tremendous impact," Drayton perceived the situation as one of "mistrust," "frustration," "hostility" and "anger"—on the enforcement staff's part—that interfered with the working relationship between CEP and DEP.

Partially in response to the enforcement staff concern about the mitigation clause and partially in an attempt to strengthen the deterrent against violation of emissions standards by sources not under order, CEP worked out a compromise which retained the clause forgiving past liability but which also maintained liability for persons who had received actual notice of their potential liability. In deciding upon this final solution, CEP used a classic device of regulatory compromise—a "grandfather" clause. In fact, the CEP draft was kind of a reverse grandfather clause: persons would be able to escape liability for past violations only if they were persons "without notice" as defined in the regulations. Specifically, the regulations provided that the exculpatory clause of Section 602(g) (4) would not apply to persons to whom the Department has,

> within the preceding five years, issued a written order . . . a warning letter . . . actual written notice that a person has been found in violation . . . [or] actual written notice of the duty to comply . . . and of the potential liability to civil penalties for failure to do so.[6]

This "notice" would be effectuated by adding "boiler plate" language about civil assessment liability on all Department orders, permits, licenses, and other forms of communication. Thus, as the Department increased its visibility and its contact with sources over the years, it would allow fewer and fewer sources to qualify for the exculpatory provision of the regulation. As the grandfather clause protection evaporated, the Department would be able to use the emissions violation civil penalty as it desired, sometimes as a plea bargaining tool, other times as a substantive penalty. In the interim, the Department would maintain the option to speed up the process by giving direct notice to all sources whenever it desired.

Unfortunately, the inclusion of the reverse grandfather clause did not end internal controversy over the exculpation granted by Section 602(g) (4). Instead, the clause prompted the enforcement staff to demand that the Department undertake a mass mailing to give all persons "actual notice" of the civil penalty regulations and thus accelerate the evaporation of the protection. To support their demand, the enforcement staff constructed a 16-foot wall chart depicting all the possible options under the emissions civil assessment and highlighting the additional complexity caused by the 602(g) (4) provision. The staff then sketched a series of hypothetical cases suggesting that one source qualifying under (g) (4) could hold up the Department for months and even years. Less dramatically, the staff stressed the large administrative costs of monitoring 602(g) (4) provisions in the absence of a mass mailing. The enforcement staff's presentation was an able one, but Commissioner Costle and Deputy Commissioner Beck felt that such a highly public move was politically unwise; in their view, support for strict environmental enforcement was waning and they did not want to provoke a major political battle with industry.*

MISCELLANEOUS PROBLEMS

Despite careful analysis and drafting, CEP was involved in a continuing process of revising and rethinking the regulatory design; as the Project members began to circulate drafts, they discovered new problems. One such problem, for example, arose from the ambiguity surrounding the statutorily-imposed assessment ceiling of $25,000 (plus $1,000 per day after receipt for an order assessing a civil penalty) per "person" per "violation." The words "person" and "source" were loosely used in many environmental statutes and Department regulations, each time in different contexts and with different implications. The $25,000 per person ceiling appeared to limit the

---

*A mailing to the 400 largest air pollution sources in Connecticut was eventually made in July 1975.

effectiveness of the regulation against the largest sources of pollution in the state, whose benefits from non-compliance easily exceeded the $25,000 ceiling.* This problem could be resolved if "person" were equivalent to a narrow definition of source as any independent point which emits pollution, i.e., each machine in a factory is a "source." However, if "source" were explicitly defined in that sense, the definition was likely to draw the attention and perhaps the hostility of the state's largest companies at public hearings. Faced with this dilemma, CEP created a new term, "unabated activity," to resolve the ambiguity:

> "Unabated activity" means the ownership or operation of any process or piece of property, real or personal, which (i) emits or causes to be emitted, any air pollutant in excess of the emission standards . . . or (ii) is not equipped or operated with the emission controls required. . . . Ownership or operation of each such process or piece of property is a separate "unabated activity" regardless of the number of identical or closely similar processes or pieces of property owned.[7]

CEP chose the language for this new definition because it seemed the most remedial-sounding of the choices available (e.g., "polluting activity") and thus seemed least suggestive of punitive intent. For this same reason, CEP eliminated all reference to "violators" or "violations" in the regulations even though the statute referred to "violations" in several contexts. "Person" was then linked to "unabated activity" in the regulations. Language similar to these examples appears throughout the regulations:

> Persons maintaining unabated activities may be assessed monthly amounts for each such activity. . . . The maximum monthly amounts set forth in the schedule represent the economic advantages a person responsible for the unabated activity could gain from one month's delay in bringing that activity into compliance. . . . [8]

Since the statute refers both to "persons" and "violations" CEP expected that this definition of "unabated activity" would assure that assessments against large corporations could be based on individual processes without the $25,000 plus $1,000 per day ceiling while remaining within the legal bounds set by the statute.

Similar problems arose in CEP's efforts to draft the provision allowing for reductions in the order assessments for those delays in compliance which were truly beyond the regulatee's control. This issue had been immediately seized on by both the Connecticut Business and Industry Association and the Department staff as being among the most critical in the regulations. The businessmen, for their part, wanted to ensure that they would not incur liability for delays in meeting Department orders which were beyond their control. Such unavoidable delays occurred, for example, in late 1974 and 1975 when many industries experienced delays in obtaining pollution control equipment. The boom in demand for pollution control equipment specifically and capital equipment generally caused severe bottlenecks in manufacturing and distribution channels throughout 1975, and CEP's enforcement survey found that 65% of all compliance overruns were allegedly due to third-party, i.e., supplier, delays.

The Department, on the other hand, was skeptical of claims of "delay beyond our control" and was unwilling to allow such an easily manufactured excuse to serve as the basis for penalty reduction. The Department had already had a great deal of difficulty trying to authenticate "third party" or supplier-caused delays: collusion between source and supplier was virtually impossible to detect; out-of-state suppliers were difficult to reach for information; and the costs of obtaining authentication were too high for the Department to bear on a routine basis.

CEP considered a number of solutions. Staff members investigated other regulatory settings for standards but found only that other agencies had faced similar problems. They then explored the possibility of tying "allowable delays" to a government-compiled index which measured delivery lag times for various industries, but this approach proved to be both unwieldy and inaccurate, since no specific information was recorded for the pollution control equipment industry. They also considered increasing the burden of proof required of persons claiming third party delays, e.g., accepted only written verification that the delay was out of the source's control "beyond

---

*CEP members heard this concern voiced by several sources. One source, a medium-sized asphalt batching company, complained that the $25,000 maximum would allow larger companies to escape significant liability, even though they might pay almost $400,000 for a year's non-compliance.

a reasonable doubt." This approach was eventually rejected too because it did not appear to resolve the collusion problem and because there were serious legal reservations over whether a unilateral shift in the burden of proof could be upheld as constitutional.

The final drafting solution appeared on its face to offer a wide range of excuses which would justify penalty reductions for "delays beyond the regulatee's control." This solution, contained in Section 22a-6b-603(g) (3), provided that

> the Commissioner shall exclude from the order assessment period such periods of non-compliance as the regulatee proves have been caused by strikes or lockouts; riots, wars, or other acts of violence; floods, hurricanes, or other acts of God; or other equally severe, unforeseeable and uncorrectable accidents; where such acts or events were occasioned directly upon the regulatee or a person under contract to the regulatee.[9]

This language, seemingly broad, had actually already been construed in contractual settings by the Connecticut courts in an exceptionally narrow manner. By their choice of language here, CEP hoped to ensure that penalty reductions would be occasioned only by truly extraordinary delays or delays which could be easily verified by the Department.

Two other sentences rounded out the provision. In the second sentence, the Department excluded from the period of penalizable delay such times "as were occasioned by delays attributable to the Air Compliance Unit of the Department in excess of routine processing times."[10] (This term was not defined; however, the sentence was really a throw-away since the Department could not in any case impose a penalty for delay that it had itself caused.) In its third and final sentence, the provision left open the possibility that problems of supplier delay could be solved by special provisions in individual Department orders. Leaving this possibility open allowed special problems to be settled in the negotiation process for the consent order, but at the same time removed any ambiguity about the status of "supplier delays"; they were not to be considered "other acts of God" and in no case would the Department be committed to reducing civil penalties on their account.

ADOPTING THE REGULATIONS

By October of 1974, Costle, other top DEP officials, and CEP had reached sufficient consensus on the various issues outlined above to begin the formal process of adopting the air pollution enforcement regulations. In Connecticut, as in most states, a variation of the Uniform Administrative Procedure Act governs this process; by requiring public notice and hearings on all regulations the Administrative Procedure Act provides several stages of public and governmental scrutiny of agency action. Public hearings on the proposed regulations were held across the state in early November.

CEP felt confident that its careful drafting of the regulations would ensure their survival. The Department, however, was still recovering from bad publicity it had received during the fall of 1973 for an announcement of proposed septic tank regulations.* Commissioner Costle was thus especially anxious that CEP prepare well for the hearings. By avoiding major controversy at a time when the strength of the environmental lobby was waning, he and CEP hoped to greatly improve the chances that the regulations would be approved by the Legislative Regulations Review Committee.

Looking to the future, Costle and CEP also wanted to use the hearing process to create a record which could be relied upon for later legal challenges. If anyone attacked the regulations' validity in the future, the record of public hearings would at least show the careful attention paid to the requirements of the Administrative Procedure Act and the constraints of the Enforcement Act. Further, extensive testimony by responsible experts supporting all the major points in the regulations would become part of the public record reviewed by any judge if the regulations were ever challenged.

---

*The septic tank regulations ran into stiff real estate lobby opposition at acrimonious public hearings, where the lobby had charged that the regulations would cost Connecticut homeowners one billion dollars. The cost figure was unsubstantiated, but the press carried the charge. The regulations were also apparently so complex that they could not be understood even by sanitary engineers. The Legislative Regulations Review Committee withheld approval of the regulations, forcing the Department to withdraw them.

As a further legal precaution, CEP created a panel of prominent Connecticut lawyers* to provide legal advice not only on general questions of regulatory design, but also on special considerations which had to be made to accommodate the peculiarities of Connecticut law. (This was especially important since none of the lawyers on the CEP staff were familiar with the Connecticut judiciary.) At the same time, the existence of the panel assured that no lawyer sitting on the panel would be able to challenge the regulations in court after they were adopted.

To promote public understanding of the regulations before the formal hearing process, CEP arranged for many formal and informal meetings with interested groups and individuals. In an attempt to reach all important groups, CEP developed a checklist containing the names of key individuals throughout the state and compiled with the aid and advice of the Commissioner, the Deputy Commissioner, several members of the Department staff, a member of the legal advisory panel, and several other knowledgeable members of the state's legal, political, and business establishments.

CEP also carefully orchestrated the public hearings which took place at four sites across the state in early November. Deputy Commissioner Beck chaired two of the hearings and Henry Beal, the Director of the Air Compliance Unit, chaired another. Perhaps most importantly, CEP scheduled in advance a number of favorable witnesses (e.g., representatives from the League of Women Voters, the Connecticut Lung Association, etc.) who agreed to testify at designated locations. CEP staff made sure that environmental and public interest groups were aware of the proposed regulations and their associated public hearings, and also notified and talked at length with industry groups such as the Connecticut Business and Industry Association. CEP proceeded on the assumption that

it was better to talk with people first rather than to await an explosion of unanticipated dissatisfaction at the hearings. In fact, the hearings were highly publicized in the media and were well-attended by industry—even though in a surprising number of cases industry representatives merely attended and did not speak.

Given the preparation that preceded them, the public hearings did not bring many surprises. To be sure, there were a few uncomfortable moments for the Department and CEP staff. In Bridgeport, for example, a local air pollution control officer took the opportunity of a public hearing to express his continuing opposition to the centralization of enforcement authority in a state environmental protection agency. In New London, a local businessman used the hearings to complain about the Department's low-sulfur fuels standards (a regulation completely unrelated to the proposed civil penalty regulations). In Hartford, the lawyer for Northeast Utilities (the state's largest utility company) had some harsh, though expected, comments on the Department's work generally and upon the proposed regulations. But overall, the hearings apparently created a favorable public impression, as evidenced by editorials and news coverage in many of the state's newspapers, as well as the national wire services. (CEP briefed many press sources before the hearings.) The *New Haven Register,* for example, in a lead editorial on the proposed regulations entitled "Innovative Plan to Fine Air Polluters" praised the regulations for their "realistic approach that would allow the State to take an aggressive anti-pollution stance without undermining the state's economy."[11]

The next step in the process was approval by an Assistant Attorney General; and although Drayton feared that James Grady, the Assistant Attorney General in charge of DEP work, might create difficulties, his fear proved unfounded. Brian O'Neil, an attorney who worked under Grady, gave the actual approval, but Grady had already studied the regulations and voiced no objections to his assistant.

The final step in the approval process was review of the regulations by the Legislative Regulations Review Committee (LRRC), composed of eight members of the House (four from each major party). Here too, Costle and Drayton feared difficulty. For one thing, the Committee had forced DEP to withdraw the 1973 septic tank regulations (see above), and Costle felt that that clash might have jeopardized relations with the Committee. However, his and

---

*The panel included a young litigator who was head of the Administrative Section of the Connecticut State Bar and who was the principal drafter of the Connecticut Administrative Procedure Act; an older, thoroughly seasoned litigator who practiced for one of the state's largest firms and represented one of the state's largest industries; a conservative, thoughtful, respected State Bar official and leading corporate litigator; and an attorney who had served as counselor to state environmental groups for over twenty years, was a leading Democratic figure, and who had recently also become a law professor.

Drayton's main concern was not LRRC disapproval but rather inaction: the Committee was a lame duck body since elections had been held in November 1974, and it could have reasonably decided that the regulations should be considered by the new legislature's LRRC.

The possibility of delay, real or imagined, worried Costle and Drayton for several reasons. For one thing, the CEP staff had been laboring for half a year in what Drayton felt was the uncongenial atmosphere of Hartford, and he worried that morale would begin to suffer unless there was something to show for those efforts. For another thing, Drayton wanted to establish CEP "credibility" by getting the regulations approved as soon as possible so that enforcement could begin. A third factor was that in Drayton's view a good working relationship had been established with the incumbent LRRC, and he was unsure whether this would be repeated with new actors.

But Drayton's principal fear was that consideration of the regulations by the new legislature in 1975 might result in their defeat. The 1974 post-Watergate election had swept in a strongly Democratic legislature, and the Connecticut Democratic Party was considered by many observers to be very sensitive to the wishes of local Democratic officials, many of whom felt that DEP had gone too far in its pollution control drive. Moreover, the national and state economies were still moving towards the depths of the 1974–75 recession, and environmental concern (in Costle's and Drayton's view) was taking a back seat to economic growth. The new legislature, Drayton suspected, would thus be much less receptive to new environmental enforcement programs.

Somewhat the same concern applied to the Governor-elect, Ella Grasso, a veteran of 25 years in Connecticut politics. The daughter of Italian immigrants, Grasso had entered state government after graduating from Mount Holyoke in the 1940's; she was later elected State Representative and Secretary of State. In 1970, she was elected to the U.S. House of Representatives and was reelected in 1972 with over 60% of the vote despite the Nixon landslide victory. Although a solid supporter of the strong patronage-oriented Democratic Party organization of State Chairman John Bailey for nearly 30 years, Grasso was perceived as being one of the more progressive issue-oriented members of the party and an able public servant. She has always had strong support from middle-class "good government" organizations such as the League of Women Voters, and her progressive image was enhanced by her opposition to the Vietnam War (and thus to Chairman Bailey and the party regulars) at the 1968 Democratic Convention. While in Congress, she had been fairly involved with the Federal Clean Air Act, but this meant that she was in Washington when DEP was created and the civil penalties program conceived. Drayton believed that she would thus be unfamiliar with the rationale for CEP's work and that "it could have been fatal" to the civil penalties program to attempt to win Grasso's support of what might be seen as a Republican and/or radical environmentalist plan.

Drayton therefore decided to attempt to "grandfather" the regulations through the lame duck LRRC, and he and other CEP staffers met frequently with LRRC members to brief them on the proposed regulations and to lobby for them. Either this effort paid off or Costle's and Drayton's fears about LRRC disapproval or inaction were unfounded, for in the first week of January 1975, the Committee approved the first batch of regulations (those requiring periodic reports from air polluters), which were sent to the Secretary of State for filing.

REFERENCES

(Unless otherwise noted, all quotations are from interviews with the person quoted.)

1. Connecticut, Department of Environmental Protection, Connecticut Enforcement Project, *Economic Law Enforcement, Volume II: Strengthening Environmental Law Enforcement: Air Pollution* (Hartford, September 1975), p. II–23.
2. Connecticut Enforcement Project, *Economic Law Enforcement, Volume II*, p. II–37.
3. Connecticut Enforcement Project, *Economic Law Enforcement, Volume I: Overview*, p. 56.
4. Connecticut General Statutes 22a-6b-4(b).
5. Connecticut Administrative Reg. 22a-6b-602(g) (1), 22a-6b-603(g) (1).
6. Connecticut Administrative Reg. 22a-6b-602(g) (4).
7. Connecticut Administrative Reg. 22a-6b-602(b) (17).
8. Connecticut Administrative Reg. 22a-6b-602(d) .(1), 22a-6b-602(d) (2).
9. Connecticut Administrative Reg. 22a-6b-602(g) (3).
10. *Ibid.*
11. "Innovative Plan to Fine Air Polluters," *New Haven Register,* November 15, 1974, in Connecticut Enforcement Project, *Economic Law Enforcement, Volume I,* p. 73.

21

The Connecticut Enforcement Project (C)

In the first week of January, 1975, the Legislative Regulations Review Committee (LRRC) of the Connecticut General Assembly approved regulations implementing a civil penalties program for enforcement of the state's pollution control laws. Authorized by the Connecticut Enforcement Act of 1973, these regulations had been drafted by a small group of consultants (known as the Connecticut Enforcement Project or CEP) working for the Department of Environmental Protection (DEP) under the direction of Commissioner Douglas Costle. In early 1975, newly elected Governor Ella Grasso replaced Costle as Commissioner of DEP with Joseph Gill, who had served as Commissioner of the Department of Agriculture and Natural Resources (DANR—DEP's predecessor) from 1955 through 1971.

THE NEW COMMISSIONER

During Joseph Gill's 15-year tenure at the Department of Agriculture and Natural Resources (originally the Department of Agriculture), he had acquired additional land for the state's parks, helped inaugurate a flood control program, introduced the 1967 Water Pollution Control Act and the Tidal Wetlands Act, and been instrumental in the creation of Governor Dempsey's Task Force on Environmental Quality. Gill was a lifelong Democrat, and when Republican Thomas Meskill was inaugurated as Governor in 1971, Gill stepped down as head of DANR, which was reorganized into the DEP in October of 1971. During Gill's 1971–1975 "retirement," he served as the first mayor of his home town of Mansfield and was a member of Connecticut's advisory Council on Environmental Quality.

Nonetheless, the announcement of Gill's selection created a storm of protest by Connecticut's decentralized environmental groups.* In response to the Gill

---

*Gill is quoted by *Connecticut* magazine as acknowledging that "I am the only commissioner in the state government today who encounters organized opposition. And I am the only one who has had organized opposition since I came into office."[1]

441

appointment and some of his early actions, over forty citizens groups, including the Audubon Society, the Sierra Club, and the League of Women Voters, formed a state Environmental Caucus to coordinate lobbying and other action. Gill's critics charged that he was too old and inexperienced in environmental affairs to run DEP and that he would jeopardize all the "progress" that Lufkin and Costle had made in the past four years. For his part, Gill described the Caucus as "engaged in a program of continued harassment . . . to 'get Gill.'" Author Peter Perl, writing in *Connecticut* magazine, summed up the Caucus' view of Gill:

> Gill was a product of thirty years in politics in an era when government believed it was working in partnership with business, rather than regulating its excesses and abuses. Gill is widely regarded as an honest, decent, and fair man, but many wondered when he was appointed whether he had the independence, competence and vision to run a regulatory agency.[2]

The criticism was not limited to environmentalists and Republicans:* one senior Democrat who had served under Gill in the Department of Agriculture called the new DEP Commissioner a weak "yes" man, charging that "Gill gives in to pressure instantly. He says yes to everyone and relies on the people underneath to say no."

Russell Brenneman, a prominent Democrat environmental lawyer and a consultant to DEP in its first year of operation, offered the following commentary on the new commissioner:

> Perhaps the criticism of Joseph Gill is too severe. I feel that Gill maybe represents a necessary breathing period or pause which rationally you could think an agency might need after going through all of this dynamic change.
>
> However, I think Commissioner Gill has not wished to grasp the significance of contemporary environmental concerns. And his close support staff people are even less attuned than he is. He's a friend of mine, but he comes at this from his own history.
>
> What Gill has not shown in my judgment is a capacity to manage well. There was clearly a quantum leap forward while he was gone and his

return merely signalled the return of the loyal party politicians who were removed from jobs or whose careers had been affected by Lufkin and Costle.

The criticism did not all run in one direction, however: before his selection, many Connecticut political observers believed that Grasso wanted to select someone who would quietly calm the situation at DEP. Lufkin and Costle had been controversial figures who were unpopular with Connecticut's municipal leaders for their failure to consult with municipalities before enforcing environmental laws. Particularly unpopular were the DEP's proposed septic tank regulations (see Part B (chapter 20)), and its attempts to force municipalities to reduce air pollution from town incinerators and water pollution from municipal sewage disposal. In a speech delivered to the General Assembly's Committee on the Environment on March 1, 1976, Commissioner Gill stated that during DEP's first three and a half years of operation,

> Municipalities, private industries and individual citizens increasingly complained of a cavalier, inimical attitude on the part of DEP representatives who were attempting to impose or enforce pollution control orders or other directives against them. DEP staff were frequently described as unreasonable, adamant, and uninterested in working with people to reach what should have been the common objective of pollution control.**[3]

In a later interview, Gill amplified on what he perceived as the modus operandi of the Lufkin-Costle era:

> Their whole philosophy was to stop development . . . zero growth. . . . If they couldn't find a way to say no [to a developer], they'd drag their feet on granting permits. . . . Directives were coming thick and fast from DEP on how you were going to run your towns.

**In the same speech, the Commissioner claimed "more than a moderate degree of success to date in instilling a more cooperative and helpful attitude on the part of these staff members who required such instruction [all with] no diminution in the level of quality of the enforcement effort, . . . in any of our regulatory sections."[4]

Connecticut magazine was owned by Daniel Lufkin, the first DEP Commissioner and a Republican; the publisher was the Republican State Chairman.

According to *Connecticut* magazine, the DEP Commissioners surrounded themselves

> ... with a predominantly young, well-educated, and dedicated staff that more often than not was criticized for being too aggressive in enforcing new laws and old ones that had been ignored. Town officials characterized DEP as "Big Brother" ordering sewers installed, wetlands regulated, and dictating local land-use policy.[5]

Mrs. Grasso's desire to appease town leaders was thus, in the view of some observers, a definite factor in her decision to choose Gill, since such leaders formed an important element in the Connecticut Democratic Party. But Gill had 20 years' experience in environmental affairs, and indeed his service had been interrupted only by the 1970 victory of Republican Thomas Meskill.

In selecting a Deputy Commissioner for the Division of Environmental Quality (under which CEP falls),* Governor Grasso rejected Gill's first recommendation that Jack Curry, former Executive Director of the State Water Commission and a DEP consultant, be appointed. Instead, acting on Curry's advice, she offered the job to Arthur Powers, the mayor of New Berlin and a former member of the State Water Commission. He declined but suggested the appointment of Melvin Schneidermeyer of Southington, the director of a regional planning group and, in Gill's words, "the best public administrator I've ever run into"; Grasso accepted this recommendation and Schneidermeyer took the post, although he did not take office until May of 1975. (In the meantime, Curry, at Gill's request, became a temporary DEP consultant and de facto Deputy Commissioner.) This appointment was unpopular with CEP staff members and some employees of the Air Compliance Unit: CEP staff members described Schneidermeyer as having little experience in public administration, despite his master's degree in urban planning and his service on a regional planning body, while some Air Compliance Unit employees felt that he was inclined to be lenient on enforcement.

OPPOSITION TO CEP?

Soon after Gill's appointment, Bill Drayton (Director of CEP) became convinced that members of the new administration were trying to persuade Commissioner Gill that there was no need for the civil penalties program. Drayton was particularly alarmed by Assistant Attorney General James Grady, who, as the Assistant Attorney General responsible for environmental affairs, had worked closely over the years with Gill when the latter was Commissioner of Agriculture and Natural Resources. Drayton, who met several times with Grady in an attempt to sound him out, described their first post-election meeting as follows:

> ... Grady made explicit what had been implied before: that he saw no need for the enforcement regulations and that he thought they were based on false representations to the legislature back in 1973 when the Enforcement Act was being argued there [a reference to the allegations by some that his office had been ineffective in enforcing the state's environmental statutes]; he confidently predicted that they would be dismantled in the new administration. He did say, however, that this would probably not be one of the earliest priorities since it was being funded entirely with federal funds and since he understood the program had EPA's support and that such a direct attack would perhaps be a mistake for the state in the light of its need for good relations with EPA. However, he also went on at length about the illegitimacy of EPA's invasion of the state's rights to manage its own affairs, EPA's inefficiency and worse, about EPA's reliance on Connecticut's initial water model.** In this conversation it was also clear that Grady had no understanding of the regulations or of the principles embodied in them or of the process they made possible. I was also left with the impression that Grady in fact had not been keeping up with recent developments in the law and, more generally, that most of his positions were positions of personal preference rather than legal reasoning.

Drayton's fear was that when the first case testing the constitutionality of the Enforcement Act and the regulations came to court, it would not be prosecuted vigorously by the Attorney General's office, since in his view "Grady had been rendering his offi-

---

**A reference to Connecticut's 1967 Water Pollution Control Act; see Part A, (chapter 19).

---

*See Exhibit 21.1 for a DEP organization chart.

cial legal opinion since 1973, that the Enforcement Act was unconstitutional and that everything having to do with it was illegitimate":

It seemed to me highly plausible that Grady [might] pursue the case with confidence or vigor. I respected his candor with me at least. However, my confidence in his capacity given a case of this complexity and given his intellectual ability and my sense of his failure to keep up with the law in any serious way, certainly in these areas was limited. [And] once a case is referred to the Attorney General's office, the Attorney General takes over responsibility for negotiations. At that stage the whole proceeding can be gutted easily and informally. [Also,] it was becoming clear that [Assistant Attorney General Alan] Kosloff was going to end up working for Grady—and since at that time he had busied himself advising, among others, [Gill's close advisor] George Russell that he felt that the department could easily get all its legal work done with only one or two lawyers and that his colleagues [in the DEP] were not necessary or not particularly competent—a remarkable display of loyalty—I had feared the worst for any test case that was to develop unless alternative arrangements were made.

Grady gave a different view of his position on the civil penalties program:

The civil penalties program is an added tool for the enforcement of the environmental laws. It is an excellent alternative tool to be used on certain occasions and for the more mechanical procedural steps [e.g., progress reports], it is an excellent tool. [But] as to major fines for major pollutors, I have reservations . . . companies will fight [a large civil assessment] almost as a matter of course.

I did not run around making a concerted effort to defeat the civil penalties program. As far as my actively pushing Gill one way or another, I simply didn't spend a lot of time with the civil penalties program . . . it was not an important issue. . . . [The question with regard to civil penalties] was how much they would be used. . . .

As Grady summarized his views of the Enforcement Act:

I was not alone in expressing questions as to the constitutionality of the Enforcement Act. . . . There are constitutional questions with regard to the Act, [namely that] an administrative act is to be given the weight of a judicial decision. . . . [But] my job is to defend the constitutionality of every statute.

In Drayton's perception, other high officials also opposed the civil penalties program:

This conversation [with Grady] was, as you may imagine, an alarming experience for me. This direct communication from Grady, an indication of the supreme assurance he had in his position's strength and our fundamental weakness, was subsequently confirmed by comments made directly and indirectly by other members of the new core groups. Thus, for example, a member of the administrative unit (responsible for processing contracts, budgets, postage allocation, etc.) with whom I had had to work closely, told me that George Russell [Gill's staffing chief and principal advisor] had told him very directly that the entire federal project on which I was working was a complete waste and would be terminated early in the new administration.

His comment to me: "It's too bad all the hard work and late nights you have been putting in will have no impact now."

However, Russell, too, contradicts Drayton's recollection:

Never, at any time, did I make any statement to anyone including the unnamed person who purported to quote me on the future of the Civil Penalties Program. I am, and always [have] been, a positively oriented person who favors trying new approaches to old problems whenever there is ever a fair chance that innovative methods may improve the existing situation. This is definitely the case with respect to the Civil Penalties Program. I have been and continue to be optimistic about the potential for this program to cure the obvious defects in our pollution control enforcement activities by providing a quick, effective and relatively simple means of making it unprofitable for polluters to continue operations which are detrimental to the environment.

Following his meetings with Grady, Drayton began to act on his perception that the regulations faced a difficult court test. Unable to influence much the handling of a test case—which would by law be in the hands of the Attorney General's office—he nonetheless attempted to line up support by contracting with expert witnesses* and obtaining outside legal advice. Among those whom Drayton arranged to be on call was Dr. William Baumol, one of America's most famous economists and an acquaintance of Drayton's family; Drayton also kept alive the panel of prominent Connecticut attorneys with whom he had dealt during the public hearings on the air regulations and this group was able to provide informal legal advice to CEP. In addition, Costle and Drayton tried to persuade former Senate Majority Counsel Robert Satter to seek appointment as special assistant attorney general for environmental affairs. However, Satter, a widely-respected lawyer and a prominent Democrat, accepted a judgeship, leaving DEP representation in the hands of Assistant AG Grady and his staff. Drayton also attempted to establish informal contacts with members of Governor Grasso's staff so that he could appeal to them in case of difficulties with Commissioner Gill.

Finally, David Tundermann, who served as Assistant Commissioner for Legal Affairs under Commissioners Lufkin and Costle, attempted during Costle's lame duck term** to create an Office of Adjudication within DEP that would have had authority to act as a court of first resort in all cases arising under DEP jurisdiction, including cases under the Enforcement Act. Establishment of this office, which had been contemplated for some time, was intended to circumvent any possible conflicts of interest that might arise from having a single office in the Department function in the capacity of hearing examiner and prosecutor. The office, however, (which consisted only of Tundermann and his secretary), was closed by Commissioner Gill because he felt it served no useful function.

STAFF REDUCTIONS

Soon after taking office, Governor Grasso, in an apparent effort to pare unnecessary spending from the state budget,*** asked George Conklin, Governor John Dempsey's Deputy Commissioner for Financial Control, to analyze the needs of DEP and other departments and recommend any expenditure cuts he thought appropriate. Conklin enlisted the help of Joseph Hickey, a "wild-eyed Irishman" in Gill's words, who had been a DANR employee under Gill and had been relegated to a minor position by Lufkin. Conklin and Hickey prepared three memoranda—later known as the "Econuts" memo—which vigorously attacked Lufkin and Costle and called for the termination of certain department employees who were characterized as environmental radicals or "Econuts." In addition, the memos described David Tundermann and the rest of DEP's legal staff as "nuts," suggesting that they were "dangerous" and should be eliminated. One memorandum made a unit-by-unit budgetary critique of DEP and concluded that the Department was a prime example of

> . . . a top-heavy bureaucracy and empire building. In addition to ordinary budget "fat," superfluous and/or dangerous categories such as lawyers working outside the AG should be eliminated, most easily through eliminating the entire category of Environmental Analysts. Any desirable exceptions can then be picked up as Special Assistants until being reclassified into more suitable categories.

The same memorandum strongly attacked the work of the Air Compliance Unit:

> Major recommendations include redrafting the Air regulations, which were drafted by environmental activists and which are both a threat to the state's economy and apparently impossible to administer.

---

*Drayton had originally contacted people to serve as expert witnesses to marshall support for the air regulations in public hearings; he maintained contact with these people and expanded his witness list for future court hearings.

**Under Connecticut law Gill could not take office until March 1, and Costle remained DEP Commissioner until that date.

***Connecticut's unemployment rate was 10% (running as high as 20% in some towns), the legislature was discussing ways of reducing the state budget, and Governor Grasso was saying that it might prove necessary to lay off 2,000 state employees. As evidence of her earnestness, Grasso cut her own salary by $7,000 and proposed a controversial "corporate property tax." (Connecticut at the time was one of a number of states that did not have a personal income tax.)

In discussing Tundermann's proposed Office of Adjudication, the memo stated:

> *Adjudication*—A new operation . . . to enforce a Civil Penalties code. Many feel this operation is unconstitutional, duplicatory of the established legal process, and duplicatory of AG. Its FY 1975–76 cost [is] estimated at $98,403 ($83,402 staff). It should be eliminated.

The "Econuts" memoranda remained secret; in fact, they were not uncovered until June 1976, during the course of an investigation of DEP by the Joint Committee on the Environment.* Commissioner Gill maintains that he never knew of them. But Governor Grasso did mandate a 500-man reduction in the state work force, of which 36 were to come from DEP, and Gill chose to "save line jobs rather than peripheral people in research and planning, which was overstaffed." Since most of the planning staff were new, younger appointees intensely loyal to Lufkin and suspicious of Gill, the firings caused some resentment among Lufkin appointees and aroused suspicions that Gill had political motives. However, Gill claimed that he could have gotten rid of many more of Lufkin's appointees but that he "never fired any of them."**

As part of the economy drive, Governor Grasso ordered the elimination of all employees classified as "Administrative Assistants" upon taking office in January 1975. Assistant Commissioner for Legal Affairs David Tundermann, despite his departmental title, held that personnel classification and accordingly should have been terminated in January. However, Curry told Gill that Tundermann needed more time to complete work on the civil penalties program (drafting regulations for Water and Water Resources and writing reports to EPA under the CEP grant), so Gill kept Tundermann on until he received an order from the Governor's office to terminate him, which he did as of May 1, 1975.*** (Tundermann's version of the story is different: he felt that Gill had terminated him to prevent his working on the civil penalties program.)

Undoubtedly, however, the most controversial staff reductions involved DEP's eight-man legal staff: in late April, Gill notified six of the eight that they would be terminated as of June 1; the remaining two were transferred into the State Attorney General's office. The firings caused something of a flap in the press, prompting Commissioner Gill to call a joint press conference with Attorney General Carl R. Ajello. His reasons for the firings, as he later emphasized, were several:

1. The DEP attorneys had never practiced law in the courts and by law could not represent the state (including the Department) in the courts or offer official legal opinions.
2. Barred from these duties, the DEP attorneys had, according to Gill, been giving municipalities advice on their obligations under the Inland Wetlands Act ("running hog wild" in Gill's words), which was also improper since each town has its own counsel.
3. Gill had no confidence in their legal or administrative ability or their judgment; he cited one (unspecified) instance when the Attorney General had had to go to court to defend the state for their actions.
4. He did not want to use them as hearing examiners, believing that it was easier and better to train "an engineer in the procedures" than a lawyer in engineering.

Ajello, meanwhile, said the action was the first move in a program to put all of Connecticut's legal services directly under the Attorney General's jurisdiction, but stressed that the decision to fire the attorneys

---

*The investigation was prompted by the charges of some environmentalists and legislators that Gill had failed to perform adequately his duties as DEP Commissioner; the charges, however, were never sustained.

**Some in the department took a different view of the firings. Water Compliance Director Robert Taylor, for example, has charged that the Department's policies under Commissioner Gill were aimed at encouraging employees to quit to save state money, and in fact more than 60 DEP employees left in the first 16 months of Gill's tenure; together with the 36 laid off, that amounted to a 12% reduction in DEP's work force. Air Compliance Director Henry Beal has called the morale in his unit during Gill's tenure "terrible."⁶

***Drayton, with the approval of Curry and Gill, arranged for Tundermann to become a part-time consultant to DEP on May 1. Apparently, however, other Grasso administration officials refused to fund the position, and Tundermann left on July 1; he was never paid for the two months of consulting.

was "Gill's alone." (The in-house legal staff of Connecticut's consumer protection agency was later fired as well.)

Answering questions from the press, Gill maintained that the four attorneys in the Attorney General's office who were assigned to DEP cases would be able to assume more responsibilities without hindering enforcement of state environmental laws. He also indicated that two new lawyers might be added to the Attorney General's environmental enforcement staff, a possibility which Ajello confirmed. Said Gill: "We can't afford two law firms. A separate DEP legal staff is an unneeded luxury."*

When questioned further by the press, Gill stated that he did not know exactly how much money the cuts would actually save and that he did not know what the DEP lawyers' duties actually had been. These admissions created a brief storm of controversy. Senator George L. Gunther (R-Stratford), a strong environmentalist since the 1960s and a potential Republican gubernatorial candidate, blasted the firings as a move "to gut the DEP" and suggested that laws would not be enforced effectively by the Attorney General's office. Attorney Haynes Johnson of Stamford, the head of the Connecticut Bar Association's Environmental Law Section, told the Hartford *Times,* "I think what they're doing is destroying the morale of the DEP. Adding more lawyers to the Attorney General's staff won't be much help."

Evon Kocohey, Director of Connecticut Common Cause, contended that Gill did not have the legal authority to "dismantle the law enforcement arm of DEP." However, Assistant Attorney General Michael Scanlon, Ajello's Executive Assistant, dismissed Kocohey's argument in a Hartford *Times* interview:

> The DEP House Counsel cannot perform the enforcement duties which some attribute to it. . . . They cannot go to court, for example.
>
> All we're doing is putting state agency legal services back within the legislative mandate. The Attorney General handles all court actions.

THE FIRST CIVIL ASSESSMENTS

Because Drayton feared that Gill opposed the civil penalties program and might terminate it as part of the Grasso administration's austerity drive, he and

the other CEP staff members had "maintained a low profile" during Gill's first few months in office, avoiding discussions of the new regulations with Gill. However, under the regulations, civil assessments could not be imposed without the Commissioner's approval, so that some discussion of the program was inevitable. Drayton decided that rather than approach Gill directly, he would use Jack Curry, a close friend of Gill's and a DEP consultant, as a go-between. Accordingly, Drayton met several times with Curry that spring to discuss the civil penalties program and to exchange ideas with Curry about how the program might be sold to Gill. These sessions were "devoid of any open political discussion," according to Drayton, who added, "I used the bridge of professionalism and common commitment to the public service as a means of communication."

Curry agreed with Drayton that the civil penalties program was a likely victim of the new fiscal austerity; as he later put it, "by the time I got there it was more than a possibility—it was a probability." In Curry's view, the problem was not that Gill was against the program, for in his long association with Gill he had never known him to be against "any valuable enforcement tool." As Curry saw it, the problem was one of priorities: as DANR Commissioner until 1971, Gill had gotten along without civil penalties; the program had been created while Gill was out of office; the concept required some study to appreciate its potential usefulness; and given the pressure of other departmental business, Gill might well decide that at a time of fiscal austerity the idea was simply not worth the expenditure of scarce departmental resources. (The EPA grant would soon expire, and continuation of the civil penalties program thus required some sort of on-going departmental commitment.) Moreover, in Curry's perception, the Attorney General's office, which by law was charged with the conduct of the state's legal business, was somewhat concerned that "a dual legal set-up was being established." As Curry summarized it, "If I hadn't recommended [the continuation of the] civil penalties [program], it probably would have died."

Curry felt that, like all new and untried ideas, the civil penalties program required close scrutiny, but

---

*The "econuts" memo on the DEP budget suggests savings of $109,000 from eliminating the attorneys' positions.

Drayton's briefings convinced him of the program's potential value. As Curry put it,

> I liked Drayton, and his presentation was a good one. It [the civil penalties program] intrigued me as a new approach; and after being in the business for thirty years, I was interested in any enforcement approach that promised to benefit the public. . . . I assessed it, I liked it, and I recommended it.

Curry told Gill that he was "impressed" with the new program and arranged a series of meetings that spring between Drayton and himself, Gill, Grady, Schneidermeyer and Alan Kosloff.* Tundermann and Drayton had earlier discussed the merits of a joint presentation but mutually agreed that Drayton should make the presentation by himself because by then the DEP lawyers had been given notice and the two felt that Tundermann's presence would only serve as an unsettling reminder of the Lufkin era.

Drayton, who had practiced his presentation in appearances before local environmental groups and the EPA, gave the same presentation to Gill and the others that he had given Curry. Four meetings were held: the first was introductory in nature, and the following sessions covered air programs, water programs, and operations and maintenance procedures.** The presentations were made in great detail and as apolitically as possible, although Gill later stated that he "did not have to be sold on the program" and was surprised that Drayton had gone the "devious" route of trying to use Curry as an intermediary. (Gill claimed that as Commissioner he had always kept "an open door" and that Drayton had never had any trouble in seeing him.)

Gill approved the continuation of the civil penalties program, although like Grady he voiced certain reservations about the use of the penalties. In Gill's words,

On paper civil penalties are great, and I have a respect for them. They are a good enforcement tool for people who are dragging their feet. But I am a disciple of due process. . . . I think a civil penalties program can provide due process if it's properly administered [if the administrator] is not arbitrary in levying the fines.

Soon after the series of meetings between Drayton and the new DEP leaders, it was necessary to take action in some cases where warning letters had had no effect on noncompliers. Drayton urged that the civil penalties program be applied to bring these firms into compliance. Curry brought Kosloff into the situation by asking him to make a report based on his evaluation of these cases: in effect, he got Kosloff involved in actually using the CEP tools. Henry Beal, Director of the Air Compliance Division and an ardent supporter of CEP, asked Kosloff to review a list of violations that Beal was recommending for early assessment of the small procedural fine for failing to submit progress reports. Like Curry, Beal wanted to persuade Kosloff that routine pathways which could be implemented faster and cheaper than litigation were necessary to achieve compliance with air quality standards.

The first fine, in the amount of $50, was levied on the Allyndale Limestone Company on June 20, 1975. The firm quickly came into compliance, paying the fine and submitting the required report. Similar penalties were assessed soon after on the American Can Company, Avco Industries, and the B. N. Beard Company, an asphalt batching company in Derby, Connecticut. While the first two submitted the required reports, the Beard Company did not. Beard had a particularly bad environmental reputation in Connecticut, even in industrial circles, and a battle began shaping up between DEP and Beard over the company's failure to pay the $50 fine and submit a progress report on its abatement of air pollution.

While the Beard case was still pending, Drayton judged his work to be done and he returned to New York; when he left Hartford in September 1975, he asked Greg Sharp, the DEP Director of Information and Education and a strong supporter of CEP, to coordinate the civil penalties program activities in the Department. During the next six months, DEP continued to impose fines under civil penalties regulation 22a-6b-601 for violators of progress report requirements. On February 27, 1976, DEP issued a civil

---

*By then an Assistant Attorney General for Environmental Enforcement under Jim Grady, Kosloff viewed civil penalties as an extraordinary remedy that could actually add delays to the enforcement process. He felt that traditional devices such as the temporary restraining order were quicker and that civil penalties would be of use principally in small cases.

**The civil penalties regulations approved up to this time were aimed at capital investment decisions by polluters; other regulations would focus on failure to properly operate and maintain pollution control equipment.

assessment of $10,539 against the B. N. Beard Company under regulation 22a-6b-603 for violating the terms of its previous order to reduce the amount of air pollution it produced from its smokestacks. The reasons for the imposition of this civil assessment were outlined by Director of Air Compliance Henry Beal in a memorandum to Commissioner Gill dated January 22, 1976, which is reprinted below.

> State Order No. 305 was served on the B. N. Beard Co. on June 13, 1974, with a compliance date of October 21, 1974. The violation was cited as Section 19-508-18(f) (2), excessive particulate emissions from a hot mix asphalt plant.
>
> Since that time, the source has taken steps toward compliance only when this department requested that the DOT* suspend purchasing from the B. N. Beard Company on the basis that its Certificate of Compliance was invalid. These actions by the Department have resulted only in unkept promises of expeditious compliance in return for having the company returned to DOT's eligible supplier list. Such is the case when after an April, 1975 meeting between yourself and company representatives, it was agreed that the company would be returned to DOT's list based upon a commitment by the company to proceed in a diligent manner to achieve compliance by November, 1975.
>
> An inspection conducted on January 9, 1976 by DEP personnel revealed that no control equipment has been delivered and no modifications or repairs have occurred to the existing, badly deteriorated equipment. Further investigation reveals that no purchase of control equipment has taken place. This initial step was to have been completed as of July 24, 1974, according to the timetable of State Order No. 305.
>
> The B. N. Beard Company is presently 18 months delinquent in achieving compliance with no clear intention of correcting its violation. In addition, B. N. Beard is the only such industry in the state which is not in compliance with this Department's Regulations.
>
> I therefore recommend that the Department proceed to issue a civil assessment under the Civil Penalty Regulations (specifically Regulation 22a-6b-603).

Beal wrote this memo for his immediate superior, Deputy Commissioner Schneidermeyer, who reviewed and approved it before passing it along to Commissioner Gill for his approval. Following Gill's approval, the fine was imposed.

Russell Brenneman was appointed DEP hearing examiner in the Beard case, and between October 1976 and March 1977, 27 hearings were scheduled. Commissioner Gill retired in December 1976**; in March 1977, Stanley Pac,*** Gill's successor, wrote to Attorney General Ajello that administrative proceedings had failed to produce compliance and that he wanted Ajello to institute legal proceedings. On April 11, 1977, attorneys for the State of Connecticut applied for an injunction, and a temporary injunction was issued on June 21. Beard still failed to comply with the Department's orders, and on October 5, 1977, the state's attorneys appeared in court to move that Beard be ordered to "show cause" why it should not be cited for contempt of court. On December 2, the court entered an order enjoining the Beard Company from operating the offending asphalt batching plant until a hearing could be held on the state's show cause motion, and the plant was closed as of the end of 1977. Meanwhile, hearings were still proceeding in DEP on both the merits and the amount of the civil assessment against Beard.

THE FUTURE OF CIVIL PENALTIES

The Connecticut civil penalties program has already had an influence on federal policy toward environmental enforcement. In 1977, Douglas Costle became Administrator of the United States Environmental Protection Agency; William Drayton testified before Congress on behalf of amendments to the Clean Air Act that would require major sources of pollution not complying with the Act's air quality standards by July of 1970 to pay a civil penalty for non-compliance after that time. The amendments passed by Congress made such penalties discretionary with EPA only for sources other than major

---

*Department of Transportation.

**Some say Gill retired at Governor Grasso's behest, claiming that she was dissatisfied with his running of the department and with his handling of the environmental lobby.

***Pac had been chairman of the General Assembly's Joint Environmental Committee and was the principal author of the bill creating DEP in 1971.

sources.* EPA also proposed the authorization of discretionary civil penalties under the federal Clean Water Law; but this proposal met with strong opposition in the House, while the Senate Public Works Committee's Subcommittee on Environmental Pollution again sought mandatory penalties. No compromise could be reached. EPA has since adopted a policy of seeking civil penalties (based on the Connecticut formula) in court for all major sources not now in compliance.

The conflict in Connecticut over allocation of environmental litigation responsibilities has also echoed on the federal level. On December 27, 1977, the Senate Committee on Governmental Affairs issued a report recommending that Congress enact legislation authorizing independent federal regulatory agencies to "conduct and control" their own lawsuits. The report stated:

> Congress intended that these particular commissions operate outside the supervision and direction of the President and other executive branch officials, including the Attorney General.
>
> The commissions are accountable to Congress for their success or failure. The practice of allowing the Justice Department to control agency court proceedings diffuse[s] that accountability by transferring an important responsibility outside the agency.

The Committee's recommendations were opposed by Attorney General Griffin Bell, who had previously stated that "we must have one Justice Department and one central unit to represent the United States Government in the courts." Other Justice Department spokesmen argued that such centralized authority is necessary to ensure uniform policies and rulings. A number of proposals to permit control of litigation by agencies were blocked in 1977 by Senate Judiciary Committee chairman James Eastland (D-Miss.), but the Committee report was being studied by the Office of Management and Budget as of early 1978.**

The Connecticut Department of Environmental Protection has continued its work on civil penalties under Commissioner Stanley Pac. Draft civil penalties regulations for the water and water resources areas had been prepared by the beginning of 1976; but several were disapproved by the Attorney General's office, and final regulations were not issued until the fall of 1977. In the meantime, DEP had imposed a number of $50 civil assessments for failure to file required progress reports (Reg. Sec. 22a-6b-601), all of which have resulted in filing of the report and payment of the assessment.

A 1976 report prepared by James Vickery, Principal Air Pollution Control Engineer in the Air Compliance Unit, compared the number of certain types of violations before and after the adoption of civil penalties and also the number of those violations corrected upon receipt of a DEP order and the time needed for such corrections. Vickery concluded that:

> The civil penalties mechanism may be credited with reasonably demonstrable effectiveness in the following areas:
>
>> making large sources face up to their correction obligation earlier by committing themselves in a timely manner to a State Ordered Compliance Timetable;
>>
>> the correction of more major violations in an expeditious manner (i.e., according to the dates of the Compliance Timetable) than was previously the case;
>>
>> the prevention and correction of violations of the procedural regulation covered under the current program; and
>>
>> the correction of minor violations where the source needed only a little prodding to comply.

Vickery also concluded that:

> Effectiveness cannot be reasonably demonstrated in the following areas (although there were some reductions in the rate of violations, they could not be clearly attributed to the civil penalty mechanism):
>
>> the prevention of both major and minor emissions violations; and
>>
>> the correction of minor violations by aggressively noncooperative sources.

In short, Vickery felt that "the merits of the program are significant and have resulted in demonstrable im-

---

*In other words, EPA must impose such penalties on major violators; it may—but need not—do so for minor violators.

**This account is based on Judith Miller's article "Control of Lawsuits Urged for U.S. Units," *New York Times*, December 28, 1977, p. 11.

provement in the rate of compliance of Connecticut air pollution sources. The demerits appear to be the result of either insufficient notification to subject sources or a program design that is a bit too unwieldy for application in minor cases. Such difficulties can be remedied." Vickery's full analysis is reprinted in Appendix A.

In 1977, the Senate Subcommittee on Environmental Pollution offered Commissioner Pac the opportunity to comment on Connecticut's experience with civil penalties. Pac's response, reprinted in full as Appendix B, contains the following assessment of the program:

> Generally speaking, the Connecticut Civil Penalties Program has been found to be an excellent tool for the enforcement of, and compliance with, small routine items, such as monthly reports submitted to the department to show progress toward compliance or for information purposes. The program, admittedly untested, appears to leave much to be desired, however, when it comes to using it for enforcement against major violators.
>
> The program, during its development, was advertised as one which would destroy the economic motive for delay in compliance with a pollution order, provide a more speedy remedy than recourse to the courts, and establish equity in the enforcement of pollution laws. This was an overly optimistic view.
>
> First, the concept that civil penalties would destroy the economic motive for delaying pollution may well be true on a theoretical basis, but it has yet to be proven that the program can be handled administratively well enough to insure this factor. . . .

> Second, we believe it is a complete fallacy that the Civil Penalties Program will bring about general compliance with pollution orders in a more speedy fashion than the other judicial and administrative remedies available to the Commissioner.

In Pac's view, the type of study of litigative enforcement that points to time lags in the enforcement process "completely ignores the historical cooperative venture between the Department of Environmental Protection and the Office of the Attorney General in negotiating with and encouraging compliance from the alleged polluter." On the reason for the limited success of civil penalties, Pac had this to say:

> It seems almost too obvious to point out that somewhere along the line the violator, as a measure of self-protection, will attack the imposition of the fines, both administratively and judicially, and of course, while this debate goes on, so does the pollution.

Meanwhile, Connecticut's air-rating by EPA remains second only to Los Angeles in dirtiness. Some experts believe that an important part of Connecticut's air pollution problem is attributable to sources such as automobiles operating in New York City, although there is as yet no way to scientifically measure the contribution of out-of-state sources. In Joseph Gill's words, "Even if we shut down every smokestack and incinerator in the state and every automobile and moved out all the people, we still couldn't meet federal air quality standards." In the view of Gill and others, the ultimate solution to the air pollution problem must lie at the national level, for it is a national problem.

APPENDIX A

An Evaluation of Civil Penalties

In the preceding section of this report the enforcement systems developed by the Civil Penalty Regulations were compared to the environmental enforcement objectives sought when the Department sponsored the enabling legislation in 1973. As discussed, these Civil Penalty Regulations were intended to cover only a limited number of the enforcement areas for which enforcement mechanisms are needed.

This section of the report then concerns itself with a focused analysis of just how effective these regulations have made environmental law enforcement as far as the "prevention" and "correction" of specific types of air pollution violations.

The time periods used here for evaluation of effectiveness of *pre*-adoption enforcement to *post*-adoption enforcement are July 1, 1974 through March 31, 1975 and July 1, 1975 through March 31, 1976, respectively.

CATEGORY I: MAJOR VIOLATIONS*

Enforcement System Implementation

As a means of implementing the Civil Penalty Program for this category of violators the Department took two broad steps. It first sent individual notices of the program to each of the four hundred largest sources in Connecticut.[1] Second, the Department discussed in each new order negotiation and included in the body of each order information concerning the recipient's liability to civil penalties for violation of the terms of a State Ordered Compliance Timetable.[2]

In the notification program each notice included a copy of the Department's *Administrative Regulations for the Abatement of Air Pollution* and a cover letter informing the source of its liability to civil penalties for failure to comply with certain of the *Regulations*. This notification program took place in two phases conducted in March and July, 1975.

The primary thrust of this notification program was to remove "ignorance of the law" as a possible excuse for violation. None of these notified sources can claim immunity from a Section 602 action if found in violation regardless of whether or not it took prompt and effective action to come into compliance.

As of the date of this report there have been *no* Section 602 penalties issued by the Department. The Department has issued *one* Section 603 civil penalty which is now under administrative appeal.[3]

Enforcement System Effectiveness

As stated, the prevention of violations and the expeditious correction of violations once detected were the dual objectives to be served by the adoption of Civil Penalty Regulations (i.e., Sections 22(a)-6(b)-602 and 22(a)-6(b)-603).

The effect that the adoption of the Civil Penalty Regulations, specifically Section 22(a)-6(b)-602, has had to date on the *prevention* of Category I violations is visually displayed in Exhibit 21.2. This exhibit shows a twenty-one percent (21%) decrease in the number of Category I violations. This analysis was done through comparing two similar time periods, one *pre*-adoption period and one *post*-adoption period (i.e. July 1, 1974 through March 31, 1975 and July 1, 1975 through March 31, 1976, respectively). While these two analysis periods are essentially identical in terms of the rate and type of inspection activity, there is one additional factor besides the initiation of the civil penalty enforcement mechanism which may be responsible for the observed decrease in numbers of detected violations. Many of the inspections conducted in the second analysis period were repeats of those source inspections conducted in the first period. The violation rate of such sources may have been affected by the fact of the initial violation detection. Thus, it is questionable whether the adoption and implementation of the Civil Penalty Regulations can account for the observed 21% decrease in the number of detected Category I violations.

---

*[Violations of emissions standards by industrial air pollution sources.]

Source: James S. Vickery, A Staff Report: Civil Penalties Regulations—Air Pollution Violations, DEP, 1976, pp. 16–25 (pages and footnotes renumbered).

The effect that the adoption of the Civil Penalty Regulations has had to date on the expeditious *correction* of Category I violations once detected can be considered in two stages:

First, the effect that Section 22(a)-6(b)-602 has had on prodding violating sources to commit themselves in a timely fashion to a Compliance Timetable which is then embodied in a State Order, and

Second, the effect that Section 22(a)-6(b)-603 has had on ensuring the integrity of any State Ordered Compliance Timetable once issued.

No specific statistical information is available on the first of these two effects. However, the Department staff in charge of negotiating timetables has estimated a sixty percent (60%) reduction (i.e. 10% of all cases now as opposed to 25% of all cases previously) in the number of those cases where the violating source has difficulty in submitting a timetable promptly. The Department staff attributes this substantial decline entirely to the adoption of the Civil Penalty Regulations.

The effect that Section 22(a)-6(b)-603 as implemented has had on ensuring the integrity of State Ordered Compliance Timetables is visually displayed in Exhibit 21.3. This exhibit shows a twenty-four percent (24%) decrease in the fraction of Category I violators who are behind schedule in meeting the deadline dates of their Compliance Timetables. This exhibit was prepared by making a before and after comparison (i.e. *pre*-adoption of Civil Penalty Regulations to *post*-adoption) of the percent of those sources under Order who completed required abatement actions on time. With no other change in the Order program or in the type or size of Order recipients over the analysis period, only the adoption of the Civil Penalty Regulations can account for the difference. The Civil Penalty Program can reasonably be credited with motivating 25% of the Category I violators who would otherwise have been expected to be behind schedule to expeditiously comply with the terms of their Orders.

CATEGORY II: PROCEDURAL VIOLATIONS*

Enforcement System Implementation

The failure of a source to submit a timely and comprehensive Progress Report while under a State Order is the only procedural violation for which a Civil Penalty Regulation has been adopted.[4] Thus, as can be seen in Exhibit 21.4, the number of other procedural violations detected by the Department remains fairly constant.

In order to implement its Civil Penalty Program for this category of violations, the Department again took two preliminary steps. It first sent individual notices of the program to each of the sources then under State Order. Second, the Department discussed in its Order negotiations and included in its written Orders informaton concerning liability for civil penalties for violation of the Progress Report requirement. Once the original notification program was complete, in March, 1975, Civil Assessments were issued to any source violating the reporting requirement.

To date the Department has issued sixteen (16) Notices of Assessment to sources under State Order for failure to fulfill the reporting requirement. Of this number of assessments, only two (2) were repeat violations (i.e., to the same source). None of these assessments has been appealed. However, for three cases the Department has had to apply to the Clerk of the State Superior Court to obtain a writ authorizing the appropriate county sheriff to initiate a collection action (typically the seizure of property with a value sufficient to cover the amount of the civil penalty). Such a procedure is provided for by statute, is administratively executed, requiring the time of neither judge nor attorney general, and has been quickly accepted by those clerks of court and county sheriffs who have been asked to use it.

Enforcement System Effectiveness

The effect that the Civil Penalty Program has had on the *prevention* of Progress Report violations is visually displayed in Exhibit 21.5. This exhibit shows that, whereas only fifty-six percent (56%) of the required reports were properly submitted prior to the adoption of this program, ninety-eight percent (98%) of these reports are now submitted in an acceptable manner.

---

*[Failure to register, to keep required records, to file required reports, etc.]

Further, the Civil Penalty Program has made the *correction* of Progress Report violations one hundred percent (100%) effective. Prior to the implementation of this program only thirty-seven percent (37%) of those reports, either not submitted or improperly submitted, were eventually submitted in an acceptable form. Presently (i.e., following implementation of the Civil Penalty Program) all reports are eventually received in an acceptable form.

CATEGORY III: MINOR VIOLATIONS*

Enforcement System Implementation

It has not proven possible to implement the Civil Penalty Program as presently written[5] so as to *prevent* any substantial fraction of the minor violations. In order to obtain significant preventive value from this mechanism for Category III violations the Department would have to undertake the monumental task of notifying, individually, each of the tens of thousands of small sources subject to the Department's *Regulations* of their liabilities for failure to comply. To date the Department has attempted the task of notification on only a limited and informal basis. In instances where a source under a Notice of Violation of an Emissions Standard fails to *correct* its violation within the allotted grace period it is informed either verbally or in writing of its liability to civil penalties. To date the Department has not issued a Section 602 assessment for a Category III violation.

The informal and limited implementation of Section 602 as described above provides the only *prevention* and *correction* effect on Category III violations.

Enforcement System Effectiveness

The effect that the current Civil Penalty Program may have had on the *prevention* of minor violations is visually displayed in Exhibit 21.6. This exhibit compares the number of detected smoking boiler and incinerator violations, fugitive dust violations and smoking motor vehicle violations during the *pre*-adoption period and the *post*-adoption period. Enforcement inspection and surveillance remained relatively constant over the period of analysis with

one exception: the elimination in October, 1975 of the mobile source surveillance program. Inspection of boilers, incinerators and sources of fugitive dust are not repeated to the degree that inspections of major sources are and reduction in the rate of observed violation cannot be attributed to the effect of previous inspections. The total observed violations in the post-adoption period is fifteen percent (15%) lower than in the pre-adoption period. It is difficult, however, to attribute this difference to the Civil Penalties Program since it is not likely that any of the potential violators knew of the program's existence.

There is no statistical information available concerning the effect that the current program has had on the *correction* of minor violations. However, the Department staff in charge of monitoring the compliance activities of such sources estimates that the Civil Penalty Program as presently implemented has made the Department eighty to ninety percent (80-90%) more effective in prompting minor violators to take required abatement action in an expeditious manner. Unfortunately, the remaining ten to twenty percent (10-20%) are the most recalcitrant cases where the source gives every impression of pushing the Department into the appeal procedure if the Department were to issue a Notice of Assessment. The cost to the Department of using the current civil penalty mechanism in such cases is considered too great to justify its application.

CONCLUSIONS

The objectives to be achieved with the adoption of the Civil Penalty Program were to provide the necessary disincentives to ensure *prevention* and expedite correction of environmental regulatory violations. These objectives were to be achieved for three basic categories of violations:

Category I: Major Violations;

Category II: Procedural Violations; and

Category III: Minor Violations

Exhibit 21.7 presents a summary of the degree of *effectiveness* concerning *prevention* and *correction* that the Civil Penalty Program has had as presently written and implemented. The civil penalties mechanism may be credited with reasonably demonstrable effectiveness in the following areas:

---

*[Smoking cars, trucks, incinerators, dust from construction sites, etc.]

making large sources face up to their *correction* obligation earlier by committing themselves in a timely manner to a State Ordered Compliance Timetable;

the *correction* of more major violations in an expeditious manner (i.e., according to the dates of the Compliance Timetable) than was previously the case;

the *prevention* and *correction* of violations of the procedural regulation covered under the current program; and

the *correction* of minor violations where the source needed only a little prodding to comply.

Effectiveness cannot be reasonably demonstrated in the following areas (although there were some re-ductions in the rate of violations, they could not be clearly attributed to the civil penalty mechanism):

the *prevention* of both major and minor emissions violations; and

the *correction* of minor violations by aggressively noncooperative sources.

The merits of the program are significant and have resulted in demonstrable improvement in the rate of compliance of Connecticut air pollution sources. The demerits appear to be the result of either insufficient notification to subject sources or a program design that is a bit too unwieldy for application in minor cases. Such difficulties can be remedied.

APPENDIX B

Conclusions Drawn from the Limited Application of a Civil Penalties Program in the State of Connecticut

The question before us is the merits of the Civil Penalties Program, the extent to which it has or is expected to work, and whether it should be used in place of or as an alternative to existing enforcement remedies.

The Civil Penalties Program has been in place in the Connecticut Department of Environmental Protection Air Compliance Unit only. This program has been operational for two and one-half years, and it has not yet been tested in court. It must be said at the outset that the program has not been given a substantial opportunity to show what can be done under it and, therefore, any comments with regard to the Civil Penalties Program at this time are conceded to be somewhat premature.

Generally speaking, the Connecticut Civil Penalties Program has been found to be an excellent tool for the enforcement of, and compliance with, small routine items, such as monthly reports submitted to the department to show progress toward compliance or for information purposes. The program admittedly untested, appears to leave much to be desired, however, when it comes to using it for enforcement against major violators.

The program, during its development, was advertised as one which would destroy the economic motive for delay in compliance with pollution orders, provide a more speedy remedy than recourse to the courts, and establish equity in the enforcement of pollution laws. This was an overly optimistic view.

First, the concept that civil penalties would destroy the economic motive for delaying pollution may well be true on a theoretical basis, but it has yet to be proven that the program can be handled administratively well enough to insure this factor. This concept also completely overlooks the punitive and remedial measures contained in the applicable federal and state statutes. Moreover, Connecticut has successfully and historically operated on the theory that we were, as a state, not looking for punishment of violators, but rather we were looking toward achieving compliance with pollution abatement orders. Perhaps,

Source: The material in this appendix was presented to the United States Senate Subcommittee on Environmental Pollution on July 15, 1977, by Stanley J. Pac, Commissioner, Department of Environmental Protection, State Office Building, Hartford, Connecticut.

unintentionally the Civil Penalties Program shifts this emphasis, and most probably to its own detriment.

Second, we believe it is a complete fallacy that the Civil Penalties Program will bring about general compliance with pollution orders in a more speedy fashion than the other judicial and administrative remedies available to the Commissioner. Recourse to the statutes of the State of Connecticut will show that the Commissioner has the authority in almost every instance to request action by the Attorney General; that the action taken by the Attorney General is prescribed by statute to be privileged in nature; and, further, that the Attorney General has the authority, when necessary, and has exercised it, to seek the extraordinary remedies of the court to do the job within days or even hours, when conditions warrant. A look at the nature of the Civil Penalties Program ought to make it obvious to the most casual observer that the imposition of large fines, which can be augmented step by step, day by day, and which, in many instances, may reach extraordinary sums (e.g., a fine of about $21,900 has been levied against a single firm and the amount increases $900 per month) are not something that the average person or corporation will sit idly by and accept. It seems almost too obvious to point out that somewhere along the line the violator, as a measure of self-protection, will attack the imposition of the fines, both administratively and judicially, and of course while this debate goes on, so does the pollution. In many cases, the goal of compliance and the theoretical speed of its achievement, may fall victim to the muddy waters of a contest over the legitimacy, constitutionality or amount of the fines.

Critics of the judicial remedies often point to time lags which occur between the issuance of the order, judical action, and compliance with the order. The so-called time lags are largely numerical myths in that merely looking at dates does not reveal the history of what occurred between the dates. This type of review completely ignores the historical co-operative venture between the Department of Environmental Protection and the Office of the Attorney General in negotiating with and encouraging compliance from the alleged polluter. Merely looking at the dates fails also, in our judgment, to take into account what in most programs has been an extraordinary percentage of compliance. Also, merely looking at the dates fails to take into account the fact that the reason for failing to achieve compliance in certain programs has been primarily the result of a lack of funds and staffing to adequately administer the program. The Civil Penalties Program does not, in our judgment, guarantee or even promise results as good as that which have been otherwise achieved. It could, in our opinion, present the potential for substantial delays in achieving compliance.

Finally, with regard to the claim that the Civil Penalties Program will provide a more equitable enforcement of the pollution laws, this is a statement which again has great theoretical value, but which may be practically impossible to fulfill. The brief use of the Civil Penalties Program for major enforcement purposes by the Department of Environmental Protection has shown that in order for its widespread, equitable and successful use, it would require of the department a vast increase in staffing. This is probably unrealistic from an economic standpoint in the near future.

We think the comparison between the results achieved by administrative and judicial remedies vis-a-vis projected results in using the Civil Penalties Program might best be compared in the Water Pollution Program of the State of Connecticut.

The Clean Water Program of Connecticut, enacted on May 1, 1967, has become one of the most successful water pollution programs in the United States. There are, of course, numerous reasons for its success, but it can be fairly said that there could have been no success unless the enforcement part of the program were itself effective. The record of the last decade greatly substantiates that the enforcement part of the Clean Water Program has indeed been highly successful and has been accomplished without recourse to the Civil Penalties Program.

The foregoing should not be construed as a condemnation or an abandonment of the Civil Penalties Program of the State of Connecticut. On the contrary, it is my stated intention to expand upon its use in the future. The above is intended to show, however, the clear belief of the Connecticut Department of Environmental Protection that the Civil Penalties Program should not be used in substitution of the proven, workable remedies as established by Connecticut statutes. The Civil Penalties Program on certain occasions and for certain reasons has and will continue to be beneficial. However, it should exist and be considered as an alternative remedy to be employed only in a selective manner and only under certain conditions.

Parenthetically, we will close this discussion with the observation that experience with the operation of the Civil Penalties Program has shown that it will probably be of very limited, if any, use against municipalities. To use this program against municipalities fails to take into account the subsequent budgetary and financial difficulties of the municipality. Municipal fines are quick to create a feeling of ill-will between the State and the municipality. Administrative actions based on the Civil Penalties Program consequently cause embarrassment to and an adverse reaction from the Municipal Chief Executive. Experience has taught us that the attempt to use the program against municipalities will accomplish virtually nothing.

Thank you for this opportunity to comment.

REFERENCES

(Unless otherwise noted, all quotations in this case are from interviews with the person quoted.)

1. Peter Perl, "Department of Half-Hearted Environmental Protection," *Connecticut* magazine, December, 1976, p. 40.
2. *Ibid.*
3. Joseph Gill, "An Overview of the Department of Environmental Protection," before the Connecticut General Assembly's Joint Committee on the Environment, March 1, 1976, pp. 5–6.
4. *Ibid.*, p. 6.
5. Perl, p. 40.
6. *Ibid.*

REFERENCES TO APPENDIX A

1. See Section 22(a)-6(b)-602.
2. See Section 22(a)-6(b)-603.
3. See the case of the B. N. Beard Co., Derby, Conn. State Order No. 305, Notice of Assessment No. 3-0001.
4. See Section 22(a)-6(b)-601.
5. See Section 22(a)-6(b)-602.

EXHIBIT 21.1:   1976 DEP Organization Chart*

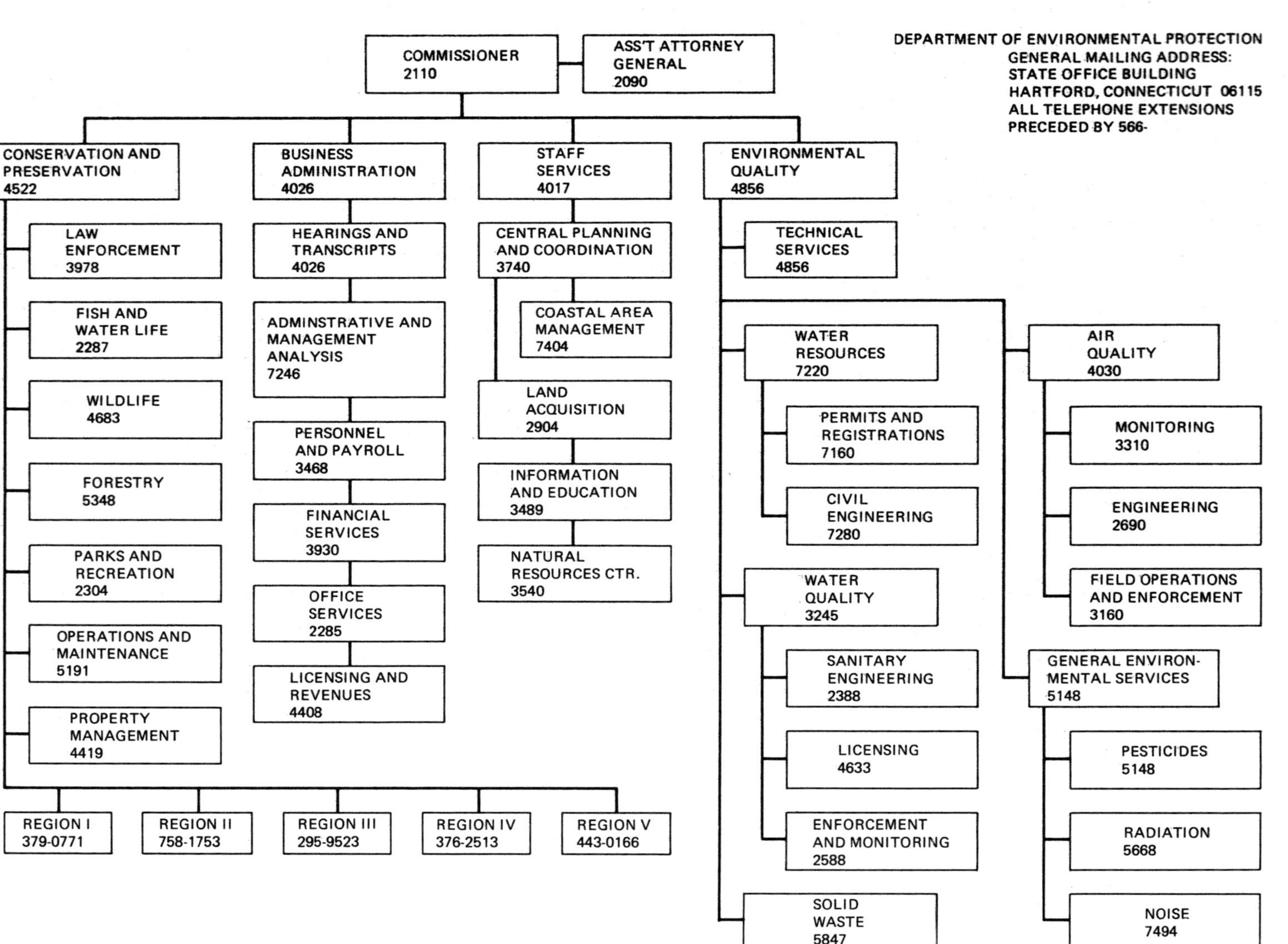

*Since Commissioner Gill made certain changes in DEP structure, this chart differs slightly from the one used in Parts A and B of this case.

EXHIBIT 21.2: Category I Violations

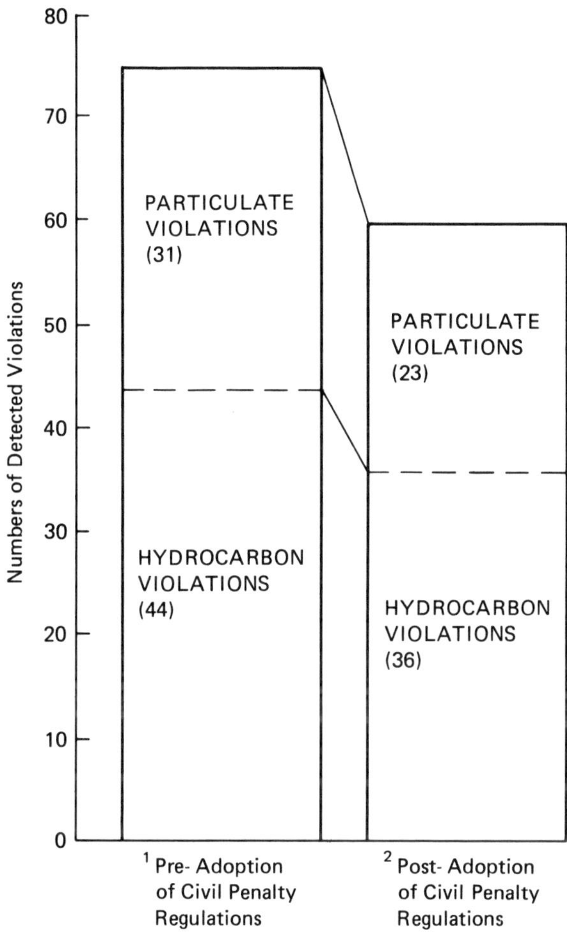

[1] July 1, 1974 to March 31, 1975.
[2] July 1, 1975 to March 31, 1976.

EXHIBIT 21.3: Number of State Orders by Percent with Conforming Compliance Timetable

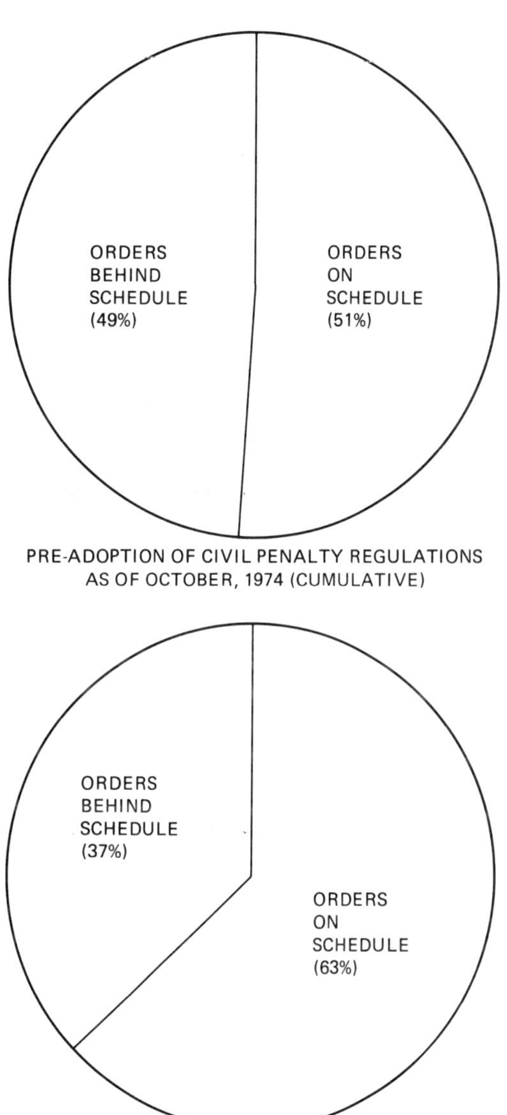

[1] As of October 1974 (cumulative).
[2] As of March 1976.

EXHIBIT 21.4:   Category II Violations

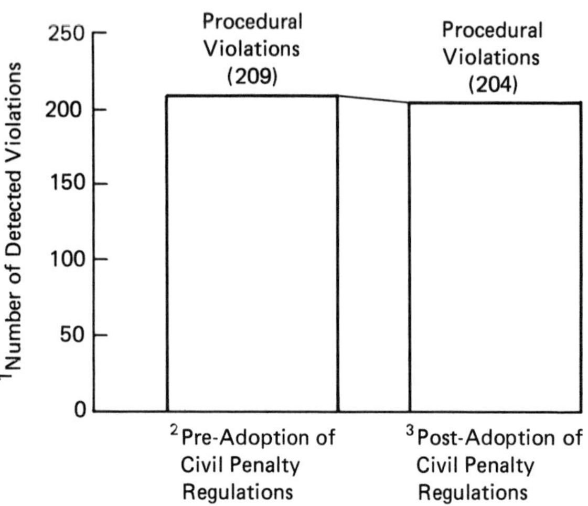

[1] Includes: Registration, Permit, Stand-By Plan, and Posting of Operating Instruction Violations [i.e., includes all procedural violations not covered by a civil penalty regulation].

[2] July 1, 1974 to March 31, 1975.

[3] July 1, 1975 to March 31, 1976.

EXHIBIT 21.5: Compliance with Progress Report (Procedural) Requirement

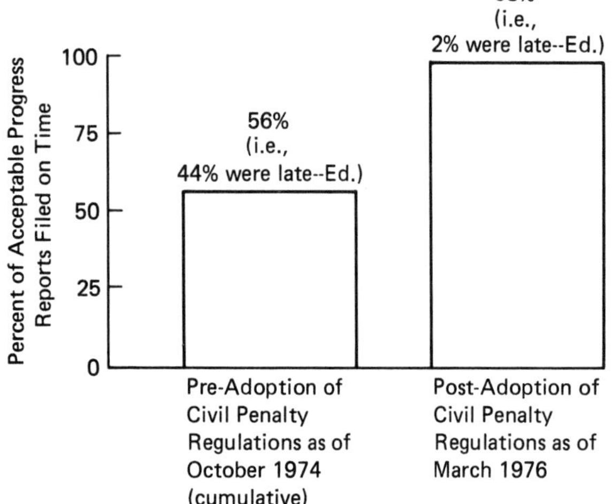

[1] As of October 1974 (cumulative).

[2] As of March, 1976.

EXHIBIT 21.6: Category III Violations

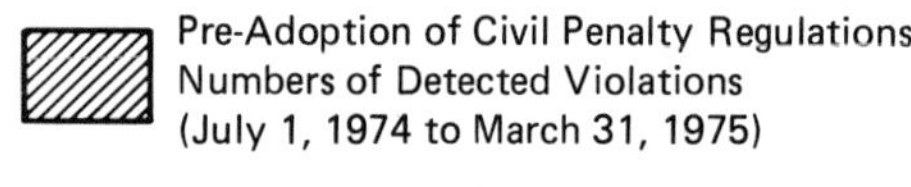

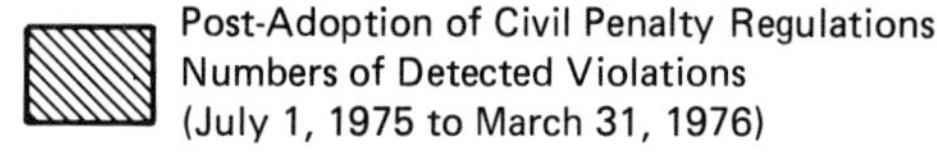

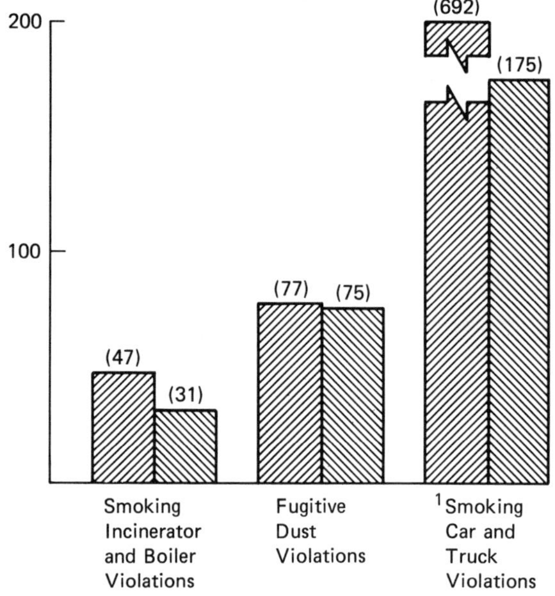

[1] Observed decrease due solely to cutback in Department surveillance.

[1] July 1, 1974 to March 31, 1975.

[2] July 1, 1975 to March 31, 1976.

[3] Observed decrease due solely to cut back in department surveillance.

**EXHIBIT 21.7: Degree of Effectiveness of
Civil Penalty Program—Summary Table**

	PREVENTION OF VIOLATIONS	CORRECTION OF VIOLATIONS
CATEGORY I VIOLATIONS	21%[a]	60%[b] Preventing Delays in Submitting Compliance Timetable
		24%[c] Preventing Delays While Under Compliance Timetable
CATEGORY II VIOLATIONS PROGRESS REPORT REQUIREMENT ONLY	95%[d]	100%[e]
CATEGORY III VIOLATIONS	15%[f]	80-90%[g]

[a]Exhibit 21.2.
[b]DEP estimate.
[c]Exhibit 21.3.
[d]Exhibit 21.5.

[e]DEP records.
[f]Exhibit 21.6.
[g]DEP estimate.

[All notes; Ed.]

22

Income Transfers vs. the Public Provision of Goods and Services In-Kind

I. INTRODUCTION

When should governments provide money income transfers? When should governments provide goods and services in-kind? In the simple world of textbook perfect economies the answer is said to be clear. Governments should provide money income transfers and collect taxes in such a manner as to achieve society's desired distribution of purchasing power. (Technically income is to be distributed so as to maximize the social welfare function.) Once this optimum distribution of income has been achieved, governments should stand aside and allow consumer sovereignty, plus perfect competitive markets to work. Any further intervention can be "shown" to lower consumer utility below what it otherwise could be. The only exception revolves around pure public goods. Technically, these goods, such as national defense, cannot

be produced and distributed in private competitive markets. This comes about since no one can be deprived of the benefits of the good if it is produced at all (exclusion is impossible), since one person's benefits does not lower the benefits of any other individual (consumption is non-rival), and since everyone must agree on some common quantity to consume (consumption must be identical). As a result, pure public goods must be provided by governments rather than sold in private markets.

Although the strong assumptions lying behind the textbook version of perfect markets (perfect knowledge, no economies or diseconomies of scale, no monopolies, etc.) are not met in the real world, this has not stopped economists from advocating the general replacement of government goods and services in-kind with money income transfers in the real world. While this conclusion may be valid, economists have generally failed to do the hard work of investigating the proper division of money income transfers and goods and services in-kind in a second best world

Source: The material in this chapter was prepared for The Department of Health, Education and Welfare and Georgetown University, in July 1972 by Lester C. Thurow, M.I.T.

where the assumptions of perfect markets are not met and where situations quickly become more complex than those analysed in textbooks.

This paper attempts to undertake this second best analysis to determine when income transfers are appropriate and when goods and services in-kind are appropriate. The aim, however, is not to give a definitive judgment on each current expenditure program or on each potential expenditure program, but to outline a set of rules that would lead one to ask for the pieces of empirical information that would be necessary to make these definitive judgments. As is usual in the analysis of the second best, very few cases can be decided from a-priori information alone. Usually a variety of value judgments and factual pieces of information are necessary before an economic judgment can be rendered.

It cannot be too heavily emphasized that this paper is examining the problem strictly from the point of view of economics and not from the point of view of politics. It does not deal with the problem of what should be done when one mode of aid is economically desirable, but another mode of aid is politically feasible. Thus, it does not deal with one of the major arguments used to justify goods and services in-kind. "Congress will vote for aid in-kind programs but will not vote for the more optimal income transfer programs." This is a problem in the second best, but not the problem to be analysed in this paper.

As a starting point, however, let us begin with the two indisputable conclusions of the simple textbook analysis. (1) To the extent that a society wishes to alter the market distribution of income to reach its desired distribution of income, the appropriate mechanism is a system of income transfer payments and positive taxes. (2) To the extent that society wishes to consume goods that have the characteristics of pure public goods, the appropriate mechanism is their public provision through government expenditures. The difficult questions spring from goals other than these two.

II. MERIT WANTS

For the sake of gradually complicating the analysis rather than jumping into the middle of a complex situation, assume for the moment that all of the assumptions underlying perfect textbook economies are in fact met in the real world. What other factors complicate the analysis? The major complication arises because of society's different preferences concerning the distribution of different private, or potentially private, goods and services.

The simple model assumes that a society has views about the desired distribution of goods and services in general, but that society has no views about the desired distribution of particular goods and services. In fact, there are some particular private goods and services where society seems to have strong preferences about how they should be distributed. Although all of the tests used to distinguish pure public from pure private goods and services would indicate that education, housing, and medical care are private and not public goods, it is also clear that most societies have preferences about how these particular goods and services should be distributed. In general, many societies seem to think that each individual should have some minimum quantity of education, some minimum quantity of housing, and exactly the same quantity of medical care. If you like, many individuals are communists with respect to medical care, quasi-communists with respect to education and housing, and capitalists with respect to goods and services in general.

Economists have attempted to strain the concept of externalities to explain social interests in the distribution of these particular goods and services, but the strain is more apparent than the enlightenment. My education does not have external non-market economic effects on others' economic positions. (While it is possible to argue that an educated literate citizenry has political externalities, such an argument applies only to the most elementary form of education. It would be difficult to prove that college graduates are better voters than high school graduates.) Neighborhood economic externalities certainly exist in housing, but these can only be used to justify neighborhood housing policies and not national housing policies. National economic externalities simply do not exist. (Social externalities rather than economic externalities are the traditional explanation. Better housing is to lead to less crime, etc. Although social externalities are widely held to exist, I am aware of very little evidence that they do in fact exist after correction is made for all other relevant factors.) With the exception of very basic public health measures, economic externalities are not produced by medical care. Death is the most private of all activities. Societies are constructed to survive the death of each of their members with little or no economic loss.

By attempting to escape into the concept of economic externalities economists have avoided facing the fact that societies do seem to have different preferences about how different private goods and services are to be distributed. Many reasons could be advanced as to why and how such preferences came about (I may be for equal health care since such a policy insures that I will get equal health care if I need it), but the reasons for the preferences are basically irrelevant to democratic governments. The only relevant fact is whether such preferences do or do not exist.

Musgrave has labeled such goods "merit wants" but the term is slightly misleading. The key factor is not that each individual merits some quantity of these goods (they also merit some quantity of goods and services in general if no one is allocated a zero income in the distribution of income), but that society's desired distribution for these goods differs from its desired distribution for goods and services in general.

Given different optimum distributions for different private goods, governments are faced with a problem. One distribution of money income is not capable of distributing different goods and services in different manners. If the general income distribution is used to meet a social goal of "equal medical care," then all income must be equally distributed. This leaves general goods and services "too equally" distributed. If, on the other hand, the general income distributed is used to generate the desired distribution of general goods and services, medical care will be "too unequally" distributed. The problem is the classic one of too many goals and not enough policy instruments.

Practically speaking, governments must provide for the general distribution of goods and services through the distribution of income and provide for the distribution of merit wants in other ways. Usually this has meant their public provision in-kind, but it need not lead to this result. Intermediate solutions exist, however, that have not been explored in the single textbook model.

There is an intermediate option of creating a second type of money (red money, chits, vouchers, whatever) that can only be used to purchase particular goods and services. This second type of money can then be distributed to generate the desired distribution for the particular good or services in question. (Market suppliers ultimately trade their red money or vouchers for normal green money.) Educational voucher plans fall into this category. Governments pay for some minimum quantity of a child's education by issuing each child a voucher worth some amount, but these vouchers can be used to purchase education at whatever school the student or his parents think most appropriate. The public pays, but it does not provide.

If the good or service in question is one where society is interested in giving each individual some minimum quantity, but is not interested in complete equality, governments can allow the purchase of such goods and services with both red money and green money. The equal distribution of red money guarantees that each person gets his minimum quantity and the distribution of green money allows him to purchase more than his minimum if he wishes. If the good or service is one where society is interested in complete equality, then it is necessary to prevent the purchase of such goods and services with green money. Only the distribution of red money can be allowed to determine its outcome. Sale for green money must be prevented.

What factors determine whether merit wants should be provided directly by government or indirectly by the issue of special money? While there are other arguments that lead to the public provision of goods and services in-kind (see below), these do not spring from the characteristics of merit wants. By themselves, the existence of merit wants would seem to argue for the creation and distribution of more than one type of money.

This conclusion is reinforced by an examination of the social preferences underlying the existence of merit wants. While merit wants usually exist, it seems doubtful that the social preferences that create them extend to the detailed characteristics of the good or service in question. A society may have a social norm concerning the minimum acceptable house in terms of safety, space per person, and plumbing facilities, but it does not have preferences about the other detailed characteristics of housing. The lack of such preferences argues for vouchers where each person can decide for himself the other characteristics of his housing. Perhaps an analogy can be drawn with the distinction between block grants-in-aid and categorical grants-in-aid. Social preferences on merit wants exist at the level of block grants-in-aid, but not at the level of categorical grants-in-aid.

The only case for the public provision of merit goods and services in-kind would seem to rest on the argument that public provision is the best method of preventing private sales of the good or service in question. This means public provision should only be used in cases where very particular distribution (such as complete equality) of the good or service is desired. Even here, however, the costs of achieving segregation through public provision in-kind must be balanced against the costs of accomplishing segregation by prohibiting the sale of the good in question for anything other than the appropriate type of money. Obviously, the relative costs are a matter for empirical analysis in each situation and will depend upon the characteristics of the good in question.

(The possible need to prohibit private sales can be seen in the British Health System. Since a few doctors have not joined the national health system, there are limited opportunities for the private purchases of health care in excess of that provided to the general population. Periodically, there are public demands that these private markets be abolished since they make it possible for the rich to buy more or better health care than that provided the average citizen.)

As a result, there are several questions that must be answered to adequately provide merit wants.

1. Is this particular good a merit want that is to be distributed in a manner different from that of general goods and services?
2. What exact distribution is to be achieved for this particular merit want?
3. Does the provision of the good in question need to be segregated from the general money market for goods and services?
4. If segregation is necessary, is provision in-kind or regulations prohibiting private sale the best method to achieve segregation?

If the good or service does not need to be segregated or if provision in kind is not the best method of segregation, merit wants should be supplied by distributing vouchers rather than by public provision in-kind.

III. LIMITED CONSUMER SOVEREIGNTY

At the heart of economists' preferences for income transfer payments lies the doctrine of absolute consumer sovereignty. Everyone is his own best judge of what should be done to maximize his own utility. In the real world the rationale behind public policies has only faced up to a slight modification of this simplistic view. The world is polarized into a world of minors and institutionalized persons who are legally incompetent to make any decisions and the remaining non-institutionalized population that is presumed to be competent to make any and all decisions. Obviously, such a polarization does not in fact exist. There is a continuum of individuals ranging from those who are competent to make any and all decisions to those who are incompetent to make any and all decisions.

Although there have been cycles in social thinking about where the line should be drawn between the institutionalized population and the non-institutionalized population, current movements in social thinking seem to be recognizing the nature of the continuum and removing sharp distinctions between competence and incompetence. Half-way houses, drug rehabilitation centers and their equivalents in personal supervision are being established for criminals, mental patients, the mentally retarded, drug addicts, and others. In addition to recognizing a continuum of individuals such centers also recognize a continuum of supervision that extends from complete decision making through all forms of decision aiding to no supervision. This means there is a need to establish where on the continuum between competence and incompetence each person lies and what degree of decision making aid is appropriate to his incompetencies.

While some of the need for decision aiding services can be provided by private individuals, much of it must rest with governmental authorities or must be supervised by governmental authorities. There simply is a need for some disinterested party to prevent the exploitation of partially competent people by other individuals. Governments have a whole range of public policies they can use to supplement or supplant consumer sovereignty. One of the mildest and least coercive of these techniques is the public provision of goods and services in-kind or the public provision of decision making services in-kind. Such in-kind aid can be used to influence, aid, or force individuals to make decisions that society thinks they would be making if the individuals had the competence to fall into the class of those with absolute consumer sovereignty.

The extent of the problems created by limited consumer sovereignty are expanded by differences in personal management efficiency. How good is one at managing and providing the normal housekeeping functions that each family provides in-kind to itself? In the simple textbook world everyone's personal management efficiency is both equal and superb. In the real world individuals and families differ enormously in family management ability. Realistically, some persons and families are simply inefficient managers. As a result, the same money income will provide very different real standards of living for different families.

When pressed on this point, the textbook economists would retreat back to the proposition that inefficient firms (families) would go broke and go out of existence—the sacred 'right to fail.' While society may be willing to let inefficient firms go out of business it clearly is not willing to let inefficient families go out of business (starve on the streets). As a result, there is a direct social interest in some minimum level of family management efficiency. This problem is clearest for those families that are so incompetent that they would go out of business if left unsupervised, but it potentially exists at all levels of income where income transfer payments are being provided.

Suppose society has an income distribution objective that calls for some minimum real standard of living above this minimum. Does it set its money income transfer payments at the level where the family who has the best family manager can reach the desired minimum, where the family who has just an average family manager can reach the desired minimum, or where the family who has the worst family manager can reach the desired minimum? Alternatively, does it give each family an income transfer payment that is designed to compensate for that family's level of inefficiency? Or does it provide public services in-kind to insure some minimum level of personal or family management efficiency?

Given the probable range in management efficiencies, income transfers would have to be impossibly large if they had to be set so that each family could reach some minimum standard of living in spite of its own inefficiencies. Realistically, there is no way to tailor income transfer payments to the level of each person's management ability. This only leaves the option of providing some kind of decision making or aiding services that constrains family management inefficiencies. The services of a home economist would be an illustration of the type of in-kind aid that might be needed.

By noting the limitations in the doctrine of absolute consumer sovereignty and by noting society's interests in limiting the right of a person or a family to fail, it is possible to focus on the question of where individuals fall on the continuum between those with no decision making competence and absolute decision making competence. Given this determination it is then possible to ask where the public provision of goods and services in-kind falls into the various techniques for rectifying limited consumer sovereignty and preventing family management failures.

While alternative distributions of different types of money (vouchers) would seem appropriate in the area of merit wants, they would seem much less appropriate in the area of limited consumer sovereignty. Generally, the individual or the family needs decision making aid and not some particular consumption good or service. These can be purchased in private markets. The private purchase of decision aiders or makers does not, however, seem to be a possibility. Decision aiders are available in the private market (investment consultants are the best example), but decision making competence is necessary to purchase a good decision aider and this is exactly the quality that has been called into question. Thus, limited consumer sovereignty would call for the public provision of decision aiding or making services. Governments need not provide drug treatment centers, but they must provide the services of someone advising or, if necessary, requiring such treatment. Correspondingly, governments do not need to provide groceries, but they may need to provide someone to advise on how to achieve some minimum of family management efficiency or, if necessary, to require some minimum of family efficiency.

Limited consumer sovereignty, however, would not call for the public provision of final consumption goods and services. Given aid in decision making, these can be provided in the private market and paid for by the general system of income transfer payments. Clearly, the appropriate public decision procedures would call for the primary use of decision aiding services to be supplemented by decision making services only when decision aids have demonstrably failed on a case-by-case basis.

The only exceptions spring from social limitations on the right of an individual or a family to fail. If some abnormally expensive item is necessary to stop an individual from failing (the best example is drug rehabilitation), the necessary service may need to be provided in-kind and cannot be paid for from general income transfer payments (they won't be large enough). If the necessary purchase is voluntary with the aid of a decision aider, voucher systems probably dominate direct provision in-kind. If the necessary purchase is involuntary and will only be made under compulsion, direct public provision is probably the only feasible solution. Private markets are just not set up to handle involuntary purchases.

Thus, limited consumer sovereignty would seem to call for answers to the following questions:

1. Where on the continuum between no consumer sovereignty and complete consumer sovereignty does each group or individual fall?
2. Given an individual or family that is not fully competent to make its own decisions, what degree of decision aiding services is necessary?
3. Given that decision aiding services have not led to acceptable decisions for the individual in question, what types of decision making services are necessary?
4. Are any abnormally expensive items necessary to prevent personal or family failure?

In general, the necessary decision aiding or making services would be publicly provided in-kind, but no final consumption goods and services would be publicly provided in-kind. Those should be purchased from the general system of earnings and money income transfer payments. The only exception would occur when abnormally expensive items were necessary to prevent personal or family failure. If the necessary purchases would be made voluntarily, vouchers probably dominate public in-kind provision. When purchases would not be made voluntarily, public in-kind provision dominates vouchers.

IV. THE CREATION OF INDIVIDUAL VALUES

Part of the mythology of absolute consumer sovereignty is the proposition that innate consumer preferences exist fully grown in each individual just as Athena sprang fully grown from the head of Zeus. Basically, economics views man as a machine with an innate set of wants who derives satisfaction from processing sets of inputs (consumption goods). Each man is to be the judge of his own welfare. Since each man wants to be "better off" he should decide when he is "better off" and when he is "better off" and no one else is "worse off" than society is also "better off."

What the simple model of "homo-economicus" fails to confront is the process whereby individual wants, preferences, or values are created. Given modern sociology and psychology, the postulate of static innate wants is simply untenable. Every society has always implicitly affected the wants of its population. As biological needs receded, sociological needs increased. As a result, it is no longer possible to maintain the fiction that the American society responds to individual wants but does not create individual wants. We must now explicitly recognize what we have always done implicitly.

J. K. Galbraith has repeatedly skirted this problem when he notes that there may be a bias against public goods because they are not advertised as extensively as private goods. This view makes two mistakes. First, advertising is only one, and not the most important, method for creating wants. Second, he implies that such advertising distorts individual preferences. The real problem is not the distortion of innate wants, but the fact that wants are generated by social pressures. There are no innate wants (other than the biological ones) to which we can appeal or to which we can return.

Directly or indirectly the American society generates the wants of American individuals. With overt persuasion purchases will differ from what they would have been without persuasion, but they will be in accordance with current preferences. What's more, their new wants have the same validity as the old wants. Both were socially determined. The only difference is that some wants may be more consciously created than others.

Although Americans have always used private and governmental persuasion to create the desired wants (belief in democracy, etc.), overt persuasion has always been associated with totalitarian dictatorships. This polarized association is unfortunate since it obscures the real problem. The real problem is not whether wants are going to be socially generated (they are), but what techniques of overt and covert persuasion are to be allowed. To what extent should the education system be used to inculcate values? Is subliminal advertising permissible? How much peer group pressure is allowable? These are the real questions that must be answered. To be against dictatorship does not solve the problem. While we often imagine the polar totalitarian extreme, the problem can be put in perspective by imagining the opposite extreme. What would society look like if there was no social persuasion? With no commonly shared beliefs and wants, anarchy would result. Any society would be impossible.

What role should the public provision of goods and services in-kind play in the creation of values? Viewed as a merit want, educational vouchers dominate public schools, but viewed as value creation, public schools may well dominate educational vouchers. Public schools allow society to insure that individuals will be inculcated with, or at least exposed to, the basic values of society. Educational vouchers permit children to be educated without being exposed to the virtues of democracy as a method of resolving conflicts of interest. Can this be allowed to any great extent if a democratic society is to survive? The obvious answer is "no."

Another example exists in the area of drug rehabilitation. A simple application of the principles of economics would allow a free market in hard drugs, allow each person the right of becoming a drug addict, allow each person to kill himself if he wished, and interfere only to prevent drug addicts from intruding on the activities of the rest of the population. (A free market in drugs and the resulting low prices might in fact be the best method of preventing drug addicts from disturbing others. They could easily earn enough money to kill themselves.) Yet society does not follow its professed 4th of July principles. Instead, it seeks to alter the values of the actual or potential drug addict, not because these are anti-social activities that harm others but because any society requires positive commitments to its values as well as the absence of negative actions.

As a result, it is necessary to ask what values the American society holds so deeply and that are so fundamental to it that it wants government programs to inculcate these values in each of its citizens. Basically, these are the beliefs where a society does not want to leave it to the accidental forces of the market place to determine whether individuals are or are not exposed to them. Such a list might include beliefs in democracy, private property, the work ethic, free speech, etc. Whatever they are, it is then possible to ask how the provision of different in-kind goods and services might contribute to the creation of these values. In the past, most such programs have been called "educational programs" but it is necessary to realize that the word "education" includes value creation in this context.

The current disputes over child care are the best illustration of the problem. If custodial child care is a merit want where the simple aim is to allow each mother an equal opportunity to go to work, then vouchered private child care centers are the appropriate answer. If child care is also desired as a method of altering values and characteristics (enrichment is our current euphemism), then the public in-kind provision of child care is appropriate. Since you want to change the values that the mothers would inculcate if they were at home, you obviously cannot allow mothers to pick the private child care centers that the public funds are to be used to support.

Thus, several questions need to be answered to determine how the public provison of goods and services in-kind could contribute to the creation of individual preferences:

1. What individual values are so important to the American society that they cannot be left to the private market place for ideas?
2. What are the limits within which government techniques of persuasion must stay?
3. What role should the public provision of goods and services in-kind play within this spectrum of allowable techniques?

V. TRADITIONAL MARKET FAILURES

The normal second best justification for government provision of goods and services in-kind rests on the existence of private market failures. Other than pure public goods or goods with aspects of pure publicness, externalities are most commonly cited. Economic externalities, however, are difficult to find in the goods and services traditionally provided by HEW. Generally, the analysis slips off into the analysis of sociological externalities (less crime, etc.) or political externalities (better voters, etc.). In these contexts the word "externalities" just does not have its technical economic meaning. If anything, sociological and political externalities refer to the creation of different values. The problem of creating values is best faced directly rather than covertly under the rubric of externalities. In any case, the appropriate solution in cases where there are externalities is a system of matching grants (matching vouchers) where the size of the grant depends on the size of the external benefits. If some purchase creates $5 worth of external benefits accruing to someone else, then governments subsidize the purchase price with a matching grant of $5. Individuals pay for personal benefits; governments pay for external benefits.

The same reasoning applies to the statement "that society should intervene since it knows the individual's own future preferences better than he now knows himself." This is an argument often made to justify compulsory education, but it is really just a disguised method of saying that society wants the individual to have specific future values. Instead of admitting this, we attempt to appeal to future innate preferences that society knows better than the individual. To pose the problem in terms of a better knowledge of future preferences than the individual himself is to confuse the problem. The problem is to create future values and not to discover them.

Economies of scale that create efficient units too big for private markets can justify government provision, but it is difficult to find instances of such economies of scale in actual or potential HEW goods and services. Similarly, traditional monopoly arguments do not seem to apply. Monopolies do not now exist and given the characteristics of the markets in question, it is difficult to see how they could be created. The only exception would seem to be in the area of medical care, but the medical monopoly, if it exists, is at the level of the medical schools and not at the level of the individual provision of goods and services. The appropriate remedy would not be public provision of medical services in-kind, but cracking the monopoly elements at the medical school level.

There are two types of market failures, however, that might lead to the need for government intervention. One leads to provision in-kind; the other leads to provision in the form of vouchers.

First, individuals may have an inadequate knowledge of the future stream of costs and benefits that flow from their actions. The appropriate response here is not the public provision of the good or service in question, but the public in-kind provision of information and advice about the costs and benefits of goods and services. Private provision does not work since there is no way to judge who should be hired to provide information. Information provision is also one of the few areas where there seem to be economies of scale at almost any level.

Second, there may be large differences between social and private discounts used to evaluate future costs and benefits. Some of the differences spring from differences in risk premiums. The problem can be seen most clearly in the area of job training programs. A low income individual who is subject to a severe budget constraint must have a high rate of time preference to allocate his limited funds in accordance with economic rationality. (The failure to recognize this is the major error in Banefield's *Unheavenly City*.) An economically rational society with its higher per capita budget constraint may have a very different rate of time preference. In addition, society may as a matter of its value judgments, place a higher premium on earning income (as opposed to transfer payment income) than that of the individual. Similarly, because of past experience, individuals may use an irrationally high risk premium to judge the outcome of any training program. Although society may know that the program has had a positive benefit cost ratio for others, he may not believe the results.

In this case, the appropriate answer is a system of matching voucher payments that can be used for the desired types of training. Ideally the vouchers would be set to pay enough of the costs (including the opportunity costs) to bring individual present value calculations into line with society's present value calculations.

Thus, several questions must be answered about market failures.

1. Are there any economic externalities, economies of scale, or monopoly arguments that justify public provision in-kind?
2. In what areas is individual knowledge too poor to make rational decisions?
3. In what areas are there large differences between individual and social rates of time preference and risk?

In general, inadequate knowledge should be remedied with public in-kind provision while differences in discount rates and externalities should be remedied with matching voucher payments.

VI. SOCIAL EFFICIENCY VERSUS GOVERNMENTAL EFFICIENCY

The pure theory of public finance does not recognize a distinction between social efficiency and governmental efficiency. Governments are supposed to do what is socially efficient and not worry about their own financial efficiency. To illustrate the problem, consider the following situation.

Suppose society decides that the average individual should purchase more education than he is now purchasing. To meet this goal the government establishes a system of educational vouchers. To some extent individuals use these vouchers to buy more education, but to some extent they also use these vouchers to reduce their own previous expenditures on education. Thus, the extra marginal dollars society spends on education may be much less than the governmental costs of the educational voucher program. From the point of view of pure public finance, this poses no problem of inefficiency. The government simply hands out vouchers and raises taxes until the desired educational expenditures take place. The gross expenditures on educational vouchers are irrelevant since the gains in general incomes can be recouped in taxes. Only net marginal expenditures on education matter. Regardless of the level of gross vouchers and gross taxes, neither the government nor the taxpayers are better off or worse off. There are simply more offsetting checks circulating around the system. From the point of view of governmental efficiency, however, a large discrepancy between net marginal expenditures on education and gross voucher expenditures can be disturbing. Programs look inefficient since the financial cost benefit ratio can be much less than 1. One dollar in educational vouchers does not yield one dollar in educational expenditures.

While it is clear that in a perfectly run world there would be no distinction between social efficiency and governmental efficiency, there may be a real distinction if it is not in fact politically feasible to recoup the funded transfer payments with higher taxes. In this case, governments may be interested in program efficiency in the government rather than social sense.

As the education illustration indicates, what looks like tied aid destined for a particular purpose may in fact be untied. In general, all aid is untied (fundable) until aid totals exceed previous expenditures for the same purpose. Only then is aid really tied on the margin. Only then can you really be forced to spend in the manner that the vouchers require. (This obviously assumes that free goods and services will never be rejected.) This is true in foreign aid, state and local government grants in-aid, and per-

sonal income transfers. The only way to avoid this problem even partially is to only subsidize expenditures in excess of those in some base period. While this avoids the problem of paying for the previous level of expenditures, it does not avoid the problem of paying for the increases in expenditures that would have occurred in the normal course of events. In theory, you could only pay for expenditures in excess of some trend rate of growth in expenditures, but defining this trend quickly becomes complex and has seldom been attended in practice.

In a socially optimal set of programs, general income transfer payments, voucher payments systems, and provision of goods and services in-kind would all be used (see above). Viewed, however, from the perspective of increasing the consumption of some specific good or service it is possible to compare the efficiency of general income transfer payments, voucher payment systems and the provision of goods and services in-kind.

The impact of general income transfer payments on the purchase of any particular commodity depends upon the income elasticity of demand for that product. The higher the income elasticity of demand, the more efficient are income transfer payments. This contrasts with a system of matching grants (matching vouchers) where governments provide some part of the cost of purchasing the commodity in question. The impact of a system of matching vouchers depends upon the price elasticity of demand for that product. The higher the price elasticity of demand, the more efficient are matching vouchers. Price elasticities, however, must always equal or exceed income elasticities. This occurs since every price reduction is an increase in real incomes and must cause at least as much of an increase in the demand for that product as an equivalent income payment. Thus, systems of cost sharing or matching vouchers are more efficient than general income transfer payments.

From this efficiency perspective provision of goods and services in-kind is exactly equivalent to a system of nonmatching voucher payments. Both provide some limited quantity of the good or service at a zero price to the consumer. By reducing previous expenditures when payments in-kind are made, payments in-kind can be turned into general income transfers just as voucher payments can be turned into cash. Since vouchers and payments in-kind are equivalent to a general income transfer payment, their impact on the purchases of a particular commodity also depends upon the income elasticity of demand. The only exception is when vouchers or payments in-kind exceed previous expenditures for that commodity. Then, either system causes a dollar for dollar increase in purchases of the desired commodity.

With this exception, matching grant systems are the most effective method of causing the greatest increase in expenditures at the least cost. On the other hand, all open-ended systems of matching grants create budget instabilities since it is impossible to predict expenditures precisely.

VII. CONCLUSIONS

As the analysis has shown, there are a wide variety of value judgments that must be made and factual pieces of information that must be determined before it is possible to specify when general income transfers, voucher payment systems, matching grant systems, and payments in-kind are optimal. Hopefully, the economic analysis in this paper, while not answering the question, helps sharpen our knowledge as to exactly what pieces of information are pertinent and exactly what value judgments must in fact be made. Obviously, the question of who and how the necessary value judgments are to be made has not been discussed. This is not because this is not an important question, but because it is fundamentally not an economic question.